CONSERVATION WITH EQUITY:

Strategies for Sustainable Development

Edited by: **Peter Jacobs** and **David A. Munro**

Contributing Editors: **Andrea Matte-Baker**
M. Taghi Farvar
L. Stephanie Flanders
Julia Gardner

Proceedings of the Conference on Conservation and Development: Implementing the World Conservation Strategy

Ottawa, Canada, 31 May - 5 June 1986

Sponsored by:

International Union for Conservation of Nature and Natural Resources (IUCN)

Environment Canada

World Wide Fund for Nature (WWF)

United Nations Environment Programme (UNEP)

Canadian Wildlife Federation (CWF)

1987

ISBN 2-88032-926-4

Citation: Jacobs, P. and Munro, D. (Eds) (1987). *Conservation with Equity: Strategies for Sustainable Development*, IUCN, Cambridge, U.K. xvii + 466 pages.

Cover design: B. Moffatt and T. Brynaert

Published by: IUCN, Gland, Switzerland and Cambridge, U.K.

Printed by: Page Bros (Norwich) Limited, U.K.

CONTENTS

TABLE OF AUTHORS

Mr. Syed Babar Ali
President, WWF Pakistan
Packages Ltd.
P.O. Amer Sidihu
Lahore 40, Pakistan

Ms. Margarita de Botero
President
Colegio de Villa de Leyva
Villa de Leyva, Colombia

Mr. Jacques Bugnicourt
Director, ENDA
Boite Postale 3370
Dakar, Senegal

Dr. Françoise Burhenne-Guilmin
Head, IUCN Environmental Law Centre
Adenauerallee 214
D-5300 Bonn 1, F.R.G.

Ms. Margaret Catley-Carlson
President, Canadian International
Development Agency (CIDA)
200 Promenade du Portage
Hull, Québec, Canada K1A 0G4

The Hon. Ms. Victoria Chitepo
Minister of Natural Resources and Tourism
Private Bag 7753
Harare, Zimbabwe

HRH The Prince Philip, Duke of Edinburgh
President, WWF International
Buckingham Palace
London SW1, United Kingdom

Dr. Jimoh Omo Fadaka
Chairman, African NGOs Environment
Network (ANEN)
Environment Liaison Centre
Post Office Box 72461
Nairobi, Kenya

Dr. M. Taghi Farvar
Senior Adviser on Sustainable Development
Avenue du Mont-Blanc
1196 Gland, Switzerland

Mr. Malcolm J. Forster
IUCN Commission on Environmental Policy,
Law and Administration
Adenauerallee 214
D-5300 Bonn 1, F.R.G.

Dr. José I.D.R. Furtado
Science Policy Advisor
Commonwealth Secretariat
Marlborough House, Pall Mall
London SW1 5HX, United Kingdom

Dr. Madhav Gadgil
Centre for Ecological Sciences
Indian Institute of Science
Bangalore, 560 012 India

Professor Johan Galtung
Department of Politics
Princeton University
Princeton, New Jersey 08544, U.S.A.

Mr. Charles de Haes
Director General
WWF International
Avenue du Mont-Blanc
1196 Gland, Switzerland

Mr. Mark Halle
IUCN Conservation for Development Centre
Avenue du Mont-Blanc
CH-1196 Gland, Switzerland

Dr Martin Holdgate
Chief Scientist
UK Department of the Environment
Department of the Environment
2 Marsham Street
London SW1P 3EB, United Kingdom.

Professor Peter Jacobs
Faculté de l'Aménagement
Université de Montréal
Montréal, Québec, Canada H3T 1T2

Dr Kenneth David Kaunda
President of Zambia
State House,
Lusaka, Zambia.

Professor Robert Keith
Faculty of Environmental Studies
University of Waterloo
Waterloo, Ontario, Canada

Mr. A.G.Kerr
Deputy Secretary
Department of Arts, Heritage and Environment
Canberra, Australia

Dr. Ashok Khosla
President, Development Alternatives
22, Palam Marg
New Delhi 110057 India

Mr. Cyrille de Klemm
21 Rue de Dantzig
75105 Paris, France

Dr. Barbara Lausche
IUCN Commission on Environmental Policy,
Law and Administration
Adenauerallee 214
D-5300 Bonn 1, F.R.G.

Professor Enrique Leff
Instituto de Investigaciones Sociales
Universidad Nacional Autonoma de Mexico
Torre II de Humanidades
Cuidad Universitaria
Mexico 20, D.F.

Professor Le Thac Can
Director
Research Institute for Higher Education
9 Hai Ba Trung
Hanoi, Vietnam

The Hon. Thomas M. McMillan
Minister of the Environment,
Government of Canada
Terrace de la Chaudière
10 rue Wellington
Ottawa K1A0H3, Canada

Mr. Jeffrey A. McNeely
Director
IUCN Programme and Policy Division
Avenue du Mont-Blanc
1196 Gland, Switzerland

Dr. J. Geoffrey Mosley
Director
Australian Conservation Foundation
Hawthorn, Victoria
3122 Australia

Mr. Namukolo Mukutu
Permanent Secretary
Ministry of Lands & Natural Resources
Lusaka Zambia

Dr. David A. Munro
Naivasha Consultants Ltd.
2513 Amherst Avenue
Sidney, British Columbia, Canada V8L 2H3

Mr. Constantine Mwale
Natural Resources Department
P.O. Box 50042
Lusaka, Zambia

Dr. John Kennedy Naysmith
Senior Advisor to the Government of Nepal
Suite 1409, Bluestar Building
G.P.O. Box 3923
Tripureswar, Kathmandu, Nepal

Mr. Marc Nerfin
President
International Foundation for
Development Alternatives
2 Place du March
1260 Nyon, Switzerland

Mr. Robert Prescott-Allen
PADATA Consultants
627 Aquarius
Victoria, British Columbia, Canada H9B 5B4

Mr. Rafael Salas
Executive Director
United Nations Fund for Population
Activities
220 East, 42nd Street
New York, New York 10017, U.S.A.

Mr. Mats Segnestam
Director
Swedish Society for the Conservation of Nature
Box 6400
11382 Stockholm, Sweden

Ms. Mary Simon
Makivik Corporation
4898 de Maisonneuve W.
Montréal, Québec, Canada H3Z 1M8

Dr. Pierre Spitz
Research Coordinator
Independent Commission on International
Humanitarian Issues
47 Bis, Avenue Blanc
Geneva, Switzerland

Mr. Maurice Strong
Special Advisor to the Secretary General
of the United Nations
Room 3627, United Nations
New York, New York 10017, U.S.A.

Professor Osvaldo Sunkel
Coordinator
Development and Environment Unit
CEPAL/UNEP
Casilla 179-D
Santiago, Chile

Dr. M.S. Swaminathan
IUCN President
Director General
International Rice Research Institute
Box 933 Manila, Philippines

Mr. Peter S. Thacher
Distinguished Fellow
World Resources Institute
1735 New York Avenue N.W.
Washington, D.C., U.S.A.

Dr. Mostafa K. Tolba
Executive Director
UN Environment Programme
Nairobi, Kenya

Professor Vo Quy
Dean, Faculty of Biology
University of Hanoi
Hanoi, Vietnam

Mr. William Waldegrave
Minister of State for the Environment,
Countryside and Local Government
Department of the Environment
2 Marsham Street
London,SWIP 3EB, United Kingdom

Mr. Brian W. Walker
President, IIED
3 Endsleigh Street
London, WC1H 0DD, United Kingdom

Dr. Jeremy Warford
Projects Policy Department
World Bank
1818 "H" Street N.W.
Washington, D.C., U.S.A.

FOREWORD

David A. Munro
Naivasha Consultants Ltd.
Sidney, B.C., Canada

The Ottawa Conference on the World Conservation Strategy was intended to evaluate progress in implementing the Strategy and to consider whether, in light of the experience of implementation, it should be revised. Convened six years after the launch of the World Conservation Strategy, the Conference reflected a fuller recognition of the place of people in ecosystems. If the World Conservation Strategy achieved a conceptual union of conservation and development, the Ottawa Conference brought forward the message of conservation with equity: how to reconcile human needs and the goal of social equity with environmental integrity and sustainable use of natural resources.

The more than 30 countries that had prepared, or were preparing, National Conservation Strategies reported on their progress. Plenary Sessions featured keynote papers on specific aspects of conservation and development, and eighteen Workshops were held on issues related to sustainable development. Each Workshop formulated recommendations, proposed ideas for action, and made suggestions as to how the World Conservation Strategy might be improved. Recommendations approved by the Plenary are included in these Proceedings.

Over 500 participants took part of the opportunity to exchange experiences and views. They came from every continent and geopolitical region. Participants represented a broad spectrum of professions and interests: they included development planners and decision makers; ministers and landscape planners; experts and policy makers in population, appropriate technology, agriculture, health, industry, human settlements, and of course, renewable resource management.

The initial sponsors of the Conference were IUCN, WWF, UNEP, Environment Canada and the Canadian Wildlife Federation. As preparations got underway those bodies were joined, as associate sponsors, by UNDP, FAO, Unesco, UNFPA, IDRC, and the bilateral development assistance agencies of Canada, Sweden, Norway, the Netherlands and the United Kingdom.

This volume constitutes the formal record of the Conference. Since the Conference was held, work has begun on a revised version of the WCS which will represent a second Conference output. Still another product of the Conference will be the Series on Sustainable Development, which will draw on the many excellent papers that were submitted to the Workshops at Ottawa.

ACKNOWLEDGEMENTS

The Ottawa Conference on Conservation and Development was convened to review progress in achieving the goals of the World Conservation Strategy. Numerous governmental, intergovernmental and non-governmental organisations as well as many individuals volunteered their good offices, funds, time and energy to assure that the Conference would successfully meet its objectives. If the spirit of Stockholm[1] was captured once again at Ottawa, it was due to the enthusiastic participants who attended the Conference and, in very large measure, to those that we are pleased to acknowledge here.

The Steering Committee was chaired by Kenton Miller (Director General, IUCN) and consisted of Charles de Haes (Director General, WWF), Reuben Olembo (Programme Director, UNEP, Nairobi), Noel Brown (North American Director, UNEP), Lorette Goulet (Assistant Deputy Minister, Environment Canada), Kenneth Brynaert (Executive Vice President, Canadian Wildlife Federation), David Munro (Secretary-General of the Conference and former Director General, IUCN), Francis Mouttapa (FAO), Bernt von Droste (Unesco), and Peter Jacobs (Chairman of the Commission on Environmental Planning, IUCN, and Professor at the Universities of Montreal and Harvard). Taghi Farvar (Senior Advisor on Sustainable Development, IUCN and Executive Coordinator of its Commission on Environmental Planning) served as Secretary of the Steering Committee.

The Steering Committee benefited from the advice of Dr B. Dietrich

1. The UN Conference on the Human Environment in Stockholm, June 1972, was the first major world gathering on the human environment and the first of the series of thematic world conferences sponsored by the United Nations. This intergovernmental Conference also included, for the first time, a parallel non-governmental component in which groups of citizens discussed the same issues in voluntary gatherings. This trend has been followed since in world conferences held on such topics as human settlements, population, energy, water, and women. In many ways, the World Conservation Strategy elaborated by IUCN, UNEP, WWF Unesco and FAO is the progeny of the Stockholm Conference, as are UNEP, IIED and many other international and national bodies dealing with environment and development.

(World Health Organization), Maurice Strong (Emergency Office of the United Nations for Africa), as well as representatives of Canadian Government agencies. These included Richard Herring (Agriculture Canada), Geoffrey Bruce and Ron Léger (Canadian International Development Agency), Richard Bill (then of Unesco) and Dawna Jones (Forestry Service, Environment Canada).

The main responsibility for the Conference Programme was vested in IUCN's Commission on Environmental Planning (CEP). It was developed by Peter Jacobs in close collaboration with David Munro and Taghi Farvar as well as with a number of CEP members including Andrea Matte-Baker, Ashok Khosla, Adolfo Mascarenhas, David Pitt, Marc Nerfin, and others. Jeff McNeely (Director, IUCN Programme and Policy Division) gave his full support and technical advice. Other IUCN staff members made numerous supportive suggestions and contributions, including Delmar Blasco, Salvano Briceño, Mike Cockerell, Pat Dugan, Danny Elder, Vitus Fernando (then of the World Commission on Environment and Development), Mark Halle, Ole Hamann, Robert Lamb (now with UNEP, Nairobi), Drake McHugh, Kenton Miller, Dan Navid, Pierre Portas, Keith Rennie, Jeff Sayer, Robert Scott, Jim Thorsell, and others. An informal CEP working group was also established in the Geneva region for consultations regarding revisions to be made in the World Conservation Strategy, consisting of Paulo Bifani (Consultant on environment and development, Geneva), Taghi Farvar, Branislav Gosovic (UNCTAD and the Economic Commission for Latin America, then of the World Commission on Environ-

ment and Development), Jeff McNeely, Keith Rennie and Pierre Spitz (Independent Commission on International Humanitarian Issues, Geneva).

The Programme was reviewed by the Programme Advisory Committee of the IUCN Council (PAC), consisting of the following IUCN Councillors: Mats Segnestam (Sweden, Regional IUCN Councillor for Europe) and the Chairpersons of IUCN's Commissions: Wolfgang Burhenne (Policy. Law and Administration); Harold Eidsvik (Parks and Protected Areas); José Furtado (Ecology); Peter Jacobs (Environmental Planning, Chairman of PAC) Jerry Lieberman (Education), and Grenville Lucas (Species Survival).

Three of our Canadian colleagues deserve very special mention for the success of the Conference. They are David Munro, Peter Jacobs and Kenneth Brynaert.

In 1981, Kenneth Brynaert asked David Munro how the Canadian Wildlife Federation might best advance world conservation. From their subsequent discussion emerged the idea that a global forum should be convened to evaluate progress on implementing the World Conservation Strategy. Support for the idea was immediately given by Mostafa Tolba, Executive Director of UNEP, and Charles de Haes, Director General of WWF. David Munro's untiring efforts in shepherding the Conference after that caused the idea to mature and bloom.

Peter Jacobs, as the leader of a volunteer network devoted to promoting sustainable development - IUCN's Commission on Environmental Planning - devoted a disproportionate amount of his time, energy and enthusiasm to elaborating the contents of the programme, and thus set a new example for the voluntary professional spirit that has been one of the major pillars of IUCN.

Kenneth Brynaert took on the endless task of managing the Conference on the Canadian side, injecting all of his business and professional know-how into the critical preparatory process there, devoting much of his own and the Canadian Wildlife Federation's time and resources to the success of this Conference. Together with the Secretary General of the Conference and the Chairman of its Programme Committee, he orchestrated a dedicated team to carry out this complex task. The host country team, acting as an efficient support system, included the following people and tasks:

Terry Brynaert asssited Kenneth Brynaert with Conference coordination, and was responsible for the graphic design of letterheads, brochures and the insignia of the Conference (the insignia for the World Conservation Strategy superimposed on the Canadian symbol, the maple leaf). Brian Moffatt handled artwork and layout, and designed the Conference Programme. Julia Gardner was in charge of preparing pre-Conference documentation, and helped extensively with preliminary editing of the papers. Andrea Matte-Baker dealt with a large volume of pre-Conference correspondence and assisted in the establishment of the Workshops. George Green was responsible for reporting arrangements for the Workshops. Stephen Hazel served as corporate counsel, handling all legal matters and contractual arrangements; William Henwood assumed responsibility for the exhibitions and overall support services

of the Conference. Luba Mycio-Mommers and Alexander Mommers were Co-chairmen of audiovisual arrangements. Andrea Hunt worked with Kenneth Brynaert and David Munro as administrative secretary. Suzanne Belaire, Cheryl Soubliere, and Pauline Giles assisted with much of the secretarial work at the Conference. Sylvie Berube and Katie Feeney were in charge of document translation (English/French). Sandi McQuillan and Margaret Pearson handled the reception and registration desk at the Conference. Judy Graham helped Kenneth Brynaert with administration and secretarial work at the Conference, while Maria Smith worked with David Munro in document coordination. Nydia McCool of Ottawa Convention Services took responsibility for Conference arrangements, accommodations, and registration. Roman Mycio helped with informal interpretation. Natalie Hamel, Marcel Hop, Brenda Morris, Jeff Ridal and Harold Stover were student volunteers from the University of Ottawa, who helped with every imaginable chore around the Conference, including running a message service. Bill Wright handled complicated computer work such as preparing the Conference participants data base. The CWF departments of mail processing and membership offered many services. Sylvia Wickes provided many support services including the much appreciated coffee and other Conference drinks.

Secretariat support was provided at IUCN Headquarters by Andrea Seagroat, Diana Gradiska-Baudraz, Béatrice Pollien, Joanna Erfani, and Sue Rallo, while Julia Tucker (Membership Administrator, IUCN) took charge of organising and tracking Conference papers and coordinating arrangements for sponsored participants. Sue Scherer of the American Express Travel Office in Geneva worked long and hard to obtain the best and most economical travel arrangements for sponsored participants from all corners of the globe.

Approximately 500 people from some 100 countries attended the Ottawa Conference. Many individuals supported their own travel and expenses through individual grants or at personal cost; many others, particularly from developing countries, were supported by travel grants graciously provided by the United Nations Environment Programme (UNEP), the Canadian International Development Agency (CIDA), the Swedish International Development Agency (SIDA), the Norwegian Agency for International Development (NORAD), the Overseas Development Administration of Great Britain (ODA), the United Nations Fund for Population Activities (UNFPA), Unesco, the Government of the Netherlands, the Department of the Environment (Environment Canada) and the International Development Research Centre (IDRC) of Canada.

Other supporters of the Conference include Bundesministerium für Wirtschaftliche Zusammenarbeit, Canada Department of Fisheries and Oceans, Canada Department of Indian and Northern Affairs, Canada Packers, Canadian Forestry Service, Commonwealth Fund for Technical Cooperation, Fur Council of Canada, Hudson's Bay Company, Imperial Oil Limited, National Wildlife Federation, Petro Canada, Polysar, Power Corporation of Canada, Safari Club International, US Agency for International Development, and Wildlife Habitat Canada. Wang Canada donated use of a complete computer system for the Conference, and Xerox Canada provided the same with photocopying systems.

Numerous organisations contributed exhibition material which was displayed throughout the Conference. Exhibitors are listed in Annex III of this volume.

The National Film Board of Canada (NFB) graciously provided a wide range of films on subjects related to sustainable development for viewing during the Conference, and the Canadian Broadcasting Corporation (CBC) provided a library of video-cassettes on relevant issues. Many other video cassettes were provided by participants and other organisations, for which we are very grateful.

Press coverage of the Conference was coordinated by The Interpress Service (IPS), a Third World news agency, and Gemini, a Third World news writing network based in London. They did an outstanding job of covering the Conference substantively, in spite of limited press facilities, thanks to a special grant from CIDA, Canada.

A particularly stimulating and entertaining session of African and Caribbean music was offered by the Ottawa University African Students Dance Group during the Conference.

Since the Conference, important grants have been accorded IUCN to implement the recommendations of the Conference, developed in Workshop sessions and approved by the Final Plenary Session. These include grants from UNEP and WWF to develop a Second Edition of the World Conservation Strategy, and grants to establish a Library on Sustainable Development from the Canadian International Development Agency (CIDA), the UN Environment Programme, the Swedish International Development Agency (SIDA), the Norwegian Agency for International Development (NORAD), and the Government of the Netherlands.

The true success of the Conference resides in the ability of each and every participant to "spread the message" of the World Conservation Strategy to those most directly involved in decision-making at local, national and regional levels, whose actions most directly affect our ability to achieve a sustainable future. Many of these are also involved in follow-up work including WCS revision and compilation of the Library on Sustainable Development.

To all of the above, and to anyone we may have failed to mention, very sincere thanks.

Publication of this volume has been supported by grants from CIDA, Environment Canada, UNEP, SIDA, NORAD and the Dutch Government.

It was designed and typeset on an IBM computer using *Ventura Publisher*, a software package recently released by Xerox Corporation. The software was donated to IUCN by Laurie Baker of Xerox's Software Business Centre in Texas, and John Meyer, software developer and President of Ventura Publisher, Inc. in California.

Finally to match the energy, effort and dedication that was put into the realisation of the Conference, our very special gratitude goes to Stephanie Flanders, IUCN Publications Unit, who spent countless days and often nights on the final editing of this complex volume, pulling it all together, designing and "typesetting" its final presentation. Sincere gratitude also extends to Morag White, IUCN Publications Unit, who provided unfailing support in final editing and publication processes; to Liz Hopkins, IUCN/CEP, for translation of French texts into English and for general support in gathering the various elements necessary to complete the volume; to Jacqueline Bradshaw-Price for illustrations; and to Sandra Woods, who assisted with volume finalisation.

OPENING AND INTRODUCTION

CONFERENCE ON CONSERVATION AND DEVELOPMENT: IMPLEMENTING THE WORLD CONSERVATION STRATEGY

Opening Address

Dr. M. S. Swaminathan
President, IUCN
Manila, Philippines

Ladies and Gentlemen, Distinguished Delegates,

All of the actions we take to survive are interdependent and of equal importance. Those actions having ecological relevance are at the heart of IUCN's mission and form the central theme of this Conference.

The Conference on Conservation and Development is a product of the collaboration of five organisations - IUCN, WWF, UNEP, Environment Canada and the Canadian Wildlife Federation. Each has had a particular role to play and the actions of each have complemented those of the other organisations. I hope that the Conference will set the pattern of action and accomplishment, not only for IUCN, but also for the collaborating organisations in the years to come.

We are grateful to the Government of Canada for the support that it has extended to this Conference. We note that Canada has made considerable progress, domestically and internationally, in achieving conservation and striking a balance between conservation and development. I venture to hope that Canadians and other participants will take from this Conference solid new ideas and the inspiration for greater achievements in sustainable development. On behalf of all the participants, I also wish to express our sincere gratitude to David Munro, Peter Jacobs, Kenton Miller, and all other scientists and staff members who have worked so hard for so many months to make the Conference meaningful.

IUCN will be completing 40 years of service to the conservation movement in 1988. In 1986, the World Wildlife Fund commemorated its 25th anniversary. These are occasions when we should look back as well as forward.

I recall that in March 1980, the then Director General of IUCN, Dr. David Munro, attended the launch of the World Conservation Strategy in New Delhi. This event was supported by the late Prime Minister Indira Gandhi, who indicated in her address that she was not launching a conservation strategy; rather she considered it to be a *survival* strategy for the billion people and the billion animals that would inhabit India at the beginning of the twenty-first century.

The preparation and publication of the World Conservation Strategy represented a significant stage in IUCN's growth. This Conference, with its opportunity to review and improve the Strategy, is another important step along the way. The fact that the Conference is sponsored and supported by so many organisations is noteworthy and encouraging.

We are meeting near the end of a week which has drawn global attention to the urgency of implementing the World Conservation Strategy. The Special Session of the UN General Assembly on the African Economic Crisis this week in New York has highlighted linkages between ecological security and economic recovery. Simultaneously in Ottawa, the World Commission on Environment and Development (WCED) received a large number of well-documented presentations which underline the importance of introducing the twin concepts of sustainable livelihood security and ecological economics as the foundation of all development planning.

An important outcome of the World Conservation Strategy has been the growing emphasis on principles of sustainable development in national plans for accelerating economic growth. National Conservation Strategies have been launched in accordance with the objectives of the World Conservation Strategy in more than 20 countries. While the papers presented at this Conference will help us to draw up an objective balance sheet of successes and failures, the next phase of the World Conservation Strategy should stress implementation, monitoring and evaluation.

The founding fathers of IUCN might not have visualised in 1948 that the Union would play a role of such breadth and significance. IUCN has, in fact, grown into its role by the imperatives of our deteriorating environment. I will not take your time to quote well-known statistics on the current harm to basic life support systems of land, water, flora, fauna and the atmosphere. Periodic reports of the United Nations Environment Programme (UNEP) and the recent report of the World Resources Institute provide the best available estimates of the quantitative and qualitative dimensions of the problems facing us today. The much publicised Sahel crisis and the impending crises of the Himalayan and Andean regions are grim reminders of the shape of things to come.

Numerous studies have shown that political corruption and commercial greed, indifference to the genuine needs of the poor for water, food, fodder, fuel and shelter, and the spread of technologies based on a one-track approach to development all contribute in varying ways to the continuing degradation of the human environment. The question is "How can we reverse current trends?"

While careless technology can cause unmitigated environmental disasters, as demonstrated by the calamities of Bhopal and Chernobyl, technologies carefully tailored to specific agro-ecological and socio-economic conditions can help to provide bread together with freedom from environmental degradation on a sustainable basis.

We can keep soil productivity at high levels today through adequate soil health monitoring and care. We can replenish soil fertility through an integrated nutrient supply system consisting of organic recycling, green manuring, scientific crop rotations and the use of the minimum essential mineral fertilizers. Because of the unusual possibilities now open for raising productivity of both crops and farm animals, we can release marginal land from annual crops and place them under sylvi-pastoral or sylvi-horticultural or other agro-forestry systems of land and water management. We can minimise or avoid the use of chemical pesticides through integrated systems of pest management.

Similarly, where water is scarce, modern irrigation methods can be modified and simplified to fit the needs of small holders. Advances in molecular biology provide scope for the development of an integrated genetic conservation strategy, ranging from biosphere reserves and other forms of *in situ* conservation, to the creation of DNA libraries. Above all, the computer and communication revolutions have given us unusual powers for effective monitoring and dissemination of environmental information.

Our Conference will strive to draw a balance sheet of successes and setbacks since the launch of the World Conservation Strategy in 1980. While we should draw appropriate lessons from all environmental disasters, we should not overlook the fact that impressive progress has been made during recent years in arousing widespread awareness on environmental issues. Awareness leads to analysis of problems, identification of solutions and thus to appropriate action.

In this context, I would like to cite the recent initiative of the government of our host country in launching an *Africa 2000* programme. By commiting financial and technical resources to this programme for a period of fifteen years, Canada is demonstrating how an ecological emergency should be dealt with by donor nations. It should be obvious that to heal the wounds caused by an ecological emergency, we must learn to labour and to wait in order to achieve meaningful, long-term results.

Canada has shown how problems for which national solutions are possible can be tackled with thoroughness. For example, concerns about the quality and quantity of Canada's water led to an inquiry on Federal water policy. The report of the Pearse Inquiry Committee entitled *Currents of Change,* published in 1985, provides a framework for the sustainable use of Canada's water resources. Similarly, a Standing Committee of the Canadian Senate recommended measures for preventing soil degradation. I would urge all delegates to this Conference to spend a little time to understand how our Canadian colleagues are giving content and reality to the concept of sustainable development.

Another significant development is the growth of regional cooperation among organisations of countries in the Sahel, Southern Africa, Southeast Asia and South Asia. In this instance, we have a growing number of instruments for concerted action at sub-national, national, regional and global levels. These could become powerful instruments in meeting such challenges as land degradation, water pollution, species extinction, acid rain, ozone depletion, carbon dioxide build-up, disposal of toxic and nuclear wastes, and the protection of Antarctica. Above all, they could help to focus attention on methods of promoting sustainable liveli-hood security for the poor, and thereby arrest the influx of environmental refugees into towns and cities.

Mrs. Gro Harlem Brundtland, Prime Minister of Norway and Chairman of WCED, reminded us that "more people will be added to the planet in the 5000 days remaining between now and the end of the century than existed at the beginning of this century." She em-phasised the need for "new concepts of management that both preserve the es-sential sovereignty of the individual, his culture, community and nation, and permit the degree of management at the regional and global level needed to guide our common destiny on our one Earth."

I would now like to share with you some thoughts on how we can convert our concerns into concrete action to promote sustainable development. Ex-amining the linkages among environ-ment, food security, agriculture and forestry, an Advisory Committee of the World Commission on Environment and Development concluded that we should strengthen the tools available to foster the *sustainable* and *equitable* use of our life support systems and natural endowments. Three recommendations of that Panel deserve the consideration of this Conference and IUCN.

International Code for the Sustainable and Equitable Use of Life Support Sys-tems

We have adequate knowledge today to draw up a code giving broad guidelines on how basic life support systems can be used in a sustainable manner. Such a code should indicate what may be done at the political, professional and public levels to achieve accelerated economic growth without harm to long-term terrestrial and aquatic produc-tivity. For the purpose of such a code, *conservation* should be defined as a *guarantee of livelihood security to all people at all times.*

Any international code will consist of elements which may not be relevant to every country. The real value of such a code will lie in the impetus and guidelines it provides for the develop-ment of national, sub-national and regional codes. A detailed national code could provide the basic founda-tion on which sustainable use of the natural endowments of that country can be promoted. Fortunately, several inter-national charters and resolutions al-ready exist, such as the World Charter for Nature and the World Soil Charter. These will be helpful in developing in-ternational and national codes for sus-tainable and equitable use of the natural assets of each country.

Implementing the Code: Promotion of grassroots-level people's associations for sustainable development.

A code by itself will have little value unless effective means to implement it are also developed. A code for the sus-tainable use of environmental assets will need the support of three major groups for its effective implementation. The first is *government*. National, and where appropriate, provincial govern-ments will have to develop incentives and disincentives to promote conserva-tion-based development. Secondly, the *mass media* will play a key role in promoting the proper use of national as-sets and preventing their abuse. Third-ly, and most importantly, the *public* will have to be the principal agents for effective implementation of the code.

Unfortunately, grassroot-level people's associations which help to mobilise community activities in the sustainable use of land and water, in the conservation of flora and fauna and in the prevention of atmospheric and terrestrial pollution, do not exist in most countries. In most developed and in some developing countries, non-governmental organisations perform these tasks with varying degrees of success. However, NGOs tend to remain unique organisations with specific limited functions and thus do not become universal. This is why we should take steps to promote *associations for sustainable development* at the village level in each country.

Schools, colleges and universities should take the lead in spearheading this movement. In most developing countries, youth below the age of 21 years constitutes over 50 percent of the population. The future not only belongs to them but depends on them. Therefore, starting with the village school, educational institutions can become the meeting places for these associations for sustainable development. The agenda for debate and decision in their meetings could include such items as:

* Promoting a symphonic system of agriculture which would lead to a continuous improvement in productivity without harming long-term land and water production potential;

* meeting village fuelwood and fodder requirements;

* substituting farm-grown inputs for market-purchased ones;

* providing safe drinking water for all;

* upgrading degraded lands;

* ensuring the livelihood security of village people who do not own land, livestock, trees or other assets; and

* organising community genetic conservation programmes such as a community seed bank.

Village-level associations can join to form provincial and national federations. National federations for sustainable development could in turn assemble to form a global federation which might meet every five years for a progress review.

Environment Amnesty

In Amnesty International, we have a valuable mechanism for monitoring and publicising human rights violations. We urgently need a similar organisation characterised by political neutrality, professional integrity and credibility to monitor natural heritage abuses. While human rights violations affect individuals, human heritage violations impair life support systems such that genetic damage may result in future generations. Natural heritage violations undermine the livelihood security of present and future populations, particularly of the poor. *Environment Amnesty* would bring to public notice prominent cases of damage resulting from the desire of some to make personal profit out of public property.

*****

IUCN, as the world's largest, most representative and most experienced alliance of conservation agencies, groups and individuals belonging to both government and non-governmental sectors should take the lead in implementing these proposals so that the World Conservation Strategy remains not a dream but an accomplishment. Today, after six years, we find that the uni-dimensional thinking and implementation structures existing both in government and in private enterprise are inadequate to meet the challenge of the multi-dimensional and multi-faceted problems we face in making development ecologically-sustainable.

This Conference will be worthwhile if we are able to identify methods of cooperative endeavour which can bring political leaders, professional experts and the public to work together in a mutually-supportive manner, so that we are able to achieve a proper match between the challenge of nature and the response of the inhabitants of spaceship earth.

CONFERENCE ON CONSERVATION AND DEVELOPMENT: IMPLEMENTING THE WORLD CONSERVATION STRATEGY

Welcoming Address

The Honourable Thomas M. McMillan, P.C., M.P.
Minister of the Environment
Ottawa, Canada

Distinguished guests and visitors, ladies and gentlemen, friends:

It is my great pleasure to welcome to Canada so many outstanding men and women from around the world. How fitting that this Conference is taking place at the beginning of Canada's celebrations of Environment Week. I am especially pleased, in the context of Environment Week, to have this opportunity to discuss the World Conservation Strategy and its implications for Canada. Canada's support of the Strategy is unswerving and enthusiastic. I urge you to read the report prepared by my Department and distributed to everyone present tonight. It details how Canada is working to meet World Conservation Strategy priorities: to maintain essential ecological processes and life-support systems; to preserve genetic diversity; and to manage resources on a sustained use basis. The report is a tribute not only to the officials of Environment Canada who worked to make it possible, but also to the spirit of cooperation and goodwill on the part of the provinces and territories which helped prepare it.

I have recently embarked on a world conservation strategy of my own: to make Canadians more aware of the international implications of the environment, by discussing both the World Conservation Strategy and the World Commission on Environment and Development, whenever appropriate. My concern is that, unless Canadians are more aware of the environment in an international context, they will be tempted to forget long-term needs and goals or to treat discussion of the long-term as implying a lack of urgency.

It does not! The natural environment will not wait. It has rhythms, logic and imperatives of its own. Indeed, one does not have to subscribe to any particular religion or, for that matter, to any religion at all, to acknowledge that the nature of our world is that it is systematic, ordered and delicate, to a degree that should inspire both awe and anxiety in us.

The environment is vulnerable to forces that we can control and to those that, with all our ingenuity, we cannot. When Mount St. Helen erupts or typhoons sweep Southeast Asia, the media tend to portray nature as being "on a rampage" or as having gone wild; not acting normally. But what if it is not? What if the ebb and flow of natural phenomena adhere to a rationale to which we are simply not privy? We certainly cannot shrug and turn away from the human consequences of tragedy; but, at the same time, we need to understand that there are limits to our ability to manipulate the world around us.

We can, of course, modify and even predict nature, but we must accept that we cannot hope to conquer it - nor should we. We can and we *must* learn to live in harmony with it. Historically, humans have indulged themselves in smug assumptions that they understood the world in which they existed. Before the 15th century, that world was conceptualised as a plate, with finite edges from which people fell into nothingness. How shattering to the collective ego it must have been to discover that the world was an orb, that it was not the centre of the universe and that it followed an assigned ellipse around a sun.

Are we really much smarter than the members of the Flat Earth Society? Or is our modern "understanding" of the planet Earth as egocentrically infantile as it was in the heyday of flat earth? It is only recently that we have begun to realise that science, which we once thought was our passport to a living heaven, has its limits. Science, after all, brought us detergents - but detergents brought us rivers and lakes foaming at the shores. Science brought us pesticides, and pesticides brought us thin-shelled bird eggs and no birds. We have been forced to trade the recklessness of a world, comfortably conceived as endless, for a sober recognition that our world is part of a system - a very strict system in which each action engenders a reaction and in which each act has a consequence well beyond our immediate experience.

But we have not even begun to explore those consequences. We can formulate chemicals that are supposed to make our lives better. We can even detect the presence of minute amounts of those chemicals in our drinking water. But we have not yet mobilised the will to find out what those chemicals, once present, actually do to us, to the water or, for that matter, the universe. Compounds that we think are beneficial could, for all we know, be harmful. We just aren't sure. And we don't know because we haven't always applied ourselves to the task of finding out.

We are finally beginning to understand that our eagerness to protect *our* atmosphere, *our* water and *our* land from the dangers of pollution, however praiseworthy, is little more than environmental ethnocentricity. It ignores the very nature of Nature - that pollution has no address and it respects no international flag. If we learn nothing else from the tragedy at Chernobyl, let us at least vow that we have finally learned the lesson of environmental internationalism. What one country does to abuse its own environment can, and often does, have profoundly harmful effects thousands of miles, even countries, away from the original source.

There is another relatively recent lesson that we have still not taken totally to heart: the earth is not a globe travelling without consequence through nothingness; it is, in Buckminister Fuller's felicitous phrase, "spaceship

Earth" - an enclosed entity swaddled in layers of atmosphere.

Accepting just that one fact remains the most difficult environmental challenge of our time - because it precedes any commitment to genuine reform. Essentially, the spaceship concept places great burdens on us, not in some comfortably remote future, but now, today, this minute. It says that everything we do on the spaceship has consequences - consequences in both space and time. In other words, our actions do affect the space beyond our space and generations beyond our own.

Nonetheless, we continue to burn fossil fuels, although it is more than ten years since scientists began warning that growing amounts of carbon dioxide, the direct result of burning those fuels, were leading to the "greenhouse effect."

Here is just some of what we can expect. On a world scale we may see, even within the next decade, disastrous flooding, heat waves and monsoons. Closer to home, in Canada, by the year 2050, the Arctic temperature may be nine degrees higher and the southern part of the country, where most Canadians live, will average about three degrees warmer. Ours is a vast land with a complex repertoire of environmental responses and we will suffer in many ways: my own province of Prince Edward Island, in the east, will be eroded as water levels rise by a metre. In central Canada there will be droughts, increases in forest fires and insect infestations, as well as more industrial problems that result from decreasing water levels in the Great Lakes. Our western provinces, already suffering from generally dry summers,

face even more tragic droughts in the future.

Perhaps most worrying of all is that change, if and when it occurs, may not be neat and orderly - it could happen too rapidly and be even more extreme than we now posit. The hard fact is that we simply don't know.

And if we did know, how would we respond? Human behaviour to date suggests that recognising a problem, even identifying its root causes, does not always mean that the means, or the will, exists to find solutions.

For example, the United Nations Food and Agricultural Organization has mapped the results of over-harvesting of wood for fuel in Third World countries - where it is still the main source of energy. Vast stretches of eastern Brazil, most of the western rim of South America north of the 20th parallel, large areas of Mexico, all of the Indian sub-continant, much of Southeast Asia - millions and millions of hectares are listed in one of three categories: likely to suffer a fuelwood crisis by the year 2000; inadequate or over-exploited; or already so depleted that it can no longer offer even a minimum supply of energy. And all of this in the part of the world with lush rain forests that have been a legend since Europeans first set foot beyond their own borders!

Here is proof, if proof is needed, of the old truism that poverty is the root of all evil. Hunger-wracked countries are forced to sacrifice their precious natural resources for urgent short-term purposes, at the expense of their immediate environment, of that of other countries and of future generations. It is a measure of the harsh realities of nature that people seeking to keep themselves warm today are, at the same time, ensuring agricultural poverty for generations to come.

We all know the litany of environmental damage being wreaked everywhere in the world: the greenhouse effect, which threatens to overheat the world by wrapping it in a layer of carbon dioxide; the dangers of a nuclear winter; arctic haze, reminding us that air-borne pollution travels long distances from its industrial origins; lessened genetic diversity; and destruction of natural heritage so essential to human survival. Mankind's life support systems - the air we breathe, the water we drink, the soil that provides our food - are under siege. A steadily burgeoning population means that more and more people will be trying to live on less environmental abundance, much of which is being squandered by sheer recklessness.

The question is: how can we stop this spiral? It would be impertinent for Canadians to lecture or moralise. It would be easy for Canada's Minister of the Environment to do so in the comfort of his own country, where the average family income is $20,000 annually, an amount greater than that of entire villages elsewhere. It is another thing to deal, as we must, with structural economic problems of countries where dire need dictates environmentally disastrous decisions.

Even if the more fortunate nations like Canada wished to lecture those less blessed, we could not do so with anything approaching a clean conscience. After all, as I have already emphasised, it is only now - very late indeed - that we ourselves, out of sheer necessity,

have begun to exercise good stewardship over our own resources.

We still have a great deal to do. Lest any person in this room doubt that, let me point out that, since I began speaking to you, more than 1200 tonnes of acid fallout have rained on Europe and North America. The rain has fallen on the Washington Monument and the Lincoln Memorial, which are already acid damaged. In Canada it has fallen on our Parliament houses, on the legislative buildings of both Ontario and Nova Scotia, on our beloved sandstone churches of Prince Edward Island. In Poland, it has fallen on the eerily blank face of a 15th century classic statue of the Virgin Mary, whose features it has already eaten away. It has fallen on the Parthenon of ancient Greece, which neither people nor nature could destroy in 2500 years, but which is threatened by acid rain in our own lifetimes.

Nonetheless, we should pay no attention to those who counsel despair. In Canada, people *are* becoming increasingly environment conscious. In fact, every serious study shows that, even in times of restraint, they are willing to make reasonable sacrifices to safeguard their shared and common resources: air, water, land.

Moreover, the country is making gains in its fight to improve the quality of the environment. The Federal Government, provinces and territories are working together, in a spirit of mutual determination, to cut pollution emission levels and to develop an increasing number of joint programmes.

Bilaterally, Canada is working steadily with the Americans to solve the two major issues facing us: acid rain and toxic-waste clean-up. The Americans, without doubt, are beginning to understand that acid rain and toxic chemical issues are more than just that - they are tests of goodwill and friendship on both sides. And if we historic, economic and even familial friends cannot reach agreement on environmental issues - when the stakes on both sides are so high and so obvious - where in this world is agreement possible? And on what issues?

Internationally, the very existence of the World Conservation Strategy means that there is a growing awareness of the global importance of the environment. It draws to world attention, in a way never before attempted, the stresses being placed on the environment we hold in common as citizens - not of any one country, but of the world community.

I believe that the Strategy and other programmes that conform to the Strategy will be successful. Why? Because they are *not* merely well-intentioned but naïve experiments in altruism: they are hard-headed, bottom-line projects based on the recognition that *every* country is entitled to operate in its own best interests - but that *every* country's best interests are served by an environment that will support life and, in time, even confer the benefits of a genuine abundance that come from clean air, pure water and healthy soil.

The Chinese have an old saying which counsels that, unless a person changes course, he will end up where he is headed. We citizens of the world have been headed where we don't want to go: close to environmental annihilation. The World Conservation Strategy offers us a better course - one that must always be firmly before us so that we can ensure that our every move is made with an eye to it.

I congratulate you all on your leadership in this most important area of public policy. I wish you continued success and I pledge Canada's unflagging support for your noble cause.

Thank you.

CONFERENCE ON CONSERVATION AND DEVELOPMENT: IMPLEMENTING THE WORLD CONSERVATION STRATEGY

Greetings

HRH Prince Philip, Duke of Edinburgh
President, WWF International
London, United Kingdom

The people of this world face many serious issues but few are as vital to the future welfare of humanity as the conservation of our natural environment.

The explosion of the human population, the consequent increasing demands on living resources, and the pollution caused by human activities are putting intolerable pressures on dwindling wild species of flora and fauna.

Conservation of nature and projects intended to achieve any kind of development are often seen as being mutually exclusive. Any development which threatens the continuing productivity of natural resources may create a short-term benefit, but will result in long-term degradation.

Most of the world's deserts are man-made by communities which outgrew nature's capacity to supply their needs. Under modern conditions, increasing demand and diminishing supply threatens the whole world with similar results on a much larger scale.

The International Conference on Conservation and Development comes at a critical point in world history; the survival of future generations of human, animal and plant populations will depend on its outcome.

CONFERENCE ON CONSERVATION AND DEVELOPMENT: IMPLEMENTING THE WORLD CONSERVATION STRATEGY

Greetings

H.E. Kenneth David Kaunda
President of the Republic of Zambia
Lusaka, Zambia

I am pleased, on behalf of the Zambian people and on my own behalf, to congratulate you on convening this important Conference. When I reflect on the great natural richness and beauty of this world, I never cease to feel a sense of awe. Within the soils of our nations, in our teeming wildlife, and in our great oceans, rivers and wetlands, lies enormous potential to bring forth benefits indefinitely: food, fuel and fibre to provide for our welfare and for our development; unique natural features to feed our imagination and our intellect. And yet, we are far from realising this potential.

In many parts of the world the productivity of our natural resources is not being tapped. In others, poverty or ignorance is leading to abuse of the very resources upon which nations must depend for the future. In our development efforts, we have at times lost that sense of balance with nature which was innate to our ancestors, and we have polluted, wasted, neglected and destroyed.

It is clear that we have made great advances in the world of science and technology, but the subtler arts of managing our natural resources have, until recently, taken second place. This is why I commend the World Conservation Strategy, the efforts applied to implement it and the principles upon which it stands.

In Zambia we have long been concerned with conserving our natural heritage, and I am pleased to state that we have taken up what we can of the far-reaching ideas of the World Conservation Strategy. A Zambian National Conservation Strategy has been prepared, and various projects deriving from this have already begun for us in Zambia. We feel this is a major step forward in developing our conservation efforts.

In order, however, to be true stewards of the earth's resources, there is still far to go in Zambia and elsewhere. My delegates at your noteworthy Conference are eager to learn from the gathered experience of implementing the World Conservation Strategy and to contribute what they can. Your Conference is indeed a great opportunity.

I wish you every success.

SUSTAINABLE AND EQUITABLE DEVELOPMENT: AN EMERGING PARADIGM

Overview

Peter Jacobs
Julia Gardner
David A. Munro

These *Proceedings* reflect a striking convergence of thought about the fundamental issues we face in pursuing a sustainable quality of life for all. The perspectives and prescriptions for sustainable development expressed at the Ottawa Conference are not entirely original. They are derived from the World Conservation Strategy but go beyond it, reflecting the experience of those who conceptualised the Strategy and tried to apply it during the six years following its publication. Conference participants signficantly enlarged the context of the Strategy to make it more widely relevant. In particular, cultural and economic aspects of sustainable development were introduced, as were issues of appropriate technology, indigenous peoples and populations. But these perspectives are not limited to simply reflecting the conventional wisdom of the day. They are, rather, at the forefront of a new way of modelling problems and solutions that is attracting an expanding group of adherents. They form the basis of an emerging paradigm that focuses on equitable and sustainable development.

The reader may be alarmed at the breadth of material covered in this Introduction. How can a single volume of papers or a week of discussion on sustainable development presume to address all the seeming problems of the globe, and all that we think about them? Conference participants would likely reply "How can it not?" Indeed, the overriding requirement for sustainable development emerging from this critique of the World Conservation Strategy was that we must view life and earth as one integrated system; if we analyse elements of that system in isolation, we seriously compromise any useful understanding of how to achieve sustainable and equitable development.

Recognising the need to provide the right tools for holistic approaches to problem-solving, the perspective advocated by those who addressed the Conference Plenary Session is particularly challenging. Meetings like the Ottawa Conference drive the evolution of new tools through the exchange of ideas among a diverse group of experts and decision-makers. Indeed, the combined experience of Ottawa participants is as close to comprehensive as might be achieved in any one setting. Every such meeting is significant as an opportunity for furthering the emerging consensus, among re-formed groups of people, in new fora and in different words. Every time nascent ideas are exchanged they become more coherent, their potential for expanding beyond current conceptual limits becomes more apparent, and more people internalise the wisdom encompassed by them. Each participant in the exchange plays a crucial role by taking ideas back to the groups to which she or he belongs, and thus, incrementally, subtly, profoundly, shapes tomorrow's wisdom. Thus societies change, paradigms shift.

The concept of sustainable development decends from two closely-related Western paradigms of conservation.[1] The first evolved from the perception that nature should be preserved; it was a reaction against the *laissez-faire* economic theory that considered living resources as free goods, external to the development process, essentially infinite and inexhaustible (Marsh, 1965). Conservation action consisted of saving pristine landscapes, untouched ecosystems and rare species from the onslaught of development (Halle and Furtado). The second was derived from the moral injunction to act as a steward of the landscape (Leopold, 1966; McHarg, 1969; Shepard, 1967) and responded to warnings of the *Silent Spring* (Carson, 1962) and *Limits to Growth* (Meadows *et. al.*, 1972). Both approaches initiated significant changes in development practices: to some extent environmental issues have been in-

ternalised in development; environment departments have been formed; and environmental impact assessment procedures developed and applied.

The adoption of these conservation institutions and processes conformed to the criteria outlined by Khun (1960) in his analysis of the structure of scientific revolutions. That is, the conservation paradigms associated with "preservation" and "regulation" were instrumental in developing new perspectives on problems that were sufficiently open-ended to attract a new group of conservation practitioners. Both approaches responded to a real and perceived crisis of confidence within the conservation community of the developed world. The emerging paradigm of sustainable development likewise responds to the demands of a crisis for new frameworks and new assumptions. In Khun's words:

So long as the tools a paradigm supplies continue to prove capable of solving the problems it defines, science (and other pursuits) moves fastest and penetrates most deeply through confident employment of those tools... retooling is an extravagance to be reserved for the occasion that demands it. The significance of crises is the indication they provide that an occasion for retooling has arrived (Khun, 1962).

The World Conservation Strategy Conference was itself the beginning of a process of retooling. As well as setting priorities and frameworks to describe the new tools, participants in the Ottawa Conference clearly acknow-

---

Note: Bracketed references to authors not followed by date refer to articles in this volume.

1.   Derived from the Greek *paradigm* or pattern, a paradigm has been characterised as a framework of thought, a scheme for understanding and explaining certain aspects of reality (Ferguson, 1980).

ledged the crises precipitating this paradigm shift as "the occasion demanding it."

CRISIS AND POTENTIAL

We find ourselves in a time of "deep and pervasive change" (Khosla) in which critical environmental problems relate to a complex network of resource uses and process (Warford). The North-South impasse is one aspect of a multi-faceted crisis related to the loss of a sense of wholeness (Nerfin; Sunkel). A sectoral, project-by-project approach to problem solving has aided and rationalised profligate resource use (Gadgil). Lack of coherent, motivating objectives has caused bureaucuracies to stagnate and has limited their response to the crisis (Walker).

The international economic order, or the "contemporary, ascendant, transnational style of development" (Sunkel) has imposed a centralised, dependent form of global development which services the political, economic and security interests of developed countries at the cost of increasing poverty and environmental degradation in developing countries (Fadaka, Workshop 15). This crisis of imbalance pervades the interconnected issues of over-population, socio-political injustice and the threat of nuclear war, as well as poverty and environmental degradation (Salas; Nerfin; Workshop 9). Even if the exploiting countries attempted to rationalise the chain of interdependence that their style of development involves, they would fail because the chain depends on increasing global prosperity, based, in large measure, on

fossil fuels that are not inexhaustible (McNeely).

With recognition of the inadequacy of current development styles and with increasing knowledge of the essential conditions of life comes hope for change (Salas, Workshop 10). As Latin American countries, for example, face structural and environmental crises, discussions of environment and development begin to converge, and the opportunity arises to create an environmental conscience able to change the thrust of development toward sustainability and an improved quality of life (Sunkel). Likewise, at the global level, this time of dynamic and complex imbalance should be exploited to support the creative development of tools for change (Khosla, Workshop 6).

The change now called for is fundamental; we need an alternative society, another type of development that is linked with structural transformation (Nerfin). The ability to practice design and management for sustainable development "will require substantially different paradigms, institutional structures and methodological tools than have been considered adequate before" (Khosla, Workshop 17). We need careful definitions of sustainable resource use so that progress toward sustainability can be measured, monitored and evaluated (Workshop 20). At the same time, previous theories will continue to be tested for their utility, and new solutions will incorporate mixtures of the old (Galtung, Workshop 12), a process characteristic of paradigm shifts. Concrete solutions to environmental problems will largely depend on a new organisational capacity of society as a whole, based on the cultural values of different communities, their creativity and their potential for innovation (Nerfin, Bugnicourt, Workshop 11).

THE PRIORITIES BEHIND THE NEW PARADIGM

The emerging paradigm of sustainable development, reviewed, expanded and embellished at the Ottawa Conference, seeks to develop strategies and tools to respond to five broad requirements:

* integration of conservation and development;

* satisfaction of basic human needs;

* achievement of equity and social justice;

* provision for social self-determination and cultural diversity; and

* maintenance of ecological integrity.

These challenges are so strongly interrelated that it is difficult, and indeed, unhelpful to arrange them in hierarchical or priority order. Each is both a goal itself and a prerequisite to the achievement of the others. The first (which in combination with the fifth provides the theme of the World Conservation Strategy), could be seen as a synonym for sustainable development, and as encompassing all others. To advance equity and social justice has been suggested to be of such importance that the concept of sustainable development, as outlined in the World Conservation Strategy, should now be expanded to "sustainable and equitable

development" (Swaminathan), a perception reflected in the title to this overview.

Integrating Conservation And Development

Disjunction and disequilibrium among socio-economic, political, cultural and environmental factors have been identified as a root cause of global crises. To seek an understanding of the linkages and to achieve balance among population, resources, environment and development can thus be seen as a necessity and a normative point of reference (Salas; Galtung). Balance and maturity in nature and in human social space override market equilibrium as indicators of appropriate development (Galtung). Indonesian authorities, for example, stress the need to redistribute population, raise the carrying capacity of the land, industrialise and develop the service sector, without increasing environmental damage or jeopardising life support systems (Salim; Workshop 16).

Meeting the requirement to integrate conservation and development may be approached in two ways. Conservation may be regarded as a by-product of a people-oriented set of overriding goals (Walker), fully recognising the productive potential of the environment (Leff), or it may be concluded that the new, sustainable orientation depends on the environment and on a "long-run ecological perspective" (Sunkel). Prescott-Allen suggests that the World Conservation Strategy takes a pro-development stand, reflecting the awareness that people and nature are interdependent and that there are many different, acceptable, ways of using nature. The two ways of approaching the conservation-development equation rarely differ substantively. For practical purposes, however, some would argue a need for the ethical perspective and positioning as a means of providing a solution to this chicken and egg problem (Workshop 11). Khosla's "science of design" presents a possible middle ground in which conservation goes beyond the requirement of not closing options toward making maximum use of the biosphere to satisfy human needs.

Satisfaction of Basic Human Needs

Recognising that interdependence of conservation and development is essential in seeking satisfaction of human needs, de Haes' "message," that nature's capital must be conserved because all human needs and concerns depend on it, is fundamental to the justification of conservation measures in most societies. In Zambia, for example, any form of conservation has to relate to "Man," to fit that country"s humanistic philosophy. The goal of Zambia's National Conservation Strategy is to satisfy the basic needs of the people by modifiying and creating development (Mukutu and Mwale; Workshop 1/2). Similarly, conservation is intended to meet the basic material, spiritual and cultural needs of the Nepalese (Amatya and Naysmith). Gadgil argues that an awareness of the benefits to be derived from "prudent" resource use in the satisfaction of long-term individual and group needs is the only viable motivation for conservation (Workshop 3). Swaminathan concurs and recommends that conservation be defined as "a guarantee of livelihood security to all people at all times."

The World Conservation Strategy could be enhanced by explicitly acknowledging requirements for improving the quality of life (Mosley). "Need fulfilment," "welfare of people and communities" and "sustainable livelihood" are all concepts that suggest the requirement for sustainable development (Keith and Simon; Waldegrave).

Equity and Social Justice

The importance of equity and social justice to the achievement of sustainable development was clearly recognised at Ottawa. In his opening address, Swaminathan set the tone by calling for an international code for the sustainable and equitable use of life support systems. Walker was among those who expressed similar views: he suggested that social justice within the rule of law should be the style of operation in all endeavours.

Beyond its obvious ethical foundations, the priority of justice and egalitarianism has both practical and motivational implications. Historial patterns of resource use repeatedly demonstrate the importance of commonality of interest and egalitarianism in environmentally prudent behaviour (Gadgil; Salas). Compared to megaprojects for energy development, recent experience with small-scale projects that are more equitable in distributing costs and benefits in the circumpolar north has shown a lessening of conflict and social risk (Keith and Simon; Workshops 4, 14). In some countries, a knowledge of the concerns of the poor and their conditions of life, combined with responsible government, has permitted an equitable response to needs of the poor which led, in turn, to a reduction of the population growth rate (Salas).

The concept of equity, social justice, and the related notion of commonality of interest also have pervasive environmental ramifications globally. In Khosla's words:

The threats to rational management of the resource base come from consumerism of the affluent and ... basic [requirements] of the poor, demonstrating the importance of the equity criterion not simply on ethical or ideological grounds but as matter of straight planetary survival.

Implications for international environmental law are complex, considering that some countries have identifiable interests in life support systems and genetic resources situated wholly within another State's territory. Burhenne and her colleagues recommend an explicit connection between duties and rights to address reciprocity and transcend issues of sovereignty. International economic influences on equity are at least as problematic as reflected in the global crisis described earlier. A recurring suggestion for alleviating inequalities of the international economic order is that developed countries should help developing countries attain the capability of managing their own resources and environmental affairs (Fadaka). This relates closely to the next challenge, that of self-determination.

Social Self-determination and Cultural Diversity

Closely connected to equity and justice, self-determination and cultural diversity are valued conditions of human life, basic to the achievement of sustainable development (Workshops 11, 12).

As illustrated in Indonesia, conservation plays an important role in development that is oriented around individual development in terms of relationships between man, God and society (Salim). From another viewpoint, self-reliance and the capacity to choose and design one's own future can be seen as a necessary precondition for sustainable development and conservation (Khosla). Aboriginal experience in the circumpolar north confirms this viewpoint, in that externally imposed systems of development, conservation and knowledge have greatly hindered sustainable development, while groups with decision-making rights have been able to influence the direction of conservation and development (Keith and Simon; Workshop 13). These experiences highlight the significance of cultural diversity, the corollary to social self-determination, by illustrating that development must be culturally appropriate to the status and concerns of local people (Keith and Simon; Workshop 3).

Several other authors identified the strategic implications of these imperatives. Suggestions include ensuring that biome-based conservation strategies promote self-reliance rather than dependence (McNeely; Workshop 7/8), that the objective of the World Conservation Strategy becomes a more people-oriented one that liberates or enhances our essential humanity (Walker), and that bottom-up, people participatory pressures should be enhanced in the WCS process (Thacher).

Ecological Integrity

The priority of maintaining ecological integrity, as it has been used in the discussion of other requirements to sustainable development, is essentially a more explicit statement of the concept of conservation. It is well-reflected by the objectives of the World Conservation Strategy in maintaining essential ecological processes and life support systems, preservation of genetic diversity, and sustainable utilisation of species and ecosystems. Little more needs to be said on this topic because it is clearly integral to the foregoing discussion, but a few observations from Conference papers are relevant.

Halle and Furtado expressed the view that goals relating to the protection of diversity and ecosystems seem to have been better covered, in practice, than the promotion of sustainable use. Mosley emphasised the role of protected areas in the maintenance of ecological integrity. McNeely urged that we not rely on reserves alone to achieve conservation, that we should give more attention to controlling human influences on local ecosystems. Regardless of whether protected areas or a more comprehensive approach to conservation dominates, we lack indicators and monitoring systems with which to evaluate progress in implementing the three objectives of the World Conservation Strategy (Prescott-Allen; Workshop 20).

TOWARD A PRACTICE OF SUSTAINABLE DEVELOPMENT

Having examined the setting for the merging paradigm of sustainable and equitable development and its broad goals and priorities, the remainder of this overview addresses the process of and frameworks for change associated with the new paradigm. These amount to an emerging design for the practice of sustainable development.

Processes and Perspectives

The five requirements of sustainable development discussed above are the broad goals of the new practice. More specific versions of these goals and definitions of processes that would lead to them must be sought. The global crisis that we face demands a period of transformation to accomodate the emergence of new paradigms. It also presents an opportunity to review the problem-solving process. Three frameworks for change will be discussed: they are analytical/strategic, ideological and institutional. Priorities and frequently-recurring methods underlying these frameworks lead to the definition below of groups of practices as goal-seeking, adaptive and integrated.

Goal seeking in this context might be defined as action that is pro-active, initiating, value-oriented, and alternative-generating. The World Conservation Strategy has been praised as adequately anticipatory but criticised as neglecting active initiatives (Sunkel; Salim). Swaminathan's "code" of sustainable development is positive in nature; it indicates what should be done. Likewise Galtung's "alternative" economic theory has a normative point of reference. An understanding of ideological frameworks is especially important in the selection, continuous refinement and re-evalution of the goals sought.

Adaptive processes are also moderating, dynamic, experimental, learning, responsive, evolutionary or interactive. They involve goal-seeking, but they go beyond that and emphasise feedback and self-reflection. Following the adaptive approach, the process of developing a strategy like a national conservation strategy is as important as the product which emerges from it (Amatya and Naysmith; Mosley; Workshop 14). In some senses, the process **is** the product. Khosla's "phase space" approach to design is a good example of this process. It allows the plotting of the evolutionary path of a system over time, showing the effects of action and feedback that lead the system toward different states - growing, static, homeostatic or developing. Aspects of these states would be combined to attain sustainable development.

Integrated processes recognise the dynamic interconnectedness of things. They are interactive and holistic, and involve dialogue and negotiation. They facilitate the maintenance of diversity or variety and are integral to processes of adaption and goal-seeking. An integrated approach recognises the need to consider the higher levels in which a problem is embedded and the lower levels, or smaller scales, which are affected (Khosla). The World Conservation Strategy has been said to inadequately support the integration of disciplines, institutions and interests, or a cross-sectoral approach to problem-solving (Sunkel; Walker; Workshop 5).

The role of these processes in the practice of sustainable development pervades the analytical/strategic, ideological and institutional frameworks mentioned hereafter.

Analytical/Strategic Frameworks

Of the three types of frameworks for the practice of sustainable development, the analytical/strategic type, with its reliance on conventional tools, techniques and theories of analysis, retains most of the vestiges of paradigms that are being superceded.

Concurrent with the search for new problem-solving tools is a reassessment of the old. Existing data are clearly of continuing use and lead to the identification of gaps in the information base. In developing countries especially, more has to be learned about the present state of the environment (Khosla). Everywhere there needs to be a greater emphasis on better information in planning and decision-making (Halle and Furtado).

Available technology is also appreciated as a tool of continuing utility:

While careless technology can cause unmitigated environmental disasters, technologies carefully tailored to specific agro-ecological and socio-economic conditions can help to provide bread, together with freedom from environmental degradation on a sustainable basis (Swaminathan).

Similarly, economic theory, if used properly, can assist in the move toward sustainable development through its inputs to policy (Warford). However, the limitations of existing economic theory and analysis are increasingly obvious, and its relevance has decreased as it has fallen behind the move toward achieving sustainable development (Galtung; Warford; Salim). In particular, economists must come to understand environmental and behavioural linkages, in order to claculate the marginal opportunity costs that resource users must bear (Warford).

The need to take account of linkages between human and environmental systems (Galtung) is a clear analytical priority for sustainable development. An understanding of networks of resource use processes is essential to the integration of environmental management into social and economic policy (Warford). The understanding of networks or systems also allows the selection of appropriate scales of analysis and development, and the tools to match (Keith and Simon). This awareness of the relevance of scale (and timing) is crucial to the new approaches to problem solving. Only a multi-disciplinary, cross-sectoral approach can achieve the holistic perspective upon which these approaches depend (Warford; Amatya and Naysmith).

The integrated diagnosis of problems and a comprehensive consideration of alternatives should provide insights for policy and strategies which the search for immediate profits or technological solutions to specific problems cannot (Leff; Galtung). In Latin America, for example, an integrated systems-approach could facilitate recognition of the socio-cultural and resource potentialities of a region in short and long-term policies. These policies could then selectively alter the style of development toward a more sustainable one (Sunkel). Some have questioned whether the World Conservation Strategy, in its emphasis on tactical and strategic actions for conservation (Prescott-Allen), or on environmental management and planning (Sunkel), provides adequate tools for the design of broad policy. It has been said to neglect the need to incorporate the environmental dimension within overall socio-economic policies (Sunkel). Although the World Conservation Strategy does not provide specific guidelines on policy design, some observers believe that its principles have proven their worth in providing a fundamental, global rationale for local or national solutions to environmental problems

(Segnestam), and in promoting a scientific awareness of the communality of interest of personkind (Gadgil). In this sense, the World Conservation Strategy is seen not as a blueprint but as a guide that must be supplemented by country-specific measures in national conservation strategies (Halle and Furtado). The latter are in turn supported by appropriate local and regional measures (Mosley; Khosla), in concert with the importance of operating at appropriate levels. McNeely's biome approach defines a new scope for conservation strategies based on natural systems that transcend political boundaries (Workshop 7/8). International frameworks for the sharing of knowledge and expertise are also evolving in Latin America, Africa and the circumpolar north (Workshop 19).

As a framework for real policy development and conservation strategies, much potential is seen in the national conservation strategy process (Halle and Furtado; Mukutu; Kerr). At this level, the emphasis is on specific tactics and strategies as well as national policy. Amatya and Naysmith maintain that a national conservation strategy "must consist of a series of action plans that are realistic, simple in style and pragmatic in substance." As well as indicating immediate actions and long-term directions, the national conservation strategy should address procedures for implementation, monitoring, evaluation and review (Mosley).

Guidelines for such procedures could be usefully included in the World Conservation Strategy (Prescott-Allen), more fully recognising the adaptive and interactive processes involved in strategy development.

Integral to evaluation and review, and indeed to the setting of World Conservation Strategy objectives, is a strong value component.   Far from being neglected by speakers at the Ottawa Conference, this is the subject of the next section.

Ideological Frameworks

While analytical/strategic frameworks are closely connected to the processes of integration and adaptation, ideological frameworks define the process of goal-seeking. Discussion of the former inevitably tends toward the technical and the supposedly objective, but ideological considerations are necessarily broad and subjective. This is not to say that they are any less important; indeed, some authors hold that the reverse is true.

Walker takes a strong value position in contending that the World Conservation Strategy should embrace the upwelling of concern in the converging areas of development, environment, population and peace. He asks that legal and technical details not be emphasised at the expense of ideas, concepts and values that may provide indicators of the global view. Consideration of values at more local levels provides standards, indices and criteria for sustainable development. In defining goals and objectives, ideological factors like culture, religion and self-fulfillment are considered alongside technical, economic and ecological concerns. The norms that are thus defined guide the selection of desirable development options and the policies and strategies to achieve those options (Salim; Khosla).

The relationship between culture and values is carefully explored by Gadgil, who observes that the World Conservation Strategy:

> *does not adequately address itself to the question of how the different segments of the world community perceive the use of natural resources, how these perceptions relate to their cultures and in turn how they determine the priorities and policies of concern to the World Conservation Strategy.*

Simon feels that aboriginal ways of life in particular should be recognised in the Strategy, because:

> *Many regional and global issues can only be fairly and effectively dealt with if the emerging realities concerning indigenous peoples are fully taken into account.*

Similarly, national and local issues can only be resolved if the values of the host community are considered. Thus, Amatya and Naysmith require that the technical aspects of a National Conservation Strategy for Nepal accord with the social, cultural and economic values of the Nepalese. This kind of approach to national conservation strategy development ensures strategy formulation which helps to maintain existing cultural elements supportive of national conservation strategy goals (Salim; Gadgil).

Unfortunately, the traditions of some of the most dominant world cultures do not support sustainable development and the appropriate understanding and attitudes that must be cultivated as precursors of conservation (de Haes; Salim). Kerr, for example, acknowledges that community awareness and the promotion of a conservation ethic is important to the successful implementation of a National Conservation Strategy for Australia. The promotion of such understanding and ethics is usually achieved through education. Indeed, education is so central that de Haes claims it should be the conservationist's ultimate goal. He outlines educational processes which go beyond the simple spreading of information to include tasks such as selecting target audiences, tailoring the message to match the audience, and monitoring and evalution. Segnestam concurs with de Haes and suggests that better use could be made of the World Conservation Strategy for educational purposes. De Haes also believes that environmental education should be built into the formal education structures of countries. This brings us to the subject of institutional frameworks for sustainable development.

Institutional Frameworks

Institutional frameworks, or social structures for sustainable development, provide the foundation for all the practices outlined under analytical/strategic, and ideological frameworks. The central role of the functional support provided by institutions was noted by virtually every contributor to the Plenary Sessions of the World Conservation Strategy Conference.

Education was seen as critical to arousing public awareness and developing support for conservation. Another way of attaining support is through maximum involvement in the processes of conflict resolution and consensus building, which are associated with the formation of strategies for sustainable development. Following this line of reasoning, national conservation strategies should adopt an approach that

uses the political process, is participatory, pluralistic and non-specialist (Walker). And the process of national conservation strategy development should involve geographical and sectoral representation of government, NGO's, science, private sector and village interests throughout (Amatya and Naysmith). But while the process of developing a national conservation strategy may be a mechanism for consensus building (Halle and Furtado; Kerr; Mosley), it cannot stand on its own. To achieve the pervasive change heralded by the new paradigm, the broader institutional environment must be carefully considered.

Gadgil explains that resource use is institutionalised through rituals, customs and the codification of knowledge. However, the inertia of social frameworks may be such that it stifles the adaptive evolution of appropriate idioms. This is the situation we find ourselves in today, as outlined at the beginning of this overview and reinforced by Swaminathan:

> The unidimensional thinking and implementation structures we have, both in government and private enterprise, are inadequate to meet the challenge of the multi-dimensional and multi-faceted problems we face in making development ecologically sustainable.

Societies must build new kinds of institutions to deal with issues that involve resources and people. Solutions to the problems we face depend on a new organisational capacity that is based on participative, collaborative, democratic and decentralised decision-making (Khosla; Warford).

Decentralisation of government and its adoption of a more supportive, less directive role is called for, to enable increased participation and the consideration of ecological factors at the centres where decisions affecting development are made (Walker; Sunkel). And yet, to implement many practices for sustainable development, some public or State intervention is necessary (Sunkel; Warford; Waldegrave). Burhenne-Guilmin, *et. al.* make clear the importance of national and international law in providing appropriate devices for ensuring the sustainable use of ecosystems. Other authors emphasise the role of government in regulating the private and corporate sectors so that resource users are required to bear the marginal opportunity costs of environmental degradation now borne by society (Warford). Waldegrave holds that governments should ensure that environmental considerations form a basic input to corporate policies and planning from the outset of economic and industrial development. He calls on government to create a climate in which economic growth can be reconciled with concern for the environment, and public opinion prevails where scientific information is lacking.

The appropriate role of scientific institutions in the practice of sustainable development is implicit in the earlier discussion of the analytical and strategic frameworks. An additional suggestion from Khosla is relevant here: that "design professions must play a leadership role in evolving an approach that is both participatory and founded in value systems."

International institutions make vital contributions in the realm of environmental law, in supporting sustainable development policies of national governments, and in promoting a global perspective on environment and development (Burhenne-Guilmin *et. al.*; Salim; Halle and Furtado). International funding agencies can be especially influential in guiding large international investments to recipients and projects oriented toward sustainable development. Fadaka suggests "a range of process-oriented actions designed to increase the attention paid to environmental issues by development assistance agencies."

Beyond funding organisations and the corporate sector - the "merchant," and beyond government - the "prince," lies the autonomous power of people - the "citizen" (Nerfin). True grass-roots participation in sustainable development can be achieved only through human agencies that do not seek governmental or economic power, but try instead to limit the power of dominant social structures and enlarge that of individuals and communities. These agencies are variously termed citizens' movements, associations, the third system (Nerfin), grass-roots people's organisations, non-governmental organisations (Swaminathan; de Haes), non-profit organisations (Segnestam), and self-reliant institutions (Salim). Their roles include carrying out projects related to sustainable development; public advocacy and the practice of solidarity; "watchdog" surveillance of goverment and industry; education and the setting of directions and goals for change (Nerfin; de Haes; Segnestam; Salim). They operate at the levels of schools, villages, nations, regions and the globe. On the international scale, Swaminathan recommends establishing "Environment Amnesty" to monitor and publicise natural heritage abuses resulting from political corruption or personal or corporate greed. Several contributors call for increased support from government and funding organisations for citizen's associations, especially in developing countries (de Haes; Segnestam; Swaminathan; Salim).

In a more cautionary vein, Nerfin notes that these associations, as mechanisms for enabling people to assume autonomous power, must themselves be accountable and their role temporary, lest they become as dominant and bureaucratic as the structures whose power they set out to circumscribe. Citizens' associations ideally should not evolve into bureaucracies because their style of operation is not pyramidal or hierarchical but horizontal. People of like values and interests are linked not by power structures but by networks of communication.

This networking principle can extend beyond citizens' associations to encompass all sectors of society if Swaminathan's advice is followed: that we "identify methods of cooperative endeavour to bring together political leaders, professional experts and the public to work in a mutually supportive manner." It is heartening that one of the most vigorous streams of convergent thinking at the Conference flowed from the recognition that networking at appropriate scales, supported by interfacing institutions and the media, can engender a sense of fraternity and commonality of interest that holds great promise for achieving all the social and environmental goals compatible with sustainable development (Keith and Simon; Khosla; Gadgil; Swaminathan; Walker).

The practices appropriate to a new paradigm have already begun. The World Conservation Strategy has been assessed as a profoundly significant first step toward the integration of conservation and development. Specific suggestions for modifications and additions to be embodied in the World Conservation Strategy II have been made. The efforts of those who participated in the Workshops of the Ottawa Conference and who spoke at the Plenary Sessions will influence increasing numbers of practitioners, and ensure a successful shift to the paradigm of sustainable and equitable development.

INTEGRATING CONSERVATION AND DEVELOPMENT

Plenary Session 1

INTEGRATING CONSERVATION AND DEVELOPMENT

Plenary Session 1

M. Catley-Carlson, Chairperson
President, CIDA Canada
Quebec, Canada

The purpose of this Plenary was to promote discussion on what has proven to be the seminal core of the World Conservation Strategy - the need to integrate conservation and development. In introducing the session, Catley-Carlson noted that while all the world knows that conservation and development should be integrated, no one is quite sure how to do it most effectively.

Sunkel's theme framework paper, using Latin America as a case study of the evolving relationship between conservation and development, explained why the World Conservation Strategy has had little impact in the region. He noted, however, that the Strategy and a new model of development now emerging in Latin America are convergent, and that the World Conservation Strategy would be more appropriate if it emphasised conservation not so much as a goal in itself but as a means to satisfy the needs and welfare of society.

Salas noted that inclusion of the population issue in a revision of the World Conservation Strategy would be an important addition, and illustrated the present status of thinking on population issues. An extension of economic theory drawing on the principles of ecology was proposed as an essential basis for improved development planning by Galtung. Warford stressed the importance of designing economic policy instruments which would positively influence environmental impacts of decisionmakers at all levels.

Sunkel stressed that sustainable development must be built on a conceptual framework that recognises resources both as assets and as flows. Salas brought to mind a world of 10,500 million inhabitants before population stabilises, but pointed out that the final story is not yet told. Bugnicourt recalled the importance of diversity and said that one must begin with the spirit at the local level in order to create a world spirit. Galtung felt that diversity and symbiosis have to be the guiding lights to formulate an horizontal theory of economics. And Warford suggested that all inputs must be considered in any attempt to realise sustainable development. The Chairperson concluded with the remark that all the interventions stressed the same thoughts in a variety of ways, reflecting the richness of positions.

BEYOND THE WORLD CONSERVATION STRATEGY: INTEGRATING DEVELOPMENT AND THE ENVIRONMENT IN LATIN AMERICA AND THE CARIBBEAN

Osvaldo Sunkel[1]
CEPAL/UNEP
Santiago, Chile

SUMMARY *The prevailing style of development in Latin America, consisting of rapid urbanisation and heavy industrial concentration, has considerable environmental repercussions. An alternative style based on ecological thinking and an expansionary adjustment policy should provide support for democracy and sustainability in responding to the current socio-economic crisis. This alternative differs from the World Conservation Strategy, which has met little acceptance in Latin America, in its emphasis on: changing the level and structure of aggregate demand; utilisation of natural and man-made patrimonies for the satisfaction of present and future generations' needs; the need for the environmental dimension to be explicitly included within socio-economic development policies and planning; and the consideration of both the natural and built-up environments as dimensions to be treated in a systematic way. A dialogue among environmental policy specialists in the United States, Canada and Latin America must be initiated to support North-South cooperation in environmental matters.*

CONFLICTING PERCEPTIONS AND PRIORITIES

Fruitful dialogue among Latin American specialists on conservation and specialists on development is hampered by misinterpretations and seeming mistrust between North and South. This has been a result of differences in perceptions and priorities. To overcome the barriers it is necessary to understand why the situation has come to this point.

The environment *problématique* emanated mainly from the North, was presented and perceived as neo-Malthusian and conservationist in nature, and was concerned mostly with pollution and population growth. It appeared to divert attention from, or to go directly against, the Latin American development effort that emphasised industrialisation, agricultural modernisation, urbanisation, and transfers of science, technology, consumption patterns and lifestyles. These goals, embraced since the 1930s, were being pursued with great determination in the 1970s when environmental concerns suddenly came to the fore. Environ-

1   I wish to express my gratitude to Mr. Santiago Torres for his help in preparing this article.

mental concerns appeared to be misplaced, elitist and a threat to Latin American development efforts. Such attitudes were shaped in public and private developmental circles in the era of the 1972 UN Conference on the Human Environment: the subject was opened to public debate and Governments had to adopt positions on the recommendations and institutions arising from the Conference.

These attitudes have been partially overcome in recent years but still prevail in some powerful circles - particularly those related to large-scale development programmes, institutions and operations, as well as among some foreign relations establishments in Latin American countries. As a consequence, conflicts arise when large projects are implemented and government officials react negatively or avoid environmental issues in international fora. Furthermore, the popularity of neo-liberal and monetarist ideologies prevalent in recent years, particularly in countries of the Southern Cone, has reinforced such attitudes among economists and government officials.

Moreover, since 1982, the foreign debt crisis has constituted a new threat against the possibility of taking environmental considerations seriously, since attention focuses on the short-term and government policies imply increasing pressure on natural resources and the environment. It is no surprise therefore that the World Conservation Strategy (WCS) has had little acceptance in Latin America, given its implementa-

tion bias toward conservation rather than the integration of development and conservation for sustainable development.[2] Negative attitudes are also influenced by some important shortcomings in the World Conservation Strategy, which will be discussed later.

Nevertheless, the environmental *problématique* has come to the foreground and continues to gather momentum despite serious socio-economic and political problems, and despite its lack of expression in decision-making. Public opinion has changed from relative indifference to serious concern, forcing recalcitrant administrators at least to pay lip service to concern for the environment. With increasing frequency they have had to engage in environmental impact assessments - even if the operational effectiveness of those assessments has not always been evident. Governments have also had to set up environmental administrative machinery and legal frameworks, which again remain weak *vis-à-vis* the departments where development decisions are taken, and ineffective in enforcing regulations.

One important explanation for the change of attitude is the seriousness of many environmental problems affecting rural and urban areas, especially large metropolitan settlements. These problems are increasingly perceived as having a negative effect on development, and that recognition changes opinions on the development-environment relationship. There is in fact

2. This is exemplified, for instance, in one of its own publications. A paperback version of the World Conservation Strategy, published under the title *How to Save the World* (Allen, 1980) and "written for the general reader," eliminated the special chapter of the World Conservation Strategy devoted to the integration between development and conservation.

ground for the hope of bringing conservation and development polarities to a
better understanding in Latin America;
an analogous process of convergence is
being observed among "conservationists" and "developmentalists" in the
North.

The President of the World Resources
Institute has recently stated that
"economic growth is needed to attack
poverty, the worst destroyer of the environment worldwide, so business and
labour leaders must make common
cause with environmentalists in promoting sustainable growth. Economists
and ecologists must cooperate if
development strategies are to promote
this goal. The development, population, and environment communities
now face the same set of problems"
(Speth, 1985). In an important statement dealing with the present situation
and future prospects of the region, the
Economic Commission for Latin
America and the Caribbean has stated
that the region "has always been
regarded as a continent with great
reserves of natural and especially of
renewable resources. Unfortunately,
this appraisal has given rise to continuous spoliation, aggravated by the
growing domestic pressure to use more
resources since the processes of socio-
economic growth and transformation
and population changes have not been
accompanied by adequate management
of the environment" (ECLAC, 1985).

This apparent convergence calls for a
special effort to clarify concepts in use
to avoid continuing misunderstandings.
But reference must be made to the
socio-economic, political and cultural
forces that determine social priorities

and the way in which development in-
teracts with the environment. It is
those forces and their international
linkage that drive consumption and
technology, influence demographic
movements, affect investments, and
shape the action of the State and other
social agents. They must therefore be
prevailed upon by policies for environmentally-sound development, since
voluntarist attitudes aimed at businessmen and government officials are not
sufficient.

Very little will be achieved without
creating an environmental conscience
to alter public and business behaviour,
value systems, social and economic
structure, the orientation of technology,
institutional organisation and juridical
normativity. While not impossible, this
is a difficult long-term task because it
must address the very roots of contemporary society; especially of capitalist
society with its underdeveloped and dependent versions.

THE RELATIONSHIP BETWEEN DEVELOPMENT AND THE ENVIRONMENT: A CONCEPTUAL BASE[3]

Development is defined as a process of
transforming society characterised by
the growth of its capacity for production, increase in average individual
productivity and income, changes in
class structure and in social organisation, transformations in culture and
values, and changes in the political and
power structure, all leading to improvement in average standards of living and
quality of life. This definition of the
process of development must be linked
to the interaction between society and

---

3   This section draws heavily on Sunkel, 1980.

nature. Increasing the labour force is only possible to the extent that necessary elements can be extracted from nature, implying some form of technology. Similarly, surplus accumulation in an expanded labour force and increasing availability of new working tools are not feasible without an increase in the extraction of the corresponding natural resources (water, food, textile fibres, wood, minerals, energy), once again calling for technical changes.

Increases in the volume and productivity of industrial materials are secured by a process of specialisation and "artificialisation." The specialisation of agricultural resources and of the rural population makes it possible to generate a surplus of food products. This surplus enables part of the rural population to move to the cities where they are needed to process the products extracted from nature. That processing in turn results in infrastructure, capital goods, and consumer goods and services. Except for services - which are necessary for the daily life of the population - the process of goods accumulation contributes to making up the artificial, "built-up" environment.

This environment, which becomes more and more concentrated in urban areas (particularly in the largest cities), constitutes a material manifestation of the evolution of technology, and also represents the accumulated and distilled product of a lengthy period of natural resource extraction. According to the conventional development approach, primary sectors lose importance to secondary and tertiary sectors, and society becomes more urban and less rural. This view of the development process has somehow created the

illusion that dependence on nature is dwindling, reinforced by a general Latin American belief of a superabundant natural resource base. The former illusion is a serious error and the latter belief is a myth.

For the artificial environment to be habitable and productive, a supply of energy is indispensable and energy comes from nature. In order for this artificial environment to be kept functioning, those elements which undergo their normal process of deterioration must be replaced. This makes it necessary to resort once again to the biosphere. All the materials and energy extracted from the environment are transformed, in terms of mass and energy, into an equal quantity of products and residues, which are eventually reincorporated into nature. No matter how many resources actually exist, their availability in a development perspective must be seen in the long-term: relative abundance is not static or absolute but depends upon how society evolves and what kind of use it makes of nature. Different stages of development have different environmental implications, and different environments influence styles of development.

Based on the foregoing, therefore, the concept of development strategy has two important corollaries: first, the environment-development equation can be solved by mutual adaptation, i.e., by changes in development style and by environmental management; and secondly, environmental management involves both the natural and the built-up environments, which are dimensions that cannot be treated in isolation from one another.

STYLES OF DEVELOPMENT AND THE ENVIRONMENT

By style of development I understand "the way in which human and material resources are organised and assigned within a particular system with the object of solving such questions as what goods and services to produce, how (where) and for whom" (Pinto, 1976), or "the specific and dynamic modality adopted by a system within a particular context and at a particular moment in history" (Graciarena, 1976).

Each national style evolves out of contradictions and struggles between social forces which endeavour to impose or defend their own ways of resolving these questions. A distinction must be drawn between "style" as a simplified interpretation of ascendant regional or world trends, and "style" as the national materialisation of complex and contradictory processes. In each country persist not only different forms of capitalism, but also pre-capitalistic and peasant forms constituting "life-styles" or "styles of survival" rather than styles of development. The combinations and interactions of activities corresponding to the **ascendant** style as contrasted with those corresponding to other forms of organising and allocating resources together make up the "structural heterogeneity" which characterises peripheral countries within the capitalist system (Pinto, 1965; Sunkel, 1974).

The concept "style of development" may also be applied not to what is, but to what, in the opinion of a given social agent, should be. In this case, what is involved is the formulation of "alternative styles," "national projects," or "relevant utopias."

The most important dimensions of the contemporary ascendant transnational style may be summarised as follows:

* the worldwide homogenisation of patterns of consumption, production, technology, design, spatial organisation and marketing, (having originated mainly in the United States);

* the dominant role of the transnational corporations in disseminating and strengthening the contemporary style, and the partial replacement of market machinery by their strategies for maximising profits on a global scale;

* the generation of near-irreversible changes in national economies and societies, and reducing the options open to governments for establishing autonomous styles of development;

* the transformation of the international division of labour, particularly through internationalisation of industrial production;

* intensified exploitation of natural resources and high dependence on oil as the most important source of energy;

* intensive and continuing technological innovation, stimulated on one hand by the need to increase and diversify the consumption of industrial goods, and on the other by the arms race;

* the generation of wastes and pollutants on an unprecedented scale which affect the atmosphere, water and soil;

* the growing spatial mobility of the population for work and recreation purposes and the insatiable demand for space and infrastructure for residential areas; and

* the formation of a transnational elite, composed not only of managers, administrators and technicians from transnational corporations, but also of government officials, university professors, scientific researchers, journalists and advertising agents, identified with the ideology of the style and its patterns of consumption and culture (Sunkel, 1978).

Within this style, the development policies of recent decades have generated considerable economic growth, intensive incorporation of technological innovations, and a significant change in the structure of consumption and production (Durán, 1982), both among economic sectors and national regions. Simultaneously there have been important changes in regional and urban-rural distribution of economic activity. The population, too, has grown rapidly, with migratory flows altering regional distribution and that between rural and urban areas. Because production and income have increased considerably more than population (despite the latter's rapid growth), per capita income levels rose noticeably, which consequently raised living standards. This can be seen in the improvements of such indicators as life expectancy, general and infant mortality and the degree of literacy. However, these averages conceal an extremely unequal distribution of the fruits of progress, because most of the increase in income has benefited middle and high-income groups (CEPAL, 1979), while sizable

sectors of the urban and rural population remain in abject poverty.

All of these changes have had considerable environmental repercussions:

* exploitation of natural resources (both renewable and non-renewable) has increased substantially and has undergone radical changes - with intensive technological innovation in traditional areas (mining, fishing, temperate zone and high-altitude agriculture) and massive expansion into frontier areas characterised by very fragile ecosystems (the humid tropics, arid and semi-arid zones) (Gligo, 1984c);

* a spatial redistribution has taken place in human activity between rural and urban areas, resulting in rapid urbanisation and heavy industrial concentration. For example, seven states or provinces in Argentina, Brazil and Mexico provide 75 percent of Latin America's industrial product (Kowaric, 1981; Uribe and Szekely, 1981; Di Filippo, 1981);

* a new and unprecedented level of waste generation and pollution has grown in all spheres. Pollution, reductions in the quality of life, and environmental deterioration are the results of lack of concern for the worsening problem of geographically concentrated, industrial, agricultural and mining wastes. The growing similarity of technology with that of the industrial countries accentuates this problem.

THE POPULATION ISSUE

The relationship between development and environment discussed in the previous section has included some population and resource issues. Here I will only highlight the complexity of the interaction between these variables which has been at the centre of the "conservation" debate. Several policy premises have emerged over the past decade which are worth mentioning (ECLAC, 1984):

First, the population issue should not be reduced to a demographic exercise, comparing projected global population growth rates with assessments of overall resources, either worldwide, regionally or nationally. Differences among population size, and the dynamics and resource endowments between areas are crucial, leading to different and variable manifestations of population and resource issues. Moreover, these differences depend on such factors as levels of development, geographical and climatic characteristics, socio-economic structures and patterns, distribution of poverty and wealth, access to resources, technological development, tradition and culture, the nature of ecosystems, and interconnectedness with the international community and global processes.

Second, population numbers, *per se*, cannot indicate much beyond the size and growth of a given society. Demographic characteristics will undoubtedly influence social organisation as well as access to and use of resources, but the multiple cultural, political, economic and international factors which shape society will finally determine the way it uses, abuses or disregards its resources. In other words, while certain demographic variables may be manipulated to some extent as independent variables to achieve particular results, overall population dynamics, including the population's

relation to resources and the environment, will depend on more profound and wider ranging socio-cultural change. Patterns of development and lifestyles play a critical role in the nature and scope of impacts on the natural resource base of a given population.

Third, environmental pollution and the use of global resources depend more on consumption patterns and lifestyles of developed countries and their diffusion to the middle and upper income groups of developing countries, than on the rates of population growth of the latter (Keyfitz, 1976).

One fact that highlights the above premises is the evolution experienced by population growth in connection with the Latin American food problem. The drop of fertility observed in the region during the 1960s and 1970s has generated a rate of population growth that is now slower than the growth rate of agricultural production. Problems of malnutrition are therefore not derived from insufficient output or from a population that grows faster than food production (ECLAC,1984). These problems are the consequence of distortions provoked by the dominant development style and power structures in production and the distribution of wealth; and thus, in the consumption capacity and preferences of different social groups.

TOWARD SUSTAINABLE DEVELOPMENT

The imitative style of development adopted in the last decades and the enormous foreign indebtedness of the late 1970s put our countries in a state of extreme dependence. Due to this vulnerable condition, the financial crisis of 1982, with associated recessive adjustment policies (that were aggravated by the joint action of the IMF and the transnational banking system), led to a profound development crisis. The region is still suffering its worst economic crisis since 1930. Per capita GNP in 1985 was almost the same as that of 1976. Urban rates of unemployment have sharply increased in all countries, as have those of rural and urban underemployment. Inflation has been accelerating, reaching hyperinflation magnitudes in some countries, hitting wage-earners, marginal groups and the unemployed. Real wage levels have been reduced to those of one and a half decades ago. Health, nutrition and shelter conditions of the population have suffered grave deterioration due to the crisis, and to prolonged reductions in investments and essential social expenditures.

The decline in long-term growth of industrial countries and of the international economy - with its increasing foreign debt - preclude any possibility of even minimum growth of the Latin American economies, let alone regaining post-war conditions of expansion (Sunkel, 1984; Griffith, Jones and Sunkel, 1986). Therefore, Latin American countries will now have to face up to their structural development crisis, which was avoided during the 1970's because of permissive financial conditions prevailing at the time. This should also constitute a starting point for a transition toward a sustainable form of development that provides strong support for democracy.

The environmental-ecological way of thinking may make a practical and conceptual contribution of the greatest value. The natural and built-up environments should be considered as social assets whose potentialities should be exploited, but only when taking into account the need for inter-generational allocation of the yields provided. The topic of environmental resources, endowments and assets may be viewed as a way of linking current short-term economic policies with medium and longer-term development policies. In other words, we should look at the crisis as an opportunity: an opportunity to mobilise resources in a way that involves change in growth style, aimed at satisfying essential needs of the population while launching a process of sustainable development.

In order to approach these questions in a positive way, it is necessary to distinguish between short-term flows and the substantial endowments which have been built-up over the longer-term. Within this latter category we may identify:

* socio-cultural heritage (the population and its demographic characteristics, its traditions and socio-cultural values, its level of education, the organisation of its institutions, ideological currents, political systems and regimes);

* the natural heritage (the territory, the characteristics of its ecosystems and the present and potential availability of renewable and non-renewable natural resources); and

* the fixed-capital heritage or "built environment" (the installed productive capacity together with infrastructure, or the man-made artificial environment).

In other words, taking a broader vision of the three classical factors of production: labour, land and capital, we must recognise that the productive capabilities and socio-political and administrative abilities of Latin American countries have reached fairly advanced levels in many cases, and will not be left idle much longer as a consequence of the external squeeze. The situation must be approached from a political economy standpoint which can establish links between socio-cultural and political capabilities; spatial, natural resource and environmental potentialities; and accumulated productive capacity. This view also constitutes a bridge to connect medium and long-term development with annual flows and short-term policies. These latter are principally connected with macroeconomic equilibria: fiscal, monetary, external, employment and income indicators with their socio-political implications and constraints. In our present crisis, the serious external disequilibrium in the short-term flows of income and expenditure requires a considerable restriction of imports but leads to a pronounced under-utilisation of the accumulated socio-cultural, natural and productive heritage potential. This means that we are in the presence of a substantial potential in terms of real resources which may be mobilised (cultural, organisational and material) insofar as such mobilisation can free itself from its dependence on imported inputs.

This approach also helps to clarify the problem of passage from a recessionary adjustment to an expansionary one, and the transition to medium and longer-term development. The recessionary adjustment essentially involves manipulation of short-term economic policy instruments so that aggregate demand is restricted, public expenditures are cut back, investments are reduced, wages and salaries are abated, money expansion is reduced and national currency is devalued. One of the main goals of such policies is to indirectly induce a reduction of imports through contraction of national income. Besides the greater or lesser success that policies may have in this respect, there are very serious negative side-effects on accumulation, production, wages, employment and utilisation of socially-accumulated endowments.

Instead of unilaterally reducing income, demand and imports, an expansionary adjustment policy would combine a selectively-restrictive demand policy with an equally selective resource-based and need-oriented supply policy, taking advantage of those idle productive assets. The objective is to change the composition of both supply and demand so that a mutual adjustment can be reached, with a much lower imported component and a greater efficiency in the use of the accumulated patrimonies. The first step would be to try to make use of this socio-cultural, natural and productive potential and available idle assets. A second step - a medium and long-term one - would involve investment, institutional and socio-cultural policies aimed at modifying the nature of this social, natural and capital heritage, with its dependent and polarised structure.

SUSTAINABLE DEVELOPMENT AND DEMOCRATIC PLANNING

While recessionary demand policies rely on the market and on aggregate macroeconomic policies, a resource-based and need-oriented strategy must rely on planning and State intervention to ensure selectivity in resource mobilisation and restriction of demand. This brings into the discussion the major issue of State policy, its repre-sentivity, effectiveness and efficiency - which I cannot begin to discuss here. But insofar as selectivity and planning aim at equitable sharing of costs and benefits, they offer the basis for strengthening concerted political proces-ses of a democratic character in which most Latin American countries are engaged.

Existing macroeconomic and socio-political knowledge, experiences and proposals, together with a more detailed knowledge at sector and project levels, permit the formulation of concrete proposals for expansionary adjustments, including specific measures and selective programmes. These involve productive and social programmes, both urban and rural, for small and medium-sized business as well as for the informal sector, with em-phasis on targets such as alleviating poverty, increasing employment, gen-erating exports and replacing imports, satisfying basic needs, and the like. Proposals must also include the cor-responding macroeconomic programme with its selective components dealing with demand, taxation and government expenditures, credits, subsidies and other policies of the public sector.

Among such measures, those worthy of mention include programmes involv-ing massive use of labour for the con-struction and reconstruction of housing, drainable works, infrastructure and col-lective equipment in popular settle-ment; for the construction, reconstruc-tion and maintenance of road systems, of public works and human settlements in general; protection against flooding and other natural catastrophes; refores-tation; the building of terraces in areas of erosion; cleaning and building protective works on rivers and canals;

drainage and irrigation works; opening-up of new land; repair and maintenance of public buildings, machinery and equipment; and other productive ac-tivities. Likewise, policies to stimulate saving and replacing fuel and other high-cost inputs should be considered.

In addition, consideration could be given to alternatives put forward by various groups, with different em-phases such as those on integrated productive systems, combined tech-nologies, ecodevelopment, etc. Each of these is centred upon production that makes use of existing know-how, labour, natural resources, wastes and residues (Sachs, 1976; 1983; Wolfe, 1979; Marino de Botero, 1983; Dag Hammarskjöld Foundation, 1975; among others). All are low-cost and highly useful activities and imply a criticism of the prevalent style of growth. They seek to restore a labour process aimed at satisfying essential needs and reinvigourating the labour force, the environment, the resource base and underutilised potentialities, while making less use of scarce factors such as capital and foreign currency. Moreover, these activities give rise to a different style of growth and a vigorous and open cultural identity. This results from the multiple links which connect them with specific geographical and resource contexts, with daily experience, with local knowledge and culture, as well as with ecosystemic relations - in short, with a long-run approach that includes the re-quirements of scientific and technologi-cal development.

Despite the opportunities presented by these measures, they tend to be adopted strictly within an emergency frame-work and under *ad hoc* circumstances. It is consequently vital, as I mentioned before, to take advantage of the present crisis to identify and stimulate the kind of policies mentioned above.

In most cases the above activities involve collective consumption or a productive infrastructure not always of interest to private enterprise. This is either because they are conceived to benefit low-income groups whose effective demand is negligible, or because they create external economies whose surplus the private investor would be unable to capture. In other words, these are activities and undertakings which normally fall within the sphere of public sector responsibility.

Because local geography plays an important role in these activities, the problems of unemployment cannot be treated in purely abstract terms; on the contrary, they must be treated with reference to concrete locations. Therefore, public activity oriented toward such local problems offers a good opportunity for decentralisation and community participation, which are issues of special interest and priority in the search for democratic planning and decision-making systems.

Even though the crisis may trigger a movement of this kind as a short-run answer to urgent problems, it is necessary to consider these activities as a starting point for more permanent, properly-financed and institutionalised programmes, especially when such activities refer to basic needs, which have been systematically neglected. In this respect, a priority area for readjustment, as mentioned above, is that related to patterns of investment and consumption, in addition to technology and resource management. It will be imperative to strongly but selectively limit all kinds of demand and technol-

ogy which directly or indirectly involve a high imported component, and to replace them with goods and services, technologies and designs based on the use of local and national, human and environmental resources.

All of these orientations will certainly result in greater use and pressure upon the environment. Thus conservation, maintenance and protection of the environment will make an essential contribution to improving the standard of living, employment and productivity. This requires greater knowledge of the environment's potential, of ecosystem conditions for its exploitation, and of the most efficient management formulae so that opportunities may be effectively used. But, at the same time, the long-run sustainability of the whole process must be assured; environmental deterioration and resource depletion must be avoided through sound management. All this requires that priority in future development strategies be given to the issues of natural resources and technology, adopting a long-run ecological perspective.

The emphasis placed on environmentally sound mobilisation of Latin American countries' resources implies a need for greater differentiation than in the past, both between countries and between regions within each country. It demands a more realistic and pragmatic level of abstraction in development strategies which considers the real availability of natural resources, technology, country size and position, the relationship between population and resources, the energy situation, the degree and features of urbanisation, and others. This means that new development strategies will be different for countries which show marked differences in these aspects; it also means that such strategies, when implemented in a particular country, shall favour regional and spatial considerations (including the urban-rural issue), as each country is made up of a heterogenous mosaic of environmental conditions.

These requirements imply a great challenge to planners, to their planning methodologies and to the institutional set-up of planning at all levels and sectors. Operational capability must be created such that natural and built-up environments are considered as resources which are scarce and have alternative uses; which can be enhanced, reproduced, depleted or destroyed depending on their use; and which are interrelated among themselves and with human activities in complex ways. The planning methodology followed in Latin America has paid little attention to these considerations, largely because - like the development strategies themselves - it was influenced by an approach which imitated development and consumption patterns of industralised countries.

It has frequently been stated that institutions and groups responsible for environmental action should play a leading role (together with the scientific and technological community) in the conception, elaboration, design, evaluation and implementation of development policies. For this role to be successful, I am convinced that the kind of environmental approach suggested above must be adopted. Ecological considerations must also be reviewed in the centres where development decisions are conceived and taken. Such action is not possible if the en-

vironmental dimension of development is kept on the sidelines or if there is no desire for a dialogue between the two viewpoints. Likewise, as mentioned in the first section of this discussion, if the World Conservation Strategy is to have an influence on Latin American development strategies, it will be necessary to discuss its major elements in the perspective of the above analysis. This will permit establishing the main convergences as well as the principal differences between the two approaches. This analysis and the discussion that may arise from it will make it much easier to filter the essential message of the World Conservation Strategy through the prism of each country's own reality, giving that message a concrete and relevant meaning.

THE WORLD CONSERVATION STRATEGY IN PERSPECTIVE

In this section major elements of the World Conservation Strategy will be discussed from the above perspective with some modifications suggested to make the Strategy more attractive, and its implementation more feasible.

Some Major Convergences

When considering the general methodology of how to incorporate the environmental dimension into the decision-making process for development, numerous convergences appear between the World Conservation Strategy and what I have discussed so far.

The World Conservation Strategy[4] states that "development that is inflexible and little influenced by ecologi-

4   Unless otherwise mentioned, all references and quotations in this section are from *World Conservation Strategy*, IUCN/UNEP/WWF, 1980. Therefore, quotations will only specify the corresponding paragraph of this publication.

cal considerations is unlikely to make the best use of available resources. By causing ecological damage it is also likely to cause economic and social damage. The most effective way society can avoid such problems is to integrate every stage of the conservation and development processes, from the initial setting of policies to their eventual implementation and operation." The World Conservation Strategy proposes that "this be done through the adoption of anticipatory environmental policies and of a cross-sectoral conservation policy" (9.1).

My argument for explicit inclusion of the environmental dimension within development planning calls for very early consideration of the environment in the planning process. Only in this way can the environment's capabilities, potentialities, limitations and risks influence, from the outset, the implementation of development policies, plans, projects - as well as the Strategy itself. This can only be done if a holistic, trans-sectoral approach is undertaken. Furthermore, I insist on the need for compatibility between those actions and policies aiming to solve short-run, urgent problems with the requirements for long-run sustainable development.

Another important convergence is reflected in the importance given in the World Conservation Strategy to promoting types of policy instruments such as "taxes, charges and financial incentives (to encourage choices compatible with the maintenance of a healthy environment); technology assessment; design and product regulation; environmental planning; and procedures for rational use allocation. The latter two instruments are regarded as crucial for the integration of conservation with development" (9.13). In support of the

effective application of these kinds of instruments, the World Conservation Strate-gy suggests that "in order for governments to take adequate account of costs of destroying, degrading or depleting living resources and of the benefits of conserving them, it is recommended that non-monetary indicators of conservation performance be selected for inclusion in national accounting systems" (9.14).

These suggestions converge, at least partially, with the instrumental and information requirements derived from my argument for a new style of development centred on the population's quality of life, with indicators that go far beyond the typical categories included in traditional national income accounts (Sunkel and Leal, 1985; Gligo , 1985).

With respect to incorporating the environmental dimension within the process of development planning, there are numerous convergences with what the World Conservation Strategy has named "environmental planning and rational use allocation." The Strategy proposes integrating development and conservation by means of ecosystem evaluation. Their focus and methods should be oriented by the following fundamental principles:

* "ecosystem suitability is assessed and classified with respect to specified kinds of use ... each with its own requirements;"

* "evaluation requires a comparison of the outputs obtained and the inputs needed for each different use." "The input-output comparison should be quantified only to the extent that quantification does not distort what is being compared and does

not attempt to compare what is not comparable;"

* "evaluation is in terms relevant to the physical, economic and social context of the area concerned (the regional climate, standards of living on the population, availability and cost of labour, need for employment, the local or export markets, systems of land tenure that are socially and politically acceptable, and availability of capital)" (10.4).

These principles are fully convergent with the fundamental importance of including regional and local input when incorporating the environmental dimension into development planning.

The World Conservation Strategy includes two other principles for ecosystem evaluation which implicitly accept my definition of development as a process of environmental transformation which should be sustainable.

These principles are:

* "suitability (of use) refers to use on a sustained basis;" under this condition the possibility of radical ecosystemic changes is accepted; and

* "evaluation involves comparison ... between an existing use, between potential uses, or between a potential consumptive use and a non-consumptive use" (10.4).

This latter principle contains the idea of alternative patterns of development if it is taken from a micro to a macro

or global level. I have emphasised this aspect when dealing with the issue of changing to a sustainable style of development.

With relation to my proposal for sustainable development based on a reasonable matching between supply and the resource base, and demand with the pattern of needs, the World Conservation Strategy states a similar criterion in a procedure for allocating uses of ecosystems and environmental resources: according to the World Conservation Strategy, allocation should be made according to a comparison of supply characteristics - as determined by the ecosystem evaluation - and demand characteristics (10.9 and 10.10).

Other relevant convergences which do not need further explanation or discussion are the following:

* the need for improvement in the capacity to manage by means of design and implementation of proper legislative and institutional settings, which facilitate and assure full incorporation of the environmental dimension (including conservation goals) within the process of planning and decision-making;[5]

* the need for a training and research process to improve knowledge of each country's natural and environmental resource base, as well as a higher capacity for their proper management among individual agents;

5   Although I have not discussed in this paper some legislative and institutional aspects which necessarily accompany most of my proposals, these are contained in the documentation (Koolen, 1985) and Final Report (ECLAC, 1985) of the Buenos Aires Seminar on "Incorporation of the Environmental Dimension in the Processes of Development Planning."

* the central importance of a more profound and generalised environmental education among the population as well as at the professional, entrepreneur and government levels;

* the crucial role of community participation in the decision-making process.

Main Differences or Discrepancies

There are two major differences between the concepts of the World Conservation Strategy and those I have summarised in this paper: one is semantic while the other deals with more substantive issues.

The semantic differences concern the term "conservation" itself, given the context of the usual and general use made of it. Considering the literal meaning of this term, i.e. "prevention of change, loss, destruction, waste, damage, etc.," it is rather one-sided when applied to complex environmental categories. It also has an ideological and political connotation in most Latin American countries, where the concept and its intention tend to be easily identified with social forces that defend the socio-political establishment and *status quo*. Applied generally to the environment, and particularly to specific natural and environmental resources, without an elaborated explanation conservationism is taken as a position aiming to keep the environment as untouched as possible. Unfortunately, most conservation movements within the region have tended to confirm this image. They have thus created mistrust in the whole concept, notwithstanding the new meaning given to it by the World Conservation Strategy.

The new definition of conservation in the World Conservation Strategy (1.4), at least at the conceptual level, suggests something quite different. As far as the natural environment is concerned, this concept fully coincides with what has been defined above as a wise and proper environmental management for sustainable development. The issue of the built-up environment will be discussed later.

Together with the semantic problem of the concept of conservation, another difficulty is the promotion of conservation, in its traditional sense, as a goal in itself, disconnected from the satisfaction of needs and the welfare of society. I therefore believe that it is more convenient not to use this term in the wider sense and that it should be replaced with a longer but more precise expression, such as "sound environmental management for sustainable development." It would be less confusing if conservation could be limited to its proper meaning, i.e., in relation to national parks, restricted areas, endangered species, etc.

In relation to the more substantive differences, there are four issues I would like to emphasise.

The first is that the whole World Conservation Strategy is essentially supply-sided. The Strategy rests mainly on proposals related to ecosystems and resource management so that conservation could be assured, implicitly assuming the level and structure of demand as an independent and autonomous variable. As I have argued, if a new alternative and sustainable style of development is to be pursued, then both the level and particularly the structure of aggregate demand must be fundamentally changed. Under present conditions any strategy aimed at making the process of growth and development environmentally sustainable which does not consider this side of the equation will be condemned to failure. I believe that any global sustainable development strategy cannot avoid this fundamental issue.

The second issue, although mainly a matter of emphasis, gives character to the difference between "conservation" and "environmental management for sustainable development" beyond a purely semantic difference. While "conservation" places emphasis on preservation, maintenance, sustainable utilisation, restoration and improvement of the natural surroundings, the concept of "environmental management for sustainable development" emphasises mobilisation and utilisation of the natural and environmental resource base for the satisfaction of present and future generations' needs, while implying the conscious achievement of conservation's main goals. Thus, the range of environmental problems within the latter approach is enlarged beyond those purely related to destruction, degradation, pollution or depletion: it also includes the existence of a great variety of unused, under-utilised, underdetected and underrated environmental resources, which is particularly shocking in the context of non-satisfaction of basic needs affecting a great proportion of the population. This means that a proper environmental strategy should be more active than reactive, without neglecting the ecological conditions for sustainability. In this

sense, conservation as it is usually understood constitutes a particular case of environmental management for sustainable development.

The third issue relates to the difference between the need for environmental management and planning (which is clearly stated in the World Conservation Strategy), and the need to incorporate the environmental dimension into overall socio-economic development policies and planning, (which *includes* environmental management and planning).[6]

The fourth issue deals with the scope of the concept of environment. While the World Conservation Strategy deals only with living resources, our approach implies consideration of both natural and built-up evironments as dimensions to be treated in an integral and systemic way. Moreover, the built-up environment is considered relevant not only because of the crucial mutual influences between urban centres and nature (particularly in a developmental perspective), but also because it is a very important element in society's quality of life, both in urban settlements and in large metropolitan areas. In this respect, the issues of rapid growth, maintenance, enhancement, protection and preservation of the built-up environment and its rapidly changing relationship to the environment in Latin America are crucially important, especially for large segments of the urban poor. Any conservation or sound environmental management strategy must include both of these aspects,

----

6   This raises the issue of the role of the State, a discussion which, as stated above, goes beyond the scope of this analysis. Yet it should be mentioned since proper consideration of environmental problems is not possible without clear State intervention through governmental planning insitutions and authorities concerned with the development process itself.

as development largely consists of transforming the natural into a built-up environment.

THE INTERNATIONAL DIALOGUE

Insofar as the World Conservation Strategy addresses the global level, it involves as a central aspect the international dimension of environmental matters. This demands international dialogue and cooperation, and eventually, international negotiations.

Conversely, I have argued for a change in the Latin American style of development so that it becomes more regionally endogenous and self-sustained in the long run. At first glance, this may give the impression that international issues become less important. The forces involved in such change, however, include a relevant international component which also calls for dialogue and cooperation within both the Latin American region itself and the North-South context.

With respect to the intra-regional level, which I will not analyse here, there is a great amount of work already done and much more to do in the future. The focus of this work has been horizontal cooperation among Latin American countries in environmental matters (see, among others, UNEP, 1982; 1983; 1984; 1985; Sunkel *et al.,* 1984; Gligo, 1984a; 1984b; 1984c; CEPAL, 1983; CEPAL/PNUMA/CIFCA, 1984).

The importance of North/South dialogue and cooperation in environmental matters has been stressed. This issue has received special attention in most international fora since the Stockholm Conference in 1972. Also, the recently created World Commission on Environment and Development (WCED) has placed international cooperation among the priority themes against which the Commission would examine key environmental issues.

The WCED has stated that actions to be taken "to ensure that development in the medium to long-term will be on both an expansive and more sustainable path ... depends less on nature than on nations, and their capacity for cooperation" (WCED, 1985). Many of the issues involved are recognised as closely related to the North/South debate.

As far as Latin America is concerned, the inter-American relationships are crucial in this debate. Nevertheless, there is no community of specialists in the international environmental policy field as there is in other fields such as hemispheric economic, social, political, military, development and international problems and relations.

There are many close and highly-specialised relations of cooperation, information and exchange regarding specific environmental issues: tropical forests, mountain ecosystems, ecosystem modelling, biogas digestors, tropical marine resources, preservation of the white whale, and so on. But there seem to be no contacts among generalists concerned with the development/environment relationship, and even less with its international and hemispheric manifestations. There are a number of United States environment/development generalists and a few Latin Americans with similar interests, but we all tend to be concerned with our own regions or the world at large, and not with each other.

If the above diagnosis is correct, it is essential to initiate a dialogue between the United States, Canada and Latin America in the areas of environment/ development and hemispheric relations. One would probably have to start with a carefully-selected group of people who are actively engaged in the development/environment field, who are or attempt to be generalists, who have an interest in this overall, "macro" relationship, who are sensitive to the international and hemispheric implications of the subject, who accept the conceptual approach of sustainable development, and therefore may be expected to share to some extent a common approach and language - essential conditions for a critical and potentially profitable dialogue.

REFERENCES

• Allen, R., 1980, *How to Save the World*, Strategy for World Conservation, Kogan Page, London.

• CEPAL, 1983, *Sobrevivencia campesina en ecosistemas de altura*, E/CEPAL/G.1267, United Nations Publication, Vols. I and II, Santiago, Chile, (15 articles).

• CEPAL, 1979, *América Latina en el umbral de los anos 80*, E/CEPAL/G. 1106, Santiago, Chile.

• CEPAL/PNUMA, 1985, *Avances en la Interpretación ambiental del Desarrollo Agrícola en América Latina*, NU LC/G, 1347 (7 articles), Santiago, Chile.

• CEPAL/PNUMA/CIFCA, 1984, *Expansión de la Frontera Agropecuaria y Medio Ambiente en América Latina*, CEPAL, PNUMA, CIFCA (11 articles).

• Dag Hammarskjöld Foundation, 1975, "What Now, Another Development," in *Development Dialogue*, No. 1/2.

• Di Filippo, A., 1981, "Distribución espacial de la actividad económica, migraciones y concentración poblacional en América Latina" in Sunkel and Gligo (eds.) 1981, op. cit.

• Durán, H., 1982, "Estilos de desarrollo de la industria manufacturera y medio ambiente en América Latina" in *Estudios e Informes de la CEPAL* No. 11, E/CEPAL/G. 1196, Santiago, Chile.

• ECLAC, 1985, Report of the Regional Seminar on the Environmental Dimension in Development Planning, LC/L.357 (SEM. 25/9), Santiago, Chile.

• ECLAC, 1984, "Development, lifestyles, population and environment in Latin America," in UN, *Proceedings of the International Conference on Population, Resources, Environment and Development*, IESA/P/ICP, 1984/EG.III/9, Geneva.

• FAO, 1974, "Studies on soil erosion in Latin America" in *Journal of Soil and Water Conservation*, Mexico.

• FAO/UNESCO, 1964, World Soil Map, Paris.

• Gligo, N., 1985, "The Preparation of Natural and Cultural Heritage Inventories and Accounts" in *CEPAL Review* No. 28, April.

- Gligo, N., 1984a, "Perspectivas ambientales del uso del suelo agricola de América Latina," in *Desarrollo y Ambiente* No. 1, CIPMA, Santiago, Chile.

- Gligo, N., 1984b, "El manejo integrado de recursos naturales agrícolas: un desafio ambiental en América Latina," in *Revista Interamericana de Planificación*, Vol. XVIII, No. 69, March 1984.

- Gligo, N., 1984c, "The Expansion of the Agricultural Frontier in Latin America," in *Journal of Public and International Affairs*, University of Pitsburgh.

- Graciarena, J., 1976, "Power and Development Styles," in *CEPAL Review*, First Semester.

- Griffith Jones, S. and O. Sunkel, 1986, *The Latin American Debt and Development Crisis*, Oxford University Press.

- IUCN/UNEP/WWF, 1980, *World Conservation Strategy*, IUCN-UNEP-WWF, Gland, Switzerland.

- Keyfitz, N., 1976, "World resources and the World Middle Class" in *Scientific American*, Vol. 235, No. 1, July.

- Koolen, R., 1985, "La organización institucional del Estado en relación a la incorporacion de la dimensión ambiental en la planificación del desarrollo," CEPAL LC/R. 438 (SEM 25/7).

- Kowaric, L., 1981, "El precio del progreso: crecimiento económico, expoliación urbana y la cuestión del medio ambiente" in Sunkel and Gligo (eds.) 1981, op. cit.

- Marino de Botero, M. (comp.), 1983, *"Ecodesarrollo: el pensamiento de un decenio,"* INDERENA/PNUMA, Bogota.

- Pinto, A., 1976, "Styles of Development in Latin America" in *CEPAL Review*, First Semester.

- Pinto, A., 1965, "Concentracion del progreso técnico y de sus frutos en el desarrollo latinoamericano," in *El Trimestre Económico*, Vol. XXXII, No. 125, Jan-Mar.

- Sachs, I., 1983, "Estrategias de desarrollo con requerimientos energéticos. Problemas y enfoques," in M. Marino de Botero (comp.) *Ecodesarrollo: el pensamiento de un decenio*, INSERENA/PNUMA, Bogota.

- Sachs, I., 1976, "Environment and styles of development" W.H. Matthews (comp.) *Outer Limits and Human Needs*, Dag Hammarskjöld Foundation, Upsala.

- Salcedo, S. and J. Leyton, 1981, "El sector forestal latinoamericano y sus relaciones con el medio ambiente," in Sunkel and Gligo (eds.) 1981, op. cit.

- Speth, J.G., 1985, "Environment, Economy, Security: the Emerging Agenda" in *Protecting our Environment: Towards a New Agenda, Alternatives for the 80s*, No. 18, Center for National Policy, Washington, D.C.

• Sunkel, O., 1985, "Some Preliminary Thoughts on Issues of Resource and Environmental Management in the Hemisphere," (mimeo), Santiago, Chile.

• Sunkel, O., 1984, "Past, Present and Future of the International Economic Crisis" in *CEPAL Review* No. 22, E/CEPAL/G. 1296, Santiago, Chile.

• Sunkel, O., 1980, "The interaction between styles of development and the environment in Latin America" in *CEPAL Review* No. 12, Dec.

• Sunkel, O., 1978, "La dependencia y la heterogeneidad estructural," in *El Trimestre Económico*, Vol. XLV (1) No. 177, Jan-Mar.

• Sunkel, O. and N. Gligo (eds.), 1981, "Estilos de desarrollo y medio ambiente en América Latina," Lecturas No. 36 (2 volumes), FCE, Mexico.

• Sunkel, O., Jordan, R. and F. Sabatini, 1984, "La crisis urbana: elementos conceptuales para una aproximación ambiental," (paper), Seminar on "Las metrópolis latino-americanas frente a la crisis: experiencias y políticas," San Pablo, 9/84.

• Sunkel, O. and J. Leal, 1985, "Economics and the Environment" in *International Social Science,* Vol XXXVIII, No. 3.

• UNEP, 1985, Final Report: Fourth Intergovernmental Regional Meeting on Environment in Latin America and the Caribbean, 18-20 Apr 85, Cancun, UNEP/IG.57/8.

• UNEP, 1984, Final Report: Third Intergovernmental Regional Meeting on Environment in Latin America and the Caribbean, 12 Apr 85, Lima, UNEP/IG.48/4.

• UNEP, 1983, Final Report: Second Intergovernmental Regional Meeting on Environment in Latin America and the Caribbean, 14-17 Apr 85, Buenos Aires, UNEP/IG.40/6

• UNEP, 1982, Final Report: Fourth Intergovernmental Regional Meeting on Environment in Latin America and the Caribbean, 8-12 Mar 85, Mexico, UNEP/IG.33/4

• UNEP, 1975, "Estudio de las consecuentcias ambientales y económicas del uso de plaguicidas en la producción de algodón en Centro America, Guatemala.

• Uribe, A. and F. Szekely, 1981, "Localización y tecnología industrial en América Latina y sus impactos en el medio ambiente" in Sunkel and Gligo (eds.) 1981, op. cit.

• Vergara, I., 1981, "El problema de la contaminación marina producida por el transporte marítimo en América Latina," in Sunkel and Gligo (eds.), 1981, op. cit.

• WCED, 1985, *Mandate for Change: Key issues, Strategy and Workplan*, WCED, Switzerland.

• Wolfe, M., 1979, "Reinventing Development: Utopias Devised by Committees and Seeds of Changes in the Real World", in *CEPAL Review*, No. 7, April.

POPULATION AND SUSTAINABLE DEVELOPMENT

Rafael Salas
Executive Director, UNFPA
New York, U.S.A.

SUMMARY Understanding the linkages between population, resources, environment and development is crucial in efforts to achieve long-term sustainable development. Earlier, the 1974 World Population Plan of Action called attention to these interrelationships. In 1984, the report of the International Conference on Population urged governments, in the context of overall development policies, to adopt and implement policies, including population policies, that will contribute to redressing imbalances between trends in population growth, resources and environmental requirements. The integration of the population issue into the World Conservation Strategy can be seen as an important contribution to international awareness of these issues.

The concern of this meeting and of the entire international community is that the 5,000 million people who will inhabit the earth next year, and the 5,000 million who will follow them in the next century, are assured the means of survival and the elements of human dignity. In order to secure continuous and even-handed social and economic development, it will be necessary to find a balance between numbers, the resources available to sustain them, the environment which protects them - which they in turn must protect - and the nature of the development process.

The interactions between population, resources, environment and development are highly complex, and have not yet been completely explored. Nevertheless, as we have discovered in many other areas of population work, they are finite in number. They can, given patience and dedication, be understood sufficiently well for meaningful interventions to be made. It is important to make the effort because a balance between these four elements is the only guarantee of a stable future.

In 1984, the International Conference on Population held in Mexico City adopted 88 recommendations for action. The first dealt with the interrelationships of these elements. It stated:

Considering that social and economic development is a central factor in the solution of population ... problems and that population fac-

tors ... have a major impact on the attainment of development objectives, national development policies, plans and programmes - as well as international development strategies - should be formulated on the basis of an integrated approach that takes into account the interrelationships between population, resources, environment and development. In this context, national and international efforts should give priority to action programmes integrating population and development.

In each of the four sectors there has been a veritable explosion of knowledge over the past few decades. Studies have provided us with new ways of looking at natural resources, and advances have been made in finding ways to develop, utilise and conserve them. In the environmental field, scientific studies and years of management experience have greatly furthered our understanding of the biosphere on which we all depend and of which we are an integral part. A growing body of knowledge of development processes has been created on the basis of years of experience, some of it trial-and-error. In the field of population, research and programme experience have dramatically increased our ability to ascertain population trends and prospects, and have added immeasurably to our comprehension of population problems and ways of dealing with them.

The world has witnessed an unprecedented demographic disequilibrium during this century, with the highest rates of population growth in human history. At the beginning of the century there were about 1,600 million people in the world. By 1985 the world population had increased to about 4,800 million. And during 1985 alone, approximately 80 million people were added to the global family. (This is equal to the number of people currently living in New York City, Moscow, London, Beijing, Mexico City and Rio de Janiero, combined.) The annual increment for the period 1995-2000 is projected to be about 90 million. Thus, by the year 2000, the world population is projected to be at 6,100 million, and by the year 2025, at about 8,200 million.

Despite the fact that the absolute numbers are on the increase, the rate of population growth appears to be gradually slowing. The early 1970s marked an historic turning point. For the first time, the human growth rate began to decline, and this global trend has continued. But however welcome, this trend should be interpreted with care. The decline is gradual, and will not lead to a stable population until the end of the next century. There is moreover no guarantee that the decline will continue, and no certainty that it will not reverse.

On a regional basis, and especially on a country-by-country basis, there are wide variations in growth rate. In Africa, the annual rate of population growth, presently about 3.8 percent, continues to rise. In Latin America, where the growth rate is 2.19 percent, and in Asia, with a rate of 1.59 percent, there is gradual decline. The developed world, which underwent the demographic transition at an earlier stage, had an annual growth rate of 0.64 percent during the period 1980-85. Thus, disparities between the developed and developing world are increasing; approximately 90 percent of the projected increase will occur in the developing countries.

A host of population-related problems has thus emerged, demanding and capturing the attention of governments, non-governmental organisations and the international community. Major population concerns of 118 countries were expressed in response to the Fifth Population Inquiry Among Governments undertaken in 1982-83. The results, published in a 1984 report, showed that 60 percent of developing countries' governments provided direct support to family planning. Approximately 70 percent of developing countries were dissatisfied with their present conditions of health and mortality; other concerns included unsatisfactory patterns of population distribution, and migration trends. The findings of the Inquiry clearly suggest that active and planned intervention is a legitimate function of governments trying to confront these problems.

When India included family planning in its first Five-Year Plan for 1951-56, it became the first government in the world to adopt a national family planning programme. At present, the majority of developing countries have introduced such programmes. Many governments that previously considered population policies to be unnecessary or even harmful have reversed their positions as the impact of population growth on socio-economic development has become more apparent. And while relatively few countries have adopted official population policies, most have formulated goals, objectives and/or strategies that serve as the basis for national population programmes. According to one estimate, 80 out of 126 developing countries had official family planning programmes in 1984. Thus, dramatic changes have occurred

in the perceptions of governments concerning the population issue.

The importance of population goals and policies has moreover been recognised in various international fora in recent years. The International Conference on Population agreed that "to achieve the goals of development, the formulation of national population goals and policies must take into account the need to contribute to an economic development which is environmentally sustainable over the long run and which protects the ecological balance."

Another of the Recommendations adopted at that Conference urged that governments adopt, in the context of overall development, specific policies (including population policies), that will contribute to redressing imbalances between trends in population growth, resources and environmental requirements.

Population pressures on the land are problematical in some areas, where attempts to put marginal or fragile land into agricultural production have resulted in erosion, desertification and in many cases, only short-lived productivity. Rapidly growing populations create demands for increased agricultural output or food imports. Although food production has kept pace with population growth in most areas of the world, food self-sufficiency has been declining in Africa. The population growth rate in the region, three percent during the period 1980-84, has been outstripping food production which increased at the rate of a mere one percent.

The increased agricultural output which must be a part of the global future will be highly dependent on the availability of fresh water supplies. Access to adequate supplies of fresh water is also a crucial element in attempts to improve peoples' health in many parts of the developing world. The global water situation thus provides a clear example of the interrelationships between population trends, the well-being of people, and resource and environmental concerns.

The scarcity of land, limited opportunities for employment, and fewer opportunities for education, health care and other social services are propelling increasing numbers of people from the countryside to the cities. As this proportion rises, rapid urbanisation is creating its own set of complex problems. The UN estimates that while about a third of the people in developing countries lives in cities today, that estimate is likely to reach about a half by the year 2000.

Some national leaders are expressing concern because high population growth rates impede efforts to attain an appreciable level of economic development. The annual rate of growth in sub-Saharan Africa is the highest in the world, with the highest rates of birth and death, as well as the highest rates of infant mortality. Approximately 45 percent of the population is under 15 years of age. As in other parts of the developing world, this young and expanding population creates rising demands for education, employment opportunities, housing, health and other services. In some areas, this creates a strain on basic socio-economic resources and institutions. It also has important implications for human resources

development, one of the priority needs of the developing countries.

Such problems associated with too-rapid population growth are increasingly being addressed by governments of developing countries. Perhaps the most recent example is a 1986 Report by the Organization for African Unity which states that: "Special importance will need to be accorded by each African country to a population policy that will, *inter alia*, address issues of high fertility, morbidity and mortality, rapid urbanisation, rural-urban and rural-rural migration, the problems of children and youth, and the protection of the environment in a manner that will ensure compatibility between demographic trends, appropriate land utilisation and settlement patterns, and the desired pace of economic growth and development."

Imbalances between population and resources, the increase in numbers of the poor, and the rapid pace of urbanisation - all of these contribute to the deterioration of the natural environment.

Set forth in this way, the problems of recreating the balance between population, resources, the environment and development appear even more daunting. Yet there are reasons for optimism, if only because of the knowledge that these problems have never before been seriously addressed. Conscientious efforts to redress these problems recognise that the groups most immediately affected by such imbalances are the poor, who comprise the vast majority of developing country populations. For a policy which will restore the balance, it is of fundamental importance to find out more about this sector's living conditions and concerns.

This has proven to be an effective approach to population concerns. Those countries which have generally been most successful in reducing growth rates are also those in which most attention has been paid to the needs of the majority of the population in education, health care, housing and employment. Also characteristic of these countries are highly effective government structures, taking the form of administrations which are in constant touch with the people and their needs. This is achieved through networks of political communication which cover the whole spectrum between village or urban neighbourhoods and central government.

Those who perceive an ethical element in this pragmatic analysis are not mistaken. To achieve and sustain the physical balance we seek will require a social balance, and a view of self-interest which reaches beyond the immediate future and the small social group, to seek the well-being of the overall community.

* * * * *

This is not an idealistic or soft-hearted approach to the problems of development, but a highly realistic assessment made on the basis of many years' experience in development and in population. The tenets of this approach have been visible in the nature of United Nations Fund for Population Activities (UNFPA) assistance, since 1969 when the Fund first became operational.

A basic aim of UNFPA funding has been to enable countries to become self-reliant in integrating their population policies and programmes with the development planning process, and to build up the capacity of national governments to implement their own population programmes.

Rather than advocating any one population policy or approach to population problems, the Fund assists in dealing with the problems identified by the countries themselves as important. Given the great diversity of population situations existing in developing countries, this may be an important factor in governmental decisions to seek assistance from UNFPA.

The Fund recognises every nation's sovereign right to determine its own population policy, based on its own cultural, religious and socio-economic situation. Equally important, the Fund operates on the principle that individuals have the right to freely and voluntarily determine their family size.

Without knowledge of the dimensions and characteristics of their population, countries' attempts to formulate and implement national development plans would be thwarted. Information on the size, structure, growth, distribution, and change over time of a country's population is essential for many kinds of development planning. UNFPA has provided assistance to many countries for demographic research and censuses. For example, 48 national censuses in Africa have been assisted by the Fund. Research and analytical studies are also supported, in order to provide decision-makers with a better understanding of the causes and consequences of population problems and their interrelationship with other factors.

Once information and understanding of a country's population situation and its relation to relevant socio-economic development factors have been obtained, the groundwork is laid for the integration of population into the country's development planning. UNFPA provides assistance to governments for the formulation of population policies and the establishment of population units in their national development planning.

Because of rapid socio-economic changes - prompted partially by high rates of population growth - there is growing interest among governments in providing information and education about population concerns. Most UNFPA-assisted country programmes include an awareness-building component, offering information about services provided through the programmes, and increasing knowledge and understanding of the implications of population issues.

The World Population Conference of 1974, the World Conference of the International Women's Year in 1975, and the 1984 International Conference on Population contributed to the recognition by many governments that family planning is important in helping to improve the welfare of mothers and children, and to increase the status of women in order to allow them to participate in national development processes. Today, UNFPA assists most countries of the developing world, at their request, by providing support to voluntary family planning programmes, usually in the context of maternal and child health care.

In addition, special programmes for women are supported by the Fund to help women acquire the ability to exercise what the World Population Plan of Action (adopted in 1974) described as their "basic right to decide freely and responsibly the number and spacing of their children, and to have the informa-

tion, education and means to do so." Projects to increase the status of women are given support in and of themselves in order to help integrate women into the development process.

In the field of population, there has been discernible and in some cases remarkable progress during the last decade and a half. Awareness and understanding have increased, programmes have been put into action, policies are increasingly being formulated, and governments have manifested a growing commitment to dealing with their population-related problems. Yet there is a long road ahead of us.

The primary and ultimate goal of population programmes is to improve the levels of living and the quality of life of the people who are reached by those programmes. This is also the goal of strategies, programmes and activities in the areas of resources, environment and development, as reflected in the World Conservation Strategy. Integrating population concerns into this Strategy is a very welcome development.

A number of efforts have been made to gain a better understanding of the inter-relationships between population, resources, environment and development. However, the task is both complicated and difficult. It demands from us a degree of knowledge about our surroundings and conditions of life which we do not yet possess. It demands a sophisticated analysis which has not yet been made with sufficient coherence. But above all, it demands a commitment from the entire international community to look squarely at the conditions of life of people in their environment, and to make a concerted and dedicated attempt to meet their needs. Experts nearly always feel most comfortable in their own fields, but the interdisciplinary approach called for here is an integrationist and interactive process, whereby the barriers traditionally existing between different disciplines are broken down and replaced by open channels of communication.

In its work, UNFPA has attempted to add substance to this approach.

Our long-range vision should be one of long-term sustainable development in a world where population, resources, environment and development have come into equilibrium.

ALTERNATIVE ECONOMIC THEORY FOR SUSTAINABLE DEVELOPMENT; SOME DESIDERATA

Johan Galtung
in cooperation with Per Svae, Ingvar Nilsson, Anders Wadeskog
Princeton University
Princeton, New Jersey, U.S.A.

SUMMARY *The roots of the environmental problem are found in economic theory as well as in economic practices. This paper is concerned with theory, and the point of departure is the division of reality by economic theory into subject matter and externalities. Environmental factors are in the latter, as costs and benefits not accounted for. The economist is inclined to "cost" negative externalities, such as pollution and depletion, and then find some way of working monetary clean-up or replacement costs into the budget. While this approach may sensitise some people to broader "costs," nature, human, social and world space have to be understood in their own right. A global and holistic language is called for, possibly modelled on principles of ecology that seem more general than those of economics. Following the objective of internalising the externalities in economic thought and practice, we could demand of economic actors impact statements as a basis for dialogue about activities with consequences far outside economics.*

The time has now come, is indeed overdue, to do more about the gap in the current debate about economic theory and practice: the need for **alternative economic theory**. Neoclassical theory has been criticised, as has current economic practice - which essentially refers to capitalist and socialist economies, the former from a (neo-) Marxist angle, and both the latter and the former from a (neo-) anarchist angle. There have also been considerable constructive attempts in the direction of building **alternative economic practice**, usually centred around a nucleus of self-reliance, combining age-old human experiences and insights with new experiments (the Green wave). Using colours rather than ideological labels, one might say that there is Blue theory and Blue practice (neoclassical), which have both been criticised by Red (or Pink) theory (neo-Marxist); and there is Red-Pink practice. All of this has been criticised from a Green (anarchist) angle. And there is Green practice. What is required is to develop an alternative to Blue, Red and Green theories.

Neo-classical theory is equilibrium-oriented, using (Aristotelian) equilibrium (particularly between supply and demand) as a reference point for further explorations. In any theory a reference point is useful, like in any human endeavour, in order to know better where one is located. However, much more interesting and useful than a market equilibrium point of reference would be **a normative point of reference** enabling us to understand better how far we are located from a possible goal of economic endeavour. Economic activity is then seen as production, distribution and consumption, whether on the basis of scarcity or abundance (usually there will be a mix, some factors and products being scarce, others being abundant and - possibly for that reason - escaping attention). A theory of choice under conditions of scarcity is a perspective that may take the form of a paradigm but should not be seen as coinciding with economic theory, being both too narrow (valid for those who have options in economic systems, not for those who have no choices) and too broad (this is a perspective that can be applied to any human activity as economists have recently done, but other disciplines have competing paradigms).

A normative point of reference for alternative economic theory would have to locate economic activity in **nature, human, social** and **world** spaces. In nature space, the theory would have to take into account the **theory of ecological balance/maturity**: diversity of biota-abiota and their symbiotic relationship as constraints on economic activity. In human space they would have to take into account a theory of human balance/maturity: **satisfaction of basic needs** (survival, well-being, identity, freedom), but in diversity and symbiosis among human beings, as a constraint on economic activity. In so-

cial space the theory would have to take social balance/maturity into account, building economic systems on diversity in sociotopes (plan **and** market, and modern **and** traditional - as two clear examples) in symbiotic relationship again as a constraint on economic activity. And in world space, alternative economic theory would have to take into account a theory of global balance/maturity, building world systems based on diversity among countries and their active symbiotic co-existence.

An alternative economic theory should see all human beings, not only entrepreneurs, as actors. The task of a good theory is to enlarge action spaces, showing as many ways as possible of obtaining reasonable goals within reasonable limits. The task is not to decide for others what they should do, under the (highly normative) injunction to be rational. Thus, following Kant, the task must also be to search for those types of economic behaviour that are both compatible with the goals indicated above (which can be described as "ecological balance" in nature space, "somatic, mental and spiritual health" in human space, "development" in social space, and "peace" in world space) **and** can, in principle, be engaged in by everybody (are universalisable). Alternative economic theory should look for classes or clusters of possibilities rather than optimal point solutions. It is then for human actors, individual or collective, to design their strategies, including challenging the goals, designing totally new processes for obtaining them, and developing new indicators of the extent to which the processes are goal-compatible. Consequently economic theory, like any other social theory, will always be in flux. There is no such thing as a final theory, nor even an approximation of that abstraction (since economic theory is always moving as economic activity moves) and certainly no asymptotic convergence toward any such abstract point in theory space.

An alternative theory will necessarily have to be global and holistic. It will take into account the effects of economic activity on actors near and remote (and not only the actor, firm, individual or country that initiated the economic activity, but also the reactors); and will imperatively take into account the effects on a broad spectrum of variables in nature, human, social and world spaces rather than being limited to classical "economic" variables, essentially coming out of the bookkeeping tradition for firms.

In this connection "global" stands for more than inter-individual, inter-firm and international; it transcends such conceptualisations into efforts to look at the systems as a whole. And, correspondingly, "holistic" stands for more than inter-disciplinary. The words "transnational" and "transdisciplinary" are better, but could also be seen as stations on the road to more total conceptualisations.

An alternative economic theory should not only be eclectic, based on neoclassical, marxist and anarchist elements, **but should ideally be developed in such a way that these three major trends in economic thinking can come out of the theory as special cases**, given certain choices in the field of assumptions, even certain values for parameters. In other words, alternative economic theory should not be identified with "green" economic theory.

Rather, alternative economic theory should be seen as an overarching theory for societies where economic behaviour would have blue, red, and green components - a "rainbow society," in other words. This is in line with the idea that the theory should expand our economic horizons and not contract them into a more or less narrow "green" corner - although, at the same time, alternative economic theory should be more sensitive to, and take more into account, green criticism and constructive practice than is possible within the blue and the red paradigms. Put differently: in alternative economic theory, there should be room for Adam Smith, Karl Marx and J.M. Keynes - as, indeed, for Kropotkin and Gandhi. The theory will certainly be concerned with how these approaches can be combined, not only in theory but also in practice within a broad range of alternatives. An eclectic theory includes a theory of optimal mixes.

An alternative economic theory would have to build in a self-understanding of economics as a science. Neoclassical theory can be seen as emerging in parallel with the emergence of the bourgeoisie on top of society: they were in need of alternative theory that complemented rather than replaced the theological-philosophical tradition of the clergy and the juridical-military tradition of the aristocracy. The behaviour of the bourgeoisie on the market became the positive point of departure for economics as an empirical science, economics *de facto* becoming "capitalistics." The bourgeoisie needed a theory for their type of power - exchange power based on buying and selling under some rules - again complementing rather than replacing normative powers and coercive power. And their basis was, of course, shop-keeping accounting theory with the shop as the unit of accounting to be followed by the enterprise, with no accounting tradition for the nature, human, social and world spaces. Epistemologically this has conditioned neoclassical theory, by contracting the theory in space, time and knowledge to the company - to the relatively immediate - and to a narrow range of variables deemed to be "economic."

However, this vision has certainly been expanded. The socialist/social democratic tradition introduced "social economics" as an effort to do "national accounting" for a society as a whole, and there are similar efforts (within the United Nations system) for the world as a whole. Such efforts may be linked to the emergence of new groups of powerful bureaucrats at the social and world levels respectively, equally in need of a theory for their own activity and legitimation of their own power. Correspondingly the range of variables has been expanded to some extent because of interaction among ministries at the national level and among agencies at the level of the UN system, although it is quite clear that a great deal of theoretical and practical work remains to be done.

However, recently the impetus toward new directions in economic thinking has come more from "below," staying closer to the ground by watching the impact of economic activity on nature and on human space (in terms of ecological imbalances and threats to the somatic, mental and spiritual health of human beings). The task of alternative economic theory is not only to try to integrate all of these efforts as mentioned above, but to do it with so much self-reflection that the forces behind these changes in economic theory are reflected in the theory itself. In other words, the cultural and structural forces and constraints are seen as determinants of the theory to be brought into the theory so as to enable us to say something about the type of **economists**, and not only the type of **economics**, that will come out of certain socio-cultural conditions, not to mention what kind of society they will try to construct.

In line with the above, **economists are then seen as a major economic factor**. If contemporary neoclassical economists tend to have blind spots for nature, human, social and world spaces; to be relatively unaware of how they and their thinking has been, is, and will be conditioned by cultural and historical factors; or are so philosophically unreflecting that they are incapable of appreciating the points just mentioned, then the net outcome may be highly counter-productive. These economists, then, serve as an input in economic systems, the moreso the more numerous and highly placed they are. (The latter factor makes them different from other social scientists who are usually, at present, in more modest social positions.) Thus, an alternative economic theory would have to see economists as an endogenous, not an exogenous factor, hoping that insight and self-reflection on that factor will change the factor.

For expanded bookkeeping, **new indicators are indispensable**, as many have pointed out. Although efforts are needed to make indications more global and more holistic, there should also be a caution against too high a level of aggregation, because it shows insufficiently where the problems are located, as effects; and from where they originate, as causes. An indicator of life expectancy for the world as a whole is interesting. But it is also important to compare the life expectancies of different age groups, genders, races, classes and nations, even if comparisons only bring out the relative aspect, not the relational aspect. This raises the interesting question of how indicators of relational aspects can be constructed. Imagine that it can be shown that the high life expectancy of nation A to some extent is due to the low life expectancy of nation B, and vice versa. Should one not, in that case, subtract something from the life expectancy of nation A? Within a firm, one branch may be in the black an another branch in the red; the total accounting would have to show the net balance between the two. Using the analogy, one might then look at nation A + B as a "dyad" and construct a measure of the "joint" (for instance, average) life expectancy. There are many ways of doing this; this little note is only to indicate a way of thinking that comes to be automatic as soon as the approach becomes more global and one refuses to draw a circle around an economic actor who accounts only for what passes the borderline to the environment, computing the balance.

A major slogan for alternative economic theory is **to internalise the externalities**. This will also have to be done at the indicator level. Across actors, in other words in the direction of becoming more global, this poses **the problem of level of integration**. In neoclassical theory, firms tend to be seen as the social atoms of inert gases because of the bookkeeping tradition. But recent advances, exploring degrees of coupling, would make it easier to reach out from the isolation of one actor to broader perpectives. Correspondingly, to think in a more holistic manner, this approach gets us immediately into **the problem of comparing across variables** that may be rather incommensurable, not to mention that some of them may not be measurable at all. In other words, there is more than enough work to do for alternative economic theory!

Regardless of the strong points just mentioned as desiderata for alternative economic theory, **there should not be any disregard in this theory for the significance of such factors as efficiency, profitability, or optimum solutions; nor for such notions as harmony and equilibrium**. More particularly, neoclassical theory has one very strong point that should also characterise alternative economic theory: not only the theory but also the economic practice is dynamic. The socialist alternative has a tendency to become more static; the planners using their combination of omniscience and omnipotence (or as much as they have of such godlike characteristics) in order to make the economy surprise-free, not only in space but also in time, achieving a certain immunity to the influence of world conjunctures through a relatively high level of self-sufficiency and by fixing goals of the economy, from above, with a relatively long time horizon. Of course, any effort to make a surprise-free society would dialectically lead to the opposite; but as bursts of unrest, as major discontinuities, rather than as a permanent state of dynamism. Capitalist economy in a certain sense has no other goal than growth, in and by itself dynamic. In addition, **dynamism in space** is guaranteed because of a high level of coupling of actors through trade in visibles and invisibles, and **dynamism in time** guaranteed through the innovative struggle of competitors to remain afloat. It is enough to visit Europe, East and West, or Korea, North and South, to appreciate the tremendous significance of this particular factor: societies close to the freezing point versus societies close to the boiling point. Of course, alternative theory should have this as a major variable and also indicate the range within which one might prefer society to be located - perhaps in a temperate zone!

Any alternative economic theory should have the concept of work as a centrepiece of the theory. A job is a setting where work, often alienated, is done against a salary on conditions decided by the labour-buyer rather than the labour-seller. A job is a special sub-category within the much broader category of work. Work is considered as normal for human beings; a prolonged situation of non-production of any kind of goods or services, material or non-material, is hardly sustainable. Leisure time only devoted to consumption may be imposed upon people as a structural necessity in a certain social formation, but empirical observation seems to indicate that even very soon the need for sustained activity that is goal-directed, in other words, "productive," in the broad sense of that term, asserts itself. To condemn a person to a life in libraries and swimming pools is no solution to the unemployment crisis, as indicated by the fact that those who prescribe such "solutions" usually do not engage in them themselves.

For growth in human space, human development may be obtained in situations of non-work, but since work to a large extent is synonymous with goal-directed activity it has to be organised in such a way that human development, that is, self-realisation, is a part of the activity. Jobs can also be socially useful and acceptable (in other words legitimate and meaningful); they may help to build social networks, develop ability to cooperate, and in addition of course, be economically "interesting." But it is in the broader category of work that self-realisation - existential meaningfulness - can be realised. As a consequence, alternative economic theory has to develop a much broader work concept than a strictly job-concept, based on the buying and selling of labour on the market.

A major task of alternative economic theory is to be helpful as a reservoir of insight from which policy implications can be drawn. The general form of the policy implication would be located in the description-prediction-prescription-strategy complex: a **description** of the present situation; a **prediction** of what will happen if trends continue unimpeded; a **prescription** in the sense of indicating a goal; a **strategy** in the sense of indicating how trends can be "bent" away from the predicted toward the prescribed course. In other words, policy implications should also countain strategies, meaning not only an analysis of **what** should be done, and **why** it should be done, but also the much more precise answers to the questions, **who** shall do it, **how, when** and **where** - and **at whose expense!** Thus, alternative economic theory should not rest content with description and prediction, but should use its postulates about those dates in order to derive strategies, as has been done for generations now within the field of welfare economics.

Alternative economic theory should not be based on any naïve assumption that one can combine all the good aspects of blue, red-pink and green economic thought and practice into a super-system, avoiding all the negative facts. Nor should it assume the pessimism of those who believe that the alternative would eliminate all positive aspects, "combining the worst of capitalism with the worst of socialism," for instance. Alternative theory should look for new solutions and not get caught in the thought prison of having to design trade-offs between old ones.

Just as ecological balance in the human-nature system is a necessary condition for sustainable development, **ecological balance has to occupy a key position in economic theory** for that theory to be realistic in the sense of reflecting reality. The problem is not only choice under scarcity but under diachronic scarcity - scarcity in the future - if ecological balance deteriorates further. Concretely this means that economic theory increasingly has to be written in the currency of nature, which is then seen as diversity *cum* symbiosis. Just as economic actors should make themselves accountable by delivering an impact statement prior to any major and/or new economic action, economic theory should provide the tools for the translation of economic activity in ecological terms.

For economic action to preserve and even strengthen ecological balance, the economic cycle probably has to be limited enough for the initator to suffer, not only enjoy the consequences of the action; and the ecological process should be cyclical rather than linear, usually meaning being more heavily based on natural, organic substances, and less on non-degradable anorganic and artificial organic compounds.

In the same vein, the second absolute in our world, humans with our **basic human needs** should occupy a key position in any theory. The basic purpose of the indicators would be to translate economic action into basic human needs "currency" so as to make impact statements, on impact in human space, more concrete.

The rest, the concrete construction of social space and world space, is abstraction. An indicator for social space such as GNP per capita should never be permitted to occupy a central position in economic theory; it should be justified in terms of ecological balance and basic human needs satisfaction, not vice-versa. Only when economic theory catches up with the action for sustainable development will it become fully relevant.

The foregoing paper is the outcome of a colloquium held at Université Nouvelle Transnationale in Paris, 29-30 June 1986, with the authors as participants.

NATURAL RESOURCE MANAGEMENT AND ECONOMIC DEVELOPMENT

Jeremy J. Warford
World Bank
Washington, D.C., U.S.A.

SUMMARY *This paper argues for the need to design broad economic policy instruments to reverse the trend toward increasing degradation and destruction of natural resources. The natural resource base, often critical for economic development, is in many cases threatened by a rapid population growth, the effect of which is compounded by inadequately controlled land and water use. Policy interventions which have a pervasive effect must be established to influence the environmentally-related behaviour of countless, relatively small-scale, resource-using activities which take place throughout a nation's economy. Natural resource management should become a standard element of macroeconomic and sector analysis, and the physical linkages between sectors need to be critically examined. Governments must overcome major institutional and political obstacles. New approaches, providing incentives and rewards to policy makers, must be developed, to increase interagency cooperation while avoiding overlapping jurisdictions, and to prevent vested interests from paralysing new initiatives.*

INTRODUCTION

The effects of poor resource management are being dramatically demonstrated in many countries in which land and water resources - in principle renewable - are declining at rates that threaten the very basis on which fragile economies rest. While environmental degradation is having a serious impact in many parts of the world, it is the poorest countries which are the most vulnerable, partly because shortages of capital and trained manpower severely limit their ability to switch to other economic activities when the natural resources can no longer sustain them. It is moreover the poorest people in those countries who suffer most from environmental degradation. Those groups are most heavily dependent upon the resource base, the problems of which are compounded by high population growth rates. There are innumerable ways in which the problem is manifested, and generalisations are difficult to make. Yet it is clear that in many developing countries the most critical environmental problems are those which relate to a complex network of events involving land clearance, commercial logging and fuel-wood harvesting, burning of crop residues and dung, over-grazing, soil erosion, sedimentation, flooding, and salinisation. Perhaps two-thirds of the world's population is thus affected. Direct consequences include severe reductions in domestic energy availability and agricultural productivity; indirect consequences have profound and far-reaching effects on human well-being. It is also clear that addressing these problems calls for approaches that question some basic assumptions about economic development, and raise generic issues including the relationships between macro-economic planning and sectoral analysis, the handling of externalities, and the welfare of vulnerable groups and future generations.

The urgency of the problem is widely recognised by governments, and attempts are being made to stem and reverse these trends: ambitious projects are underway to replace trees which have been cut down; to clear dams that have silted-up from soil erosion; to pump groundwater for irrigation to help contain the advancing desert; to clean-up poisoned ground and polluted air. However, in many developing countries the situation is worsening, and many efforts to remedy the problems are failing. In addition to lack of resources (with poverty itself being both a cause and a consequence of environmental damage) there are a number of reasons for this, including political and financial vested interests, institutional overlap and bureaucratic inefficiencies, and the myopic view of decision-makers. But perhaps the most important reason is the sheer difficulty of dealing with a myriad of relatively small-scale natural resource-using activities which together are responsible

for the bulk of environmental degradation.

The traditional approach to environmental management is to invest in projects which have primarily environmental objectives, such as reafforestation or sewerage schemes, or to ensure that components of other projects contain elements designed to mitigate adverse environmental impacts. This essentially project-by-project approach is important, and must be continued. Alone, however, it is clearly inadequate, and needs to be supplemented by more powerful, wide-ranging policies. By concentrating on curative, piecemeal solutions rather than on the underlying causes, the traditional approach - in industrialised as much as in developing countries - fails to confront the real issues which have more to do with the way society works and less with the technical aspects of natural resource degradation. Environmentally-related behaviour and our policy toward it is in fact at the very heart of our social, macro-economic and sector policies relating to agriculture, energy, industry, domestic and foreign investment, fiscal, monetary and trade policy, income distribution, and regional planning.

It appears therefore that the project-by-project approach should be supplemented by one which integrates environmental and natural resource management directly into economic and social policy. This can be done in two ways: (a) through the design of investment programmes supporting environmental and natural resource objectives, and (b) through promoting economic, social and institutional policies and incentives that influence environmentally-related behaviour of government agencies, major resource users, and the countless small-scale resource-using activities which occur throughout a nation's economy. While our understanding of technical ameliorative measures is imperfect, and continued efforts are needed to improve it, the foregoing also implies a need to devote much more effort to developing our understanding of:

* the nature and severity of natural resource degradation in light of economic and social criteria, including the welfare of vulnerable groups and future generations;

* the underlying causes, both human and those occurring naturally, of natural resource degradation; and

* the range of feasible economic, social and institutional policy interventions appropriate to the situation.

These issues are elaborated in the remainder of the paper.

THE COSTS OF NATURAL RESOURCE DEGRADATION

National Accounts and Resource Degradation

The problem of inadequate land and water management is acute not only in ecological terms, but also in terms habitually used by economists; indeed, the disciplines of economics and ecology should be seen as mutually reinforcing. In developing countries, the effects of high debt-burdens and deteriorating terms of trade are being compounded by the severe economic costs of resource degradation, and there are abundant examples of individual environmental protection measures - both policies and projects - which show acceptable returns even according to narrowly defined benefit-cost criteria. Unfortunately, the status of renewable natural resource stocks is rarely considered in a systematic, comprehensive way at the macro-economic level, where major strategic planning decisions are made. It is even more rare for explicit linkages to be established between national income accounts and the renewable natural resource base upon which so many economies depend.

It is, however, increasingly being recognised that conventional measures of national income, such as GNP per capita, give misleadingly favourable estimates of economic well-being or economic growth. These measures do not recognise the diminishing of natural capital stocks (be they renewable or non-renewable), and instead consider the depletion of resources, i.e., the loss of wealth, as net income. Growth built on resource depletion is clearly very different from that obtained from productive efforts, and may be quite unsustainable. Unless net capital formation is larger than natural resource depreciation, the economy's total assets decline as resources are extracted or degraded: this appears to be exactly what is happening in many of the poorer, natural resource-based economies.

By definition, while exploitation of non-renewables such as oil or coal involves depletion, land and water use does not necessarily do so. The complexity of the physical linkages between activities, and uncertainty as to the ability of land and water resources to regenerate, have previously masked what has been happening. Costs of natural resource depletion have not been estimated and, together with all other forms of depletion, have certainly not been reflected in national income accounts. Policy makers, relying upon GNP as a criterion for national well-being (and perhaps being preoccupied with short-term considerations), may therefore have been lulled into a false sense of security. Indeed, the numbers may be large: for example, rough estimates show the economic costs of unsustainable forest harvesting in major tropical hardwood exporting countries ranging from 4 to 6 percent of GNP, offsetting any economic growth that may otherwise have been achieved.

The point of the foregoing is not to suggest reform of national income accounts (although they have a number of serious shortcomings in addition to the one noted here). Rather, it is to emphasise the importance of natural resource depletion in an overall country planning context. That is to say that the macro-economic impact of natural resource utilisation and depletion calls for macro-economic policies to regulate it. A critical step in this process is to refine our understanding of relationships between physical events and their economic consequences. Attempts need to be made to quantify the physical nature and extent of the degradation processes to the greatest extent possible, and to express them in monetary terms where feasible. This would help to highlight the consequences of different patterns of resource utilisation for future economic growth, and provide a better basis for making strategic decisions concerning resource conservation, augmentation, or even further exploitation.

The Marginal Opportunity Cost of Resource Depletion

A useful tool for conceptualising and measuring the physical effects of resource depletion in economic terms is the marginal opportunity cost (MOC). This refers to the cost borne by society of depleting a natural resource, and ideally, would be equal to the price that users have to pay for resource-depleting activities. A price less than MOC stimulates over-utilisation: a price greater than MOC stifles justifiable consumption. Marginal opportunity cost may be described in terms of its three elements:

* the direct cost to the user of depleting the resource;

* the benefits foregone by those who might have used the resource in the future (applicable to renewable resources if they are not harvested on a sustainable basis); and

* the costs imposed on others, either now or in the future (so-called external costs).

Although the concept has been extensively employed in analysing the costs of depletable commercial energy resources, calculation of marginal opportunity cost is never easy. This is particularly true of the kind of natural resources discussed in this paper. Nevertheless, several useful efforts have been made, including estimates of the value of agricultural output losses due to deforestation, and of foregone electricity output from dam sedimentation. Of greater importance than the final result itself, however, is the discipline that is required to painstakingly evaluate all physical interrelationships and analyse each of the effects of resource use. This applies in particular to the importance of making explicit the tradeoffs or value judgements involved regarding impacts which cannot be evaluated in monetary terms. These include decisions about the income distributional consequences of alternative patterns of resource use, the impact on vulnerable groups such as indigenous peoples, the preservation of antiquities, irreversible effects, genetic diversity, and the welfare of future generations. The proportion of marginal opportunity cost that may be estimated unambiguously in monetary terms will sometimes be large, sometimes small; the analytical framework for arriving at the point of decision-making appears, however, to be of universal applicability, and marginal opportunity cost may be used effectively as a benchmark to help make judgements about such things as:

* the merits of conservation or protective measures, including investments, regulations and laws;

* taxes, subsidies, and prices of natural resources or their complements or substitutes.

Discount Rates, Irreversible Effects, and Future Generations

Economic analysis has a critically important role in determining appropriate investments and policies in the environmental area, if its limitations are recognised. In highlighting the consequences of certain events that cannot themselves be measured in monetary units, and making those consequences explicit in its own narrowly defined terms, economic analysis may be an indispensable aid to good decision-making, but it may fail as a discipline if it is pushed too far.

The limits of economic analysis are illustrated very well in the treatment of equity considerations, of which the welfare of future generations is a special case. It is often claimed that traditional benefit-cost analysis fails in that discount rates used are too high, resulting in inadequate weight being given to the costs of resource depletion or the benefits of conservation measures to future generations. In fact, manipulation of discount rates is not the answer, for it is inconceivable that one could arrive at a specific discount rate which satisfactorily reflects the various value judgements and technical parameters (e.g., private and social time preferences, welfare of future generations, productivity of capital, economic growth and savings rates) that are involved. It is much too blunt an instrument for that.

There are circumstances in which intertemporal choices can be made quite satisfactorily by the use of discount rates that reflect returns to capital in alternative uses based upon fairly short-run market criteria. This applies where there is no reason to expect one generation to be very much worse or better-off than another, or where irreversible effects are not involved. Gains resulting from projects or activities which pass standard economic tests could, if future societies so choose, be reinvested for the benefit of generations still further in the future. In these circumstances, marginal opportunity cost alone, using market-based discount rates to estimate future costs and benefits, may be used as an adequate benchmark to evaluate investments or policies. However, where irreversible effects are involved, or where future societies are expected to be significantly richer or poorer than the present one, marginal opportunity cost must be supplemented by analysis of likely physical and income distributional consequences. Uncertainties involved in making predictions about events that will take place many years hence should not deter us from taking such analysis at least as seriously as we now take conventional benefit-cost analysis.

The future generations issue is important, not only in itself, but also because it is a good illustration of the role and limitations of economic analysis in natural resource management. In practice, however, we should not allow it to obscure or become an obstacle to the resolution of more immediate environmental concerns. The urgent problems of the Sahel, for example, suggest that priority should be given to resource management (including externalities) which have an immediate impact, because irreversible effects are already taking place, and the welfare of future generations will depend largely upon measures that improve the well-being of those now living.

THE CAUSES OF NATURAL RESOURCE DEGRADATION

Physical and Behavioural Linkages

The calculation of marginal opportunity cost requires a systematic effort to trace through the often highly complex interrelationships between resource-using activities. Underlying causes of environmental degradation are often related to activities that at first sight are only remotely connected to the observed effects. If project and policy measures are to be viable, they should be based upon a sound understanding, not only of the physical linkages between events, but also the equally complex economic, financial, social and institutional linkages which parallel them. This requires still further refinement of our understanding of the magnitude and extent of interdepen-

dence between man-made activities and natural resource systems, e.g., between deforestation, land clearance, and overgrazing on one hand, and soil degradation, erosion, watershed destruction, and sedimentation on the other. Efforts should be made to quantify impacts at each stage of the interlinked ecological and economic system, in physical and/or monetary terms, to determine the points at which it would be most socially profitable to intervene through explicit policy measures. One essential element of this exercise would be to separate out the contribution of naturally-occurring events to environmental degradation which may dwarf the impact of human activities.

Improvement of Physical Data

Establishing the link between economic analysis and environmental considerations has typically been frustrated in the past by the inadequacy of physical data. This situation is changing rapidly: recent developments in geographic information systems not only allow us to assess current natural resource endowments and use trends, but also to better project future endowments under various scenarios of economic growth and sectoral output. In particular, in assessing physical linkages and long-term trends, remote sensing from space may offer the benefit of a broad synoptic view, repetitive coverage, and uniformity with respect to the way information is collected. Combined with traditional methods of collecting physical data, and by integrating such information with socio-economic data (on population, land tenure systems and so forth), these developments suggest that systematic linking of macro-economic and resource planning can indeed become a reality. Economic planners therefore have a major role in helping to ensure that the collection and analysis of technical information is well focused, and geared to operational or policy requirements.

Improved Understanding of Behavioural Factors

Along with better understanding of physical data, we also need to develop a better understanding of individual and institutional behaviour as it relates to resource use. This very much requires a multidisciplinary approach, and analysis of causes that are even more fundamental to the way society works than those already discussed. The range of variables that potentially affect environmentally-related behaviour is awesome. Taxes, prices and subsidies relating to agriculture/forest products, their substitutes and complements; income distribution, land tenure and property rights arrangements; the government and private sector institutional structure; population pressure; education levels in general, and of women in particular; and the political power structure may all play a role in determining the rate of environmental decay. In addition to the range of expertise in the physical sciences, determination of policies therefore calls for the involvement of the economist, political scientist, sociologist, and anthropologist, as well as for legal and institutional expertise.

POLICY INTERVENTIONS

Project and Policy Intervention

As noted, the traditional approach to environmental problems is for public authorities to engage in projects such as reafforestation and pollution control, which are aimed at remedying past abuse of the environment, or to prevent degradation by building ameliorative components into industrial projects or irrigation schemes. The kind of technical, economic and social data, and the nature of the value judgements needed to make sensible decisions about such investments, is also required in designing policy interventions. The kinds of empirical and conceptual problems encountered in determining appropriate economic incentives parallel very closely those related to the conduct of benefit-cost studies, and estimation of marginal opportunity cost is equally important in project as in policy analysis. In one area however, the design of policy interventions is more complex than project analysis: while the success of projects rests heavily upon behavioural issues, the success of policy interventions depends even more heavily upon them, and in particular upon the prospects for changing them.

Elimination of Existing Subsidies

Much work also needs to be done in this area, but already considerable evidence for optimism exists as to our ability to make concrete recommendations about feasible policy interventions. Examples abound of instances in which government policies, typically in the form of direct subsidies to environmentally harmful activities, are also unwarranted even in narrowly defined, traditional economic terms. This is particularly true with regard to forestry policies. Governments have frequently established inappropriate forest revenue systems that leave enormous profits to the timber industry and provide little incentive for sustainable long-term forestry. Such profits result from a variety of subsidies and tax concessions, including:

* free provision of infrastructure, such as roads and port facilities;

* reduced or waived export taxes on processed wood;

* subsidised credit and export financing;

* tax holidays and unlimited loss carry-over provisions; and

* concessional leases.

Problems are compounded by short-term leases (sometimes for as little as one year), which encourage concessionaires to exploit forests without concern for future productivity. In a number of countries, property rights are automatically conferred upon those who clear the land and use it, thus providing further incentive not to leave standing forest untouched.

Inappropriate incentives affect more than forest use. Encouraged by subsidies, excessive use of pesticides has led not only to increased exposure to toxic substances, but also to more resistant strains of mosquitoes and to a resurgence of malaria in many parts of the world. Resistance of other insects to pesticides is also growing, and net economic losses - even in the short-term - may be a direct consequence of subsidies. Returns have frequently been found to be higher when use is made of integrated pest management practices, involving minimal applications of pesticide, combined with more resistant crop varieties and naturally-occurring pesticides.

There are many more examples of incentives that lead to resource degradation. The typical means of providing irrigation water, for instance, tends to encourage wasteful use. Introduction of user charges covering full economic costs rather than simply operating costs may do much to improve the situation. We perhaps accept too readily the argument that the administrative difficulties of charging for irrigation water on the basis of use presents an insurmountable hurdle. Pricing of electric power is another interesting and illustrative case: governments typically require electricity consumers to pay charges which cover the financial costs incurred by the utility. These costs, however, frequently underestimate economic and social costs; they are lower than marginal opportunity cost, for example, when future resource exploitation costs more than previous schemes (typically true of hydro systems), or when pollution costs are not fully borne by the utility. Subsidy may be said to exist if the price paid for publicly provided goods or services is less than marginal opportunity cost; it will often be the case that increasing prices beyond those required to meet the financial objectives of power utilities will improve the efficiency of resource utilisation and enhance environmental objectives.

The foregoing examples all have a common characteristic: they represent cases in which government policies have perverse effects in both environmental and standard economic terms. They also represent fairly direct incentives for wasteful environmental management. Greater reliance upon natural market forces and removal of the distorting influence of government interventions will in these instances be the appropriate policy stance. Determination of the appropriate policy prescriptions in such cases is in principle straightforward, although since vested interests are involved, policies may not be so easy to determine in practice.

Externalities, the "Commons" Problem and Naturally-Occurring Events

Quite appropriately, the emphasis of policy reform in the agricultural sector over recent years has stressed the importance of reliance upon market forces to provide correct signals to producers and consumers. However, as we all know, the free market is a good servant but a bad master; it is characteristic of environmental problems that they frequently cannot be resolved in an efficient or equitable manner by unregulated market mechanisms, which leaves no alternative but some form of public intervention. Indeed, the subsidies referred to in the preceding paragraphs might justifiably be replaced by taxes.

Interference with market processes is currently somewhat unfashionable, but examples of situations calling for it are abundant: the "commons" problem, in which exploitation of a resource such as grazing land may continue to appear profitable for additional users while actually being disastrous for all, frequently warrants public intervention. Common ownership does not necessarily imply a problem: tribal ownership of property is frequently characterised by sustainable farming methods. The most serious problems tend to be associated with the use of land or other resources for which ownership is not clearly defined. Measures designed to induce prudent management of such communal resources may include physical restrictions, pricing policies, or the introduction of a variety of property

rights, land tenure and leasing arrangements. The financial and technical assistance and water rights protection given to private pastoral associations in some West African countries are examples of public interventions aimed at the "commons" problem.

Central to the natural resource management issue is of course the presence of external effects; thus it is frequently in the private interest of individuals to act in such a way that costs are imposed upon others who are not in a position to demand compensation. Examples are legion: the complex physical linkages between various types of resource-using activities referred to earlier typically imply a series of external effects that can only be controlled by government intervention.

The types of incentives to deal with externalities may require extremely indirect methods. For example, a tax levied on livestock production might reduce over-grazing leading to a reduction in land clearance, and by stemming the rate of soil erosion, exert a beneficial influence on agricultural productivity many miles away. Ideally, the tax should be such that the livestock producer faces total input costs equal to the marginal opportunity cost of his activity, which is determined, *inter alia,* from the effects on soil erosion and consequent impact on agricultural output elsewhere in the system. Export taxes on logs; taxes or subsidies varying by crop (according to their soil conserving characteristics); and subsidisation of energy-efficient woodstoves or of kerosene are further examples of possible interventions that call for careful weighing of costs and possible perverse effects against the economic and environmental benefits that might result.

Finally, public intervention may be required to manage or ameliorate the effects of naturally-occurring resource degradation, including both gradual and catastrophic events. Measures should be designed in light of the costs and benefits (broadly defined) of the ameliorative action. The contribution to damages made by natural forces and by human activity needs to be disentangled and incentives or other policies designed accordingly. For example, avoidance of flooding caused by naturally-occurring soil erosion and sedimentation might be assisted by incentives to induce industrial or residential location in less damage-prone areas; on the other hand, to the extent that commercial logging is responsible, the focus should be on incentives designed to improve the management of forest resources.

The Administrative Costs of Incentive Systems

One of the basic arguments in favour of an approach to natural resource management which relies upon pervasive incentive systems is an administrative one. The costs of dealing with widespread environmental degradation on a case-by-case basis are likely to be excessive. However, designing and implementing incentive systems are also not costless, because all systems to a greater or lesser degree involve monitoring, policing, and regulation. A system of stumpage fees, for example, may require extensive monitoring; irrigation water charges may need metering; the bureaucratic and legal costs of administering land-reform schemes may be overwhelming.

The decision as to whether a system of incentives or regulations is worthwhile may be assisted by, and subject to the usual limitations of, a benefit-cost approach. The cost of the incentive system itself (e.g. the cost of measuring water consumption and collecting fees from water users), should be compared with the estimated benefits, i.e., the savings from the change in resource use resulting from introduction of the incentive scheme. The magnitude of the savings would depend upon the reaction of the users to the price change (price elasticity of demand), and the marginal opportunity cost of the activity to which the incentive scheme is formally applied.

THE NEED FOR PARALLEL ACTIONS

Distribution of Income and Wealth

The types of intervention discussed in the previous section, some quite direct, some less so, could all conceivably be introduced within existing social and institutional systems. Other influences are also of critical importance but represent more fundamental characteristics of the societies concerned, and therefore are likely to be more difficult to change. One of these is the great inequality in income and wealth that tends to characterise many developing countries. This is often reflected in an extremely skewed distribution of land which in itself may be an obstacle to sound natural resource management.

As population pressure grows, the poor tend to be marginalised onto areas of low agricultural potential and which are frequently ecologically sensitive (semi-arid savannas, erosion-prone hillsides, tropical forests). The situation is aggravated where large farmers respond to growing pressures to expand primary commodity exports and thus enlarge the areas on which cash crops are grown. At the same time, there is evidence that large land-owners - particularly those engaging in monoculture - do not protect the quality of their land and soil as much as do small farmers who own their land. Intuition also suggests, although hard evidence is not conclusive, that security of land tenure exerts a positive influence on conservation. With inadequate control over the land they farm and little political weight, the poor cannot easily obtain the capital, external information and technology by means of which to reverse their plight.

While the issue of land reform is a central question of natural resource management, it is also one of the most difficult to address. In developing countries the relevant decisions are frequently made by a small, politically influential group with interests in commercial logging, ranching, plantation cropping, and large-scale irrigated farming operations. As a result, the prevailing systems of investment incentives, tax provisions, credit and land concessions, and agricultural pricing policies tend to favour those in power, causing losses for the economy as a whole, while damaging the environment and resource base.

Institutional Structures

Another obstacle to improving natural resource management may be the government institutional structure, in which the activities of public agencies may impinge on parties whose welfare is of no concern to them. For example, the costs of a hydroelectric scheme to farmers or indigenous peoples may not be adequately taken into account by a power utility; downstream flooding caused by a river development scheme may not influence a provincial government if the damage occurs outside its borders. Coordination and control of resource use to implement incentive systems which impact on several sectors may require the creation of new agencies with authority over certain functional ministry operations in a given region. Also required are incentives to induce public servants to act for the common good, in addition to the goals of their own agencies. The complexity of achieving such changes is obvious, but this represents one of the most important public sector management issues facing developing countries today.

Population

Population pressure is one of the root causes of poverty in general and of natural resource degradation in particular. Accordingly, the success of economic and other incentives will depend largely on the success of family planning and other population-related policies. For purposes of the present discussion, there is little to add: virtually all governments recognise the problem of population growth, and major efforts are being made on both the supply side through provision of family planning facilities, and on the demand side primarily by education, to address this fundamental issue. Economic considerations, whether we like it or not, play some role in individual decisions about family size and spacing. The role that governments should play in influencing choice by economic incentives or other means is a highly controversial subject, which goes well beyond natural resource management issues.

The Role of Women

One aspect of the population issue which does concern us directly is the role of women as household and small-farm decision-makers. In many developing societies, women carry the major burden in supporting the household and in performing agricultural work. Without their involvement, resource-related policies are unlikely to succeed. In Africa, about 80 percent of subsistence agriculture is carried out by women; men increasingly are involved in attending to cash crops or have migrated to urban areas. Women normally do not have title to land, nor adequate access to credit. They may therefore be in no position to take the steps necessary to protect the quality of the land and water resources within their control. The fact that women generally also have less education than men compounds the problem. Equality of educational opportunity, of land ownership, and of access to credit are therefore required if decision-makers at the household and small-farm level are to be able to respond effectively to incentive systems.

CONCLUSION

Approached from the perspective described in this paper, an agenda for action is emerging; within it economics has a major role to play in bringing together and mutually reinforcing environment and development. On the basis of broad natural resource assessments, economic tools may be employed to help determine the desirability of environmentally-related projects, their design and location. Economic analysis may be vital in pin-

pointing the need for new incentives, or the removal of misguided existing incentive systems. Used properly, economics can identify the policy instruments which are necessary if sustainable development is to be achieved.

At the same time, the broader policy focus requires that the traditional economic approach be reassessed, and that methodologies be improved and refined. In fact, much could be gained if the tools and concepts already offered by economic theory were to be applied systematically and correctly. Economic analysis must avoid taking a static view, focusing instead on the dynamic nature of the complex environmental and natural resource problems with their multitude of linkages and indirect effects. Many of these effects either show up at far-away locations (e.g., downstream effects), or in the distant future (e.g., gradual depletion of soil nutrients), posing a major challenge to economists who must learn first to understand the many co-evolutionary processes - the physical interactions plus the human impact - and then to apply suitable economic methods.

Moreover, if economic methods are to be successful, it is crucial that their limitations be understood and continually kept in mind. In particular, it should be recognised that value judgements about distributional and irreversible effects are unavoidable, but quantification in monetary terms of as many variables as possible is important in crystallising those issues involving implicit value judgements which may otherwise be ignored.

Economic assessments and projections will necessarily be fraught with uncertainty, given the complexity of the various physical and behavioural linkages involved in natural resource management. This makes it imperative that economists recognise the technical limitations of their profession and collaborate actively with specialists in many other areas, including: engineers, agriculturalists, natural and social scientists, lawyers and management experts. This is, above all, an activity that calls for a multi-sectoral and multi-disciplinary approach.

An agenda for action, to be developed at the individual country level, should consist of work in the following areas:

* assisted by new technologies, assessment of the existing natural resource base, trends and patterns in resource utilisation, and prospects for the future under various scenarios of economic growth by major sector;

* estimation of the impact of resource depletion on net national product to highlight the magnitude of the problem;

* estimation of the economic and social consequences of major categories of resource use, based upon the marginal opportunity cost framework;

* use of such information to make judgements about the merits of resource conservation, augmentation or further exploitation strategies at the country planning level;

* in light of the foregoing, identification of investment programmes, and areas where widely-impacting policy interventions need to be introduced;

* elimination of those goverment policies (typically subsidies) which are clearly perverse, not only in narrow economic terms, but also in terms of their direct environmental impact;

* design and introduction of more complex interventions, calling for incentives - price, tax and subsidy policies - which have an important, but often indirect impact on resource use, and which address externalities and the "commons" problem;

* continued efforts to address major underlying causes, not only of natural resource degradation, but of development problems generally, including income and land distribution; population growth, education and the status of women; and institutional reform.

The logic underlying the above agenda is applicable to the handling of environmental problems in general, and is clearly consistent, for example, with some of the arguments used to justify the "polluter-pays" principle. The experience of developed countries in trying to get to grips with industrial pollution provides no grounds for complacency about the task that lies ahead; indeed, a massive effort - analytical, empirical, and persuasive - will be needed to implement the agenda. However, there are feasible ways of integrating natural resource issues into economic planning at the national level to give "equal time" to environmental concerns. It has been noted that the case for certain types of intervention is fairly straightforward; their impacts will be direct and easily justifiable in conventional economic terms, as well as being environmentally beneficial. Given progress in these areas, there are grounds for optimism that steps involving the design of more complex, indirect interventions, and even of policies which address the underlying causes of natural resource degradation will be successful.

The views expressed in this paper are those of the author, and should not be attributed to the World Bank, to its affiliated organisations, or to any individual acting on their behalf.

The author is, however, indebted to many colleagues in helping him to formulate the ideas contained in this paper, and for comments on earlier drafts of the paper itself. He is especially grateful to R. Ackerman, D. Anderson, T. Blinkhorn, D. King, D. Pearce, N. Myers, R. Repetto, R. Goodland, R. Overby, A. Sfeir-Younis, J. Spears, L. Squire, P. Thacher, and J. van Holst Pellekaan.

REFERENCES

- Anderson, Dennis and Robert Fishwick, 1984, *Fuelwood Consumption and Deforestation in African Countries,* Staff Working Paper No. 704, World Bank, Washington D.C.

- Baumol, William and Wallace E. Oates, 1975, *The Theory of Environmental Policy: Externalities, Public Outlays and the Quality of Life,* Prentice-Hall, Englewood Cliffs, N.J.

- Mishan, Ezra J., 1976, *Cost-Benefit Analysis,* Praeger, New York.

- Noronha, Raymond and Francis J. Lethem, 1981, *Traditional Land Tenures and Land Use Systems,* Staff Working Paper No. 561, World Bank, Washington D.C.

- Page, Talbot, 1977, *Conservation and Economic Efficiency,* "Resources for the Future," Johns Hopkins Press, Baltimore, Maryland.

- Pearce, David W., 1975, *The Economics of Natural Resource Depletion,* Macmillan, London.

- Repetto, Robert, 1986, *World Enough and Time*, Yale University Press, New Haven and London.

- World Resources Institute and International Institute for Environment and Development, 1986, *World Resources 1986,* Basic Books, New York.

CULTURE, PERCEPTION AND ATTITUDES TO THE ENVIRONMENT

Madhav Gadgil
Indian Institute of Science
Bangalore, India

SUMMARY *Homo sapiens is the only species known to practise ecological prudence, i.e. restraint in the use of resources to ensure their availability at a stable or higher level in the long run. However, the question remains as to how cultures come to assume prudent or profligate patterns of resource use. Cultural behaviour has been conditioned by the long history of mankind as members of well-knit social groups to further interests of one's own group and show antipathy toward interests of alien groups.*

Over history, cultural groups whose resource use was affected by extensively-shared interests were more likely to evolve practices of prudence while others have demonstrated more profligate practices. The response of the World Conservation Strategy to the latter group, especially in the Third World, needs to be broadened to take account of how cultures affect resource use. This would include an attempt to retain and nurture prudent practices of the non-Western world, although these must now be incorporated in the idiom of science. The ultimate solution lies in a new, genuinely egalitarian social order within nation states as well as between them, since only this can create the commonality of interest among world peoples, eventually giving rise to a new culture of prudent resource use.

INTRODUCTION

Homo sapiens is a species unique in many ways. Through the use of tools, symbolic language and cultural transmission of information, we have acquired an unprecedented level of control over the environment. We are also the only species definitely known to display ecological prudence, i.e. restraint in resource use to ensure its availability at constant or higher levels over the long-term (Gadgil, 1985a). Such prudent behaviour is not however universal; many human groups utilise resources at their disposal in a profligate fashion. This uneven incidence of ecological prudence, in time, in space and in respect to different kinds of resources, is among the most intriguing questions facing the student of human behaviour; it is also a question of vital practical import.

Resource use patterns adopted by human groups are affected by earlier use patterns of those groups, as well as by other groups with whom they are in contact. Thus, resource use patterns are conditioned by culture, which we define here as patterns of behaviour that are learned from other members of the population through cultural transmission (Bonner, 1980; Cavalli-Sforza and Feldman, 1981; Boyd and Richerson, 1984). It is evidently these cultural patterns of behaviour that cause human groups to act beyond immediate biological needs of survival and reproduction, sometimes encouraging them to refrain from immediate resource consumption in the long-term interests of the group.

What then are the forces that mould these culturally-prescribed patterns of behaviour? Opinions diverge widely on this issue, ranging from the position that cultural behaviour is totally free of biological constraints, to the belief that cultural behaviour takes forms which enable individuals to maximise their genetic fitness (Alexander, 1979; Sahlins, 1977). We adopt here the syncretic position taken by Boyd and Richerson (1984) who argue that while cultural behaviour will not necessarily help maximise individual genetic fitness, it will be conditioned by certain broad genetically-prescribed tendencies. These would undoubtedly include a propensity to pursue selfish interests. However in addition, they suggest that selection at the level of groups must have played a significant role in moulding man's innate tendencies and therefore group loyalty. The tendency to conform to behaviour patterns of other group members, as well as antipathy toward interests of other groups may

be part of our genetically-prescribed bias. It is also plausible that willingness to establish bonds of cooperation based on reciprocity would be a part of man's innate genetic tendencies (Axelrod, 1983).

So far, these suggestions of innate tendencies are merely based on theoretical arguments and anecdotal evidence; there is no firm empirical basis for any of them. Nonetheless, they are highly plausible and provide us with a useful framework within which to explore human cultural behaviour. This essay will attempt to further develop that framework, exploring human cultures, perceptions and attitudes to the environment. Special emphasis will be placed on one particular expression of these perceptions, namely the World Conservation Strategy.

SOCIAL ORGANISATION

A Hierarchy of Groups

Much human resource-related behaviour is a function of our organised social activity. In other words, mankind deals with environmental resources in groups of variable size and composition, ranging from nuclear families and hunting bands to nation states and multinational corporations. Their adopted patterns of resource use may thus be expected to reflect the tendency to further interests of their own group, and be indifferent to or even inimical to interests of alien groups. Restrained resource use would serve the interests of a group provided that greater resource availability later on benefits the group concerned. This would happen if the group continued to depend on use of that resource at the later time, and if other groups were unlikely to usurp the benefits of its prudence. On the other hand, profligate use of a resource would serve a group's interests when restraint is unlikely to benefit it in the future or restrained use may benefit groups that are in competition with it.

We suggest that individuals, as well as people acting in groups, perceive group interests in this fashion and that these perceptions in turn affect their attitudes toward environmental resources. Everyone simultaneously participates in groups at numerous social levels, which may include a family, tribe or caste, a professional group, a corporation, a nation state, or even the entire biosphere. The interests of these various groups may often diverge. The relative weight that an individual attaches to divergent interests of groups depends on the extent to which he shares in benefits accruing to the group. Thus, an individual will strongly identify with interests of a relatively homogeneous group whose well-being benefits him, but do so less in the case of a heterogeneous group which only benefits him marginally. Moreover, an individual will strongly identify as alien a group in whose well-being he does not share at all. We may then expect an individual to perceive as appropriate the prudent use of resources when such prudence benefits a group with which he has a strong commonality of interest. Conversely, profligate use of resources will be seen as proper when prudence will only benefit other groups with whom he has little commonality of interest.

Perceptions and Culture

While perceptions and attitudes may respond quickly to an individual's interest as a group member, culturally-determined patterns of behaviour would respond somewhat differently. This is because behaviour patterns are based on an integration of conditions over long time periods and over a large number of individuals. Hence, culture is influenced strongly by the earlier history of groups as well as by interests of more dominant groups within the society. The emergent behaviour of individuals is an outcome of the prevalent culture, as well as their individual perceptions.

Commonality of Interests

Consider a specific resource, for instance the population of blue whales in world oceans, a particular stand of forest in the middle Himalayas, or water flowing in a Kenyan stream. Consider such a resource over a reasonably long time-scale, say a few generations. We can then propose the set of individuals that will have some access to and measure of control over any given resource during the extended time-scale. We suggest that these individuals would perceive prudent use of the resource as appropriate only if they possess a broad commonality of interests. On the other hand, if they strongly diverge in their interests, they would tend to consider profligate resource use as proper. Such perceptions would be translated into elements of cultural patterns of behaviour if they persist over time, and especially if they are maintained by dominant groups within the society.

INSTITUTIONALISING RESOURCE USE

Idiom of Ritual

Human cultures have adopted a variety of devices to institutionalise either prudent or profligate use of resources. These employ three kinds of idiom: ritual, custom and codified knowledge. Of these, the idiom of ritual is oldest and based on a model of nature that treats hills, rivers, trees and snakes as creatures with which humans are bound in a social relationship. Since most positive human relationships are woven out of kinship or reciprocity ties, these entities are treated as kin (especially as mothers) or organisms in a mutualistic relationship. In this idiom they are either offered gifts of value (sacrifices) or are promised protection from excessive harm at the hands of humans. Thus, traditionally in India, the Peepal tree (*Ficus religiosa*) is never cut, nor any cobra killed; no fishing is allowed in sacred ponds; no breeding heron, stork or crane is disturbed, and poisoning of rivers for fishing is restricted to a few ritual occasions. Such restrictions, likely to have arisen during the hunting-gathering time, have undoubtedly contributed toward sustainable resource use (Gadgil, 1985b).

Idiom of Custom

The more complex societies of agricultural pastoral times retained a number of such ritual restraints on resource use; they added others in the idiom of custom, i.e. an agreed pattern of behaviour within relatively-small social groups. For instance, there are two communities of basket weavers in western Maharashtra (India): Kaikadis and Makadwalles. Of these, the former uses only bamboo and the latter only palm leaves. Of three endogamous groups of nomadic hunters in the same region, only Phasepardhis snare blackbuck and deer, Vaidus concentrate on trapping small carnivores, while Nandiwallas seek out wild pigs and monitor lizards. In consequence, tradi-

tionally, Phasepardhis had a monopoly over blackbuck populations of a certain region. They report that they also had the custom of releasing any fawns or pregnant does that they snared, a practice that undoubtedly helped maintain the blackbuck populations (Gadgil and Malhotra, 1983).

Ritual and custom were also turned toward decimation of resources as well as their sustainable use. The Indian epic Mahabharata, dated around 1000 b.c., describes an episode in which an entire forest on the bank of Yamuna was burned to appease the fire god, Agni. Those offering this sacrifice drove back every animal and tribal member attempting to escape from the burning forest. This is perhaps a real life episode depicting the struggle between forest dwelling hunter-gatherers and agricultural/pastoral people for land, with the latter justifying themselves in the idiom of a ritual sacrifice to the fire god (Gadgil, in press).

Christianity too attacked nature worship and related taboos, cutting down sacred groves of oak trees to construct churches. The nineteenth century custom of wearing egret plumes (womens' hats), or the still persistent wearing of fur coats from wild mammal skins, or the demand for rhino horn as a supposed aphrodisiac, provide striking examples of customs responsible for resource decimation.

Codification

Systemisation of resource use must have begun with urbanisation when demands of trade and taxation introduced measurement and recording. An early example of codified resource use is the setting aside of special elephant forests prescribed in Kautilya's Arthasastra, a third century b.c. Manual of Statecraft from India (Kangle, 1969). Elephants were captured from such forests for use in armies by the king. There was to be no other capture or killing of elephants under threat of capital punishment.

Application of codified knowledge for regulating resource use has increased significantly with the rise of modern science. Issues addressed range from maximum sustainable yields of exploited fish populations to the destruction of life on earth following a nuclear war. Again such codified knowledge has been harnessed to promote prudent as well as exhaustive use of resources.

PATTERNS OF HISTORY

Hunter-gatherers

Historically, dramatic changes have occurred in resource use patterns as well as in human social organisation. For much of its history, the human species was organised in territorial tribal groups of hunter-gatherers using environmental resources in a relatively modest way. In this phase members of a tribe, controlling resources over a given territory, had a strong commonality of interests. As suggested above, this should have favoured prudent resource use. Prudent use was, in fact, institutionalised through various ritual restraints, permitting these societies to remain in equilibrium with their resource base over tens of thousands of years.

Farming Societies

With the introduction of plant cultivation and animal domestication, human societies substantially increased their use of living resources. Simultaneously they became much more heterogeneous. The ruling elite that emerged in these societies claimed control over increasingly vast terrains. The response was twofold: Smaller, more homogeneous groups such as nuclear families now controlled resources in restricted areas, for example as individual farms. Resource control over uncultivated land and waters, on the other hand, came to be vested in a much larger, more heterogeneous group of people. While farms thus came to be managed with considerable prudence, common resources have in many cases been managed profligately. This is perhaps best reflected in the rise of religions such as Christianity and Islam which debunked nature worship and with it the prudent use of resources.

Indian Caste Society

The Indian agricultural/pastoral society responded differently to the complexities of resource use. The society remained organised in a number of tribe-like endogamous groups, the castes. Caste society regulated resource use in such a way that each group acquired monopoly over particular resources of a specific locality, for instance, Phasepardhis over blackbuck or Kaikadis over bamboo, as described above. Furthermore, different village caste groups tended to retain common interests in the careful use of their local resources due to a variety of arrangements for resource sharing - in spite of the highly inegalitarian nature of caste society. This society had therefore elaborated a whole system of rituals and customs encouraging prudent use of resources, up until the British colonial period.

Conquest of Nature

The European society, by contrast, discarded ritual systems of prudent resource use without elaborating any system of social customs promoting prudence. This society developed an ethic of man as free to conquer nature and to use resources as he desired; an ethic which has been traced to the Greek stoic tradition through at least one thread of early Christian Protestantism (Passmore, 1977). The European response to the gradual exhaustion of its resource base was to develop codified knowledge - science and technology - that permitted more intensive and effective use of resources. It also permitted substitution of new resources for exhausted older ones; i.e. coal for wood in iron smelting. These technical advances further reduced expectation of benefits from sustainable resource use and prompted the ethic of profligate resource use so characteristic of the European age of expansion (seventeenth to nineteenth centuries).

Science and Prudence

The latter half of the nineteenth century witnessed a maturation of scientific understanding in the European civilisation. It also witnessed the emergence of more egalitarian societies in the Western world. This meant that the larger human groups controlling resources within European nations now had a much greater commonality of interests. This catalysed emergence of the modern, science-based conservation movement first in Switzerland, then so ravaged by deforestation and landslides, and later in other parts of Europe and the Americas (Thomas, 1956.)

Rape of the Colonies

Yet prudent resource use practices, grounded in the scientific understanding that thus emerged in Western civilisation during the late nineteenth and early twentieth centuries, were not applied to other parts of the world under direct or indirect control by the West. Western control over resources of these areas was relatively new and apparently temporary. Furthermore, there was little commonality of interest between indigenous populations of the Third World and their colonial or neocolonial masters. One result has been that while the Japanese and Americans have maintained excellent forest cover on their native lands, they have shown little concern for liquidation of forest cover in Southeast Asia or in Latin America. A similar scenario holds within a country such as India which has absorbed much Western science and technology. There is little commonality of interest between the group that benefits from the country's forest-based industries and the rural and tribal populations traditionally controlling, and still largely dependent upon, forest resources. The result is non-sustainable use of forest resources by both of these segments of the society, despite the supposedly scientific management of forests that is believed to be in operation.

EMERGING INSIGHTS

World Conservation Strategy

However, a greater commonality of interest is now emerging in the world as a whole. This has its origin in the scientific awareness that what happens in one part of the world is bound to affect all others over the long-term. The World Conservation Strategy (WCS) is one of the consequences of this awareness. It emphasises the interconnectedness of ecological systems and the need for a common approach toward prudent use of resources worldwide. It draws attention to the value of biological diversity, and in a sense to the need to recapture the mutualistic relationship with other living creatures which underlay the practices of nature worship in "primitive" times. Clearly the WCS is an important step toward generating a new culture of prudent resource use worldwide.

Managing Living Resources

The World Conservation Strategy adopts an essentially managerial posture. It argues that in the common long-term interests of humanity, we must be concerned with maintaining essential ecological processes and life support systems, preserving genetic diversity and sustainable utilisation of species and ecosystems. It then lists the major obstacles to achieving these objectives, not in terms of the socio-economic order with the perceptions and policies that flow from it, but rather in terms of managerial limitations due to a lack of appreciation and information about the issues involved. It goes on to suggest how we could manage ecosystems and genetic diversity by developing proper policy, legislative and technical tools.

Moulding Cultures

While this is an exercise of tremendous value, it does not adequately address itself to the question of how different segments of the world community perceive the use of natural resources, how these perceptions relate to their cultures and in turn how they determine the priorities and policies of concern to the Strategy. In this context we may pose two broad questions: "How do we develop existing perceptions and culture that support the goals of the WCS?" and "How do we overcome the elements of perception and culture that are antagonistic to the goals of the WCS?"

A NEW CULTURE

Kinship with Nature

Among the most positive aspects of cultural heritage is the feeling of kinship, or at least, ties of mutual interest with other living organisms. Such an attitude is widely encountered among primitive cultures and must have prevailed throughout the long history of man as hunter-gatherer. It provided the rationale for a whole spectrum of cultural traditions in restrained use of living organisms. Many cultures, including that of India, have retained at least some elements of this attitude: A majority of Indians believe in rebirth and passage of the soul through a whole series of other organisms. Incidentally the number of organisms is given as 8.4 million, a figure remarkably close to the current estimates of the total number of biological species. They also worship trees, especially those belonging to the genus *Ficus*, snakes, peafowl, elephants and monkeys. Again, it is notable that tropical ecologists now consider *Ficus* as a keystone resource for the conservation of a whole catalogue of other species. Another tree considered to be sacred is *Prosopis cinerarea* in parts of the Indian desert. This is economically the most valuable of desert trees, although rather slow growing. Its preservation is therefore a great boon to desert dwellers who eat the pods; feed pods and leaves to their animals; use the thorns to fence their fields; and use the wood for fuel and construction.

Scientific Rationale

This attitude of kinship or mutualism toward other living creatures was rejected by a dominant school of Christian thought, setting man apart from the rest of creation. This is why the notions of evolution have been so abhorrent to Christian dogma. Our modern scientific understanding evidently takes us closer to the more primitive position. The human species is as much a product of 3,000 million years of evolution on the earth as other living organisms, and shares much with them. In fact, one estimate puts the homology of the chimpanzee genome with that of human species at as high as 96 percent. The science of ecology also tells us that man is a part of the web of life, and very much dependent on it. This understanding has promoted a vigorous debate on rights of other species in the Western world (Ehrenfeld, 1978).

This perception of biological kinship of man with other species of living organisms, and their interdependence, must become a common element of mankind's perception. I believe that such a perception should be incorporated in the idiom of science and not in that of ritual; for ritual veneration and ritual protection of living creatures as an element of culture is quickly vanishing everywhere. On the hill chain of the Western Ghats, Peninsular India, the natural vegetation has largely disappeared in its climax forms, except for small pockets in sacred groves. I have been involved for more than a decade in attempts to identify such

pockets and protect them (Gadgil and Vartak, 1975, 1981). This exercise has revealed that in many areas local people realise the practical value of these groves for protection of stream catchments, as plant medicine reservoirs, and so on, and often would like to protect them. Forest managers however view these as stands of overmature timber, and merchants, as sources of profit. In this complex situation, a majority of local people no longer perceive these groves as something to be protected as sacred, and have joined the merchants in exploiting them. While quite a few groves still persist and are protected, this aspect of culture is bound to vanish in the next decade or two. The sacred groves could be protected in the long run only if society comes to value them as the reservoirs of genetic diversity that they are, offering economic incentives to the local population to protect them.

Need for a New Idiom

Any attempt to perpetuate ritually-based protection of living creatures is not only impractical, but may have negative implications as well. For Indians have not only preserved sacred groves or Banyan trees (*Ficus bengalensis*), but have also permitted the cattle population to explode, at least partly because of our veneration for it. Overgrazing cattle has serious consequences in much of the country, including loss of diversity over vast areas which have come to be dominated by a few unpalatable species like the exotic weed *Parthenium*. One must therefore attempt not to perpetuate respect for other living creatures under the old idiom, but aim at preserving the desirable attitudes and practices suitably rationalised in the modern scientific idiom.

Toward a New Social Order

Not only should the World Conservation Strategy address itself to the question of how to build upon perceptions and cultural elements supportive of its aims, but also on how to overcome elements antagonistic to its objectives. As argued above, I believe that the main cause underlying all such antagonistic perceptions is the absence of perceived commonality of long-term interests among those controlling most of the world's resources today. This has two basic effects: it causes increasing disparities within societies and between nations; and also causes technological progress which has permitted a small elite to acquire a hold over many of the earth's resources. One approach could therefore be restoration of control over resources to small, largely homogenous local communities. This is the approach advocated by Mahatma Gandhi and attempted by some of his followers. Another notable example of such an attempt is that of Chandi Prasad Bhatt, a leader of the Chipko movement in the Himalayas. Chandiprasad has organised village after village in the Alaknanda valley to manage their own resources prudently. It is however, an uphill climb, for powerful commercial and bureaucratic interests continually try to sabotage these attempts. His success has therefore been limited (Agarwal *et al.*, 1982).

The real solution has to come from a new genuinely egalitarian social order, both within and between nation states. Only then can commonality of long-term interests prevail on a global scale, and only then will there evolve a worldwide human culture which is truly sympathetic to the objectives of the World Conservation Strategy.

REFERENCES

• Agarwal, A., R. Chopra and K. Sharma, 1982, *State of India's Environment : A Citizen's Report*, Centre for Science and Environment, Delhi.

• Alexander, R. D., 1979, *Darwinism and Human Affairs*, Pitman Publishing Limited, London.

• Axelrod, R., 1983, *Evolution of Cooperation*, Basic Books.

• Bonner, J. T., 1980, *The Evolution of Culture in Animals*, Princeton University Press, Princeton, New Jersey.

• Boyd, R. and Richerson, P. J. 1984, *Process of Cultural Evolution*, University of Chicago Press, Chicago.

• Cavalli-Sforza, L. L. and M. Feldman, 1981, *Cultural Transmission and Evolution: A Quantitative Approach*, Princeton University Press, Princeton, New Jersey.

• Ehrenfeld, D., 1978, *The Arrogance of Humanism*, Oxford University Press, Oxford.

• Gadgil, M., 1985a, "Cultural Evolution of Ecological Prudence," *Landscape Planning*, 12:285-299.

• Gadgil, M. 1985b, "Social Restraints on Resource Utilization: The Indian Experience," in: J. A. McNeely and D. Pitt (eds.) *Culture and Conservation: The Human Dimension in Environmental Planning*, Croom Helm, Dublin, 135-154.

• Gadgil, M. and K.C. Malhotra, 1983, "Adaptive Significance of the Indian Caste System: An Ecological Perspective," *Annals of Human Biology*, 10:465-478.

• Gadgil, M. and V. D. Vartak, 1981, "Sacred Groves of Maharashtra: An Inventory," in: S. K. Jain (Ed.) *Glimpses of Ethnobotany*, Oxford and I.B.H., New Delhi, 279-294.

• Gadgil, M. and V. D. Vartak, 1975, "Sacred Groves of India: A Plea for Continued Conservation", *J. Bomb. Nat. Hist. Soc.*, 72 314-320.

• Kangle, R. P., 1969, *Arthashastra. An English Translation with Critical Notes*, III Parts, University of Bombay, Bombay.

• Passmore, J. 1977, *Man's Responsibility for Nature*, Unwin Brothers Limited, London.

• Sahlins, M., 1977, *The Use and Abuse of Biology*, Tavistock Publications Limited, London.

• Thomas, W. L. (ed.) 1956, *Man's Role in Changing the Face of the Earth*, Chicago University Press, Chicago, Vols I & II.

CULTURE(S) AND ENVIRONMENT(S)

Jacques Bugnicourt
Director, ENDA
Dakar, Senegal

SUMMARY *Although we may often be unaware of it, the relationship between culture and environment enters into everyone's daily life; as, for example, when we notice certain aspects rather than others of a room, a street or a landscape; when we read; when we speak. Or when we act upon the environment through our choice of how we move from one place to another, the kinds of food we eat, the construction materials we use, and so on. When we reflect upon our habits, we become aware of the numerous forms taken by this unavoidable relationship. This paper will demonstrate the relationship more concretely, with the help of some examples, first showing the link between culture and perception of the environment and, secondly, the link between culture and action for managing nature and its resources.*

CULTURE(S) AND ENVIRONMENTAL PERCEPTION(S)

In order to establish the relationship between culture and the environment, we must be aware that landscapes vary, that approaches are not transferable and that certain conflicts are inevitable. We often act under the false impression that we can analyse a landscape anywhere in the world by identifying its topography, vegetation, agricultural practices and man-made structures.

An expert or a qualified observer would use "universal scientific terms" in describing the landscape in Figure 1: the village is depicted by dwellings (A); stands of trees represent forestry (B); the river shows water flowing from west to east (D). The hills (M) are taken in at one sweep from base to summit.

Figure 1.

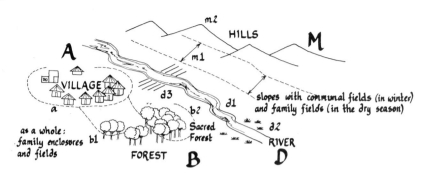

* *within the "universal" culture: different terms indicate the overall topography and apparent use;*
* *within the local culture: specific local terms describe vegetation, relief, soil type, legal status*

The expert or town-planning graduate attempting to manage this landscape would soon encounter difficulties in communicating with the inhabitants. The dwellings interest villagers only to the extent that they represent family enclosures inseparable from the family plot (a). The forest, for the villagers, is not a homogenous unit even when all species of trees are the same.

Certain trees mark field boundaries to the southwest of the village (b1). Separate from these is the sacred forest (b2), the boundaries of which have been indefinable probably for centuries. It is not possible to assess the sacred forest only in terms of square metres of wood, as the expert would do, for it is the dwelling place of "spirits." As such, it is the place appointed to raise myths and stories of the human group, and serves as a fauna and flora preserve. Villagers look upon the sacred forest as a temple or church.

Is there at least a common perception between the "universal" point of view and local inhabitants' opinion concerning the river? Looked at externally

(universal standpoint) the fact that there *is* water is most important. Yet from the villagers' point of view, three different terms describe use of the river (d1, d2, d3). Upstream, the river is mainly for irrigation (d3); further down, livestock is watered (d1); and the marshy river banks at the boundaries of the village provide fishing (d2). Beyond the river, the alluvial plain and foothills are considered as a single unit by the villagers (m1). There, the sloping fields are used communally in winter and exploited by each family for its own particular needs during the dry season. In this case, one single term is used by the villagers to describe slope, colour of the soil, communal use during the winter and family use during the dry season; like many toponyms, one single word describes vegetation, relief, soils, use, and legal status.

The example given above, taken from an actual Sudanese landscape, could be applied theoretically to the majority of Third World rural areas. Such a landscape can be read in several ways.

Each culture divides, analyses and defines its environment in a particular manner; it perceives and understands the landscape according to its own vision. Thus, the above observations are not as trivial as they might appear. The shortcomings of perception have implications that go well beyond a simple divergence in descriptions about the same landscape. The perceptions are, in fact, non-transferable; they represent cultural/environmental relations that cannot be directly transposed from one population to another.

In following the course of the Senegal river from the villages of the *Toucouleur* to those of the *Soninké*,[1] the arrangement and type of dwellings change, as does the vegetation. The shapes, colours and even the sounds that characterise human settlements are not interpreted in the same way from one culture to another. It is not easy to visualise what the basic word "house" means from one part of the world to another. The *galle peul* of the Sahara or the *bororo* hut of Amazonia do not conjure up the slightest hint of what is suggested by the words *home*, *heim*, *foyer*, and so on. The streets in an Arab market have nothing in common with the wide avenues in European or North American cities. The word "garden" can bring the image of a French or English park, of Chinese or Japanese mini-gardens, the reality of the *allées canaques*, or the household gardens found all over sub-Saharan Africa. The desert, which seems so monotonous when viewed from a distance, is dotted with named localities; Tuareg or Moorish nomads recognise "invisible" characteristics there. Water too has very different meanings. In the Muslim countries of North Africa, water is "pure" when it has flowed through the reservoir of a mosque, regardless of its taste or the germs it harbours. Within a few score kilometres of the coast, the *lébou* fishermen of Senegal call the sea by names that echo its colour, depth and the fish that are found during different periods of the year.

In each of these cases we are dealing with a categorical and logical division, specific to each language. The perception of elements in the environment includes historical and poetic aspects, positive and negative nuances. It includes, in sum, an emotional loading and references to value systems unique to each culture.

This diversity of spatial approaches becomes clearer when they are compared to the variations of environmental perception over time. The extent of the synchronic and diachronic irreducibility of cultural/environmental relations can help to reach an understanding of the nature and importance of latent or apparent conflict.

For those who feel closely integrated with nature, the symbiosis between society and the environment is regulated by religions. The notion of a cycle, often underlying such a position, includes human beings, animals, vegetation, water, and so on. As the earth is the common denominator of all these elements, it is not possible either to discard or alienate it. Then came God who initially created Nature, then Man, the first being a gift to the second. After the Fall, Man was condemned to difficult labour. Herein lies the source of the dominant direction of thought:

1. People living in, respectively, the middle and lower Senegal valley.

Judaism, Christianity and Islam look to Man's domination of nature. In the contemporary world, there are other currents. One, in the uncompromising name of short-term profit, allows everything in the environment to be ransacked and abused. Another looks toward modelling and transforming nature, even beyond what is reasonable: Saint Simonism, Marxism or even a kind of "great works" conception.

Against these lines of thought, nineteenth and twentieth century romanticism and the vogue for "untouched nature" led to a gradual rediscovery of and appreciation for nature. This later developed in a wider sense, to an even more acute awareness of myriad "environmental" forms.

The village greening projects, the creation of national parks, and various movements - notably scouting - which revalued forests, the jungle and wild animals, progressively brought about a new way of looking at the environment in European and North American societies, as well as in their outposts on other continents.

Figure 2.

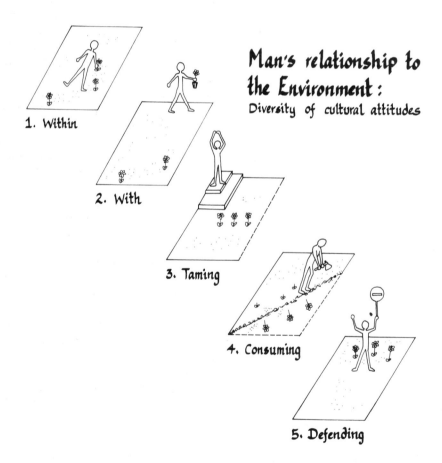

Man's relationship to the Environment :
Diversity of cultural attitudes

1. Within

2. With

3. Taming

4. Consuming

5. Defending

This development of Western ideas shows how, depending on which cultural element is dominant in a given sector of society, Man's so-called "normal" attitude with regard to nature differs profoundly.

In assigning Man's place in the environment, each culture brings interpretations, opinions and specific attitudes that inevitably give rise to contradictions in time and space. On the one hand then, the numerous conflicts of interest between different socio-economic categories competing for a given environment is explained. Groups hold to images and projects that are incompatible with those of rival groups.

On the other hand, many cultural conflicts emerge and are perpetuated, particularly between those who make decisions about the environment according to "universal" norms and groups of people who espouse the "traditional" or "local" concepts of the area in which they live.

Conflicts are exacerbated because "universal" concepts are themselves ambivalent. They insist on solidarity on a regional, continental or international scale, while defining that solidarity in terms of **one** environmental concept developed by Euro-American culture. Differences and conflicts are thrown into even sharper relief when the focus moves from the realm of ideas to that of action.

CULTURE(S) AND ENVIRONMENTAL ACTION

Distortions between culture and the environment become clear in "projects," or economic or administrative actions that ignore the cultural reality of the beneficiaries or go against it, often leaving environmental disaster in their wake. The following cases provide examples:

One tree does not make a forest. Is it possible that such a simple sentence can explain the failure of a forest reconstruction effort in a degraded hill zone of the developing world?

An account of what happened three years ago in northeastern India is convincing enough. In order to combat erosion and improve the tribal economy of the Bihar Hills, Mrs. Gandhi launched a vast programme to reconstitute the forest environment. She had hoped to carry it out with the help of the forestry services and the population. An Indian association, and *Enda Tiers Monde*[2] with some *Murda, Santal* and others, immediately organised a meeting to consider how common administrative and population initiatives could effectively undertake reforestation and landscape reconstruction in the area. The session began in a lodge in the hills; tribal people spoke little and listened to the successive presentations by officials about the advantages of reforestation.

At the end of two days, the silent acquiescence began to appear suspect and the peasants were urged to speak their minds among themselves. They spoke the whole day and into the night and, under the light of hurricane lamps, presented their report. The eldest among them rose and declared: "One tree does not make a forest" and then sat down. There was a short wait. Nothing. He was asked to elaborate a

---

2. *Environnement et Développement du Tiers Monde,* a non-governmental organisation.

little. The old man rose again and this is what he said:

> These hills have always been ours. Since the world was the world we have lived in the forest. One day, a rumour circulated that the English were leaving. The forest guards stayed with the same uniform and the same insignia. They brought contractors from the town. We told them not to touch our forest. They replied that we did not have titles to the land, that everything belonged to the State. Then they brought trucks and workers from the town who, to begin with, cut down the trees around the villages and then later further away. Some of the good soils slipped into the valley. The young men too went to the valley. Soon, only the forest at the horizon remained. We now need a permit to collect wood and we hunt only on one day a year.

Figure 3.

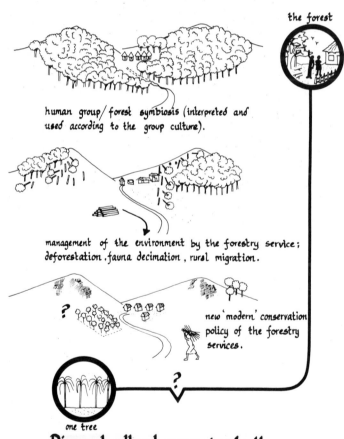

the forest

human group/forest symbiosis (interpreted and used according to the group culture).

management of the environment by the forestry service; deforestation, fauna decimation, rural migration.

new 'modern' conservation policy of the forestry services.

one tree

Divergent cultural approaches to the Environment—"One tree does not make a forest".

Then the same forestry officials using the same language, came to tell us that from now on they are our friends; they were going to plant trees around us that we could tend ourselves and that would eventually bring us money. In truth, the equivalent of one single tree was planted but in thousands upon thousands of seedlings, like soldiers on parade. This 'tree' they called 'technically' the best. What is this tree, this stranger, this intruder? We do not even have a name to describe it.

*This is nothing like the forest that was taken from us. We need certain trees to give us beams for our houses, others to provide fencing and others, tools. Some are used as firewood. Not **one** tree around us: dozens of **different types** of trees, some bushey, others of intermediate size and others reaching to the sky. At each of these stages, the bark, leaves and birds with their eggs feed us. At each season, the fruits and berries, the leaves, again, the bark and roots heal us when we are ill. In such abundance, our women find the products they need to make themselves beautiful. And it is in those trees that our Gods frolic. All of this has been destroyed and in its place they ask us to accept that this monopolistic and foreign tree be planted. This tree, in truth, is not the forest.*

A long silence followed. "So, what do you want?" The answer: "That, perhaps we work together among our tribes and look for an area to rebuild."

Reconstruction of the forest environment according to the technical and economic criteria of the administration was clearly incompatible with the view that the tribes held of the way in which their environment should be developed.

What may be a decisive environmental improvement in the eyes of some may in fact offend cultural conceptions of the intended beneficiaries. Another example comes from the Sahel, situated at the border of Mali and Niger. It concerned a village and a territory populated by Bella, formerly "servants" of the Tuareg but now freed. The problem in this case was drought and to determine the elements of environmental development, according to the needs of the population.

A team went to the area to listen to groups of men, women and young people. The discussions quickly revealed that high mortality and morbidity, especially among young children, was the main concern due to poor water quality. Polluted water kills. In addition, the water source was distant from the village and fetching it each day was hard work. Wells were needed close by for drinking, for the animals and for irrigating small gardens which would yield additional food in the dry season. But with what means could the water be extracted? (See Figure 4.)

Extraction of the water by hand was not a popular idea (Fig. 4, sketch 1), whereas using a motor pump was initially greeted with much enthusiasm (Fig. 4, sketch 3). After two days of discussions, however, the idea of using a motor pump was finally rejected. "Who would supply the engine, the spare parts, the fuel?" the peasants asked. "Wouldn't that kind of pump soon take over our lives and make us dependent upon it? Would the water

Reasoning of the Engineer and of the People with regard to technical choice

☐ **What are the priority needs?**

Children sick or dying from bad water.

Water far away and difficult to collect.

☐ **What should be done?**

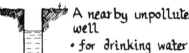

A near by unpolluted well
• for drinking water
• for small gardens

☐ **How should the water be drawn up?**

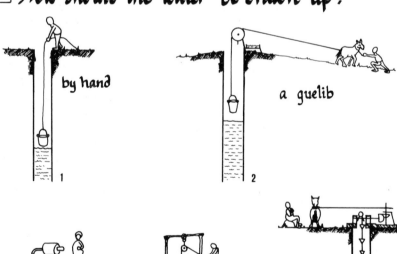

by hand
1

a guelib
2

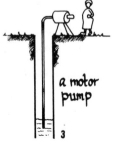

a motor pump
3

by pulley
4

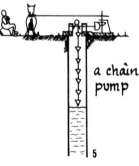

a chain pump
5

"flow have to be managed each day, and if so, who would do it?"

The discussions finally centred on a choice between a hand-operated pully (sketch 4), the *guélib* operated by a donkey, bullock or camel (sketch 2) and the chain pump (sketch 5). The technicians in the contact group thought the Bella's choice should clearly be the chain pump. The villagers hesitated for a long time. They consulted the women and children. Then, against all opposition, they opted for the *guélib*. The outsiders were very disappointed: "You could have had a much greater flow with the chain pump."

"Perhaps," replied the villagers "we understand that, but if a large quantity of water flows, the news will spread for miles around. Herds will come from all directions, changing their routes in order to be watered here for long periods. Each beast that drinks also eats. Before and after being watered, the herds would feed on the fragile carpet of vegetation around us. Wider use of our water would bring rapid destruction of our pastures."

"Is that not avoidable?" asked the team members "Can you not refuse access to the wells by sending away the beasts that do not belong to you?"

"That would be impossible" replied the Bella. "Water belongs to God. Our fathers and forefathers never refused anyone. We would never accept an abundance that excluded our neighbours, or breach our rules of hospitality. We prefer to have less water and keep our friends."

Rejection of the motor and chain pumps demonstrates that the villagers'

technical choice was not made according to usual "universal" profit motives, but rather on the basis of the culture and religion of the group.

Yet it is not only in rural areas that a biased or inaccurate interpretation of the environment may lead to ill-adapted action; urban areas suffer similarly.

The frame of reference of most decision-makers in large urban centres of the Third World is that of the "beautiful city" with multi-storeyed buildings, often air-conditioned, and wide asphalted avenues. The influence of ecologists is moreover favourably felt in the importance given to parks and gardens as well as in the efforts to reduce pollution of all kinds. The predominance of the "new town" vogue facilitates the manipulations of dominant interest groups which seek to divert most of the available urban investments and operational loans into the "beautiful city."

The poorest of the urban population, however, are often consigned to the interstices and periphery of the "beautiful city." They live in poor, inter-city environments where community organisation, dwelling types, materials, food, nutritional deficiency, illness, general and infant mortality rates, life expectancy and so on, are often much worse than in the better areas of the city.

The notion that a "street environment" exists is not recognised. Nevertheless, young people live according to its rhythm, shoulder the limitations it imposes, exploit the opportunities it offers and develop, without anyone noticing, new urban cultures. Most of the solutions put forward for "street children" by public authorities and non-governmental organisations ignore this reality and thus are destined to fail. Environmental policy in most Third World cities is drawn up and applied without enough recognition of the cultural concerns and behaviour of the poorest and youngest groups in the population.

Yet it is not easy to decide **how** the cultural component should intervene in the structure and application of both urban and rural environmental conservation and management....

CONCLUSION

In reviewing the relationship between culture and environment there are more questions than answers. But perhaps the following will lead to a re-examination of certain approaches and practices.

* A major dilemma is evident: would reintegration of the cultural dimension into environmental policies lead to a manipulation of people from different cultures, causing them to acquiesce in choices made without their participation, or, on the contrary, diversify the bases, substance and methods of the selected policies?

* Incompatible imperatives confront each other. The first imperative is never to lose sight of the indispensable solidarity needed on a world scale: "One earth." Certain perspectives are valid for the whole planet and there is a certain common denominator underlying national conservation policies. The other imperative looks in the opposite direction;

a uniform environmental policy, drawn up according to so-called universal criteria but in reality obeying a single cultural norm, should not be imposed on countries and populations. Methods habitually applied in Europe and the United States should not be employed. How should a compromise be engineered between common management at the macro-environmental level, and localised application of national or regional norms at the micro-environmental level?

* The "environmental compromise" will not be easy to install. It will be difficult to take different cultures into account as **components** of conservation strategies and of environmental policies at the local, national and international levels. It is not too soon to admit, with all its consequences, that there are as many "natures" as "cultures."

* In the Third World, protection and management of the environment can only be successful if popular participation is extensive; neither financial aid nor laws are sufficient by themselves.

* Populations will not genuinely take environmental policies into account until they are stripped of Euro-American ethnocentricity, and until they are conceived and applied through the specific culture of the people. Is it not time that the World Conservation Strategy became *A People's Strategy for Environmental Development?*

BUILDING BLOCKS FOR IMPLEMENTING THE WORLD CONSERVATION STRATEGY

Plenary Session 2

BUILDING BLOCKS FOR IMPLEMENTING THE WORLD CONSERVATION STRATEGY

Plenary Session 2

Hon. Victoria Chitepo, Chairperson
Minister of Natural Resources and Tourism
Harare, Zimbabwe

This Plenary Session was organised to focus attention on the significant roles that may be played by major institutions external to the process of implementing the World Conservation Strategy.

At the opening of the Session, the Chairperson explained how strong and comprehensive government policies could serve as instruments for promoting both evironmental values and development. She illustrated the organisation of government institutions in Zimbabwe, and how they deal with forestry, agriculture, education, and population planning, in relation to conservation and development.

Ensuing discussions dealt with institutional structures and mechanisms favouring conservation procedures, implementation of the World Conservation Strategy and possible revisions to it.

Walker's theme framework paper sets forth a provocative collection of ideas and observations aimed at placing the World Conservation Strategy in a broad social context. He draws attention to the fortunate confluence of popular movements concerned with conservation, development, population and peace, and suggests that it represents an unprecedented potential for action. Overview papers deal with: the relationship between development assistance programmes relating to conservation and development, and the needs and aspirations of recipient countries (Omo-Fakada); progress in developing domestic and international law that could support implementation of the World Conservation Strategy (Burhenne-Guilmin, de Klemm, Forster, Lausche); and the characteristics of the flow of investments and loans from donors to receivers (Thacher). Prescott-Allen's paper outlines his particular perspective as the compiler of the World Conservation Strategy, noting aspects of its evolution and suggesting how it could be improved and used to greater advantage.

STRATEGY NEEDED TO ESTABLISH INSTITUTIONAL BUILDING BLOCKS

Brian W. Walker
President, IIED
London, United Kingdom

SUMMARY *This paper deals with the* **strategy** *and* **concept** *needed to create an effective World Conservation Movement and the* **philosophy** *most appropriate to current and future needs. It argues that people's fulfillment must form the raison d'être of an effective World Conservation Strategy. A bottom up, participatory approach must bring into relationship four great movements of public concern integral to a strategy for global conservation: development, conservation, population and peace. The relationship derived could foster the exchange of ideas and political and institutional changes in favour of community-biased conservation. The strong would aid the weak in building peoples' movements which would shape and implement National Conservation Strategies, while national governments would stand in a supportive role. Dependency and determinist frameworks must give way to a plural, holistic and open movement whose purpose is to liberate men and women to be fully human, finding their place within the order of the planet earth.*

INTRODUCTION

In the main this framework paper is written to stimulate ideas. It concentrates on those concepts critical to the evolution of a successful (i.e. sustainable) strategy for world conservation, before discussing institutional building blocks which would service such a strategy. At certain points this paper will be found to be at odds with the current World Conservation Strategy, although it remains to be seen whether such differences are substantive or a matter of interpretation and emphasis. Yet before turning to these issues I shall briefly identify four characteristics pertaining to the nature of institutions, as a starting point for our debate.

SOME INSTITUTIONAL CHARACTERISTICS

First, institutions are the means to an end. Too often, however, they become ends in themselves. This can happen for a number of reasons, not least of which is people remaining in office for inordinately long periods of time. Ten years is long enough for anyone to hold high office, with six or eight years a healthy compromise. This allows enough time for the institution to benefit from officers' experience, but not enough to permit dullness, repetition or boredom to take hold.

Secondly, institutions degenerate when their objectives are unclear, ill-defined, or contradictory. This point is critical to a strategy for world conservation and I shall return to it as my principle argument.

Thirdly, an institution ceases to be dynamic when the body politic is no longer interested in its objectives. Eventually, people lose heart when they believe that those objectives are unattainable.

Fourthly, ample research describes how all institutions pass through a constant process of ossification leading ultimately to atrophy. This accelerates when the original energy and creativity of the founders is lost, because they move on, die, or are removed from office. Most people in this audience will have experienced, during college days, the "new society" set up under the passionate conviction of one or two founding members, which flourished vigorously until key individuals left three years later, student days over. They take with them the creative leadership essential to a healthy institution. This same process occurs in areas of religion, politics, education, or areas of ethical concern, although they normally have a longer life span. Enthusiasm for "causes" can stimulate spiritual commitment from one generation to the next, but invariably signs of ossification are apparent within a decade of

birth. The management of such institutions is largely concerned with opposing inertia, limiting the growth of dull bureaucracy, and countering the waning interest of members or supporters in the core subject. Where such management is effective, the institution is said to be vigorous and even successful.

It may seem odd that I have not included in this four-part list either the need for funds to stimulate the organisation, or the plant and machinery, buildings, equipment, staff or other infrastructure to achieve the objectives of the group. I do not underestimate the importance of income generation in the attainment of objectives. But my own experience, both as a businessman and as an NGO activist, is that if the product is right and the vehicle designed to promote or sell it is effective, then income will be generated. In this sense income generation, while essential to institutional success, is secondary, flowing as it does from the former considerations.

COMMENTS ON THE WORLD CONSERVATION STRATEGY

Let us turn from these general comments to a specific analysis of the World Conservation Strategy. Of the four characteristics described above, the second and third are of strategic importance.

The identification of dynamic objectives will make or break a successful strategy. And here I have a serious quarrel with what I consider to be the inadequacy of the World Conservation Strategy. I believe that people and their communities should represent both the starting and the finishing points for conservationists. Only insofar as that is made explicit will governmental commitment maximise its potential in support of our objective for global, sustainable development. It is not difficult to recognise the connection between the ill-fated Union Carbide plant in Bhopal and the poverty and slum conditions of high-density living areas prevailing in that district. Those people had been politically neutered by poverty. They had no voice. It is not surprising that disaster struck. Similarly, the suppression of pastoralism and the imposition of a market economy in the African Sahel zone, without the cash infusion from nineteenth century colonialists to fuel that economic model, contributes to today's environmental bankruptcy of this huge land mass. While there are other factors, that act of colonial folly is central to the human suffering and land degradation of sub-Saharan Africa.

I do not believe that people are, or ought to be, supportive of conservation for its own sake. Conservation is a tool: a means to an end and not an end in itself. That end, like music, art, literature, education, or any of the good things in life, should relate to a process which liberates or enhances our essential humanity, enabling people to realise their potential - regardless of the physical environment in which they find themselves. For men or women of religion, this has been best expressed in the philosophy of medieval scholars that everything we do or refrain from doing should be "to the glory of God." Beethoven, searching within himself to define the impulse which gave rise to his great passion, observed that "Music is a great and glorious gift of God." There is something within us - which is also beyond us - that cries out for ex-

pression and, when encouraged to grow, expresses our essential humanity, as well as that of our community structures, whether family, village, nation state, or of humanity itself.

If this is true then it follows that "conservation" is not so much a by-product of legal processes, rather it is a by-product of human or community development. It does not precede it, nor is it separate from it. We care for this planet not simply because it is here but because it is the cradle and home of the human species. It enables people to grow to their full potential. If conditions are repressive, it diminishes and brutalises them. The explosive growth of cities and towns in the South demonstrates how pressure on local ecosystems is generated.

A strategy for conservation is futile, therefore, unless it embraces a strategy for human settlements. But policies for human settlements cannot be agreed without issues of population, health and family planning featuring prominently. Nor can those issues be tackled themselves without reference to the reasons why the rural poor flock to the cities. So agrarian reform - and hence development policies - are brought into play. But these too are bound to fail unless they are culturally sensitive and give rise to rural communities which are stable because livelihoods are sustainable. Thus, the circle is complete. And the pivot on which everything turns is the inter-relatedness of all phenomena. In particular the human species is dependent on all created matter. In his essay on Man, Pope captured this idea:

> *Nothing is foreign.*
> *Parts relate to the whole;*

and later

*All served, all serving; nothing stands
alone: The chain holds on, and where
it ends, unknown.*

What matters then is not so much the environment, but the **interplay** between the most dominant product of that environment, humankind, and its environment. "If you would learn the secrets of nature," Thoreau remarked, "you must practice more humanity than others." It is this commitment which encourages the key creative relationship.

The basic building block of matter identified by the physicist, the protected flora and fauna of the conservationist, the industrial enterprise of the entrepreneur, the artefacts we design, the biosphere which surrounds us, or the mantle of green on which we stand, are all important insofar as they relate to the human community now and in the future. By definition, conservation cannot be authentic if it presupposes the human animal standing at a remove and contemplating something called "nature." Our species has relevance by being intimately woven into the tapestry of life. If the warp or the weft of that tapestry breaks down, we break down; our potential is curtailed. Ultimately our survival is jeopardised.

This is not simply a piece of abstract philosophy. It led Barbara Ward to insist on a name change of our own organisation before she would accept its office of President. The "International Institute for Environmental Affairs" had to become the "International Institute for Environment and Development." Its original priorities were inadequate. For my part, I would prefer those last two words, Environment and Development, to be reversed, for that would reflect the proper ordering of

our thinking and planning. Neither point is pedantic; it is the authentic product of experience.

I find the dry and arid concepts of "sustainable agriculture" or "sustainable development," which tend to dominate the vocabulary in this field, deficient for our purposes. What we are really seeking is surely something akin to the concept of "sustainable livelihoods" as advocated by Mahatma Gandhi. Dr. Robert Chambers has researched and is now promoting this idea in terms of development aid: or, how the welfare of people and community wealth can be developed so as to be sustainable within habitats. We might describe this as the "new economics." If livelihoods are sustainable, then by definition, nature is safe from earth's most powerful predator.

The notion of "sustainable livelihood" is an attempt to weave together a number of ideas. Creation of wealth based upon the prudent stewardship of resources is one. The touchstone of sustainability as the foundation of economic and social decisions is another. The participation of local people in determining, directing and evaluating their own development is another crucially important thread in the process. The needs and priorities of people and their communities, rather than the needs of elites and their bureaucracies, is a central concern. The use and maintenance of inherited knowledge and traditional wisdom, especially when handed down from mother to daughter, has an equal place with technology. The implications of such a style are immense, not only for mainstream development and conservation policy, but also for research and ultimately the reassessment of social values and social justice. How is that concept to be put persuasively to Ministers of Finance and Treasury officials? This is the real challenge.

As people develop and as they build their communities in the process, so must we protect the whole of our heritage, not least the natural environment, for, if I may borrow a theologian's phrase, it is the "ground of our being" and of those yet to come. We do not have the right to destroy it. Balance and harmony, not disorder or chaos, are woven into the very nature of matter. Surely reverence for life is essential to our well-being. One of the central purposes of human experience must be to secure the reconciliation of all created things, one to another. Yet we deny this central theme in procreating beyond sustainable levels, in removing tree cover and exposing fragile soils to wind and rain, in exhausting water tables or reversing river flows, in crowding our own species into megalopolises, and in imposing inequitable structures on those without power. The ultimate result is to reduce man to the role of an irrelevant spectator wandering aimlessly in the dark. He takes up residence in the "City of Dreadful Night" described by James Thompson in these haunting words:

I find no hint throughout the Universe
Of good or ill, of blessing or of curse,
I find alone Necessity Supreme.

Inevitably, when humans deny their own potential and reject this elixir of balance and harmony, then disaster is the consequence: Bhopal, the Sahel, the Himalayan Watershed, the slums of Calcutta, ultimately Hiroshima and Nagasaki.

I have laboured this point because if the need for such a strategy is accepted, then the institutions we create must strive to reflect that ethos, giving shape and form to those objectives. Institutionally, we must seek to create sinews within society which respond faithfully to those kinds of insights. The direction in which I am pointing is fraught with problems for humankind which can be a difficult, perverse and aggressive species. Gandhi was right to note that there is enough for everyone's needs, but not for everyone's greed. Too often greed is the motivator and energiser of human action.

THE FOUR GLOBAL MOVEMENTS CRITICAL TO A SUSTAINABLE STRATEGY FOR WORLD CONSERVATION

What implications flow from the foregoing progression? Beginning with a reductionist analysis, four key concerns may be identified. They are the disciplines or activities represented by the words development, environment, population, and the peace movement. These are the four great issues dominating the end of the twentieth century, causing vulnerability to the same extent that their concerns remain disconnected or their purposes unattained.

These four themes capture what is essential to humanity and the environment in our time. Each has now become a complex, technical discipline of its own. While there are overlapping constituencies, each has tended to develop its own adherents, followers and intellectual leaders. However, taken singly each is inadequate. In none resides a settled body of opinion or corpus of conventional wisdom. The hallmark throughout is one of intellectual ferment and conflict. In aid and development we struggle with the necessity of short-term relief versus the imperative of sustainable development; the growth of GNP often militates against the pursuit of individual welfare and happiness; the individual frequently conflicts with the state; the "trickle down" with the "bottom up." In the environmental field we applaud the political activists of Green Peace and Friends of the Earth on one hand, and the science-related advocacy of, say, IUCN or IIED on the other; we have those who wish to protect and conserve, and those who wish to develop sustainably. In population there are those who would restrict the size of the family by State decree and those who brook no interference by either State or contraceptive device in procreation. Arguments over abortion, euthanasia and the right to life rend these groups asunder. In the peace movement absolute pacifists are suspicious of those who support a first-step freeze on nuclear weapons and those who point away from nuclear war to biological or psychological warfare, or to that brand of violence yielding social inequities and legalised injustices.

It is neither my role nor our concern at this Conference to argue the pros and cons of any of these positions. The point I am making is simple. Across these four areas of concern - for the safety, stability and development of our global system - there is now great public concern for and commitment to our future. It ranges from the enlightened best to the fanatical worst, but it is there; its time has come. How then do we exploit this opportunity and give it institutional form?

RE-STATING A STRATEGY FOR WORLD CONSERVATION

First we need an intellectually coherent restatement of a world strategy for conservation which explicitly embraces these four areas of concern. It would need to be based on sound scholarship and yet strive to be visionary, while sensitive to the tensions and differences of view.

Secondly, that statement (and the institutions it projected) should carry the vision forward from the Cartesian to the interdisciplinary in its ethos and structural disciplines.

Thirdly, large areas of activity would need to be popularist; projecting a "bottom up" approach which encourages local communities to determine national and international strategies. We are talking about *Homo Sapiens* - people - not governments or Prime Ministers or Presidents. It is thus quite insufficient to claim that the "prime responsibilities for conservation action undoubtedly lie with national governments." Of course there is truth in that statement. But more true I believe is that people and their communities should be the focus of our strategy for world conservation if we are looking for sustainability. Anything less is unsatisfactory. I do not wish to be misunderstood here. The political and legal processes are essential and need to be maintained until we devise something better. But they must reflect politics for people and their communities, and not politics for elites and their bureaucracies. They must lean heavily, therefore, on a "bottom-up" process and not the "trickle-down" approach. People and their communities should be encouraged to design and plan for their own sustainable development and the lasting enhancement of their environments. The implications of such a style for existing conservation movements are enormous.

Fourthly, I would like social justice within the rule of law to be the style of the operation. We cannot forget that at the root of our assault on the environment lies cupidity, profligacy and the dominance of one species, one group, or one person over another, as well as sheer ignorance. If that is to be changed then two revolutions are necessary - the one ethical and intellectual, the other political and pragmatic.

In our catalytic role we advocate change. But change always exacts a price; a journey to be undertaken, energy to be expended. For the bees of a hive to produce one pound of honey they must fly the equivalent of twice the circumference of the earth. Nothing of value is likely to be created without energy, patience, commitment and visionary planning.

Institutionally, therefore, the leaders of these inter-related areas of concern - development, environment, population and peaceful co-existence - must rethink their respective positions, not only in the light of their separate, institutional targets, but more importantly in their common objectives and the identification of common means for achieving those objectives. This process of course has to accommodate the competitive nature of the NGO world where everyone is clamouring for the same purse, column inch, media slot, political advantage and liquidity. We are naturally suspicious of others who talk of cooperation: "What's their game," we wonder. Perhaps we could take the initiative and propose a conference designed to explore how all four groups might share their thinking, design common campaigns for the attainment of agreed objectives, target one anothers' constituencies with promotional or advocacy material and break down the barriers which divide us. We could try throughout to create a global groundswell of public opinion, pluralist and open, which will not be distracted from securing its political objectives.

Within this global framework, and on the basis of a new holistic discipline in which cultural sensitivities rank high and fora are created for listening to each other, many such elements might be identified. I argued at the beginning that income would flow from having a good product and promoting it with appropriate skill. But risk capital, venture capital, capital to explore new ideas or to help a new institution to "get off the ground" are not easy to come by. The movement has tended to spend too much time on legal or technical particulars, and not enough on manifestos, ideas and concepts. This is partly because Anglo-Saxons still tend to dominate these movements. Anglo-Saxons are expert in data identification, accumulation and storage. These are important and valuable contributions, but inadequate in and of themselves. The crucial task is to relate data to values through philosophy and ideas via the use of indicators. By indicators I mean insights which are illustrated through the use of clear and compelling images of the total world system, the global view, the cosmic view if you like, which is the central reality of our era. That seems to me to be the crucial step we still need to take. Could we look, therefore, to agencies like Oxfam, the World Resources Institute or World Wildlife Fund to consider seriously their responsibility for priming new groups, ideas or campaigns across the four areas I have delineated, in a language which is compelling to ordinary people? Do we need a central independent fund created just for these purposes and sustained by relatively wealthy agencies? Such a fund could provide scholarships and fellowships to enable young people to explore the potential offered by a holistic approach to the global problems of the twenty-first century.

In the same vein there should be more evidence of joint campaigns between the constituent parts. Five years ago in the United Kingdom, sixty separate groups from these movements joined together to finance the Independent Broadcasting Trust. The aim was to exploit new television opportunities for separate and collective presentations of our respective messages through modern, professional television programmes and documentary films. Could this be done internationally? Could we set up a satellite and create an NGO electronic network to talk to people in their homes and across the oceans of the world? Given the explosive growth of videos, could we combine cash resources, ideas and filming skills to create our own supply of videos for the mass market? Another excellent example of cooperation was the process that resulted in the United Kingdom Conservation Strategy, the biggest single exercise in public consultation the UK has ever seen. Could that be repeated in countries of the South? Perhaps Germany's "Green Movement" has gone furthest in integrating common concerns from dif-

ferent perspectives. But other regional or continental structures should reflect this approach more fully, not only in the donor countries - but in the Third World as well. We need to support, with hard cash as well as with experience, in partnership with each other, the proliferation of voluntary agencies and indigenous peoples' movements in the South which are dedicated to the attainment of our common objectives.

Of course there are dangers; there are problems to be overcome. The peace marcher may find difficulty in giving top priority to saving whales; those who wish to preserve our tropical forests may be apprehensive of the implications of community development with all their political and cultural consequences; the relief worker in Ethiopia may be impatient with the biologist who dedicates his life to studying *Asellus acquaticus* (the water louse); the family planner may be uncertain of the meaning of the nuclear winter, or bored with the science of water tables in Java. But this is part of the problem. Our disciplines, institutions and interests are too specialist and too little integrated to ensure a response from those who hold political power and from whom decisions might yet be drawn in favour of the causes we advocate. And yet success will be measured politically in the first instance. We must be serious in engaging the political process and using it dynamically to secure our objectives. Risk ventures, therefore, will be a real feature of a new strategy.

THE STRENGTH IN PLURALITY AND DIVERSITY

I am not looking for the development of one, large, amorphous institution, for there is both strength and resilience in pluralism and diversity. Nevertheless, it would help in breaking down institutional barriers if we could agree, for example, to a staff exchange - not only between the four areas of concern, but also between the large, powerful agencies, and smaller, struggling agencies which, despite their poverty, are often highly creative, and frequently set the pace for the larger agencies.

Furthermore, while many donor agencies, trusts and foundations argue for mergers and rationalisation in our movements, I take a contrary view. More important, I believe, is the need for greater cooperation between large agencies and bilaterals on one side, and the smaller NGO's on the other. It is not that there are too many agencies; rather that they work too exclusively in their own small corners and have not learned how to "professionalise" the ethic of sharing ideas, people, wealth, experience. The failure of development aid, especially in Africa with its appalling environmental consequences, is the direct result of this stiff-necked policy. Surely we must look for more dynamic ways of working together. This is why I welcome the initiative taken by the World Bank which has invited IIED to act as the honest broker in hosting a meeting between it and their NGO critics later this year in London. The progress will be catalytic and will provide a learning experience for all of us.

I mentioned at the outset the importance of and need for a body of management expertise and professional practitioners if we are to be effective in securing our objectives. Where does that expertise come from, and are we content merely to rely on the infusion of a few individuals from industry or commerce to galvanise our ranks and improve our efficiency? Institutionally how do we train our staff in management skills? What structures does this require? Amateur enthusiasm, while generating the necessary commitment, is no longer adequate as the basis from which to engage in dialogue with politicians, industrialists, scientists, or city planners. We need professional as well as scholarly skills. We need practice as well as theory. These do not come by accident. They presuppose planning, resource allocation and a definition of accountability. All of this ought to be tackled from an international platform. It is on this basis that common codes of conduct, or a corpus of "professional" wisdom, can be defined and promoted. In this context I think that Professor Johan Galtung of Princeton University raises an important challenge to us in saying that scientists who sign Official Secrets Acts cease to be scientists - they become civil servants. If that is true, and if the world's top ten percent of scientists are in government employ, then our scientific human resources are seriously depleted.

CONCLUSION

I have argued that we cannot work for an effective World Conservation Strategy unless people and their communities are its *raison d'être*, and their fulfillment its goal. Historically we are privileged to live at the confluence of four great movements of public concern, each of which is integral to a strategy for global conservation: development, conservation, population and peace. Our first task is to bring these four movements into some kind of relationship, essentially so that we can listen to each other and learn from each other. The style should be "bottom up" and people participatory rather than "top down" and elitist. There is considerable potential in exploiting the concept of "sustainable livelihoods" and the wealth of ideas which flow from it. Given such a foundation, political changes in favour of community-biased conservation can be attained, and a host of sub-activities from public advocacy to the stimulation of professionalism can be given shape. It follows that the strong would aid the weak and particularly that the "North" would help the "South" in building and supporting peoples' movements sympathetic to our cause. Such a people's movement would shape, formulate, and implement national conservation strategies from the bottom up. National governments would stand in a supportive role, as would legislators and their legal instruments. In particular, we have to learn how to argue persuasively the merits of our case with Treasuries and Ministers of Finance. It is central that in each of the areas discussed: development, conservation, population and peace, a stable and sustainable planet will be secured "by" people and not "for" people.

Dependency is the arch inhibitor to progress. Even as we can bend plants to suit the arid zones of Africa instead of trying to bend the environment to our needs, so must we bend the political process to the needs of people and their communities, instead of the other way around. Nor would we wish any of this to be within that determinist framework enshrined in Hardy's epic poem, "The Dynasty," in which he describes

Things mechanised
By coils and pivots set to
foreframed codes......

but rather as a plural and open movement whose style is holistic and whose purpose is to liberate men and women to be fully human, finding their place, within the wonder of Earth's majestic order.

ENVIRONMENTAL LAW - PROGRESS AND PROBLEMS

Françoise Burhenne-Guilmin
Cyril de Klemm
Malcolm Forster
Barbara Lausche
IUCN Environmental Law Centre
Bonn, Federal Republic of Germany

SUMMARY The World Conservation Strategy (WCS) calls for both national and international legal action to implement its objectives. At the national level, each country is called upon to review and consolidate its legislation on living resources to ensure that it makes adequate provision for conservation, to develop legislation specifically providing for sustainable utilisation and protection of living resources and their support systems, and to pay particular attention to enforcement and implementation. At the international level, the World Conservation Strategy calls for the development of legal mechanisms to achieve or contribute to conservation goals. This paper provides an overview of environmental law, both at the national and international levels, in order to identify the legal requirements for implementing the Strategy and the inadequacies of the existing law.

CONTENT AND EVOLUTION OF ENVIRONMENTAL LAW

There are two aspects of environmental law. The first deals with relationships and conflicts between legal persons touching on the environment; the second concerns relationships between legal persons and the environment itself, consisting largely of preventive or remedial measures. These two elements are interlinked, but only the second, resource-related aspect touches directly upon implementing the World Conservation Strategy.

Resource oriented environmental law is composed largely of elements of classical law disciplines, both public and private. For example, administrative law governs environmental decision-making; tax law provides fiscal incentives for conservation; conservation associations' rights to seek redress fall under general rules of procedure; remedies are awarded according to ordinary civil law, etc. Like all other fields of law, environmental law is dependent for its effectiveness upon its institutional background and will not function efficiently unless appropriate infrastructure exists.

Although some aspects of environmental law have been known for centuries, it has only been recognised as a discrete body of law in the last twenty years. The earlier "reactive" process led to piecemeal development of the subject, which has only given way to a comprehensive body of law as awareness of accelerated environmental harm has heightened. This process has been mirrored by the growing number of constitutional provisions and basic laws relating to the environment.

Among the factors which hampered this development was the necessity, in the early stages, of employing legal devices originally developed for other purposes. Many of these hinder environmental matters as, for example, when the general law obliges a landowner to cultivate or drain fallow land.

Environmental law has also suffered from its perceived antithesis toward short-term economic and social development, which have too frequently been preferred. Thus, exceptions are frequently made from legislation for certain activities such as agriculture and forestry. Even when environmental factors are taken into account along with social and economic factors, they are generally so vaguely described that their relative weight is unclear. This often results in difficulty in rendering a decision on the grounds that environmental factors have not been properly considered. Finally, while economic and social factors invariably impinge on environmental law, the converse is rarely the case.

ENVIRONMENTAL LAW AND THE OBJECTIVES OF THE WORLD CONSERVATION STRATEGY; THE NATIONAL DIMENSION

Classes of Environmental Laws

Environmental laws form two basic types: those which directly regulate or control potentially harmful human activity, by prohibiting it or subjecting it to a permit process; and those which indirectly influence such activity by inducing certain forms of conduct (by incentive or disincentive).

Direct regulation of activities. Direct regulation measures may in turn take one of two forms:

* regulation of land use, by which the site of activities affecting the environment can be controlled; or

* controls over the conduct of activities themselves, e.g. by a permit with operating conditions attached to it.

An important element of control is the issuance of some sort of permit. As this is not usually entrusted to conservation agencies, it is essential that procedural safeguards exist to prevent activities from causing grave or irreversible environmental harm, and to ensure that ecological considerations are taken into account by the authority.

Sometimes this is achieved by removing the authority's discretion entirely in certain areas. This has occurred in the United States Endangered Species Act (which prohibited Federal agencies from authorising, financing or conducting activities that may jeopardise species); and in the Wilderness Act's prohibition of road construction or use of motor vehicles in wilderness areas. But such examples are rare. It is more usual to ensure that information about the ecological values at stake is presented to the authority. Environmental agencies may, for example, have to be consulted prior to the decision-making process. In some countries, the procedure for including ecological factors has been formalised by requiring that certain proposals undergo an environmental impact assessment before the decision can be taken, with content and timing of such assessments set forth in legislation. Frequently, procedures are mandatory so that, if they are not complied with, decisions can be reviewed or overturned for that reason.

Moreover, once decisions of this sort have been made, some legal systems provide mechanisms for challenging them. In a few countries, the conservation agency concerned has the right to veto a decision on certain grounds, although it is more usual to find a system of appeal. This may be to a higher administrative authority (even to the responsible Minister in countries such as the United Kingdom), or it may be to the courts. Courts are rarely prepared to review a decision on its merits, but their function as guarantors of procedural correctness and due process ensures them an important role in reviewing environmental decisions. Thus, an emergency power often resides with the court to halt any activity which may result in irreversible environmental damage, pending an enquiry into the decision-making process. It also assumes that someone has *locus standi* to bring the matter before the court in the first place.

Influencing or inducing an attitude. There are two general means of achieving this effect, either through economic incentives and disincentives or through legislation.

Economic incentives and disincentives

Incentives to promote environmentally sound behaviour by private persons usually take the form of subsidies or favourable tax treatment. Thus, a recent European Community regulation provides, under certain conditions, for subsidy payments to farmers to maintain the natural environment on their land. Examples of favourable tax treatment are capital allowances in respect to pollution abatement technology, and the granting of land-tax credits for preservation of wetlands, natural prairie areas, or for the conservation of river banks.

Disincentives, by contrast, seek to penalise environmentally undesirable activities. This is the principle behind imposing charges for effluents, for example. In practice, however, these require considerable care lest they become regarded as licences to pollute at a price. The United Kingdom Wildlife and Countryside Act employs a variation of the disincentive model by envisaging the refusal of agricultural subsidies on activities adversely affecting the flora, fauna, geological or physiogeographical features of lands.

Legislation reflecting social and consumer pressures

It is clear that attitudes (including those of public authorities) may be influenced by social forces. In some countries, social pressures are harnessed by legislation to encourage reactions which are favourable to environmental objectives. For example, sales of electrical appliances may be affected by requirements to bear labels stating their energy efficiency; goods labelled as containing asbestos meet with consumer resistance while recycled paper products do not, and so on.

Problems Facing Environmental Law in General

Dependence on adequate scientific information. The quality of both decision-making and environmental law implementation is determined by the quality of information upon which they are based. In this context, not only must scientific input (in the form of ecological inventories, maps, and habitat assessments) be of a high standard, but it must be available to decision-makers. Too frequently, this condition is not met. Timely and appropriate adjustments in implementation cannot be made unless adequate monitoring is correctly carried out.

The threshold of acceptable harm. A perennial difficulty for environmental regulation is to define the level of activity which sets the regulatory process in motion. This threshold varies with its subject, but may be based upon emission levels;[1] on the size of the area concerned;[2] or even upon the cost of the operations in question.[3] Most frequently, however, the threshold relates to environmental damage and, although precise values are sometimes used, it is common for the threshold to be defined in terms of "significant" or "undue" harm; notions in which a degree of uncertainty is inherent. In addition, the "threshold" approach itself risks overlooking the cumulative effects of innumerable small actions, which in aggregate may have a severe effect upon life support systems, genetic resources and overall environmental quality.

The problem of ensuring compliance. It is necessary to ensure that environmental regulations are respected by private persons and by public authorities. Failure of public authorities to comply with environmental law (e.g. in issuing regulations, in the grant of a permit, or by failure to observe procedural requirements) is, in many countries, subject to investigation under administrative law, often by court action.

It is largely the responsibility of public authorities to secure compliance of permit holders and of the general public. This is usually achieved by imposing penalties, many of which have increased markedly in recent years. Penal sanctions however, are only truly effective if sufficient effort is directed at detection and prosecution of offenders, and environmental law requires both trained personnel and equipment for this purpose. In a few jurisdictions, voluntary assistance (including that of individuals and conservation groups) has been accepted.

The problem of remedies.[4] Most legal systems adhere to a traditional concept of damage which is direct, personal and capable of being expressed in monetary value, thus virtually excluding any possibility for recovering true ecological damage. This obtains

---

1.   In the case of air or water pollution.

2.   As in Denmark where activities affecting fragile ecosystem elements require a permit if the area in question is above a certain size.

3.   As with the preparation of environmental impact assessments in France.

4.   In this paper, attention is paid only to remedies for damage to the environment itself, and not to remedies for physical injury, damage or economic loss. Thus, while monetary damages may compensate fishermen for loss of income caused by damage to a fishery, these fall outside the scope of this paper, which is concerned exclusively with natural resources matters, such as the cost of restoring the stock and its habitat.

for two reasons: (a) it is often difficult to identify anyone suffering sufficiently directly and substantially as a result of the destruction of a wetland or species and, (b) because of the difficulties in assessing the amount of damage or costs involved in restoring the environment to its pre-existing state.

The measure of damages should ideally be the full cost of restoration. But because many legal systems set strict limits upon the power to award punitive damages, assessment remains difficult; hence the trend toward imposing civil penalties which bear no relation to real restoration costs. From the environmental point of view, it would be preferable if that part of the damage which is restorable (e.g. restocking, restoration of habitats to the extent possible) could be recovered. This should, however, not prejudice the imposition of civil penalties for those cases of irreparable loss.

*****

An attempt will now be made to assess the extent to which the objectives of the World Conservation Strategy have been achieved in national laws.

Maintenance of Life Support Systems and Essential Ecological Processes

Although the legal processes discussed in this section are also relevant to others (particularly to the conservation of genetic resources), the problem here is a broader one. The goal is not only to maintain areas in a natural state, but also to maintain vital functions and to preserve a sufficient number of differing ecosystems of a quality adequate for the production of living resources.

In principle, these goals may be achieved, *inter alia,* by any legal mechanism which controls development activities so as to allocate land and water use in the most ecologically rational manner possible, and so as to reduce degradation to a minimum. Thus, the planning and permit systems referred to above are essential to maintaining life support systems and ecological processes. The effective operation of such systems contributes largely to the conservation of the most important and most threatened life support systems identified by the World Conservation Strategy (agricultural, forest, coastal and fresh water systems).

In addition, these general regimes may be reinforced by provisions relating to particular life support systems. These may seek to:

* regulate conflicting uses (and ensure the maintenance of natural functions) e.g. coastal zone legislation, legislation on mountainous areas, arid zones (grazing) legislation, estuarine legislation;

* provide for the maintenance of certain types of life support system maintenance at a level consonant with the importance of the ecological and biological values involved. In a few countries, such special provisions exist for wetlands, coral reefs, mangroves, and free-flowing rivers as well as in those forest laws which require that a certain proportion of existing forest area be retained;

* maintain elements essential to the life support system concerned (e.g. protection of forests for water catch-

ment areas, vegetation for stabilising dunes);

* combat a particular threat (such as the effect of acid rain on forests).

Yet, even given these general or specific devices, the maintenance of life support systems and ecological processes can only be achieved if attention is paid to the quality of air, waters and soils by means of pollution control legislation.

Such legislation exists (albeit at differing degrees of sophistication) in virtually all developed countries and in a growing number of developing ones. The most common approaches are based on the determination of standards, which may take a wide variety of forms, such as ambient, emission, process, material or management-use standards.[5]

Some of the problems posed by standard-setting have already been addressed in the discussion of the concept of thresholds. There is, however, an additional series of problems, which may be economic (what is economically tolerable for a particular class of industry), technical (what is technically feasible in a particular country at a particular moment) or both (how standards evolve dynamically to reflect progress in the state-of-the-art without causing

undue economic burdens or distortions). All of these elements have their place in the standard-setting process which unavoidably leads to a decision based on a compromise between the advantages and disadvantages involved.

Some reference should also be made to the practice of establishing "special areas" for pollution control. Presently, these tend to be directed toward the reduction of pollutant levels in highly polluted areas, but there may be great value in extending their use to areas which are ecologically sensitive or important, where the concept should work in tandem with special applications of the planning controls mentioned above.

It is clear, however, that pollution control laws are insufficient in themselves to protect basic life support systems and essential ecological processes. As scientific appreciation increases on the interrelationship of impacts throughout an entire natural system, it will be necessary to develop legal mechanisms which can accommodate management planning on a system basis, and coordinate controls over activities affecting the overall natural system. Pollution laws are currently confined to specific problems.

Conservation of Genetic Diversity

The protection of individual species. Almost all countries have legislation to

---

5. Ambient or quality standards refer to the maximum permissible concentration of a pollutant in the recipient medium (air, water, soil, etc.), while emission standards are usually expressed in terms of the permissible level of a given pollutant per unit of discharge. Both, however, may be expressed in more general terms; ambient standards by reference to a particular purpose (such as waters capable of sustaining fish life) and emission standards by being linked to the best available abatement methods. Both approaches have advantages and disadvantages and, as they are by no means mutually exclusive, a combination of both might well be optimum. Other forms of standards aim to prevent or reduce the amount of a given pollutant reaching the environment by indirect means, such as the determination of produce characteristics (as in the case of unleaded petrol), the prescribing of rules governing the use or application of certain products (such as pesticides), or by insistence upon certain industrial processes (for instance generating less waste than others.)

protect individual species. Originally designed to preserve endangered or spectacular species of mammals and birds, such laws have been extended to cover many other vertebrates in need of protection from taking. Thus, many countries now protect all species of birds except a small number of game and pest species, a principle known as "reverse" listing. With regard to invertebrates, although some countries have been protecting certain species since 1937, it is only recently that long lists of protected species, especially insects, have begun to appear in legislation. Similarly, although certain plant species have been protected for some time, and although some countries have compiled long lists of protected plants, protecting individual species by law is a relatively recent phenomenon which is almost completely confined to industrialised countries.

The effectiveness of species legislation is, however, severely limited in that, in a majority of cases, prohibitions only apply to taking in the narrow sense of the term (i.e. killing, capturing, collecting, etc.) and to trade. Yet except for animals which are slow breeders, taking is seldom the major or only threat to survival. Although protecting essential or critical habitats is universally recognised as a basic requirement for species preservation, it seldom appears in legislation. If it does, it is usually in terms so general that implementation or enforcement are difficult, if not impossible. A notable exception is the United States Endangered Species Act of 1973 which prohibits all actions that may harm a listed endangered species and protects their critical habitats from harmful Federal activities. In addition, each species so listed must be the subject of a recovery plan taking into consideration all factors likely to affect its conservation status.

Legislation prohibiting or restricting the taking of plants is, in most cases even more ineffective, as the destruction of protected plants by legitimate activities such as farming or construction remains generally authorised. In addition, in many common-law countries, there are constitutional impediments to prohibiting land owners from taking or destroying plants on their own land. As an example, the United States Endangered Species Act only protects from taking those specimens of an endangered plant which grows on Federal property.

It is probable also that few forest laws take account of the need to protect species diversity in forest practices.

The protection of ecosystems. There are four general mechanisms through which this is achieved:

By establishing protected areas

Almost all countries have now enacted legislation on the establishment of protected areas, the definition of which may cover a wide variety of areas. These may range from strict nature reserves (where all human activities, except scientific research, are prohibited) to areas where only certain activities are regulated. Whereas the initial purpose of many such areas was to protect spectacular scenery and provide outdoor recreation facilities for the public, in recent years the concept has evolved to encompass preserving species-rich ecosystems and endangered species' habitats. This was based on the recognition that if protected areas were allowed to become mere ecological islands, a large fraction of their plant and animal species would be lost.

The prohibition or control of certain activities, which is the essence of a protected area, may be achieved in a number of ways.

Where large tracts of public lands are available, the establishment of protected areas under public ownership is easy, at least in theory, and may be achieved at little cost. (Land management departments may, however, be reluctant to relinquish their rights over areas under their jurisdiction.) If land requiring protection is in private hands, however, its acquisition by a public body may be extremely expensive. If possible, agencies have tried to avoid the expense of outright land acquisition by seeking to acquire a lesser interest or only those interests in the land which are necessary to protect the ecological value of the area (such as the right of drainage), where such rights are separable.

Governments are usually reluctant to use their expropriation powers against unwilling owners for conservation purposes. Alternatively, a government may, by order, impose strict restraints on activities carried on in a specified place, even though the land remains under private ownership. All forms of detrimental activity, including (where necessary) farming, may be prohibited by law. The owner is usually compensated for his loss, and this procedure is extensively used in many European countries. In other legal systems, such as those of the United Kingdom and United States, the government cannot establish a reserve on private land except under a management agreement with the owner or under the terms of a lease or similar instrument.

Management agreements are contracts concluded between a landowner and a public authority. The landowner commits himself not to do certain things, such as drain the tract or clear its natural vegetation, in exchange for a lump sum or periodic payments. An example appears in the United Kingdom Wildlife and Countryside Act which authorises the Nature Conservancy Council to enter into such agreements with owners of Sites of Special Scientific Interest.

In some countries, protection orders containing restrictions on land-use are filed with title to the land, thus constituting a public servitude for which compensation is usually provided. Although some activities such as hunting (which would normally be prohibited in a reserve) may be allowed, the protection against habitat destruction may be very effective. Examples of this exist in Danish conservation legislation and the Massachusetts coastal wetlands protection law.

Protected areas may also be established on private lands under an agreement with a government conservation agency, or by voluntary dedication.

Reserves may also be established under the private law of property by private persons. In some countries, such as the United States, the United Kingdom and the Netherlands, the acquisition and management of such lands by private persons (including conservation organisations) receives considerable public assistance in the form of subsidies or tax concessions. In general, reserves do not enjoy privileges other than those directly deriving from ownership of the land, although in some cases government-approved private reserves are protected by law against encroachment by third parties. It may also be necessary to preserve these areas against government action, such as expropriation for public purposes. In certain US states, there is, for example, a procedure called "dedication" which ensures that no interference by a government agency may take place except with the consent of the legislature, the State Governor, or the court, as the case may be. In the United Kingdom, the National Trust may declare any of its land unalienable, with the result that encroachments may only be sanctioned by Act of Parliament.

Another method of securing protection through the private law is to enter into contracts with other landowners imposing servitudes running with the land. In most legal systems, this is only possible where the land in question is adjacent to land owned by the organisation seeking the benefit, but there are some exceptions such as Switzerland and certain US states.

By land-use controls and permits

While in many countries controls over land use (including zoning) extend to rural areas, agricultural and forestry operations are usually exempted from their provisions. Thus, existing controls are insufficient to stop the destruction of natural habitats, particularly as a result of extensive farming methods. Some jurisdictions (including Switzerland, Luxembourg and certain US states) have recently required any alteration to certain types of habitats to be the subject of a permit. Thus, the Danish Conservation Act of 1969 (as amended) sets up a very strict system of land-use controls and permits applying to any activity which may affect

river beds, lakes, peat bogs, heaths, salt marshes or coastal vegetation. An extension to cover natural grasslands is proposed for the near future. No compensation is payable if a permit is refused. In many countries, however, farmers' interests continue to oppose the introduction of such a system.

In the case of forestry, restrictions on the felling of private forests have long been imposed in a large number of countries at the request of forest departments, although felling and other management restrictions are not generally applicable to those departments themselves. A notable exception is found in the United States Federal Forest and Rangelands Renewable Resources Planning Act of 1974, as amended in 1976, which severely restricts the discretionary authority of the Forest Service in National Forests.

By providing incentives or disincentives

Such devices, discussed above, also have applications in the preservation of genetic diversity.

By controlling the introduction of exotic species

Strong preventive measures are essential to prevent harmful introductions of new exotic species, particularly to lakes and islands. Legislation controlling deliberate introductions has now been adopted in many countries and permits are generally required for the introduction of exotic species. The prevention of accidental introduction, especially of small invertebrates and plants, is much more difficult to control except by stringent quarantine controls at borders. To deal with escapes of plants and animals kept in gardens or in captivity, some countries now prohibit any import of certain potentially harmful species.

Sustainable Exploitation and Use

Legal regimes governing exploitation reflect its three main forms: subsistence, commercial and recreational.

Subsistence exploitation was traditionally balanced with ecological capacity, as over-exploitation would have been detrimental to the exploiting group. As a closed system it generally caused no harm, but has now all but disappeared from developed economies and elsewhere; the advent of modern weapons and equipment has led to a tendency to take more specimens and to market the surplus. In many cases, disruption of clan or ethnic bonds has removed the self-regulation of such systems, which have been replaced by regulations imposed by governments. These may contain severe restrictions. Where it is still authorised at all without a hunting licence (as in many African countries), subsistence hunting may only be conducted with traditional weapons and protected animals may not be taken.

As a result of the depletion of many animal populations and the changes which have taken place in international trade, commercial hunting is of less importance than formerly. It is strictly limited in many countries, often being subject to a special permit requirement, and is even prohibited in some countries.

Commercial fishing, on the other hand, especially in the sea, continues to be of considerable economic importance. Originally, fisheries administration imposed increasingly complex restrictions on the taking of fish (including closed seasons and closed areas), limitations

on gear (particularly mesh sizes of nets), on the size and power of vessels, etc., thus affecting the economy of fishing operations. Global quotas based on maximum sustainable yield were later introduced, but proved to be ineffective and difficult to enforce. Extending the "exclusive economic zone" to 200 nautical miles, however, as provided for in the Law of the Sea Convention, does offer an opportunity for coastal States to achieve rational management of fisheries in something approaching a closed system.

As a result of the depletion of wild populations and other threats such as habitat destruction, considerable restrictions have been imposed on recreational hunting and fishing. Although legislation in many countries has introduced traditional controls on over-exploitation - in the form of closed seasons, hunting and fishing licences, prohibition of hunting or fishing in closed areas (such as game reserves) - these proved insufficient and were supplemented by other devices, including hunting examinations, bag limits, overall quotas and trade prohibitions. In several European countries and in North America, attempts have been made to limit the number of hunters, for instance by drawing lots or by restricting the number of permits), and to provide for a more rational management of game populations through the development of shooting plans.

Whatever the form of exploitation, ecological management will always remain an essential requirement. Restrictions on taking are not sufficient, although quotas and bag limits should obviously be based on the optimum sustainable productivity of the resource and the result of population dynamics studies. Yet in the large majority of cases, it is equally important to analyse all causes of potential depletion and to take remedial action where possible. Habitat preservation for exploited species will, in most cases, be crucial. Oddly enough, hunting and fishing legislation hardly ever takes this matter into consideration, except in very recent laws and then only in vague terms. Until management plans which integrate all the factors necessary to ensure sustainable production are required by law, measures limited to the control of taking, however valuable in themselves, are bound to fail.

As indicated above, national law rarely provides appropriate devices to ensure sustainable use of ecosystems by planning multiple uses sustainably. Resource and ecosystem evaluation play, at best, a rudimentary role in most domestic systems.

ENVIRONMENTAL LAW AND THE OBJECTIVES OF THE WCS - THE INTERNATIONAL DIMENSION

The Nature of International Environmental Law

International law governs the conduct of States and other international persons. Thus, environmental and conservation matters fall within the ambit of international law in a number of instances. First, many resource and environmental questions can only be properly addressed if a number of States adopt common rules for solutions. Such questions may be global (it is hard to imagine sulphur dioxide emissions into the atmosphere or the protection of the ozone layer being dealt with in any other manner), but the principle applies equally within a narrower geographical scope. Thus, proper management of any shared resource (such as a fish stock) can only be achieved by action at the regional or sub-regional level. In this manner, the scope of the legal response is determined by the nature of the issue to be addressed.

Secondly, actions taking place within one State may produce effects which impinge on resources or environmental quality beyond the limits of national jurisdiction. These results may be direct and apparent, as in the case of air pollutants affecting a State downwind of their sources, or they may illustrate more complex consequences, as when a lower riparian State suffers from flooding or siltation caused by deforestation in a neighbouring State upstream.

International law derives from a number of sources, principal among which are international conventions or treaties, international customary law (insofar as it reflects the general practice of States), and the general principles of law recognised by civilised nations. In recent years, each of those sources has displayed features of interest to international environmental law.

The usual medium to establish new international obligations, especially those which involve the elaboration of some detail or complexity, is the treaty. These instruments (sometimes referred to as conventions, agreements, etc.) represent agreements entered into by sovereign States (or other international persons) and thus do not create legal obligations for States which are not parties to them.

This inherent reservation notwithstanding, treaties have made a major contribution to developing international environmental law in the last 15 years. They enable new principles to be introduced into this body of law with the minimum possible delay and, as the treaty derives from the will of sovereign States, it is not essential that its principles depend on pre-existing international law, so radical changes can be introduced. (See, for example, the virtual exclusion of national territorial claims from the implementation of the Antarctic Treaty regime.)

In recent years, however, one of the principal benefits claimed for the treaty, namely that it provided for rapid reception of new principles in the international law, has appeared to be more in doubt, as the time taken for treaties to come into force has increased markedly. Treaties are normally subject to a two-stage process of acceptance by States. The first stage consists of the signing of the treaty by State representatives and usually takes place immediately upon concluding the text (whether by international conference or otherwise). In most cases, signature must be followed by ratification, the precise form of which varies according to the constitution of the State. It is only upon completion of this second stage that the State becomes bound by the terms of the treaty in international law.

The reason for the increased delay in bringing treaties into force may derive from a number of factors. Treaties to which a number of States may become parties have traditionally come into force only when a significant proportion of the potential parties have ratified. As the number of States has increased enormously over the past two decades, treaties of global application

tend to require a correspondingly greater number of ratifications to come into force.

This problem has been exaggerated in some fields by a desire to ensure acceptance of treaty provisions over a broad geographical area. Uniform obligations dictate differing speeds of acceptance among States at different stages of development.

Furthermore, on occasion, excessive attention to detail in the text of a treaty has proved counter-productive. In some instances, before a treaty could come into force, economic or technical developments had overtaken the detailed provisions and rendered them inappropriate. (See the oil pollution annex to MARPOL.)

All of these shortcomings have occurred in the field of environmental law. While States having ratified a treaty could agree among themselves that, until such time as the treaty attracts enough ratifications to bring it into force, they will conduct themselves toward one another as if it were already in force, this has not found much favour in practice. Yet in recent years, States have resorted to a number of devices to avoid delay in the coming into force of treaties; devices which have sometimes also improved the appropriateness of the international law's response to the problem addressed by the treaty.

One such device (which is also used widely in regional agreements) is to supplement a treaty that has its substantive part confined to a statement of general principles, with subsidiary agreements in the form of protocols. Such protocols contain more detailed provisions on aspects of the subject matter of the treaty. A familiar example is provided by the numerous Regional Seas Agreements. These commit State parties in general terms to abate dumping at sea or land-based marine pollution, but leave the elaboration of how these objectives are to be achieved to protocols to which States may become parties. Frequently, the parent treaty will oblige a State becoming party to the treaty also to accept one of the protocols. Protocols consequently have the potential to develop almost as if they were sub-conventions devoted to very precise questions, of a kind unlikely to be developed independently, even on a regional basis. Occasionally, protocols may be developed to accommodate the desire of some parties to extend or strengthen provisions of the treaty, when that desire is not shared by other parties. In such a case, the protocol may be used to create binding legal obligations between the first group of States thus avoiding stagnation of the treaty, without the necessity of persuading reluctant States to concur. An example of this two-tier system is provided by the recent "Thirty Percent Protocol" to the Convention on Long-Range Transboundary Air Pollution.

Another device is to remove technical references from the body of the treaty and relegate them to an appendix or technical annex. This is coupled with a provision enabling parties to the treaty to amend the appendix or annex, not by formal ratification and acceptance, but by some less solemn means such as a decision at the periodic meeting of the parties. Thus, lists of species to be accorded various degrees of protection or substances whose disposal is to be controlled under the treaty may be amended with a minimum of formality and delay. Naturally, States which dissent from the amendment are not bound to respect it if their dissent is appropriately manifested, e.g. by reservation or objection. The device, while of real utility in applications such as those illustrated, does have major limitations and is not appropriate for large-scale, substantive amendments to treaties. In certain applications, it can even present constitutional difficulties for some States.

Some treaty systems have also begun to operate on the basis of arrangements between parties to the treaty, which are less formal than amendments to the treaty or its annexes, but which effectively extend the treaty obligations. This may be through an agreed interpretation of the application of treaty provisions to disputed or doubtful areas.

Some treaties display far more radical departures from traditional treaty practices. One of these is the Convention on the Conservation of Migratory Species of Wild Animals (the Bonn Convention), to which the World Conservation Strategy makes express reference. In some respects, the Bonn Convention is a perfectly ordinary convention of the "framework" type. Under its terms, parties commit themselves to conclude agreements subsidiary to the Convention to protect certain migratory species. What distinguishes this provision from similar ones elsewhere is that the Convention expressly envisages the participation in such agreements of States which are not party to the parent Convention itself. It thus creates an independent legal obligation with a group of States which are bound to one another (but not to the non-Convention State) by a particular legal instrument. This device would enable States, party to the Bonn Convention, to conclude an agreement on a particular species, even though one of the range States of that species was unwilling to ratify the Convention as a whole, as long as the State agreed to enter into the agreement regarding the species in question.

In some instances, States have even been prepared to abandon the traditional treaty format altogether and to allow their relations to be governed by mere *ad hoc* agreements, thus dispensing with almost all formality, except for a memorandum of the decisions adopted. While it is arguable whether this process differs in principle from any other form of international agreement, it is undeniable that in manner and form it represents a marked change in procedure. It should perhaps be noted, however, that such *ad hoc* agreements often occur under the "umbrella" of an international organisation, itself established by a convention of the (usually very) formal type which may thus be said to underlie the agreement.

It is sometimes superficially difficult to distinguish between agreements of that last type and the myriad declarations, resolutions, recommendations, proclamations, guidelines, statements of principles and so forth which issue from international meetings, particularly from those of international organisations. In order that an international agreement may constitute a source of international law it should establish **rules** of international law expressly recognised and accepted by the contracting parties. It is on this point that much "soft law" fails. That is not to say, however, that "soft law" principles may not pass into the international law, merely that they cannot do so as international agreements.

One of the other sources of international law is custom, insofar as States accept the rules of that custom as obligatory. Thus, the principles of a declaration, emanating from a meeting of an international organisation (such as those set forth in the Stockholm Declaration), while not binding in themselves, may become part of the customary international law if subscribing States implement those principles. Thus, the principles are incorporated into international law not by virtue of their mere promulgation, but of their being honoured in practice by a sufficient number of States. Arguably, a similar result may be achieved by the principles being approved of in other binding instruments, e.g. in the preamble to a treaty.

An attempt will now be made to examine the extent to which the objectives of the World Conservation Strategy have been accomplished in each of these areas of international activity.

Acceptance of Common Rules to Regulate Common Problems

The preservation of essential ecological processes. In some respects, achievement of international law may be said to be most impressive in this area. Concerted efforts have been made at both global and regional levels to tackle threats to such processes in a considerable number of areas. Thus, conventions regulate ocean protection from vessel-source pollution. These cover pollution by oil and by certain chemicals, and they have achieved a considerable degree of sophistication, both in the technical sense (in that States have specified with remarkable precision the engineering standards and equipment requirements necessary to achieve the degree of protection aimed at) and in the legal sense (in that they do not confine themselves to mere prohibition of polluting acts, but also provide for enforcement mechanisms of notable effectiveness, together with civil liability for damage in some cases). On a broader scale, the Law of the Sea Convention creates an international legal framework for ocean protection from degradation arising from a much wider range of sources, including land run-off, atmospheric transfer, etc. Some of these sources have also been the subject of particular attention from regional groupings of States. Thus dumping of wastes into the sea is regulated under one Convention which is truly international in its potential membership, and also under a number of regional agreements - some of which are Protocols to UNEP Regional Seas Agreements.

In areas other than marine pollution, attempts to achieve this degree of sophistication are hindered both by existing interests relating to current use of national territory (especially economic interests) and by the restraints imposed by States' anxiety to maintain national sovereignty. Thus, while States may be willing to compromise with regard to the high seas or outer space, there is less room for manoeuvre in regulating the pollution of international rivers or the atmosphere. These are often the very places where industries have traditionally disposed much of their waste. Nevertheless, there is evidence of progress in these areas, as may be seen in numerous treaties on the management of international watercourses. At one time these treaties concerned themselves almost entirely with regulating the *volume* of water to be received by downstream States; they now usually include some stipulation as to quality as well. Even in the notoriously complex field of atmospheric pollution, two major conventions have been concluded in recent years, one addressing the problem of long-range transboundary air pollution, the other concerning protection of the ozone layer.

It must be admitted, however, that these represent almost the only substantial successes in this field to date. Even in marine pollution, striking success is confined to the vessel-source question (especially if this is deemed to include dumping conventions). Marine pollution from other sources has barely been addressed in international instruments. Land-based pollution of the sea, for example, is the subject of only two regional agreements and one set of controls, all centred in one highly developed and industrialised region. The problem of marine pollution through atmospheric fallout has not been addressed specifically in any international agreement. No international agreement exists to govern protection of the marine environment against pollution from offshore installations' exploitation of mineral resources (although the framework for such control is provided for in the Law of the Sea Convention). Attempts to deal with atmospheric pollution on an international basis may be criticised as being pious in intent, but hesitant and insufficient both in their extent and in their approach.

The preservation of life-support systems. In this area, the pattern referred to in the preceding section is intensified. There are few international instruments in which States have undertaken the defence of life-support systems protected by an international agreement presently in force and specifically directed to that end; and no such instruments relate to tropical moist forests, northern polar regions, tropical semi-arid rangelands, coral reefs, temperate woodlands, etc.

There are some exceptions to this general statement. In addition to the ocean protection measures mentioned above, the Ramsar Convention (also expressly mentioned in the World Conservation Strategy) provides a framework within which major wetlands of international importance, especially waterfowl habitats, can be protected. The Antarctic Treaty provides perhaps the best-known example of a comprehensive attempt to apply conservation management to a large, cohesive, ice-covered area; an attempt which has been highly successful. On a rather more restricted level, the 1971 Amendments to the International Convention for the Prevention of Pollution of the Sea by Oil, concerning the Barrier Reef, proposed to complement one of the most widely accepted marine pollution conventions by providing stringent standards for vessels trading in the area of the Great Barrier Reef.

Preservation of genetic diversity. Here again, the substantial achievements of international law present results which are patchy at best. There is no international instrument which promotes the preservation of genetic diversity *per se*. The nearest approximation is the recent International Undertaking on Plant Genetic Resources concluded under the auspices of the UN Food and Agriculture Organization. This is a "soft law" document *par excellence* and applies only to plant resources. It is moreover seriously flawed by its heavy bias toward *ex*

situ conservation and cannot be regarded as other than a severely limited response to the problem.

Nevertheless, attempts have been made to protect particular species or groups of species and their habitats. Examples are the 1973 Agreement on the Conservation of Polar Bears, the 1972 Convention on the Conservation of Antarctic Seals, the Convention for the Protection and Conservation of the Vicuna (Buenos Aires, 1981), and the Convention on International Trade In Endangered Species of Fauna and Flora (CITES). These agreements and conventions, together with the network of biosphere reserves established under the Unesco Man and the Biosphere Programme and perhaps the Bonn Convention, may truly be described as global responses. Additionally, it should be noted that Article 196 of the Law of the Sea Convention contains express provisions relating to the introduction of alien species, and Article 194(5) makes express reference to the habitats of endangered species.

Also, to the extent that instruments concluded for the purpose of promoting conservation generally achieve the preservation of genetic diversity, a number of regional agreements should be mentioned. These not only contain controls on taking, but also envisage the establishment of protected areas. These conventions provide a framework which allows the problem to be dealt with in the round, thus approaching most nearly the aim of the World Conservation Strategy. An example of this is the African Convention on the Conservation of Nature and Natural Resources. The provisions of the Bern Convention on the Conservation of European Wildlife and Natural Habitats are here worthy of note, especially as to endangered species. In recent months, a striking development has been the attachment of a protocol to a Regional Seas Agreement for East Africa providing for wildlife and habitat conservation in the marine environment and coastal areas of the region. Similarly, a number of treaties exist for the protection of birds, many of which include unexploited species.

These treaties, however, (with the exception of those relating to the vicuna) usually fail to cover the entire range of the species concerned and so fail to provide any mechanism for managing the species as a unit.

To some extent, the preservation of genetic diversity is also achieved as a result of instruments with other or additional objectives. Thus, the World Heritage Convention (to which the World Conservation Strategy makes reference) seeks to protect sites which are of importance for a whole range of reasons, some of which (like those of aesthetic, historic or cultural importance) have no relation to conservation whatsoever, but do provide for the protection of sites which are valuable in conserving genetic resources.

This piecemeal approach to genetic diversity, through instruments which traditionally have been largely species-specific, may be explained by the fact that the subject is one which is only now becoming recognised as calling for a global legal solution.

Maintaining sustainable use of species and ecosystems. In connection with species use regulation, most existing international instruments do not adequately ensure the sustainable nature of such use. Even in the numerous international fishery agree-

ments (most of which make some reference to the necessity of calculating allowable catches to avoid marked depletion), the practice of these agreements makes it clear that, while such calculations may be made, they tend to consider exploited stocks in isolation, without taking into account their interdependence on other parts of the ecosystem, a classic example of which is the International Convention for the Regulation of Whaling. The very different approach adopted by the Convention on the Conservation of Antarctic Marine Living Resources in this respect is a striking but almost unique departure from this principle. Provisions of the Law of the Sea Convention, relating to exploitation of living resources of the exclusive economic zone (within which are located over 90 percent of commercial fishery stocks), also provide an opportunity for management of those stocks in a manner which is both rational and sustainable. It remains true, however, that protection of exploited species' habitats is almost entirely unprovided for under the Convention.

Similar shortcomings may be seen in international instruments dealing with terrestrial living resources, many of which are bilateral agreements. Most such agreements make some attempt to set "closed seasons" (during which the species may not be taken) and contain a general exhortation to States' parties to cooperate in scientific research or information exchange. In general, however, they do not display any evidence of a common decision by the parties sustainably to manage affected populations. Even where the agreement covers the entire range of the species or population involved, there is usually no express obligation in the agreement to manage that species or population as a unit. A recent and pronounced exception to this is the Bonn Convention, which is entirely premised upon the recognition of a need for all States to participate in whose territory a species is regularly to be found at any point in its life-cycle.

International agreements concerning sustainable use of ecosystems are even more rare, although some attempts have been made to arrive at international management of the Waddensee. The European Outline Convention on Transfrontier Cooperation between Territorial Communities or Authorities provides a framework for cross-boundary collaboration, while, in the field of "soft law," the UNEP Principles of Conduct in the Field of the Environment for the Guidance of States in the Conservation and Harmonious Utilisation of Natural Resources Shared by Two or More States, have had a discernable influence on subsequent international agreements.

Response to Transnational Effects

Many of the instruments for preserving essential ecological processes referred to above also relate to cases of transfrontier effects, but such cases have also given rise to other important international law developments. This is particularly true of procedures to be followed when transfrontier effects may be foreseen. Although these procedures also form part of customary law, they are best illustrated by reference to conventions, but it should not be assumed as a result that they depend upon the existence of treaty relations between concerned States.

Thus, a State planning to carry out some activity on its own territory, which will or may affect the environment of other States should give those States prior notice of what is intended. Further, it should make available to those States such information at its disposal which would enable them to form an impression of probable effects of the activities. An example of such provision occurs in the 1974 Nordic Environmental Protection Convention. In addition, a practice is developing of requiring States to carry out a prior examination of the likely effects of activities, to ascertain whether any transnational effects may arise. This trend is particularly noticeable in some of the Regional Seas Agreements, especially those governing the West and Central African Region and the Wider Caribbean. Notification systems are also provided for by instruments emanating from other international organisations, often in connection with particular subjects. Thus, a recent Decision and Recommendation of the Organisation for Economic Cooperation and Development (OECD) requires that States exporting consignments of hazardous waste ensure that the competent authorities of other States receive adequate and timely information concerning it. Notification provisions also form part of EEC Directives on major industrial hazards and the introduction of new chemicals into trade.

Furthermore, States are obliged, when such a transfrontier effect is foreseen, to enter into consultations with one another on the matter. Some recognition of this obligation appeared in the African Convention on the Conservation of Nature and Natural Resources as long ago as 1968 and has subsequently become not an uncommon element in treaties, appearing in many of the Regional Seas Agreements, in the Paris Convention for the Prevention of Marine Pollution from Land-Based Sources and in the Long-Range Air Pollution Convention.

These information and consultation provisions represent merely a specialised form of the general duty of States to exchange information and cooperate with one another in ensuring that transfrontier environmental interferences do not occur. This broader obligation is referred to in numerous regional agreements, in the Long-Range Air Pollution Conventions and also appears in the Law of the Sea Convention.

Problems Faced by International Environmental Law

The recognition of liability. One of the most striking developments of recent years has been the growing acceptance of the obligation on those whose actions gave rise to environmental damage to pay compensation for it. On the international plan, this represents a particularly significant aspect of the treatment of transfrontier effects, although in general only States may claim compensation in international law.

As mentioned above, compensation in the sense of monetary damages (although not unknown in international law) is of little value in environmental damage cases. Indeed, the simple recognition of such a concept from national law is actively unwelcome, as it presents particular difficulties when applied to environmental quality. A prime example in national compensation laws is the insistence that the plaintiff show a proprietary or other legally recognisable right in whatever has been damaged, the value of which can be accurately calculated. In general international law, neither the recognition of the right nor calculation of damage accruing as a result of its infringement are matters which not are subject to uniformity of view. Thus, in international law actions for damages are surrounded by all the pitfalls which exist in national law, many of which are rendered infinitely more difficult than in any national system (such as establishing a chain of causation).

Thus, the question of legal standing presents a difficulty at the international level. Yet a recent development may present a method of avoiding some difficulties. A recently negotiated Protocol to the Convention on Civil Liability for Oil Pollution Damage abandons the idea of "environmental damage" in favour of "the costs of restoration of the marine environment." This shift not only emphasises a rejection of the "payment for pollution" concept in favour of something more closely connected with the ideal of *restitutio ad integrum*, but also replaces the imprecise concept of damage and the wrangle over State's interest with an easily ascertainable figure representing the amount actually incurred by a State in restoration. While there may still remain some areas for dispute (such as causality questions and whether or not the steps taken by the State were reasonable and necessary), these are essentially matters of fact. Of course, as in the national law, no remedy exists respecting irreparable losses.

Lack of reciprocity. Treaties, to which so much reference has been made in this paper, are often loosely spoken of as the international law equivalent of legislation. While this analogy is understandable, it is better to think of treaties as contracts by which otherwise applicable international law is varied. Thus, international law may be regarded as not unlike a private law system, in which parties are bound to one another, either by their contractual relations or by common law obligations.

At this point, however, an important practical difference between the two systems is apparent. If a party to a contract to build a house in return for payment fails to perform his part of the contract, the other party has a simple remedy; he merely refuses to make the payments as they fall due. As the obligations of the parties are reciprocal - in that the consequences of one's failure may be made to rebound upon him directly by the other party there exists a possibility for enforcement which may make it unnecessary to resort to any tribunal. This consideration is of particular importance in international law, where enforcement mechanisms of a formal nature are lacking, although they are well-established in other international law fields (such as commercial treaties). There is little value in threatening that, if State B continues to fell its tropical moist forests, State A will retaliate by polluting the Rhine! It is because of this factor that national law has occasionally been resorted to in order to "import" sanctions for failure to observe international treaty rules. Well-known examples of this are the Pelly Amendment to the United States Fisherman's Protective Act and the Packwood-Magnuson Amendment to the United States Fishery Conservation and Management Act. These use national law to remove economic benefits from other States deemed to be undermining the effectiveness of international conservation conventions.

The pernicious doctrine of sovereignty. The almost fundamental proposition of international law is that States are possessed of virtually unlimited authority to do whatever they think fit with respect to activities taking place within their national territory. This basic principle is, of course, subject to some qualifications. States must not use this right to injure other States, and, in recent years, a growing body of international law on human rights has imposed further limitations. It nevertheless remains the point of departure for considering the application of international law to any new problem.

In the field of conservation, obstacles posed by the doctrine of sovereignty are immediately apparent. Resources, especially representative life-support systems and genetic resources, may be entirely located in areas which are subject to national sovereignty. In these cases, the classical international law provides no effective solution should the host State begin destroying the resources, at least in the absence of discernible effects within the jurisdiction of other States.

A possible solution. These two obstacles may seem to be only remotely connected, but it is conceivable that a solution to the doctrine of sovereignty may also dispense with the lack of reciprocity.

No suggestion is more likely to raise unconsidered outcry than the proposition that State sovereignty over natural resources situated within their territory is not absolute. Yet, increasingly, the conduct of States (even of those which most loudly promote the theory of permanent sovereignty) has tended to lean in the opposite direction. It is no longer accepted that the practice of torture or apartheid is entirely an internal matter and those matters, grave as they are, are not essentially different from the obliteration of major life-support systems as described in the World Conservation Strategy.

On such a basis, it may be predicted that international law will come to recognise that other States do have identifiable interests in life-support systems and genetic resources situated wholly within the host State's territory. The rights derive from imperative interests of the world community which the doctrine of sovereignty was developed to serve, and are a direct product of the world heritage concept which has done so much to advance the cause of conservation in other respects.

Yet, it is a fundamental principle of jurisprudence that rights are to be balanced by correlative duties. If the world community is to be accorded right over "sovereign" resources, it is clear that it must also accept some responsibility for their conservation, not as a gesture of good will or voluntary aid, but pursuant to an obligation which is as binding as that placed upon the host State to protect the resources. If this proposition is accepted, the difficulty caused by lack of reciprocity in conservation agreements also disappears, since the new relationship contains a sufficient element of reciprocity to ensure that the agreement is respected.

It has not hitherto been possible to claim that international law has reached this position. History, however, abounds in examples of its develop-

ment through the influence of reason and natural law. Yet it may be that the first stirrings of response, prompted by the Stockholm Declaration, have found expression in the World Charter for Nature, adopted and solemnly proclaimed by the United Nations General Assembly in 1982. The Charter, which might be described as a blueprint for implementing the World Conservation Strategy, spells out an intricate network of obligations (and, by implication, rights) incumbent on both States and individuals. These obligations may be regarded as the germ of acceptance of higher rights and duties of the world community toward essential resources; rights and duties which transcend the doctrine of sovereignty. This acceptance represents the greatest single challenge facing the international legal system in the next decades, and its greatest opportunity to serve mankind.

CONCLUSIONS

For the most part, the foregoing discussion has centred upon what has been achieved by the law in implementing the World Conservation Strategy. This final section will seek to identify lacunae, both as to the specific objectives of the Strategy and generally, for the removal of which the conservation community should continue to press.

At the National Level

Essential ecological processes and life support systems. While it is true that pollution control laws are highly developed in many countries (although markedly less so in the developing world), these are subject to the grave reservation in that the standards they employ are overwhelmingly related to human health and not to broader ecological factors.

A general criticism of national laws is that they still tend to demonstrate a sectoral approach to environmental control, concentrating on air quality, waste disposal, and so on. Little evidence exists of a cross-sectoral approach or of the institution of mechanisms for multidisciplinary coordination and ecosystem management. A particularly striking feature of many national legal systems is the lack of legislative provision for soil protection, whether in the pollution or erosion control context.

Perhaps as a particular manifestation of this failure, the broad concept of ecosystem management is only just beginning to appear in legal instruments, for example in connection with mangroves. It must be recognised, of course, that progress in this direction goes beyond purely legal responses and depends upon the achievements of real advances in the structural planning process.

Preservation of genetic diversity. Legislation protecting species remains essentially haphazard, as a result of isolated reactions to threats to particular species. Furthermore, laws tend to be highly selective as to the species protected, and plants and invertebrates are frequently ignored. Legislation tends to address itself largely to endangered and controlled species, leaving a broad spectrum of others wholly unprovided for in the law.

A major shortcoming is the failure to integrate species protection with other aspects such as habitat conservation. Controls over taking of species are common, but consideration of taking in the context of preserving the amount and quality of available habitat or of the preparation of a comprehensive recovery plan for a species is much more rare.

Sustainable use. Almost invariably, it is still the practice to regard stocks or species as independent units and to pay little or no regard to the inter-relationship between the species with other stocks or with the environment at large. Although prudence dictates that whenever a species is subject to utilisation, exploitation should be governed by a scientific management plan, such plans are required by law only in a very few cases. It should also be stressed that insufficient provision is made for protecting the habitat of an exploited species and for considering the exploitation in respect to impacts upon the species throughout its entire range.

As with the preservation of genetic diversity, however, the legal system can do no more than provide a framework within which to carry out improved management. The achievement of that higher degree of management lies in other hands.

General issues unrelated to particular World Conservation Strategy objectives. Three general issues warrant discussion here:

Control of public actions

A method of ensuring that public authorities comply with the requirements of environmental law is essential. It is by no means clear that an effective system of control over administrative action exists in many countries. In particular, the law relating to *locus standi* militates against effective enforcement of environmental law in many countries by insisting on traditional requirements of property damage or direct injury, and by its reluctance to accept that interest groups should be entitled to seek enforcement or implementation of laws affecting their concerns. The result is usually to hamstring public interest litigation in environmental cases.

Remedies

Broadly similar considerations apply in respect of remedies. Recognition of environmental restoration costs as a legitimate measure of damages (instead of striving to establish the economic value of the "loss" incurred) might present a method of establishing some system of civil liability for general environmental harm. While restoration should always be regarded as the first resort, consideration should be given to imposing some kind of fixed civil penalty in respect to irreparable losses, in order to avoid these being regarded as "free goods."

Instruments for planning

In almost every aspect of implementing the World Conservation Strategy, the existence of an effective planning instrument, capable of taking into account ecological as well as social and economic factors, is a *sine qua non*. In many countries, however, even the rudiments of such a system can hardly be said to exist, let alone to deal with such a sophisticated assessment. A further *sine qua non* in this connection is the availability of adequate scientific information.

At the International Level

Essential ecological processes and life support systems. With regard to essential processes, the pattern is very similar to that obtaining at the national level. Although there are areas in which great strides have been made, these are centred upon ship-borne marine pollution, which is at once far from the most important source of marine pollution and refers to sources which are relatively easy to control.

A number of truly global issues, such as protection of the ozone layer, have only recently been recognised as matters calling for international legal response. Although these often involve much more serious environmental problems, they are intrinsically more difficult to resolve, and little effective progress has been made in tackling them.

In the context of life-support systems, the Ramsar Convention represents the only attempt to deal with such systems on an international basis.

Preservation of genetic diversity. International legal response in this context has hitherto been patchy. The matter is only now achieving recognition as being a fit subject for a global solution. Indeed, it may still be questioned whether it is so recognised insofar as it extends beyond the *ex situ* preservation of plant resources.

Sustainable use. In the sense given to that term in the World Conservation Strategy, sustainable use remains a concept in the course of international law development restricted to "shared resources." At present, there is little evidence of widespread adoption of the ecosystem approach or of instituting a system under which resources are subject to common decisions regarding their management and an agreed regime of information-gathering and monitoring.

General issues unrelated to a particular World Conservation Strategy objective. Five additional international issues are described in closing:

Regional and global responses

Increasingly, the international community is prepared to permit the scope of international legal response to be determined by the nature of the problem addressed, with the result that global conventions are reserved for truly international problems.

Integrated approach

As in national laws, there is a tendency to deal with international environmental issues on a sectoral basis. A pronounced exception is found in the regional conservation conventions (and especially in the ASEAN Agreement), which attempt to grapple with several aspects of the problem. The same is true of the Regional Seas Agreements in connection with marine and coastal areas. Attention should be given to extending this approach to other areas.

The hardening of "soft law"

The environmental law field has seen numerous examples of "soft law" principles developing into international law properly so called by virtue of their becoming part of States' practice. The importance of this trend should not be underestimated.

The emergence of global principles?

At least in the area of traditional sources of international law, it can hardly be said that developed principles already exist which would serve to implement the World Conservation Strategy. There is, however, in the World Charter for Nature, a comprehensive declaration of what those principles might look like and in which they may forseeably pass into the general customary law.

Institutions and financing

Although these matters are too vast to be discussed in this paper, it is important to mention the rudimentary state of international institutions dealing with conservation matters and the almost total absence of sources of finance specifically directed to those purposes.

INTERNATIONAL INSTITUTIONAL SUPPORT: THE INTERNATIONAL SYSTEM, FUNDING AND TECHNICAL ASSISTANCE

Peter S. Thacher
World Resources Institute
Washington, D.C., U.S.A.

SUMMARY *Following a review of the kinds and magnitudes of international investment flows, current efforts are described to improve the relationship between conservation/environment activities at the donor end, and the planning and decision-making function at the receiver end. The critical roles of national conservation strategies and sectoral approaches are addressed in this context. Suggestions are made for action at both ends of the process to increase amounts of investment flows in countries providing international finance, and to improve human and institutional capabilities in the developing world, where natural resources are at greatest risk.*

INTRODUCTION

Those of us gathered here, and the institutions with which we are affiliated, have new and significant opportunities to influence financial flows at both the supply end (in what I term the "metropolitan" countries), as well as in the receiving or "frontier" countries. Developing countries would reap the greatest benefits if national conserva-tion strategies could be drawn up to effectively guide domestic and foreign investments toward sustainable development. It is there that key pressures must be exerted, and these must be "bottom-up," people-participatory. The focus of my remarks is on what we can do to advance this process through familiar institutional channels at the international level; or, in other words, how to improve the "top down" flows whose impacts on natural resources are often decisive.

First, let me explain why I use the terms "metropolitan" and "frontier" countries.

Yale University historian William Cronon reminds us of two approaches to understanding the historical development of North America: the explanation of United States history as a "moving frontier" of settlements, as portrayed by Frederick Jackson Turner; and the explanation of Canadian history in terms of Harold Innis' "metropolitan thesis." In the latter, events in the "frontier" are seen as extensions of economic, social and political influence - "an expanding metropolitan economy centred on a handful of cities ..." (Cronon, 1984).

Today, many more than a handful of "metropolitan" cities exercise strong influence over the "frontier," which for our purposes is primarily developing countries in the tropics. The modern "metropolitan" system consists of a variety of international institutions composed of individuals who, like the early North American settlers, view natural resources as "commodities" to be bought and sold according to monetary values. Until now, such evaluations have not taken into account the value of watershed management functions of forested slopes, for example, or the biological productivity of marshed and estuarine areas. To this day, the economist lacks the means by which to assign value to a standing tree (See Repetto, 1986).

And because of technological advances, the scale and intensity of investment impacts on natural resources have also increased greatly. Rates of destruction per unit of energy may not have changed, but the number of people wielding chainsaws has; fisheries continue to multiply, but not as fast as the size and horsepower of fishing fleets. Twentieth century agricultural practices in the temperate zones are being applied throughout tropical regions where both the soils

and the culture can collapse, as we see so vividly in Africa today (See Walker, 1986).

MODERN METROPOLITAN FLOWS

How large are the funds flowing into "frontier" regions from "metropolitan" states? How much comes from which public or private sources? What mechanisms determine the use of those funds? How might we influence them to support the World Conservation Strategy?

World Resources 1986 demonstrates (Table 11.5) that the total net receipts of developing countries from all sources in 1983, measured in constant 1982 dollars, was just over $100 billion. Some 34 percent of this amount consisted of public funds known as "Official Development Assistance, (ODA).[1] Two percent was in the form of grants from private voluntary organisations and 63 percent is described as "nonconcessional flows." Of that $63 billion, about one-third is officially supported as export credits and in other forms, while close to two-thirds are private, mostly in the form of commercial bank loans.

More recent data (which will be analysed in *World Resources 1987*) reflect dramatic changes in the size of

1. Official Development Assistance is defined by OECD's Development Assistance Committee (DAC) as those flows to developing countries and multilateral institutions provided by official agencies, including state and local governments, or by their executive agencies, each transaction of which meets the following tests: (1) it is administered with the promotion of the economic development and welfare of developing countries as its main objective, and (2) it is concessional in character and contains a grant element of at least 25 percent. To calculate the grant element of an official development assistance transaction, a 10 percent discount rate is used. Current economic support, humanitarian assistance and emergency relief including food aid are included, but any kind of military assistance is excluded as are various types of indirect forms of aid such as price support measures or price subsidies connected with the movement of goods in trade (OECD, 1985, p.171).

these flows and their composition. Yet, regardless of their size, each of these components of "metropolitan" flow into the developing world plays a different role in relation to the goals of the World Conservation Strategy.

In general terms, technical assistance and other grant or concessional loans provided by official development assistance may be seen as the "engine starter" of development: if they succeed in improving the human and structural resources of a country, they help to attract larger sums from the private sector in the form of investment and commercial loans. "Pre-investment" activities funded under official development assistance not only prepare the ground for larger local and foreign investments, but also set the course of future development, influencing decisions and actions yet to come. Many training and other "infrastructure" programmes supported by official development assistance thereby help to shape the future more than their size might suggest. This characteristic is what makes the policies governing the use of these funds critical in terms of the World Conservation Strategy.

An important distinction needs to be maintained between ODA funds transferred to developing countries as a part of "foreign aid," and loans made by the World Bank.

The term "official development assistance" is limited to highly *concessional*

funds for development objectives. It includes credits advanced by the International Development Association, but excludes loans by the World Bank and regional development banks (because these loans remain below the 25 percent grant element) (OECD, 1985). World Bank and other multilateral development bank (MDB) loans may be advantageous to developing countries - and the value of related services provided, such as project identification, monitoring and evaluation, should not be overlooked - but they are loans for repayment that are not given on "concessional" terms; thus they do not qualify as official development assistance. Conversely, the International Development Association (IDA) was established in 1960 as the "soft loan" affiliate of the World Bank to provide credits to governments with the lowest GNP per capita. International Development Association credits carry 10-year grace periods, 50-year maturities, and no interest; they thus qualify as official development assistance.

To date the International Development Association has issued a total of $34 billion in credits to poorer developing countries. These flows show up as official development assistance from "multilateral agencies."[2]

Official Development Assistance and Multilateral Development Banks: Critical Flow for the WCS

In view of the central coordinating role of multilateral agencies and the size of

---

2. In recent years officially supported funds have become more critical in flows to less-developed countries, whether part of official development assistance or not. The term "official development financing" has been introduced to recognise the development value of lending by multilateral development banks. It includes (1) bilateral official development assistance, (2) multilateral disbursements that correspond to official development assistance (such as grants or concessional loans from the International Development Association and other institutions) and, (3) other non-official development assistance disbursements by multilateral development banks (OECD, 1975, p.173.)

funds flowing through multilateral development banks, some ten years ago the UN Environment Programme (UNEP) and the Canadian International Development Agency (CIDA) sponsored a study on development fund transfers, implemented by the International Institute for Environment and Development (IIED). The study surveyed environmental attitudes and practices of nine international development financing institutions, with findings published in 1979[3] under the title *Banking on the Biosphere?* (Stein and Johnson, 1979). In her foreword to this book, which played a key role in subsequent policy decisions of these institutions, Barbara Ward (Lady Jackson) noted that the study had uncovered "many voids in perception about environmental impacts and a general absence ... of systematic attention to environmental impacts of all stages of project conception, design, and execution."

Less than a year later, the Executive Heads of those same nine institutions, joined by the UN Environment Programme, signed the "Declaration of Environmental Policies and Procedures Relating to Economic Development." The Declaration set forth the means by which they would execute their responsibility "to ensure the sustainability of economic development activities financed by them." They formed the Committee of International Development Institutes on the Environment (CIDIE) to establish a continuing mechanism for review of progress toward agreed policies and procedures.[4]

How effective has the exercise been? An authoritative answer can be found in a statement by Dr. M. Tolba, Executive Director of the UN Environment Programme, at the opening of CIDIE's sixth session in June 1985. Taking stock of CIDIE's activities during its first five years, Dr. Tolba pointed to signs of its "potential effectiveness" in such areas as information exchange, particularly in forestry and pesticides; education and training; and increased awareness in financial circles of the issues involved. Bilaterals too have taken note of the environmental dimension of their work, and "a number of NGOs have been brought into the sustainable development fold." But "CIDIE has not yet truly succeeded in getting environmental considerations firmly ingrained in development policies. There has been a distinct lack of action by several multilaterals." CIDIE members have "gone along with the Declaration in principle more than in major shifts in action.... Environmental impact assessments are not yet an integral part of all or even major development projects." Dr. Tolba concluded that "without a radical realignment of CIDIE's direction, its future could be really limited. We should be doing less talking and more action."

In characteristically blunt terms, Dr. Tolba put his finger on the heart of the problem: "Until developing countries ...

---

3. The nine institutions were the African Development Bank, Arab Bank for Economic Development of Africa, Asian Development Bank, Caribbean Development Bank, European Development Bank, Inter-American Development Bank, World Bank, Organization of American States, and United Nations Development Programme.

4. CIDIE has since held annual meetings hosted by these members and, most recently, by a new member, the European Investment Bank in Luxemburg.

themselves can do the job of integrating environmental considerations with planning, that job must be done through major assistance on the donors' side. The tendency is for developing countries to rush head-long into projects for immediate return; the task of development institutions is to clarify and help prevent the long-term damage that can result from such a rush. Clearly, the best time to forestall such harm is at the beginning - as early on in the conceptual state of project planning as possible."

By what means can "development institutions" assist in the task Dr. Tolba has identified? They will suggest ways in which multilateral users of official development assistance can be influenced to support dynamic national conservation strategies.

Multilateral Institutions

Among international development institutions, the World Bank exercises strong leadership and is usually the best example to cite. For example, in fiscal 1984 the Bank invested some $800 million - about five percent of total lending - in large-scale environmental projects. These funds were largely devoted to water supply, sanitation, and reforestation. A further $150 million was committed to preventive and ameliorative measures associated with development projects in agriculture and industry (World Bank, 1985a). But, the Bank notes, despite this systematic, albeit relatively-small effort, environmental degradation continues: not usually because of highly visible, internationally-funded development projects, but more typically as the result of a myriad of individual, small-scale activities, which account for the bulk of environmental degradation. Because of

their sheer numbers, they are impossible for responsible public agencies to control individually."

Valuable although this approach has been, the Bank concluded that the incorporation of environmental measures on a project-by-project basis has not prevented the problems from worsening; "thus, the establishment of policies, regulations, and incentives that will focus environmentally rational behaviour throughout national economies is required if economic development is to be sustained" (World Bank, 1985a).

The World Bank is now developing the use of digital analysis and remote-sensing techniques to improve understanding of environmental systems that support national economies. The purpose of this new approach within the Bank is to incorporate information into country development programming on a systematic basis. This is done through the Global Resource Information and Database (GRID) methodology, now available at UNEP facilities in Geneva and Nairobi. Yet combined with enhanced computer capabilities at low prices, this new technique is within easy reach of all sorts of developing country institutions: governmental planning offices, universities and the private sector.

A very different approach than the Bank's has been taken by the Organization of American States, a non-UN member of CIDIE, whose Department of Regional Development prepared a report based on experience relevant to the World Conservation Strategy (OAS, 1984). This report holds that, "if resource management considerations are built into the planning process at an early stage, playing a role in the identification, selection, formulation and harmonization of projects, then environmental impact assessments - with their high cost and adversary nature - can be avoided."

A combination of Bank and OAS experience, when applied in strengthened national institutions, would bring about the conditions necessary so that, in Dr. Tolba's words, "developing countries themselves can do the job of integrating environmental considerations with planning."

The UN System Within the "UN Family." There are important differences between the "UN System" (composed of the many United Nations agencies and programmes) and the larger collection of institutions which meet from time to time under the chairmanship of the UN Secretary-General. The larger group, including the World Bank and the International Monetary Fund, is known as the "UN Family" (See Bertrand, 1975).

Looking at metropolitan states' use of official development assistance funds in relation to the goals of the World Conservation Strategy, we note that most such funds are distributed through bilateral agencies, rather than through the multilateral agencies and programmes of the UN-System. Since the mid-1970s, the United States has taken the lead in cutting back on multilateral funding in favour of bilateral. In principle, donors remain committed to a "strong centrally-funded system of UN technical cooperation," but in practice, the trend has reflected the opposite, with many UN agencies operating at reduced levels. Because technical assistance funds help to set the course of future development more than project support still dominating bilateral assis-

tance, the implications of this reduction on sustainable resource management are ominous.

First among the multinational institutions of the UN System (excluding multilateral development banks), in terms of potential to help or hinder the World Conservation Strategy, is the UN Development Programme (UNDP).

UNDP's central purpose is to provide systematic and sustained assistance in fields essential to technical, economic, and social development of developing countries. It does this through small-scale projects which provide technical assistance to governments in formulating their development plans, and in building-up responsible administrative machinery in agricultural and industrial production, health, education, power, transport, communications, etc.

Additionally, through its larger-scale projects, the UN Development Programme provides governments with a bridge between advisory/training projects and development capital. These projects take the form of resource surveys, research to locate investment opportunities, and training programmes to develop competent personnel to carry on development work.

Since 1971 UNDP has sought to work on the basis of a "country programming" system intended to coordinate UNDP assistance with the recipient countries' own development plans and with other external development aid. The move away from project preoccupation toward a more integrated approach to development planning was begun in the Agency for International Development (AID). This initiative spread to the international level in 1970, when the UN General Assembly

tional Development (USAID). This initiative spread to the international level in 1970, when the UN General Assembly adopted what is known as the "Consensus" and laid out "new dimensions" relating to technical cooperation.[5] The 1970 formula made the countries concerned responsible for establishing a "country programme" and, as far as possible, the implementation of projects themselves.

In theory, both UNDP and the World Bank are well placed to assist developing countries in formulating coherent development strategies and the development of domestic programming capacities. In fact there has been a significant growth in their function as external fund coordinators for development.

Regional and sectoral mechanisms have also been established to coordinate aid efforts: the "Club des Amis du Sahel" was established in 1976, the Southern Africa Development Coordination Conference (SADCC) in 1980, and a sectoral forerunner, the Consultative Group on International Agricultural Research (CGIAR) in 1971.

Increasingly, these international mechanisms are used by the providers of official development assistance to improve coordination of aid to individual countries.

Starting in 1958 when the first Aid Consortium was set up for India under Bank auspices, mechanisms known as "Consortia," "Consultative Groups,"

and "Round Tables" are now active under the World Bank, regional development banks, and UNDP in most recipient countries. The Organization of African Unity (OAU) submission to the Special Session of the UN General Assembly on Africa cites the experience of 29 African States with consultative groups or roundtables. It called for joint committees composed of senior representatives of concerned governments, as well as from major donor countries and financing institutions. The OAU proposes co-responsibility and regular meetings not only to review work underway but to "assist in revising and updating the national action programme" in each country (United Nations, 1986).

These mechanisms represent efforts to improve programme performance in social and economic conditions. This is achieved by exchanging ideas and experience and through better coordination at the level of the intended beneficiaries. Although closely identified with the "top down" aspects of official development assistance, they offer opportunities to help recipient countries improve their ability to coordinate and better control external funds (from the bottom up) assuming the existence of a national development plan or overall strategy at the national level.

Outside the UN Family. Over the years, States providing official development assistance have concentrated efforts to coordinate bilateral aid policies in the Development Assistance Com-

5. The United States started to make widespread use of country programming in the 1960s and, since the late 1970s, USAID has prepared for each major recipient a Country Development Strategy Statement (CDSS). The CDSS includes an analysis of specific development problems, recipient government policies regarding them, and the approaches to be adopted by AID in addressing them (from DAC 1985 Report). Among the bilaterals, Sweden and Switzerland also draw up country programmes with recipient governments as a basis for future bilateral assistance.

mittee (DAC) of the Paris-based Organisation for Economic Cooperation and Development (OECD). The Committee's Review, "Twenty-Five Years of Development Cooperation," maps the totality of experience of the bilateral aid agencies that originated and funded the bulk of official developmental assistance. The DAC Report addresses outstanding problems in light of a quarter-century of experience, and plots the future course of action as seen by key actors dominating development assistance flows. This Report shows great sensitivity to resource issues as well as the need to engage NGOs more actively in the development process, especially in developing countries. It should be required reading for anyone seriously interested in our subject.

OECD's Environment Committee has increasingly turned its attention to environmental impacts outside member States and to better resource management. A project recently approved by the Environment Committee is intended to promote the capabilities of developing countries to manage their environment and to monitor activities which can be detrimental to the environment."[6]

Many other such mechanisms are available, and their use by donors and recipients would help to accomplish the aims of the World Conservation Strategy. But none can serve as a substitute for strengthening national capabilities in the developing world so that countries themselves can meet Dr.

Tolba's goal of "integrating environmental considerations with planning."

"Development" Policies - Bilateral and Multilateral. A study of environmental policies, procedures, and performance of the largest United States bilateral development agency, the Agency for International Development (AID), was issued in 1980. This report, "Aiding The Environment," was part of a follow-up study to the earlier IIED multilateral study and focused on six bilateral assistance agencies (Blake, *et. al.*, 1980).[7]

The report cited growing concern in the 1970s that apparent rates of tropical deforestation prompted a redirection of USAID support for timber projects, on the grounds that "destruction of forests hampers economic growth in developing countries" (Sullivan, 1977).

Under this new mandate, USAID was authorised to assist forestry projects and to emphasise "community woodlots, agroforestry, reforestation, protection of watershed forests, and more effective forest management." Comparable language was included in the House Appropriations Committee Report that year. USAID was urged to increase staff and attention to "forest management considerations within the framework of their environmental assessment policies, procedures, and reviews" and, whenever appropriate, to incorporate a forestry/fuelwood component within rural development projects (US H.R., 1979).

6.   OECD internal documents approved at the May session of the Environment Committee in Paris.

7.   The five other bilateral agencies studied in the IIED report, "The Environment and Bilateral Aid" by Brian Johnson and Robert O. Blake were of Canada, Federal Republic of Germany, Netherlands, Sweden, and the United Kingdom.

In 1979 Congress amended the Foreign Assistance Act to read:

> ...The Congress recognizes that the accelerating loss of forests and tree cover in developing countries undermines ... efforts to improve agricultural production ... and otherwise to meet the basic human needs of the poor. Deforestation results in increased flooding, reduction in water supply for agricultural capacity, loss of firewood and needed wood products, and loss of valuable plants and animals (U.S.C., 1979).

A Presidential directive to AID followed, calling for evaluation of existing forestry projects and for new projects to preserve natural forest ecosystems and their multiple uses. Funding for forestry has greatly increased since then, but the development of a comprehensive approach to tropical forests did not get underway until six years later, when a unique combination of governmental and non-governmental organisations brought it all together.

Carefully researched testimony to Congress by United States NGOs in 1983/84 about poor environmental performance of international development institutions led Congress to broaden the scope of its concern in a key report, "Multilateral Development Bank Activity and the Environment" (US House Subcommittee, 1984). This report was addressed to the United States Department of the Treasury. Even though the Senate Banking Committee and the United States Treasury do not have an environmental orientation, sensitive awareness of environmental and natural resource issues is reflected throughout the Committee Report:

> These recommendations reflect a growing Congressional concern that sustainable, ecologically sound development must be a basis for international development assistance efforts. Global environmental problems have intensified at an accelerating pace in recent years. As the pressures of population, pollution, natural resource exploitation and environmental degradation have increased, attitudes toward international development assistance have changed. Sustainability of economic growth, local participation in project formulation, application of appropriate levels of technology are all becoming watch-words of current development thinking.

In presenting its recommendations, the Congressional Committee stated that they are intended to encourage economic growth and to protect the investment made by donor nations by helping to assure that projects funded by the multilateral development banks form a basis for sustainable development."

Besides calling for strengthened staffing to cope with environmental and natural resource problems, the report recommends increased training in environmental planning and programme development by the World Bank's Economic Development Institute, expanded use of NGOs in borrower nations (including organisations of indigenous people, environment and health ministers). Also recommended are "small-scale and environmentally beneficial projects" including, specifically, "mixed farming, afforestation and development of high-yield wood-lots, dune stabilisation, integrated pest management strategies, improvement of energy efficiency, and improvement of irrigation system operation and management."

Recommendation 14 specifies that:

Country program planning and strategy activities of each of the development banks should reflect and conform to the 1980 World Conservation Strategy forged by the International Union for Conservation of Nature and Natural Resources and the United Nations Environment Programme. Where programs deviate from the precepts of the World Conservation Strategy program, documentation should be justifying the need for other strategies.

The Congressional Committee also exhorted the banks to adhere more closely to the precepts of the 1980 Declaration of Environmental Policies and Procedures Relating to Economic Development, noting that the Declaration complements the World Conservation Strategy.

In addition to studies and annual reporting, the Committee report "recommends that [the] Treasury instruct US Executive Directors to oppose any project that:

a) results in use of natural resource harvests (such as forest, fish, grasslands, or wildlife) at an unsustainable level within a population or ecological unit;

b) threatens to cause species extinction or to endanger species survival;

c) causes environmental degradation beyond recipient country boundaries (unless and until agreement is obtained from the country suffering this impact);

d) is expected to significantly convert or degrade the minimal and already overtaxed designated natural areas including national parks, wildlife reserves, world heritage sites and biosphere reserves which serve as the last vestiges of sanctuary for many forms of life;

e) threatens to significantly impair the land and resource base upon which indigenous peoples depend;

f) fails to adequately provide for management and control of pesticide use..."

The report also calls on US Executive Directors at multilateral development banks to "convene a meeting of other Executive Directors at each of the multilateral development banks to share information and to develop an environmental oversight process which can be widely supported within each Board of Directors."

Many here may be inclined from past experience to dismiss these recommendations as pious but lame words, yet within the year the US Treasury had surveyed all recommendations and exchanged views within the government and the concerned banks. It responded both extensively and substantively in writing and in formal testimony to both Houses of the Congress.

In his testimony before the Senate Committee on Appropriations, the Assistant Secretary for International Affairs in the Treasury, Mr. David Mulford, reviewed current hydroelectric, irrigation, and flood control projects that pose risks to water quality, siltation problems, and threats to human health and well-being. These and other substantive problems led the Assistant Secretary to conclude that although environment considerations can be systematically incorporated into multilateral development bank planning, the "conspicuous absence of environmental considerations" in some projects and their inadequate treatment in others has been the central problem (US Senate Subcommittee, 1985).

Since then, in December 1985, Congress enacted Section 540(a), which charges the Secretary of the Treasury to "instruct" US Executive Directors of multilateral development banks to carry out virtually all of the actions earlier recommended in the House Committee Report: to increase staffing for environmental review of projects; to promote procedural changes so as to involve environmental and health experts, including NGOs; to increase support for environmentally beneficial projects and training, and to carry out internal actions to improve performance and work with other donor nations (US H.R., 1985).

This Congressional enactment carries weight in the United States Government because it arises in the appropriations process and enjoys broad support by both political parties. It furthermore enjoys explicit support by the Administration.

Beyond Official Development Assistance

Officially-Supported, Non-Concessional Flows. Official development assistance, while critical in terms of influencing future capabilities and choices, is only part of the picture. Non-concessional funds are a mix of officially supported and private funds that in 1983 amounted to more than 60 percent of the total metropolitan transfer.

If growing demographic pressures will be destructive to a fixed resource base in the absence of economic and social advancement, then official, non-concessional flows - such as through export credits - can play an important part in the economic well-being and resource conservation of developing countries. But because I view these flows as having only secondary effects on the goals of the World Conservation Strategy, mostly in relation to technology choices, I will move without further comment to the private sector.

Flows from the Private Sector. To many of us, the enormous funds that traditionally flow from the private sector have often appeared to be more a part of the problem than of the solution. This is partly because reverse flows in the form of repayments and profits are sometimes larger than incoming official development assistance. This is often because the corporations involved have been reticent about the beneficial relationship between environment and development. Most of the corporate world seems indifferent to their governments' endorsement of the Word Conservation Strategy in 1980 (United Nations, 1980).

In addressing private flows, it is useful to bear in mind distinctions between multinational corporations and commercial banks, and between various industrial sectors, such as manufacturing processes (with their continuing preoccupation with pollution problems), and extractive sectors like mining and timber.

Direct Investment

World Resources 1986 shows that "direct investment" in developing countries has fallen from a high of almost $17 billion in 1981 to less than $8 billion in 1983. More recent data show that it climbed to $9.5 billion in 1984 (OECD, 1985), and under present conditions modest growth can be expected in this hemisphere and in Asia.

Papers prepared for the World Bank's Development Committee last year highlight the characteristics of direct investment which make this sector critical in terms of World Conservation Strategy goals: "Unlike commercial lending," it reads, "the funds provided are always part of a package of technology and management, both of which can enhance the productivity of the capital transfer. In addition, like portfolio investment, direct investment shares in both the risks and rewards associated with the project financed. It is these qualities - the combination of technology, management, and capital with risk sharing - that give direct investment a special role in developing country financing. Accordingly, the measured volume of direct investment will normally significantly understate the importance of this type of capital to the recipient country" (World Bank, 1985b).

In testimony to the US House Appropriations Committee (Whitten, 1986), Secretary Baker explained the function of the Multilateral Investment Guarantee Agency (MIGA), which was endorsed in the Tokyo Summit Declaration in May, 1986. This Agency is to encourage growth of direct investment in developing countries by insuring against political risk. But more than an insurance agency, MIGA will be "the first multilateral institution designed to deal in concrete ways with policy reform in developing countries, with the aim of encouraging a greater recep-

tivity to investment flows," and will have close links to the World Bank Group. Secretary Baker believes it will be "better placed than a national insurance agency to promote policy reforms" because it will focus on broader questions and its advice will be seen as more impartial than advice given by bilateral agencies.

Given the sensitivity to environmental and resource matters in the Treasury, I think we should watch this new mechanism for opportunities to influence future direct investment flows into paths set out in the World Conservation Strategy.

Bank loans

The "Baker Initiative," which was largely endorsed at the Tokyo Summit, was launched to restimulate private investment and to help both developing and metropolitan countries "grow their way" out of their problems. This was designed to bring hope to the impoverished while heading off the danger of loan defaults to metropolitan banks.

We may have wished for more prominence in the Tokyo Declaration but surely welcome, and will look for opportunities offered by, the language adopted in its final paragraph:

> *We reaffirm our responsibility...to preserve the natural environment and continue to attach importance to international cooperation in the effective prevention and control of pollution and natural resources management.... We also recognize the need to strengthen cooperation with developing countries in the area of the environment.*

Such initiatives may tap the flexibility of many multinational corporations that are looking beyond short-term gains in ways that even commercial bankers may understand. After all, bankers want to get back into the business of lending funds for investment, but under present conditions they also need "insurance" protection against loans to less-developed countries. This may open up the possibility that CIDIE-like principles could be applied by legislative bodies of the metropolitan countries as a condition for such Federal insurance. As noted in the Congressional Report, moves to incorporate environmental conditions need *not* be motivated by environmental considerations *per se*, but rather, "to encourage economic growth and to protect the investment made ... by helping to assure that projects funded ... form a basis for sustainable development."

Having come perilously close to a collapse of international credit, which could have brought down the entire banking system, leading bankers are today beginning to explore how economists can best take environmental and natural resource factors into account. At the international level, leadership in establishing "the technical linkages between environment-affecting activities and their effects ..." (World Bank, 1985a) continues to be shown by the World Bank, as is reflected in the paper presented here by Mr. Jeremy Warford.

Flows from Private Voluntary Non-Governmental Organisations

Finally, in this survey of metropolitan funds moving into the developing world, we come to the smallest portion - grants by private voluntary agencies.

This sum grew from $2.2 billion in 1983 to $2.5 billion in 1984.

These estimates come from the authoritative 25-year review of development activities by the OECD Development Assistance Committee. They are based on activity surveys known to bilateral agencies that are in large part jointly financed projects "at the grass roots level ... fostering self-reliance by helping communities to help themselves" (OECD, 1985). While no one would assert that such projects could substitute for officially-supported activities, their growing value needs no explanation to this audience. The point I would like to make is that the amounts involved are considerably larger than $2.5 billion when one adds the non-reported funds devoted by NGOs to activities supporting better management of natural resources for conservation and sustainable development.

For example, the Development Assistance Committee probably did not count the funds of the more than 3,000 non-governmental organisations listed with the Environment Liaison Center (ELC) in Nairobi. While many of these are small NGOs in developing countries, their funds are often more than matched by outside support. A good portion of the tens-of-millions of dollars raised by organisations participating in the World Wildlife Fund and IUCN itself is similarly dedicated, although probably not counted. And foundations play an increasing role.

Less than a month ago one of the largest NGOs, the US Rockefeller Foundation, increased its funding for work in developing countries to $300 million over the next five years. Adding together existing support from such US Foundations as Ford, Carnegie, and Kellogg, one soon reaches a significant fraction of this year's $600 million in US bilateral aid (Teltsch, 1986). Those of us who stay in touch with IUCN's Centre for Conservation and Development (CDC) and other IUCN activities know how much these are dependent not only on support from bilateral aid organisations but on private funds as well.

And of course the value of NGO contributions cannot be measured by funds alone. Many of you are aware of Bob Rodale's AID-supported work in Tanzania. In this "Regeneration" project, agricultural productivity can be enhanced without reliance on high-energy inputs that has characterised development aid in past decades - to so little benefit in Africa.

THE ROLE OF "METROPOLITAN" NGOS

New and significant opportunities exist for institutions in the metropolitan states to influence the annual flow of some $1 billion to developing countries. What are the key pressure points? To survey those which have emerged so far I will use the same three main categories: Official Development Assistance, Private Sector and Voluntary NGO Funding.

Official Development Assistance and Multilateral Development Banks

Better known to conservation groups than the work of banking committees, at least in Washington, are the ongoing efforts of such groups as the Environment and Energy Study Institute. The work of this group is summed up in the title of their first report, "A Congressional Agenda for Improved Resource and Environmental Management in the Third World: Helping Developing Countries Help Themselves." Its recommendations address many of the same issues, but are wider in scope, giving attention, for example, to suggestions on how to support the conservation of biological diversity through existing programmes, under Congressional surveillance.[8]

Just as banking committees get into environment issues, so this group got into banking when it suggested that Congress investigate the broader debt situation in developing countries and its relationship to environment and development issues. The idea was to assess the feasibility of rescheduling part of the debt owed to the United States Government in exchange for developing-country efforts to undertake environmental projects that improve long-term prospects for sustained growth and debt repayment.

In some environmental quarters, criticism of foreign aid is so pronounced as to call the entire effort into question. Considering the growing needs for better resource management in precisely those areas where the natural resource base is being destroyed fastest, I think it would be tragic if such groups added their voices to others seeking to suppress international development efforts.

8. The Environment and Energy Study Institute is an independent, non-partisan organisation that works closely with the Congressional Environment and Energy Study Conference. Its Task Force Report was printed in October 1985 and is available from EESI, Suite 200, 410 First Street, S.E., Washington, D.C., 20003.

For example, those who favour full reliance on the free market mechanism point to current "success" stories in such countries as South Korea. But it was successful aid programmes in the 1960s that made this growth possible. It is as irresponsible for "free market" proponents to decry the need for foreign aid as it is for environmentalists and conservationists to do so. The goals of both groups will be set back if official development assistance funds are reduced. So both groups should call for more funds, put to better use, rather than for funding cuts.

It is particularly encouraging to see NGO coalitions forming in Washington and in other metropolitan capitals. A good example is the broad-based United States NGO Steering Committee on Development, Environment and Population. Its brochure "Making Common Cause" was presented only last week to the World Commission on Environment and Development here in Ottawa and is available for discussion in a Workshop at this Conference.

My point in reviewing evidence of successful work for more than a decade is to show the alignment of current metropolitan influences with the concepts of the World Conservation Strategy. Eighty percent of official development assistance comes from OECD member States enjoying free elections and active non-governmental organisations. It is surely not coincidental that only in these countries are radical changes underway to reduce the historic resource-destructive nature of metropolitan influences in the frontier regions.

Assuming we want to increase the contributions that official development assistance can make to the World Conser-

vation Strategy, how might we identify the pressure points by which to accelerate these new tendencies?

We might start by noting that while the United States remains the largest contributor of official development assistance funds ($8 billion in 1983-84), its contribution is less than a quarter of total official development assistance. Other OECD member states contribute more than $20 billion; OPEC and CMEA states add 14 percent and 9 percent respectively; and a group of developing countries 1 percent (OECD, 1985). Thus, conservation and development-oriented NGOs working together in OECD capitals to support foreign-aid funding, and to ensure that it is directed toward sustainable development, could influence more than $28 billion.

One of the most active members of the United States NGO community in this field, Bruce Rich of the Environmental Defense Fund, recently completed a round of discussions with senior civil servants, members of parliaments, and non-governmental organisations in the United Kingdom, the Federal Republic of Germany, Netherlands, Belgium, Denmark, France, and the EEC. These discussions focused on the "package of reforms" for the World Bank and other multilateral development banks (endorsed by United States Congress and Treasury), and on the effort to protect tropical forests and their native peoples. These initiatives are beginning to bear results; for example, the Belgian Minister of Finance agreed to call the attention of Belgian representatives of multilateral development banks to the broad issue.

Many European NGOS are aided by the fact that the European Development

Fund is governed by the Lome III Convention between the Community and 66 developing countries. This Convention contains general articles on environment as well as specific items on reforestation, desertification, and sustainable yield management (ELC, 1986). Additionally, Council resolutions were adopted in 1984 which explicitly bind European Community bilateral programmes to CIDIE principles, most specifically in the areas of tropical forest conservation, desertification, water management, agricultural and energy use systems.

Consequently, I urge any not involved to become active in exerting pressures to increase and improve foreign aid from their countries, whether bilateral, through the Community, or multilateral.[9]

In addition to working at domestic pressure points to raise official development assistance funds and influence policies for their use, there are a number of international pressure points where many of us could begin to exert influence along lines supportive of the goals of the World Conservation Strategy. I have shown the influence brought about over the past ten years by organisations such as the International Institute for Environment and Development, working directly with bilateral aid-agencies, the World Bank, and other multilateral development banks.

Increasingly, we have seen these international development institutions come together in various fora to improve their own policy coordination, such as the multilateral development banks in CIDIE, and the bilaterals of OECD's Development Assistance Committee and the Environment Committee. National representatives at these meetings operate under instructions from home offices, the location of which is often in foreign ministries. Each of these should be studied in concerned metropolitan countries so that influence can be brought to bear on officials responsible for determining national policy and authoring appropriate instructions.

Overall policy for the use of appropriated official development assistance funds is often vested in parliamentary groups. These, too, come together internationally to make common cause. Just two weeks ago parliamentary leaders from 29 African States met in Harare under sponsorship of the Zimbabwe Parliament and the Global Committee of Parliamentarians on Population and Development. They agreed on a number of national measures which can contribute to sustainable development in ways that supporters of the World Conservation Strategy would welcome (Scheuer, 1986).

These are some of the obvious steps that metropolitan countries should be systematically taking to improve the official development assistance contribu-

---

9. As indication of priorities, OECD members pledging $10 million or more to UNDP in 1984 (in millions of US dollars) were: US $160; Canada $52; Norway $48, Netherlands $48; Sweden $45; Germany $43; Denmark $42; United Kingdom $28; France $27; Italy $26; Switzerland $18; and Belgium $11. (Figures from US Department of State Report to Congress for fiscal Year 1984, "U.S. Contributions to International Organisations.")

tion to sustainable development. Analysis of aid recipients quickly identifies those countries where official development assistance is particularly significant. For example, the 1985 DAC Report lists 50 "aid-reliant" countries where net official development assistance receipts represent between 5 and 58 percent of GNP (OECD, 1985).

Private Funds

As *World Resources 1986* reports, the confrontation between business and environmentalists that characterised the early 1970s is giving way to a new willingness on both sides to work together constructively. Evidence for meaningful cooperation can be measured in terms of activities flowing out of the level of agreement reached in late 1984 at the World Industry Conference on Environmental Management (WICEM). While the impact of this development on the goals of the World Conservation Strategy was weakened when industry limited WICEM's environmental scope to pollution, I think we should be encouraged by the willingness of industry, particularly the manufacturing sector, to be forthcoming about environmental issues of direct concern to them; issues about which they have considerable experience and insights to offer.

We should take advantage of this willingness on the part of "the principal agents through which environmental correction and prevention must take place" (Strong, 1985) to expand the scope of dialogue and bring new corporate sectors into the discussion. Yet efforts must be made in frontier countries as well: commerce and industry - ever on the lookout for areas in which to invest - will be attracted to those countries in which an effective, ongoing National Conservation Strategy gives confidence that local governments are overcoming poverty and coping with rising population demands in ways that do not threaten either the resource base or social stability.

How should we draw up a strategy, targeted at institutions where policy changes might influence direct investment in ways that promote the World Conservation Strategy?

We could start at the principal metropolitan sources. Today, investment is concentrated in four countries that have supplied more than three-quarters of the direct investment in developing countries: the United States, the United Kingdom, the Federal Republic of Germany and Japan.

Sectoral and geographic composition of this investment should also be studied in relation to the World Conservation Strategy. For example, while all four - especially the Federal Republic of Germany - invest heavily in manufacturing, the United States and Japan have favoured extractive processes in developing regions nearest to them. The United Kingdom has gone into other sectors including services, agriculture, public utilities, transport and construction, and like France, has concentrated geographically on former colonies.

National pressure points will vary from country to country, but an approach to a top official in a key corporation may be more productive than the associations where industry groups come together, largely for defensive purposes. At the global level, the International Chamber of Commerce and its associated industry groups represent good targets for those seeking to influence direct investment to advance the goals of the World Conservation Strategy. In many countries colleagues in the World Wildlife Fund national chapters can often be of major assistance.

We should not neglect national level commercial banks. Michael Sweatman, former President of the Mercantile Bank of Montreal, is encouraged by a recent statement by David Rockefeller:

> *...Just as our world is increasingly interdependent, so are the problems. Health, hunger, overpopulation, and economic stagnation are all complexly intertwined. Our air and our oceans recognise no borders, and your neighbors' acid rain or pollution is soon your own. Faced with desperate poverty, nations will, understandably, do almost anything to survive - even if this involves decimating their natural resources and the environment. Given the fragility of our planet's ecosystem, poverty that forces such actions is to the final detriment of us all (Rockefeller, 1987).*

Can these concerns, which are being recognised in the banking community, be translated into a new financial institution devoted to conservation? Sweatman's proposal for a World Conservation Bank deserves close study here in Ottawa and in the months ahead.

Private Voluntary Organisations and Non-Governmental Organisations

A number of avenues are well known to this audience. Some have been highlighted by the Development Assistance Committee, among other official development assistance-oriented institutions.

Several DAC members are tapping national skills hitherto not involved in development activities, for example Norway in the agricultural sector, Australia in agricultural research, France in agricultural and medical research, industrial technology and urban engineering. The Netherlands, on the other hand, is increasingly making use of local consultants.

Well-established procedures are available in most bilateral agencies for cofinancing NGO projects with official funds covering up to 100 percent of the costs. Some bilaterals involve national non-governmental organisations to seek out developing country NGOs for support (OECD, 1985).

Only last week at the Special Session on Africa in New York, Canada proposed a "new mechanism within the multilateral aid system...to make available to local communities, village councils and volunteer organisations in Africa, funds and technical expertise to help them to carry out projects of their own choosing to meet their needs in the fields of desertification, conservation of ground cover, and food production" (Vezina, 1986).

In making this proposal, External Affairs Minister Monique Vezina cited Canada's conviction that local communities, volunteer agencies and NGOs "can play a strategic part in mobilising Africa's human energies." She restated Canada's objective of introducing 2000 small cooperation projects in Africa before the end of next year. Appropriately, Canada has turned to UNDP to develop the details of the new mechanism.

The sub-theme of forests, which has run throughout my remarks, illustrates how "metropolitan" non-governmental organisations are capable of influencing, and even mobilising new funds in ways beneficial to the goals of the World Conservation Strategy. A current example in which the World Resources Institute (WRI) has played a leading role is the preparation of a comprehensive approach to tropical forests. The history of strong policy backing from the US Congress and USAID for increased efforts to strengthen forestry may have prepared the base, but did not produce a comprehensive approach to the problem until metropolitan non-governmental organisations became active in drawing up the Call for Action on Tropical Forests (WRI, 1985). This was developed by a task force convened by the World Resources Institute in cooperation with the World Bank and UNDP. However, this document would not have advanced to its current status, as the basis for FAO's Tropical Forestry Action Plan, without active national and international NGO participation alongside major intergovernmental institutions. It is particularly encouraging to see recognition of the utility of this work expressed by the principal intergovernmental agency involved, FAO, whose Deputy Director General commended the initiative (Walton, 1986).

Similarly, in his recent testimony in Congress, Secretary Baker states: "The World Resources Institute study offers a large number of interesting project ideas. Tom Clausen has agreed that the study is useful. He has consented to further meetings with senior Bank staff to examine the feasibility of specific investment proposals in the coming years. After discussing the proposals with the World Bank staff, we plan to have similar discussions with management and staffs of the regional development banks. I am hopeful that these discussions will identify development bank lending commitments which contribute substantially toward achieving the objective of protecting tropical forests in developing countries" (Whitten, 1986).

Looking at the current phase of this project, it is unimaginable that the country-by-country sectoral reviews can lead to lasting results unless local NGO participation in each developing country is actively promoted. Participation by IUCN, and metropolitan NGOs like WRI and IIED, among others, throughout this process has been welcomed by FAO, the World Bank, and UNDP. What is now needed, and I hope will be pursued in workshops here, are specific steps to encourage the "bottom-up" participation of developing country NGOs in this programme.

This brings me to a related point. One of the first steps in drafting a national conservation strategy is a collection of resource and environmental information as a basis for a sensible national strategy which will meet present and foreseeable needs. Sectoral reviews can provide much of the data needed for developing national conservation strategies. Contributions could be generated from foreign assisted projects in forestry, desertification, water and sanitation, health, or other areas. Opportunities exist in many developing countries for NGO involvement in all of these areas. It may be that non-governmental organisations have a unique contribution to make due to their interdisciplinary nature.

It will be through efforts of these groups that the information base will be generated and political basis mobilised. These should help to ensure that national conservation strategies are built from the ground-up in frontier States. Metropolitan non-governmental organisations can assist this process both by direct support and by seeking foreign support to strengthen indigenous institutions.

In my experience, a useful comparison can be made between the "Tropical Forest Plan of Action" and the earlier "Plan of Action to Combat Desertification." The comparison illustrates the central role of institutions in the frontier States.

Both plans are equally sound and both have high price tags for work which would make profound differences. The Desertification Action Plan, however, never got moving because of two weaknesses: the inability to mobilise external funds to support agreed actions; and the lack of priority concern on the part of developing countries.

The Tropical Forestry Action Plan, the authors of which included the World Bank, UNDP, and several bilateral agencies, carries with it the strong implication that if developing countries request external assistance to support needed actions, the assistance will be forthcoming. Thus, the key to whether or not action will be taken is a political question - one of domestic priorities - and rests on the political and governmental institutions of the countries affected. The role of local NGOs thus becomes vital if significant external funds are to be applied. And we should not overlook the value of allied group efforts which do not deal explicitly with environmental questions; for example, many NGOs focusing on women's issues may also be in the forefront of national conservation strategy issues.

SUMMING UP

Anyone familiar with the history of North America knows that deforestation is not a new process, but a continuation of century-old habits of land clearing. Nor is fuelwood shortage a new crises.[10] What is new is not the process, but the fact that with today's technology and population, the rate of deforestation is accelerating rapidly at the frontiers.

But today we have the means to measure and understand the consequences, as well as the procedures by which to make better choices for the future. There is moreover no real shortage of financial resources if we - promoters of the World Conservation Strategy - work with key institutions to influence policies governing the use of funds. In his authoritative review of a decade of

---

10.   In "Changes in the Land," William Cronon quotes the Swedish naturalist Peter Kalm as remarking with horror that, "an incredible amount of wood is really squandered in this country for fuel: day and night all winter, or for nearly half of the year, in all rooms, a fire is kept going."   By Cronon's calculations a typical New England household probably burned more than an acre of forest each year. "In 1800, the region burned perhaps eighteen times more wood for fuel than it cut for lumber."   Local firewood scarcities often became a cause for concern within ten or fifteen years of a town's establishment.   Boston experienced shortages as early as 1638 and private cutting of wood on common lands became a perennial source of dispute.   By 1794 timber and wood had reportedly "doubled in price, in every part of New England, within ten years."   This trend in most cities of the East Coast led to the eventual shift to coal in the nineteenth century.

notable progress in "International Environmental Policy," Lynton Caldwell concludes with these disturbing words:

Barring unforeseen events, the ecological quality of the environment for all living things seems almost certain to suffer a net decline in the decades ahead...Were it not for the international programs just described, and the conservation efforts in many countries, the losses could be much greater. It is difficult to believe that a change in human perceptions and values could occur on a scale and within a period of time to reverse this pessimistic conclusion. Yet human history has recorded abrupt and unpredicted changes in social behaviour. Events of the decade 1972-1982 suggest that peoples and their governments are, with relative rapidity, developing an appreciation of the consequences of continuing along the path of ecologically heedless exploitation of the earth. This consideration reinforces the significance of the World Conservation Strategy which, as Thomas E. Lovejoy of the World Wildlife Fund has declared, is also a strategy for survival (Caldwell, 1984).

Caldwell's challenge, and ours, is to translate the World Conservation Strategy into "practical political action." I hope my remarks will suggest some of the steps we can take to influence the vast metropolitan funds flowing to developing, frontier states. A good use of "top down" funds is to strengthen the capacities of these States to draw up well-based national strategies. This will advance the goals of the World Conservation Strategy, and help ensure that the resource base can be protected for an expanding population.

REFERENCES

• Benedick, Richard E., 1986, "Environment in the Foreign Policy Agenda," address before the Ecology Law Quarterly Symposium on Environment and International Development, Washington, D.C., March 27, 1986.

• Bertrand, Maurice, 1975, "Some Reflections on Reform of the United Nations," UN Joint Inspection Unit, United Nations, Geneva.

• Caldwell, Lynton K., 1984, "International Environmental Policy" Duke University Press.

• Cronon, William J., 1984, "Boundaries and Ecosystems in US and Canadian History," address to the October, 1984 Workshop on Transboundary Monitoring, Philadelphia, Pennsylvania.

• ELC, 1986, Environment Liaison Center publication as cited in *World Resources 1986*, p. 200.

• Lovejoy, Thomas E., *Uniterra*, UNEP, Vol. 8, 1980.

- OAS, 1984, "Integrated Regional Development Planning: Guidelines and Case Studies from OAS Experience" published by OAS in cooperation with the US National Park Service and USAID, presented to the 1985 CIDIE meeting.

- OECD, 1985, "Twenty-five Years of Development Cooperation," Report by OECD reviewing efforts and policies of the Development Assistance Committee, published by OECD, Paris.

- Repetto, Robert 1986, *World Enough and Time*, a World Resources Institute book, Yale University Press, New Haven.

- Rockefeller, David, "Help wanted: Apostles of Aid" as printed in the *Prospectus for the 4th World Wilderness Congress*, 11-18 September 1987, Colorado.

- Scheuer, James H., 1986, "Finally, Africa Looks to Itself" *New York Times,* OpEd page, 28 May 1986.

- Stein, Robert and Brian Johnson, 1979, *Banking on the Biosphere?* Lexington Books (D.C. Heath & Co), ISBN 0-669-02734-0.

- Strong, Maurice, 1985, keynote address in "Sustainable Development: Report of the Proceedings of the Global Meeting on Environment and Development" (Environment Liaison Center, Nairobi, 1985), as quoted in *World Report-86*, p. 187.

- Sullivan, John H., 1977, Statement as quoted in "Aiding the Environment" NRDC.

- Teltsch, Kathleen, 1986, "Rockefeller Unit Doubles Its Third-World Aid" *New York Times*, 4 May 1986.

- United Nations, 1986, "Africa's Submission to the Special Session of the UN General Assembly on Africa's Economic and Social Crisis," Paragraphs 58-59; attachment to General Assembly document A/AC. 229/2*, 23 April 1986.

- United Nations, 1980, UN General Assembly resolution 35/74 adopted unanimously 5 December 1980.

- US H.R. 96-273, 1979, 96th Congress, 1st Session, 22 (June 14, 1979).

- US H.R. 99-450, 1985, House Joint Resolution 465, "Further Continuing Appropriations for Fiscal Year 1985," Sec. 540, 99th Congress, US House of Representatives.

- US House Subcommittee, 1984, "Multilateral Development Bank Activity and the Environment," Committee Print 98-20, Subcommittee on International Development Institutions and Finance of the House Committee on Banking, Finance and Urban Affairs.

- US Senate Subcommittee, 1985, "Environmental Considerations in Multilateral Development Bank Projects" - Special Hearing before the Subcommittee on Foreign Assistance and Related Programs of the Senate Committee on Appropriations.

- USC, 1979, Section 103(b), 22 *U.S.C.* Section 2151a(b)(3).

- Vezina, Monique, 1986, Statement at UN Gen. Assembly, 27 May 1986.

- Walker, Brian W., 1986, "Authentic Development in Africa" No. 274 in the Headline Series by Foreign Policy Association, New York.

- Walton, 1986, Statement by FAO Deputy Director General Walton at the opening of the Eighth Session of the FAO Committee on Forestry.

- Whitten, Jamie L., Chairman, US House Committee on Appropriations, 30 Apr 1986, Written testimony of Secretary Baker to questions submitted for the Record transmitted by US Department of the Treasury 30 April 1986 to Chairman Whitten.

- World Bank, 1985a, Annual Report, Washington, D.C.

- World Bank, 1985b, "Direct and Portfolio Investments: Their Role in Economic Development," *Development Committee Report Number 4, Resources for Development* and, in revised form, in *World Development Report 1985*.

- World Resources Institute, 1985, Tropical Forests: A Call for Action, Vols. I, II, III; Washington, D.C.

ADDITIONAL READING

On official development assistance, the World Conservation Strategy and general aspects of the paper:

- *Ecology Law Quarterly*, special issue on Environment Law and Policy in Developing Countries, published by Boalt Hall School of Law, Univ. of California, Berkeley.

- *World Resources 1986*, IIED and IUCN, Basic Books, 1986.

On techniques to incorporate resources in economic planning:

- *Alternative Environmental Assessment and Management*, (ed.) C.S. Holling, 1978, John Wiley and Sons, ISBN 0-471-99632-7.

- *Ecology in Practice*, 1984, Tycooly, ISBN 0-907567-78-9, 2 volumes;

- *Natural Systems for Development - What Planners Need to Know*, (ed.) R. Carpenter, 1983, West-West Environment and Policy Institute, Macmillan, ISBN 0-02-949290-4.

- *Resource Inventory and Baseline Study Methods for Developing Countries*, 1983, American Association for the Advancement of Science, ISBN 0-87168-258-3.

- *The Environment, Public Health and Human Ecology - Consideration for Economic Development*, 1985, James A. Lee, Johns Hopkins University Press, ISBN 0-8018-2911-9.

- *Integrated Regional Development Planning: Guidelines and Case Studies from OAS Experience*, published by Organisation of American States (OAS), Washington, D.C.

On international institutional aspects:

- *International Environment Policy*, Lynton K. Caldwell, Duke Press Policy Studies, Duke University Press, 1984.

INTERNATIONAL COOPERATIVE PROGRAMMES

Jimoh Omo-Fadaka
Environment Liaison Centre
Nairobi, Kenya

SUMMARY *In their own interest, developed countries should be looking for ways of assisting developing countries' efforts to implement sustainable development strategies. New openings for action are in the spheres of leadership, intergovernmental exchanges and multi- and bilateral cooperation. One way of providing assistance would be to take a more forgiving approach to developing countries' debt problems. Of crucial importance is the need to resist imposing solutions on developing countries; instead, the focus should be on strengthening those countries' institutions.*

INTRODUCTION

Most of the developing countries are in the midst of an environmental and natural resource crisis which is undermining their drive for sustained economic growth. Problems involve the management of dangerous chemicals, dependence on expensive energy imports, pollution levels, the loss of forests and biological diversity, and land deterioration from deforestation and desertification. Moreover, because the struggling economies of the developing countries are generally closely-tied to the use of natural resources, the widespread deterioration of the renewable resource base has serious implications for the future, particularly when viewed together with rapidly expanding populations and the increasingly intricate economic and security interconnections among all nations.

A new environmental agenda should emerge for the developed countries which represents global policy and political challenges for developing countries. Current issues are the spread of deserts, loss of forests, soil erosion, growth of human populations, exhaustion of ecological communities, waste accumulation and alteration of the planet's biogeochemical cycles. These environmental concerns transcend borders, national laws and local customs. As a result, the politics needed to meet present and future challenges require a new vision and a new diplomacy, new leaders and coalitions.

The issues demand attention from developed countries because they are inextricably linked to pressing international goals; expansion of international trade and markets, improvement of North-South relations, promotion of sustainable economic development and ensuring long-term stability in developing countries.

The developed countries should have a direct and, as the situation worsens, a growing interest in the environmental and natural resource problems of developing countries. The tragic accident in Bhopal, India, and the famine that continues to afflict many African countries underscore that need. Humanitarian and environmental values are at stake, but so are developed countries' economic and security interests.

Events like Bhopal can fuel anti-American sentiment and provide support for efforts to unduly restrict the operation of United States companies, thus diminishing prospects for mutually beneficial direct foreign investment. Yet less dramatic than the Bhopal accident, although inestimably more serious globally, is continuing environmental degradation which reduces the capability of nations to support their people. Resource challenges that are not met lead first to economic and social stresses and then to political instability or authoritarian measures which undermine free institutions and may trigger armed conflict.

Environmental degradation in developing countries affects industrialised countries in other ways too. In addition to development assistance from developed countries, for example, the banking community of those countries has also loaned many billions of dollars to developing countries. Continued environmental and resource degradation, coupled _with heavy

reliance on energy imports, reduces developing nations' ability to pay back their outstanding debts.

Increasingly, leaders of developing countries are showing concern about environmental and resource deterioration. And rightly so. Conservation of the productive resource base - soils, fisheries, forests - is particularly critical in developing countries which, on average, are six times more dependent than industrial countries on those natural resources.

Yet, while legislation to protect the environment in developing countries is now virtually universal, implementation, enforcement and monitoring are often grossly deficient. Even where the political commitment is present, lack of information, staffing shortages, poor training, inadequate technical and financial resources all create special vulnerability.

Fundamentally, countries should manage their own resources and environmental affairs. Unfortunately, with all too few exceptions, developing countries do not have the needed capability. In light of the seriousness of the global resource situation, and its importance to the interests of developed countries, a concerted effort is now urgently needed to help developing countries manage their own resources and environment. The key questions are: What can developed countries do to strengthen the capability of officials and other leaders in developing countries to better cope with their environmental and resource challenges? How can developed countries help them to achieve sustainable agricultural, energy and industrial development?

A guiding principle behind such help should be that developed countries do not impose their environmental systems on developing countries. Instead, they should act to bolster and support institution-building efforts designed to strengthen the ability of developing countries themselves to make informed decisions and carry-out effective policies.

A FRAMEWORK FOR ACTION

Provide Leadership. Occasionally, developed countries can provide a leadership role in improving environmental and resource management in developing countries. For example, the United States played a leading role in managing renewable resources such as forests, rangelands and wildlife, which led to the development of principles, policies and programmes often followed by other countries.

Especially in the early 1970's, the US took the lead in international environmental and resource deliberations. For example, her role was instrumental in establishing the United Nations Environment Programme, in securing the Washington Convention (on control of trade in endangered species) and other international agreements, and in calling world attention to environmental concerns. Such initiatives are crucially needed now, and ought to be focused on such issues as population, poverty, agrarian reform and renewable energy. The general aim should be to ensure that developing countries achieve truly sustainable development based on sound environmental and resource management - which ultimately must be based on self-reliance.

Set an Example at Home. Most people in developed countries do not realise the impact that their domestic policies and programmes have abroad. When the United States established domestic policies and institutions in the early 1970's and took vigorous domestic actions to deal with environmental and resource issues, her example was emulated by many other countries, both developed and developing. Partly as a result of United States domestic action, environmental and resource issues were placed high on the agendas of many other countries. Similarly, in the early 1980's, when the United States was seen to be pulling back from these issues, the loss of momentum had international repercussions.

Provide Intergovernmental Assistance. This can be done through international programmes that can contribute significantly to improving environmental and resource management in developing countries. Developed countries can also make important contributions to international development through such multilateral organisations as the World Bank and the United Nations Development Programme.

Provide Other Forms of Assistance. In addition to assistance through bilateral and multilateral development assistance institutions, developed countries can facilitate and encourage improvement in the capabilities of developing countries to manage their own environment and resources in other ways. These include, but are not limited to, provision of experience and information, training, scientific and technological exchanges, and support for non-governmental organisations in the countries involved.

Support International Cooperation. The participation of developed countries in, and their support for, international environment and resource conventions and other agreements may be crucial to the success of such instruments, and would contribute significantly to their effectiveness. The same is true of their participation in such international organisations as the United Nations Environment Programme.

SUGGESTIONS FOR ACTION

It is suggested that developed countries should:

Strengthen Environmental Authorities in Developing Countries

Development assistance agencies should help strengthen environmental authorities in developing countries by promoting institution-building efforts designed to bolster the authorities; and by requiring countries receiving assistance to submit comments assessing the environmental and natural resource aspects of any development project.

Although many developing countries have governmental environment agencies of some sort, many of these are new, inadequately staffed and lacking in political power. Some are one-person offices or interagency coordinating committees without independent authority. Lack of an adequate institutional infrastructure is a major impediment; in the majority of cases, the result of conflict with other government agencies typically has been that the newly-created environmental institutions have been forced to focus on narrow pollution issues, thereby minimising friction because no usurpation of powers is involved. In the worst cases, agencies are consulted late, their views are ignored or they are overruled.

Institution-building is admittedly a difficult task for a donor agency, but development assistance agencies have been deeply involved for many years in assisting major ministries such as agriculture, health, and housing. However, more needs to be done by development assistance agencies to help countries improve their national policies on environment and natural resources and to strengthen their institutional and scientific capability. They need to address much more explicitly the question of the institutional capability of the host country's environmental arm. Central to that assessment is the question of the environmental agency's authority and its ability to exercise cross-cutting policy management on important environmental or natural resource matters.

Strengthen Indigenous Non-Governmental Organisations

Developed countries should improve their efforts to strengthen environmental and resource-related non-governmental organisations in developing countries.

The major weaknesses of private organisations generally in developing countries are poor management, poor fundraising capabiliy, lack of understanding of public affairs techniques, all of which add up to a failure to create the pre-conditions for self-sustainable ability. Developed countries should expand their efforts to assist indigenous non-governmental organisations by paying more attention to management questions as well as the environmental programme of such organisations; and providing assistance with fundraising and public affairs techniques.

Review Options for Using Foreign Debt to Encourage Sustainable Development

Developed countries and their private sector commercial banks should investigate the debt situation in developing countries to assess the feasibility and desirability of cancelling or rescheduling part of the debt, in exchange for developing countries' efforts to undertake environmental and natural resource projects which will improve the long-term prospects for sustained growth and debt repayment. In addition, policies of the International Monetary Fund that may result in environmentally unsustainable development should be examined. The foreign debt load removes scarce capital from economic development initiatives, undermining developing countries' long-term ability to grow and repay the debt.

Debt rescheduling or forgiveness could be used to promote the economic growth so necessary in alleviating the international debt problem, and simultaneously augment the developing countries' environmental and natural resource programmes. Debt rescheduling or forgiveness could be used as an incentive for a developing country to undertake needed environmental and natural resource management projects, for example, in soil conservation, dune stabilisation, tree planting and/or protection of globally strategic areas in which all nations benefit. Other kinds of projects could include the creation of alternative employment opportunities for people dependent on fragile ecosystems. By conserving and restoring the resource base on which development depends, such projects would contribute to long-term growth and eventually strengthen a country's ability to repay its debts.

Support for the United Nations Environment Programme (UNEP)

All member States of the United Nations could continue to support, at the current level of funding, the United Nations Environment Programme. It is an independent agency of the United Nations family and is funded by voluntary contributions from member governments.

Among the UN agencies, UNEP serves as an advocate for protection of the environment and natural resources, and encourages the integration of environmental criteria in development projects to avoid unnecessary economic and social costs. It is largely due to UNEP's catalytic role that over 110 countries now have national environmental agencies. UNEP has made an immense contribution to the protection of our global environment.

The above suggestions stress the need to take environmental and natural resource factors into account in development activities to ensure their long-term success. Comprehensive assessments of environmental conditions have proven invaluable to developing country officials in the planning, execution and management of development efforts.

This approach to environmental assessment and management indicates opportunities for sustainable use of natural resources in systems of development, as well as adverse impacts which can undermine the development effort itself. It is this positive approach which the recommendations envisage.

Since this paper has concentrated its effort on actions to help developing countries help themselves, the suggestions do not address other entitites or policy issues. Of course, the private sector, non-governmental organisations, industry and academia have much to contribute and should be involved in implementing many of the suggestions.

Taken together, the suggestions recognise that there is no simple way to promote environmentally sustainable development in developing countries. Rather, the suggestions encompass a range of process-oriented actions designed to increase attention to environmental issues by development assistance agencies, and to enhance the ability of developing country leaders to better manage their resources for sustainable development.

THE WORLD CONSERVATION STRATEGY: A SECOND LOOK

Robert Prescott-Allen
PADATA Consultants
Victoria, B.C., Canada

SUMMARY *This paper describes the evolution of the World Conservation Strategy, some of its achievements, and how it could be made more effective. Because the enormous potential of the Strategy to advance conservation and contribute to sustainable development has not been realised, it should be revised to build upon its strengths and correct its weaknesses. The strengths of the Strategy are found in its scope, its orientation toward development, its balance, its cross-sectoral approach and its concentration on "quick-acting" strategic actions. Its weaknesses are a lack of explanation of main strategic actions of the WCS; the absence of a plan to marshall and deploy resources required to ensure implementation; the omission of detailed provisions for monitoring and evaluating; and the need for guidelines on WCS implementation, and guidance on sustainably developing living resources.*

INTRODUCTION

The enormous potential of the World Conservation Strategy (WCS) to advance conservation and contribute to sustainable development has not yet been actualised. This suggests a flaw in the Strategy that should be corrected. This Conference provides a timely opportunity to reflect the aims of the World Conservation Strategy, assess their achievements, and consider ways of making the Strategy more effective. This paper will describe why and how the World Conservation Strategy was prepared, explaining key decisions on scope, content, and orientation toward development; review its achievements; and suggest some changes to the Strategy so that it can achieve the results that may realistically be expected of it.

WHY THE WCS IS WHAT IT IS

The World Conservation Strategy was prepared because IUCN, UNEP and WWF wanted to be sure they were tackling the priority conservation problems in the most effective ways. Conventional conservation projects were either not succeeding or their success was only temporary. The three organisations therefore wanted to know:

* Where they should be concentrating their efforts and resources (i.e., to

distinguish priority regions, ecosystems, and species groups); and

* what additional actions they should take to enhance the effectiveness and long-term success of their standard conservation actions (such as establishment and strengthening of national parks and reserves, protection of endangered species, and improvement of conservation legislation).

The World Conservation Strategy took two years and six drafts to prepare. (The published version is a modified sixth draft).1 The first phase (1977-78) produced a consensus document on nature conservation. Its scope reflected the traditional concern of IUCN and WWF: conservation of wild species and natural ecosystems. The second phase (from the Ashkhabad General Assembly to completion of the published version) produced a negotiated document on biosphere conservation between IUCN, UNEP, WWF, FAO and Unesco. During this phase, the scope of the World Conservation Strategy was enlarged, its orientation toward development was made more positive, and the number of potential users greatly increased.

FROM NATURE CONSERVATION TO "LIVING RESOURCE" CONSERVATION

At the Ashkhabad General Assembly, developing country members of IUCN urged that the scope of the Strategy be expanded to include all living resources so that their most pressing conservation problems, such as soil loss and degradation of farmland, could be addressed directly. They asked that agriculture, forestry, fisheries and rural development be made as much a part of the Strategy as wildlife and nature conservation. UNEP strongly supported this recommendation, and the scope was duly enlarged.

This change meant that conservation results the Strategy was intended to achieve could no longer be measured exclusively in terms of species and ecosystem diversity. A long list of other desired results became at least as important, including maintenance of biogeochemical equilibria, organic waste degradation, nitrogen fixation, soil and water conservation, and sustainable production of crops, livestock, timber, fish and other resources. A succinct definition of what conservation was trying to achieve required reducing this list to the fewest categories possible. Thus, three objectives of conservation were formulated: maintenance of ecological processes and life-support systems; preservation of genetic diversity; and sustainable utilisation of species and ecosystems.

Expressing conservation goals in terms of these three constituent objectives had a most important consequence for the World Conservation Strategy. It

---

1   A consensus of the nature conservation constituency was obtained by consulting the IUCN membership of governments and NGOs (including WWF) and its network of Commission members through a poll on conservation priorities; circulation of the first and second drafts; and debate of the second draft at the Ashkhabad (USSR) General Assembly. Substantive work was done by four review panels appointed by the IUCN Council. Initial drafts of the WCS were co-written by Duncan Poore, WCS Senior Ecologist, and Robert Allen; drafts 5-6 were compiled by Robert Allen.

made it easy to show that conservation "is a process - to be applied cross-sectorally - not an activity sector in its own right" (WCS 1.6), and to argue more cogently that conservation is the responsibility of every sector and not just of those sectors designated "wildlife" or "parks and reserves." The three conservation objectives are crucial integrators, since a great many sectors (including agriculture, forestry, fisheries, health, energy, natural resource-based industries, and recreation and tourism) depend on maintenance of ecological processes, biological diversity and harvested resources as much as do traditional wildlife and nature conservation.

Unfortunately, the word "objective" was ill chosen. It has confused a number of Strategy users, who have misinterpreted it as a motivating objective (why we conserve) rather than as a constituent objective (what we must do to achieve conservation). To avoid further confusion along these lines, the three objectives might best be referred to as the three "components of conservation."

CONSERVATION STRATEGY OR SUSTAINABLE DEVELOPMENT STRATEGY?

The Ashkhabad General Assembly also discussed broadening the Strategy's scope to include full treatment of the socio-economic context of conservation, with special emphasis on the ecological effects of human population increase, as well as other major influences as poverty, economic growth, energy and raw materials consumption, inappropriate technologies, and human need satisfaction. Under protest from some members (including references to a "conspiracy of silence" on population), it was decided that adequate treatment of these issues would greatly increase the time needed to complete the Strategy, and should therefore be deferred until its next revision.

In retrospect, this was a wise decision for two reasons, in addition to those of time and logistics. First, the actions recommended by the World Conservation Strategy represent actions that would still have to be taken even in a world at peace, with stable human numbers, and no socio-economic inequities. It was and it remains essential that clear guidance be given on these actions, and that people concerned with conservation and sustainable development continue to press for them. Second, the credibility of the World Conservation Strategy stems from its concentrating on matters within the expertise and mandates of its authors and sponsors. It required a year to achieve a consensus by the members of IUCN and WWF on "nature conservation" aspects of the Strategy. It required another year to reach agreement between IUCN and WWF on the one hand and UNEP, FAO and Unesco on the other - on resource conservation aspects of the WCS (agriculture, fisheries, forestry, etc.); on the balance between resource conservation and nature conservation; and on the balance between conservation and development. To prepare sections of equal authority and credibility on population, peace and disarmament, a new international economic order, poverty, human rights, and so on, would have required negotiation with many more national and international agencies.

An unintended but highly beneficial result of the decision to keep to conservation and its integration with development was that it resulted in a strategy, and not just a manifesto. A manifesto is a public declaration of objectives, intentions and opinions. But a strategy is itself one of the principal means by which the objectives and intentions it expresses are carried out. It is addressed not to a passive audience or readership but to groups of active users who are supposed to act on it. Therefore, to be effective (that is, to be a strategy, not a manifesto), a strategy must be shaped by and carry with it the user groups which are expected to act on it. Decisions on the scope of a strategy are in practice decisions on who should participate in its preparation - and so are highly strategic, since they largely determine the prospects of the strategy's implementation, and hence of its eventual success or failure.

ORIENTATION TOWARD DEVELOPMENT

The World Conservation Strategy is pro-development.   This represents a radical shift in position by IUCN, one that is still being resisted by much of the conservation movement it represents.   The shift came after the fifth draft, following detailed review by the UN Environment Programme.   The idea that conservation is necessary for development had been a theme of IUCN at least since the United Nations Conference on the Human Environment (Stockholm 1972); the theme of the IUCN General Assembly in Banff (Canada) that year was "Conservation for Development." All drafts of the World Conservation Strategy reiterated this theme, asserting that development will not succeed without conservation. The published version of the Strategy goes further. It states that conservation

will not succeed without development (WCS 1.10-11;14).

UNEP pointed out that non-conservationists were by far the larger and more powerful group of potential users of the WCS.   The Strategy was intended to influence government policy makers and their advisers, development practitioners (including aid agencies, industry, commerce, trade unions) and resource users (some of whom may be conservationists, but most not). To succeed, the Strategy had to be free of rhetoric, and worded in ways that showed that we were aware of the development constituency's main concerns, in order to enable them to see what we were trying to say, rather than the stereotype of what they thought we would be saying. This advice was in accord with two cardinal strategic principles: find allies whenever and wherever you can; and avoid confrontations unless they are absolutely necessary (Stebbins, 1984).   As a consequence, changes to the World Conservation Strategy text included:

* elimination of inflated claims of the importance of conservation;

* balanced presentation of the underlying causes of unsustainable development and environmental destruction;

* recognition of lack of development as the main immediate obstacle to conservation in the rural areas of developing countries (WCS 14);

* restriction of non-negotiable conservation positions to the absolute minimum and expressing them as pragmatically as possible without softening the position. For example: "...we should not knowingly cause the extinction of a species" (WCS 3.3);

* recognition that most decisions concerning conservation are matters of relative advantage and disadvantage, balancing costs and benefits, risks and rewards; that socio-economic factors generally matter quite as much and often more than ecological factors; and that with increasing demands by different interest groups on the same ecosystems, there is often competition and conflict among conservation components and among socio-economic objectives;

* grasping the nettle and proposing which conservation components should have priority under particular circumstances.

Widening the scope of the Strategy from nature conservation to living resource conservation (biosphere conservation) and re-positioning conservation with respect to development resulted in an enormously expanded constituency of support for the conservation community. But these two actions led to a risk of alienating not only the ideological preservationists (for whom development is an anathema) but the conservers of biological diversity who are the heart of the conservation movement and the core constituency of both IUCN and WWF. The concern of this group is that the cause of biological diversity will suffer - that the *rapprochement* with development is the thin end of a utilitarian wedge that will lead to nature conservation being thrust still deeper into the shadow of resource conservation. By (1) giving prominence to the maintenance of biological diversity (it is, after all, one of the three constituent objectives of the WCS); (2) allying it with the other two components of conservation; (3) showing that the three components are interrelated and that all three are needed for sustainable development; and (4) proposing ways in which they can be integrated into the development process, the case for conserving biological diversity will be greatly strengthened with a potentially more lasting effect and on a wider scale than hitherto.

The perception that biological diversity has received short shrift seems to be based on the following:

* the misconception that the strategic actions recommended by the World Conservation Strategy (for example, preparation of national conservation strategies and adoption of cross-sectoral conservation policies) are meant to be "instead of " rather than "in support of" conventional conservation actions (such as habitat protection);

* neglect of biological diversity by many of the national conservation strategies prepared so far;

* an adversarial attitude to "government," "industry," "development," etc., that precludes any accommodation between conservation and development, since no outcome is considered possible other than victory or defeat;

* the rise of the animal rights movement and the emergence of the "deep ecology" philosophy, reinforcing anti-utilitarian feelings among conservationists and leading to a hardening of the adversarial attitude mentioned above.

The first of these points is a simple misconception. The second problem can be corrected quite easily. The third and fourth problems are symptomatic of the widespread failure (found in both the conservation and the development communities) to come to terms with two key features of human relations with the biosphere.

TWO PARADIGMS OF CONSERVATION AND DEVELOPMENT

Two complementary paradigms - one traditional, the other modern - describe the features of human relations with the biosphere that support the approach to conservation and development taken in the World Conservation Strategy. The traditional paradigm is expressed by the Fijian word, *vanua*, which means both "land" and "people." The concept of nature and people being one and the same is found in the belief-systems of many indigenous peoples and is far older than that of conservation (as it is generally understood). It reveals a basic fact of life: that human beings are simultaneously modifiers, beneficiaries and integral components of the biosphere. To survive we need to modify the biosphere and we need to maintain it. Development and conservation together result in happiness, while one without the other results in misery. Hence we need to integrate conservation and development, and the species with which we share this planet are both companions (with intrinsic rights and values of their own) and commodities (consumable sources of food, medicines, raw materials, income and employment). Any environmental ethic must accommodate this dichotomy. Those of many indigenous people have done so, expressing strong spiritual bonds with animals and plants that feed, clothe and cure them,

as well as with species whose value to them is purely symbolic.

The modern paradigm is expressed in a Latin motto, *ex uno plura*: "out of one, many." One ecosystem can supply a wide range of different goods and services to an equally wide range of people. As societies develop they diversify their demands on the environment, requiring a greater range of goods and services from the same ecosystem. For example, the coastal forest of Pacific North America provides a great many commodities (and hence substantial income and employment); essential ecological services (watershed protection, conservation of soil and water, moderation of local climate); recreation and amenity; and genetic resources for silviculture, agriculture, horticulture and aquaculture (Prescott-Allen C. & R., 1986). The beneficiaries of a given ecosystem include subsistence users, commercial users, recreational users, non-comsumptive users who are "against use" and sectors that are simply not aware that they are users. The great variety of ways in which people benefit from particular ecosystems is a reflection of the biological diversity of the ecosystems, of the complexity of modern economies, and of the pluralism of modern societies. When ecosystems supply goods and services of great importance to many different interest groups, reconciliation of conflicting uses becomes crucial for both development and conservation. Hence the need for cross-sectoral policy-making and coordination, and for an approach to conservation that accommodates many different ways of relating to nature - the antithesis of the intolerant ideological approach of "deep ecology" and the extreme animal rights movement.

Our unity with the biosphere (*vanua*) and the diversity of our demands on any one component of the biosphere (*ex uno plura*) call for a concerted effort to bring people together and help them identify the mutuality of interests between society and nature and among different sectors of society. The World Conservation Strategy has shown the way by re-positioning conservation with respect to development and by recommending ways of integrating conservation and development and achieving better cross-sectoral coordination.

THE STRATEGY OF THE WCS

As the Strategy progressed, the second of its two tasks (identifying actions to enhance the long-term effectiveness of standard conservation actions) became much more important than the first (identifying priority regions, ecosystems and species). Seven of the nine chapters (78%) of the first draft were devoted to particular ecological regions and groups of species. This proportion is reversed in the published Strategy, where only four of twenty sections (20%) deal with priority regions and species. Experience suggests that we should have taken this trend to the limit, and dropped all discussion of priorities, since this can be done better and more flexibly through the regular programming procedures of IUCN, WWF and the UN System. Had we done so, we could have devoted more attention to the two problems that the WCS identifies as being at the root of the failure to achieve conservation: the separation of conservation from development; and narrow sectoral approaches to living resource management (WCS 8.6).

The actions available to conservationists and developers alike are of two kinds: tactical (or technical) and strategic. Both are needed and the two should be mutually supportive. Much of the World Conservation Strategy is concerned with the main tactical actions needed to achieve the three components of conservation. In the course of preparing the Strategy (well toward the end of the second phase in fact), it was realised that strategic actions themselves fall into two groups: slow and quick-acting actions. Those that may take years to implement and produce results are slow-acting strategic actions. The WCS simply acknowledges that such actions must be taken for both conservation and development to be sustainable and calls for additional strategies to achieve them: "a strategy for peace; a strategy for a new international economic order; a strategy for human rights; a strategy for overcoming poverty; a world food supply strategy; a population strategy" (WCS 1.8. See also WCS 20.1-6).

There is also a group of quick-acting strategic actions - actions that can be taken and produce results within normal planning periods (five years) of most governments, and that are needed to facilitate and support tactical conservation actions. These are capable of removing those obstacles to conservation and sustainable development which are caused by the way human institutions work (but not deep-rooted structural problems such as population growth, poverty, or socio-economic inequity). Such quick-acting strategic actions include:

* actions to integrate conservation and development and achieve cross-sectoral coordination;

* actions to enhance the effectiveness of agencies with responsibilities for living resources (WCS 11.10-11);

* rural development projects, especially those with a conservation component (or undertaken in association with conservation projects), such as those outlined in WCS 14.

* actions to build support for conservation and sustainable development;

* actions to facilitate the above, including the preparation and implementation of national and sub-national conservation strategies (WCS 8);

* action to identify national and sub-national priorities among the many strategic and tactical actions needed to achieve conservation and sustainable development.

The strategy of the WCS is to re-position conservation with respect to development (by showing humanity's dependence on development and conservation combined into a single equitable, sustainable endeavour). In addition, it must promote quick-acting strategic actions (listed above) to facilitate conventional technical measures, remove institutional and other immediate limiting factors, and to "buy time" for strategic actions dealing with deeper and less tractable problems (such as socio-economic inequity and population growth).

WHAT THE WCS HAS ACHIEVED

"The results of the World Conservation Strategy amount to the sum of what can be done locally all over the world: a bit more or a bit less here or there." (Thomas Blohm, Venezuela, in a letter to IUCN, March, 1978, in response to the first draft of the WCS.)

Since the immediate aim of the World Conservation Strategy is to achieve the three components of conservation (maintenance of ecological processes, maintenance of biological diversity, maintenance of harvested resources at sustainable levels), these are the results by which the effectiveness of the strategic actions should be judged.

Evaluating the World Conservation Strategy therefore involves answering the following questions:

* How widely have the strategic actions recommended by the WCS been implemented?

* How well have they been implemented?

* Have they achieved results?

Evaluation depends on monitoring. Unfortunately, monitoring of the World Conservation Strategy has not been adequate. IUCN has pledged to "monitor implementation as closely as possible" (WCS 20.7). Following the launch of the Strategy, there was a good deal of discussion by the IUCN Secretariat and by IUCN's Programme and Planning Advisory Group (PPAG) about how IUCN should meet this commitment. It was recognised that monitoring implementation of the World Conservation Strategy was needed to:

* indicate the effectiveness of efforts to promote the WCS;

* reveal gaps in implementation and show where promotion of the Strategy is most needed;

* stimulate, through publication of the results of monitoring, further and more widespread implementation of the WCS;

* provide the information needed to evaluate the World Conservation Strategy.

In turn, WCS evaluation is needed to test whether the Strategy significantly advanced conservation in several countries; and suggest ways in which it could be improved in subsequent revisions.

It was proposed to the IUCN Council that the progress report on WCS implementation, to be submitted to the 1981 General Assembly of IUCN (Christchurch, New Zealand), should do three things:

* report on national and international promotion of the World Conservation Strategy;

* analyse the report to distinguish real progress from lip service and "business as usual;"

* make proposals on monitoring achievement of the three components of conservation for an eventual evaluation of World Conservation Strategy effectiveness.

Only the first of these was done. Since then reporting has remained rather superficial. The IUCN Bulletin carries regular progress reports (at first in the body of the Bulletin, later as a supplement, "WCS in Action"), but these are essentially promotional, to praise those who have acted and stimulate those who have not yet acted: a useful and necessary function, but no substitute for analysis and evaluation.

As far as I know, there is no monitoring of indicators of conservation progress that would enable eventual evaluation of the effectiveness of national conservation strategies, sub-national conservation strategies, and other strategic actions in response to the WCS.

Indicators of conservation progress that could be monitored include:

Maintenance of Ecological Processes

(1) Distribution of ecological processes:

* extent of most suitable agricultural land (prime farmland) that remains available for agriculture, rates of loss of farmland to non-agricultural uses, and quality of land reserved for agriculture;

* areas and rates of conversion to agriculture, livestock rearing or forestry of land that is marginal for these activities;

* areas and rates of conversion to incompatible uses of land required for watershed protection, particularly in upper catchment areas.

(2) Land quality, notably areas of land where soil loss and degradation are occurring, and rates of soil loss and degradation are high (including silt load of rivers and sedimentation of reservoirs, areas of desertified land and rates of desertification).

(3) Areas of coastal wetlands, seagrass beds and coral reefs that remain able to support fisheries, waterfowl and other wildlife resources; and rates of removal, degradation or, conversely, protection.

Maintenance of Biological Diversity

(4) Ecosystem diversity: proportion of representative ecosystems (ecosystems representative of each of the main biogeoclimatic zones of the country or region concerned) and unique ecosystems given secure long-term protection in parks or reserves.

(5) Species diversity: recovery rates of endangered species; proportion of monotypic families and genera, endemic genera and species and culturally important species given secure long-term protection in parks or reserves.

(6) Genetic diversity: extent to which traditional and advanced cultivars (cultivated varieties), breeds and special genetic stocks of established and incipient domesticates are given secure long-term protection (in seedstores, *in vitro* collections, field genebanks, etc); extent to which the major genetic variants of wild relatives of domesticates and wild resource species are given secure long-term protection primarily in parks or reserves (genebank areas) but also in zoos, botanical gardens, seedstores, etc.

Maintenance of Harvested Resources at Sustainable Levels

(7) Extent to which harvesting of species and ecosystems is sustainable (in balance with the species' or ecosystem's capacity for recruitment or recovery), especially with respect to fisheries, forestry, and rangeland management.

This is a partial list of possible indicators of conservation progress, the final choice of which would require careful thought. One most important set of variables - those relating to the global ecological processes by which the biosphere regulates the chemistry of the planet and sustains life - is not listed above. Some of the proposed indicators may be unreliable or may be difficult to ensure. For example: the relationship between area of coastal wetland and dependent fisheries is obscure (a 50% reduction in wetland area may not lead to a halving of the fishery) and the productive/recovery capacities of many fisheries (especially multispecies ones) remain a mystery.

Two points are clear however. First, monitoring implementation of the World Conservation Strategy requires the cooperation of many agencies (IUCN, the UN System, SCOPE, and in particular, national agencies). Second, monitoring should focus on those countries where there are concerted efforts to implement the Strategy. It would be logical to concentrate on countries undertaking national or sub-national conservation strategies, since a programme to monitor indicators of conservation progress could be set up in conjunction with the national or subnational strategy - and indeed **should** be, so that the effectiveness of national and sub-national conservation strategies can also be evaluated.

HOW TO MAKE THE WCS WORK

This Conference has been called to evaluate and improve the World Conservation Strategy. It was intended from the start that the Strategy be revised regularly, to build on its strength, correct any weaknesses, and respond to new problems and concerns (The IUCN General Assembly at Ashkhabad even resolved that the World Conservation Strategy be revised every three years, at each

General Assembly. That was before we realised how much time and effort were required to negotiate a worthwhile Strategy.)

Six years after the launch of the World Conservation Strategy, some of its apparent and real strengths include the following:

* Its scope: living resource conservation (a synonym for biosphere conservation), or maintenance of ecological processes, biological diversity and harvested resources. The scope is large enough to involve all sectors and interest groups and small enough to permit a workable consensus;

* its orientation toward development: The WCS has greatly increased the potential constituency of support for conservation by adopting a human-centred approach and by making practical proposals for integration of development and conservation;

* its balance: The World Conservation Strategy is both human-centred and biosphere-centred, recognising that as people and as components of the biosphere we have to be both. The WCS also stresses the obligation to balance the needs of different interest groups, both among present generations of people and between the present generation and posterity. This balance is expressed in the Strategy's cross-sectoral approach, in its emphasis on the poor and disadvantaged among present generations of people (WCS 1.10-11; 14; 20.2-4), in the ethical positions it takes toward future generations of people (WCS 1.5; 3.1-2) and toward other species (WCS 3.1-2; 13.1)

* its cross-sectoral approach: Because of the need to combine conservation and development and to balance the interests of many different groups of people, a cross-sectoral approach is mandatory;

* its strategy: its emphasis on national and sub-national conservation strategies, and other "quick-acting" actions to facilitate and support conventional technical measures, remove those obstacles to conservation and sustainable development caused by deficiencies in human institutions or other limiting factors, but "buy time" for strategic actions dealing with deeper and less tractable problems.

Some of the weaknesses of the Strategy are focused on:

* a lack of explanation of the main strategic actions of the World Conservation Strategy, how they relate to each other, and how they relate to other actions;

* the absence of a plan to marshall and deploy the resources required to ensure WCS implementation, including deepening commitment to its implementation by member governments and organisations of IUCN, WWF and the UN System;

* a need for guidelines for WCS implementation (to provide more detailed explanation and guidance than can otherwise fit into the format of a strategy);

* the omission of detailed provisions for monitoring and evaluating the Strategy; and

* lack of guidance on sustainable development of living resources, in contrast to maintenance of living resources.

This list includes only those aspects of the Strategy that I believe have prevented full advantage being taken of the strength of the World Conservation Strategy - and hence limit its value as a strategy. There are a number of important issues that the WCS does not discuss, nor even mention. Many of these issues have been organised as Workshops within the context of the WCS Conference and include:

* Sustainable Use of Energy (Workshop 6/18);

* International Cooperation for Peace and Development (Workshop 9);

* Ethics, Culture and Sustainable Development (Workshop 11);

* Economics of Sustainable Development (Workshop 12);

* Indigenous People and Sustainable Development (Workshop 13);

* Managing Common Property Resources (Workshop 14);

* Environmental Rehabilitation (Workshop 15);

* Population and Human Settlements (Workshop 16);

* Appropriate Technology and Sustainable Development (Workshop 18).

Discussion of some of these issues could be included in a revised World Conservation Strategy without sig-nificantly enlarging its scope (so main-taining one of its strengths), while ad-ding to some of its other strengths, such as balance and orientation toward development. Others - if treated with the depth that a strategy requires - would substantially enlarge the Strat-egy's scope especially in terms of Workshops 6, 9, 12 and 13.

With respect to this second group of is-sues, achieving the degree of consensus necessary to generate the concerted ac-tion implied by the term "strategy" will be extremely arduous, not just among conservationists and environmentally-aware members of the development community, but with the many other bodies whose support and participation are needed for action to be effective.

REFERENCES

• Australian Ministry of Planning and Environment, 1984, Draft *State Conservation Strategy for Victoria*, Overview statement for public comment, East Melbourne.

• Bramble, B. 1985, Evaluation of Project 3044*, Conservation Strategy Development*, Photocopy, WWF, Gland.

• Committee for Rational Utilisation of Natural Resources and Environmental Protection, 1985, *Vietnam National Conservation Strategy* (draft).

• Haribon Society, 1983, *Philippine National Conservation Strategy: A Strategy for Sustainable Development*, Manila.

• IUCN, 1980, *World Conservation Strategy: Living Resource Conservation for Sustainable Development*, IUCN/UNEP/WWF, Gland/Nairobi.

- IUCN, 1979, 14th Session of the IUCN General Assembly and its 14th Technical Meeting, Ashkhabad, USSR. Sept/Oct. 1978, *Proceedings,* IUCN, Morges.

- IUCN, 1978a, "1st Draft: World Conservation Strategy," IUCN, Morges.

- IUCN, 1978b, "2nd Draft: World Conservation Strategy," IUCN, Morges.

- Prescott-Allen, C. & R., 1986 (In press), *The First Resource. Wild Species in the North American Economy,* Yale University Press, New Haven.

- Prescott-Allen, R., 1986, "National Conservation Strategies and Biological Diversity," Report to IUCN Conservation for Development Centre, Photocopy, IUCN, Gland.

- Public Advisory Committees, 1986, *Prospectus for an Alberta Conservation Strategy,* Public Advisory Committee to the Environmental Council of Alberta, Environment Council of Alberta, Edmonton.

- Stebbins, G.L. 1984, *Rare Native California Plants: Famous, Obscure, and Humble,* In: P.E. McGuire & C. O. Qualset (eds). Proceedings, Symposium and Workshop on Genetic Resources Conservation for California.

- Sunkel, O, 1985, "Beyond the World Conservation Strategy: Integrating Development and the Environment," Framework paper for Conference on Conservation and Development: Implementing the World Conservation Strategy, Ottawa, May/June 1986.

ALTERNATIVE STRATEGIES TOWARD SUSTAINABLE DEVELOPMENT

Plenary Session 3

ALTERNATIVE STRATEGIES TOWARD SUSTAINABLE DEVELOPMENT

Plenary Session 3

Margarita de Botero, Chairperson
President, Colegio de Villa de Leyva
Villa de Leyva, Colombia

In introducing the session, the Chairperson spoke warmly of the ideal of a democratic and participatory society based on ecological principles, aimed at social justice. She said that diversity was more important than homogeneity and proclaimed the right to be different. She suggested that the political and economic system must expand to embrace the new ecological perception, becoming in effect, a different, innovative political alternative. She stressed the need to reflect both science and ethics in our development patterns, and recalled how Ivan Illich has hoped for a new future, one in which creativity would be unfettered.

It is clear that means other than the preparation of national conservation strategies are essential in implementing the World Conservation Strategy. National conservation strategies are but one, albeit the most prominent, of several different approaches to environmental management for sustainable development. This plenary session enabled persons who have worked on other approaches in achieving sustainable development to share their experiences and insights.

The papers presented showed clearly that there are vitally important lessons to be learned by looking at conservation and sustainable development from different perspectives. Khosla's theme framework paper noted that each society must learn to design and manage its future in light of its resources and aspirations. Broad and novel concepts of environmental planning are essential in the achievement of sustainable development and each country must adopt concepts that suit its circumstances. Farvar's presentation demonstrates the benefits and contributions of local community-based developments; Spitz explores the usefulness of looking at sustainable development from the viewpoint of a particular resource or activity; and McNeely suggests applying ecological principles that are biome-based within a number of similar-but-different ecosystems. The case study on sustainable development in the northern circumpolar regions by Keith and Simon pays particular attention to the social and political aspects of sustainable development in a distinct geographical region shared by several nations.

ALTERNATIVE STRATEGIES FOR ACHIEVING SUSTAINABLE DEVELOPMENT

Ashok Khosla
President, Development Alternatives
New Delhi, India

SUMMARY *National conservation strategies are but one of the alternative approaches to achieving sustainable socio-economic development. This paper identifies principles and tools for design and management which apply across many of the transitions now faced by mankind, at all levels of decision-making. A framework draws connections among: the characteristics of a system supporting sustainable development, operating concepts for good design, and fundamental criteria for economic, social and environmental design. The effects of administration, conservation, preservation and assessment processes on a system are conceptualised in a model expressing the transform grammar of design, while a decision-making model describes the selection of a transformation process to move a system from its present state to a desired future state. The concepts expressed in the framework and models point to the need for trans-disciplinary design professions to help societies build institutions that will deal with specific issues within the requirements of sustainable development and the broad objectives of each society.*

INTRODUCTION

At a time of deep and pervasive change, the present era offers unique opportunities for developing the tools of creative management for the inevitable, inexorable transitions now taking place on almost every front: resources, technologies, institutions, and development approaches. We can deal with such transitions, as most societies have historically done, reactively and adventitiously making piecemeal adjustments which allow us to cope with change - at least temporarily. Alternatively we can, as the World Conservation Strategy recommends, restructure our affairs at a more fundamental level and develop the means to shape the course of change itself to be of benefit for all, now and in the future.

By identifying "sustainable development" as the basic goal of society, the 1980 launch of the World Conservation Strategy was able to make a profound contribution toward reconciling the interests of the development community with those of the environmental movement. It was, in this sense, a major milestone if not the culmination of a long, peripatetic international debate which started at Founex in 1970, and continued throughout the following decade under various topical guises in such places as Stockholm, Bucharest, Vancouver, Rome, Mar del Plata, Nairobi. With this historical lineage, it was not difficult for the Strategy document to demonstrate a clear and undeniable advance in development thinking over the decade; its unique position in this debate lies in the broad acceptance it received at the hands both of development agencies and of conservationists.

Even so, the Strategy was bound to some degree by the perceptions and organisational constraints of its time and was not able fully to address some important environment and development issues. It restricted itself largely to living resources, and while the document presents an unusually fine and comprehensive appreciation of the interconnections among different resource uses, its primary focus was on the necessity for maintaining genetic diversity, habitats and ecological processes.

While the Strategy clearly recognised the need for injecting the concerns of sustainability into development planning, it could not propose more than a few simple methodological tools for achieving this. It was also unable to deal adequately with certain issues which were considered too controversial or sensitive, but which can nevertheless have profound impacts on the sustainability of development - including particularly those relating to the international economic and political order, war and armed conflict, population growth and urbanisation. Since the launch of the Strategy, other, similar issues have appeared which were not foreseen at the time, including

major new uncertainties in the economies of developed countries, and an endemic debt crisis which threatens to undermine the ability of developing countries to manage their resources in an environmentally-sound manner.

The Strategy took care to identify, for each major type of actor and decision-maker, action needed to achieve its objectives. These included the formulation of more detailed strategies at international, national, sectoral and other levels by planners and policy-makers at each of those levels. The three organisations which sponsored the preparation of the Strategy, IUCN, UNEP and WWF, have of course extensive programmes dealing with precisely these issues. However, with very few exceptions, the efforts of these organisations or others to implement the Strategy have concentrated primarily on promoting national conservation strategies, with little effort devoted to other types of action in this context. The time has now come to pursue initiatives on other fronts as well.

With the growing reliance on decentralised systems of governance, which is becoming possible by rapid advances in technology and imperative based on the complexity of society's needs, it is necessary to identify the prerequisites for decision makers to "think globally and act locally." These certainly include clearly-articulated and widely-accepted societal objectives which are in consonance with the requirements of sustainable development, and the design of institutions, planning instruments and technologies needed to achieve such development.

Over the past two decades, the worldwide effort to incorporate environmental concerns into the development process has led to the evolution of a series of policy and planning concepts which successively improve the ability of society to manage its future. This effort has progressed from early attempts to cure ill-effects of poorly-conceived development projects (e.g., through reactive pollution-control measures), to the prevention of major environmental damage (through impact assessment), to the fostering of projects specifically aimed at improving environmental values (through administrative measures). If the development aspirations of all are to be met, the means must now be found not only to minimise environmental damage, but to optimise the manner in which resources can be used for the greatest possible overall benefit; a concept which has come to be known by the term "environmental management" in recent years.

The central thesis of this paper is that to achieve development which is sustainable, each society must learn to design and manage its future in the light of its resources and aspirations, and that the ability to practise such design and management will require substantially different paradigms, institutional structures and methodological tools than have been considered adequate before. This paper identifies concepts of design and management, which appear to have direct application across many of the transitions now faced by mankind. Moreover, the concepts are applicable at all levels of development decision-making, from political leadership to the individual citizen. Within the context of this broader view of design and management processes, development planning becomes one of a large number of activities amenable to a common set of meta-tools and methods. The same meta-tools and methods apply broadly to the design of objects, products, settlements, spaces, industrial plants, social institutions, and a host of other concerns. And while the specific tools and substantive issues vary from one sphere to another, the common principles underlying them are quite similar, if not invariant.

In broadening design and management concepts, and by incorporating into them criteria which satisfy both private and public objectives, we attempt to show that national conservation strategies are but one type of numerous alternative approaches available to institutions, individuals and society as a whole, to work together for sustainable socio-economic development. Starting from the basic premise that good design leads to sustainable development, we demonstrate that it must also, **necessarily** contribute to a more just, equitable, economically viable and ecologically-resilient development. Our analysis further shows that to achieve such a goal, design must be:

* adaptive, self-regulating and evolutionary, and should not close options valued or likely to be valued by society;

* based on a convergence of individual and societal interests, and should in turn reinforce these;

* in tune with the variety, scale and institutional environment of the problems;

* able to synthesise opposing objectives into an integrated whole;

* collaborative and multidisciplinary to handle the complexity of issues involved;

* participative, enabling people to choose and progressively guide their future rather than having it imposed on them.

To help introduce these principles into the theory and practice of sustainable development, we propose a general framework for understanding and managing the design process.

NEW DIRECTIONS FOR DESIGN

While few would deny that development should be sustainable, the concept of sustainability itself is subject to many different interpretations. The variety of definitions possible is implicit in the number of different lifestyles and development paths that societies, consciously or otherwise, have chosen. Yet, despite a great apparent diversity among and within the nations of the world, the paths taken by most demonstrate at least one underlying commonality. In a nutshell, they tend to indicate two basic assumptions: considerable basic faith in the ability of the biosphere to recover from gross ecological insult; and in human ingenuity to find technological solutions to the unintended effects that societal, economic strategies themselves may create.

It is our view that these assumptions are not justified, and that a framework is needed within which the designer can identify, for each problem, clear objectives consonant with the requirements of sustainable development. To be useful the framework must, further, enable the designer to generate plausible alternatives for meeting these

objectives, and to develop the tools for selecting the best possible option among them.

The average designer will, of course, need tools which are much more specific than a generalised "conceptual framework," and these do not presently exist. This is perhaps the major reason for the little progress made in implementing conservation-based design. At the same time, the nature of the design problem and its inherent complexity also require methods which cannot be simply reduced to rules of thumb or formulae of convenience. The trade-offs implicit in most conservation issues are rarely simple, and the ability to design for sustainable development must be built on the solid foundation of a capacity to innovate.

Some of the existing methodologies are quite actionable, and give the designer useful operational guidance. They are, however, good primarily for solving the immediate problem given to a designer, generally by a client. They help him very little in anticipating or pre-empting situations which are not predefined in the design brief. They help him even less in designing a solution which satisfies the less-tangible criteria of sustainability, such as rational management of resources, equity and self-reliance. Most of these methods are too literal and mechanistic to provide a theory of the underlying causal factors without which the design process can only address a narrowly-conceived, specific and usually superficial problem.

On the other hand, the environmental concerns which have become increasingly visible over the past decade have led to the evolution of paradigms which place more direct emphasis on global, societal and resource issues. Among these, perhaps the clearest definition of the preconditions which must be satisfied for living resources to be managed for sustainable development is given in the World Conservation Strategy. None of these efforts has, however, yet led to the development of methods or tools which are adequately operational.

What are needed now are tools, and the meta-tools to shape them, which allow the designer to identify and solve the specific problem posed to him, while at the same time satisfying the requirements of sustainable development.

The approach we propose here does not, in its present form, entirely fill this gap. Based on methodologies currently being developed by Development Alternatives in India, it is simply intended as a first step toward the development of a new process for design which can reconcile the imperatives of the immediate with our obligations to the long term, the needs of people with the constraints of natural resources, and the interests of the client with those of society.

SUSTAINABLE DEVELOPMENT

Figure 1 presents a simple taxonomy of the factors which must underlie design for sustainable development. It attempts to connect (rather than logically deduce) such factors at successive levels of increasing operationality.

It is the patterns and rearrangements of the underlying structures and functions of a system which determine whether changes in it are likely to be sustainable, not the immediately observable phenomenal behaviour it exhibits on the surface. These structures and functions are represented by the variables and flows within the system and the number of possible states, flows and connections among them represents the "variety" of the system.

The basis of sustainable development lies in change (for development), and resilience (for sustainability). To represent the concept of change through regulation, adaptation and moderation, we use the term "Modulation." "Resilience" is used with its ecological connotation of an ability to deal with perturbations without major structural change. (See Figure 1.)

Modulation depends on the "Variety" of the system being designed and its environment, and to some extent on the method by which changes in this variety are selected. By contrast, resilience is achieved by the "Selection" process, within the general constraints set by the potential modulation on the system/environment complex.

Variety in turn consists of two component factors, "Diversity" and "Connectedness." In simple terms, diversity is the number of states, and connectedness is the number and strength of the flows or links.

Selections of desirable options are made on the basis of the information received through "Feedback" loops in the system, using "Values" (and criteria) chosen so as to increase the likelihood of sustainability. Feedback loops provide information on the performance of the system, often in response to external inputs. The values provide the basis for selection in terms of predefined objectives, aimed at achieving resilience and modulation.

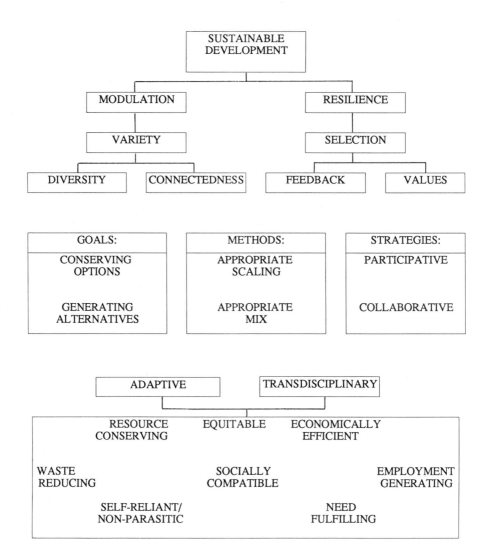

Figure 1: Factors which must underlie design for sustainable development.

We therefore have four fundamental variables which are necessary bases for good design: diversity; connectedness; feedback; and values.

DESIGN FOR SUSTAINABLE DEVELOPMENT

From the point of view of design methodology, the application of selection procedures (feedback and criteria) to the variety variables (diversity and connectedness) lead to three pairs of operating concepts for good Design: the first for its Goals, the second for its Methods, and the third for its Strategies.

In the short space available here it is not possible to demonstrate the full operationality of these concepts but we will attempt to give, by reference to some well known examples, some indications of cases where some of these concepts have been tried out. It should be noted, however, that because of the complexity of real-world problems, most examples can be used to demonstrate a variety of lessons, and any conclusions drawn here are meant only to serve the purpose of illustrating a specific issue. The Sahelian drought, for instance, provides a host of examples underlining the need to implement sustainable development practices not only at the regional and national level, but also within the local community.

Design Goals

The two fundamental goals of design for sustainability appear to be the generation of feasible and desirable "Alternatives" and the conservation of "Options."

An alternative can be seen as one possible set of states which in itself constitutes an entire development path and contains a viable range of potential for change and flexibility within it. Each alternative contains within it a complete set of options which are feasible within the constraints of society and resources. The art of design lies in generating the maximum possible set of meaningful alternatives - ones which are in broad consonance with the objectives of the design. Existing design methodology has addressed this issue in some depth, although it has not yet been able to incorporate the broader societal issues adequately into the definition of the design objectives.

The conservation of options, in close analogy with the conservation of genetic resources, is a matter of keeping open any option which is currently, or might in future be of value. In addition to the basic requirement of not closing important options, particularly those which may be irreversibly lost, conservation also implies making maximum use of the potential of the biosphere to satisfy human needs. This is the part of a designer's work which might be called the science of design.

The Jataka Kathas of ancient India are fables much like Aesop's, but which stress the oneness of humanity and environment. In an ancient society these were probably the best tools available to ensure that future options were conserved for succeeding generations. The retention in India (until very recently) of practices in tune with the conservation of environmental options are vestiges of such traditions built into the religious practices of communities such as the Jains and Bishnoys.

Design Methods

Two basic methods for effective design, often overlooked, are the application of appropriate "scale" in matching tools to problems, and the conjunction of a viable "mix" of final solutions. The concept of scale is relevant to the generation of feasible alternatives, and the term mix pertains to an appropriate combination of options. At the simplest level of spatial scale, the planning of land use employs tools extending from garden design to regional planning as appropriate at different scales of planning, from the micro level to the macro.

Our concepts of scale and mix are even more general, and refer not only to spatial, temporal, quantitative and organisational variables, but also to levels of aggregation in information analysis and hierarchy in the decision-making process. Many design problems are mishandled because the tools chosen are inappropriate at the actual scale and mix of the problem. Others can be made trivial or non-existent by viewing them from a vantage point of higher-level policy.

The quest for appropriateness should not be seen as an exercise in finding a single "correct" scale, but as a resonant combination of different levels, all of which take part in providing a resilient, viable solution, not unlike Bohr's Complementary Principle in Physics which sees the wave and particle as equally correct, co-existing facets of the same electron. For the designer, this concept offers important new insights and opportunities, and will be explored further in the discussion below on our proposed transform grammar.

Designers have all too often ignored the higher levels of design and decision-making within which their own design activity is embedded and the levels below them which will be affected by the product of their work. Unless the flows of information up and down between the different levels are substantially improved, design from the societal point of view can be sub-optimal at best. A transport systems designer who ignores the possibilities of reducing peak loads through interventions at the community level such as staggered working hours, and at the operating incentive schemes, may well improve the routes and schedules but will still fall short of the possible improvements in overall service.

In the field of agriculture, Fukuoka's "One Straw Revolution" demonstrates the possibility of a natural agriculture based upon high diversity and high productivity by the use of diverse species at the correct scale and in the proper mix.

Design Strategies

The two work strategies which the designer needs today are Participative design and Collaborative design. The interplay of variety and selection make it increasingly necessary for the designer to work in a cooperative environment. The needs of the client and the complexities of satisfying large numbers of societal criteria, many possibly conflicting, and the necessity of feedback in selection and operation, require the closest possible participation of those who will be affected by the outcome of the design effort.

The increasing variety of societal considerations and technical information which must be accessed now make it virtually impossible for the single designer to manage the data he requires and the criteria he has to use. Design must therefore necessarily involve an increasing amount of team work and collaboration. Collaborative teams also carry the responsibility of representing interests, usually of longer-term values, not likely to be represented by participation alone.

A variable which designers most often ignore, yet perhaps the most important, is the institutional environment within which the design is to be created, implemented, maintained and evaluated. Unless carefully incorporated into the design or appropriately circumvented, external factors ranging from narrowly defined political objectives to operational realities such as frictional losses, time delays, and cost escalations, result in risks which can neutralise the benefits that the design was originally expected to produce. The risks can only be avoided if the complete man-machine-resource-nature-society nexus is taken as the basis of the solution to be designed.

It is for this reason that we have come to believe strongly that the principles of design elucidated here have as much relevance to the design of institutions as they have for the design of landscapes, industrial products or agricultural projects. Equally important, the concepts of scale and mix underlie our contention that the (quite valid) emphasis on the formulation and implementation of national conservation strategies must now be increasingly supplemented by like-minded measures at other levels, and lead to the internalising of sustainability considerations in strategies for: regions (supranational, subnational); biomes; sheds; sectors; institutions.

Correct scaling is essential to meaningful participation (and, of course, vice versa). For example, large centralised municipal corporations cannot expect participative feedback from citizens if they do not set up the intermediate levels which can connect them through proper information flows with the people. It is for the lack of these interfacing institutions that municipalities so often make regulations at the micro-level, and then set up wasteful and futile policing systems to enforce them.

As a process for the creation of alternatives, diversification, appropriate feedback, and values for sustainable development, the participative use of human resources appears to hold great promise. The Chipko movement in the foothills of the Himalayas is a people's movement largely fueled by the environmental values of village folk. "Chipko" in Hindi literally means to stick to or to cling. In order to thwart large-scale deforestation, individuals of the local community cling to trees as government contractors approach them for felling.

The concept of adaptive management attempts to develop an operational methodology based on transdisciplinary, non-competitive and collaborative strategies for the generation of alternatives and the conservation of options. It offers excellent opportunities for developing solutions whose variety matches that of the problem, and to anticipate and design rather than to react.

Design Criteria

In view of the foregoing argument for the integration of goals, methods and strategies, it appears to us that the concerns of the professional designer must be broadened and made more inclusive.

Our experience as designers in Third World countries shows that to meet the goals, and develop these methods and strategies for design, we need to generate and choose alternatives which fulfill the economic, social and environmental criteria listed in the final box of Figure 1.

The derivation of these criteria from the axiom of sustainability is not difficult. For instance, threats to the rational management of the resource base come from both the consumerism of the affluent and the satisfaction of basic needs of the poor, demonstrating the importance of the equity criterion - not simply on ethical or ideological grounds, but as a matter of straight planetary survival.

Any design that is likely to succeed in fulfilling both the expectation of the client and the requirement of sustainability must in some way optimise its contribution to these criteria. A fundamental requirement to achieve this is that the design and management processes be adaptive and trans-disciplinary.

MODELS

Study of the behaviour of a real world system (physical, social or any other) can be greatly aided by the use of models which describe its evolution in terms of the interaction of the variables and parameters which constitute those models. For a model to be useful, it must at least be able to describe faithfully the system's known behaviour; for values of the variables outside the ranges for which empirical data exist, it must be able accurately to predict its behaviour.

The great success of science comes from the ability it has developed to map the real world onto continually improving abstract images (models). The growing capacity of scientists and engineers to transform information from real world systems to ever more abstract spaces, and then to retransform them back into operational reality has made possible extraordinary contributions to human welfare.

The higher-level models are not ends in themselves, but means of expanding the designer's horizons, to enable him better to cope with higher level effects, increasing complexity, proliferating variety and the broad sweep of time. Such models do not always depend on abstruse formal mathematical constructs, and they are often most useful simply for heuristic and communication purposes, to generate insights and to make interactive collaboration and participation possible. Self-regulating systems must have the ability to use feedback on error as a method to avoid failure. Indeed, since the test of a model can be based only on falsification, the designer must be able to handle error without ignoring it. This concept is fundamental for the design of adaptive techniques for designing and managing the development process.

The Transform Grammar of Design

Among the models we have found most useful in our work is one based on an analogy with the phase-space approach, which has been so successful in the physical sciences. It draws on recent theoretical advances on several fronts, and in a number of different disciplines, particularly including information theory, cybernetics, fuzzy sets, cluster analysis, non-equilibrium statistical mechanics and dissipative systems.

Our own practical experience in the fields of appropriate technology, building design, and organisational development has helped us gain some understanding of the practical constraints within which such models must work. Our model is still clearly far from complete. As yet, it might be more accurately described as an approach rather than a model. But even in its present, rather rudimentary state of development, the model clearly offers considerable potential for illuminating the processes which affect sustainability in a great many types of systems.

Figure 2: Processes affecting sustainability in environmental systems

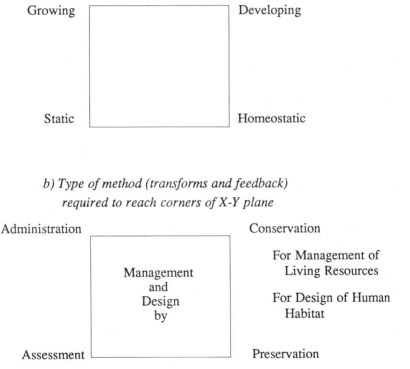

a) State of system at the corners of X-Y plane

Growing   Developing

Static   Homeostatic

b) Type of method (transforms and feedback)
required to reach corners of X-Y plane

Administration   Conservation

Management
and
Design
by

For Management of
Living Resources

For Design of Human
Habitat

Assessment   Preservation

In its simplest form, our model describes an environmental system by four independent variables: variety (along the X-axis), productivity (Y), wealth (Z) and time (t). The meaning of these variables are summarised below, and also shown in Figure 2. This model provides a means for plot-ting variables of importance to the design objectives over time on a volume in X-Y-Z space, each point of which denotes a different situation. When projected on the X-Y plane, the four corners of the box are repre-sentative of extreme states of the sys-tem which are named in Figure 2a.

AXIS	X	Y	Z
GENERAL	VARIETY	PRODUCTIVITY	WEALTH
ANALOGY	"Quality"	"Rate"	"Quantity"
MEANING FOR DESIGN	Options	Connectedness	Resilience
ECOSYSTEM (States)	Number of Species	Net Production	Standing Biomass
ECOSYSTEM (Processes)	Number of Links in Trophic Chains	Change in Quantity of Flows	Quantity of Flows
SOCIAL SYSTEM	Number of Infor-mal Structures	Degree of Dynamic Change	Social Capital or Heritage
ECONOMICS	Mix of Technologies Creating GNP	Addition to GNP	Total Wealth, Assets, or Resources

The four corners of the boxes in Figure 2 have specific meaning, both in the states they represent, and in the transforms needed to reach these states:

X,Y	1.0	0.0	0.1	1.1
VARIETY (X)	High	Low	Low	High
CHANGE (Y)	Low	Low	High	High
TYPE	Stable	Stable	Dynamic	Dynamic
SYSTEMIC LEVEL	Structural	Operational	Operational	Structural
TYPE OF TRANSFORM	PRESERVE	ASSESS	ADMINISTER	CONSERVE
STATE OF SYSTEM	HOMEO-STATIC	STATIC	GROWING	DEVELOPING

The interesting feature of this space is that the evolutionary path of a system over time can be plotted on it to yield valuable insights into its behaviour and potential. The space is characterised by gradients which represent various forces of nature and society, and these can be modified by policy interventions, institutional mechanisms and technological advances. A system acted upon by such a field would tend toward the state with the lowest potential.

The transforms which act upon the system and attract it toward any one of the four corners are also named in the figure. These transforms, which are like the topography which can channel and direct the movement of the main course of a river, are simply the combined effects of different combinations of action and feedback. The Y-Z plane, viewed alone, represents the general perception of the feudal/industrial society and may be adequate when X (variety) is small and changing slowly. However, where X is large or changing rapidly, a view limited to the Y-Z plane cannot explain the stagna-tions or catastrophes which can easily be understood by looking at the X-Y plane. At a time of transition such as the present, the previously neglected view along the Z axis at the X-Y plane becomes imperative, and the basis for any design for sustainable development.

To make the foregoing analysis more concrete, and demonstrate the application of this model, consider the possible proposals for the use and management of a tract in the hinterland of a large city. The solid curve in Figure 3 represents the natural development of a general terrestrial ecosystem. The hinterland under consideration will have to be characterised on the X-Y plane by an appropriate point (state), in this case say the point A. The options available can then be analysed in terms of the effect that their respective transforms have on this initial state.

For example, a decision to use the site for a landfill will be retrogressive, taking the system "Assessively" back to the more Static and therefore less valuable state D (see Figure 3).

Figure 3: Ecosystem development on the X-Y plane. The contours are a representation of the natural transform and feedback mechanisms operating in the absence of external intervention. In its first stage of development, the ecosystem is Growing and Conserving; in its second stage, it is Preserving. Point A represents the state of traditionally harvested agricultural lands and pastures. B is the situation created by chemical agriculture (Administration), e.g. the Green Revolution. C is the area into which the ecosystem is guided by natural agriculture (Conservation) e.g. the One Straw Revolution.

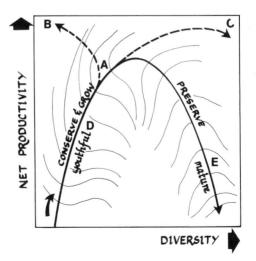

The decision to convert the land to a Eucalyptus plantation for fuelwood would Administer the system to the Growth (boom) state B. Preservation by fencing the site would allow the system to mature into stable Homeostasis E. By a well-designed mix of compatible uses, such as recreation, fuel-generation, aquaculture, cropping, land-fill and protection, the area can be Conserved into a Developing system C, which is likely to be more sustainable than most other options.

Incidentally, the generality of this method is demonstrable by a completely different example to which this figure applies, where B represents the "Green Revolution" in the Punjab, C the "no-till agriculture" of Wijewardene in Sri Lanka or the "One Straw Revolution" of Fukuoka in Japan, and the slash-and-burn of Papua New Guinea tribes.

Do the requirements of sustainability imply static states in the X-Y plane? A more detailed analysis shows that a single "solution" which can be represented by a static point on the X-Y plane rarely satisfies the conditions of sustainable development. Generalising the concept of resonating states alluded to earlier in the discussion on design, it is likely that good design draws strength from the particular advantages of each of several possible states. It is for this reason that while the upper right corner might appear, to development-oriented conservationists, to represent the ideal to be aimed for, often a more sustainable situation exists in the form of a stable combination of states some distance from this corner.

A Model for Decision-Making

In arriving at a decision, the decision-maker needs to have some concept of what the present state of the variables (issues) to be acted upon is, the possible states to which they should be transformed, and the options available to achieve this transformation.

In a simplified but useful scheme this may be represented in symbolic terms as:

where A is the present state, Z is the desired future state, and T is the set of transformation process options available to the decisionmaker. f is the feedback of information on system performance.

Needless, to say, the realities of decision-making are quite complex, and the present model must be understood within their context. Each of the above symbols, and the dynamic links which connect them can, in fact, represent such complexity.

First, the present state, A, comprises a host of variables A(i), many of which may be relevant to the decision at hand. Furthermore, each component A(i) is a dynamic variable, changing with time and circumstances.

Second, the desired future is also a set of variables Z(j), themselves evolving over time with changes in perception, aspiration and understanding of the resource base.

Third, the transformation process cannot be a single intervention, but rather a matrix of interventions $T(i, j)$ which together define a reliable path from the $A(i)$ to the $Z(j)$.

Fourth, and perhaps most important, development-related decisions can rarely take society directly from its existing state to the final one, but rather through a series of intermediate states, say B, C, D, ...W, X whose sequence may not be obvious, but must be understood by designers and decision-makers if they are at some point to achieve their goals.

Thus the limitations of this model should be recognised. However, even in such a simplified form, this model is helpful in identifying the information and methodological needs of the designer, especially when visualised on the X-Y plane.

THE DESIGNER AS A PROFESSIONAL

Why should the designer subscribe to the values of sustainable development, for which the tools described above have been designed? Ultimately, the answer to this question lies in the values held by society, and in how well its educational and reward systems help the designer incorporate these values into his own.

Sustainable development on a global scale can only be achieved if each society chooses development options which respond to its aspirations and needs within the opportunities and constraints of its resources. Countries of

the Third World have now, therefore, to evolve their design priorities in the light of their own realities, instead of continuing to use borrowed ones either from other traditions whose context is entirely different, or from former colonial masters whose aim was to exploit resources, not conserve them. It is for this reason that self-reliance, the capacity to choose and design one's own future, becomes a necessary precondition for sustainable development. In other words, a country must be able to formulate clear concepts in its own terms regarding A, Z and T.

The more advanced economies have been relatively successful in understanding A, and in developing their responses T. The environmental *problématique* has now increasingly brought home to them the need to define more explicitly and carefully their future choices, Z.

In developing countries, particularly those with a national planning machinery, the situation is largely reversed. Many of them have been able to formulate a reasonably clear (although not necessarily appropriate) idea of where they wish to go, but they neither have adequate access to information regarding their present resources or needs, A, or regarding the means to transform these to the desired state, T.

For a society to design its development path, in other words, to formulate its own A, Z and T, it must build new kinds of institutions which deal with administrative, scientific, and technical issues. Foremost among these is the need of all societies to establish responsive systems for education, information exchange and research. In this effort, it is the more powerful agents of change, and particularly the design professions which must play a leadership role.

In both developed and developing contries, the existing professional systems tend to legitimise design practices which are:

* **Sub-optimal**: The designer operates with a narrow design brief to satisfy his client, even if that means consciously or unconsciously sub-optimising the larger system in which he works;

* **non-systemic**: The designer is not expected to anticipate, adapt, or innovate for changed circumstances or threshold effects, and he can acceptably blame these on "chance;"

* **non-collaborative**: The designer does not consult other specialists, nor offer his special knowledge to them, either because of contractual obligation or professional insecurity;

* **non-participatory**: The designer avoids participation of manufacturers, users, and operators of his products and society at large by claiming to know better, to save costs, or simply to avoid information overload. He also cuts off longer-term feedback loops, since his design brief is generally narrow and short-term;

* **unsustainable**: The designer does not work for a term longer than or a frame of reference larger than that given by his immediate client. He need not take the burden of acting on behalf of a future society for a sustainable future.

Some good design practices, on the other hand, discouraged by the existing professional systems are: giving priority to societal and environmental values; designing for variety; designing through collaboration and participation.

As shown by three centuries of Western science, a reward system administered by the pressure of peers is perhaps the most effective way to ensure quality and integrity, without hurting creativity. But even the scientist has not been totally successful in internalising societal values into his enterprise. What both the scientific and design communities now have to develop are value systems, enforced if possible by their own internal mechanisms, to ensure that their work does not undermine the objectives of the wider society within which they operate, but rather reinforces them.

What are the rewards (or punishments) which motivate the individual designer? In a developing country, they certainly include, in rough order of influence, job opportunities (or loss of them), publication in the scholarly press (or non-publication), development of personal and intellectual integrity (or its erosion). Probably at a lower level, but still important, is recognition by various constituencies ranging from government, actual or potential clients, peer groups and the public.

CONCLUSIONS

National conservation strategies are but one of the types of action needed to make the precepts of sustainability integral parts of the development process. Other, complementary approaches are also needed which develop the capacity of societies at all levels to design their own, more sustainable future.

The interlinkages and complexities of environmental issues cannot be dealt with by the prevailing knowledge systems, which are based on compartmentalised disciplines unable to deal with the totality of a natural or social system. While the need for multi-sectoral, trans-disciplinary, and cross-cutting approaches has been a commonplace statement for some decades, the exigencies of designing for sustainable development makes this, perhaps for the first time, a concrete imperative.

Educational institutions responsible for professional training in some developing countries are beginning to recognise this, and to make provision for a broader education, but the process has a long way to go. A central component of the education of an environmental designer will necessarily have to stress the ethical basis of his responsibility as a professional.

No doubt the process of shifting educational objectives will be accelerated as the demand for broad spectrum but technically competent designers grows.

Throughout the world, and more particularly in the developing countries, there is an urgent need to reorient the design professions so as to make them more responsive to social reality, and more attractive to the most creative minds. When the professional institutions, such as the value and reward systems, succeed in reorienting the designer's basic approach toward issues of sustainability, the types of tools developed in this paper become useful, and even necessary. They might even be of some help in designing the institutions themselves.

SUSTAINABLE DEVELOPMENT IN THE NORTHERN CIRCUMPOLAR WORLD

Robert F. Keith
University of Waterloo
Waterloo, Ontario, Canada

Mary Simon
Makivik Corporation
Montreal, Quebec, Canada

SUMMARY The circumpolar world supports small indigenous societies that depend on the traditional harvesting of wildlife. Section I of this paper explores lessons learned from political controversy concerning resource development in this region, and draws conclusions about what development and conservation strategies will most likely contribute to the goals of sustainable development. Exclusion of local peoples from the decision-making process for both development and conservation initiatives will lead to rejection and failure of these initiatives. Had the circumpolar nations seen their "norths" as part of a distinct region rather than as unique domestic hinterlands, they could have learned from one anothers' experiences, avoided imposing "southern" national patterns of development and conservation, and avoided unnecessary political controversy. Section II contributes an Inuit perspective on these themes. It emphasises the need to understand and to integrate aboriginal ways of life into the World Conservation Strategy, and the increasing role and activities of indigenous peoples in international affairs.

SECTION I: DEVELOPMENT STRATEGIES, CONSERVATION AND POLITICAL PERSPECTIVES

Introduction and Setting

In international debates surrounding global development issues, the word "north" has come to mean "developed," and the word "south" to mean "un-" or "underdeveloped." Yet, within the wealthiest of the developed nations, the domestic connotations of these two words is reversed. In nations such as Canada, the United States (Alaska), Denmark (Greenland), and Norway, the "south" is the highly populated and industrialised metropolitan region containing most of those nations' political and economic power. The "north," by contrast, refers to the remote hinterlands "laden with resources." In these regions, small culturally-distinct populations live a less-privileged and influential life, still based in large part on the traditional hunting, fishing and trapping that have sustained them since time immemorial.

The northern circumpolar world consists of the top of the world, i.e. those regions commonly referred to as

"Arctic" and "the sub-arctic." There are no fixed physical or geographical coordinates that define the circumpolar world; the region may be defined differently depending on whether one is using climate, vegetation, wildlife, or cultural distinctiveness as reference points. For our purposes, the area under discussion includes Alaska, the northern half of Canada, Greenland, northern Scandinavia, and the tundra regions of the Soviet Union. The center of the circumpolar world is the Arctic Ocean, covered for much of its area by a permanent ice cap. Until this century, much of the circumpolar world was virtually inaccessible and regular communication within the region was all but non-existent. But it is far from being the empty, useless wasteland it is often assumed to be.

The climatic pattern of the entire northern hemisphere is largely determined in this region. While circumpolar ecosystems are far simpler than those in temperate and tropical regions, they are rich in minerals and deposits of oil and gas. Arctic Quebec and northern Norway are important sources of hydroelectric power for areas to the south. The entire circumpolar region is of great military and strategic importance, for the Soviet Union and NATO countries face each other directly across the North Pole.

The circumpolar world is also a homeland, or more correctly, a series of homelands. Peoples such as the Indians and Inupiat of Alaska, the Indians, Dene, and Inuit of Canada; the Inuit of Greenland; the Sami of northern Scandinavia; and the "Small Peoples" of the Soviet Union co-exist, in various degrees of harmony, with the majority populations of nations to which these regions belong. Their

populations may be small, but these northern aboriginal peoples are still the majority in many regions of the circumpolar north and exert an important political and economic influence. Few still pursue an exclusively subsistence lifestyle such as pre-dated their "discovery" by southern societies, but most continue to rely heavily on traditional hunting, fishing, trapping and herding to support their communities, to provide the bulk of their nutritional needs, and to provide a modest cash income.

Environmental sensitivities of the circumpolar world stem largely from its low carrying capacity and wildlife populations. Because of its severe climate, the region has limited ability to recuperate from environmental damage or to absorb pollutants. Vegetation grows slowly and therefore the herbivorous wildlife of the region, including huge caribou herds, muskox, and (domesticated) reindeer, must migrate great distances to find food. Before the northern circumpolar peoples came into contact with "southern" societies, they led a nomadic existence, following the wildlife upon which they depended for survival.

Environmental characteristics of the circumpolar region, having led to the wide dispersal of human settlements, also require that local resources (primarily fish and wildlife) continue to play an important role in sustainable development. Until recently, northerners were almost completely dependent on wildlife for their basic needs. A nomadic existence, low population density, and periodic starvation ensured an equilibrium between man and nature. The establishment of permanent settlements, rising populations, and adoption of industrial technologies are now up-setting this equilibrium, creating the need to manage wildlife more actively and to find new patterns of sustainable development that support less limited and harsh lifestyles.

During the past 15 years, much of the circumpolar world has experienced bitter conflicts between northern peoples and southern national governments over the development of renewable and non-renewable resources.[1] In the late 1960s and early 1970s a combination of high prices for resources on international markets, the search for secure sources of energy in developed countries, and improvements in technology made large-scale extraction and development of northern minerals, oil, gas, and hydro-electric power both feasible and profitable. The discovery of oil at Prudhoe Bay, Alaska; the plans to build a large-diameter pipeline through the Mackenzie Valley in Canada; the proposal to transport liquified natural gas by tankers through the Northwest Passage; the opening of Black Angel mine in Greenland; and the James Bay (Quebec) and Alta River (Norway) hydro-electric projects all served to warn circumpolar peoples that southern pressures were about to increase dramatically on northern resources. These projects gave rise to fears that the effects of development would damage the delicate northern environment and wildlife upon which these peoples rely.

The immediate effect of each of these initiatives was to push the hitherto unor-ganised northern peoples to organise and protest. In some cases developments were halted or changed substantially, while in other cases the protest had no effect. But in all cases the disputes received considerable national attention and generated much sympathy for northern peoples. Much official attention was diverted by national governments toward finding appropriate development patterns for these regions which would balance the national need for northern resources with that to protect the northern environment and respect the rights of northerners.

In some circumpolar regions, disputes over resource management have been more or less settled. While Greenland has settled a number of its disputes with Denmark, there has been strong resistance to tourism development. Inuit have feared that tourism debases traditional cultural values and can destroy the environment. On the other hand, some planners have come to see that the very pristine quality of the arctic environment and the breathtaking beauty of Greenland's coast, as well as the unique blend of traditional and modern elements in the society and the prolific artwork produced, are themselves attractions to foreign visitors of the sort who would not wish to see these lost. Thus Greenland authorities are now looking at the possibilities with new vision in their search for sustainable economic activity and job-creation.

In northern Norway, inland Sami reindeer herding, as opposed to the mixed

1 Contacts between the northern peoples of the Soviet Union and the rest of the circumpolar world have been few and sporadic and therefore the remainder of this paper addresses the non-Soviet circumpolar north. There are encouraging signs that cooperation and exchange among the northern nations will increase in the future, and it is to be hoped that the Soviet experience in its north can contribute to how these regional challenges are approached.

(fishing, farming, gathering) lifestyle of coastal Sami, has become an item of controversy in the heart of an ancient culture due to development pressures. As habitat is lost and providing a living from traditional sources becomes harder, political tensions rise between different Sami groups. This has created a highly unstable situation in which governments and special commissions, attempting to provide a better framework for respect of Sami culture and aboriginal rights, are bemused. Both coastal and inland interests have demanded strong new protections for their livelihoods, but an overall social and political settlement in the region seems more difficult than ever.

In Alaska the search for a comprehensive management plan for the Inupiat lands of the North Slope was long and difficult. It was marked by high degrees of tension between the local people on one side and industry and government on the other. Through creation of their own "home rule," borough government for their homeland, the people were able to develop a comprehensive coastal zone and borough-wide plan. In a process which involved public hearings, local research, planning workshop sessions, the rejection of plans at higher levels and a return to the drawing board, the people learned a great deal about the needs and interests of industry and government, while other forces learned much about the legitimate concerns of Inupiat for the living environment. Today, much more understanding and mutual support characterises development planning on the North Slope. Local people receive significant benefits through revenues accruing to their borough government, through employment opportunities and the new

skills brought by large industry. The era of confrontation and direct opposition which stopped development and sometimes halted the borough government itself, has ended. Yet those years of conflict generated a great deal of valuable scientific research which might never have otherwise been undertaken.

The experiences of northern peoples in all these regions are similar enough to establish a regional pattern of conflict over development and conservation and to invite hypotheses about which development and conservation strategies work in the circumpolar world and which do not. Most northern peoples find the phrase "sustainable development" meaningful and attractive in the context of their needs. The Inuit Circumpolar Conference, which represents the Inuit of Canada, Alaska, and Greenland, has officially endorsed the World Conservation Strategy, albeit with some reservations. The circumpolar world offers some important insights into what the phrase "sustainable development" means in remote regions where renewable resources support culturally-unique populations.

Development Strategies in the Circumpolar World

Development driven by national and international demand for arctic resources could play an important role in economic development and a sustainable livelihood for northern peoples. Oil and gas exploration and production in Alaska and Canada, base metal mining in the arctic islands of Canada, commercial fishing in the waters off Greenland, and hydroelectric power generation in Canada and northern Norway are examples of such development. Most of these activities have been supported by national governments.

Because of the limited ability of wildlife to support growing populations and modern lifestyles, externally initiated development is an important part of the mix of economic activities necessary for sustainable development in the circumpolar north. However, such development has important implications for conservation. Whether such development in northern regions can be made compatible with the goals of conservation will, at least in part, be a function of the scale and timing of development.

Until the recent decline in prices on international resource markets, externally-driven resource development proposals in the circumpolar region have tended to involve large-scale projects, constructed, or intended to be constructed, over relatively short periods of time. Examples include the Mackenzie Valley pipeline in Canada, the large-diameter Alyeska oil pipeline in Alaska, the James Bay hydro-electric development in Quebec, Canada, and the proposed Alta River hydro-electric development in Norway. Resource industries and governments both have argued that the remoteness of arctic and sub-arctic resources from southern markets requires that economies of scale be utilised and that development proceeds rapidly once the resource potential of an area has been proven.

However economically sound such arguments may have been (and in the case of many proposals for oil, gas, and mineral development they were eventually proven unsound), in all circumpolar nations these large-scale proposals were met with forceful opposition from northern peoples and con-

servationists. The striking feature of this opposition was its frequent success in delaying or even halting the projects despite millions of dollars spent by industry on preparatory research and official support from governments. Promises of jobs and benefits for local people, elaborate environmental assessment processes, and large investments in environmental studies and technologies for habitat protection or rehabilitation, were not sufficient to allay fears of major environmental and social damage. These projects were seen by many northern peoples as too large and too short-lived to have positive benefits sufficient to outweigh the perceived high risks. Consequently, the delays and failures in implementing these projects were costly and politically divisive.

An alternative to large-scale, quickly constructed projects is those undertakings which are smaller in scale, are phased over a longer period of time, offer fewer apparent risks and provide greater social learning. It may be helpful to compare and contrast a number of characteristics of large-scale short-term construction developments in the north with those of smaller-scale, phased projects in order to suggest a broader strategy for sustainable development. Key characteristics are: risk associated with development; duration of benefits; distribution of benefits and costs; and level of conflict.

Risk can be divided into four categories: environmental, social, technological, and financial. Environmental risk involves pollution, loss of wildlife habitats and disturbance of arctic marine species. These risks are borne directly by local residents but indirectly by the international community because of the global importance of the

Arctic. Social risks are borne by local residents in the form of loss of livelihood or creation of community related social problems. Technological risks associated with the use of new, unproven technnologies are borne by the developer and by the environment; financial risks are borne by investors.

How do the risks of large- and small-scale, phased development strategies compare? Two projects may provide useful insights.

Mackenzie Valley Pipeline Project

In the early 1970s, a consortium of Canadian and United States oil and pipeline companies proposed a large-diameter pipeline to transport natural gas from Alaska to southern Canadian and United States markets. The proposed route was through the valley of the Mackenzie River, the largest Canadian river flowing into the Arctic Ocean. Small communities throughout the valley were populated largely by indigenous Indian and Inuit peoples. Many millions of dollars were spent on feasibility studies, engineering designs, and environmental studies before an independent government-sponsored inquiry recommended a 10-year moratorium on development in the Mackenzie Valley. The National Energy Board of Canada rejected the pipeline proposal, supporting recommendations of the inquiry. Its reasons for rejecting the proposal were the potential environmental and social risks of the project to native peoples and their traditional resources, such as caribou, along the pipeline route. The communities in the valley were unprepared for such a large-scale development and were negotiating a legal agreement with the Canadian government on the recognition of land rights and the protection of their tradi-

tional ways of life. These "land claims" were intended to determine ownership and rights of use for land and resources on those lands that had been traditionally used by the native peoples. The project was also seen to threaten the Porcupine Caribou herd of Yukon Territory, an international wildlife resource.

In the end, government regulatory authorities concluded that the social and environmental risks outweighed the purported economic benefits expected of the project. Most instructive, however, is that three years after the project was turned down, it became apparent that the pipeline would not have been economically viable because of a worldwide surplus of natural gas. In retrospect, developers could see that the financial risks of the project had been far greater than they had anticipated.

The Mackenzie Valley Pipeline project brought to light an important argument in favour of smaller-scale, phased development: The level of financial risk often converges with the high level of environmental and social risk which is associated with large-scale, single effort projects in the remote circumpolar region. For reasons of less financial risk together with preferences of local residents and national and northern conservation interests, developers and investors often favour smaller-scale, phased projects with more manageable environmental and social impacts.

Norman Wells Pipeline Project

A proposal for a smaller-scale oil pipeline along the southern part of the Mackenzie River Valley was put forward by Esso Resources Ltd. at approximately the same time as it became apparent that the Mackenzie Valley gas pipeline was not financially viable. The proposed pipeline, known as the Norman Wells Pipeline, was intended as the first phase of what might eventually become a multi-phase oil development in the Mackenzie Valley. The proposal offered lower technological, social and environmental risks because of its smaller-scale and because the first phase was to be built in an area considered less environmentally-sensitive than the Mackenzie Delta and lower river valley.

The smaller-scale would result in less social disturbance because the influx of outside workers from the south would be substantially smaller. Perhaps most importantly, the project offered an opportunity to test sub-arctic pipeline technology. Considerable effort was made by the developer and government regulatory agencies to design and implement environmental and social monitoring procedures in the project construction and operation phases. The opportunity for all interests - local residents, government, and industry - to learn from experience and use the results of monitoring to make decisions about future development was crucial to the usefulness and acceptance of the phased development approach. Advantages accrue to all interests. For the developer, considerably lower financial risk provides the incentive for phased development. Phased development reduces risks to the environment and to people. This sharing of interest in a common development strategy provides a strong driving force for its adoption in the circumpolar region.

The Norman Wells Pipeline proposal was not immediately accepted by nearby Dene Indian communities. It was, and still is, controversial to some de-gree, particularly with respect to the involvement of the Dene communities in decisions relating to the construction and monitoring of the project. Yet the project has served to allay some of the more dramatic fears of the consequences of oil and gas development in the Canadian North. Moreover, the small scale of the project has opened new opportunities for Northern participation in non-renewable resource development, through jobs and training and through joint ventures between Esso and Dene-owned corporations.

Main Characteristics of Alternative Circumpolar Development Strategies

The smaller risks and greater opportunities for local participation in phased developments like the Norman Wells Pipeline serve to increase the acceptability of externally-driven development in the northern regions and to show northern peoples that such development can play an important role in a sustainable, mixed economy. The duration of the flow of benefits from development is a second key factor in a project's acceptability. In the past, national planning policies and large-scale development projects have led to a "boom and bust" cycle in the northern areas of circumpolar countries, characterised by a large influx of capital, technology, and workers from the developed south, temporary inflation, a short period of construction or of non-renewable resource extraction, and the subsequent collapse of the economies of communities that had rapidly become reliant on the short-lived prosperity.

Pipeline, mining and hydro-electric developments have all followed this pattern. Phased development, however, permits non-renewable resources to be extracted over a longer period of time, contributing to a more sustainable economy and wiser utilisation of the resources.

The third characteristic of alternative circumpolar development strategies is the distribution of benefits. A majority of the benefits from large-scale, externally driven development accrue to the developed southern parts of circumpolar countries in the form of energy and mineral products and profits. Social and environmental risks and costs are incurred in the north. Smaller-scale, phased developments provide opportunities for increased local benefit through greater local participation in various aspects of the project and retention (rather than leakage) of project related monies.

The final characteristic of alternative development strategies that we will consider here is the degree of conflict created by development. Conflict between northern peoples, developers, and governments has been an important aspect of most large-scale development proposals in the circumpolar region.

Development projects such as the Alyeska pipeline in Alaska and the James Bay Hydro Development in Quebec, although ultimately realised, caused northern Indian and Inuit in the surrounding regions to organise an effective, strong opposition and contest the projects in court. Other projects such as the Mackenzie Valley Pipeline, the Alta River hydro-electric proposal in northern Norway and the Arctic Pilot Project (a Canadian proposal to ship liquified natural gas from Arctic Canada to Europe causing an international circumpolar incident) were eventually refused by government regulatory bodies, stalled, or abandoned, at

least in part because of the opposition of northern peoples.

Externally-driven developments that are small-scale and phased will not be automatically welcomed by circumpolar peoples, but the reduced environmental risks and the greater benefits accruing to the project region help to increase perceptions among northern peoples that they have the potential to contribute to a sustained economic future in the region. Perhaps more important, however, is the central involvement of circumpolar peoples in development project planning, approval, and monitoring. In this regard, the attitude of northern peoples who have secured some legal right to participate in the decision-making process for development projects is markedly different from those still fighting for such recognition.

In Alaska and Canada, the settlement of aboriginal land claims recognised secure land rights and provided large amounts of capital to the aboriginal groups. In some cases, these settlements have created decision-making structures that gave the aboriginal claimants a right to participate in decisions on development. The exercise of these rights has led to a sense of security and influence among the aboriginal claimants, who are more interested in participating in externally-driven development than those aboriginal groups still seeking settlements. The Greenland Home Rule Government (representing a population of 80 percent Inuit, or Greenlander), has recently supported exploratory drilling for oil in an environmentally-sensitive region in East Greenland. The power Greenlanders won under the 1978 Home Rule arrangement allows them to control most aspects of this kind of development and to set regulations that reflect the extremely high sensitivity Greenlanders felt about environmental issues. The Home Rule government was implacably opposed to the Canadian Arctic Pilot Project, about which they were consulted very little. The fierce and violent opposition of the Sami of northern Norway to the Alta River proposal can be explained in part by the little formal influence the Samis have in a highly centralised national decision-making process.

Because the indigenous populations of the circumpolar world are small, national governments of the circumpolar nations tend to view their concerns as secondary to a "national" interest that supports large-scale, short-term resource extraction projects. This approach has been proven false, shortsighted, and wasteful many times over in the past 15 years. The circumpolar world is a distinct geographical, environmental, and cultural region. There are many similarities in the development strategies of circumpolar nations and in their "we" versus "they" attitudes to northern development conflicts. Their shared experiences demonstrate that regional development strategies aiming to sustain development in northern regions ultimately serve national, as well as northern, interests.

Southern and Northern Approaches to Conservation

The political and social stresses that have existed throughout the northern circumpolar world for the past 15 years cannot be attributed entirely to ill-conceived and inappropriate industrial development initiatives. It is true that large-scale resource developments planned and driven by southern interests were the catalysts for northern peoples' political organisation and opposition in Alaska, Greenland, northern Canada, and northern Norway, and that these peoples responded first with concerns about the threat of large development projects to the delicate renewable resource base upon which they traditionally based their livelihoods. However, as the larger "southern" societies moved to address the environmental concerns of northerners by proposing various mitigative measures, policies, and conservation initiatives, it became increasingly apparent that northerners' concerns were more far-reaching. They objected to their exclusion from the decision-making processes that guided industrial development projects, as well as entire development strategies. In many cases, northerners were no more receptive to southern instigated conservation initiatives and processes than to the development projects that spawned them.

The phrases "externally driven" and "southern-driven" development suggest a monolithic imperative overwhelming the circumpolar regions with a single-minded resolve to develop northern resources at all costs. This simplistic characterisation ignores the importance of conservation and the environmental ethic in most nations constituting the circumpolar world. In most cases, "southern-driven" development initiatives in the circumpolar region were opposed or contested by southern environmental interests. These can be defined broadly to include not only non-government conservation groups but also national government officials and politicians responsible for protecting the environment and wildlife in the northern regions of their respective nations.

The setting aside of conservation areas, such as national parks and wildlife preserves, and centralised planning policies were the initial principal goals of those who feared the consequences of widespread, large-scale industrial development in the North. In some regions, such as the Yukon and Alaskan North Slopes, Lancaster Sound in the eastern Canadian Arctic, and eastern Greenland, the setting aside of lands for conservation became national causes that thwarted or modified industrial plans to extract oil and gas.

A second thrust of "national" environmental efforts to protect the circumpolar regions, especially in North America, was the attempt to implement land-use planning and coastal zone management policies in marine areas. These were seen as vehicles through which some semblance of order could be given to industrial development, either by designating various land and water uses before industrial projects were proposed or by establishing regulatory regimes through which approvals for industrial projects must be sought. The idea was to find some way to protect the environment from the cumulative efforts of numerous unplanned *ad hoc* developments.

Centralised planning policies and initiatives to set aside protected areas were seen by their proponents as responding both to protests of northern peoples and to national concerns. However, as the conservation versus development debate continued into the 1980s, it became apparent that circumpolar peoples, especially northern aboriginal peoples, were as resistant to southern conservation strategies as to southern

industrial imperatives. Neither seemed compatible with the future that northern peoples were seeking to guarantee for themselves, i.e. the sustainable utilisation of all resources to the advantage of their communities.

The preservationist philosophy that underlies the setting aside of national parks, wildlife preserves, and other conservation areas is, in itself, foreign to northern peoples who regard themselves and their activities as an integral part of the environment that sustains them. In Canada and Alaska, northern aboriginal peoples have fought many battles with public officials seeking to set aside as much land as possible as a check on or complement to large-scale industrial development. In Canada, the establishment of Wood Buffalo National Park caused bitter relations for years between the Dene of the South Mackenzie River, and Parks Canada, the national parks agency, over the question of aboriginal hunting rights. Disputes such as this eventually led to a change in Canada's national park policy for the North, to permit aboriginal hunting and trapping in parks. But as recently as last winter, the Inuit of the Eastern Arctic withdrew their support for a new park in Ellesmere Island to protest against bureaucratic interference with their land claims negotiations. In Alaska, disputes between native peoples and those seeking to create parks and to withdraw lands for conservation have resulted in unusual alliances between oil companies and aboriginal peoples to oppose such withdrawal of lands. Both groups are fighting for access to resources, even if the uses may be incompatible.

In Canada, two aboriginal organisations (the Dene Nation and the Inuit

Tapirisat of Canada) are advocating an innovative mechanism for their involvement in wildlife management through land claims negotiations and through discussions concerning aboriginal rights in the Constitution. The principal element of this mechanism would be a joint government-native wildlife management board that would make all management decisions in the claims area. This approach has four important characteristics:

* The boards would be bound to operate according to conservation principles. The preliminary agreement establishing the Inuit board refers to the World Conservation Strategy.

* The management regime to be established would be more comprehensive than existing government requirements which are divided sectorally and sometimes limited goegraphically. Proponents of this approach, which the Canadian government recently endorsed, have pointed to practical, as well as aboriginal, reasons to institute joint management boards.

* Current government regulations are often difficult to enforce because northern people have had limited input in their preparation.

* Local users have an incentive to manage wildlife resources prudently because they stand to benefit or suffer most directly from their decisions.

The desire of northerners, particularly native northerners, to share fully in wildlife management should not be seen as an atavistic urge to recreate a traditional lifestyle. Tomorrow's local-ly-controlled, renewable resource economy will only faintly resemble yesterday's subsistence economy. The modern renewable economy no longer exists in isolation: it is becoming integrated in broader national economies from which it derives support either through transfer payments or wage employment. The renewable resource economy also depends on trade to procure the goods (guns, fuel, food, etc.) needed to support it.

It is important to understand that conflicts between northern peoples and those seeking to implement conservation strategies are not merely philosophical. The behaviour of public officials - most notably of wildlife biologists and marine biologists - in conservation debates and disputes often displays a detached arrogance, offensive to northern aboriginal peoples by its insistence on Western scientific methods as the sole measure of accuracy and a thinly veiled disdain for traditional knowledge of northern people. Dr. Peter Usher, a Canadian consultant, has written extensively on the pressures that lead professional wildlife managers to distance themselves from the human milieu in which they operate, and eventually to oppose the interests of northern aboriginal peoples. They defend a competing and antithetical system of knowledge that is not only inaccessible to northern peoples, but is used as a tool to interfere with their traditional livelihoods.

In 1982, the Inuit of the south-central Canadian Arctic were pressured to restrict their annual kill of caribou because government officials claimed that herds were declining sharply. Their protests and assertions that these government officials had underestimated the size of the herd went unheeded, until the following year's count proved that the restrictions had been unnecessary. Incidents such as this lead to years of bitterness and northerners' resistance to "official" wildlife management schemes.

Conflicts between traditional and modern systems of knowledge have probably done more to discredit conservation efforts in the circumpolar regions than any other factor. For years the gap seemed insurmountable, but recently the northern peoples themselves have begun taking exciting initiatives to make competing systems support each other. Makivik Corporation, which represents the Inuit of Arctic Quebec, has established two research centres where young Inuit are being trained in modern research techniques integrated with traditional knowledge. These and other experiments offer an important source of experience and expertise to implementors of the World Conservation Strategy in areas where populations seek a modern existence based upon traditional lifestyles.

That conservation, or more properly, conservationists, can oppose sustainable development in remote, resource-based regions is evident from the damage caused in the circumpolar world by the worldwide anti-harvesting movement. Obstruction of the world market for seal pelts has had catastrophic consequences in communities in Alaska, the Canadian Eastern Arctic, and Greenland. Resolute Bay in the High Canadian Arctic saw its cash income from seal pelts drop from just over $50,000 (CDN) in 1982 to about $1000 (CDN) in 1983.

The worldwide anti-trapping campaign led to the formation of "Indigenous Survival International," an international body of northern aboriginal groups from Alaska, Canada, and Greenland, to defend traditional hunting and trapping economies threatened by this new movement. For the peoples of the circumpolar world, the anti-harvesting movement is a direct attack on their very existence as unique societies trying to forge a link between traditional subsistence lifestyles and the current economic limitations and demands of their communities. The northern economy has always been based on renewable resources and will be for the foreseeable future. The anti-harvesting movement has left unanswered the most basic question of how these people can lead other than a welfare existence without the commercial use of renewable resources.

For the northern peoples of the circumpolar world, the key to survival and social and economic well-being is sustainable development. The Inuit Circumpolar Conference has endorsed the World Conservation Strategy and is seeking to devise a comprehensive Arctic policy based upon it. The goal of sustainable development is not expressed merely in reaction to large-scale, externally-driven industrial development, but also to conservation ethics, practices, and strategies that leave northern peoples on the periphery of decision-making, that disdain their traditional knowledge, that seek to preserve rather than to conserve, and that attack the ethical basis of their existence. In our judgement, industry has come further in understanding and respecting the needs of northern aboriginal peoples than have the established conservation interests in the circumpolar nations.

Sustainable Futures Through Political Development

The northern circumpolar regions of Canada, Alaska and Scandinavian countries have passed through a turbulent period during the last 15 years. A political awakening of northern peoples in these countries grew, in all cases, from specific industrial proposals that were seen to threaten traditional lifestyles. That these small populations were so frequently successful in halting or modifying industrial development is a testament not only to the democratic nature of the circumpolar countries but to the tenacity and determination of the circumpolar peoples themselves. The political upsurge of northern peoples appears to be at an early stage with many more accommodations needed in national capitals before stability is ensured.

Development/conservation issues sparked this unrest, but neither national development nor national conservation strategies and initiatives have successfully resolved these resource-use conflicts in the circumpolar world. In all of these countries, the conservation concerns that motivated the original protest against development evolved quickly into political concerns, which are being addressed through political solutions such as Home Rule for Greenland, land claims settlements in Alaska, royal commissions in Norway, and a combination of land claims and constitutional negotiations in Canada. These processes are in many respects desirable, but they owe their existence in part to the failure of southern-based conservation strategies to answer the demands of remote, culturally-unique regions.

Circumpolar peoples are trying to build a sustainable future on an uncertain and variable resource base. They will require innovative technologies, training, and some integration of their economies with southern economies to succeed. Whether assistance to build their economies comes from development initiatives or conservation initiatives, it will meet with much resistance if the welfare of these peoples and their communities is not seen as a primary goal.

As in all regions of the world that share a common ecology, wildlife base, and cultural composition, there is a need in the circumpolar north for bilateral and multilateral cooperative efforts among the nations it comprises. Some needs, such as treaties governing polar bears, caribou, and other migratory species have been implemented or are being negotiated. But regional strategies should not be limited to this kind of cooperation. If the nations of the circumpolar world had seen their northern regions as part of a distinct international region rather than as hinterlands, it is possible that they would have been more attentive to the experiences of their neighbours, that they might have avoided protracted political disputes, and that they might have seen solutions to resource-use conflicts with more vision. These lessons are just beginning to be understood in the capitals of the circumpolar nations, but they are the bitter and unforgettable experiences of northern circumpolar peoples. Through initiatives such as the Inuit Circumpolar Conference and Indigenous Survival International, circumpolar peoples are exploring a regional approach to building a lasting and sustainable future.

SECTION II: AN INUIT PERSPECTIVE ON ACHIEVING SUSTAINABLE DEVELOPMENT

Introduction

This international forum provides a welcome opportunity for a wide range of interests to make their views known, and it enables us to focus on global and regional strategies. The central theme of this Conference is "Implementing the World Conservation Strategy." As this might suggest, there is a growing realisation of global interdependence. As a result, peoples and organisations everywhere are seeking new paths toward transnational consensus. The cross-cultural alliances, which are in the process of forming, will hopefully give new meaning to the basic principle of international cooperation. This could lead to more appropriate regional actions.

As an Inuk from northern Quebec, I would like to share with you an Inuit perspective on "Achieving Sustainable Development in Circumpolar and Other Regions." Although I will specifically refer to the Arctic, my remarks will at times go beyond the North and have broader application.

The main thrust of this presentation is as follows: many regional and global issues related to sustainable development can only be fairly and effectively dealt with if the emerging realities concerning indigenous peoples are taken fully into account. These issues, which involve the rights, status, customs and concerns of aboriginal peoples, cannot remain on the periphery. Nor can they be put aside.

In the Arctic and other regions inhabited substantially by aboriginal peoples, implementation of the World Conservation Strategy will only be successful if the status and concerns of distinct local peoples are respected. Existing perceptions and assumptions, on the part of non-native organisations and governments involved, will require re-evaluation.

Some of the principles I am emphasising are expressed or implied in the foregoing section. I would like to highlight some significant points from that discussion. In addition, I will briefly cover the following:

* the need to understand and appropriately integrate aboriginal subsistence activities and way of life into the World Conservation Strategy; and

* the increasing role and activities of indigenous peoples in international affairs. In particular, Inuit initiatives toward a transnational Arctic policy will be described.

Conservation and Sustainable Development

Harold J. Coolidge, Honorary President of the International Union for Conservation of Nature and Natural Resources (IUCN), wrote the following in favour of a sustainable future:

Conservation and development are not only compatible, they are two expressions of the same need - to keep the earth as a sustaining home.[2]"

---

2   See Foreword in Thibodeau and Field (ed.), *Sustaining Tomorrow: A Strategy for World Conservation and Development*, University Press of New England, Hanover, 1985.

For countless years, many Inuit and other native peoples have asserted virtually the same values and precepts in their own way. Too often developers and governments have violated aboriginal homelands. They have distorted the goals of development, so that they are neither equitable nor sustaining from the aboriginal point of view.

The previous section examines "sustainable development" in Arctic regions. It concludes that phased development is generally preferable to large-scale resource development projects driven by southern interests, and that notherners need to be included in decision-making processes. The reasons for favouring phased development include the following:

* the risks associated with such development are often lower for both the developer and local native communities;

* the duration of benefits to the northern region tends to be longer and may allow for more meaningful involvement by local peoples;

* the distribution of benefits and costs may well be more equitable from an aboriginal viewpoint; and

* the level of conflict between local populations and project proponents is likely to be reduced.

In addition to "equitable" and "sustainable" development, it is important to promote development that is "culturally-appropriate" to northern regions.

It is also worth noting that the United Nations has concluded that there is a strong relationship between human rights, peace and development. None of these objectives is said to be truly realisable in isolation from one another. Without greater use of the world's human, financial and material resources for peaceful and safe purposes, many efforts toward sound conservation and sustainable development may fall short.

The United Nations is working on evolving concepts such as the right to peace and the right to development. Although these emerging rights are highly complex and multi-dimensional, the World Conservation Strategy might eventually integrate principles of peace with those of conservation and development. These principles should also be applied at the regional level.

Aboriginal Subsistence and the World Conservation Strategy

In discussing sustainable development, one of the primary issues of concern to indigenous peoples is the lack of a clear, appropriate reference to aboriginal subsistence in the World Conservation Strategy. This omission not only affects regional strategies, but also has global implications that are serious and adverse.

Those who oppose such reference maintain that the Strategy must remain culturally neutral. As a result, it is said that no specific mention of aboriginal peoples and our traditional way of life is warranted. After all, everyone must be treated equally.

This perspective of equality and cultural neutrality does not appear to be justified. Equality does not always mean that all peoples must be treated the same. It is a well-known principle that in order to treat some peoples equally, we must treat them differently. Otherwise majorities would always oppress those lesser in number and the inevitable result would be assimilation.

Also, it is a fallacy to believe that continued inaction would be an act that is in any way neutral. The World Conservation Strategy is intended to be a comprehensive document. If it fails to recognise an important element of the global ecosystem, like aboriginal subsistence, there unfailingly occurs a subtle but definite devaluation of the activity itself. Inadvertently, you would help those who see the world in simplistic, absolute terms - those who seek to eliminate our food sources and traditional practices.

In explaining the World Conservation Strategy, some people have remarked that the Strategy's philosophy regarding conservation and development essentially applies an aboriginal perspective to all the world's people. If this is the case, it would be a sad irony that the global practices of indigenous peoples would at the same time be denied full and fair recognition within the Strategy itself.

Since time immemorial, native peoples throughout the world have engaged in traditional harvesting. These subsistence activities are clearly a part of our aboriginal rights. They are fundamental cultural and human rights, unique to indigenous peoples. As it is declared in the *International Bill of Rights,* "in no case may a people be deprived of its own means of subsistence."

The profound spiritual and cultural significance of our own means of subsistence and the intimate ties to conservation are not always well understood by outside observers. But all of these cultural, legal and other differences set us distinctly apart from other peoples.

The indigenous peoples of the world, and our relationship to the land and its renewable resources, merit appropriate inclusion in the World Conservation Strategy. Therefore, it is my hope that you will actively support efforts, at this Conference, to add a new section on indigenous peoples and our subsistence way of life.

Role and Activities of Indigenous Peoples in International Affairs

There are a number of key initiatives by aboriginal organisations at the international level that may be of interest to the Conference. These evolving elements could have a significant, positive impact on regional and global strategies, both present and future.

These new developments include the following:

* A possible new section for the World Conservation Strategy has been drafted by Indigenous Survival International (ISI) on native peoples and subsistence. ISI should be commended for its leadership and the vital work it has done in this area. The proposed text will be submitted to this Conference and to IUCN for further consideration;

* a "Body of Principles on Indigenous Rights" is being prepared by aboriginal organisations, in collaboration with the Geneva-based Working Group on Indigenous Populations. It is hoped that an international covenant will be adopted. The covenant would set international standards concerning the recognition of our rights and status as aboriginal peoples;

* an Inuit Regional Conservation Strategy is being formulated for

northern circumpolar regions. The Inuit Circumpolar Conference (ICC) is working closely with persons affiliated with IUCN, to elaborate a strategy appropriate to the Arctic and its peoples; and

* the future development of a comprehensive Arctic policy is being planned by Inuit from Canada, Alaska and Greenland. As a first step, draft principles for such a policy are currently being prepared under the direction of the Inuit Circumpolar Conference. Inuit will be reviewing these principles at the July 1986 General Assembly of the Inuit Circumpolar Conference to be held in Kotzebue, Alaska.

With regard to Arctic policy-making and international agreements, a growing number of issues affecting Inuit rights and interests are increasingly being regulated at the international level. Examples include ocean dumping, acid rain, arms control, fish, whales, migratory birds, endangered species and resource development in marine areas. In these and other instances, national or local initiatives alone are not adequate to protect Inuit communities and our northern regions.

If issues related to sustainable development in the North are to be properly addressed, it is essential to develop a comprehensive foreign and domestic Arctic policy. Too often, these two aspects lack sufficient coordination. In reference to foreign affairs, I and other Inuit fully appreciate the role of the national governments. However, when international agreements directly affect Inuit and the circumpolar regions, it is impor-

tant that we be more meaningfully involved. Such participation could readily be accommodated in at least the policy-making and implementation stages.

Conclusion

Increased international collaboration among indigenous peoples, governments and conservation organisations could be invaluable in planning for our global future. However, it would only seem fair that this cooperation be based on principles which recognise our fundamental rights and status as native peoples. Full and proper recognition must not be limited to regional approaches or strategies. Such rights and status should be clearly confirmed by organisations and governments at all levels.

Aboriginal cultures, practices and rights have existed for centuries. Yet, the actions of individuals and governments often seem to suggest that our presence and its implications are only an emerging reality.

If we are to attain our collective goals of sustainable development and a more secure future, each of us must be committed to learning from past mistakes and expanding our horizons. It is only in this way that we can help to build and maintain that delicate, crucial bridge of common understanding.

This paper is a joint presentation of the Canadian Arctic Resources Committee and the Inuit Circumpolar Conference. Section I was written for the Canadian Arctic Resources Committee by P. Burnet, F. Bregha, G. Green, P. Jull and R.F. Keith. Section II was written by Mary Simon.

ENVIRONMENT AND DEVELOPMENT IN LATIN AMERICA: TEN ISSUES

E. Leff[1]
Universidad Nacional Autonoma de Mexico
Mexico

The crucial problems of environment and development in Latin America can be summarised in the delineation of ten central issues. These are as follows:

* In Latin American countries, the present International Economic Order has led to a style of development which has caused ecosystem degradation and impoverishment of the majority of the population. Natural resources have been exploited in ways that have eliminated any possibility of natural recuperation. The style of development generated by this International Economic Order is established through the mediation of local social sectors which share the same benefits, passing on the growing social and environmental costs to majority sectors of the population.

* The financial mechanisms of the International Economic Order have deepened the structural crisis of the region. The most evident proof of this is the foreign debt. Raw materials are increasingly exported from Latin America in order to cover the high interest on an unpayable debt. The vast majority of Third World countries are in the same position and are gradually coming to realise that they are paying, to their own detriment, both the price of the highly industrialised countries' economic imbalance as well as the price of war economies, which inhibit development and threaten human existence.

* Latin America has sufficient natural resources to cover the basic needs of its population as well as sufficient human and ecological potential to sustain a development process. However, inadequate handling of its resources has led to the elimination or drastic alteration of its natural ecosystems throughout areas covering between 35 and 45 percent of the continent.

* Degradation of the environmental potential for development results, then,

1. This Manifesto is referenced to E. Leff on behalf of the Consortia of Latin American delegates.

not from excessive demographic pressure on the land, but from incorporating technological patterns based on a dependent, centralised, standardised style of development.

* Because the causes involved in the origin of environmental issues are complex, they should be seen as a set of interrelated natural and social processes. A structural diagnosis of their causes is therefore needed in order to find alternative solutions.

* The environment is seen as having productive potential in the context of a more egalitarian and sustainable alternative style of development, based on an integrated management of its ecological, technological and cultural resources. This perception of the environment contrasts with predominating ideas which see the environment as a limiting factor or as an available natural resource which will inevitably deteriorate as part of the cost of development. Latin America is thus beginning to develop its own way of thinking in relation to environmental issues.

* The emergent concept of sustainable development in Latin America transcends the limits of environmental policies, which are aimed at technical controls and prevention of specific eco-destructive effects. The sectoral analysis of some of these effects or of technical means to their solution (preventing acid rain, gene-

tic improvements, antipollution measures, etc.) prevents an integrated diagnosis of the causes of environmental degradation and does not allow for alternative processes capable of reversing the negative effects.

* In the emergent proposals, the productive system aims principally to satisfy the basic needs of the population and to improve the standard of living. This implies the need to substitute a new productive rationale, capable of bringing about both social and environmental benefits, for that of reaching the highest immediate profits.

* The implementation of this rationale implies scientific and technological policies which take into account the natural, social, economic and cultural conditions of each country or region in order to reach an integrated exploitation of its resources.

* Concrete solutions to environmental problems ultimately depend on a new organisational capacity of society as a whole, based on the cultural values of different communities, their creativity and their potential for innovation. Such solutions can only come about within a political framework which breaks with economic, ideological and technological dependence and promotes conditions for democratic and participatory management of resources.

FROM RELIEF TO REHABILITATION: THE CRISIS IN ENVIRONMENT AND DEVELOPMENT

David A. Munro[1]
Naivasha Consultants Ltd.
Sidney, B.C., Canada

SUMMARY This special session was planned in recognition of the African crisis in environment and development, manifested in extensive environmental degradation and widespread famine. Insufficient agriculture, severe shortages of fuelwood and water, and diminishing numbers of livestock and wildlife are indications that the crisis is continuing. The purpose of the session was to provide a forum for discussion of ways to surmount the crisis and minimise the possibility of recurrence. All of the participants have had personal experience with environment and development in Africa. Taken together, their assessments provide a comprehensive overview of factors giving rise to the African crisis.

The presentations recognised that a total systemic breakdown has occurred in arid and semi-arid parts of Africa, the product of a deteriorating ecological situation which is interwoven into broader economic, socio-cultural and political issues. Intensified human activities, population growth, and destruction of resources; the mounting debt crisis; institutional inadequacy; rural deterioration and urban migrations are all indicators of the continuing decline. The crisis has moreover been drought related, which has triggered a downward spiral of environmental degradation that has given Africa a different ecological character from earlier times. Experts now recognise that the interactions between man, society and political systems on one hand, and the environment on the other, have given the catastrophe its structural characteristics.

Certain historical trends show that in parts of the Sahel, roots of the crisis go back many centuries. Ecosystems of the West African Sahel have been depleted by interventions such as recurrent burning and the introduction of livestock. As well, the area suited to pastoralism has shrunk as a result of centuries of trans-Saharan caravan trade, which placed a continuing demand on fodder and fuelwood. Prevailing winds and the movements of

---

1. This summary includes reference to materials prepared by David Runnalls at the Sunday afternoon session.

wildlife and livestock during the dry season have displaced plant seeds southwards, without any compensating northward movement. This has caused a compression of the usable zone of the Sahel and thus greater intensification of use in that region. The introduction of firearms and later, open field cultivation - which replaced more complex, traditional agro-forestry systems - have also substantially contributed to environmental deterioration of the region.

The most immediate consideration, however, is the present inability of many African countries to produce sufficient food for their needs. Subsistence farming receives low priority and little support, while export crop cultivation has been encouraged. Many governmental agriculture departments have attempted to transplant agricultural systems from developed countries that have little to do with the socio-economic and ecological realities of Africa. Thus, anomolies continue to exist such as, at the height of the Sahelian crisis, several countries affected by the drought, whose inhabitants suffered from famine, continued to import grain and food relief while exporting large quantities of their own fish, ground nuts and other foodstuffs.

Increasing human populations and the consequent demands on resources constitute another immediate factor in environmental degradation. Arid areas of Africa, traditionally inhabited by pastoralists, cannot support settled land use; these pastoral areas cannot remain productive unless grazing pressure is spread out over time and space by periodic movements from place to place. Yet as a result of political boundaries established during the nineteenth cen-

tury partition of Africa, traditional movements of nomadic, pastoral people have been blocked. Ecological support systems have thus broken down, and with them, social systems have deteriorated.

New political organisations and forms of government have not taken root in tribal cultures of rural Africa. Governmental organs are not stable entities; they cannot respond to needs of the people, nor of the environment. People do not see these institutions as providing them with support and protection; they are rather something alien to their understanding and needs. In fact, people do not believe that outsiders are responding to their problems. Institutionalised famine relief, although based on humanitarian motives, is itself part of the problem. Aid which never ends is demoralising; it saps the will on which self-help depends.

Behind these aspects lies almost constant political instability, warfare and civil strife. Land which was once considered as developed has been degraded and abandoned as a result of armed conflict. Seeking a greater degree of security, many rural residents have moved to already overcrowded cities which lack the infrastructure to support the population influxes.

There was general agreement that the primary causes of the African crisis are political and economic, and that they produce both severe ecological and social distortions. This consensus represents a real advance. The need now is to move from an understanding of links between social and economic pressures and economic degradation to that of the need to integrate conservation and development, establishing a continuing partnership between the conservation and development communities.

Essential elements to any long-term solutions are: first, that these solutions must come from Africans themselves. Solutions proposed and implemented by outsiders have often been ill-adapted to African conditions. Furthermore, African governments have come a long way toward making the hard political choices necessary for rehabilitation. Both the Lagos Plan of Action and the series of concrete steps resulting from the recent meeting of African Environment Ministers bear witness to this effort.

Secondly, external donors have a major role to play in providing money and technical skills. However, caution must be exercised against returning to the large, capital-intensive projects of past years. Small community-based projects planned and managed by local people must be the target.

Thirdly, there is a need for trained technicians to learn from and adopt time-honoured, traditional agricultural methods; for instance, in the use of root crops rather than grains as foodstuffs, or in learning traditional grazing techniques. These techniques must be developed within the parameters of ecological stability.

* * * * *

Participants referred to a number of policy actions and activities that should be important elements in rehabilitation. The crisis is considered to offer a unique chance for change. But Africa is still at the survival stage. Rehabilitation will lead to a stage of equilibrium, and only from there can Africa hope to proceed on the path to development.

Developmental activities must take place within the parameters of ecological stability; economic planning must be oriented toward meeting people's needs. Policies and action must be centred on people, on households and their survival. The will to survive is the most powerful weapon in the arsenal of the poor, and should be used as a tool for rehabilitation. Human dignity, hope and trust must be restored, and the needs of the most vulnerable met.

Effective sustainable development policies in Africa must be rural development policies; policies directed to peoples' needs, not only to provide better incentives, knowledge and infrastructure, but also to enhance the overall attractiveness of rural life. Self-reliance is fundamental to any approach toward rehabilitation. Education and instruction are necessary for improved food production, health care, water usage, forestry and energy.

Broad policy instruments are required which emphasise decentralised decision-making and action at the grassroots level. Positive pricing and marketing policies for agricultural products, and extension and research programmes for providing credit are particularly important. And development expectations must be related to the environmental productive capability. The tendency to see development as a transformation of ecosystems should be replaced by recognising the complementarity of indigenous knowledge and Western science. In this way, rather than transforming systems, the strengths of local adaptations to ecosystems and the capabilities of the local human communities can be built upon. It has now been clearly demonstrated that development without conservation is limited, short-sighted and short-lived.

Specific programmes are fundamental to restoring critical ecological processes in the western Sahel. Development of shelter belts are particularly important and have been readily accepted by people of the region. There is an urgent need in certain areas to provide substitutes for charcoal or fuelwood for urban markets. Preservation of wetlands can provide the basis of support for dryland ecosystems as well as refuge areas in periods of stress. Major river systems and natural forests could be better managed.

The session concluded with recognition of the positive partnership which has developed between Africa and the international community in the rehabilitation process. The recent Canadian *Africa 2000* Programme, involving the Canadian International Development Agency in collaboration with other federal and provincial departments and NGOs, demonstrates one aspect of this partnership. The International Union for Conservation of Nature and Natural Resources (IUCN) is also adopting a network strategy in its African programme for small ecodevelopment projects in the Sahelian zone. The thrust of these initiatives will be to ensure proper integration be-

tween projects and that information derived from each is made broadly available. A second element of IUCN's approach will be to see that National Conservation Strategies are built-up from local networks of ecodevelopment projects. This will provide an opportunity for different organisations and professions to come together to ensure a truly cross-sectoral approach so necessary to achieving conservation. Continuing development efforts must be sustainable and systematic.

- *Special mention is made of the participants to this Session. Brief biographies have been included in Annex I with those of authors contributing to this volume.*

Mr. Geoffrey F. Bruce
The Hon. Mrs. Victoria Chitepo
Mr. Jeffrey Gritzner
The Hon. D. G. Lwanga
Dr. Walter Lusigi
Professor Adolfo Mascarenhas
Professor Ophelia Mascarenhas
Dr. David A. Munro
Professor Reuben Olembo
Mr. David Runnalls
Dr. Pierre Spitz
Dr. Maurice Strong

LOCAL STRATEGIES FOR SUSTAINABLE DEVELOPMENT

M. Taghi Farvar
IUCN Senior Advisor on Sustainable Development
Gland, Switzerland

SUMMARY *A number of examples are used in this article to show the emerging principles of ecodevelopment, which can be characterised as a strategy of local equitable and sustainable development. This means that people are involved in decision-making at the grassroots (community) level, relying primarily on local resources, community-based institutions and creativity. The entire process is meant to help meet their needs, on the basis of social justice and equity, in ways that protect the environment.*

This formulation implies a new approach to development, including the fundamental relationships between people and their environment. It also means finding new mechanisms for policy-making, designing, planning and executing programmes in the field.

Enough worldwide experience is now available to begin to characterise the ecodevelopment approach. This article is not intended to be exhaustive or overly conceptual. It is rather illustrative and anecdotal, drawing on local experiences.

DEVELOPMENT AT THE LOCAL LEVEL

Local Needs

Local strategies for sustainable development have to start by addressing basic needs. These needs are partly material, partly spiritual. They are mainly to be determined by the local population and coordinated with the needs of other areas. Any strategy for long-term sustainability and environmental protection must be able to satisfy local needs at an acceptable level. Part of the coordination problem at the national and regional levels must therefore be devoted to solving problems of inter-regional disparity.

An interesting example of this is provided by the *Kuala Juru* project near Penang in Malaysia, where a university-based team helped poor traditional fishermen define their needs and defend their resource base. Scientists from the University of Science of Malaysia in Penang helped them analyse the main problem and understand its source. The problem was water pollution by industrial and chemical plants in the region which was threatening the community's fisheries. Once the local fishermen had been encouraged to organise themselves into cooperatives, they were able to exert group pressure in stopping or reducing the pollution. The cooperatives also began to use improved methods for exploiting their oyster fisheries and for storing, processing and marketing the products to the advantage of the community.[1]

Another example of systematic need identification at the local level is provided by the Lorestan Endogenous Development Project in Western Iran. In the mid-1970s several groups of development workers were selected from among the local population for training in methods of endogenous development based on community needs. The approach used was group dialogue among trainees. The trainees were selected at the rate of 1:1000 out of some 35,000 recently sedentarised nomadic tribes, settled in their summer mountain pastures. Agriculture was recent there, therefore animal husbandry and its related cottage industries constituted the main subsistence activities, supplemented by seasonal labour at urban construction sites.

The dialogue method used was based on a reiterative process that began with a free-floating discussion of local problems and needs (a record was kept by the trainees writing on a paper board), followed by an attempt to organise the information thus obtained. Subsequently categories relevant to the trainees' area of work were retained and subjected to the same reiterative process for more detailed identification of both problems and needs. It was found that trainees' perception of their needs moved from a superficial to a deeper and more analytical level. The main role of the project experts at this stage was to provide the method and promote frank discussion.

That unique empirical knowledge-base, systematised through the approach described above, and also through dialogue, was then used as the foundation upon which to construct a training curriculum (Farvar, 1984).

Need identification is an important part of the ecodevelopment approach, provided it is done at the outset and through truly participative methods. It must be based on community interaction and discussion, since a list of "needs" obtained through conventional social science methods (such as formal questionnaires and interviews) is likely to be not only superficial, but also misleading, as too many external elements intervene. Experience with dialogue shows, however, that the very process of involving the community in identifying its needs helps to give the community self-confidence in planning and undertaking the action to follow.

1. This information is based on a visit in 1979 to the *Kuala Juru* fishermen and on various reports presented by Dr. Lim Teck Ghee (then at the University of Science of Malaysia) and colleagues to the UN University Project on Goals, Processes and Indicators of Development. Some published information can also be obtained by writing to the *IFDA Dossiers,* International Foundation for Development Alternatives, 4 Place du Marché, 1260 Nyon, Switzerland.

Self-Reliance at the Community Level

Self-reliance is an effort to minimise the dependence of the population on external factors beyond its control, and to maximise reliance on its own capacities and resources in their own development. It is a graduated and progressive concept in which the principle is to assume responsibility, thereby meeting needs at as low a level of integration as possible, unless other overriding factors intervene. In China, where the concept has received more systematic attention in recent decades, it was conceived as a way of meeting community needs at the work-team and village levels, before going to the level of the commune, which was a collection of several dozen to several hundred villages. In like fashion, needs would be met at the level of the commune and the district before going to the province or the national government.

Tanzania is another example of a society that has tried to be self-reliant. Self-reliance was the fundamental ingredient of *u-jamaa* or Tanzanian socialism based on the community and the family. Coming from the Arabic root *jamaa* (society, community, togetherness), it is defined by its architect, former President Nyerere as follows:

> *Ujamaa is an African word and thus emphasizes the Africanness of the policies we intend to follow. Second, its literal meaning is "family-hood".... By the use of the word ujamaa, therefore, we state that for us socialism involves building on the foundation of our own design. We are not importing a foreign ideology...(Nyerere, 1968).*

The people were asked to participate in the construction of a new self-reliant society:

> *We may decide to spend some of the resources we have... on buying imports of skills or machines from abroad. But our real emphasis will be on using the skills that we already have, and on developing the natural resources that we now possess. In our situation this means that the emphasis of our development will be in the rural sector, and particularly in agriculture (Nyerere, 1968).*

In many ways, self-reliance can be said to be a very old concept, and even a natural state, in both social and natural systems. It is basically modern and Western economic systems that have managed to replace it by dependence on large, monopolistic and often centralised systems (See McNeely's article in this volume for a discussion of self-reliance from a centralised versus decentralised structural point of view.)

In most of the examples given in this article, self-reliance has been one of the pillars of the approach.

Local Planning

The World Conservation Strategy attempts to unify the meeting of human needs (use of species, ecosystems and natural resources) with the concepts of sustainability, maintenance of biological diversity and essential ecological and life support systems.

In most countries, planning is a centralised process, often descending from a national planning commission or ministry down to province and district levels. In such a system local populations, usually looked upon as the *objects* of development, will not feel any incentive to look beyond their immediate, short-term interest. One cartoonist portrayed that clearly in the words of a peasant looking with awe at a planner who was trying to convince him of the need to protect the land by long-term planning: "To me *long-term planning* means having something to eat for tomorrow's lunch!"

How then do we make it possible to conserve while meeting the need for tomorrow's lunch?

Planning for sustainable development must take place first and foremost at the level of the local community. This is possible, as shown in the case of the Lorestan project in Iran if a process of *dialogue* is used as the basic methodology. In a process of dialogue, barriers between today and tomorrow tend to break down, and traditional wisdom about social and ecological processes has a chance of fusing with what modern science and technology may be able to contribute. Later on in this article (see the section on local institutions), we shall show some other essential ingredients of successful local planning.

In this manner, once appropriate ways of approaching sector-based strategies have been identified, they can help satisfy needs identified by the community through dialogue.

THE LOCAL ENVIRONMENT

The process of development based on local definitions of needs and local planning to meet those needs through self-reliance, then acts on the local environment, that is, on the complex of local resources such as land and soil, water, pasture, fisheries, forests and wildlife, as well as the sometimes less tangible ones such as ecological relationships, renewable energies, or even minerals.

To exploit those according to twin socio-ecological criteria of sustainability and equity is the topic of the rest of this article. This section shall primarily address sustainability in resource use, and is followed by a discussion of issues relating to equity and people.

Environmental Resources

Having determined needs through a process of dialogue and participatory planning as described above, local resources can then be harnessed to meet them.

The sun and the earth's gravity can be used in the form of solar, wind, hydro- and biomass energy, including the use of wastes for energy extraction.

Solar energy, which was used in ancient times, is one of our ultimate sources of energy on earth. Its applications today are no longer considered technologically out of reach; the main questions that remain are those of its economics, and how to use them at the community level so that all have access to them. Great progress has been made in reducing the cost of solar energy use. Solar photovoltaic energy cost thousands of dollars per watt when it found its first use in aerospace applications two decades ago. Today it costs a mere $5 per watt of peak energy capacity in easy-to-use and reliable photovoltaic solar panels, and costs are ever-decreasing. They are already economic for many applications including pumping water from shallow to intermediate depths in isolated areas, rural lighting, relay stations for telecommunications, and refrigeration for vaccines in isolated rural areas. The main factor still impeding more widespread use is probably the artificial pricing system applied to conventional energy resources, such as petroleum, natural gas and nuclear energy.

To give an example: just before the recent destabilisation of the oil market, kerosene and diesel fuel purchased by Iran from countries such as Japan cost on the order of $45 per barrel in hard currency. The same barrel was sold at the retail level in Iran for a mere $4.50, a subsidy level of 90 percent in hard currency. Adding the cost of transport, distribution and government overheads, one could easily reach or surpass a 95 percent subsidy level for petroleum derivatives in Iran. If we further consider that the official exchange rate used for imports is only about 10 percent of the free market value in that country, it will not be hard to see that these products are subsidised in the neighbourhood of 99 percent or better![2]

Any new and renewable technology would be far more economic if it received such subsidies!

Although the case of Iran is a little out of the ordinary due to the recent economic convulsions as a result of revolution and war, the basic fact remains that conventional energy resources are subsidised heavily by governments faced with the problem of satisfying the insatiable appetites of urban dwellers for energy and other oil products. There are no doubt hard political and social realities involved in a government's inability to break the vicious circle of dependence on what everyone knows is a depletable and highly polluting resource. Yet, by showing that alternatives do exist and would be economical with a little government attention, we may be able to pave the way to the great social and technological transformations needed to protect our resources in the long run.

Dung and other organic matter, often burned in villages for fuel, can supply excellent soil-building fertilizer as in India, China and Brazil after having yielded considerable quantities of energy.

India has a few hundred thousand biogas units at the village level. China has up to eight or nine million in Sechwan Province alone. Many other countries are adopting biogas programmes which are a natural way of producing methane gas and organic fertilizer, with the added bonus of improved sanitation.

In New Caledonia, the Philippines and China, new resources have been found by combining integrated resource management systems. Fertilizer from biogas plants is channelled to algae, fish and duck ponds, while the rich waste water from these is further used to irrigate and nourish crops. At the same time methane produced in the first stage is used to run diesel and

---

2.   These calculations are hardly less valid today given the recent crash in the price of crude oil.   Crude oil has gone from some $30 per barrel to about $15 per barrel.   Refined products are affected much less, perhaps by only about 10 to 20 percent.

petrol engines for irrigation pumps, flour mills, industrial machinery, tractors, or electricity. In one giant biogas plant near Los Angeles, USA, sewage from about a million inhabitants is used as raw material to produce about 21 megawatts of electric power for the public grid, finding a multitude of uses down the line.

Wind energy is also becoming extremely attractive. Besides the numerous small-scale applications most people have heard about or experienced, "wind farms" have become a reality. A large number of small- or medium-scale wind machines are installed so that together they produce an impressive amount of electricity that is then fed to a local or regional grid. In 1984, California alone produced about $20 million of wind-generated electricity for public use, using some 8500 small (50 to 70 kw) wind machines in windfarms to obtain some 610 megawatts of electricity.

The dominant economic system and development style of a country have a profound impact on land allocation and other resource use at the local level. In most countries much of the best land is devoted to the cultivation of cash crops, especially for export. Naturally the opportunity cost of this land-use pattern is great in that the land is no longer available for meeting local needs.

For example, foreign agricultural experts who have worked in Tanzania have not usually studied indigenous or environmentally sound agricultural techniques. Instead, they have introduced soil-exhausting alien high-yield varieties and chemical methods. This transfer of technology is a Trojan horse that takes along its ideological basis, creat-

ing economic and technical dependence on the industrialised nations. In the villages themselves, the land is usually divided between private, communal and *ujamaa* plots. Whereas subsistence agriculture is practised in the clan-owned fields, *ujamaa* agriculture produces almost exclusively cash and export crops. Replacing food crops with cash crops for exports turns many countries into sources of raw material for industrialised countries. What is left behind is often a depleted and poisoned landscape, and missed opportunities for taking care of local needs (Semiti, 1973).

Central America is a dramatic demonstration of such a state of affairs. (Farvar, 1972). In countries such as Nicaragua, Guatemala, El Salvador and Honduras, the best lands are devoted to export crops such as cotton, coffee, sugar cane, cattle, and bananas. The dominant system of production there is still the large plantation, sometimes extending over several hundred thousand hectares, except in Nicaragua where such estates were taken over by the State after the revolution. Cotton is easily the worst offender for the environment, as it is sprayed up to several dozen times each season in a seemingly losing battle against ever more resistant pests.

Although total contamination of the environment in cotton-growing regions has been a problem of unprecedented magnitude about which the population has been highly aware and concerned, an equally serious problem has been the low price of raw cotton shipped for export. The latter has meant that the countries of the region are earning very little foreign currency for the amount of good land they are devoting to the crop. Guatemala, for example, pays out three-quarters of its foreign exchange earnings from cotton in order to import pesticides, fertilizers, spray planes, tractors, and the many other external inputs for cotton growing, leaving it with some $10 million net out of gross annual earnings of $40 million.

To correct this situation, two approaches are needed simultaneously. On the one hand, chemical pesticides must be replaced by biological and other non-chemical control methods, and on the other, natural products grown in developing countries should be processed locally in order to increase their added value, and therefore decrease the amount of land and resources needed to produce a given amount of foreign currency.

The first solution is already possible. Experiments in Central America (at such institutions as the FAO and the Universities of California and Nicaragua) show that great hopes exist for breaking out of the vicious circle of chemical pest control. It is even possible to grow cotton in Central America without any reliance on synthetic organic pesticides at all, with great economic (and of course environmental) benefits.

It is, however, more difficult to convince the world to buy processed goods (shirts instead of raw cotton, cookies and syrups instead of sugar, soluble packaged coffee instead of coffee beans). Some countries, however, such as China, India, Pakistan and Korea are succeeding in penetrating the Northern markets, to great advantage. Our calculations for the Central American case show that selling shirts instead of raw cotton could result in a reduction of the area of land needed under cotton to only 1 percent of the current acreage,

in order to earn the same amount of foreign currency. This would, of course, mean that 99 percent of the land could be saved and used for other needs including conservation.

Adapting to Local Ecological Systems

Much depends on the local ecosystem in terms of the appropriate styles of development and need-satisfaction. In Sri Lanka, conservation farming is helping local people do away with the need for shifting cultivation while achieving far greater productivity by going with the "grain" of ecological systems. In this system of conservation farming, ploughing, which is responsible for most of the erosion in humid tropical lands is avoided as much as possible; a crop mix is selected involving grains, pulses, fruits, vegetables, forage and firewood trees, and others on the basis of symbiosis and commensalism. Pest populations are kept down by maintaining high and stable species diversity. This approach has also been tried successfully in Nigeria and other countries (Wijewardene, 1985).

Somali camels, farmed in northern Kenya, are enabling the local population to take much greater advantage of the local arid and semi-arid ecosystems at higher rates of energy conversion and greater environmental resistance than cattle. Although nomadic pastoralism based on camels (such as among the *Rendille* people of the Kaisut Desert, Marsabit District, or the *Ariaal* mixed camel-cattle pastoralists of the Ndoto Mountains, Kenya) is well known, the idea of camel farming is quite new. This approach has been tried in the desert regions of Israel with great success (Yagil, 1986).

There are also many examples of people being helped to take better advantage of ecological resources in or around a protected area. One example is provided by the Plitvice National Park in Yugoslavia, where a cooperative that is in charge of the Park is maintaining economic self-sufficiency by engaging in compatible agricultural and animal husbandry activities around the park in addition to managing its tourist resources.

Likewise, the Zhdyarske Hills Protected Area in Czechoslovakia, an area of national artistic inspiration, manages to keep one of the cleanest rivers in the world flowing through it while maintaining sixteen agricultural production cooperatives and two State Farms totally or partially within its boundaries.

The Choice of Appropriate Technology

The discussion above, particularly under "Environmental Resources" pointed out many of the major issues related to the choice of appropriate technology. It is amply clear that without consideration of the economic system and development styles in a country, it is not possible to succeed in the choice of appropriate technology.

Most developing countries are dual societies composed of the wealthy "modern" sector and the poor "traditional" sector and what little technological research and development (R&D) there is often serves the former. For example, most entomological research in the Third World is devoted to trying out imported pesticides on the local cash crops to see what dose should be applied. Little, if any, R&D is applied to solving the problems of pest control in non-chemical ways, especially in the poor sectors of peasant farming. Most of what is done is at best imitative and adaptive, and devoted to the needs of

the small percentage of elites in the country.

There have been notable islands of exception. Among these are the ASTRA programme of the Indian Institute of Science in Bangalore, where such people as Amulya Reddy, Madhav Gadgil and their colleagues are involved in intensive R&D programmes in favour of the poor. Also in India, Development Alternatives, with Ashok Khosla and his many dedicated colleagues, is a non-profit organisation doing intensive technology development for mass applications through a franchising system. They have worked on improved looms and woodstoves, mud-based building technologies, transport and many other socially useful technological innovations.

China is another large country with lengthy experience in attempting to solve rural technological problems. Some recent examples have involved the use of biogas technology and small hydro-electric power stations, village or commune level production of microbial insecticides such as *Bacillus thuringiensis*, useful predators and parasites such as the tiny parasitic wasps (*Trichogramma species*), praying mantids (*Mantis religiosa*) and ladybugs (*coccinellidae*).

Experiences of the Bu-Ali Sina University in Hamadan, Iran, showed how local level need assessment can help in the design of appropriate technologies for local needs, taking advantage of both traditional and modern science and technology. With such an approach, the specificities of the local environmental conditions can be used to full advantage. One such example was helping revive *canats*, which are a network of underground canals dug horizontally at a very slight slope (usually less than 1 percent), connected by a series of vertical shafts or wells. They are the traditional means used for tapping underground water in hilly or mountainous regions where the phreatic (sub-surface) water table is higher, and gently leading it by gravity to where it emerges from the ground without the use of any special devices or energy. Many of these have fallen into disrepair as a result of ill-conceived land reform schemes and the subsequent "modernisation" of the country under the Shah. At the University, programmes were designed with the help of students, faculty and peasants to revive some of the *canats*. That trend continued and intensified in the country after the Revolution of 1979.

THE LOCAL PEOPLE

Traditional Knowledge

Canats, plant medicines, and natural dyes are only a few of the examples drawn from indigenous knowledge that have sometimes been integrated into local strategies for sustainable development. In some cultures there is an extensive repertoire of written traditional technology and science. Among these are traditional medical texts in Amharic, Arabic, Greek, Persian, Sanskrit, Thai, Tibetan and Turkish; Aztec, Inca and Mayan science and artifacts; and books in Persian on the geohydrology, chemistry and architecture of *canats,* and on agricultural techniques.

The local population is also usually one of the best sources of information on the local ecological systems taxonomy (the Inonu tribe of the Philippines can recognise some 1600 plant species and cultivate up to 400 of

them), and some of the empirical "do's and don'ts" of resource management.

It is becoming an increasingly accepted fact in both the development and conservation communities, that combining traditional knowledge of the local people with what can be judiciously sifted out of modern technology, can bring about a much richer contribution from both.

Community-based Institutions for Resource Management

Where resources and people have coexisted over the centuries, people have evolved their own institutions for community-based management of natural resources. Forests, water, land, fisheries, wildlife and pasture are all often managed communally in traditional societies, and systems of management and decision making have evolved, such as the *boneh* system in Iran and the *hema* system in Arabia that can now be used for participatory planning and sustainable development.

In the *boneh* system, designated representatives of the local peasants with small-holding or usufruct rights, form an irrigation council with the power to allocate water resources and insure their maintenance and equitable distribution. The *boneh* has also acted as a unit of collective planting and harvesting, often holding the means of production in joint ownership, and deciding on such issues as crop composition, peasant-landlord differences, and other matters related to production and resource management.

The *hema* system exists in Arabia and Syria, with close parallels in other societies, with local variations in name and function. It is primarily a system of community imposed rotation and access to common pastures. Among the nomadic societies of southwest Asia, an institution known as the *maal* or *tash* is composed of a number of units of tent-holds, and their animals and grazing rights, headed by an elder (*rish-sefid*). The *maal* migrates together, grazes livestock together, milks and processes the dairy products together. They have also joint responsibility for protecting their pasture-lands.

Similar institutions exist in most traditional societies, including the *subak* of Malaysia for rice cultivation, the *zanjeras* of the Philippines for irrigation management, the *sar-panj* system in northern India for irrigation and agricultural coordination.

Experience in applying these community-based resource management systems to ecodevelopment and local participation is limited, but what little exists shows that they may well be the *conditio sine qua non* of success in the field.

Enabling Ecodevelopment

The Lorestan project referred to at the beginning of the article provides an example of local level training and education for self-reliant development, based on the approach of dialogue.

A similar approach was used at the Bu-Ali Sina University in Hamadan, Iran, as referred to above, in which a combination of traditional and modern science and knowledge was used to train ecodevelopment workers from the barefoot peasant and tribal worker to the specialist in ecodevelopment planning, biological control and habitat management (both Master level courses), rural engineering (consisting of rural water supply, rural energy supply, rural construction, and rural industries: four university level Bachelor of Engineering courses).

CONCLUSION

Ecodevelopment is a powerful means for implementing sustainable development for local communities and ecosystems. It involves helping local people decolonise and then define their own perceptions of community needs. Finally, applying a judicious mixture of old and new knowledge they can embark on the management and further development of their natural resources to fulfill their needs.

For a society that does not base its development on solid local foundations, the experiences culled here suggest that it will probably face serious social and natural crises sooner or later. The case of the Sahelian inability to protect itself in the recent droughts is one such warning.

The experiences mentioned here, and many others too numerous to mention in this article are an indication that many people are beginning to heed the signs. It can be said that a potentially healthy movement of ecodevelopment that holds much promise for the future of mankind, has started.

REFERENCES

• Farvar, M. Taghi, 1986, "Ecodevelopment - A Tool for Involving People," *Ecoforum*, 4-5 (11), August/October.

- Farvar, M. Taghi, 1984, "Politics of Ecodevelopment: The Cart before the Horse?" and "The Horse that Jumped the Cart: Trials and Tribulations of Ecodevelopment in Western Iran," in: Glaeser, Bernhard (ed.), *Ecodevelopment and Ecofarming: Projects, Prospects,* International Institute for Environment and Society, West Berlin.

- Farvar, M. Taghi, 1976, Interaction of Social and Ecological Systems," in: W. Mathews (ed.), *Outer Limits and Human Needs: Resource and Environmental Issues of Development Strategies,* Uppsala, Dag Hammarskjöld Foundation, 1976.

- Farvar, M. Taghi, 1972, *The Ecological Impact of Pesticides in Central America: Agriculture, Public Health and Development,* Ann Arbour, Michigan, University Microfilms.

- Gritzner, *et. al., Proceedings of the Conference on Common Property Resource Management Systems,* In Press.

- Nyerere, J. K., 1968, Freedom and Socialism, Oxford University Press, Dar es Salaam.

- Semiti, G A., 1973, "Cash Crops versus Food Crops and Their Comparative Effects on the Human Environment," *African Environment,* 8, Dakar, ENDA. Also, Sandberg. *Ujamaa and Control of the Environment.* BRALUP paper No. 5. Dar es Salaam, BRALUP, University of Dar es Salaam, 1973.

- Wijewardene, Ray, 1985, *Conservation Farming,* GTZ, Colombo.

- Yagil, 1986, pers. comm.

SECTORAL APPROACHES TO SUSTAINABLE DEVELOPMENT

Pierre Spitz
Independent Commission on International
Humanitarian Issues
Geneva, Switzerland

SUMMARY *Ministerial decisions to act or not to act concomitantly influence development and the environment. Because solutions to development problems will be found through appropriate ministries rather than in pastoral locations, State ministries need more opportunities to thoroughly examine alternatives. Alternatives are often impeded by powerful interest groups, thus national conservation strategies and sectoral strategies can play a fundamental role in protecting the resources upon which the State and pastoralists depend. Within each environmental ministry there should be a conservation strategy department whose task would be to widen as much as possible the range of choices and study their consequences on the environment and development. Technological memory is becoming increasingly important in this regard as it provides a store of possible solutions which are adaptable to specific situations.*

It is not without reason that economics has become the dominant discipline in the development field and that scientific ecology has such a struggle to penetrate the seats of decision-making at ministries, banks and companies. Ecological thinking too often assumes an unmonnied universe without prices, costs and profits; the very elements that unfortunately weigh heavily in the evolution of human societies. Even the etymology of the words "economy" and "ecology" marks the unequal contest: the *nomos* of economy signifies administration while the *logos* of ecology signifies science. In developing his new concept, Haeckel thus opposed the science of relations between organisms and their habitat, to the administration of wealth.

When, in 1972, Maurice Strong proposed the term "eco-development," he cast a major challenge in asking for the reconciliation of two apparently antagonistic processes: that of nature conservation for its own sake, without consideration for people, versus that of economic growth without consideration for the environment.

What has happened since 1972? Pessimists will say that the development dialogue has changed but that the practices of governmental and intergovernmental organisations have been little affected. Optimists will maintain the opposite: that given the opportunity to express itself, public opinion is more aware of the environment and the long-term; that economists are more aware of the complexity of managing living resources; that ecology better reinforces and integrates economic factors; that cultural dimensions of development are better recognised; that traditional knowledge is treated with less suspicion; and that the scientific community better appreciates the necessity of interdisciplinary, systemic and holistic approaches. Finally, the optimist would say that development planners at different levels better perceive the benefits of intersectoral actions and the value of popular participation in the search for local rather than universal solutions. Local solutions are more closely suited to ecological, social and cultural specificity than to the chronological, spatial and social homogeneity approach. Yet, planners have long cherished the latter because it simplifies their task.

All kinds of pollution, degradation of tropical soil fertility, desertification, and irreversible loss of genetic resources are some of the processes, becoming ever more evident, that are forcing changes in the development debate. But why do practices not change more quickly? Clearly, certain interest groups see no advantages in change and are powerful enough to oppose it. But to become immobilised because of this alone would be defeatist and would even call the usefulness of our Conference into question.

We should recognise that the need to study links between elements of a complex system, in order to decide how to proceed and to identify probable consequences, is ill-suited to State management. The same remark applies to the multiciplicity of decision centres that follows from community participation. Nevertheless, the role of the State, whether it be strong or weak, is essential and too often neglected. Ministerial decisions to act or not to act concomitantly influence development and the environment. (Development here refers to improving the living conditions of less-advantaged groups in the population, now and in the future.) Let us then consider certain ministries and ask ourselves how a national conservation strategy could not only be reconciled with development imperatives and the struggle against poverty, but also constitute, in itself, the best possible path to development.

To take an example: A transport minister makes decisions which have direct implications both for long-term conservation of natural resources and for development. The plan for a road is a choice that has a direct impact on the environment, and the construction methods of the road will influence drainage, movements of fauna, etc. Where there is a minister of the environment who is stimulated by informed public opinion, such choices can be debated. However, no environmental minister would challenge the issue of road-building. Acceptance of road transport is so deeply embedded that alternatives are not seriously taken into consideration. Under certain conditions, the construction of a railway, for example, could bring energy and foreign exchange savings while yet causing less damage to the environment.

A sectoral approach to sustainable development necessarily depends on examining the widest possible array of options, under which each must be examined from two points of view: from the viewpoint of national independence, and from that of improving the long and short-term living conditions of the poorest people. In case of conflict there are, of course, political arbiters but at least the different options would be examined.

An interesting historical example of the above point is the proposal made in nineteenth century India by Sir Arthur Cotton about the management of rivers and canals for combined irrigation and navigation purposes. In spite of detailed studies which showed that, for the same investment, the proposal was much more profitable for the British and for the Indian peasants than the construction of railways, the British industrial establishment carried the day and railways were built. Sir Arthur Cotton's experience does not only offer historical relevance; current proposals to combine irrigation with navigation in Bangladesh and West Bengal are not the object of serious consideration.

A finance minister in a developing country who stimulates the export of agricultural products to improve the balance of payments often accelerates environmental degradation without bringing real benefits to the poorest. Who profits from meat or wood exports? Essentially, a few privileged groups. Have the alternatives always been thoroughly examined? Unfortunately they have not. Rather, industrialised countries imposing unequal terms of exchange, and the interest groups in developing countries who act as their agents, discourage the study of alternatives. The most powerful agents draw the greatest profit from the destruction of natural resources. When desertification and deforestation associated with internal inequalities and external dependence lead to famine, it

cannot be said that ecological concerns and the struggle against poverty are opposing forces.

A team from the University of Wageningen who studied a group of herders in Mali, concluded that they were using optimal methods given the resources at their disposal. Over the last few years, however, a new practice in relation to herding has emerged. Businessmen and officials have been investing their savings in livestock herds that are looked after by a third party. Traditional logic no longer functions in this new situation; the herds are growing in size and damaging the environment. The usual simplistic refrain: increase in herd sizes; overgrazing; degradation; etc. is entirely overturned by careful studies carried out in traditional settings.

But solutions will not be found in pastoral locations. The struggle against desertification must be waged through ministries of finance and industry which should adopt fiscal measures to divert savings into more productive uses that are less damaging to the environment. Environment ministries thus often appear to be dealing with secondary effects rather than principle causes. Within each environmental ministry there should be a conservation strategy department whose task would be to widen as much as possible the range of choices and study their consequences on the environment and development, including questions of foreign trade, finance, transport, health, housing, and of course, agriculture.

Such a department would also be an ideal link for non-governmental organisations by providing informed contacts within the government structure. It would of course be necessary to ensure that such contacts were sufficiently committed to environmental issues to want to make their voices heard. Perhaps it would be useful to require that such people would have spent several years in an environment ministry as well as having previous experience in several other ministries. Their position would be reinforced and the experience acquired would only strengthen the environment ministry.

An ideal ministry of agriculture would organise its departments in such a way that economic, ecological, social and cultural diversity would be taken into account. It would make the needs of those groups lacking power or voice a priority. In developing countries, the majority of these groups are found among cultivators and pastoralists. The 5, 10, or 20 percent of farmers possessing the most land and capital already have the economic and political means to influence decisions in the directions they desire. They can influence the agricultural structure, the organisation of markets and prices, the direction of research, extension services and credit. The means must therefore be given to others to make their opinions heard, through farmers' organisations which are not dominated by the powerful.

There are an infinite number of possible productive combinations in the areas of cultivation and livestock farming but only a few, largely influenced by the historical development of agriculture in Europe and North America, are applied. In the nineteenth century, the overriding problem confronting Canadian and United States agriculture was to improve productivity of labour against a background of labour

scarcity in comparison with the vast areas of land available. Europe had the opposite problem: limited land was coupled with an excess of labour and required attempts to raise productivity of surface unit of land. The technical solutions were thus very different. North America turned to mechanisation, symbolised by McCormick, and Europe improved crop rotation and soil sciences, after Liebig. The two techniques merged after the Second World War and it is this Euro-American approach which is for the most part applied in developing countries today.

In spite of increased land productivity and the absence of mechanisation in Europe, Osvaldo Sunkel has shown that 60 million Europeans, out of a population of about 300 million in 1900, left their continent between 1840 and 1920. That migration occurred during a period of healthy agricultural development, low mechanisation and no motorisation against a heavily labour-intensive industrial development that was dominating the economy.

Policies which bring about rural unemployment, migration to towns and urban unemployment are partly decided with short-term interests in mind, and partly in ignorance of the range of possible solutions. The two are not independent of each other. Ignorance influences the perceptions of urban decision-makers with regard to their own short-term interests. In addition, their general lack of knowledge of the management of living resources hides the contradictions between their perceived short-term, and their real long-term, interests. Yet an increase in agricultural and food production without increased employment is not an answer to hunger. As history has shown many times, grain stocks can exist alongside famine.

The history of agricultural research has been entirely focused on the quest for homogeneity and the spatial and temporal separation of production processes. Agricultural research, instruction and extension must therefore be careful-ly re-examined in the light of sustainable development imperatives. Yet not only in agriculture but in all areas, the failure of technological memory is becoming ever more pronounced because of the proliferation of new techniques. However, it is for that very reason that technological memory is becoming increasingly necessary as a store of possible solutions or ideas best adapted to each situation.

LEARNING LESSONS FROM NATURE: THE BIOME APPROACH TO SUSTAINABLE DEVELOPMENT

Jeffrey A. McNeely
Director, IUCN Programme and Policy Division
Gland, Switzerland

SUMMARY *"Biomes" are the largest land community units which ecologists find convenient to recognise, with most authorities distinguishing ten to twenty terrestrial biomes for the world. In a given biome, the climax vegetation formation is superficially uniform, although the species composition of plants and animals will vary from place to place; there is virtually no species overlap, for example, between tropical moist forest biomes in Brazil and Zaire. Ecologists have often felt that lessons learned in one part of a biome may be applicable to those of another, so a number of biome-based guidelines and strategies have been developed. These have stimulated comparative studies and increased awareness of the problems; they have provided a framework for interdisciplinary cooperation; and have promoted international collaboration. They have been less successful in prescribing specific action related to development planning, especially when the biome is treated as a generalised whole rather than as a complex collection of smaller inter-related ecosystems which must be managed locally. Biome approaches must provide practical solutions to real problems at the local level; they must be integrated with other programmes, and administrative responsibility must be assigned to a specific entity. The time-frame within which biome-based strategies operate is a criticial factor. This paper suggests that the "post-petroleum" and "post debt-crisis" period is the one for which we should be planning, although our plans also need to see us through the coming transitions to new sources of energy and capital.*

INTRODUCTION

As the human population inexorably approaches the 5,000 million mark and per capita GNP continues to expand globally, exploitation of the planet is ever-increasing. Many "natural" ecosystems are being converted into agro-ecosystems, which leads to increased productivity for people and some of their domestic animals, but reduced productivity for a large number of other species.

This may seem an inevitable process, even a desirable one from a human perspective. All ecosystems in the world are significantly affected by man - even penguins in Antarctica have DDT in their tissues. But along with man's global impact comes an ability and responsibility to consider the consequences of human actions on ecosystems. People can decide what are desirable or undesirable objectives in ecosystem management, and devise ways and means to put their value judgements into action.

While all ecosystems are modified by human activity, nature still holds many lessons for our species. Many lines of evidence suggest that the long-term survival of *Homo sapiens* depends on a reasonable balance between natural, semi-natural, and agricultural ecosystems. But what is "a reasonable balance," and how can it be attained in a period of increasing resource scarcity and higher demands? How can nature contribute to human welfare in a sustainable way?

This paper offers a perspective for looking at large natural systems and considering how such a perspective may contribute to development. It defines fundamental concepts in the ecology of sustainable development, discusses benefits of the perspective, outlines some problems, provides examples of how approaches to development based on natural systems are being applied in different types of large natural systems, and suggests general principles which might be more widely applicable.

DEFINING BASIC CONCEPTS

Within the **biosphere** - the entire global ecosystem capable of supporting living organisms - ecologists have a number of ways of looking at smaller divisions of nature. They subdivide the biosphere into terrestrial, marine and freshwater ecosystems, and further into biomes. A **biome** is the largest land community unit which ecologists find convenient to recognise (Odum, 1971). It refers to a biogeographical region or formation; a major regional ecological community characterised by distinctive life forms and principal plant or animal species. The term is often applied to the theoretical climax plant and animal community, so that even areas which have been thoroughly altered by human action may be considered to be part of, for example, the tropical forest biome. A **biotope** is the smallest geographical unit of the biosphere or of a habitat that can be delimited by convenient boundaries and is characterised by its **biota** (the total flora and fauna of a given area) (Lincoln, Boxshall, and Clark, 1982).

Biogeographers and ecologists have spent considerable time and effort trying to classify the various habitats of the world and to make sense out of the worldwide distribution of the biota. There is still no clear consensus (see, for example, Allen, 1877; Wallace, 1876; Merriam, 1894; Sclater and Sclater, 1899; Hesse, *et al.*, 1951; Dansereau, 1957; Darlington, 1957; Good, 1964; Holdridge, 1967; Simmons, 1979; Bailey, 1982). However they might be distributed, the major units of distribution of the biota are composed of **natural communities,** assemblages of populations of animals, plants, bacteria, and fungi that live in an environment and interact with each other. They form together a distinctive living system each with its own composition, structure, environmental relations, development, and processes. An

ecosystem comprises a natural community and its abiotic environment, treated together as a functional system of complementary relationships in which there is transfer and circulation of energy and matter (Odum, 1971). The ecosystem is probably the most useful level of analysis for development practioners because its scale is small enough to deal with effectively.

The modification of the biosphere and the application of human, financial, living and non-living resources to satisfy human needs and improve the quality of human life is **development**, as defined in the World Conservation Strategy. Such modification of ecosystems can be positive or negative, depending on the eye of the beholder. Clearing a tropical forest to grow a maize monoculture replaces a complex system with a much simpler one and reduces the biomass, but in some cases the crop shows greater biomass productivity. In the eyes of the farmer this is preferable, indeed it enables him to survive in the short-term. But to the conservationist interested in maintaining biological diversity and ecological processes for long-range benefits to humanity, the ecosystem change is fraught with danger.

One of the most useful insights provided by the World Conservation Strategy is that for development to be sustainable, it must take account of social, ecological and economic factors of the living and non-living resource base; and of the long and short-term advantages and disadvantages of alternative actions. But sustainability is only a necessary quality; it is not sufficient by itself to justify a land-use decision. Other important decision-making criteria also enter into the question, such as the value of the forest proposed for con-

version as an intact ecosystem. By stressing the criterion of sustainability, the World Conservation Strategy provides a reasonably objective first foundation for decision-making.

BENEFITS OF THE BIOME-BASED APPROACH

The biome approach will be the focus of this paper. The classification of natural systems is somewhat arbitrary and depends largely on the purposes to which the classification is to be put.

Irrespective of how many biomes are used to divide the world, these very large international units serve as useful levels of analysis for certain applications. Strengths of strategies and plans for promoting sustainable development over an entire biome include the following considerations:

* Biome-based plans overtly recognise that development must be based on natural systems of renewable resources. They thereby emphasise to development planners the importance of considering the overall functioning of large natural systems when weighing options for resource utilisation at the ecosystem level. By establishing a broad perspective for comprehensive consideration of ecosystems, planners can avoid the danger of defining ecosystems too narrowly to justify a particular sort of utilisation.

* Biome-based plans identify the major common ecological relationships, processes, potentialities, and vulnerabilities of the biome.

* They identify major common problems facing various parts of the

biome, thereby helping to identify common solutions.

* They provide a basis for applying lessons learned in one part of the world to similar biomes found in another part of the world; facilitate communication among those concerned with the biome; provide a framework for interdisciplinary co-operation both within a country and between countries; and stimulate comparative studies and increased awareness of the common problems.

* They enable the priorities of conservation to be clearly identified and defended on scientific grounds, which are valid regardless of the location of national frontiers. Biome-based approaches provide a tool for objectively deciding where the limited resources available for international conservation can be applied to the highest priorities, free of the constraints imposed by nationally-based planning and programming activities.

As stated clearly in the World Conservation Strategy, the goals of regional development must be more closely tied to the problems of ecosystem conservation. Because biomes (and many of the ecosystems of which they are composed) extend spatially across political boundaries, development and conservation efforts which address modern global problems must eventually be regional and international.

EXAMPLES OF BIOME-BASED APPROACHES TO SUSTAINABLE DEVELOPMENT

The strengths of the biome-based approach have appealed to quite a num-ber of international agencies - indeed, this approach helps many such agencies justify their existence. IUCN, for example, uses biomes as its largest level of analysis, with programmes on tropical forests, coastal and marine ecosystems, mountains, islands, and arid lands. Unesco's Man and the Biosphere Programme has major activities in biomes such as tropical forests, deserts, mountains, islands, and chapparal. FAO's Forestry Department has concentrated for many years on the tropical forest biome, with other departments working on arid lands.

Here I would like to briefly describe some of the biomes addressed, the means used, and the lessons that might be drawn from them.

The Desert Biome

Perhaps the most dramatically de-graded biome is the desert or "arid land," especially in the Sahel region of Africa. The situation in the Sahel has received considerable attention in recent years from a multitude of international agencies. In brief, the Sahel is losing productivity because of rangeland deterioration, degradation of rain-fed croplands, waterlogging and salinisation of irrigated lands, deforestation and destruction of woody vegetation, declining availability and/or quality of groundwater or surface water supplies, and growth and encroachment of mobile sand dunes.

Over the past ten years, considerable research in arid lands from North America to Australia to Mongolia has contributed to UNEP's major programme on Integrated Regional Schemes to Combat Desertification (UNEP, 1982). This research has revealed that deteriorated arid rangelands are quite resilient and are able to regenerate, once live-stock pressures are removed. One surprising finding is that arable agricul-ture is often more significant in disturb-ing the environment than livestock-raising: while over-grazing obviously devastates arid grasslands, cattle, goats and other animals graze on marginal lands because they have been displaced by crops grown on land which is more appropriate for livestock. Groundwater in many parts of the desert biome is also being over-exploited. By the year 2000 the desertification of rain-fed lands will be significantly worse in the subsistence farming regions of the Sahel, as well as in other arid lands de-pendent on ancient aquafers.

Ironically, relatively dense human populations once lived in balance with the Sahelian ecosystem, with flourish-ing agriculture and animal husbandry producing surpluses, and plenty of un-exploited land remaining for what would today be called wildlife conser-vation. But traditional forms of land and animal husbandry, often involving seasonal pastoralism, have been replaced by cash crops. As a result, small farmers have been pushed onto lands formerly used by nomadic pas-toralists, causing them to become over-taxed, impoverished, and neglected. In most of the Sahel, because of demand from expanding urban populations, em-phasis on "green revolution" technol-ogy, and artificially-maintained low food prices through government pricing policies, the small farmer is en-couraged to adopt "technological agriculture," but does not obtain the fair market price for his produce. Meanwhile the pastoralists are starving. A vicious cycle of increased penury and increased social and political in-stability in rural areas of the Sahel has

been established without any sig-nificant improvement of urban life.

Scientists, planners, and politicians have failed to recognise that the economic and ecological bases of small-scale peasant farming systems in the Sahel depended on the continued exist-ence of the natural woodland vegeta-tion. The appalling consequences of habitat degradation for people simply were not foreseen. Similarly, the cru-cial role of wetlands during the long dry season has. received little attention; as a result the problems of drought have been exacerbated by agricultural conversion of these natural dry season refugia. Sahelian degradation has its roots not in drought, which is not an unusual condition there, but in inap-propriate forestry, agricultural, and water management policies (IUCN, 1985).

The problems of desertification have been known for quite some time, and in 1977 the United Nations adopted an anti-desertification programme. Ac-cording to the World Commission on Environment and Development, the programme was largely ignored by donor and recipient governments alike. That programme was estimated to cost US $4.5 billion per annum to the year 2000 for the entire globe. "A break-down of this figure," says the Commis-sion, "reveals that the estimated cost for Ethiopia was US $50 million per year to the year 2000. Neither the political will nor the money could be found to implement this programme. Yet, eight years later, faced with a human drama beyond precedent, the world community had to divert an es-timated US $400 million for crisis-response measures to date for Ethiopia alone, and this figure will undoubtedly exceed $500 million before the next harvest" (quoted in WRI, 1985).

In the long-run, the "crisis mentality" of development and disaster relief agencies needs to be replaced by an "anticipatory mentality." Once ecosystems become so degraded that they reach the headlines of the world's newspapers, it is often too late to take effective remedial action. In the Sahel, it is only in the occasional good rainfall years that meaningful work can be done to contain desertification and build the ecological infrastructure necessary for stable agriculture. As IUCN President M. S. Swaminathan has pointed out, "Unfortunately, in normal rainfall years, neither national nor international sources of additional funding become available. Consequently, unique opportunities for ecodevelopment are lost" (IUCN, 1985).

As in so many other areas, prevention is better than cure. But prevention is not nearly so dramatic, and requires that development agencies be shown very clearly how and why their budgets are going to yield real benefits.

The main lessons to learn from the Sahelian part of the desert biome are that:

* Decision-making must be built on the potentialities and limitations of natural systems, and governments need to recognise the interdependence of agriculture, animal husbandry, forestry, and "nature."

* Government policies should give full consideration to traditional land-use techniques, offering useful lessons and inspiration for new solutions to age-old problems.

* The value of prevention is almost always persuasive, but politicians and international development agencies need to be convinced that crisis management must be replaced by crisis prevention.

* Resource management should be removed from urban-based planners and aid agencies and placed in the hands of people who live with the resources.

Tropical Forests

Tropical forests provide an excellent example of the strengths and weaknesses of the biome-based approach. Some 76 countries contain tropical forests: 23 in Tropical America, 37 in Tropical Africa, and 16 in Tropical Asia (FAO-UNEP, 1982). The great majority of tropical closed forests occur in just three countries: Brazil, Zaire, and Indonesia.

Covering just six percent of the earth's land surface (about 7.5 million square kilometres), the parts of the tropical moist forest biome which still have closed forest may harbour more than 40 percent of all living plants and animals. Tropical forests are being converted - for timber, fuelwood, and agricultural land - at a rate of about 200,000 square kilometres per year, a bit over 2 percent of the entire biome. As the area of tropical forest is reduced, the rate of destruction is likely to become even greater. Demand for wood, especially firewood, is estimated to grow from 2,500 million cubic metres in 1976 to 4,000 million cubic metres by 1990, and FAO estimates that 7 million square kilometres of tropical forest lands will be cleared for agriculture in the next twenty years.

Most tropical forests on fertile soils have already been cleared; those remaining are on sandy or acidic soils, or on hilly terrain, with forestry being the most appropriate land use for such situations. Although large areas of tropical forest exist in a few countries, in places such as East and West Africa, Madagascar, South and Southeast Asia, and Central America, the forests of the biome have been reduced to mere remnants.

In response to this alarming situation, efforts have been made to use a biome-based approach when including conservation elements in tropical forest development activities. IUCN produced ecological guidelines for development in tropical rainforests (Poore, 1976) based on conferences held in Indonesia and Venezuela. IUCN was not particularly effective at promoting the guidelines, and it has been difficult to establish whether they were being used. From all appearances, exploitation has proceeded as usual.

Into the 1980s, concern about tropical forests increased as trees were felled. Most of this concern originated from consumer nations while those countries having major tropical forest resources were concerned primarily about how to exploit them most effectively. Nevertheless, protected area systems were also established in most tropical countries. Progress was particularly encouraging in the major tropical forest countries - Zaire, Brazil, and Indonesia. By 1982, no less than 355 protected areas had been established in the biome, covering some 6 percent of the global biome area (Harrison, Miller and McNeely, 1984). In the face of expanding resource exploitation in their periphery, many of these protected areas are now threatened, and new approaches are being sought to ensure their long-term viability.

In 1983, an international task force was convened by the World Resources Institute, the World Bank and UNDP, with participation by a wide range of institutions (including IUCN). The task force produced a document entitled *Tropical Forests: A Call for Action* (WRI, 1985), and in the process stimulated FAO's Committee on Forest Development in the Tropics into action, leading to the "Tropical Forestry Action Plan" (FAO, 1985). Both of these biome-level documents spell out what the forest sector must do to tackle the problem and will go a long way toward more appropriate development of tropical forest lands.

Useful as these documents are, it is apparent that the economic and political basis of tropical deforestation needs to be further considered as a framework for fundamental changes in the application of international development assistance. For example, both FAO and WRI "action plans" call for an expansion of existing sectoral aid programmes but give insufficient attention to the fact that the forestry sector has only a relatively small impact in terms of both the real magnitude of deforestation and its fundamental social and political causes.

The main lessons learned from actions within the tropical forest biome are:

* Activities deriving from biome-based tropical forest strategies need to be carefully focused on a specific target if they are to have an impact.

* Strategy documents need to consider the overall biome, not just sectoral activities in the biome. The linkages

between forestry and agriculture, forestry and energy, and forestry and people, among others, should be included in biome-level strategy documents.

* Much more work needs to be done on applying research to on-the-ground management problems. Managers and researchers are still not communicating as well as they should, and the "implementation gap" seems to be growing rather than narrowing.

The Island Biome

Islands have received attention through the years from a wide range of organisations, but relatively seldom on a "biome basis" which considers islands as a unit of analysis. Islands differ from larger land masses in many ways which are important for conservation and development:

* As a result of isolation, evolutionary processes on islands yield many species of endemic plants and animals.

* Many island species, especially plants, invertebrates, and birds, have evolved in relative isolation and display adaptations which ill-equip them for survival in the face of habitat changes, new competitors, new predators, or human intervention. Thus they are more vulnerable to extinction.

* Natural resources of islands are scarce in both variety and quantity, so they cannot tolerate mismanagement to the extent that continental resources can.

* Because of the scarcity of natural resources, islands require different approaches to ensuring the continuing flow of raw materials, goods and services required by their inhabitants.

* Island people tend to develop their own ways and means to conserve natural resources, and can show an exceptionally sensitive appreciation of natural processes.

* While many island peoples have developed traditional means for conserving their resources and environment, new pressures from cash-crop agriculture for export (e.g., sugar cane, bananas), population growth, tourism, and political factors have surpassed the capacities of these traditional methods to maintain a balance between people and resources.

Many island territories, notably in the Pacific and Caribbean, have recently gained independence and now require assistance to develop their own capacity to manage resources. While many islands are overpopulated relative to their current land uses, development policies, and resources, they seldom have the critical mass of people needed to develop strong conservation institutions and resource management specialists. This problem is exacerbated by the fact that their isolation makes pooling of human resources and institutions expensive and difficult. At the same time the new Law of the Sea Treaty greatly expands the area of jurisdiction of these nations, bringing new management responsibilities and opportunities to ensure proper use of coastal and marine resources.

While islands face important and unique difficulties, they can also provide a resource for improving approaches to conservation management. They represent microcosms of problems faced on larger land masses, thus allowing pilot or demonstration projects to be carried out under relatively simple conditions where ecosystem limits are clear. The problems are common to most islands, so a worldwide approach which unites Caribbean, Pacific, Indian Ocean, Mediterranean, and Atlantic islands could be both effective and welcome. Finally, many traditionally-used island approaches to conservation management could be applied in promoting sustainable development in continents and in other island groups far away from their origins.

In short, islands have many problems and opportunities in common, which merit common discussion and sharing of experiences. An opportunity thus exists to bring together island nations and territories to explore, determine, and implement a common agenda for cooperative action in conservation and development. Interested parties in such a programme might include industrialised island nations (Japan, New Zealand, United Kingdom), nations in the tropics dominated by a single large island (Madagascar, Sri Lanka, Cuba, Papua-New Guinea), industrialised nations with tropical island territories (United States, United Kingdom, France, Netherlands, Spain), archipelagic States in the tropics (Indonesia, Philippines), small island nations (Seychelles, Vanuatu, Jamaica, others in the Caribbean, Pacific, Atlantic, and Indian Oceans), and nations with significant islands as part of a larger mainland country (Greece, Australia, Chile, United States).

Lessons to be learned from the islands biome include:

* Biome strategies need to be sensitive to variety, quality and availability of natural resources.

* Solutions to environmental problems will be more readily attained in smaller, well-defined systems.

* Biome strategies should recognise contributions from traditional forms of resource use.

* The more that common factors are shared by the same biome in different parts of the world, the more useful is a biome-based approach likely to be.

* A biome-based approach is likely to be most useful when it involves expertise from all parts of the world where the biome occurs.

Based on these considerations, islands could provide an excellent example of how a biome-based approach could work, provided the involved government agencies, NGOs, and international organisations are determined to collaborate.

The Mountain Biome

Mountain biomes might be called the Cinderella of the ecological world, especially in the Third World, despite being widespread and dominant (by area). Mountains have been the focus of specific intermittent action. The Unesco Man and the Biosphere (Project 6) and several NGOs, notably the International Mountain Society, have called attention to problems of the biome, but conservation in mountains still suffers from considerable uncertainty (Thompson, 1984).

Some general points can be made about the special characteristics of mountain biomes in developing countries:

* Mountains are very fragile, complex ecosystems, which can become rapidly degraded particularly through deforestation, erosion, and seismic events (although the interrelationships among these perturbations are not well understood).

* Rather like islands, mountain valleys are often biologically isolated and contain endemic species; such narrowly-endemic species are threatened by site-specific mountain catastrophies.

* Mountains are an integral part of the wider highland-lowland system, so that environmental changes upstream can have major adverse consequences downstream (notably flooding).

* Again like islands, mountain areas have pluralistic social structures, but unlike islands they are also zones of social confrontation and convergence producing both conflict situations and a rich cultural mosaic.

* Although mountains have often been on the periphery of large political structures, mountain societies have also developed strong local, independent political structures. Some of these have been strongly unifying over large areas of the biome (e.g. Inca Empire) while others have been isolationist and self-reliant. Transport problems are central to the latter condition.

* The resource base for development in mountain areas is scarce and concentrated, often in just a few fertile valleys surrounded by steep areas of depauperate soils. These low-productivity lands are often sparsely inhabited common areas. Traditional resource use has evolved on a basis of sophisticated local knowledge, including techniques such as terracing, shifting cultivation and skillful adaptation to micro-climates.

* While population pressure has developed in some areas, the dominant pattern for high mountains has been depopulation which seems to be associated in some areas with the decline of terracing and increasing erosion. Health problems are acute in many mountain areas, with very high infant mortality rates.

* Ironically, poverty in recent years has intensified in parallel with a shift from subsistence agriculture to cash cropping. Due to fluctuations in commodity prices, rises in interest rates and inflation, the cash economy has often brought lower standards of living.

* Mountain areas have been particularly vulnerable to development pressures determined far outside the mountain areas. Examples include tourism, military installations, roads (especially on unstable slopes), and dams.

Conservation management in the mountain biome faces many challenges. In developing countries, these tend to be heightened by a weak institutional development infrastructure, lack of training facilities and general limitations of resources. The programmes that do exist have often been scattered, poorly-coordinated, and insufficiently communicated to others interested in the approaches being tried. Too few links have been formed between sectors - e.g. watershed management, agriculture, and forestry. The urgent need to mount research and training programmes, as well as specific demonstration pilot projects in some of the inaptly named "hot spots," and building on success stories is now being recognised in the international community and by mountain States. A number of integrated action experiments are underway with backing of international consortia in the major mountain areas. These include the International Centre for Integrated Mountain Development (Kathmandu Unesco, Swiss and West German Governments), the Integrated Management of Soil and Water Resources Training Courses in the Caucasus (UNEP, Soviet Union, Bulgaria), the African Mountain Training Workshops (UNEP, IMS, Unesco) and several others. Mountain areas have also fostered many vibrant community level NGOs and movements, the best-known being Chipko, which is becoming increasingly involved in conservation and development activities.

But there remains a need for a framework through which all the interested parties (IGOs, NGOs, mountain States and community organisations) may communicate and move ahead cooperatively in promoting conservation and development. Such a framework would need to cover the different characteristics of various biome parts, including relatively well-known cases such as the Himalayas, Andes, Caucusus, Alps, and Rockies, as well as other mountain areas where conser-

vation and development problems are acute - for example, the mountains of eastern and western Africa, Ethiopia, Lesotho, and Papua New Guinea.

Lessons to be learned from the mountains biome are that:

* Conservation plans in mountain areas need to be closely related to local needs and popular wishes. Implementation must be designed in a pragmatic and flexible way.

* The diversity represented by the various isolated mountain communities should not be replaced by monolithic forms of development. On the contrary, appropriate development in mountains should be based on the micro-level adaptations which farmers have been making for thousands of years. Local expertise of great value may be contributed by semi-literate farmers, so development practitioners need to find ways and means of tapping that expertise.

* Local adaptions are integral parts of local cultural systems, thus individual elements of the systems can be interchanged only with considerable care.

* The concept of diversity is central. Mountain peoples have long recognised that diversity is their key to survival so they use numerous means to wrest a living from a reluctant environment. Mixed systems involving transhumance, terraces, agroforestry, local varieties, hunting and fishing, and the forestry-agriculture-wilderness interface are essential to many mountain cultures. This diversity needs to be maintained; what works in one place is not neces-

sarily appropriate for the next valley. A series of local adaptations based on local cultural diversity is more likely to succeed than a "universal elixer" designed to solve all conservation and development problems (McNeely, 1985).

Wetland Ecosystems

Wetlands do not really constitute a "biome" as usually defined by ecologists. Rather, most biomes include wetlands within them, and many types of wetlands occur in several biomes. Important lessons can be learned by treating wetlands as a unit of analysis and a focus for certain types of conservation and development action. In particular, the often diffuse character of wetlands and the array of complex benefits provided by them underline the need for broadly-based approaches to developing this "biome."

The wetland "biome" is one of the few having its own convention. The Ramsar Convention defines wetlands as "areas of marsh, fen, peatland or water, whether natural or artificial, permanent or temporary, with water that is static or flowing, fresh, brackish or salt, including areas of marine water the depth of which at low tide does not exceed six metres." Thus defined, wetlands include mangroves which are particularly noteworthy in that their boundaries are clear and many genera are common to mangrove forests (e.g. *Rhizophora, Sonneratia, Avicennia, Bruguiera*).

Wetlands provide a wide range of products and services, including support of major fisheries, regulating flood levels, and helping to provide pure water supplies. Sustainable uses and products of mangroves alone include: firewood, charcoal, construction materi-

als, paper and woodchips, tannins, foods and drinks, medicines, stock grazing, honey, fish, crustaceans, shell-fish, recreation, education, flood assimilation, shoreline and riverbank protection. Yet despite these myriad benefits, wetlands are often considered as wastelands to be drained for more "productive" purposes. Before such radical ecosystem alteration is carried out, planners need to consider the complex functioning of the wetland as an intact ecosystem.

Species of fish which spend part of their lives in wetlands account for two-thirds of the world's fish harvest. Yet most of these are caught offshore, often by fishing fleets from centres spread widely along the coast, and even by foreign fleets. Many of the functions served by wetlands, such as flood and erosion control, as well as their role in regulating water quality, also bring benefits to communities living hundreds of kilometres from the wetland in question. In these and in many other ways the wetlands of one biome can yield significant benefits to peoples of another.

In a similar way changes occurring in one biome can influence wetlands in another. Thus while the construction of a dam in the tropical forest biome in Nigeria or in the savanna biome of Latin America may have little impact upon the dominant ecosystems of these biomes, resulting changes in hydraulic regime can lead to a major reduction in the productivity of the coastal wetlands which depend upon a regular supply of river-borne water and nutrients. Similarly, siltation caused by inland deforestation is a major source of damage to coral reefs throughout the world.

Further, such impacts can, in some instances, greatly exacerbate existing resource-use problems in a second biome. Thus in the Sahel (as in other parts of arid Africa), wetlands have traditionally provided a reserve of water and pasture for use during critical periods of the dry season. Now, as a result of dam construction in the savanna and forest biomes to the south, the flooding regime of many Sahelian rivers has been seriously altered. In the resulting absence of many traditional wetland refugia, dry season grazing on arid pastures has intensified and has played a major role in degrading the rangelands which is so apparent today.

Pollution is also a serious problem in the wetland biome. Rivers and other wetlands have traditionally been used as disposal sites for industrial and domestic waste. But water draining from agricultural land into lakes and rivers now increasingly carries with it pesticides and fertilizers which lead to eutrophication, and to mortality of aquatic life. Although measures have now been taken to improve water quality in several major river systems, less well-known small water courses, lakes and marshes have received little attention. Similarly it is these smaller sites which are increasingly subject to alteration and drainage. In many cases the combined value of small sites is greater than that of any major wetland, so danger of loss for these "minor" sites requires greater attention. Thus, while in the past wetland conservation efforts have focused upon wetlands of international importance, there is now a major realisation that broader emphasis needs to be directed toward maintaining wetlands as a *unit in the landscape*, rather than simply conserving a few wet museums.

These are but a few of the threats facing wetlands. The list for mangroves is particularly distressing. Threats include: mining and mineral extraction, diversion of freshwater, conversion to agriculture and aquaculture, salt pond construction, construction of channels and harbours, solid and liquid waste disposal, oil and other hazardous chemical pollution, and over-exploitation of plant and animal species (Saenger, Hegerl, and Davie, 1983).

Numerous additional examples from all parts of the globe could be provided. But there is one common and alarming feature: all of these threats have impacts which can reach well beyond the biome or region in which they occur. Wetlands everywhere suffer from what Kahn (1966) has referred to as the Tyranny of Small Decisions. The piecemeal destruction of wetlands does not reflect all the consequences of the cumulative effects of many small wetlands alterations.

From this brief overview of wetland ecosystems three major lessons emerge:

* There is constant flow of goods and services between many biomes. Environmentally-sound management requires that the decision-making process takes full account of this flow.

* Biomes consist of many individual ecosystems, many of which are thinly distributed within the biome. Appropriate biome conservation strategies therefore need to consider not only the dominant ecosystem (or best example of each ecosystem within each biome), but must take full account of minor yet important ecosystems and sites.

* The full value of any ecosystem can only be properly assessed by means of determining the combined contribution of individual sites.

SOME LIMITATIONS OF THE BIOME APPROACH

While the previous discussion has indicated the utility of biome-based approaches, several evident limitations should also be discussed if development practioners are to have a balanced understanding of what the biome approach can and cannot do. Its major limitations are that:

* Discussing problems at the biome level may tend to over-generalise solutions. The danger lies in assuming that because ecosystems are similar, solutions will be likewise. Since each biome is a complex collection of smaller semi-independent but inter-related ecosystems, it is at the level of the smaller unit that solutions need to be applied.

* While a biome strategy is essential to provide a framework within which to assess local conditions, the biome scale is usually too large to prescribe specific action.

* Because the scale of analysis is so large and general, biome-based strategies often tend to advocate central planning approaches rather than promoting local adaptations for sustainable use of locally-available resources.

* Biomes are seldom reflected by an administrative structure within governments, so responsibility for implementing biome-based strategies is often diffuse.

I would now like to address a more fundamental concern: the conflict between what our distinguished colleague Ray Dasmann has called "ecosystem people" and "biosphere people" (Dasmann, 1976). While this dichotomy is perhaps better visualised as ends of a spectrum, ecosystem people generally live within the constraints established by local environmental conditions, while biosphere people draw support not from any one local ecosystem but from the entire capital of the world's living matter. Consuming planetary resources through rapid, inexpensive trade and communications, biosphere people can bring great amounts of energy and materials to bear on any one ecosystem, abandoning it when it is no longer sufficiently productive.

Over-exploiting the tropical forests of Thailand, for example, is no problem for biosphere people because there are still many tropical forests in Indonesia. And when the Indonesian forests are depleted, the world can draw on Zaire or Brazil. But what happens to the local people who remain dependent on the now-depleted living resources, who indeed had developed ways and means of using these resources sustainably, without depletion?

The answer is easy. Like the people of the drought-stricken Sahel, they must become biosphere people and draw on the resources of the rest of the world, even if they cannot always pay for them. No problem.

No problem, that is, until the intricate chain of interdependencies begins to break down. People in the Sahel can starve while exporting vegetables, cotton, and peanuts to Europe. But surely, we all hope, the more we multiply our interdependence, the less likely we are to let the chain break through inadvertence, mis-handling of the debt crisis, manipulations by oil cartels, or even, heaven forbid, through a major war.

Is there a rational basis for this hope of increasing inter-dependency? There is indeed: modern history. Over the past 200 years, world prosperity has steadily increased with only a few disruptions along the way. This long, steady growth in prosperity has been very comforting, and in fact has enabled us to come from all around the world to meet in Ottawa today.

Unfortunately, a hard look at the ecological basis of this prosperity is shockingly sobering. We are prosperous fundamentally because we have been able to tap a "new" source of energy which has enabled us to grow, process and distribute far more food than ever before. The fossil fuels - coal and oil - are non-renewable; once they are gone, they are gone forever. And long before they are truly gone, they will be so expensive that they will no longer play much of a role in the human ecosystem.

Without cheap and plentiful energy, the "global ecological niche" of biosphere people cannot be sustained for very long. Gever, *et. al.* (1986) have carried out a very thoughtful analysis on the impact of declining oil supplies on the economy of the United States. In sum, they have found that by 2005 at the latest, and perhaps as early as 1995, it will take more energy on average to explore for new US oil and gas than the wells will produce; United

States oil will be virtually exhausted by 2020. Neither the supply of alternative fuels nor the nation's energy efficiency can be increased quickly enough to completely offset the effect of declining supplies of oil and gas, which now account for 75 percent of US fuel use. Therefore, a long-term downturn in US GNP is likely soon, they report, probably starting in the 1990's. Most disturbing from the global perspective (given that the United States is by far the world's leading food exporter), is the probability that the United States may cease to be a net exporter of food within the next 20 to 35 years. The dependency of US agriculture on oil for fertilizers, pesticides, tractors, pumps, drying, storage, and transport has led to great vulnerability both for the United States and for countries dependent upon United States food exports.

Clearly, this study has important implications far beyond the United States. The "green revolution," for example, is generally unsustainable because its major inputs - fertilizer, pesticides, pumped water, storage and transport facilities - depend on oil. So the green revolution, which has saved the world from the chaos of famine, has enabled the human population to reach levels which may not be sustainable.

What then? No one can predict the future, but perhaps we can agree that the best we can hope for is relative stability and a calm, peaceful evolution to a new ecological niche. This will have to depend on locally-available resources for most of the basic requirements of life. This need not necessarily mean a radical reduction in quality of life, but social, economic, and environmental conditions will surely be fundamentally different without oil. By stressing the importance of developing new and sustainable ways of using renewable resources now, while we still have the luxury of considerable surplus wealth and maybe even sufficient time, an approach to development based on natural ecosystems could help lay the foundation for the future. But we had better hurry, before the debt crisis reveals that the "surplus" wealth is only a paper tiger.

SYNTHESIS: GETTING THE MOST OUT OF THE BIOME APPROACH

Drawing from the preceding discussion, it is evident that **the major concern about biome-based conservation strategies is to ensure that they promote self-reliance rather than dependence**. This requires that steps be taken to ensure that ecological integrity of the biome is maintained.

Derived from this primary concern are several other considerations:

* The biome should be treated as a complex collection of smaller, semi-independent but inter-related ecosystems which must be managed locally, and also as part of a generalised whole. Management strategies need to be based on ecosystems and habitats, perceived as inter-related components of a biome. The complex network of links, feedbacks, species, nutrients and biomass flowing **between** the various ecosystems keep the biome working as a whole, which is far more than the sum of its parts.

* Biome-based strategies must promote local adaptations for sustainable use of locally-available resources, rather than relying on central planning approaches. But these local adaptations are most likely to lead to lasting benefits when they are implemented with the most knowledge possible of component parts of involved ecosystems. Ignoring linkages between local ecosystems and the rest of the biome risks producing unexpected, undesirable, and counter-intuitive perturbations in other parts of the biome.

* Biome approaches need to be practically relevant to real on-the-ground problems, which require local application; and they must be integrated with other types of programmes where administrative responsibility can be assigned to a specific implementing agency.

In short, biome-based strategies are most useful when they are used as broad frameworks which provide a comprehensive perspective for action at the local ecosystem level. However, interconnections between biomes need to be considered as well. As Riklefs *et. al.* (1984) have pointed out, planning for development projects should be approached at the level of large natural units, such as major watersheds and coastal areas, which circumscribe the movement of materials and populations in the areas in question. All resource management programmes - including agricultural systems, forestry, water resources, and national parks - within such areas are inevitably linked and cannot be considered apart from one another. In addition, the costs and benefits of development programmes can be realistically assessed only on the scale of the total system affected. As emphasised in the case of wetlands, costs or benefits may otherwise be transported from one part of the system to another and not properly weighed in decision-making processes focused on small areas.

A primary principle of integrating development and the conservation of ecological processes is that **management should work within the framework of natural patterns and cycles, not seek to change them.** This requires identifying appropriate use for various regions and habitats on a sustained level with minimal management, i.e., that which leaves the maximum number of natural regulatory mechanisms intact. The importance of learning from natural mechanisms in development and management programmes argues strongly for preserving large tracts of relatively intact ecosystems so that their natural self-regulatory mechanisms may be understood, and later applied to specific management problems within the same biogeographic unit (Riklefs, *et. al.*, 1984).

CONCLUSIONS

As oil is replaced by other forms of energy, we, as a species comprised of many local populations, will need all the information we can gather about how to adapt to local ecosystems. The transfer of knowledge from one part of a biome to another may well yield important new insights on how to manage living resources, often drawing on traditional knowledge. New ways of controlling agricultural pests through biological means, producing natural fertilizers, adapting domestic plant breeds to local conditions, and developing sustainable cropping systems may well be discovered through a biome approach which builds on the ways people can

adapt to the limitations of local ecosystems.

Realising that the "global ecosystem" is here to stay (at least as long as the oil lasts), the biome approach makes it easy to adapt sectoral and local strategies to biome-level requirements. Conversely, biome strategies can also, if handled properly, provide guidelines for local action which can be further refined and adapted to local needs.

While the best biome-based strategies are aimed at solving problems we face today, they also have the ultimate potential of greatly contributing to present needs for improved management, and to our post-petroleum future when renewable resources become the mainstay of human civilisation.

Logically, there is no long-term alternative to mankind living in balance with the living environment. Short-term over-exploitation of individual ecosystems may delude us into believing that all is well, but the time will come when the human species must find ways to become a productive part of the various world biomes. How difficult and painful this process of adaptation will be in the future depends very much on three main factors:

* How well we are able to maintain diverse and productive ecosystems;

* How well we are able to develop new and improved agricultural technology which fundamentally creates new types of agro-ecosystems; and

* How well we are able to learn lessons from the diverse human cul-

tures which have found ways to live in balance with their local ecosystems.

In the short-term, the types of actions which could be relevant at the biome level include:

* Rehabilitation programmes for threatened or degraded ecosystems, such as areas in the wet tropics which have lost their forests or areas of the Sahel that have lost their woodlands or wetlands;

* Demonstrations of alternative management approaches which are sustainable and promote productive ecosystem functioning;

* Programmes to record the ways and means of people having lived in harmony within ecosystems, and to apply this knowledge to modern requirements;

* Compilation of inventories on the contents and functioning of ecosystems within various biomes, to provide a basis for conservation and development action;

* A major awareness programme for senior government officials which would promote human adaptations to local ecosystems, ensure that impacts on ecosystems and ecological processes are considered in all development projects, and provide material for the government to convince the urban public of the wisdom of conservation policies.

The planet Earth is a human ecosystem and its balance cannot be maintained by isolated preserves no matter how well they are managed. Instead, a spectrum of more knowledgeable, carefully controlled and carefully tailored human influences on local ecosystems needs to evolve to allow both the maintenance of biological diversity and the continued prosperity of *Homo sapiens*.

ACKNOWLEDGEMENTS

This paper was prepared with the assistance of my colleagues in the IUCN Programme and Policy Division. Contributors included Robert Scott, Delmar Blasco, Ole Hamann, Jeff Sayer (tropical forests), David Pitt (mountains), Patrick Dugan (wetlands), Taghi Farvar, James Thorsell, Simon Stuart, Frederic Briand, and George Frame. Advice, comments and contributions were also received from Mark Halle and Keith Rennie of IUCN's Conservation for Development Centre, and from Jerry Harrison, Mark Collins and Sue Wells of IUCN's Conservation Monitoring Centre. Norman Myers provided his usual incisive comments. However, none of the above are responsible for the final form of the paper, nor does the paper represent official IUCN policy.

REFERENCES

- Allen, J.A., 1877, "The Geographic Distribution of Mammals," Bull. *U.S. Geol. Geogr. Survey*, 4,339-343.

- Bailey, Robert G., 1982, "Classification Systems for Habitat and Ecosystems," pp. 16-26 in US Environmental Protection Agency, *Research on Fish and Wildlife Habitat*, EPA, Washington, D.C.

- Brown, Lester R., 1981, *Building a Sustainable Society*, W. W. Norton and Co., New York, London.

- Colinvaux, Paul A., 1973, *Introduction to Ecology*, John Wiley and Sons, Inc., New York.

- Croizat, Leon, 1958, *Panbiogeography*, L. Croizat, Caracas.

- Danserau, Pierre, 1957, *Biogeography: An Ecological Perspective*, Ronald Press, New York.

- Darlington, Philip J., 1957, *Zoogeography: The Geographical Distribution of Animals*, John Wiley and Sons, New York.

- Dasmann, Raymond F., 1976, "Lifestyles and Nature Conservation," *Oryx*, 13(3), 281-286.

- Dasmann, Raymond F., 1975, *The Conservation Alternative*, John Wiley and Sons, Inc., New York.

- Dasmann, Raymond F., 1959, *Environmental Conservation*, John Wiley and Sons, Inc., New York.

- Dasmann, Raymond F., John P. Milton, and Peter H. Freeman, 1973, *Ecological Principles for Economic Development*, John Wiley and Sons Ltd., London.

- Dasmann, R.F. and D. Poore, 1979, *Ecological Guidelines for Balanced Land Use, Conservation and Devlopment in High Mountains*, IUCN, Morges.

- Dieren, van W. and M.G.W. Hummelinck, 1979, *Nature's Price: The Economics of Mother Earth*, Marion Boyars Ltd., London.

- Eckholm, Erik P., 1982, *Down to Earth*, W.W. Norton and Company, New York.

- FAO, 1985, *Tropical Forestry Action Plan*, FAO, Rome.

- Frankel, O.H. and Michael E. Soulé, 1981, *Conservation and Evolution*, Cambridge University Press.

- Furtado, J. I. (ed), 1980, *Tropical Ecology and Development*, The International Society of Tropical Ecology, Kuala Lumpur.

- Gever, John, Robert Kaufmann, David Skole, and Charles Vorosmarty, 1986, *Beyond Oil: The Threat to Food and Fuel in the Coming Decades*, Ballinger Publishing Co., Cambridge, Massachusetts.

- Golley, Frank B. and Ernesto Medina, 1975, *Tropical Ecological Systems*, Springer-Verlag, New York.

- Good, Ronald, 1964, *The Geography of Flowering Plants*, John Wiley and Sons, New York.

- Hadley, Malcolm and Jean-Paul Lanly, 1983, "Tropical Forest Ecosystems: Identifying Differences, Seeking Similarities," *Nature and Resources*, 19(1), 2-19.

- Harrison, J., K.R. Miller, and J.A. McNeely, 1984, "The World Coverage of Protected Areas, Development Goals and Environmental Needs," pp. 24-33 in McNeely, J.A. and K.R. Miller (eds), *National Parks, Conservation, and Development: The Role of Protected Areas in Sustaining Society*, Smithsonian Instition Press, Washington D.C.

- Hamilton, Lawrence S. and Samuel C. Snedaker (eds.), 1984, *Handbook for Mangrove Area Management*, IUCN/UNEP/East-West Centre.

- Hardin, Garrett, 1982, *Naked Emperors*, William Kaufman, Los Altos.

- Hesse, Richard, W.C. Allee, and K.P. Schmidt, 1951, *Ecological Animal Geography*, John Wiley and Sons, New York.

- Holdridge, L.R., 1967, *Life Zone Ecology, Tropical Research Centre,* San José.

- IUCN, 1985, *The Sahel: Environmental Degradation and Rehabilitation,* Diagnosis and Proposals for IUCN's Response, draft report, Gland, Switzerland.

- IUCN, 1980, *World Conservation Strategy,* IUCN, Gland, Switzerland.

- IUCN, 1975a, *Ecological Guidelines for the Use of Natural Resources in the Middle East and South West Asia,* IUCN, Gland, Switzerland.

- IUCN, 1975b, *The Use of Ecological Guidelines for Development in the American Humid Tropics,* IUCN, Gland, Switzerland.

- IUCN, 1975c, *The Use of Ecological Guidelines for Development in Tropical Forest Areas of South West Asia,* IUCN, Gland, Switzerland.

- Kormondy, Edward J., 1969, *Concepts of Ecology*, Prentice-Hall, Inc., Englewood Cliffs, New Jersey.

- Lincoln, R.J., G.A. Boxshall and P.F. Clark, 1982, *A Dictionary of Ecology, Evolution and Systematics,* Cambridge University Press.

- Lovelock, J.E., 1979, Gaia, *A New Look at Life on Earth*, Oxford University Press, London.

- McEachern, J. and E.L. Towle, 1974, *Ecological Guidelines for Island Development*, IUCN, Gland, Switzerland.

- McHarg, Ian L., 1971, *Design with Nature,* Doubleday-Natural History Press, Garden City, New York.

- McNeely, Jeffrey A., 1985, "Man and Nature in the Himalaya: What can be done to ensure that both can prosper" pp. 25 - 31 in McNeely, J.A., J.W. Thorsell and S.R. Chalise, *People and Protected Areas in the Hindu Kush-Himalaya*, King Mahendra Trust and ICIMOD, Kathmandu.

- Merriam, C.H., 1894, "Laws of Temperature Control of Geograhic Distribution of Terrestrial Mammals and Plants," *National Geographic Magazine*, 6:229-238.

- Myers, Norman, 1983, *A Wealth of Wild Species*, West View Press, Boulder, Colorado.

- National Research Council, 1982, *Ecological Aspects of Development in the Humid Tropics*, National Academy Press, Washington, D.C.

- National Research Council, 1980, *Research Priorities in Tropical Biology*, National Academy of Sciences, Washington, D.C.

- Odum, Eugene P., 1971, *Fundamentals of Ecology*, W.B. Saunders Co.

- Odum, W.E., 1976, *Ecological Guidelines for Tropical Coastal Development*, IUCN, Gland, Switzerland.

- Ophuls, William, 1977, *Ecology and the Politics of Scarcity*, W.H. Freeman and Company, San Francisco.

- Poore, D., 1976, *Ecological Guidelines for Development in Tropical Rain Forests*, IUCN, Gland, Switzerland.

- Riklefs, R.E., Z. Naveh, and R.E. Turner, 1984, "Conservation of Ecological Processes," *IUCN Commission on Ecology Papers* 8, 1-16.

- Saenger, P., E.J. Hegerl and J.D.S. Davie, 1983, *Global Status of Mangrove Ecosystems*, IUCN, Gland, Switzerland.

- Sahlins, Marshall, 1972, *Stone Age Economics*, Aldine Publishing Co., Chicago.

- Schonewald-Cox, Christine M. and Steven M. Chambers, Bruce Mac Bryde, Larry Thomas, 1983, *Genetics and Conservation*, The Benjamin-Cummings Publishing Co. Inc., Menlo Park, California.

- Sclater, W.L. and P.L. Sclater, 1899, *The Geography of Mammals,* Kegan Paul, Trench, Trubuer, and Co., London.

- Simmons, I.G., 1979, *Biogeography: Natural and Cultural,* Edward Arnold, London.

- Soulé, Michael E. and Bruce A. Wilcox, (eds.) 1980, *Conservation Biology,* Sinauer Associates Inc., Sunderland, Massachusetts.

- Southwick, Charles H., 1976, *Ecology and the Quality of our Environment*, D. Van Nostrand Co., New York.

- Udvardy, Miklos D.F., 1975, *A Classification of the Biogeographical Provinces*, IUCN Occasional Paper 18, Gland, Switzerland.

- UNEP, 1982, *Intergrated Regional Schemes to Combat Desertification*, UNEP Centre of International Projects, Moscow.

- Wallace, A. R., 1876, *The Geographical Distribution of Animals*, Harper, New York, (2 vols.).

- Whittaker, Robert H., 1970, *Communities and Ecosystems*, The Macmillan Co., London.

- World Resources Institute, 1985, *Tropical Forests: A Call for Action*, WRI, Washington D.C.

NATIONAL CONSERVATION STRATEGIES

Plenary Session 4

_____

NATIONAL CONSERVATION STRATEGIES

Plenary Session 4

Maurice Strong, Chairperson
Special Adviser to the Secretary General
of the United Nations
New York, U.S.A.

In his introduction, the Chairperson noted that while the World Conservation Strategy can be implemented only through sound national conservation strategies, it is equally true that it cannot be planned or effectively implemented in a purely national context. He noted that the Conference, like the World Commission on Environment and Development, was a manifestation of the growing realisation that environment and development were inextricably linked. Ecological as well as economic factors have a significant impact on growth and development. A conservation strategy is clearly a sensible growth strategy which accurately reflects the systemic nature of the issues which must be addressed. It is through economic policies that we affect the environment, and it is only by informing those who command the levers of economic growth and development that we will ensure the conservation of environmental and natural resources and maintain environmental resources as our most important capital stocks. We must shift our emphasis from conventional development to sustainable development.

The World Conservation Strategy prescribed the formulation of national conservation strategies as the primary means of achieving conservation. The case studies and theme framework paper of this session indicate not only the variety of ecological, social and political conditions that must be taken into account in preparing national conservation strategies but also the spectrum of useful approaches. Common and diverse elements of national conservation strategies are identified and discussed by Halle and Furtado in the theme framework paper. Case study presentations relate to Australia (Kerr and Mosley); Indonesia (Salim); Nepal (Amatya and Naysmith); Vietnam (Le Thac Can and Vo Quy); and Zambia (Mukutu and Mwale).

The Chairperson also emphasised that conservation strategies were not for conservationists alone; they must be implemented by those who establish and carry out economic development policies. But we should note that there are neither national nor international institutions that combine both approaches in their mandates. Thus conservation and development together must become the central theme on the global agenda.

THE ROLE OF NATIONAL CONSERVATION STRATEGIES IN ATTAINING OBJECTIVES OF THE WORLD CONSERVATION STRATEGY

M. Halle
IUCN Conservation for Development Centre
Gland, Switzerland

J. I. Furtado
Commonwealth Secretariat
London, United Kingdom

SUMMARY *The World Conservation Strategy, as one of its priority recommendations, urges the preparation of strategies to integrate conservation with development at national and subnational levels. This is in recognition of the fact that, whereas many environmental issues are of a transboundary nature, most decisions affecting the use or conservation of natural resources are made by national or local governments, at least in less-advanced countries. National conservation strategies (NCSs) are now underway or completed in over 30 countries and a great deal has been learned from the experience. This paper explores the nature of national conservation strategies, what they aim to do and how the NCS process can best be designed to achieve its objectives. In doing so, it underlines some of the strengths of the NCS process as well as some of the obstacles still to be overcome. Finally, it discusses certain issues relating to the formulation of a national conservation strategy which, it is hoped, will serve as a point of departure for debate.*

INTRODUCTION

The launching of the World Conservation Strategy in March 1980 was a significant turning point in the history of the conservation movement. It marked the transition from a fragmented local approach to nature preservation that was somewhat divorced from the realities of human and natural resource development, to one involving the integration of nature conservation with natural resource and human development, both globally and locally. The need for this change in perception emerged as a scientific issue at the Intergovernmental Conference of Experts on the Scientific Basis for Rational Use and Conservation of the Resources of the Biosphere. The Conference was convened in 1986 by the United Nations Educational Scientific and Cultural Organisation (Unesco) in Paris, to review international scientific programmes concerning nature and natural resources. The International Biological Programme (IBP), which received special attention, focused research and training on biological productivity of various natural and man-made ecosystem or biome types.

Four years later, that same need was articulated politically at the United Nations Conference on the Human Environment (UNCHE), convened by the United Nations in Stockholm (1972). Both of these international meetings led to action programmes: the Man and the Biosphere (MAB) Programme of Unesco, and the United Nations Environment Programme (UNEP), respectively. While the recommendations of the Stockholm Conference (UNCHE) have been endorsed by all countries and the MAB Programme by most, the World Conservation Strategy has yet to receive global endorsement, although its counterpart, the World Charter for Nature, has been broadly adopted.

The change in the perception of conservation as concerning the health of the biosphere may be attributed to a number of factors:

* International development under two United Nations Development Decades failed in the tropical and arid zones because emphasis was placed on sectoral economic growth and industrialisation following models used in the temperate zone.

* Development assistance emphasising economic and industrial growth failed to address the questions of wealth distribution, environmental protection and the quality of life in the less-advanced countries, resulting in increased malnutrition, poverty, environmental hazards, graft and debt.

* Institutional structures inherited historically by less-advanced countries of the tropical and arid zones (the "South") failed to integrate technology transfers from the advanced countries of the temperate zone (the "North") because of the inappropriate nature of technology transferred and of inadequate local scientific and technological capability for development. (Rapid scientific advances and technological innovations resulting from investments in research and development in the North have heightened this technological gap with the South).

* Extensive transformations of nature and natural resources demonstrated the ecological linkages between natural communities, habitats, and ecosystem or biome types at regional and global levels.

* Space science, technology and cultural exchange increasingly reinforced notions of a common global heritage, destiny and unity.

Conservation in its new form embodies three significant modifications to the traditional Western understanding of the concept. Conservation has traditionally been regarded in the industrialised countries as a rearguard movement, saving and preserving pristine landscapes, untouched ecosystems or habitats, and rare species from the relentless onslaught of human and natural resource development. The task of the conservationist was to muster as much influence as possible to counterbalance development which, while regarded as a necessary evil, had to be prevented by conservationists from "going too far." The scope of this concern and action was essentially at local and national levels.

Secondly, and related to the first, conservation had a strong moral emphasis embracing the notions of respect for nature and of Man's duty to protect it - usually in the interests of future generations. Species and habitats were thus protected, not because they offered a potential for natural resource development, such as a potential cure for cancer or a potential guarantee of a viable irrigation system, and not even because "they were there" - but because it was a moral imperative not to destroy what nature had created. The conservation component of most major religions and belief systems has been noted elsewhere, and is certainly significant in many human cultures.

Thirdly, the protection of species and habitats was undertaken largely at the local and national levels, with international concern only for the spectacular or unique species, habitats, or ecosystems. The unequal global distribution of species or habitat and ecosystem types, and their international significance as a common resource for all humanity to share, use and protect, were not perceived as being important even though most agricultural economies have flourished on exotic species and the tropics have been known to harbour a wealth of species of potential economic use.

The rationale for conservation thus clearly involved a number of elements which were not normally taken into account in decision-making processes on society, technology, resources and the economy. The Western notion of conservation was essentially part of a dualism in opposing resource development - the Manichaean black and white. It was steeped in Teutonic logic that had influenced Western civilisation and religions for centuries, and was regarded as the antithesis of the so-called "Protestant ethic" of development. This ethic advocated the exploitation of all environmental and natural resources so that Man could subjugate Nature. It was treated with considerable circumspection in Asia where cultures founded on ancient civilisations were based on the notion of Man as an integral part of nature. The ideal world represented a balance between these elements: enough development to ensure an improved quality of life but enough conservation to ensure that the natural environment was worth living in, without specifying the balance in space, time or technology.

How did the World Conservation Strategy change this? Conservation as understood by the World Conservation Strategy (WCS) has not totally abandoned traditional Western views, but has broadened its scope considerably and, in so doing, has changed its perspective. Conservation still embraces nature preservation so that sound conservation action can, in many cases, mean a strong and active opposition to resource development. However, conservation and development are no longer regarded as separate and opposing issues. The World Conservation Strategy defines development as "the modification of the biosphere and the application of human, financial, living and non-living resources to satisfy human needs and improve the quality of human life;" and conservation as "the management of human use of the biosphere so that it may yield the greatest sustainable benefit to present generations while maintaining its potential to meet the needs and aspirations of future generations." It is immediately evident that conservation and development embrace the same elements. Development, by and large, is predicated on the transformation of natural resources for human needs; conservation is concerned with managing that process of transformation in the interests of long-term sustainability. The relationship is recurring with conservation performing a regulatory role in the resource transformation process.

While the opposition to conservation has not altogether disappeared, it now means that "good" development incorporates conservation; whereas "bad" development ignores the realities of conserving resources. **Has the moral content of conservation disappeared?** On the contrary, it has been permeated and reinforced by sound ecological and economic principles, so that conservation can hold its own position in the development debate.

The World Conservation Strategy provides guidelines on the essentials of conservation and on how to bring about "good" development; that is, development which integrates conservation concerns and which uses resources in a sustainable manner over the long term. It suggests a range of actions at local, national and international levels; provides the conservation components for sustainable development; and points to a number of considerations for decision-makers who subscribe to its philosophy. It is not a blueprint and does not provide the answer to issues and conflicts pertaining to everyday decision-making on conservation and development, nor is that its intention. It is a starting point from which many paths will radiate leading to differing approaches to conservation and development at local, national and international levels, depending on social and cultural perceptions about the quality

of life and on the stage of human development reached.

This paper explores one of these paths: the notion of implementing the World Conservation Strategy at the national level through the formulation of National Conservation Strategies (NCSs). Its analysis is based on experience in more than 30 countries. It provides a tentative evaluation of the extent to which the NCS formulation has led to improvements in the sustainability of resource transformation; notes some of the obstacles encountered and the ways in which these obstacles have been overcome; and outlines a number of issues requiring further debate and discussion on NCS development. It is, in particular, the statement of these issues which we hope will guide discussions at the Conference.

HISTORY OF THE NATIONAL CONSERVATION STRATEGY

The World Conservation Strategy (WCS) recommends *inter alia* that each country "review the extent to which it is achieving conservation, concentrating on the priority requirements and on the main obstacles to them." It further suggests that such a review should form the basis of a strategy to overcome the obstacles to, and meet the requirements of, conservation for sustainable development. Such national strategies are intended "to provide the means of focussing and coordinating the efforts of government agencies, together with non-governmental conservation organizations, to implement the World Conservation Strategy within countries." It also suggests that these strategies "would serve the purpose of focussing the attention on relative priority requirements for conservation, stimulating appropriate action, raising public consciousness and overcoming any apathy or resistance there might be to taking the action needed."

While offering perfectly sound advice, the World Conservation Strategy does not provide any particular guidance on such practical measures as who should take the lead in formulating strategies, what steps should be taken, how the different partners should be involved, what the final outcome should be, and many other questions essential to successful formulation and implementation of National Conservation Strategies. Clearly, there can be no detailed guidelines as to what NCS documents should contain since they must be closely related to the policy-making structure of each country, and must respond to the realities of each country's level of environmental, technological and political awareness, and infrastructure for development. Nevertheless, it has been clear from the start that, in promoting NCSs, the International Union for Conservation of Nature and Natural Resources (IUCN) and its co-sponsors of the World Conservation Strategy were embarking in new directions, especially in providing a focal integrating theme for governmental and non-governmental sectors.

Following the launch of the World Conservation Strategy, World Wildlife Fund (WWF) and IUCN made a clear commitment to support its implementation, in particular, through the formulation of national conservation strategies. This was given a high priority as the principal means of ensuring that the WCS would not remain a pious compendium of wishes but instead would be rapidly transformed into a cultural and interactive process. With this in

mind, IUCN established the Conservation for Development Centre (CDC), a specialised operational centre within the IUCN Secretariat, to respond to requests from countries for assistance in implementing the World Conservation Strategy. In 1981, IUCN's Commission on Environmental Planning also focused on the subject of publishing "Guidelines." WWF agreed to support a major effort to implement the WCS and sponsored a "World Conservation Strategy Follow-Up" project through CDC, beginning in 1982. The first priority of this project was to promote the establishment of national conservation strategies in certain less-advanced countries.

IUCN and WWF received requests for assistance in formulating NCSs almost immediately. Nepal and Zambia were two of the earliest countries to respond, and IUCN missions visited these countries in 1982 and 1984 to initiate the NCS process. Further assistance was provided to other countries either directly or indirectly. WWF's National Organisation in Malaysia also initiated work on a series of State strategies and several advanced countries, such as the United Kingdom, Italy, New Zealand and Australia, launched national conservation strategies without direct involvement of either IUCN or WWF. Other countries, such as Norway, Spain and The Netherlands undertook projects aimed at determining the relevance of the World Conservation Strategy to their own policies and practices.

In 1983, IUCN organised a seminar to take stock of NCS activities in the less-advanced countries and to prepare a guide on NCS formulation based on this experience. This document, *National Conservation Strategies - A*

Framework for Sustainable Development was published in January 1984.

The second purpose of the WWF-sponsored project in CDC was to interest other funding sources in endorsing NCS formulation and related project work in less-advanced countries. Sweden and The Netherlands were early supporters of this work, followed closely by the United States. Since then, several other sponsors have provided funds for NCS work, including Canada, Norway, the European Economic Community and the United Nations Environment Programme.

LESSONS EMERGING FROM THE NATIONAL CONSERVATION STRATEGY EXPERIENCE

Although a detailed listing of countries having developed an NCS depends on the definitions used, more than 30 countries have formulated (or are in the process of formulating) national conservation strategies or strategies at a sub-national level. This slow pace in initiating NCSs is attributable to a number of factors, notably the potential policy conflicts between nature conservation and environmental protection, the lack of national capability or infrastructure, and/or the lack of financial resources. At this rate, a generation appears to be required for initiating national conservation strategies in all countries. Hence, alternative mechanisms need to be explored for implementing the World Conservation Strategy, and these are reviewed elsewhere. Of the NCSs executed, the majority are in the African and Asia-Pacific regions. Less-advanced countries have principally undertaken them, with Fiji and St. Lucia being the only small island States.

There appears to be a correlation between development of the NCS process in low-income countries and the availability of development assistance funds. There is a need to assess the significance of ecological priorities to these countries and to explore how the NCS process could be incorporated into development planning. Most are located in the tropical and arid zones, which are rich in biological diversity although environmentally fragile. For sustainable development, therefore, these national conservation strategies need to be reinforced by transnational interests of the industrialised and newly-industrialised countries - as the greatest consumers of natural resources within these zones - and by the traditional informal consultative process of decision-making.

Although there can be no such thing as a "typical" NCS because of the strong links between the form and content of policy-making on one hand, and national cultures, political systems and institutional arrangements on the other, the experience gained in formulating NCSs has yielded a number of lessons which may be more generally applicable. The purpose of a national conservation strategy is to build consensus among actual or potential users of natural resources about optimal use of those resources on a sustainable basis. It may also be used to adjudicate between cases where one form of use calls for total exploitation of resources and another for total preservation. Thus, in brief, the aim of the NCS is to achieve consensus on optimal use of natural resources in promoting sustainable patterns of development. However, no document in itself can achieve the ambitious goals of conflict-resolution and consensus-building, both of which are vital if conservation and development are to be integrated as proposed by the WCS.

The first lesson from various NCS experiences is that the formulation of a national conservation strategy is an important yet complex process. Just as national policies must be published and endorsed, it is essential that, at a suitable stage in the NCS process, a national conservation strategy document be published, adopted by government, and endorsed by the public. Thereafter it should be used as a benchmark against which to review achievement in integrating conservation with development. The NCS document can serve as a useful sourcebook and reference, providing material for environmental education and public information. However, the essential point is that *the NCS process rather than the product* is of paramount importance.

The continuity of this process is based on the assumption that human development is characterised by perennial social and technological change although actual realisation of that change may not always take place. Various factors pertaining to development affect conservation as a regulatory mechanism, especially in the less-advanced countries of the tropics and sub-tropics:

* rapid population growth with a doubling rate of about 35 years, resulting in differential impacts on natural resources, the environment, capital, technology and infrastructure;

* youthful demographic structure creating demands on a range of social and welfare services and on the distribution of wealth;

* demands on natural resources necessitating a global reorganisation of production systems to combat the differential impacts of poverty, malnutrition, starvation, epidemics and natural hazards;

* environmental degradation and hazards resulting from careless use of good and marginal lands, and the unpredictability of global climatic changes;

* economic crises reflecting, in particular, unequal access to capital formation and the inability to sustain high economic growth rates;

* technological disparities due to marked differences in technical expertise, research and development investments, the increasing pace of scientific discoveries and the stream of technological innovations generated by each discovery.

The second lesson is that successful strategies cannot be carried out wholly by national governments, no matter how broadly based their mandate nor advanced their infrastructure. In almost all cases, the most effective approach appears to be that government takes the lead and overall responsibility for formulating the NCS, since it determines the principal policies and decisions on allocation and use of natural resources. Furthermore, in any process of consensus-building aimed at change, those who are responsible for policies and decisions must play a central role. At the same time, NCSs generally call for a significant shift in the way policies and decisions are made and in view of the re-orientation of perspectives on conservation and development. Government bureaucracies generally favour compromise and stability which makes them disinclined to radical change. Therefore, they should be effectively counterbalanced by strong participation from non-governmental organisations whose role often includes that of a "watch-dog" or lobby. The role of the agricultural, industrial and commercial sectors is critical for formulating an effective NCS, since development is sponsored largely by private enterprise or initiative. The degree to which national conservation strategies are linked to national planning is uncertain in many cases, especially since a significant proportion of the less-advanced countries with weak infrastructures have no Five-Year Development Plans. This weakness in the planning infrastructure is reflected in the recruitment of foreign consultants to undertake NCSs in least-advanced countries; it will have to be addressed wherever necessary to ensure the continuity and national nature of the NCS process. Thus the second lesson is that *successful national conservation strategies rely on expertise from governmental and non-governmental sectors*.

The third lesson to be learned is that successful national conservation strategies are those which involve participation of all sectors in formulating, implementing, monitoring and review of the NCS. It may be necessary to treat a strategy document as highly confidential when it is initiated, but finalising it for implementation by its supposed beneficiaries needs participation from all sectors. Consensus building is a slow and difficult process requiring substantial debate and education within the public and private sectors. Only by continuous interaction in seeking solutions to resource use and allocation conflicts will the value of each contributory viewpoint be judged. It is par-

ticularly important to dispel the impression that an NCS is an "environmental sector study." Too often this impression has prevailed, especially when the lead has been taken by a Ministry of Environment or its equivalent, so much that other Ministries or sectors regard the NCS as the domain of that Ministry rather than as an initiative of concern to them as well. Thus, there is value in establishing a clearly-identified and independent secretariat for the purpose of formulating the Strategy, in which there is strong and balanced representation from both the development and environment sectors. *A national conservation strategy regarded as an environmental sector study misses its essential purpose*: that of determining the conservation limits of development.

The fourth lesson concerns the duration of the NCS process. It begins with initial discussions on the value of the NCS process to the country, continues through adoption of the consensus document by government and concerned public, and leads to implementation, monitoring and review. Within this sequence of events, IUCN's role is that of a catalyst. There are few examples so far of national conservation strategies having reached such an advanced stage that they are nearing implementation. In this respect, the case of Zambia is almost unique and serves as a good example. Far from resting on the formal adoption of the NCS by the Cabinet, the Zambian Government immediately pushed ahead with the implementation phase, ensured the continuing existence of an NCS Secretariat and Steering Committee and, through these mechanisms, has worked vigorously to develop a "National Conservation Investment Programme." This Investment Programme, consisting of projects aimed at implementing the principal recommendations of the Strategy, is designed for submission to Zambia's international development partners - principally, the bilateral and multilateral development assistance agencies. If and when this process is completed, it will mark a highly significant precedent. It will, in effect, signify that *the government has declared conservation to be a priority form of development*, and that an investment in conservation is equivalent to an "insurance policy" taken out on development itself. With this commitment, the World Conservation Strategy can be said to have served its purpose. However, in order to address the long-term sustainability of development, NCSs need to be re-examined so as to adapt to natural resources and emerging technologies. Constant reference to an NCS will allow for a balance between development planning and socio-economic objectives at local, provincial, national, regional and international levels, and at various levels of technocultural impact (small- and large-scale, low and high technology). Alternative mechanisms may be needed to complement national conservation strategies, such as sectoral strategies, to achieve the integration of conservation with development. The NCS thus appears to be *a never-ending process*.

CONTENTS OF NATIONAL CONSERVATION STRATEGIES

Each NCS must adopt a form that favours its ready acceptance and implementation by the government. It has frequently been the view that an NCS should be in effect an "environmentally sound" National Development Plan, or that an NCS should be incorporated into the National Development Plan to the extent that in time it may not require an independent existence. For reasons mentioned above, this is not always desirable at the outset: the notion of an NCS as an essential "companion volume" to the National Development Plan only enhances the gulf between conservation and development. Yet, central planning plays a different role in each country. In countries where the National Development Plan is the principal guide in allocating natural and financial resources, linking the NCS to development planning is clearly of value. In other countries where decision-making concerning resource use devolves upon sub-national units or takes place in an *ad hoc* manner through decisions of individual families, corporations or political organs, linking the NCS to development planning can also be of value.

NCSs should comprise three general components:

* a national conservation and development profile;

* an analysis of resource demands of development and the constraints on sustainable development; and

* a mechanism for consensus building.

The World Conservation Strategy defines conservation as the sound management of natural resources in the interests of a development that will yield sustainable results. It is clearly essential, therefore, to have a detailed understanding of the nature, extent, distribution and status of the natural or environmental, human and financial resources on which national development is based, as well as current and potential threats to these natural resources. It is equally important to have a clear picture of development priorities, both locally and provincially, and the existing and planned alternative development patterns. Finally, it is essential to have an understanding of the social and institutional mechanisms that exist or could exist, and which determine how development is implemented and monitored, and how the resources on which development depends are used.

In the opening section of an NCS, it is useful to have a description of the natural resources of the country, particularly to the extent that these affect development. A clear and comprehensive profile of the country's natural resources is a necessary starting point for the NCS process. Environmental profiles exist in a number of different forms. Some are extremely comprehensive (for example, the USAID country environmental profiles), others are more sketchy. However, they all share the characteristic of gathering, analysing, and presenting environmental information relevant to development in ways that are most useful to the decision-maker. Similarly, it is essential to understand the principal development priorities of the country, i.e. its policies, current development patterns and principal areas for investment. This section should outline the extent to which national development is dependent on the natural resources described in the environmental profile, and indicate, at least in a preliminary fashion, the linkages between the two.

Each country has established policy, legislative and institutional mechanisms designed to translate developmental decisions into action on the ground, and to regulate and monitor this process. These are clearly essential in determining how conservation can best be integrated with development. A thorough analysis of these mechanisms is an essential component of the initial, descriptive part of an NCS. It should review the legislation applying to conservation and development, the country's policies in this respect, and the institutional mechanisms through which responsibility for conservation and development are distributed.

The above sections together form what might be called the *NCS Prospectus*. This document outlines the resource base on which the country's development depends, its current status and related major environmental issues. It also describes the nature of the development process, the demands made by development on the natural resource base, and the institutional mechanisms which exist to regulate the process. *In many countries, this document is regarded as the NCS itself.* In the majority of such cases, however, the strategy has remained a document and has had little long-term impact on decision-making. In order to implement the WCS, the following further steps are necessary to ensure not only the existence of a clear and cogent analysis but also the impact of the NCS on the management of natural resources locally, nationally and internationally:

Analysis of the Resource Demands of Development

Once the national profile has been established, it is possible to examine it seriously for existing and potential conflicts in the manner in which the country's natural resource base contributes to a sustainable development pattern. In other words, the developmental challenge is *to design a process which will optimally improve the standard of living of the country's popula-*

tion without undermining the capacity of the country's resources to sustain transformation in the future. This is not simply a question of calculating what level of exploitation a given resource will sustain; it is, rather, a question of formulating a mechanism for adjudicating between conflicting demands on a given resource or set of resources, in particular where one use calls for the protection of that resource and the other its exploitation.

As an example, one may consider a forested watershed in a less-advanced tropical country. The forest, to the Forest Department, may represent a volume of timber with a total revenue value calculable in precious foreign exchange terms. To the manager of the water resources and supply systems, it may be an invaluable source of potable water for the capital city and/or of hydro-electric power which could offset imports of petroleum products. It may thus also be worth valuable foreign exchange. To the agriculturalist or pastoralist, it may represent potential farm land of considerable value. To the agency responsible for resettling landless peasants, it may potentially be sub-divided and allocated in order to improve living conditions for the poorest segment of the population. To the wildlife enthusiast, it may harbour an endangered species. To the university researcher, it may provide a field laboratory. To the city dweller, it may serve as a place to escape the tensions of daily life. Each of these uses is valid in itself and none is intrinsically more valid than another. However, few countries have a satisfactory means or capability of determining which use or combination of uses is most likely to lead to the best develop-

ment, sustainable over the longer term. As a result, decisions are often based on which sector first identifies use of the area, has the most political or economic power, and is *heavily biased in favour of exploitive use* rather than preservation. Too often such a resource, which could otherwise be made productive, is considered wasted. Therefore, one of the most important tasks in a national conservation strategy is to design mechanisms to resolve conflicts between existing and potential users of natural resources.

Analysis of Constraints to Sustainable Development

In order to promote sustainable development, it is important to have a clear understanding of the factors rendering this form of development difficult under current circumstances. Thus, a central function of an NCS is to identify these constraints and to design specific projects or mechanisms to remove or overcome them. Frequent internal constraints relate to: the lack of coordination and communication between government ministries, inadequate or unhelpful legislation, lack of published policy, of trained personnel and of access to credit and extension. External constraints, equally if not more important, concern conditions attached to international financial assistance, policies governing trade and tariffs, commercial agreements, and opportunities for capital formation.

It is often these factors, rather than fundamental resources and development priorities, that determine the extent to which natural resources contribute to sustainable development. This is especially true in view of the disadvantaged position of less-advanced countries in terms of:

* lower levels of natural resources per capita;

* lower prices per unit of natural resources harvested;

* lower wages per unit of human effort;

* inheritance of artificial boundaries set by the resources-partitioning interests of former colonial or metropolitan countries;

* internal differences about developmental patterns, which are not founded on indigenous cultural attributes or perceptions;

* lower levels of resource consumption per capita;

* lower levels of capital, technology and infrastructure per capita;

* high population density and population growth rates;

* higher levels of responsibility for nature preservation in the tropical and arid zones.

This part of the analysis is thus most important since it facilitates the formulation of a realistic framework or strategy for pursuing sustainable development at local and national levels. This reality must include the politicisation necessary to ensure the dynamism and sustainability of development.

Consensus Building

Understanding the nature of conservation and development problems is quite different from designing realistic solutions to them. Such solutions must involve the concurrence of people at a wide variety of levels if development is to be sustainable. It is insufficient for the central government to enjoy a consensus on a certain standpoint if resource users at the local level are in fundamental disagreement. It is, therefore, an important exercise to assess to what extent and how decisions on resource use are determined by the central government. In most non-centrally-planned countries, centralised decision-making occurs only to a limited extent; resource use is determined by a combination of public sector decision-making at the central, provincial and local levels and by *ad hoc* decisions taken by agricultural and industrial families or private enterprise. Frequently, the most significant factor in resource use is commercial interest, and often this is only loosely circumscribed by policy, legislation or government directive.

Thus, for an NCS to be successful, it is essential that there be a consensus at all levels of management and interest on how resources can best contribute to the overall good of the country and its people. Consensus-building is the most difficult, but also the most challenging, part of NCS development. The most important factor in seeking consensus is to ensure a broad level of participation in the formulation of the NCS itself. This is best brought about by involving in the NCS process local groups, community and non-governmental organisations, as well as the widest possible range of government ministries at both the central and the provincial level. The NCS project in Botswana has designed a series of village surveys and, in selected areas, even household surveys to determine public perceptions of conservation and development, and to ensure that issues of central importance to villagers and individual households are taken into account in the NCS process.

Also of essential importance is public information and education on conservation and its link with development. The absence of a general understanding of this link is, in almost every case, a fundamental obstacle to sustainable development. Public information in the form of radio and TV programmes, films, suitable publications, classroom education, and the like, is important at every level from elementary education to the professional training received by civil servants. This is an aspect of NCS formulation that is often neglected and must be strengthened.

NATIONAL CONSERVATION STRATEGIES AND IMPLEMENTATION OF THE WORLD CONSERVATION STRATEGY

The World Conservation Strategy formulates three basic objectives: sustainable use of species and ecosystems, protection of essential ecological systems and processes, and maintenance of biological diversity. The NCS process is designed to ensure full implementation of the WCS at the national level. How effectively does it carry out this task when seen from the perspective of the three WCS objectives?

Promoting the sustainable use of species and ecosystems has been the central objective of the NCS process. However, a number of factors have made realisation of this objective difficult:

* the dominance of sectoral planning with little integration of techno-cultural and infrastructural development;

* the uncertainty of scientific advances and technological innovations and their impact on resource development;

* the lack of critical information on biological diversity, habitats, ecosystems and ecological processes, and trade-offs necessary for sustainable use of natural resources with particular reference to species and habitat or ecosystem types;

* the uncertainty of transnational planning on resource use and its impact on national self-reliance and global interdependence;

* the centralised control of information which makes decentralised and flexible management of natural resources difficult.

In order to secure the long-term future of the World Conservation Strategy, a critical path approach may be necessary for linking NCSs to international development plans. The environment and development profiles, taken together, identify the principal natural resources on which development must be based. The second part, leading to an assessment of the resource demands made by development, gives an indication of the relation between these demands and the carrying capacity of the resources. This in turn requires an understanding of those resources essential to supporting life and maintaining the viability of ecosystems, and of the impact of technocultures on carrying capacity.

The protection of biological diversity and ecosystems appears to be better covered in the NCSs, since species and protected areas have been the major thrusts of the conservation movement. However, only a small fraction of biological diversity and ecosystems are known in the tropics, and this is a major constraint. Apart from micro-ecological processes such as the hydrological cycle, there appears to be a poor understanding of large-scale ecological processes, both natural (e.g. air and water circulations, animal migrations) and man-made (e.g. human migration and trade). The understanding of symbiosis in all its manifestations (species-species, animal-plant, animal-animal interactions, or profession-profession interactions) is rudimentary in terms of conservation and development, both at micro and macro levels.

A recent review of NCSs and biological diversity, carried out for IUCN and WWF by Robert Prescott-Allen, principal author of the WCS, concluded that biological diversity concerns tended to be under-represented in the NCS process, largely due to a misunderstanding of the meaning of biological diversity and an underestimation of its importance to conservation and development. The report recommends a series of guidelines aimed at correcting this imbalance. Given the growing support within the development assistance community for the preservation of biological diversity, those agencies supporting NCS formulation are likely to welcome this renewed emphasis and balance between the three objectives of the WCS.

ISSUES FOR DISCUSSION

The following issues highlight major points for discussion on National Conservation Strategies in relation to the World Conservation Strategy:

Who Really Determines How Resources are Used?

It is important for decision-makers to constantly re-examine their assumptions, especially concerning the extent to which decisions taken by central and regional governments actually determine the way a particular resource contributes to development at the local level. It is often difficult for decision-makers to be self-critical in this respect. Frequently, the psychology is: "We plan - it is up to others to implement." But this does not change the fact that resources are often used in an unplanned fashion by family or communal enterprises. This is not usually a result of faulty or ill-considered plans on which resource use is based. It is rather that resource use is determined by immediate individual or communal needs at a certain time and not by a plan designed by and for a community or a country.

The peasant in the rural area, without access to credit or extension services, finding his land exhausted, might move up the hill and transform another piece of forest into agricultural land. This is not part of a long-term plan. It is a response to an immediate need. Planners and decision-makers must examine the role of planning in addition to its expected scope. There is probably a correlation between a country's level of development and the extent to which its decision-makers actually determine how resources are used. There is probably also a correlation between the importance of planning in a social and economic system and the extent to which resource use patterns correspond to plans. It would be worth examining this correlation further but, more important, it is necessary to recognise to what extent resource use lies temporarily or permanently outside the control of planners and decision-makers. The role of the peasant family or the small-scale craftsman or businessman in stimulating the transformation of natural resources in NCSs, appears to have been underestimated. So too has the role of transnational organisations especially when less-advanced countries are endowed with weak infrastructures.

The actors in the decision-making process will vary considerably at the local level depending on religion, beliefs, values, culture, basic needs, education, understanding, levels of economy and short- and long-term interests. Expressions of belief (faith, hope and charity) will vary according to levels of economy (survival, subsistence and surplus), as will basic needs (food and shelter, security and fellowship and organisation).

What Mechanisms Exist to Resolve Conflicts?

Conflicts arise when there are competing demands for the same resource - a situation that planners are well equipped to deal with. However, there is a particular range of problems related to this issue which are generally not examined in sufficient detail. As suggested above, such problems frequently arise when one potentially legitimate demand on a natural resource calls for its exploitation, and another equally legitimate demand on the same resource calls for its protection. Most planning and decision-making systems are ill-equipped to deal with such conflicts, particularly when they are sectoral by nature. The coastal waters of a small less-advanced country may provide an example. The quality of the coastal waters may be a principal determinant of a country's ability to attract tourists to its shores. However, to the manager of the city's sewage system these same waters provide a convenient and inexpensive dump for the city's wastes. Clearly, at a modest level of development, this will not necessarily lead to an irresolvable problem. However, at some point, decision-makers must make an honest attempt to find solutions which work for all concerned.

Planning itself is inadequate for resolving such conflicts, although it is a useful tool. Decision-making is an art form and thus not totally rational. It needs to take cognisance of formal and non-formal, overt and covert mechanisms; of trade-offs and benefits including graft and favours; and of the distribution and stratification of wealth and advantage. The substance for consideration depends on beliefs, values, understanding and levels of economy. Mechanisms for resolving conflicts must acknowledge the value of opposing views for promoting human development, and

of ideological differences in the basic approach, so much so that resolving one conflict may generate another.

The Long-Term Versus the Short-Term

Planners, like the decision-makers who act on their advice, must assess the costs and benefits of various development alternatives. Certain problems arise in this respect which have a significant bearing on natural resources management and, therefore, on the ability of the natural environment to support development. Planning and decision-making, for example, are seriously biased toward actions with short-term benefits. The reasons for this are well known and include electoral cycles, immediate pressures on the economy, lack of macro-ecological understanding and of a basic hope for future solutions to present problems. Yet a strong argument can be made for the long-term potential of natural resources to support and sustain development besides short-term benefits derived from their exploitation. What mechanisms exist for planners to accord value to the needs of future generations, the need for ensuring the ability of natural resources to renew themselves indefinitely, the need not to undermine the natural resource base or take unnecessary risks which consequently lead to real human and natural hazards?

The assessment of long-term and short-term benefits and costs needs to take into account both quantitative and qualitative information. These assessments will vary according to the survival, subsistence or surplus levels of the local economy,

and trade-offs for development alternatives. They will also have to take into account the desire for self-reliance and interdependence, for safety and security, and for fellowship and cooperation, at the national and regional as well as the global level.

Handling of Qualitative Information in Planning and Decision-Making

Economic planning has relied hitherto on partial models based on quantitative data. This reliance is unrealistic for overall socio-economic development in view of the complexity of the development process. Yet numbers somehow have a "magic" about them. They suggest that issues are clear-cut and that decisions can be taken on the basis of arithmetic rather than judgement. This badly skews decision-making and the understanding of science, and is a problem which planners must face squarely. Returning to the forest example, it is possible to quantify the value of hydro-electric power produced as a result of the watershed forest being intact and providing so many hectolitres of water per day. It is possible, in addition, to assess the replacement cost of exploiting other energy sources if that forest were to be destroyed. Similarly, it is possible to compute the value of a known volume of timber or the value of the resulting agricultural land if the forests were cleared. What is much more difficult to assess is, for example, the amenity value to the harassed city dweller of a place where he can recover from the stress of city life. Further, without calculating the value of wildlife in the form of meat, leather or trophies, the knowledge that they share their land with other creatures can be of real value to people. Because it is impossible to quantify these values, however, they are too easily brushed aside.

While economic analysis has emerged from the study of human societies, ecological analysis stems from the study of natural communities. Although the units of measurement differ in these two analytical systems, there are homologues related to energy, matter, space, time and information diversity. The scale of analysis, i.e. country or region, with its heterogenous structure and function, requires a new approach that can address short-term benefits and costs together with the long-term. The mathematics appear to be in place for some pilot-scale application.

Externalities

Much has been said about the debt crisis and the stringent conditions laid down by international financing institutions which essentially dictate the economic direction of certain less-advanced countries. Yet not enough has been written about the real consequences of this situation, in terms of the scope of planners and decision-makers from the advanced as well as the less-advanced countries, to manoeuvre on resource management or, indeed on other issues. The largest economy in the world is potentially the largest debtor. There is no point in imagining an utopian scenario where elected officials of a country sit down quietly to plot objectively the best course for their country's future. There are too many factors, many beyond the control of the country itself, which render this scenario at least partly unrealistic. The

obligation of a country to earn foreign exchange can be a major, if not *the* major, determinant in deciding between options for natural resource management and use. Each country must evaluate its international agreements and obligations against the extent to which it risks undermining the natural resource base on which the future of several countries depends. An international perspective to conservation and development is, therefore, urgently needed.

Yet this debate is rarely, if ever, conducted with sufficient openness and honesty because of the structure of international financing institutions, dominated by interests of the advanced countries. To what extent do the conditions of the International Monetary Fund render it practically impossible for countries like Costa Rica to assign their forest reserves to conservation - fundamentally their most beneficial use - and to provide the forest service with the resources to manage these reserves for long-term productivity? To what extent do the policies of Peru's aid partners restrict its options and make impossible what, from Peru's viewpoint, might be the ideal approach to resource management? To what extent do trade agreements close the doors to solutions which, overall, would be in the longer-term interest of the country and its people? International trade, financing and management appear structured to negate the conservation interests of less-advanced countries in the tropical and arid zones, where the representative preservation of nature is of significance to the global community.

A Strategic Approach

While advanced countries might have the infrastructure and financial resources to formulate and implement their own national conservation strategies, most of the less-advanced countries do not have such a capability. It is necessary, therefore, for those countries to take a critical and strategic approach toward implementing the World Conservation Strategy. Such an approach is necessary if conservation is to ensure sustainable development, and thus function as a continuous regulatory mechanism. Initially, it may not entail a formal national conservation strategy but this could be achieved through first focusing on major commodities that earn foreign exchange significant to development. It may entail an examination of the formal and non-formal sectors of the economy, of trade-offs that ensure the stratification and distribution of wealth, of traditional symbolism and social organisation that could foster conservation, depending on the key attributes of the country for conservation and development. Inevitably, such an approach will have to consider religious virtues (faith, hope and charity) and natural virtues (fortitude, perseverance and temperance) that determine national identity. It will also have to examine self-reliance, global interdependence, and factors that govern technological and social innovations necessary for sustainable development. This will have to take place at the survival, subsistence or surplus levels of the economies of various types of countries.

THE ZAMBIA NATIONAL CONSERVATION STRATEGY

N. Mukutu
Ministry of Lands and Natural Resources
Lusaka, Zambia

C. Mwale
Natural Resources Department
Lusaka, Zambia

SUMMARY This paper outlines the formulation of the Zambian National Conservation Strategy to meet particular needs at a time when the Government decided to shift its emphasis in development from mining to agriculture. Such a decision has serious implications for a country where agriculture is not yet highly developed and where there is evidence of negative effects from unplanned and uncontrolled use of the environment. The Strategy has been designed to set realistic priorities which acknowledge the importance that Zambia attaches to conservation as it relates to mankind, and provides meaningful benefits for people.

The Government of the Republic of Zambia has prepared and is beginning to implement a National Conservation Strategy. The following discussion outlines the experience gained to date in undertaking this worthwhile venture.

Zambia's reliance on copper, constituting one of the highest levels of dependence of any country on a particular commodity, has become a severe constraint to national development. In recognition of this, the Government has reassessed its development position with new emphasis on agriculture. This has two important aspects: First, since agriculture in Zambia is not yet highly developed and requires the opening up of virgin lands, it is important to determine what those lands are capable of producing. A second consideration is that the natural resources upon which agriculture depends are renewable if they are conserved and destructible if they are not; therefore, we need to define ways of ensuring their renewability if we are to sustain our agricultural development.

Sustained development of other sectors of our economy also depends upon the proper management of natural resources. We recognise that use of natural resources in one sector has consequences for the environmental condition of others. Thus we consider the role of conservation to be the wise management of natural resources so they continue to produce sustainable benefits indefinitely.

Formulation of the National Conservation Strategy came at a time when Zambia could point to a number of conservation successes, but also to evidence of deteriorating available resources. This has been a result both of ill-planned development activities which ignored environmental considerations, and of other uncontrolled activities arising from population pressure on natural resources. In some parts of Zambia, these have included:

* deforestation, leading to cyclical environmental problems such as flooding and drought, a result of land clearing for fuelwood, for commercial agriculture, and for Chitemene shifting cultivation;

* soil erosion, caused by inappropriate cultivation practices on arable land, overgrazing and badly-controlled burning;

* the degradation of traditional pastures, resulting from poor cattle management. Excessive numbers of livestock on available pastures have meant unproductive and unmarketable animals, together with soil erosion which has further contributed to reduced availability of adequate grazing lands; and

* pollution, which, although not yet widespread, has been present in certain localities, particularly around copper mines and factories. This is an indication of poor site planning and design.

Before outlining how Zambia formulated her National Conservation Strategy (NCS), it must be emphasised that our national philosophy is based on Humanism. We believe that any form of conservation must relate to mankind. Conservation and development activities should, therefore, have meaningful benefits for our people. In this respect, we believe that natural resource-related development projects should not only meet biological and economic criteria, but must also satisfy social needs.

FORMULATION OF THE STRATEGY

In 1980, His Excellency the President Dr. K.D. Kaunda took up the "conservation for development" initiative with the former Director General of the International Union for Conservation of Nature and Natural Resources (IUCN), Dr. Lee Talbot, and together they considered preparing a National Conservation Strategy for Zambia. This discussion took place during a ceremony at which the Director General presented a copy of the World Conservation Strategy (WCS) to His Excellency.

Four years later, the Zambian National Conservation Strategy was launched as a project of the Ministry of Lands and Natural Resources, with technical assistance from IUCN, and funding from the Governments of Sweden and The Netherlands. Following its feasibility study, the document was prepared by a thirty-man Technical Group which represented the interests of various government, parastatal and private organisations. It was aided by a full-time, two-man Secretariat from the Ministry of Lands and Natural Resources and IUCN, and was prepared under the guidance of a fifteen-man Task Force which represented various sectors in Zambia. The Task Force was chaired by the Secretary General of the National Council for Scientific Research, a good "neutral" forum for such work.

The first stage involved technical studies and the preparation of background papers by each member of the Technical Group. This was followed by seminars and discussions on both the technical and policy aspects of this initial work, as well as the results of separate working group sessions on special topics. It should be noted that we made every effort to challenge Technical Group members, examining critically the way in which natural resources were being used in their respective sectors. Discussions were designed so that the resultant Strategy would be as practical as possible, devising the most feasible ways of putting Zambia on the path toward sustainable development through wise use of its natural resources. Priorities were analysed, realistic goals defined, major constraints identified and practical suggestions made which took into account current financial, technical and manpower limitations. The Strategy document was completed in a few months. This enabled us to keep up momentum and forced us to concentrate only on the priorities. Because the Strategy was completed rapidly, it should be viewed more as a statement of commitment and a plan of action than as a scientific study.

A CONSERVATION STRATEGY FOR ZAMBIA'S DEVELOPMENT

The theme of the Strategy reflects that of the World Conservation Strategy: it stresses that conservation and development are two sides of the same issue. Conservation can aid development because it nurtures the productive capacities of natural resources as well as the environment in which people live and work. Development can contribute to conservation by ensuring that people's needs are adequately supplied, so they are not obliged to over-exploit and damage soils, forests, fisheries, and other natural resources in an effort to survive. The goal of the Strategy is to satisfy the basic needs of all Zambians - both present and future generations - through careful management of the country's natural resources.

Its objectives are similar to those of the World Conservation Strategy. The National Strategy emphasises two areas: first, a way of building an Environmental Planning procedure into Zambia's development process; and simultaneously, a Natural Resources Development Plan. In other words, we are not just talking about modifying development to meet environmental criteria, but are also concerned with creating development - a new kind of development which is based on a sustainable harvest of natural resources, and a continued regard for ecological processes.

IMPLEMENTATION

In July 1985, the National Conservation Strategy was presented to the Cabinet and approved with very few changes to the Task Force document.

The Strategy proposes the establishment of an Environment Council which will manage Strategy implementation and oversee the preparation of environmental legislation to be incorporated in an Environment Council Act. However, because of financial and other problems, we have decided to set up an interim National Conservation Committee which will usher in the Environment Council when the Act is passed, and when other preparations (such as defining environmental standards) have been completed.

The role of the National Conservation Committee is to:

* coordinate conservation planning for all Government and non-government agencies concerned with conservation and environment matters;

* liaise with development aid agencies to ensure their support for the programme of conservation activities under the Strategy;

* advise the Party and its Government, through the Ministry of Lands and Natural Resources, on policy and legal aspects of natural resource management;

* plan (in consultation with the National Commission for Development Planning), identify projects for which Environmental Impact Assessments would be required, and develop potential conservation measures for development projects.

Emphasis so far has been on developing projects which focus on priority actions defined in the National Conservation Strategy. We are following this up by instituting the environmental planning procedures which are required as a part of the central development planning process. Projects already underway include:

* community environmental improvements in squatter areas around Lusaka: activities such as fruit and fuelwood tree planting, more efficient house design, etc. (Most of the population is urban and many environmental problems - particularly deforestation - are urban-based.);

* multi-purpose development including sustainable community use of wildlife in the Luangwa Valley;

* creating a conservation education and information unit in the Ministry of Lands and Natural Resources;

* research in the conservation and use of indigenous plants in drought-prone areas;

* developing a farm and community forestry capability;

* setting up a Natural Resources Data Bank; and

* establishing small pilot projects using the resources immediately available to the National Conservation Committee. Especially important here is the pool of Zambian expertise which we have recognised and built-up during the period of National Conservation Strategy formulation.

In fact, the process of preparing a National Conservation Strategy has been most valuable in showing us just how much expertise we have in Zambia, and how to put it together effectively in order to deal with our diverse environmental problems.

If we can become effective at addressing our own development problems, then the possibilities for working with friendly organisations such as IUCN, UNEP and many others appear to be more fruitful in the future.

A NATIONAL CONSERVATION STRATEGY FOR NEPAL

Devendra Amatya
Nepal Conservation Strategy Group
Kathmandu, Nepal

John K. Naysmith
Senior Advisor to the Government of Nepal
Tripureswar, Kathmandu, Nepal

SUMMARY Nepal's rapidly growing population is faced with sustaining itself on a land base that is steadily declining in productive capacity. The National Conservation Strategy will link conservation (resource management) policy with other major policy sectors such as population, energy development and industrial development. It will contain a series of interlocking and practical recommendations developed from locally prepared background papers that describe pilot programmes for physiographic regions. A series of working symposia including local government and non-government participants will review the background papers and the draft Strategy. Provision has also been made for effective participation by the public, village and district leaders and national level policy makers in preparing the document. It is expected that such participation combined with the direct involvement of senior government officials in Strategy fomulation will ensure its successful implementation.

The National Conservation Strategy for Nepal stresses the relationship between conservation and development, considering conservation to be the managed use of natural resources to ensure maximum sustainable benefits for present and future generations.

The principal objective of the Strategy is to alleviate problems resulting from Nepal's increasing population and the diminishing productive capacity of its land, water and forests. To be successful, technical aspects of the Strategy must accord with the social, cultural and economic values of the Nepalese. It is being designed to meet basic material, spiritual and cultural needs of the people of Nepal, now and in the future.

The Strategy will emphasise the judicious use and appropriate allocation of natural resources in a series of Action Plans that are simple, practical and capable of implementation. These Plans will link conservation, or resource management, with other major government policy sectors such as population, energy development, industrial development and decentralisation.

Conservation and development are mutually dependent. Without development, Nepal cannot add to its collective wealth and, hence, cannot afford to undertake necessary conservation measures. Conversely, without conservation, the productive capacity of Nepal's land and renewable resources will progressively diminish, thus development will not be sustained. For this reason, the objectives and Action Plans of the National Conservation Strategy for Nepal, and the Objectives and policies of the Development Plans, should be mutually supportive.

CONSERVATION/DEVELOPMENT PROBLEMS AND PROGRAMMES

The population of Nepal, currently 17 million, has been increasing at the rate of 2.66 percent annually. It is expected to reach 25 million by the year 2000. The present mean population density of 115 persons per square kilometre will become 170 persons in 15 years.

During the period 1971 to 1981, the population rose by nearly 30 percent whereas the production of food grain rose by only 10 percent. An important phenomenon in the food supply situation is that, of the total cultivated land, only one-third is found in the hills or mountains, whereas these areas support slightly more than half the population. A further complication is the fact that many of the areas to which food must be transported are remote and not easily accessible.

Based on current population projections, present management practices and present levels of dependency, it is estimated that to meet the population's need for firewood, fodder and timber, Nepal's current forest will be converted to shrubland within 30 years.

Erosion is a natural phenomenon in the mountainous regions and on the steep slopes of hill regions. Much of the erosion that occurs throughout Nepal, however, results from over-exploitation of forest land, pressure to expand cultivated lands into unsuitable areas, and the adoption of detrimental land-use practices.

In addition to the major social and economic costs incurred by the loss of valuable agricultural and forest land, serious indirect problems are also apparent. For example, increased sedimentation disrupts irrigation systems and damages hydro-power plant structures and equipment. Widespread conversion of forest land is moreover seriously detrimental to Nepal's rich biological diversity and its potential to realise development objectives.

In spite of the serious problems facing Nepal, there are also real opportunities for overcoming them. Although considered as one of the world's poorest countries in economic terms, it is rich in its diversified culture, social traditions and natural heritage. There is also evidence of considerable development possibilities. The installed hydro-electric capacity is 129 MW, whereas the estimated potential that can be economically developed is 27,000 MW. The extent of its hydrocarbon potential is also now being examined. If more intensively managed, Nepal's forests and shrublands are capable of producing substantially greater volumes of fuelwood, fodder and timber than at present. There is similar potential for increasing agricultural production in spite of limited opportunity to increase the 20 percent of Nepal's land area now under cultivation.

His Majesty's Government has made considerable progress in addressing such conservation/development issues. Several policy areas of the current Five-Year Development Plan are related to conservation or natural resource management, including:

* massive afforestation and forest conservation programmes;

* conservation of watershed areas in villages, hill settlements and agricultural areas;

* forest farms to supply domestic forest product needs, to provide raw materials for forest-based industry and to produce industrial forest products;

* food production programmes to ensure self-suffficiency of food grains in the hill areas within ten years;

* agriculture and irrigation programmes that better utilise small-scale irrigation works and tubewell borings;

* measures to diversify agricultural crops and increase rural income;

* low-cost small and medium irrigation projects in the hills and Terai;

* small hydro-power projects in remote areas, and alternative energy sources such as bio-gas, solar energy and wind power;

* a decentralised and integrated planning process that incorporates appropriate land use and conservation policies.

THE NATIONAL CONSERVATION STRATEGY PROCESS

Current Status

The first phase in developing the National Conservation Strategy for Nepal was the preparation of a *Prospectus* which was published in 1983. The *Prospectus* includes a brief description of the country's main environmental problems and a statement of the Strategy's objectives and principles.

In 1985, Phase II was initiated and the Secretariat established. Located in Kathmandu in leased commercial office space central to most of the government agencies with which it must deal, the Secretariat provides the focal point for day-to-day activities involving the National Conservation Strategy. Secretariat staff consists of an officer seconded from the Department of Soil Conservation and Watershed Management, a local forestry consultant who previously worked for His Majesty's Government and the National Conservation Strategy Senior Advisor. Other staff include an administrative officer, a secretary/word processor operator and a voluntary librarian/executive assistant.

An outline of the central document of the Strategy was drafted and a series of subject areas identified for which background papers would be written. A work plan and schedule for the preparation of all documents and the Strategy were also developed.

A series of 16 bilateral meetings were held with government executive officers including the Vice-Chairman of the National Planning Commission and Secretaries and Directors-General of the key Ministries, Commissions and Departments, to discuss the overall approach to Strategy preparation and to identify contact persons and prospective authors of various papers. Those selected later attended an inter-agency meeting convened by the Secretariat, at which details concerning the preparation of some 30 background papers were discussed and agreement was reached on how to proceed.

The background papers will form the basis of the Strategy. Each paper is being written according to clearly defined terms of reference prepared by the Secretariat. Together, these papers will cover all of the resource sectors as well as subjects such as drinking water and sanitation, irrigation, cultural heritage, and the role of women in resource conservation.

The papers are being prepared by the best-qualified local people available. Since the Strategy is, in effect, a major policy initiative of His Majesty's Government, it is essential that senior government officials be fully involved in its preparation. In some instances, however, the most qualified contributors are from the university, non-government organisations or the private sector.

Effective public involvement is also of primary importance. There must be practical channels, for example, for those who work and live on the land to contribute in a significant way to the development of the Strategy. Active participation by various groups such as the panchayats, the conservation committees at the village and district levels, and district line-agency personnel is essential for its successful implementation.

As a first step in the critical area of public involvement, the Secretariat has initiated a public information programme. Articles have been prepared for, and appeared in, the press in both Nepali and English and have received wide distribution. Interviews conducted by the Royal Nepal Academy for Science and Technology have been translated and broadcast throughout the kingdom by Radio Nepal.

The Secretariat undertook an initial analysis of current or recently completed resource management or conservation-related projects. The survey identified the scope and nature of such projects and their relationship to the Strategy and its Objectives. Coordination of such projects within the context of the Strategy once it is implemented is considered to be essential. This review is seen as a first step towards attaining that goal.

Future Action

The background papers will be rigorously examined by a team of highly-qualified local reviewers during a series of six symposia. They will be subsequently finalised by the authors. The Secretariat will then prepare the first draft of the central document, drawing substantially from the background papers.

The central document will describe current major obstacles to achieving the

National Conservation Strategy objectives under such headings as: financial and manpower resources, institutional arrangements, village and district capacity to undertake programmes, availability of trained personnel, management capability, consumption patterns, cultural attitudes, and access to information. It will also analyse the conservation-development interactions and the cross-sectoral implications of development.

Taking into account the above considerations and the success or failure of current conservation measures, the Strategy will describe a series of action plans necessary to realise the objectives based on categories of programme, policy, organisation and institutions, including relevant legislation. Finally, it will describe a series of pilot programmes which will include as many of the action plans and recommendations described in the Strategy as possible. They will be part of the implementation phase and will provide the basis for the future extension of the Strategy throughout the country.

A key step in preparing the first draft of the central document will be a series of district and village meetings. Five districts representing most, if not all, of the conditions found in Nepal's five physiographic zones will be selected. Village and district panchayats, or locally-elected governments, will also be consulted on all aspects of the Strategy including problems and solutions related to such subjects as agricultural production, fuelwood and fodder acquisition, soil conservation, and off-farm employment. These meetings will also provide an opportunity to receive valuable local advice concerning the prospective pilot programmes.

This draft of the central document will be subjected to a two-phase review, by authors of the background papers and then by a panel of highly-qualified local people which will include representatives of the private sector, non-government organisations, aid agencies and the university. The Secretariat will then prepare a second draft of the central document on the basis of the comments received.

The third and final review stage will involve an inter-agency meeting of Ministry Secretaries and other executive officers chaired by the National Planning Commission. A series of bilateral meetings between the prospective participants and the Secretariat will ensure that the former are fully conversant with the contents of the Strategy before the inter-agency meeting.

Comments received at this meeting will be taken into account when the Secretariat prepares the final draft of the Strategy, which will then be translated into Nepali and officially presented to His Majesty's Government.

Following approval, the various Action Plans not already incorporated into line-agency programmes during the preparation and formulation stages will be implemented together with the pilot programmes described in the Strategy.

POINTS IN PREPARING THE NATIONAL CONSERVATION STRATEGY FOR NEPAL

Cross-sectoral Impacts

A key requirement in formulating the Strategy is an acknowledgement of the critical cross-sectoral impacts inherent in resource development. Without such acknowledgement, consideration of environmental degradation, for example, would tend to be limited to the effects and to ignore the causes. Therefore, linkages, such as those between energy development and forestry, urban development and agriculture, population and the carrying capacity of the land, and biological diversity and economic development, will be examined and taken into account.

It is important to note that the approved final version of the National Conservation Strategy will not be merely an amalgam of key issues raised in the background papers. It will be a document in which the respective positions and policies of government ministries and line-agencies are modified where necessary in order to minimise any cross-sectoral effects. Thus it will be a government-wide statement based on a policy of integrated resource management.

Use of Existing Data and Expertise

In formulating the Strategy, every effort must be made to utilise relevant existing data. For example, the extensive map coverage related to soil systems, land capability and land utilisation, prepared by the Land Resource Mapping Project, provides a valuable tool for determinimg optimum future land use patterns and land allocation. The highly-trained multidisciplinary teams at Nepal's National Remote Sensing Centre can also provide inventory data required for resource planning. Subsequent monitoring would provide a scientific basis for modifying and refining aspects of the Strategy during implementation.

It is also important to capitalise on the expertise of government officials and on the experience gained in rural development projects. The latter, in particular, will provide effective and practical means for implementing many parts of the Strategy.

Local Involvement

A concerted effort will be made to raise the level of understanding concerning the Strategy and its specific relation to the needs of local people through the local panchayat system and the operation of the decentralisation policy. The first step will be to clarify the point that the Strategy emphasises the wise use, rather than the preservation, of natural resources. As a corollary, working with the panchayat system during the preparation and development stages of the Strategy will enable people at village and district levels to make the maximum contribution.

The Strategy and Action Plans must reflect the fact that the cost of conservation measures cannot be borne by subsistence farmers and that they must be provided with realistic alternatives if the desired objectives are to be achieved.

It will also be necessary to ensure that non-government organisations, the university community, professional associations, business and industry adopt a resource conservation orientation and that conservation societies within Nepal actively participate in the preparation and implementation of the Strategy.

Government Participation and Political Will

At the government level, executive officials must be encouraged to play a key role in formulating the Strategy through the preparation of background papers, for example, since their participation will greatly increase the chance that they will promote its implementation.

A further consideration is the need to engender the political will necessary to implement the Strategy by demonstrating that a conservation policy must be equal in status to other major policy sectors such as population, energy and industrial development and that the success of any of these policies is dependent on the recognition of their inter-relationship.

It is also important to develop an awareness of the opportunity presented to politicians to show the merits and effectiveness of decentralisation and local decision-making by involving them in the preparation and implementation of the Strategy.

CONCLUSION

There is more than one kind of National Conservation Strategy. There is also more than one way it can be produced.

In Nepal, the problems related to resource use are real; so too must be the solutions. The National Conservation Strategy for Nepal must consist of Action Plans that are realistic, simple in style and pragmatic in substance. Such a Strategy must be built with painstaking care. In developing the Strategy, the process will be as important as the the product. At the outset, there must be widespread understanding of what the Strategy is, followed by effective means for extensive participation in its formulation and implementation.

The pitfall to be avoided is a Strategy consisting of a series of theoretical constructs and imprecise recommendations which may satisfy the author unfettered by circumstances, but which will guarantee failure in terms of implementation and achievement of the stated objectives.

Government, the private sector, the scientific community, special interest groups, and the public at large each has a substantial role to play. Only such a collective effort of energy, ideas and will can produce the necessary breadth of practical solutions to Nepal's resource-related problems.

CONSERVATION STRATEGY: BASIS FOR A DEVELOPMENT STRATEGY

Le Thac Can
Research Institute for Higher Education
Hanoi, Vietnam

Vo Quy
University of Hanoi
Hanoi, Vietnam

SUMMARY *For Vietnamese working on the rational use of resources and the protection of the country's environment, development means an attempt to improve the spiritual and material quality of life. This definition applies to the individual, the community and the nation as a whole. In a country characterised by low income, a weak material and technological base, and an environment ravaged by war, the success of a development strategy will depend on detailed knowledge of the current status and likely future utilisation of resources. Experiences gained in the initial stages of preparation of the Vietnamese Conservation Strategy and the activities undertaken provide interesting pointers for those in other countries facing similar problems.*

INTRODUCTION

In 1980, the year in which the World Conservation Strategy (WCS) was published, a team of researchers at the University of Hanoi proposed a national programme on the rational use of natural resources and protection of the environment. A more rapid economic and social development in the five years of post-war reconstruction made implementation of such a project both important and urgent. The programme was officially inaugurated in 1981. During the first symposium held in December 1983, preliminary ideas for a National Conservation Strategy were reflected in reports discussed there. Coincidentally, a copy of the World Conservation Strategy, circulated by an IUCN representative participating at the symposium, revealed a remarkable similarity of approach and objectives between the World Conservation Strategy and Vietnam's programme. Toward the end of 1984, IUCN and the Programme Committee began collaborating in the preparation of a National Conservation Strategy (NCS) for Vietnam.

Vietnamese scientists concerned with the problem of rational use of resources and protection of the environment look upon development as a means of improving the material and spiritual quality of life at individual, community and national levels. For low-income countries with weak physical and technological infrastructures, as is the case in Vietnam at the moment, development must be based on the natural resources of the country. The success of a development strategy rests on an accurate identification of objectives concerning the quality of life, and a feasible path for their realisation within the limits of available resources. Therein lies the crux of a development strategy: its logic and feasibility depend on knowledge about current status, future trends, and the likely short- and long-term utilisation of resources which raises the question of conservation. Close links tie the two strategies together to form a complex system in which a conservation strategy becomes a scientific base that provides the objective conditions for determining the development strategy.

Drawing on those concepts and IUCN recommendations, Vietnam's National Conservation Strategy group has published a preliminary report on its first year's work which provides a general outline of the Strategy. It is hoped that the report will stimulate discussion among a wider public about the country's conservation problems.

Features emerging from the studies so far are described below.

A PRELIMINARY ASSESSMENT: ABUNDANCE AND DIVERSITY OF COUNTRY RESOURCES

Vietnam, covering an area of 330,000 square kilometres, is situated along a peninsula. Climatically, the country is relatively humid, ranging from tropical in the southern lowlands to temperate in highland areas. The climate is also subject to monsoon influences. Natural resources are remarkably abundant and varied, the most important being: over 10 million hectares of agricultural land; 16 million hectares of forest; 1 million hectares surface area of fresh and brackish water available for fish farming; a hydro-energy potential of over 60 billion kwh per annum; diverse mineral resources including coal, oil and gas, iron, bauxite, other non-ferrous metals and construction materials; a flora of 7000 species, a fauna of 2400 vertebrates, and thousands of other species. All of these resources indicate a vast development potential (Le Ba Thao, 1977, *La Nature de Vietnam*).

Disadvantages of the Natural Environment

There are, however, some negative aspects related to the resources mentioned. Floods, droughts and typhoons are frequent. High temperatures and humidity create conditions which result in disease and epidemics, the contamination of fresh products and the corrosion of metal and technical instruments. Certain minerals, needed for agriculture and industry, are only available in insufficient quantities, and the wide dispersal of mineral deposits makes prospecting and exploitation difficult and costly.[1]

DESTRUCTIVE TRENDS IN THE USE OF NATURAL RESOURCES

High population growth rates (over 2 percent per annum during the last few decades) in an economy that is still essentially at subsistence level, have created in Vietnam, as in many other

---

1 General Report, First Symposium on Resources and the Environment.

developing countries with low incomes, disastrous trends in the use of natural resources. The most serious are:

* deforestation to provide construction materials, heating fuel, or other forest products and to permit agricultural expansion, resulting in a decline in forested areas from 43 percent in 1943 to 21 percent in 1983;

* soil loss through erosion estimated at 100 million tonnes per year over all drainage basins;

* deterioration of arable land fertility due to poor cultivation and irrigation methods;

* over-exploitation of fish stocks in certain coastal regions and estuaries;

* waste of minerals during prospecting, exploitation and use.[2]

LONG-TERM EFFECTS OF WAR DAMAGE

The legacy of the war waged against the Vietnamese people between 1945 and 1975 has been serious damage both to natural resources and to the environment. Between 1961 and 1971, the United States Air Force dropped 13 million tonnes of explosives and 72 million litres of defoliants and herbicides on Vietnamese territory, contaminating two million hectares of forest and 1.5 million hectares of land in rural areas. About one million hectares of forest and hundreds of thousands of hectares of agricultural land were rendered unusable.[3]

Much of that damage has been repaired by the Vietnamese people since the war. However, complex problems concerning reforestation of badly affected zones, restoration of local fauna, monitoring the health of the population and improvements in environmental conditions, still remain to be solved.

ALTERNATIVES TO IMPROVE CONSERVATION, NATURAL RESOURCE USE AND THE ENVIRONMENT

In spite of the gravity of the picture rendered above, present conditions affecting both natural resources and the environment in Vietnam are still reversible. Central government organisations, local authorities, scientists and much of the population are aware of the situation and are doing their utmost to halt further deterioration. They are helped to the extent that certain conditions favour the restoration of natural resources, a large proportion of non-renewable resources remains unexploited and urban and industrial centres are still underdeveloped.

Currently, there are numerous programmes aimed at the improvement of environmental management. These include new approaches to the use of marginal zones and to the management of waste land; pilot projects that will demonstrate the effectiveness of ecodevelopment; and the planning of a system of 87 natural reserves and national parks based on land use models adapted to each region. Over the last few years, efforts to intensify cultivation of paddy rice, based on ecological

2. *ibid*

3. *ibid*

principles of low energy input, have resulted in food self-sufficency.

A mass tree-planting campaign has led to the reforestation of 120,000 hectares of hills and mountains in 1985 and to the planting of 450 million trees in rural areas - the equivalent of over 400,000 hectares of forest. Fertility control programmes have reduced the population growth rate from 2.55 percent in 1976 to 2.10 percent in 1984. Campaigns against urban and industrial pollution and for the conservation of genetic resources have also been successsful. Recognising the importance of education, the subject of conservation has been introduced into the curriculum in secondary schools.

A Vietnamese National Conservation Strategy is still a long way from completion. Of the 21 necessary preparatory operations recommended by IUCN, only seven have been incorporated to date. However, in view of the need to gain time in the struggle for conservation, the Programme Committee has continued to prepare the National Conservation Strategy while implementing those measures that have already been agreed on by the population.

DEVELOPMENT OF NATIONAL AND SUB-NATIONAL CONSERVATION STRATEGIES: AUSTRALIAN CASE STUDY

A.G. Kerr
*Deputy Secretary, Department of Arts,
Heritage and Environment
Canberra, Australia*

SUMMARY *The National Conservation Strategy for Australia, while drawing on the objectives and framework of the World Conservation Strategy, is a document adapted to Australian conditions. These include a highly-diverse environment, a federal system of government, and a constitution which assigns primary responsibility for land use and resources management to the State and Territory Governments. The National Strategy was developed during a two-year period of collaboration involving extensive public consultation and culminating in a National Conference. Endorsed by the Federal Government in July 1984, and by some States and national organisations since then, it is a document based on consensus. It is also grounded in the assumption that the National Conservation Strategy should provide a permanent framework for formulation and review of environmental policies and programmes, particularly where highly-developed Federal, State and Territory infrastructures and legislative bases already exist. Specific examples of recent major environment programmes reflecting the application of National Conservation Strategy principles are also cited.*

INTRODUCTION

Australia was one of more than thirty countries which participated in launching the World Conservation Strategy on 6 March 1980. At that time, the Prime Minister accepted the Strategy on behalf of the Australian people, pledging Federal Government support for a more focused approach to managing living resources.

THE AUSTRALIAN ENVIRONMENT

Australia has a land area of 7.9 million square kilometres with a coastline of 36,000 kilometres. It spans more than 30 degrees of latitude, from 10°S to 43°S. The natural forces which have shaped the country over geological time have produced regional environments of great variety, ranging from vast arid lands to complex rainforests and alpine heaths, and from enormous coral reefs to large sand islands and ancient coastal landforms.

Aboriginal occupation of the Australian continent has been traced over 40,000 years, during which time human activities established an equilibrium with the environment. It is only in the last 200 years that the situation has changed. Australia is approaching the bicentenary of settlement by European immigrants which commenced at Sydney in 1788. Since that date, many land-use practices adopted by the settlers, such as vast programmes of land clearing for agriculture and grazing, have altered the natural landscape over large areas almost beyond recognition, and have proved to be unsustainable.

THE AUSTRALIAN CONSTITUTIONAL FRAMEWORK

Australia is a Federation of six States, the self-governed Northern Territory and other territories administered by the Federal Government under a Constitution which makes no specific reference to environment or conservation and which assigns primary responsibility for land use and natural resource management to the State and Northern Territory Governments. Federal Government responsibilities for conservation, therefore, arise from or are incidental to other powers such as the power to legislate with respect to external affairs, trade and defence. However, consistent with its national role and responsibilities, the Federal Government is prominent in nationally significant conservation activities, in spite of its limited prescriptive powers in relation to resource development and conservation.

The Federal, State and Territory Governments share many conservation objectives, and have established mechanisms to develop and pursue them. Collaboration on environment and conservation matters occurs, in particular, through two Ministerial Councils - the Australian Environment Council and the Council of Nature Conservation Ministers - which bring together Ministers responsible for general environment matters and for nature conservation, respectively.

DEVELOPMENT OF A NATIONAL CONSERVATION STRATEGY

Three weeks after the launch of the World Conservation Strategy, the Prime Minister announced that the Federal Government, the States and the Northern Territory had agreed to collaborate in utilising the World Conservation Strategy to develop a National Conservation Strategy for Australia (NCSA).

The task of developing a national strategy clearly required consultation outside established mechanisms between governments, because the use and management of the country's renewable natural resources are matters of concern not only to governments and their agencies, but also to business, industry, community groups, conservationists, scientists, educators, land owners and many members of the public. Australia had had extensive previous experience with public participation in environment and conservation decision-making, through various Parliamentary inquiries, advisory bodies, environmental impact assessments, public conferences and other procedures established to address particular issues. However, the development of the NCSA was the first occasion on which a national consensus had been sought on a wide-ranging subject and through such extensive public participation.

A National Steering Committee of Federal, State and Northern Territory officials was appointed to coordinate the development of the National Conservation Strategy for Australia. The Committee's responsibilities included establishing guidelines and defining broad principles of the Strategy. In particular, it clearly recognised that the document would have to be based on existing constitutional responsibilities.

A Consultative Group comprising representatives of industry and conservation groups was set up to advise the National Steering Committee. Administrative support was provided by a small Task Force established in the Federal Department of Home Affairs and Environment (now Arts, Heritage and Environment).

The NCSA was prepared through a process of extensive public consultation. The first stage involved collection of information, ideas and views from the widest possible Australian sources. Twenty eminent Australians, representing a broad range of disciplines and interests, were invited to submit papers for discussion at a National Seminar in November-December 1981. At the Seminar, 200 participants from many organisations and walks of life discussed matters to be included in a National Conservation Strategy. Proceedings of the Seminar formed the basis for preparation by the Task Force of a discussion paper entitled "Towards a National Conservation Strategy,"

which was widely distributed for public comment in 1982.

Over 550 written submissions received from a wide range of organisations throughout Australia were systematically analysed. A Draft Strategy was prepared by the Task Force from these pubic comments, under the guidance of the National Steering Committee and with advice from the Consultative Group. In June 1983, 150 delegates and 50 observers assembled for a four-day Conference in Canberra to refine the Draft Strategy for presentation to governments.

The Federal Minister responsible for the environment, the Hon. Barry Cohen, in his opening address, reminded the Conference that:

A new generation of people has emerged which is constantly questioning every new project that is labelled 'development.' They want answers to a whole range of questions such as: Who are the major beneficiaries? What is the cost and who will bear it? What will we lose in gaining this development?' We owe a great deal to those who have asked these questions with increasing persistence.

However, the Minister pointed out, Australians have become used to, and demand, a rising standard of living. This demand, in turn, places heavy demands on Australia's natural resources.

The main objective of the Conference was to reconcile conservation and development viewpoints. After lengthy debate and difficult negotiations, the Conference agreed on the text of "A National Conservation Strategy for Australia."

THE NATIONAL CONSERVATION STRATEGY FOR AUSTRALIA

The NCSA adopts three objectives from the World Conservation Strategy:

* to maintain essential ecological processes and life-support systems;

* to preserve genetic diversity;

* to ensure the sustainable utilisation of species and ecosystems;

and sets an additional objective:

* to maintain and enhance environmental qualities which make the earth a pleasant place to live and which meet aesthetic and recreational needs.

Five Strategic Principles for achieving these objectives are identified:

* to integrate conservation and development;

* to retain options for future use;

* to focus on causes as well as symptoms;

* to accumulate knowledge for future application; and

* to educate the community.

The Strategy sets out 12 Major Goals and proposes 60 Priority National Actions as specific measures for achieving the objectives of the NCSA. Priorities are identified for: education and training; policy planning and coordination; legislation and regulations; research; international activity; reserves and habitat protection; controlling pollution, wastes and hazardous materials; use of living resources; and conserving soils and water.

Some examples illustrate the level of detail addressed in the Priority National Actions:

* Conduct thorough environmental and socio-economic assessments, proposals and policies that are likely to have significant effects on living resources;

* encourage governments to examine existing legislation which may promote activities inconsistent with the NCSA;

* improve taxonomic and ecological knowledge of plant and animal species and their distribution, impacts and inter-relationships;

* develop and encourage the use of fisheries techniques that minimise incidental take;

* take an integrated whole catchment approach to the management of water and related land resources;

The National Conservation Strategy for Australia does not spell out in detail how these actions should be undertaken. It represents commonly agreed objectives and principles, identifying, in generic terms, actions intended to be implemented in a variety of ways, in line with the constitutional responsibilities of the various tiers of government. It also provides a framework for business, industry and community groups to develop specific actions for application in their own areas of responsibility and according to their own needs and priorities. At the time that the NCSA was produced, many actions of governments were, of course, already consistent with it.

The strength of the Australian National Conservation Strategy lies in the fact that it represents a consensus of a broad cross-section of the Australian community. As the Chairman of the 1983 Conference, Sir Rupert Myers, pointed out in a message published with the NCSA, a few items of interest to particular groups have not been addressed because consensus had not been reached on them. If even one item not agreed by consensus had been included, the credibility and authority of the whole NCSA as a consensus statement would have been jeopardised.

Three States, Victoria, Western Australia and South Australia, have now decided to produce State conservation strategies. Progress at the sub-national level is reported in the next section by Geoff Mosley.

NCSA Endorsement

In July 1984, the Federal Government endorsed the National Conservation Strategy for Australia in the following terms:

The Commonwealth has endorsed the strategy on the understanding that endorsement implies agreement with the Objectives and Strategic Principles of the document agreed at the National Conference. The endorsement shows the Government's willingness in principle to implement the Priority National Actions, in co-operation with development and conservation interests, taking account of Australia's federal, constitutional, legislative and administrative framework, and the general economic climate.

Four of the six State Governments and the Northern Territory have joined the Federal Government in endorsing the NCSA. The other two States, Tasmania and Queensland, have accepted the National Strategy as a broad statement of philosophies relevant to the conservation and development of living natural resources. The Australian Committee for IUCN has endorsed the Strategy, as have a number of other national organisations, including the Institute of Engineers, the Australian Council of National Trusts, the Australian Council of Local Government Associations and the Australian Institute of Foresters.

Application of the World Conservation Strategy Model

The conservation strategy framework recommended in Chapter 8 of the World Conservation Strategy has proved to be a useful model for the preparation of Australian national and sub-national strategies. The model has been adapted in significant ways to take account of Australian political, institutional and administrative arrangements.

The wide acceptance of the World Conservation Strategy in Australia, and the close collaboration achieved between governments and non-government bodies in the development phase have been crucial factors in obtaining wide support for the National Conservation Strategy for Australia and ensuring its success as a model for complementary sub-national strategies. Flexible use of the WCS framework has enabled the various levels of government to respond to the WCS in ways which are mutually complementary, are consistent with the principles and objectives of the World Conservation Strategy, and reflect the priorities of individual governments and their constituencies.

IMPLEMENTATION OF THE NCSA

In accordance with the Resolution of the 1983 NCSA Conference, an Interim Consultative Committee was established by the Federal Government to advise the Minister for Arts, Heritage and Environment how best to promote the objectives and principles of the NCSA and to implement, monitor and evaluate it. The Committee reported to the Minister in August 1985. The report recognised that it would not be possible or sensible to attempt to address simultaneously all of the NCSA's 60 Priority National Actions. The relative priorities will change from time to time and are unlikely to be the same at local, State and national levels.

The report recommended that the Federal, State and Northern Territory Governments should cooperate in identifying and implementing those Priority National Actions which could best be undertaken on a national scale, and that responsible agencies begin to implement the Priority National Actions regarded by them as most urgent in their particular contexts. It was the view of the Interim Consultative Committee that implementation of selected Priority Actions which have com-

munity support will have a multiplier effect and will create a climate in which other actions may follow incrementally as priorities and resources determine.

The Interim Consultative Committee regarded the development and maintenance of a conservation ethic among the Australian community as being of equal importance to undertaking specific practical conservation tasks. The Committee's report contains recommendations aimed at publicising NCSA objectives and promoting such a conservation ethic. These include establishing a broadly representative National Conservation Strategy Advisory Council to act as a high-level forum for consultation, and a source of expert advice on matters relating to the NCSA such as promotion, research and monitoring. The Council would also report publicly and independently on the state of Australia's living resources and supporting ecosystems.

The Committee's report was released for public comment and recommendations, the comments of which will be considered by the Federal Government this year.

The Interim Consultative Committee also considered the value of specific, practical demonstration projects in promoting a conservation ethic and acting as catalysts to other practical activities designed to harmonise conservation and development. In this context, land degradation was identified as a critical problem amenable to local solutions which would provide an opportunity for considerable public participation and information. The Committee recommended undertaking initially a series of local, highly visible tree conservation and establishment projects to combat salinity and land degradation in selected catchments along Australia's largest river system, the Murray and Darling Rivers and their tributaries.

Development of the Australian National Conservation Strategy, and its endorsement by the Federal Government, created unrealistic expectations on the part of some conservationists of massive Government expenditure on conservation. Such thinking is based on a view of the Strategy as a plan for a one-off programme. In conveying the NCSA to governments, the 1983 Conference Chairman described it in terms of "objectives and guidelines for future policies and actions." Its purpose is to provide to governments and agencies an all-time framework for the formulation and review of conservation and environmental policies and programmes.

By applying the National Conservation Strategy for Australia in this way, governments and agencies are able to build on the foundation of highly-developed Federal, State and Northern Territory infrastructures and legislative bases which have been in place since the early 1970s. Since that time these respective Governments have strengthened the legislative base for conservation of flora and fauna, protection of cultural and natural heritage, environmental impact assessment, control of pollution and regulation of various other aspects of the environment. Much of this legislation establishes specialised conservation and environmental protection agencies.

In the six years since the World Conservation Strategy was launched and the NCSA conceived, many major environmental programmes have been introduced involving all levels of government and the community at large. In particular:

* Federal legislation was enacted in 1983 to provide for the protection of property that Australia has identified as "natural heritage" or "cultural heritage" within the meaning of the Convention for the Protection of the World Cultural and Natural Heritage. This legislation was used to prevent the construction of the Gordon-below-Franklin Dam in South-West Tasmania.

* The Federal, New South Wales, Victorian and South Australian Governments have adopted a collaborative approach to promote effective planning and management of the water, land and environmental resources of the Murray-Darling Basin. Activity is being coordinated by a newly-established Murray-Darling Basin Ministerial Council comprising Ministers responsible for water resources, planning and environment in the four Governments.

* The Declaration of the Great Barrier Reef Marine Park, the largest marine park in the world with an area of 340,000 square kilometres, has been completed. Zoning Plans for the Park are being progressively introduced and administered through cooperation between the Federal and Queensland Governments. Oil drilling in the Great Barrier Reef Region has been prohibited by legislation and further legislation is being developed to control the construction and use of offshore platforms and artificial islands in the Marine Park.

* Income tax legislation has been amended to remove tax incentives for primary producers to clear land.

* A National Tree Programme has been established to arrest and reverse the decline in tree cover, especially in rural areas. The programme operates through a National Coordination Committee, through a network of State and Territory committees, and through links with non-government organisations. It sponsors projects at government, community and private levels. Several million trees have been planted under the auspices of the programme to date.

* A National Soil Conservation Programme has been established to develop and implement national policies for the rehabilitation and sustainable utilisation of soil and land resources, aimed particularly at halting soil erosion, salinity, desertification and habitat destruction and at repairing degraded land. It complements other soil conservation programmes administered by State and Territory Governments. A major proportion of the funds provided by the Federal Government under the National Programme are disbursed through State and Territory Governments for projects within their jurisdiction. Projects with a national perspective are funded directly through a Federal component of the Programme.

* An Australian Biological Resources Study, which coordinates research aimed at collecting, describing and classifying Australian plants and animals, and determining their distributions, has been expanded, and work on a programme of documenting all Australian fauna and flora is well advanced.

* A programme has been established to control the use and transport of hazardous chemicals. A National Chemicals Notification and Assessment Scheme is being developed to evaluate new chemicals before they enter the Australian market, and to review chemicals already in use which may be hazardous to health or to the environment.

* Unleaded petrol has been introduced, and all vehicles manufactured after 1 January 1986 must be designed to run on this petrol.

* In 1985, the first national "State of the Australian Environment" report was published by the Federal Government. Complementary reports will be published soon by some State Governments.

* The Australian Forestry Council (comprising Federal, State and Territory Ministers responsible for forestry) is currently developing a national forest strategy which reflects NCSA principles.

* A widely representative Working Group has prepared a comprehensive set of recommendations for a National Rainforest Conservation Policy and Programme. The Federal Government is currently considering the Working Group report, with a view to developing arrangements for implementing it in cooperation with the States and Territories.

Implementation of objectives of the National Conservation Strategy for

Australia is a continuing task. Community awareness and public participation will be the keys to continuing success, and thus promotion and education will be principal roles for Governments.

The Prime Minister of Australia, the Honourable Bob Hawke, in his Forword to the NCSA, wrote:

My personal view of conservation is a pragmatic one. Renewable resources provide the basis for much of our national income today and we are relying on them to continue to do so in years to come. Unless we conserve them for sustainable development it will be our children and their children who will pay the price of our neglect.

There would be few Australians who could not identify with those sentiments.

FURTHER READING

- Department of Home Affairs and Environment, 1982, "National Conservation Strategy for Australia: Proceedings of the National Seminar, Canberra, 30 November - 3 December 1981."

- Department of Home Affairs and Environment, 1982, "Towards a National Conservation Strategy: A Discussion Paper," Canberra.

- Department of Home Affairs and Environment, 1982, "National Conservation Strategy for Australia: Conference Draft, February 1983," Canberra.

- Department of Home Affairs and Environment, "National Conservation Strategy for Australia: Summary Record of Conference held in Canberra, June 1983."

- "A National Conservation Strategy for Australia: Proposed by a Conference held in Canberra in June 1983," 1984, Australian Government Publishing Service, Canberra.

- Department of Arts, Heritage and Environment, 1985, "National Conservation Strategy for Australia, Interim Consultative Committee: Final Report to the Minister for Arts, Heritage and Environment," Canberra.

- "Guide to Environmental Legislation and Administrative Arrangements in Australia," 1984, Australian Environment Council Report No. 16, Australian Government Publishing Service, Canberra.

- Department of Arts, Heritage and Environment, 1985, "State of the Environment in Australia 1985," Canberra.

- Department of Arts, Heritage and Environment, 1985, "Objectives, Achievements and Priorities in Environment, Conservation and Heritage," Canberra.

These publications may be obtained from the Department of Arts, Heritage and Environment, GPO Box 1252, Canberra, ACT, 2601 Australia.

AUSTRALIAN CASE STUDY: STRATEGIES FOR THE FUTURE

J. Geoffrey Mosley
Director, Australian Conservation Foundation
Hawthorn, Victoria, Australia

SUMMARY As a federation, Australia presents an interesting example of the challenges of implementing a National Conservation Strategy where diverse conservation strategy activities have already been undertaken at the sub-national level, and where the Constitution assigns control of the environment and resources to State Governments. This paper discusses the reactions of individual States to the development of State strategies, outlines some sectoral, regional and local strategies and argues for the need to promote a comprehensive network. The network would link these conservation strategies with one another and with other major strategies concerning, for example, the economy, industrial development and population, in the interests of consistency, efficiency and achieving the optimum value from such activities.

One particular difficulty cited has been the very general nature of the World Conservation Strategy and the National Conservation Strategy for Australia which leaves room for differing interpretations of the text. Sub-national strategies, therefore, need to be more specific, concerned with long-term goals and plans which remain viable regardless of changes in government but which are, nevertheless, seen as evolutionary documents subject to monitoring and review.

INTRODUCTION

Australia has made initial progress in introducing the conservation strategy concept at Federal, State and local levels. The Australian case may thus serve as a model for other national policy planners considering strategic environmental planning.

The general problem confronting those concerned with pioneering the conservation strategy is how to promote its usefulness as a planning tool. Rather than anticipating a single solution to this problem, it is more appropriate to recognise that parallel action will be necessary on various fronts. These will include the development of a wide range of strategies for different areas and resources; the linking of these strategies; careful consideration of the content of each; and explicit provisions for implementation, monitoring and review.

As a federation, Australia can already point to diverse and widespread conservation strategy activities but most of the work in developing an extensive network of successful strategies still lies ahead. In this context, the relationship of the strategies to one another is of particular interest. Also of interest is the opportunity now presented in Australia for fostering public awareness of the value of conservation strategies by closely involving the community in their development.

This paper discusses ways and means of developing a set of related long-term plans to conserve the Australian environment. It deals with strategy development at all geographic levels.

DEVELOPING A COMPREHENSIVE NETWORK OF STRATEGIES

Because of its concern with long range future goals, considerable governmental promotion will be needed to bring a conservation strategy to public notice. However, promotional activities in themselves are not sufficient to achieve widespread acceptance of the strategy tool; effort will also be required to encourage the development of strategies for specific resource sectors at smaller geographic levels. Involving the greatest number of individuals and organisations possible in strategy development and implementation is probably the most effective way of creating public awareness and support. This has been demonstrated in the State of Victoria. As far as can be ascertained, Victoria is currently the only region in Australia where strategies are being

prepared at the local level. In this instance the interest developed as a result of the circulation of State strategy discussion papers and drafts.

The World Conservation Strategy recommended that every community review the extent to which it is achieving conservation (WCS 8.1). The review would form the basis of a strategy to define priority requirements and overcome obstacles to them. The strategy, the WCS states, "may be at the national level or at one or more sub-national levels (provincial, state, municipal), or there may be separate (but, it is hoped, complementary) strategies at several levels, depending on the division of government responsibilities for the planning and management of land and water uses." (International Union for Conservation of Nature and Natural Resources, 1980).

The National Conservation Strategy Conference held in Canberra in June 1983, which proposed the National Strategy subsequently endorsed by most Australian governments, also expressed the view that, among other things, success would require action to develop and implement conservation strategies complementary to the National Strategy "for States and Territories, local government areas, regions and specific sectors such as manufacturing, industry, mining, forestry, agriculture and fisheries" (Dept. of Home Affairs and Environment, 1983).

The National Strategy

The development of the National Conservation Strategy for Australia is described in detail in the preceding chapter by A.G. Kerr of the Department of Arts, Heritage and Environment.

The long period between the finalisation of Strategy text by the Strategy Conference in Canberra in June 1983, and the Federal Government's decision to establish a body to oversee its implementation, has been strongly criticised by conservation NGOs. The conservation groups feel that because some momentum has been lost, it is now important for the Government to take decisive measures on the specific proposals of the Interim Consultative Committee, which produced its final report in August 1985.

State Strategies

The Australian Constitution located the main responsibilities for environmental and resource control with State governments, so there is strong reason to develop State-level strategies which are specific to their needs and problems. However, three years after the Strategy Conference in Canberra, State strategies are yet to be completed by any of the six States, and three of these and the Northern Territory have yet to commence work on one.

The Tasmanian and Queensland Governments, which have consistently expressed concern in recent years about what they believe to be an intrusion of the Federal Government into their environmental affairs, have not endorsed the National Conservation Strategy for Australia, yet they are two of the Governments which are not proposing to develop State strategies.

In Tasmania (Bennett, 1986), policymakers have not decided whether to prepare a State strategy, but do not consider the matter a high priority at present. The Queensland Government has not announced a position on the development of a State strategy but agrees to consider the principles of the National Strategy in Government policies and programmes as they are received from time to time (Wilcox, 1986).

The view of the The Northern Territory Government is that further strategy documents at the State or regional level could be of some value but that the more immediate task is to apply the NCSA within the Territory in order to promote broader understanding of the concept (Hatton, 1986).

The Government of New South Wales is not convinced of the need for a State strategy, in spite of the personal involvement of the Premier in strategy development decisions. It is endeavouring, however, to set up a Committee to oversee and report on implementation of the National Strategy within the State. Terms of reference of the proposed Committee largely relate to the implementation of priority national actions of the National Strategy and do not include any reference to State or local strategies. As a consequence, the Nature Conservation Council of New South Wales, an NGO body, has declined membership in the Committee until such time as the State formally decides to prepare a State strategy. According to the Head of New South Wales' Department of Environment and Planning, the Committee will discuss and report on the advisability of a State strategy. Discussions with Department officers indicate that resistance to the introduction of State and local strategies might be due to concern about committing further resources when an elaborate system of State environmental policies, regional and local plans already exists. Yet these same plans and procedures (which incorporate project assessment as part of the overall process) could readily be adapted to the conservation strategy approach.

The three remaining States present a somewhat different picture. South Australia, after some hesitation, is now strongly committed to the preparation of a State Conservation Strategy (Hopgood, 1986). The Environment Protection Council is to prepare a draft Strategy by the end of 1986 and this will be circulated for public comment. The Strategy is intended to be a practical document containing clear references regarding its implementation (Caldicott, 1986). Initial reservations to preparing a State Strategy related to concern about achieving agreement on a text, but the Environment Protection Council feels that this problem may be overcome by using the National Strategy format, thereby building on the consensus reached by that document.

Western Australia is even further along than South Australia but completion of its State Strategy is proving to be a protracted affair. It is hoped to have a "definitive draft" version ready for public discussion later this year (Hodge, 1986).

The most promising development at the State level in Australia is the Victorian State Conservation Strategy. The hallmark of this process has been the strong involvement of the public and a determination to produce a document which will be thoroughly operational. The action part of the proposed final Strategy is highly specific, with implementation procedures being incorporated in the Strategy itself. If the Strategy receives final approval, it is projected to be a most effective measure and a model for conservation strategists worldwide.

Sectoral Strategies

By the cumbersome nature of strategy development processes at national and local levels in Australia, it was anticipated that activity at the sectoral, regional and local levels would be limited. This has proved to be the case. Although the Commonwealth Government endorsed the National Strategy in July 1984, there have been many instances of Federal departments preparing policies and plans which are not relative to the objectives and principles of that document. In other instances, opportunities have not been optimised. However, notwithstanding limited encouragement at various levels, a number of individuals and organisations recognise the merits of the strategy approach.

The draft National Forestry Strategy, published and circulated for comment by the Standing Committee on Forestry, Australian Forestry Council, is a good example of the use of a sectoral strategy. Another is the development of a Salinity Control Strategy, which represents a major step forward in implementing a priority action in the Victorian State Strategy and the National Strategy. Both Victoria and New South Wales have, in previous years, incorporated formal statements on conservation policy for particular sectors into their planning machinery. Those statements are easily adaptable to the conservation strategy model.

Antarctica is a promising area for strategy development. At the conclusion of the Fourth Meeting of the Commission for the Conservation of Antarctic Marine Living Resources, the Australian delegation announced that a conservation strategy was needed for Antarctic Marine Living Resources (Australian Conservation Foundation, 1985). Preparatory work on this, including a proposal for interim catch limits, is proceeding. In response to the request by the Australian Government at the Twelfth Consultative Meeting of the Antarctic Treaty Consultative Parties, Canberra, 1983, for a comprehensive review of Antarctic conservation measures, the meeting noted that there was a need "to consider whether further coordination was necessary of the various elements of environmental protection and conservation contained in the Antarctic Treaty system" (Dept. of Foreign Affairs, 1984). Clearly these developments provide a basis for the development of a Conservation Strategy for Antarctica and the Southern Ocean, which has been an objective of IUCN since its 15th General Assembly in October 1981.

Regional Strategies

While regional planning has always had a somewhat precarious existence in Australia, successful examples exist in several States. Regional strategies require State initiative and local enthusiasm for progress in the implementation of these strategies. Generally, the developments to date have been special purpose strategies for a regional context.

* In New South Wales, of 11 Regional Environment Plans (REPs), seven are primarily concerned with areas which have higher than usual amenity value. Two refer to areas affected by extractive industries and another is aimed at protecting prime crop land.

* In Victoria, a number of regional planning authorities have been established under the Town and Country Planning Act in areas of high amenity value. Comprehensive strategy plans have since been developed for these (Upper Yarra Valley and Dandenong Ranges Authority, 1982, and Western Port Regional Planning Authority, 1975). The proposed Victorian State Conservation Strategy will encourage the development of regional and local strategy plans.

It is natural that initial regional conservation strategies would be hybrids between sectoral and regional strategies because these are focused on particular problems such as the conservation of visual values, or high-quality agricultural soils. Ultimately, however, the regional strategy will need to deal with all areas of the State, be more comprehensive in character, and receive input from the strategy processes at both local and national levels. Regional environment plans, being special purpose in character, are prepared at the level of the State Government, whereas long-term local initiative is essential for regional conservation strategies.

Local Strategies

At present, Victoria is the only State engaging in local conservation activity. One municipality has completed a strategy and several others are preparing similar plans. The Shire of Mornington document (Shire of Mornington, 1986) has been developed in two volumes: one for authority officials and the other for residents. Interestingly, the Shire has decided that in order to ensure that the Strategy is treated as a dynamic tool, it will always term the document a draft (Corbett, 1986).

In New South Wales, the district Town and Country schemes under legislation are termed "Local Environment Plans," and little modification will be needed to adjust them to the conservation strategy system.

DISCUSSION

In the Australian situation, it is becoming increasingly clear that the development of conservation strategies at the sub-national level will help to promote the entire conservation strategy approach. The circulation of 20,000 copies of the Commonwealth Strategy Discussion Paper (Dept. of Home Affairs and Environment, 1982) and 5,000 copies of the Victorian draft Strategy, along with the preparation of many hundreds of submissions on these and other documents, have encouraged awareness of the merits of the strategy approach.

If a strategy provides an effective measure for planning conservation initiatives at Federal and national levels, it is reasonable that such an approach would have intrinsic value at the more local levels. An important reason for this is the opportunity it provides for direct citizen participation in environmental planning. It also permits an exchange of ideas which may originate as well at the community level as within policy-making bodies. While each strategy may have individual merit, they will most likely be optimised into

an overall interconnected system, provided that close attention is paid to the linkages.

LINKING THE STRATEGIES

Considerable attention has been given to the use of common logos, terminology and formats in developing the National and some State conservation strategies. This is appropriate since uniform formats provide continuity and the ability to interlink strategies, while permitting attention to be concentrated on content as it varies from area to area.

The proposed Victorian State Conservation Strategy provides that the Ministry of Planning and Environment will ensure consistency of all local and regional planning schemes with the State Conservation Strategy.

Since sensitivities often exist in the relationship between different tiers of government, sub-national strategies should not be regarded solely as a means of implementing broader strategies. Nevertheless, it is important from the standpoint of efficiency that reference is made in each conservation strategy to other strategies with which it is linked. This is an aspect of strategy development where assistance from a special State or national body would be helpful.

As yet there is little recognition of the need at any level of government in Australia to link conservation strategies with other fundamental strategies such as those dealing with the economy, industrial development, energy, social justice and population. An early opportunity for this will present itself in Victoria when the three basic strategies on conservation, the economy and social justice have been approved. At the national level, the National Population Council is preparing a paper on population options but the Government is not presently considering linking and integrating long-term plans and policies in different sectors. This is something that the Commission for the Future could assist with, although at present it is concerned with preparing citizens for the impact of new technology.

IMPROVING THE CONTENT

The general nature of the World Conservation Strategy and the National Conservation Strategy for Australia texts has caused certain difficulties. While the strategies have found easy acceptance among developers who welcomed the position that development is not necessarily incompatible with conservation, the same generality has created concern and reservation among some conservationists who observed developers' reactions and witnessed the strategies being used to avoid genuine conservation options. The situation could be rectified to a large extent by developing more specific sub-national strategies. This is probably one of the main reasons why several Australian States have taken no steps to produce State strategies.

The main difficulty in the wording of the World Conservation Strategy and Australia's National Conservation Strategy is that it leaves open the questions of what constitutes "sustainable utilisation," as well as the circumstances under which species and ecosystems should be reserved against removal of materials for consumption purposes. As a result, frequent instances have occurred in Australia where development interests have claimed backing of the National Conservation Strategy for their activity, on the grounds that they are either simply "utilising" resources, or (regardless of the facts) "sustainably using" them. The Victorian Sawmillers Association, for instance, quoting the World Conservation Strategy and the NCSA position that conservation and development are compatible, claims priority for its proposal that forests in the Victorian Alps should continue to be used for logging rather than be included in the major National Park plan proposed by the State government (Victorian Sawmiller's Association, 1985). These interests are assisted in such an interpretation of the Strategy by WCS objective No. 4:

to ensure the sustainable utilization of species and ecosystems.

This reads like an exhortation to utilise resources (sustainably) even though there may be other conservation options for a given situation which do not involve cropping or harvesting a species, or otherwise removing material resources. The interpretation by readers of the Strategy has been that, according to the WCS, species such as kangaroos and whales *should* be harvested, as long as this can be done sustainably. IUCN itself has encouraged this interpretation by some of its own statements, particularly with regard to whales (International Union for the Conservation of Nature and Natural Resources, 1985). The WCS should not be quoted as implying that the moratorium on whales should end once population levels are such that sustainable utilisation can be achieved. There is a clear option of "letting the whales go free" regardless of whether sustainable utilisation is attainable. One proposed resolution of this dilemma is to reword Objective No. 4 as follows:

to ensure that the utilization of species and ecosystems is sustainable.

National parks and protected areas as well as the conservation of some species from harvesting serve cultural and recreational needs. There is insufficient protection in the existing three "Objectives" of the World Conservation Strategy for the "setting aside" of areas and species for non-consumptive purposes. Considerable recasting of this important introductory section of the WCS is therefore suggested, although it should not be limited solely to the addition of phrases such as that mentioned above.

The problem relating to the general nature of the Strategy will remain if national strategies are not more specific than the WCS and if the sub-national strategies are not more specific than national ones. State governments will be tempted to make their strategies slightly enlarged translations of the Australian National Strategy because this leaves their discretionary powers unaffected. These are unfortunately often exercised in favour of development interests meeting short-term needs.

Too great an emphasis, at the national level, in the promotion of State strategies as a means of implementing the National Conservation Strategy for Australia could also encourage this thinking. The State strategies, while maintaining some similarity of format, should be based primarily on local initiative and be designed to play a meaningful role in long-term planning. It is encouraging to note that Victoria has shown independence from the NCSA

model by adding a fifth objective concerning non-renewable resources.

A conservation strategy should, by definition, be concerned with long-term goals and plans since there may be difficulties in maintaining the viability of a given strategy if it is seen as being a publicity document for a particular term of government. If this should happen, it is unlikely that such a strategy would continue in force after the next change of government.

In general, the strategy should indicate long-term directives; the "shopping list" of action items should not be confused with the strategy itself. Greater emphasis should be placed on causes of environmental problems in the World Conservation Strategy and the National Conservation Strategy for Australia, including escalating resources consumption as a result of increased per capita demand and growing population. Amendments relating to the requirements for improving the quality of life are needed in both the Australian National Strategy and the World Conservation Strategy (where they are presently not mentioned).

IMPLEMENTATION

The arrangements proposed to be used for the implementation of the Victorian Conservation Strategy should be widely studied by conservation strategists around the world. The proposed draft Strategy details implementation procedures to be followed, both with regard to actions and policies, and for the implementation of the Strategy itself. The latter aspect is particularly important because it relates to the establishment of the status of the conservation strategy.

Implementation provisions are designed to "lock" the strategy into the decision-making systems of Government Departments, Ministers and Cabinet. In Victoria the Conservation Strategy is one of three strategies. An Economic Strategy was released in April 1984 and a Social Justice Strategy is also being produced. All Cabinet proposals must be consistent with the State Economic Strategy and a similar arrangement is proposed for the other two State Strategies. The proposed conservation strategy states that the Ministry of Planning and Environment will ensure consistency of all local and regional planning schemes with the State Conservation Strategy. As far as possible, strategies should nominate responsibilities for each action and procedure; the Victorian strategy may not go far enough in this regard.

Monitoring

A conservation strategy is only as good as the impact it has, and the arrangements for monitoring its effects should be a vital aspect of the procedure. This monitoring capacity should be detailed in the strategy document. One approach is to link the strategy closely with impact assessments and environmental reporting systems.

Already the Commonwealth, South Australia, and Victoria have produced State of the Environment Reports (Dept. of Arts, Heritage and Environment, 1985; Minister for Environment and Planning, SA, 1985; Ministry for Planning and Environment, Victoria, 1985a). These in time will be more closely related to the strategies, including the strategy revision process.

Review

The World Conservation Strategy and the National Conservation Strategy for Australia both mention the need to be further developed and updated. At national and sub-national levels in particular, the fact that strategies involve a compromise between competing viewpoints about resource allocation creates some resistance to review. It is important to overcome this problem by stressing in strategy documents that they will need to be reviewed from time to time, to take account of changing conditions and new priorities and to incorporate new information and insights. In this context, it will be helpful if the disagreements which occur during the strategy development process are carefully recorded and published, since these provide a focal point for further discussion and government leadership.

CONCLUSION

The Australian conservation strategy has taken only a few steps of its long march, but useful experience has already been gained about the best way to travel.

To promote the conservation strategy, it is essential to encourage involvement in its development - doing as well as preaching. It matters less that minor mistakes are made than that the work is begun. The experience in Victoria has shown that the State strategy process can have a cumulative effect. There is no reason why work should not commence at all geographic levels simultaneously. As an evolving document, adjustments can be made later to ensure complete consistency.

The development of a comprehensive network of conservation strategies should be a community process. Leadership from government, especially central government, is essential. But for strategies to become living documents, they will depend greatly on local initiative, on the development of a conservation ethic and on civic pride.

For a new idea offering the potential to achieve a healthier, safer and more fulfilling society, government must ask itself whether the process is proceeding quickly enough. There is a particular need, at this stage, to set-up bodies which provide encouragement, giving advice and guidance on development of the strategies and on their linking, monitoring and review. Such bodies, relevant Ministers and government departments, need to become aware of the obstacles so that they can be overcome. In New South Wales, for instance, pride in an existing system needs to be replaced by a realisation of benefits from developing a State Strategy of high conservation standards, thus keeping it in the vanguard of conservation policy in Australia.

The use of the World Conservation Strategy format is obviously helpful in overcoming apprehension on the part of a government or agency, concerned about the difficulties of obtaining approval by disparate groups. In cases where governments show little or no interest, non-governmental organisations can play a major role in educational campaigns which lead to decisions to introduce strategies. Such bodies will have to be vigilant about State Governments which use token endorsement of the National strategy to sanction local action, or alternatively produce a non-operational version of a National strategy.

The linking of strategies at various levels offers other advantages in optimising their effectiveness. Similarly, there is scope for linking conservation strategies with other major strategies at each level.

With regard to content, it is important for the strategies to be treated as evolutionary documents containing both long-term goals and action plans. The detailing of immediate plans should not be allowed to overshadow the long-term strategic intentions, otherwise there is a risk that they will be too closely associated with the political ambitions of particular officials or governments.

It is important that the means for implementing, monitoring and reviewing the strategy should all be stated in the strategy document. This will reduce the likelihood of mere lip-service being paid to such a vital document.

Because of the complex system of Australian Government, many suggestions are presented in this paper for progress with conservation strategies. Other considerations will undoubtedly come to light in the context of other government applications. It is clear that in most situations the task will be easier if some group or individual has the task of developing a framework for the optimum employment of conservation strategies.

REFERENCES

• Australian Conservation Foundation, 1985, "Strong Australian Statement to Antarctic Commission," *ACF Newsletter*, 17 (10), p.7.

- Bacon, G.J., President, Institute of Foresters of Australia Inc., Pers. Comm., 28 Apr 1986.

- Bennett, J.M., Minister for National Parks, Tasmania, Pers. Comm., 17 Apr 1986.

- Buxton, M., Ministry for Planning and Environment, Victoria, Pers. Comm., 13 May 1986.

- Caldicott, R., Secretary, Environmental Protection Council, South Australia, Pers. Comm. 15 May 1986.

- Conservation and Environment Council and Department of Conservation and Environment, Western Australia, 1982, *Towards a Conservation Strategy for Western Australia, Report on a Meeting held at Yanchep National Park*, July 1982, Government Printer, W.A.

- Conservation and Environment Council, 1983, *A Conservation Strategy for Western Australia*, Draft, Department of Conservation and Environment, W.A., Report 12, July 1983.

- Corbett, D., Conservation Officer, Shire of Mornington, Pers. Comm., 14 May 1986.

- Coutts, L., Director, Australian Council of Local Government Associations, Pers. Comm., 26 Mar 1986.

- Department of Foreign Affairs, 1984, *Antarctic Treaty, Report of the Twelfth Consultative Meeting Canberra, September, 1983,* Australian Government Publishing Service, Canberra.

- Department of Home Affairs and Environment, 1982, *A National Conservation Strategy for Australia, Living Resource for Conservation for Sustainable Development, Towards a National Conservation Strategy - A Discussion Paper*, Dept. of Home Affairs and Environment, Australian Government Publishing Service, Canberra.

- Department of Home Affairs and Environment, 1983, *National Conservation Strategy for Australia, Living Resources Conservation for Sustainable Development. Proposed by a Conference held in Canberra, June 1983*, Dept. of Home Affairs and Environment, Australian Government Publishing Service, Canberra.

- Department of Arts, Heritage and Environment, 1985, *State of the Environment in Australia 1985*, Australian Government Publishing Service, Canberra.

- Ecofund Australia, 1986, "Habitat Protection for Threatened Species and Wild Genetic Resources - A Proposal for a New International Treaty," Unpublished.

- Hatton, S., Minister for Conservation, Northern Territory, Pers. Comm., 27 Apr 1986.

- Hodge, B., Minister for Environment, Western Australia, Pers. Comm., 5 May 1986.

- Hopgood, D., Minister for Environment and Planning, South Australia, Pers. Comm., 21 Apr 1986.

- International Union for Conservation of Nature and Natural Resources (IUCN), 1980, *World Conservation Strategy*, Gland, Switzerland.

- International Union for Conservation of Nature and Natural Resources (IUCN), "Submission to International Whaling Commission, Bournemouth, 15-19 July 1985."

- Lord Howe Island Board, 1986, *Draft Regional Environmental Plan*.

- Madigan, M. and Harris, C., Department of Environment and Planning, South Australia, Pers. Comm., 7 May 1986.

- Ministry for Conservation, Victoria (State Conservation Strategy Task Force), 1983, *Conservation in Victoria - A Discussion Paper on a State Conservation Strategy*, Ministry for Conservation, Aug 1983.

- Minister for Environment and Planning, 1985, *Preliminary State of the Environment Report for South Australia*, Adelaide.

- Ministry for Planning and Environment, Victoria, 1984, *Ensuring our Future: Draft Conservation Strategy Overview Statement for Public Comment, December 1984*, Ministry for Planning and Environment.

- Ministry for Planning and Environment, Victoria, 1985(a), *Report of the State Conservation Strategy Community Workshop, Lorne, May 1985*, Ministry for Planning and Environment, Sept 1985.

- Ministry for Planning and Environment, Victoria, 1985(b), "Ensuring Our Future - State Conservation Strategy", Draft, Nov 1985.

- National Conservation Strategy for Australia Interim Consultative Committee, 1985, *National Conservation Strategy for Australia Final Report to the Minister for Arts, Heritage and Environment,* Department of Arts, Heritage and Environment, Canberra.

- Shire of Mornington, *Conservation Is Ensuring Our Future,* Residents' Manual, Second Draft, Apr 1986.

- Smyth, D., Director of Environmental Planning New South Wales, Pers. Comm., 21 Apr 1986.

- Standing Committee on Forestry, Australian Forestry Council, 1985, *National Forest Strategy for Australia, Draft*, Department of Primary Industry, Canberra.

- Upper Yarra Valley and Dandenong Ranges Authority, 1982, *Regional Strategy Plan*, Oct 1982.

- Victorian Sawmillers Association, 1985, *Victoria's Alpine Region: Preserving a Vital Resource*.

- Western Port Regional Planning Authority, 1975, *Conservation Plan Mornington Peninsula*, May 1975.

- Wilcox, S., Acting Under-Secretary, Department of Arts, National Parks, and Sport, Queensland, Pers. Comm. 10 Apr 1986.

- Working Group on Rainforest Conservation, 1985, *Rainforest Conservation in Australia, Report to Minister for Arts, Heritage and Environment,* Department of Arts, Heritage and Environment, Sept 1985.

INDONESIA'S NATIONAL CONSERVATION STRATEGY

Emil Salim
Minister of State for Population
and Environment
Jakarta, Indonesia

SUMMARY *In Indonesia, conservation plays an important part of development oriented toward individual fulfilment. Conservation measures are designed to prevent jeopardising life-support systems while confronting the need to control and redistribute the population, increase the carrying capacity of the land, industrialise, and develop the service sector. Environmental law in Indonesia needs to be supported by a re-examination of economic theory (e.g. recognising that development is not an end in itself), by improved environmental impact assessment procedures, and by more stringent environmental standards based on indices of improvement in the quality of life. Examples of factors necessary for policy making in sustainable development are reviewed, including institutional support at the international level, attitudinal changes through education, people's participation, and networks ensuring cooperation between industry and other interests. Especially important in Indonesia is the growth of self-reliant institutions (NGOs) to help maintain the existing traditional environmental awareness during the period of change.*

INTRODUCTION

The Indonesian National Conservation Strategy, an integral part of the overall development strategy, is aimed at the development of the individual Indonesian.

Indonesia was colonised for centuries and it is only since independence in 1945 that its people have been able to develop their own identity. The basic characteristics of such an identity are the establishment of a harmonious relationship between Man and God the Creator, between Man and society, and between Man and the natural environment. This relationship, achieved only over a long period of time, provides direction for development programmes and it is in this context that conservation plays an important role.

But how is conservation integrated into Indonesian development policies? What are its strengths and weaknesses? And what lessons can we learn for the future, not only for Indonesia but for other countries as well?

THE CHALLENGES OF DEVELOPMENT

According to the World Bank, Indonesia's Gross National Product per capita in 1983 was US $560 compared with the Canadian GNP per capita of US $12,310. The country's infant mortality rate is 101 per 1000 births compared with 9 per 1000 in Canada. Life expectancy is 54 years compared with 76 years in Canada. In other words, Indonesians have a lower income, a higher mortality rate and a shorter lifespan than Canadians.

The reasons for this situation lie in the fact that Indonesia was a late starter in development, a continuous development process having begun only in 1968. The country lacks capital and skills, and depends primarily on natural and human resources for its development. This combination produces an economy based mainly on primary products, where raw materials are usually exported, processed abroad and are then imported.

Such an export-oriented and primary-sector-based economy is strongly affected by economic fluctuations outside Indonesia's borders. When Americans buy fewer cars, the demand for tires declines. This reduces the demand for rubber, negatively affects Indonesian exports and results in a lower income for the rubber farmer. With technological advances and economic growth, the world is getting smaller and countries are becoming more interdependent. Developing countries, however, are more dependent on industrialised countries than vice-versa.

Under these circumstances, it is necessary for Indonesia to change its economic structure and to become less vulnerable to international price fluctuations. This means the acceleration of development, exploiting resources and changing the environment. Such development will need to be both intensive and extensive in order to meet the demands of 163 million people - a figure which is expected to grow to 223 million by the year 2000. The problem is complicated by the fact that 60 percent of the population inhabits the island of Java while the remainder is dispersed over other islands, many of them still under-populated.

To meet these challenges, Indonesia is following a five-pronged programme of development.

First is the programme of family planning to reduce the number from four or five children per family to two over the next 14 years, both through medical means and socio-economic incentives.

Second is the programme of transmigration opening new frontiers in Indonesia outside Java where the man/land ratio is lower. To maintain the population on Java at its current level of 96 million people, approximately 1.5 million need to be transmigrated annually. The current level of programmed and spontaneous transmigration is almost half this rate. Thus Java's population will be more than 110 million by the year 2000.

Third is the programme designed to increase the carrying capacity of land, either through intensification of agriculture or other techniques such as hill terracing. In many parts of Indonesia shifting cultivation still exists. While this gives scope for improved agricultural development, it also opens the door for the increased use of fertilizers, pesticides and chemicals.

Fourth is the programme of industrialisation to increase employment opportunities per unit of land. In densely populated areas, agriculture ceases to absorb the unemployed while development offers a better chance. Industrial development also enables Indonesia to process its own raw materials into finished goods.

Fifth is the programme of development in the service sector, such as the improvement of trade, banking, insurance, education and health services, at both a formal and informal level. According to statistics, the capacity of these service sectors to absorb the unemployed is greater than that of other sectors.

This then is the development programme launched in Indonesia to meet the challenges of population growth and unequal distribution, poverty, and unemployment, by changing the economic structure and improving the quality of life.

All these efforts, however, also mean modifying Indonesia's environment, thus jeopardising life support systems and biological diversity. How can Indonesia simultaneously solve its development problems while preventing environmental destruction? This question will have to be addressed if the long-term objectives enabling Indonesians to live in harmony with God, society and the natural environment are to be achieved.

Conceptually and legally, the answer lies in the Environmental Impact Assessment Law promulgated in 1982. It stipulates that Indonesia shall adhere to basic principles of environmental management, emphasising that sustainable development assumes the obligation to use resources wisely in support of the continued process of development. This law has the unanimous approval of all political parties and organisations, and is widely accepted throughout the country. It indicates the existence of a political will to follow a pattern of development which reflects genuine concern for a healthy environment for future generations in Indonesia.

TOWARD SUSTAINABLE DEVELOPMENT

The basic thinking behind this Environmental Impact Assessment Law is the integration of environment and development. This implies the inclusion of environmental considerations at all stages of development, such as planning, implementation and evaluation. It also means that environmental management, encompassing, among other principles, sustaining natural resources and maintaining environmental quality, is to be considered as a development objective in itself.

The integration of development and environment is impelled, first of all, by the recognition that development can only be sustained to the extent that the environment and natural resources can equally be sustained. Secondly, it is guided by the recognition that quality of life is very much a function of the quality of both physical and social environments. Since achieving the best possible quality of life for all is the ultimate objective of our development efforts, the pursuit of that ideal provides the impetus and focus for integrating development and environment.

Such an integration affects Indonesia's perception of conservation in general, and the issues explored in the World

Conservation Strategy in particular. In other words, an apparent neglect of a conservation issue should not be attributed automatically to a lack of awareness or a lack of concern. There might be considerable concern and awareness but the significance accorded an issue will depend on its perceived place in the overall development of the environment.

While an environmental-development outlook has been promulgated by law, integration requires new concepts, new approaches and new analytical tools. It also requires a review of present development and economic theories. For too long such theories have regarded development as an objective in itself. To accept development as a self-validating goal means that it would be all too easy to relegate other considerations, such as environmental and social questions, to subordinate positions. All current development and economic theories brand these other considerations as "externalities" which should remain outside economic calculations and which should be evaluated only in terms of "social costs."

Over and above the lack of new concepts, new approaches and new analytical tools in support of the integration of development and environment is the communication gap between environmentalists - including conservationists - and economists. The two groups are speaking on different wavelengths.

The concepts of "biological diversity" and "life-support systems" consider natural resources as capital stocks. Such natural wealth should be considered not only in terms of derivable incomes, but also in terms of stocks to be safeguarded lest we become poorer

despite increasing incomes. The maintenance of that wealth, sustaining natural resources, safeguarding the quality of our life-support systems and maintaining biological diversity, should be examined from the point of view of cost as well as investment.

This view does not prevail in most countries in the calculation of National Income. The formulation of Gross National Product and National Income indices does not take into account the depletion of natural wealth. Only the income derived from natural stocks is considered. Exports of forest products, while reducing forest stocks as a part of the natural wealth, are only registered in the National Income Account as income and are, therefore, seen as desirable. This is one of the many reasons why concepts advocated in the World Conservation Strategy have failed to enter the mainstream of economic policy formulation, in both developing and developed countries, as well as in development agencies such as the World Bank, Regional Development Banks and the United Nations organisations.

In addition to a re-examination of the theory, we are also in need of concepts and approaches to form the basis of practical policies and operational procedures. These needs include better analytical tools such as extended cost/benefit analysis referring to development as well as environmental considerations; better ways to establish thresholds of environmental sustainability and to measure environmental carrying capacity.

We could extend the list of needs even further and refer, for instance, to the need for improving the procedures for environmental impact analysis (EIA). Procedures should ensure that such an assessment should not be a mere addendum to a project proposal. It should rather be an integral part of a project's feasibility study, applied as early as possible (at the project development stage) to all projects, whether public or private, having significant destructive or constructive impacts on the environment. Environmental impact analysis should consider both the physical and social environment because both affect the quality of life, which, therefore, becomes the common reference point.

Project development based on agreed environmental standards affects environmental quality. The more stringent the environmental standards, the more possible is the achievement of a healthy environment. Only on this basis can mortality rates be reduced, life expectancy lengthened and quality of life improved.

It is in considering quality of life that environmental improvement and economic development merge. But in this context we are still faced with the task of developing appropriate quality of life indicators, which encompass both physical and social environmental indicators and those for economic development.

The difficulties of implementing the World Conservation Strategy are that it does not indicate appropriate standards for biological diversity, life-support systems and indicators of sustainable development. At present, translation of the Strategy objectives into specific operational targets to permit their inclusion in major economic development objectives remains unrealised.

INDONESIA'S ENDEAVOURS TO ACHIEVE SUSTAINABLE DEVELOPMENT

In light of these difficulties, Indonesia has attempted to implement the concept of sustainable development through five broad approaches.

The country has established regional resource use plans at the provincial level as the basis for regional resource management. For each of the 27 provinces throughout Indonesia, a regional environment/population balance sheet is produced which serves as a baseline for sustainable development. It reveals the state of the environment and population in each province through the use of various statistical data and population censuses of 1971, 1980 and 1985. It also indicates trends in population movement, resource use and structural changes, both economic and social. Based on these data, the major question that emerges is what resources need to be exploited on a sustainable basis to improve quality of life for the population over a 20-year period? Following a consultation process within and between central, regional and district governments, a regional development plan with a common focus is submitted to the District representative body for formulation into law. This sustainable resource use plan then serves as a guide for all Ministries and Regional Government agencies to launch their respective development programmes.

Indonesia is also implementing an Environmental Impact Assessment Law, which requires those projects with significant impact on the physical and social environment to combine technical and economic feasibility studies with environmental impact studies. Each province is obliged to determine environmental standards which are consistent with the Regional Development Plan and which give full consideration to factors affecting the quality of life.

"Quality of life indices" have also been established. These include income per capita, infant mortality rate, crude mortality rate, fertility rate, life expectancy, literacy rate, enrollment ratio of the population for various age groups, accessibility to clean water, sanitation facilities per thousand persons, and human settlement space per capita, among other criteria. These are extensions of the "physical quality of life index" as developed thus far. Through such an index, development and environmental considerations can merge. This index is closely linked with the setting of environmental standards mentioned before. It is through these standards that objectives of the World Conservation Strategy are incorporated into development plans, enabling conservation to achieve its proper place in the development process.

An effort to encourage, stimulate and promote peoples' participation in the development process is also underway. The Environmental Impact Assessment Law provides the legal basis for this participation as well as the growth of non-governmental organisations, which we prefer to call "self-reliant institutions." Promotion of these institutions is based on the recognition that sustainable development requires changes in people's outlook and perception of development; changes which can be achieved most effectively through peoples' direct involvement in the process. Almost 80 percent of Indonesia's population is concentrated in rural villages. Typical of agrarian societies, most have lived harmonious-

ly with the environment. The present need is to maintain that awareness of nature in the face of change, since development to meet people's basic needs and overcome poverty is increasing. Participation of the people in determining the direction of that change is vital if the harmonious balance between Man and the environment is to continue.

It is also through the involvement of these self-reliant institutions (SRIs) that market imperfections are to be corrected. If environmental considerations are not revealed through the price mechanism of the market economy, it is expected that SRIs can act as a substitute in indicating the proper path toward sustainable development. In this context, peoples' participation is important not only to obtain political support, but also to articulate environmental considerations which are not revealed through market forces. Through the involvement of SRIs, the harmonious relationship referred to above can be maintained.

Lastly is the development of supporting elements, such as further elaboration of the Environmental Impact Assessment Law; adopting educational curricula (with emphasis on value formation conducive to sustainable development); developing research projects that contribute to combining conservation and environment issues with development activities, and so forth. In all of this, perhaps the most crucial need is to develop new yardsticks for sustainable development. The Gross National Product concept is necessary but not sufficient as the only tool. Incentives must be generated to produce behaviour conducive to sustainable development. Economic planners and policy makers must be made more aware of sustainable development concepts. This applies equally to political leaders, parliamentarians, mass media, the press and the public at large. Sustainable development requires broad attitudinal changes; all groups need to participate in this process of change.

Given this brief outline of Indonesia's efforts to launch development along the sustainable path, there are various achievements worth citing. For example, 230 elephants trapped in a transmigration area in South Sumatra have been saved; efforts have been undertaken to protect the "Puncak area" (a mountain resort) from encroachment by people in search of land; river basin management has been improved through better coordination; conservation areas have been enlarged throughout the country; laws have been promulgated which incorporate environmental considerations, such as the Industrial Law of 1985; and self-reliant institutions dealing with environmental problems have grown rapidly, from about 70 in 1980 to 450 in 1985.

There have also been setbacks, such as destruction of the rich East Kalimantan conservation area from forest fire; destruction of coastal areas for economic purposes; and river and sea shore pollution by industries and human settlements.

Indonesia is still struggling to find the proper balance between environment and development. The task of giving substance to the notion of sustainable development is most challenging. However, low income, poverty and population pressures are severe obstacles which make these efforts crucial. But concepts, and tools of analysis and policy-making to assist planners meet these challenges are still inadequate, particularly in the field of conservation.

This is even more evident in the international setting where agencies are still compartmentalised, separating agencies concerned with development from those focusing on environment and conservation. There is no single international body with the leverage of the International Monetary Fund or the World Bank to enforce requirements for sustainable development. Nor is there a proper counterpart to the International Union for Conservation of Nature and Natural Resources (IUCN) at the intergovernmental level. There is not even a thinking process consistent with the World Conservation Strategy at the intergovernmental and international level. In fact there is no common endeavour among governments to incorporate environment, including the basic concepts of the World Conservation Strategy, as a priority consideration for political leaders. The Strategy is still seen as a private contribution to the debate.

While working on the politics of conservation is important, we must continue to build the foundations of sustainable development throughout the world. To achieve this goal, a similar approach on an international scale to that implemented by Indonesia is perhaps worth considering.

In this context, I propose that IUCN take the initiative to stimulate development of broad regional resource use plans to serve, within the next decade, as guidelines for sustainable development for national governments in a region; secondly, to introduce the use of environmental impact assessments worldwide, to be initiated by project originators, industries and multi-national corporations whether or not requested by national governments; thirdly, to develop a "quality of life index" containing components applicable to all nations and serving to improve on the GNP index; fourthly, to promote "self-reliant institutions" or non-government organisations in environment/conservation fields to articulate the arguments for sustainable development; and to enlarge the network of cooperation between environmentalists/conservationists and those engaged in development.

This meeting will produce many ideas, and it will record experiences of many countries. It is hoped that out of this Conference the message will traverse the globe: that in an increasingly interdependent world, sustainable development can only be successful if we work together to build a common future.

Through sustainable development we may survive together and move from the "World Conservation Strategy of Words" to the "World Conservation Strategy of Action."

SPREADING THE MESSAGE

Plenary Session 5

SPREADING THE MESSAGE

Plenary Session 5

Syed Babar Ali, Chairperson
President, WWF Pakistan
Lahore, Pakistan

This session was intended to provide an improved basis for effective communication of conservation and sustainable development principles. De Haes' framework paper establishes a useful operational framework for communication and stresses the significance of environmental education. These topics are also developed by Segnestam on the basis of experience of the Swedish Society for the Conservation of Nature. Waldegrave draws on his experience as Minister of the Environment in discussing how corporate, community and government priorities can be influenced.

In introducing the session, Chairperson Babar Ali stressed that there would be no single message, but a multitude of messages, coming out of discussions. Many different ideas must be communicated, and different audiences must be targeted. This in turn would call for public awareness and education campaigns that must be carefully planned to respond to the different needs.

The session agreed that the availability of and access to information was a crucial factor in implementing conservation principles. Waldegrave notes that the possibility of influencing industrial, governmental and other priorities rests on the assumption that the citizenry has enough information on which to make judgements and build national campaigns. Therefore, it must become established practice - and should even constitute a principle of law that governs enterprises and government - that all information on activities having an environmental impact should be made public. Only in cases of genuine security risks should it be withheld. Segnestam adds that liaison between different environmental sectors was also important.

Waldegrave calls for greater efforts to be directed toward reaching compromises acceptable to all parties, citing the example of those between local groups and central governments. It was suggested that dissemination of information about environmental disputes and their resolution could help create greater awareness and understanding of the rationale for certain environmental actions. Segnestam holds that public understanding is the result of a country's "environmental maturity" a feature of such maturity being that political parties must vie with each other in taking environmentally-responsible positions. Political debate favours clear definition of the issues and attracts media attention, thereby serving an educational purpose.

SPREADING THE MESSAGE

Charles de Haes[1]
Director General, WWF International
Gland, Switzerland

SUMMARY   For the conservation movement to be successful, the connection between conservation and vital human concerns such as peace and economic stability must be made clear. The effective spread of this message depends on the systematic application of professional communications expertise in the following steps: analyse problems to identify priorities and target audiences, including conservation and development interests; tailor the message to target audiences; select the most effective medium; encourage participation and two-way communication; assign the tasks and train personnel for a sustained education effort; monitor and evaluate the process. Techniques should emphasise the positive aspects of conservation and the spread of relevant data. National and local non-governmental organisations should play a major role in spreading the message, especially in the area of broadly-based environmental education.

INTRODUCTION

The success of the conservation movement will depend not on the quality of its science, not on the dedication of its practitioners, not even on the funds allotted to its cause, vital though these factors are. It will depend on how widely and compellingly this message is spread:

> *The foundation of life*
> *and all basic human needs*
> *is in nature, but nature's*
> *capital is not inexhaustible.*
> *Each of us must*
> *use it caringly and*
> *sparingly.*

All conservationists know that this sustainable development message, at the heart of the World Conservation Strategy, is a solemn truth. But conservation is too important to be left to conservationists. The daily violence to our life support systems and natural resource base are acts of men who do not know, or do not care about, the consequences of their actions - or have no alternative to them. The most important thing that conservationists can do is to reach these people with versions of the basic message that will engage their fundamental interests and con-

1.   This paper was presented for Charles de Haes by Dr. Luc Hoffmann.

vince them that conservation is a necessity in their lives.

As the Senegalese poet Baba Dioum put it:

In the end, we will conserve
only what we love. We will love only
what we understand.
We will understand only what we are
taught.

Spreading the message is not just wholesale broadcasting of alarming facts and figures; it is using selective information to educate specific groups of people. The lesson to be taught is that conservation is everyone's serious business, alongside eating and breathing and raising a family; as fundamental as peace, jobs, inflation and security; as elemental as air, water, earth and energy. Vital human needs and concerns must be shown to rest on their foundations in nature as solidly as our feet are planted on Mother Earth. This does not refer only to abstract human needs, but the needs of you, of me, of every individual and every community. The conservation message must resonate with "This means **you**!"

Whether the motivation is love, as Baba Dioum writes, or a commitment arising from enlightened self-interest, as others put it, it is certain that individuals and their institutions will conserve voluntarily only when they understand the links between conservation and what they value in life, and are convinced that they can actually help solve the problem. Some of the links are obvious, such as that between air pollution and breathing. When Japanese children had to wear masks in school for protection against polluted air, the country was shocked into action. Japan now has some of the best pollution-control legislation in the industrialised world. Other links, such as soil erosion and food production, are publicised in times of famine. Some connections are less obvious, but no less direct: the relationship of inflation to scarcity of natural raw materials, for example.

If these are basic issues, then so are natural-resource management and conservation. Yet when the world's leaders meet, conservation only makes the agenda in its most overt forms - transboundary acidification, perhaps, or rights to water from international rivers. Rarely does its significance for such agenda issues as debt repayment or development assistance appear. It is crucial to bring such links into view in order to establish conservation among the top priority issues of our time.

WHAT ARE THE STEPS TO THIS UNDERSTANDING?

The classic steps in spreading a message, whether internationally, nationally or at the community level, are as follows:

* Identify and study the target audience;

* formulate and test appropriate versions of the basic message according to the special self-interest and culture of the audience;

* identify and test the most effective methods or media for reaching the audience;

* assure that your method enables two-way communication so that the audience participates actively (rather

than listens passively), and the message-sender can learn from the audience;

* enlist efficient, credible people and groups to do the job; train where necessary and provide regular support;

* monitor the programme systematically so that results can be measured, adjustments made and the audience can be further convinced and enlarged through evidence of progress.

There is nothing new in these steps, which require meticulous planning. Taken together, they constitute a campaign. We have been following them in the conservation movement for some time, with growing success.

We do not have to invent entire new systems to improve message dissemination, although there is always room for improvement and for incorporating rapid advances of communications technology. We do have to intensify and coordinate our efforts as a movement, sharpen our techniques and apply them systematically, for time is not on our side. Let us look at these steps with that fact in mind: we have little time left to reach and educate vast, scattered and widely differing audiences before the natural resource base that supports us all literally erodes beneath our feet. We must select our priorities with a view to both short- and long-term results.

SELECTING THE TARGET AUDIENCES

The process of selecting target audiences begins with problem analysis. What human behaviour is responsible for the problem? Why do people engage in this behaviour? What are the alternatives? Who is involved, and who needs to know what in order to improve the situation? Which problems should be dealt with most urgently? The answers to these questions will identify priorities and target audiences, but they can be extremely complex.

THE RIDDLE OF "COUNTRY X"

Almost any case history will demonstrate this complexity. Let us take the problems of tropical forest destruction in Country X and try to identify who needs to be reached with what messages. In seeking the origins of deforestation in Country X, and the concomitant loss of soil, watersheds, plant and animal genetic resources, nutrient recycling, air and water purification capacity, siltation, flood control, and the like, we find that rural poor are often responsible. They must therefore be a priority target audience.

Further analysis will show, however, that some of these rural communities have been forced into the forest area from better farming land and do not know how to survive by other means. Perhaps population pressure caused the push because family planning information was lacking. Perhaps families were evicted from small farms that the government converted into cash crop plantations to repay foreign debts or to finance or replace imports. Perhaps an international lending agency has insisted on this policy. Perhaps a development aid agency has financed projects that displaced these families.

Analysis may quickly add new target audiences for messages to counteract the deforestation "caused" in Country

X by rural poor. At a certain point one begins to wonder whether deforestation is the problem, or a symptom of the familiar (and bogus) conservation versus development conflict.

The same process that drove certain rural families to encroach on the forests will have forced others to look for work in the cities, creating restless, unhealthy urban slums. This has a destabilising effect on the political scene and on internal security. To avoid urban riots, the government may hold down food prices in both the markets and in the prices paid to farmers. This disincentive to farmers may produce food shortages which become famines in times of drought, requiring an influx of external free food and seed aid, further weakening the local farmer. And so it goes, in an ever more intricate web of cause and effect where additional target audiences emerge as influential in some aspect of the original problem or its side effects.

The politicians and general public in Country X, affected by watershed failures, floods, food shortages, inflation and civil unrest, need to be able to relate these events to environmental situations in order to determine appropriate political and social solutions. So, too, the publics in countries financing development aid, relief, foreign lending, military assistance and so on, must make the connection between the environmental situations in Country X and their own high taxes, the weakness of export-market jobs, and feelings of frustration and insecurity concerning the Third World. More target audiences appear.

All of this happens without considering the role of trans-national industry in the wholesale exploitation of timber

lands in Country X which needs hard currency; or that of international consumers who provide the market for luxury hardwood, or the legacy of colonialism that did not educate and train the resource manager that Country X now requires. And let us not forget that the conservationists (often externally based), who created reserves to protect forest flora and fauna and perhaps attract income-producing tourists, then have to arm rangers to keep out rural poor just over the boundary, who are desperate for the once free plant and animal products.

By now the list of target audiences is almost as long as the Amazon, and where are the priorities?

JOINING FORCES WITH DEVELOPMENT

The answer is that they are all priorities, but for different members of the conservation movement. Ideally, a planned division of labour within the movement would assign target audiences to those best qualified to deal with them. Practically, however, our movement is relatively young and far from able to direct the energies of its independent operators so logically. Nevertheless, this should be our aim. IUCN has the nucleus of a very broad movement in its ranks. Its plan to coordinate the efforts of members to achieve common programmes based on the World Conservation Strategy priorities is an important focal point for coordination.

The scenario of Country X dramatises the message of the World Conservation Strategy that conservation and development issues are often interdependent. Plans for a campaign to attack deforestation or any environmental problem must involve target audiences of the organisation promoting development as well as those promoting conservation. The sooner the two groups begin to work in tandem, the better for both. Their final goals are the same. The parties that sponsored and collaborated in the World Conservation Strategy - IUCN, UNEP, WWF, FAO, and Unesco - could consider creating a mechanism for coordinating at least the information and education efforts of the two movements and their support troops in the NGO community.

Sharing the workload of reaching audiences will also mean sharing resources, especially from the more solvent international groups in the North, to strengthen the capacities of national and community-based NGOs in the South. The latter often are best situated to reach their rural target audiences. But their work may be hampered by something as basic as lack of money or an import permit to buy bicycle tires. They are understandably impatient with rhetoric and showcase international conferences when the kind of material help they need in the field is so scarce. In its 25th anniversary campaign to develop local will and skill and combat environmental illiteracy, WWF is giving special attention to support from community-based NGOs.

TAILORING THE MESSAGE

Formulating and testing appropriate versions of the basic message, tailored to the interests and culture of the identified target audiences, is the second step. The industrialised world has brought this activity to a super-professional level. It is called **marketing** by

that world, not "spreading the message." It is time that the conservation movement paid more attention to the implications of these different phrases. They are revealing. "Marketing focuses on the needs of the buyer," according to one definition. "Spreading the message" is definitely focused on the desires of the seller. It is the language of evangelism, and here is where the conservation movement risks going wrong.

Some conservationists resemble the door-to-door missionaries who warn that the world will come to an end soon and only true believers will be saved. Conservation missionaries share an apocalyptic vision and a rather smug confidence that they are an elite, the custodians of the message. They are not discouraged by failure to make any converts. Too much popular success would end the satisfaction they derive from being elitists fighting the good fight against great odds. To such people, all too prominent among conservationists, the act of "spreading the message" becomes an end, not a means. They are far too preoccupied with what they want to say to consider what their audience needs to hear.

Most conservationists, to be fair, are trained in science, not communications. They may indeed have facts and figures the world should urgently heed, but their language - phrases such as "genetic diversity" and "sustainable utilisation of natural resources" - goes over the heads of important target audiences. Even the word "conservation" is so laden with different meanings as to be a handicap in addressing many of the audiences identified in the Country X scenario. One man's "deforestation" is another man's "fuel wood problem."

The key is to formulate versions of the basic message according to the special self-interest and culture **of the audience**, not the messenger. This is the job of marketing experts, not evangelists. Professional communicators should form an integral part of the team of any conservation organisation. They may be recruited from the ranks of professional marketing and communications specialists, or at the rural community level from successful extension workers.

The point is, spreading the message should involve message-spreading professionals. Conservation scientists need not worry about over-commercialising. There is less danger that this course will lead to hucksterism in market-reseach and "selling" conservation than there is in continuing a purist approach that preaches only to the converted.

CHOOSING THE CHANNELS

The professional communicator will combine the third step - **selecting the most effective medium** for delivering the message to a given audience - with the steps of message formulation, for the message must suit the medium as well as the audience.

When the World Conservation Strategy was launched in 1980, the communications goal was to make as big a splash as possible so that the maximum number of target audiences would become aware of its existence. Of particular importance among these audiences were top-level political leaders, industries, and the media. The launch was organised to take place simultaneously in some 30 world capitals in the presence of chiefs of State, thereby assuring resounding media impact and

the involvement of decision-makers. It worked. The same technique has since been used to launch national conservation strategies, sponsored in the United Kingdom, for example, by the Prince of Wales. Good documentation accompanied these attention-getting events, so that they were followed for a time by thoughtful discussion in the press and other fora.

At the outset, then, the World Conservation Strategy had a good combination of target audience, message formulation and medium selection. It made no effort to give a blueprint on how to spread the message further, leaving this to national and local organisations. The World Conservation Strategy has sunk considerably from public view since then, with notable exceptions in Nepal, Senegal, Zambia and a few other countries. This has disturbed many conservationists who would like the World Conservation Strategy to be a household word or a golden rule. Actually, at this stage it is not necessary for the man in the European street or in the African *boma* to have heard about the World Conservation Strategy and only slightly more important to have heard about his national conservation strategy, if any. On the other hand, it is very important for certain levels of political leadership and administration to be familiar with these conservation tools. This is the mission of all those engaged in promoting national conservation strategies.

Who needs to know what? Answering this question will also help answer the question of what medium to select.

WWF's President, HRH the Duke of Edinburgh, exemplifies the effectiveness of the direct one-on-one approach when he travels around the world, meeting rulers and presidents face to face in private discussions. Other organisations also effectively use special ambassadors, arranging for leading scientists or industrialists to hold private talks with their influential counterparts in target countries. Extension workers do the same thing with village headmen, farm cooperative leaders and others.

At the other end of the spectrum is the press conference, covered by radio, television and newspapers, which carries a message to a potential audience of hundreds of millions by a combination of electronic, print and word-of-mouth repetition. The advances of communications technology and its rapid extension around the world make it possible to cover the globe with similar messages at virtually the same time. Of course, very few messages are appropriate for an audience of hundreds of millions, but there are some. Our environment is also planetary. Messages about the quality of air, water, soils, and climate can lead people wherever they are to think and act constructively toward nature. And communication technology exists for the conservation movement to exploit.

The variety of media at our disposal is great and underutilised. Northern conservationists are wedded to the printed word, whereas many important target audiences read very little. This is true whether we seek to influence legislators or rural farmers. Analysis of our target audiences will reveal where each gets its information and indicate the channels best suited to reaching them. National and local NGOs perhaps know the terrain better than international organisations, which is another good reason for strengthening NGO capacities and working closely with them in a

coordinated fashion. WWF-India, for example, uses story-tellers with traditional illustrated scrolls to reach illiterate villagers; soap operas on radio (radio is still the best medium to reach millions of rural poor) have been effective in Latin America and Sri Lanka; satellite television is opening up new audiences around the world.

A fundamental rule of press officers is to **relate what is news to a conservation element**; the Sahel famine, Bangladesh floods and tidal waves, debt repayment crises, food price-riots in Third World cities, a picture of a movie star wearing a leopard skin coat - an information specialist must always be alert to linking conservation to the news of the moment.

PARTICIPATION

We have said that man will conserve what he has been taught to understand and to value. A good teacher knows that lessons are retained best when instruction is a two-way process with the learner actively participating. This brings us to the fourth step: **providing two-way communication** and being open to learning from the audience.

The disastrous effects of many large-scale, internationally-assisted development projects in the Third World have increasingly made both the development and the conservation communities more sensitive to the need for dialogue with people on the ground. The famine in Africa has made planners re-think their approach to food production. Small farmers and herdsmen possess traditional wisdom and hold the key to production, yet for a long time they were largely unconsulted and given little material support. The notion of listening to the people, instead of constantly preaching at them or ordering them about, is currently fashionable. We should give it more than lip service.

Natural resource managers have much to learn, for example, from the way tribes have protected communal grazing land in the Middle East (e.g. the *hema* system of rotation) or community water source and irrigation management in Africa and Latin America. And whether we are interested in changing the ways of motorists, petrol refiners and auto manufacturers in Europe, or the fuelwood gathering and plowing habits of subsistence farmers in a developing country, we will increase chances of success by engaging in dialogue.

This two-way communication step is often overlooked, just as testing materials on sample audiences before going into full-scale information campaigns is often neglected. Both pay big dividends when properly employed.

ASSIGNING THE TASKS

When campaign planning has identified the target audience and the most effective message and medium to reach it, including an element of participation, the decision must be taken on **who will do the work?**

The small, community-based conservation and development groups have few alternatives to doing the work themselves. Their problem is in resources and finance, material and skills. Large international - and many national - organisations, seeing the weakness of grass-roots groups, often bypass them. They hire expatriate consultants or academics from the cities. Many of these are truly dedicated, unusually experienced field people, whatever their

origins. But history shows that consultants rarely seem to work themselves out of a job or bring their counterparts up to the level of replacing them.

In the short-run, bringing in expertise to get a job started is often justified. In the long-run there is every reason to develop local will and skill and strengthen national and local capacities to do the job with a minimum of outside help. This is the only way that it will be sustained, keeping in mind that "sustainable" is our watchword.

It is obvious that enlisting efficient and credible people to do the work is good management in any situation. Credibility in spreading the conservation message means having a reputation for honesty and balanced judgement. Spokesmen should be on guard against exaggeration. Credibility also includes sensitivity to the culture of the target audience - as true when dealing with urban consumers in industrialised countries as with nomadic herdsmen in Africa. It includes, as we have noted above, the ability to listen.

Involving prominent personalities is a good way to get media attention; names carry authority and make news. Marketing professionals know that statements from "satisfied customers," especially role models, make audiences listen and believe.

Getting people to do the job right will usually involve training. Small NGOs, best able to do some of the most important message-spreading to crucial target audiences, will need continuing support just to stay active on shoestring budgets. This financial support on a reliable, continuing basis is the least the international organisations should give.

Finally, staying on the job for however long it takes is essential. Efforts should be concentrated, consistent and sustained. It is important to recognise from the start that changing people's attitudes and behaviour can be a lengthy, painstaking process. Budgets should be calculated accordingly.

MONITORING AND EVALUATION

Once a World Conservation Strategy message campaign is underway, the communicators cannot turn their backs and start thinking about the next assignment. Vital to the success of any information and education effort is a built-in systematic process of **monitoring and evaluation**. Were the messages and the media choices right? Is Jones doing his job effectively and happily? Is the project meeting its time and budget projections? Is anything going wrong that ought to be corrected?

In Somalia a few years ago, a poster by the Ministry of Health, illustrating how to dig a latrine, had to be withdrawn because many back-country people interpreted the drawing of a man holding a shovel as showing him urinating. Proper testing would have caught this before thousands of posters were printed, but at least monitoring corrected the situation.

Once drawn into an activity, people will want to know what is happening. Reporting the findings of monitoring and evaluation can to help motivate participants, from legislators to villagers, by keeping them informed when progress is being made, and by reassuring them that solutions are possible and their own contributions are indispensable. This will be necessary for fundraising and political support of the work as well.

Evaluation should also include a survey of what others are doing in conservation and development with the same, or similar, target audiences. This will encourage cooperation, division of labour, multiplication of impact and avoidance of duplicating the errors of others.

These are the basic steps in spreading the message of conservation and making it stick. They must all be planned in advance, budgeted for adequate staff and supervised from start to finish.

A LOOK AT PROGRESS

This is the textbook version of how to spread a message. Most of us know these steps and have put them into practice. If this is the case, are we satisfied?

We should not be complacent, but we can take satisfaction in how the conservation message has spread in the last few years. We should not despair at the magnitude of the job still to be done. Ours in many ways is a success story and where some progress has been made, energetic follow-up will assure more advances. Consider these facts:

* The poll-taker George Gallup has said "commitment to the environment is the most deeply and widely held value his research has ever uncovered among Americans," according to Environment Magazine.

* At the end of World War II there were no environmental ministries. Today there are several score such ministries and department-level agencies. In the last 25 years, 21,100

texts have been adopted as national conservation-related legislation; 225 multilateral and 345 bilateral environmental treaties have been concluded.

* Green parties are springing up and electing parliament members; established parties are recognising the public commitment to the environment and polishing and publicising their own environmental policies.

* Development aid agencies, at least on paper, increasingly require environmental impact studies before proceeding with projects.

* Major newspapers and magazines have begun to feature regular correspondents and columns on the environment, and environmental television programmes have set audience records.

Perhaps the most effective force for spreading the message has been the stress by man on nature itself, resulting in calamities that horrify the world - the famines, floods, death of forests and chemical pollution of air and water endangering human life. We may feel that conservationists should not be "prophets of doom" and should spread a message of hope. But let's face it - disaster is news. We can and should make known the gravity of the threats to our only environment. This said, we should always accompany these warnings with the message that solutions exist, provide practical action advice and insist that **each one of us can and must play a part in conservation**.

Many techniques can be brought into play: associating conservation with admired role models - famous personalities, respected religious leaders, entertainment and sports stars; offering awards and honors for industries and individuals who have made conservation achievements; turning the spotlight of publicity on wrong-doers and making them socially unacceptable; levying stiff penalties for infractions of environmental laws; advertising in all forms for conservation objectives; arranging field trips for legislators, journalists, businessmen and others to provide direct exposure to problems and solutions. The adoption of confrontational tactics can attract publicity and mobilise action, but confrontation is a double-edged weapon and must be handled with care.

Most of these techniques, as well as marshalling data, are useful in lobbying political, economic and social institutions. And lobbying does help spread the message and achieve concrete results.

A service vital to spreading the message is the maintenance of a reliable, continually updated data base that has its key indicators reported to the public. As Lester Brown, President of the Worldwatch Institute, remarked in introducing his "State of the World 1984" report:

> *Observers generally agree on the principal actions needed to put society on a sustainable footing ... but confusion persists on how well the world is doing in meeting these goals ... policy makers now often lack [two things] ... a sense of direction, showing where we have made important gains and where we are falling behind [and] ... a set of guidelines to evaluate policy options and budgetary priorities.*

Provision of such data goes beyond the monitoring and evaluation needed to spread the message. Collecting the data, making them available to the conservation movement's members and the public, and releasing them to the media in a timely and attention-getting fashion establishes the authority and public-service role of an environmental organisation at any level. It creates news from original facts. It is an indispensable information tool in both the short and long run.

THE ROLE OF EDUCATION

How nice it would be if presenting facts and figures to a target audience would have the same effect of producing heat and light as applying a match to a well-laid hearth fire! How nice it would be to think, as many optimists do, that if people are given the facts, they will act according to common sense! Alas, reliance on such hopes has led to much sad disillusionment.

Over the long-term, the surest way to influence human attitude and behaviour is through education, from infancy to adulthood. Even though it is an activity quite distinct from information, any discussion of "Spreading the Message" must finally come to education, both formal and informal. It is the best hope for arriving at the process poetically described by the Senegalese Baba Dioum: teaching leading to understanding, leading to love, leading to conservation. It all begins with **teaching**.

The education systems of a culture are as difficult to change as traditions in diet. They do respond to the needs of society, however, and end by placing a stamp on society's attitudes and governing its reactions to stress. The World Conservation Strategy declares that education should produce an entire new

ethic uniting man with the rest of creation.

Experience shows that the role of international organisations in environmental education should be as generators and processors of theory, as clearing houses of new information and research, and as catalysts and supporters of local efforts. Education is by nature a national, local and even family-based activity. Therefore, one must recommend conservation action to **strengthen capacity of non-govern-mental groups at the national and local levels** to produce appropriate environmental educational materials, offer training to teachers and promote environmental education as a priority for the education establishment of their country.

If education is a preparation for life, then environmental education and an understanding of life-support systems is an essential element in preparing youth for life in a world that has had its faith in technology and notions of "progress" shaken; is alarmed by deterioration of the environment - yet has no possibility of returning to Arcadia.

The youth of today is turning to the environment as a cause for its idealism to champion. Youth, in fact, is often ahead of the mainstream conservation establishment in its dynamism and creativity. Youth should be encouraged as one of the movement's greatest assets.

Proper environmental education will reconcile the debate of whether man is a part of nature or apart from nature. (He is both.) Whether environmental education comes as a separate element in the curriculum or permeates all subjects across the board, or both, is for local authorities and parents to decide. But it must be **environmental** education, relevent to the environment of the students, whether rural or urban, and not purely conservation education.

CONCLUSION

A framework paper is obliged to tick off rather cursorily the items that specialists' papers will deal with in more detail. The purpose here has been to state a conviction, shared by many, that the success of conservation depends on spreading a message, and doing so through professional communications expertise. It has indicated the steps for organising and executing an information campaign and mentioned some techniques and services that have proven useful. It has noted that the long-term success of conservation requires incorporating a broad environmental education into the formal pedagogy of countries and the informal traditions of communities. And it has recommended that support be given to non-governmental organisations which are in the best position to pursue information and education objectives at national and community levels, but are typically starved for resources.

As conservationists, we are impatient to see these principles become woven into the fabric of our society. Much progress has in fact been made. But the progress has no short-cuts. It must be one of steady persuasion and education until the day arrives when, in the words of Max Nicholson, "Everyone must be able to say that we are all conservationists now."

THE WORLD CONSERVATION STRATEGY, EDUCATION AND COMMUNICATION

Mats Segnestam
Director, Swedish Society for the
Conservation of Nature
Stockholm, Sweden

SUMMARY   *The principles of the World Conservation Strategy have provided a good basis for a conservation message by defining a fundamental global rationale for local or national solutions to environmental problems. In Sweden, the World Conservation Strategy has acted as a springboard for lobbying and discussions with people involved in forestry, acidification, education and Swedish foreign-aid.   The Strategy has also been utilised in a range of educational settings in Sweden. However, statements in the World Conservation Strategy on communication and education have generally not been useful in spreading the conservation message; existing potential of the World Conservation Strategy for spreading that message has been under-used.   Swedish experience suggests that the task could be simplified and its success enhanced by identifying the roles to be played at different levels, supporting non-profit organisations in their efforts at all levels, recognising the importance of spreading the message, reaching the right audience, and linking ideas with practice. The importance of education must be better recognised and acted upon, with help from the International Union for Conservation of Nature and Natural Resources.*

INTRODUCTION

The field of communication, information and education is an extremely difficult one to discuss in overall, summary terms: it is all-embracing; it can be sub-divided in any number of ways; most people's views on the importance of its concepts and on related approaches appear to diverge; and finally, without exception, we all in our several ways consider ourselves experts in the field.

Another factor adding to the difficulty of summarising the field in a brief discussion, particularly in the context of the World Conservation Strategy, is that the Strategy represents a partial breach with some of the world's great religions, with widespread beliefs regarding human beings' power of manipulating their environment, with masculine ideals of strength and superiority, with economic theories, with people's reluctance to admit gaps in their knowledge, with the need of politicians for short-term survival and with human egotism and egocentricity - in short, with most human behaviour and understanding.

At the same time, this breach may be said to underline, more clearly than anything else, the crucial role of education and communication in conservation. It also suggests that, in any discussion of the multiplicity and depth of the problems, at least in my part of the world, a loaded and sensitive term such as "indoctrination" cannot be avoided.

The World Conservation Strategy takes up the question of education and communication in Section 13, entitled "Building support for conservation: participation and education." It stresses the importance of determining target groups, and describes some essential aspects of formal education, such as current school curricula and conservation education areas. The Strategy summarises "environmental education campaigns and programmes, particularly for the users of living resources, legislators and decision-makers, schoolchildren and students" in the checklist of priority requirements.

THE WORLD CONSERVATION STRATEGY AS THE BASIS OF A MESSAGE

The World Conservation Strategy has played a vital part in promoting conservation worldwide. It put the global situation in a nutshell; it was a global vision and it captured the imagination. Any of the most daunting environmental problems can illustrate the Strategy's significance. Issues such as acidification, world hunger, desertification, and erosion demonstrate that the

Strategy is of fundamental significance to world environment problems and that conservation is something that must be taken seriously. This is necessary for us to understand the problems and tackle them before they become acute, thus economically much more painful, and politically, perhaps impossible to solve. But while the Strategy has been of inestimable importance in spreading the conservation message during the 1980s, the opportunity and potential it provides have by no means been exhausted.

The Strategy has been invaluable for many people who, in the years before its inception, discussed the vast and overwhelming problems of environmental conservation in a global perspective and sought solutions to these problems. The Strategy activated and boosted world conservation, giving it a far more positive role. Psychologically, this achievement has been invaluable. Conservationists must increasingly adopt a positive approach and be able to take part in discussing constructive solutions to the world's problems. Thus, as a source of encouragement and guidance, the importance of the Strategy, in providing a concrete framework for reference, cannot be underestimated.

The World Conservation Strategy has proven to be a useful way of getting the environmental message across, because it has also served as a bridge between the global situation and national or local problems. The fundamental principles and overall targets of the Strategy have sometimes been more readily acceptable than the imperative local solutions which are economically or politically awkward in the short-term. Having accepted Strategy principles, it is easier for people to explain, to themselves and others, why the local solutions are necessary.

The Strategy's linkage of conservation and development has also been a fundamental precondition to making its message effective, or giving it the capacity to reach broad social groups. However, a notable difficulty relating to the Strategy and the conservation message is that awareness and debate concerning important issues are frequently subject to the whims of fashion. The mass media are always on the look-out for something new; people's attention is turned from one subject to another. Possibly, we must accept this as a natural component of human behaviour, but we must bring about a lasting advance: we cannot allow the imperatives of conservation to be relegated to the sidelines. This suggests some important points of departure for strategic thinking when it comes to disseminating the message.

THE WORLD CONSERVATION STRATEGY AS A GUIDING PRINCIPLE FOR EDUCATION

In some respects, Section 13 of the World Conservation Strategy is somewhat vague and general. Nevertheless, it contains important guidelines, worthy of considerably more attention than they have received so far. Because there has not been enough follow-up to Section 13, either internationally or nationally, the Strategy's rather general pronouncements on communication and education have had limited decisive impact on worldwide efforts to spread the message. We must ask ourselves why, although information and education in the conservation field are so often emphasised, it is still so hard to make a

concerted attempt to achieve these ends.

The importance of education is still grossly underestimated, despite all assertions to the contrary. The long-term view often pales beside the burning issues of the day. This is a very serious strategic error on the part of conservation, something which will delay and obstruct our dealing effectively with the big problems, and exacerbate the difficulties of even reaching the growing numbers of people who must think about day-to-day survival. A systematic analysis of the weak points in the dissemination process is absolutely essential.

One can, of course, plead that propagating the environmental message is a tremendously complicated undertaking, since the issues themselves are so complex and the target groups include everyone on earth. And, in a sense, it is wrong to talk about one message, when there may be thousands of messages, depending on the time and on the circumstances. It is also wrong to talk about spreading the message as if it came from one centre with a supreme knowledge. But at the same time, the issues involved in spreading the environmental message can be simpler and more straightforward than they often appear. Discussions of the message and its dissemination have frequently been confused by educators themselves. In the last six years, I have listened to several exchanges of views in which so-called experts on communication and education have held theoretical, complicated, jargon-filled and confusing discussions of what conservation is, what educational concepts in various forms stand for, and how models for propagation of the

conservation message can be constructed.

Few things have caused so much
frustration in international conservation
circles as this very question: education.
The gap between theory and action has
been far too wide. We should now ensure that the discussions are turned into
concrete plans and active measures.

A fundamental mistake of many
people who have become involved in
educational questions worldwide is that
of attempting to apply local or national
approaches in the international sphere.
The World Conservation Strategy does
not address this issue adequately. Internationally, limited resources must be
concentrated more on strategic guidelines and other measures supporting the
development of national and local
educational activities.

Enthusiastic amateurishness in spreading the message is still common in conservation circles, both nationally and internationally. The World Conservation
Strategy does not provide any guidelines but IUCN should play a more active leading role than it has done to
date.

THE EXAMPLE OF SWEDEN:
VARIOUS APPROACHES

Several world conservation and environmental organisations, including
the Swedish Society for the Conservation of Nature, have found the World
Conservation Strategy useful in discussing their own programmes. This is, of
course, one of the most important ways
of indirectly propagating the Strategy's
message - using its principles as the
basis of action programmes worldwide.

The Swedish Society for the Conservation of Nature has also made use of the
Strategy by constantly and deliberately
reminding others of the principles it
embodies, whenever conservation and
development problems, both national
and international, are engaged in; the
Society has also promoted the attitude
that anyone who is unfamiliar with the
Strategy or does not think along its
lines is "behind the times." This slow
but unrelenting approach also helps to
boost the power of the message.

We have deliberately utilised the
Strategy in contacts with political
leaders - not least those we know to
have focused on international matters.
When our Society met with the late
Swedish Prime Minister, Olof Palme,
we pointed out connections between
peace and environmental preservation,
and described the major role of conservation work in preserving world peace.
It was natural in that instance for us to
use the Strategy's three chief objectives
to describe the implications of global
conservation.

Because the starting point is international, we have, in dialogues with
politicians, been able to agree more
quickly on fundamental values relating
to the husbanding of natural resources
in Sweden. It has also been easier,
with reference to the Strategy, to suggest the long-term political advantages
which a more open attitude to natural
resources conservation can bring. The
Strategy has been presented to members of the Swedish legislature (the
Riksdag) at the invitation of the
Speaker of the Riksdag. In addition to
an account of the Strategy, four fields
were selected to illustrate the implications of the Strategy for Sweden.

These areas were forestry, acidification, education and Swedish foreign aid.

It is also of the utmost importance who spreads the message. Human preconceptions are one of the biggest stumbling-blocks to those who want to tell the world about conservation. We must take this into account, and try to find a way around it. In Sweden, those involved in conservation have tried to enlist the help of other organisations not normally associated with conservation issues. A good example is the Swedish Red Cross, whose cooperation has been most valuable. When the Red Cross linked the well-known issues of mass starvation and other human disasters to environmental destruction, people suddenly began to listen - people who had previously been deaf to the same message when it came from the conservation organisations.

The Swedish foreign-aid agency, SIDA, was also a natural point of liaison for us when the Strategy was launched. At a very early stage we had the opportunity to tell SIDA staff about its principles and assumptions. The Strategy facilitated our work of making the case, in discussions with SIDA's management, for environmentally-sound Swedish aid. Reality - in the form of erosion, desertification, population growth and hunger - has also "simplified" our task: it is generally easier to explain the Strategy's principles and gain acceptance for them when one can relate them directly to a reality powerfully experienced by recipients of the message themselves.

Another lesson from experience is that the Strategy's demands should be adjusted to match the audience. In discussions with the Swedish Ministry of Foreign Affairs, for example, we have presented the concept of a "foreign environment policy" based on the Strategy, which would enable the environmental conservation approach to penetrate many aspects of foreign policy. Integration with everyday bureaucratic terminology and concepts gives the Strategy message a completely new impact; without that linkage, the message may not get across at all.

A similar example is the conscious effort we have made to use the Strategy in our discussions with the Swedish forest industry. Since Swedish foresters are concerned about the world forest situation in general, especially in the tropics, it has not been difficult to create an understanding of the Strategy's general principles. The next step was to scrutinise Swedish forestry with reference to the same principles. We on the conservation side have been able to explain our aspirations relatively easily and it has been correspondingly difficult for the industry to reject, for example, the demand for biological variety. With the Strategy's principles as a starting point, it has also been easier for us to formulate conservation requirements for Swedish forestry. And when a large Swedish forest company (SCA) recently drafted a conservation policy on its own initiative, the policy began by quoting the three main principles of the Strategy, and was thereafter based on these.

A corresponding discussion between conservationists and farmers is now underway in Sweden; here too, our springboard has been Strategy principles.

We have tried to build on Strategy principles as well on the issue of acidification. We have divided the work into two parts: internationally-oriented and nationally-oriented. The former has been based on a flow of information on the status of countries affected by acidification, and is directed primarily toward groups which can in turn spread the message further: environmental organisations, journalists and politicians in other countries. Work has also been aimed at creating joint environmental policy platforms through cooperation with other environmental organisations. We have provided some information material, such as posters, but the basic aim has been for material on the issues to be produced locally. The national work has focused on the provision of information to the public via books, radio, TV and newspapers, but also through discussions with sectors affected, such as forestry, and with politicians who must bear responsibility for measures taken. The great - and only - boon of the acidification question has been its vindication of the Strategy's principles. A clearer illustration would be hard to find in our part of the world.

These are only a few concrete examples of how the World Conservation Strategy has been used to spread the conservation message in one country. Additional examples follow of how the Strategy has been used in Sweden:

* In touring exhibitions based on the Strategy;

* in fact sheets and discussion material for schools in connection with the exhibitions;

* in lectures on the Stategy throughout the country;

* in a Swedish translation of the WCS Executive Summary and of Robert

Allen's book *How to Save the World*;

* in study material for use with the book in local discussion groups and study circles;

* in seminars to train study-circle leaders, who have in turn led country-wide study circles;

* in a popular version of the Strategy for school use, produced jointly by the Nordic (Danish, Finnish, Norwegian, Swedish, Faeroese and Icelandic) Societies for the Conservation of Nature;

* in repeated references to the Strategy through conservation periodicals and deliberate use of the World Conservation Strategy logotype in their articles;

* in presentation of the Strategy to selected groups of influential industrialists and representatives of trade and industry;

* in the use of Strategy principles as a springboard for discussions on national strategies in fields of natural resource management, energy policy, and the like.

In discussing the responsibility of education for conservation issues, we, in the field of conservation, have demanded objectivity on the part of schools, pointing out that educational material is more often taken from institutions with a non-conservationist approach. The objectivity requirement makes it necessary for schools to include conservation material in teaching.

Linking the Strategy's ideas with practice has also proven to be tremendously important. Failure to make the ideas concrete and recognisable by this linkage, preferably through familiar examples, makes it difficult to get the message across.

SOME FURTHER REFLECTIONS AND PROPOSALS

The World Conservation Strategy must continue to be used as a starting point for educational efforts. The document has a great deal to offer. We should therefore try to ensure that it is used more often, and with greater awareness in all conservation and natural resource management discussions. It is vital to inform the right people in a country on the Strategy, and to encourage them to speak for and about it.

We should continue our efforts to give the Strategy the highest possible status. When the document is known at high levels in society and treated with respect, it is considerably easier to get other social groups to accept proposals, approaches and conclusions.

The Strategy message has not always hit home. One must analyse the reasons why, in each case, and consider whether recipients regard the message as irrelevant to their own situation, or as relevant but unimportant, or as insufficiently concrete or reliable. The fundamental aspect of the Strategy, namely its linkage of conservation and development, has not always penetrated in the diffusion of its message. This essential point must not be lost. This is where the tremendously important link with employment and the economy comes into play. We should strive to make the Strategy the basis of a new holistic approach to several of the most pressing social is-

sues, encouraging a new attitude toward the surrounding world. This underlines the importance of integrating Strategy approaches with schoolteaching at an early stage. It is more difficult to absorb a new philosophy of or attitude toward life when one has grown up with other fundamental concepts and values, and when one's working situation is based on old, exploitative ways of thinking. This is why we must systematically follow-up the sections of the Strategy dealing with information and education. The IUCN should be able to provide help and direction.

When a national conservation strategy is created in a country, it should include a strategy for that country's education in conservation. In any case, the national conservation strategy should recommend and lay the foundations for a full programme of education in the conservation and care of the environment.

I am not proposing here any details of a conceivable national strategy of conservation education. Points for consideration have been suggested in other parts of this paper, and other proposals have been made in connection with this Conference. Nevertheless, one must analyse the weaknesses in existing systems of formal education in order to know how to devise a national conservation education strategy and what kind of resource input we should make. Here, IUCN can help on the international level by drawing up a model programme of national endeavour, including a checklist of what it will take for the educational system to be acceptable from all standpoints. Where formal education is concerned, the checklist should contain such things as: In-service training for teachers; curricula (for pre-school, primary and secondary, upper secondary school, technical training); textbooks and teaching aids; timetabling and timescales; opportunities for laboratory work; existence of excursions and study areas; financial leeway for exploiting the practical resources, and so on.

Regarding education, we must distinguish more clearly between that which can and should be done at the international and at the national level. Internationally, we can contribute guidelines, basic ideas and background material, but education, training and information must, in all essentials, be provided nationally or locally. Every international effort must be analysed with extreme accuracy; there is an overwhelming risk of resources being wasted in a confusion of national and international approaches if we are not careful.

Discussions of national strategies and programmes of conservation education can be supported via IUCN on a regional basis. Activation of the regional level would permit a more systematic, country-by-country review of a "checklist" of key factors in formal education.

National investments in formal education are essential. The aim is a complete programme of conservation education for every country. Conservation must not overlook this opportunity and this vital contribution, which is necessary in order for information to reach the citizens early. By the time a child is ten years old, and often before, many basic ideas have already been established. We must therefore admit of the process of "indoctrination." A feeling for conservation must become a reflex; the countervailing forces in modern -

and especially industrialised - society are so immensely powerful. We should not underestimate the need to teach pure natural science. A knowledge of nature often leads to a feeling for it; an emotional commitment to nature, which in turn may be one of the strongest pillars for an understanding of what conservation requires.

We should also use the formal apparatus of education to disseminate the message, for the simple reason that using the apparatus which society has developed is the obvious course to take. Alternatives to teaching apart from formal schooling are difficult as a rule; talk of a school system's inertia can only mean that a greater effort is needed to exploit it as a medium. We must begin to reinforce conservation teaching in the country, in pre-school and early elementary-school education, and in study programmes with a crucial bearing on natural resource use, such as courses in agriculture, forestry, and technological studies.

There must also be room in the message for moral/ethical elements both in formal education and in more informal learning. Facts are insufficient, since the environment is too complex for us to comprehend in full, predict, master or manipulate.

In the area of informal education, the checklist may contain definitions of key target groups, ways of approaching them, and good examples of useful material:

* For conservation information to be more effective in many parts of the world, non-profit organisations must receive considerably more support. For example, non-governmental organisations in the industrialised

world ought to be capable of, in cooperation with foreign-aid agencies, augmenting resources available for their counterparts in developing countries.

* More deliberate efforts should be made to politicise conservation when possible and appropriate. Information-wise, the opportunities will then come automatically.

* National and local radio and television stations could appoint environmental staff units. Employees in such units then have a vested interest in trying to keep the debate alive and find new angles on environmental issues. Far too often, information on the natural environment and its conservation is now presented solely as entertainment, especially in the television medium.

* Concrete, everday examples of the aspirations of conservation can be demonstrated through behavioural changes, improving learning and understanding, since children imitate adults.

* Lastly, we should bear in mind two ever-present difficulties: when it comes to spreading the conservationist message, conservation does not have all the answers to the complex and intractable problems of the environment, and it is difficult or impossible to assign a monetary value to much of what we want to protect or maintain. We must say this loudly and clearly when we spread the message, but we must simultaneously compel the people with whom we are communicating to adopt a moral stand and a long-term view. And if people protest against the fundamental principles of the World Conservation Strategy, we must demand to know what alternative principles would be better. With the world as it is today, the tone of our message should be explanatory but also aggressive and challenging, not defensive or apologetic.

NEITHER PRINCE NOR MERCHANT: CITIZEN
AN INTRODUCTION TO THE THIRD SYSTEM

Marc Nerfin
President, International Foundation for
Development Alternatives
Nyon, Switzerland

SUMMARY *The North-South impasse is part of a general crisis which reflects the global changes of the last forty years. Humankind has begun to recapture its wholeness, but the hegemony of North over South and under-development persist in a multi-faceted crisis. Aspects of the crisis include the permanent threat of nuclear holocaust, the ongoing severe impacts of hunger, and the growing fracture of societies. The way out of the crisis is "another development" which is concomitantly need-oriented, self-reliant, ecologically sustainable, and joined with people-empowering structural transformations. Governmental or economic powers are unable to offer solutions or alternatives. Thus, there is a need to discern in the fundamentals and functions of human agencies those who are able to ensure life on this planet. On the basis of the IFDA experiences, this paper examines the development of the citizen's movement, discusses "the third system" - citizens and their associations acting without government or economic power - and advocates global networking as a tool of people's empowerment.*

INTRODUCTION[1]

There is indeed a North-South impasse, but to understand it, it is necessary to analyse its underlying causes and to consider the role of different social actors, since the problem may not be the same for different actors.

First, the "impasse" is only one aspect of a general crisis, itself reflecting the historical changes which have occurred over the last forty years. To put it bluntly, the world as seen from San Francisco in 1945, at the founding of the United Nations, was essentially white, Western, Christian and elitist; its basic paradigms were Newtonian (Capra, 1983). Today, largely as a result of the "great awakening" of the Third World, but also because we can now see our planet from outer space, humankind is recapturing its wholeness. What has not changed, however,

---

1   All letter citations refer to the IFDA Dossier; corresponding reference list follows.

is the unequal exchange (whatever the innovations in its mechanisms), the hegemony of North over South, and under-development. The crisis is at the same time economic, financial, environmental, social, cultural, ideological, and political.[2]

In terms of the human condition, the crisis fundamentally means the permanent threat of the nuclear holocaust and the already real, daily, hunger holocaust, which kills 40,000 children every day; Hiroshima every week.[a] This will never be repeated often enough: do we really understand the meaning of these four words, *an Hiroshima every week?*

But one must be aware of what underlies this massacre of the innocents, the growing fracture of every society into two, much worse than the traditional East-West or North-South rifts: the two Indias, the two Chiles, the two Netherlands, the two USAs; the world of the powerful, of the rich, of the employed, of those who participate; and the world of the powerless, of the poor, of the unemployed, of the dispossesed - worse, of those who are no longer economically useful.[b] This fracture is the result of under-development, mal-development and other poisoned fruits of the same misdirection of human affairs, everywhere on this planet.

The only way out of such a crisis is a new, alternative society, or another development (Dag Hammarskjöld Foundation, 1975), which could be described as concomitantly need-oriented

(but by no means limited to so-called "basic needs"), self-reliant, endogenous, in harmony with nature, ecologically sustainable, and linked with people-empowering structural transformations. In other words, another development means that people are organising themselves so as to develop who they are and what they have, by themselves and for themselves.

Second, governmental or economic powers have often proven unable to offer solutions to the crisis and even less to contribute to the search for alternatives. They have also proven unable to respond to the cry for peace and another development. They are more part of the problem than of the solution. There is thus a need to go to the fundamentals and discern in the human agencies those who may be better able to ensure the continuation of life on this planet.

As a modest contribution to the debate, this paper defines human agencies and, on the basis of the IFDA experience, examines the world development of the citizens' movement, discusses the relations between people and the third system and advocates global networking as a tool of people's empowerment.

A Definition

Contrasting with governmental power - the Prince, and economic power - the Merchant, there is an immediate and autonomous power, sometimes patent, always latent: people's power. Individuals develop an awareness of this, associate and act with others and thus

---

2. Rather than dwelling here on the matter, may the author refer readers to his paper "The Future of the United Nations System: Some Questions on the Occason of an Anniversary."

become citizens.[3] Citizens and their associations, when they do not seek either governmental or economic power, constitute the "third system." Contributing to make patent what is latent, the third system is one expression of the autonomous power of the people.

A SNAPSHOT OF THE THIRD SYSTEM CONSTELLATION

Associations are legion.[4] The 21st Edition (1984/85) of the *Yearbook of International Organizations* describes 7,109 international non-governmental organisations plus 5,577 internationally-oriented national bodies. The 1981 *Directory of Non-Governmental Organizations in OECD Countries Active in Development Cooperation* includes the profiles of 1,702 such bodies. There are many times more in the national and local spheres. In India, a 1978 questionnaire on participation in development was sent to 1,400 "NGOs" - of which more than 90 percent had no effective international links.[c] In France, associations were in the hundreds in the 1930s, in the thousands in the 1950s, 10,000 in 1960, 30,000 in 1977 and anywhere between 300 and 500,000 in 1981, a year during which some 100 new associations were established every day.[d]

In this magnitude, numbers only invite and at the same time defy categorising.

For the purpose of this introduction, a snapshot of that part of the galaxy of associations which could be considered as the third system may suffice to discern some structure and trends.

Third system associations are formed by citizens who are anxious to improve their lives and those of others, individually or collectively, either because of their situation in society, or for personal reasons, whether intellectual, moral or spiritual. Social history suggests that the former motivation is more important; people motivated by the second reason are more ardent; and the combination of the two is the strongest motivation. A worker usually remains a worker, and his or her reasons to be active in a trade union are part and parcel of her or his social existence. Parallels can be found for members of ethnic minorities (or majorities) and a woman who becomes a life-long feminist activist. But not all workers, all women, and so on, become citizens, and the personal motivation is always essential. Motivations are many, but observation of the third system as it unfolds (beyond its "traditional" manifestations such as trade unions) suggests that there are a few deep-seated mobilising themes, notably peace, women's liberation, peoples' rights, environment, local self-reliance, alternative lifestyles and personal transformations, consumer self-defence. Additional themes in some industrialised

---

3. The author must confess here an ethnocentric shortsightedness: the concept of "citizen" is probably meaningful only in a Western (including Latin American) context and in the "modernised" fringes of the world polity. There may be equivalents in other cultures - as for instance the "Mwananchi" in Swahili - but the question remains open and the author would be grateful to interested readers, especially those of African, Buddhist and Moslem culture, for advice on the matter.

4. Words are never innocent. The phrase "non-governmental organisation" is politically unacceptable because it implies that government is the centre of society, and people its periphery. To insist on people's autonomy also requires some semantic cleaning-up. Except in quotations, we will use instead of "NGO," the expressions "association," whose sense is wide enough, and "third system," in the precise acceptation proposed in this introduction.

countries are solidarity with people of the Third World including refugees and migrants, and, in Eastern Europe (or at least in Poland), a new form of trade unionism (Zielonka, 1983).

The multiplicity of forms under which these associations appear correspond to the diversity of motivations and circumstances. Because they reflect peoples' autonomy, associations are often allergic to forms defined by the establishment. The term is thus purposely used here in a rather loose sense.

Many associations are officially recognised and/or registered through formal constitutions, organs, membership, reporting, accounting, and the like. Others are *ad hoc* gatherings of like-minded individuals who occasionally share ideas and experiences through a "round-robin" letter. The spectrum in between includes all other possible configurations: some are underground; others are not concerned about their legal status and simply exist; a few even resemble political parties, such as the Greens in Western Germany[e] (Capra and Spretnak, 1984), and still are part of the third system as long as they stay out of executive power. There may also be groups of marginal shareholders who try to voice social concerns in a transnational corporation. Many others, especially in Buddhist and Christian cultures, have a spiritual foundation. Some are limited to a few members; others constitute vast movements, occasionally assembling several hundreds of thousands of people. In short, third system associations are as diverse as societies themselves.

Citizens and their associations usually act in a determined space - local, regional, national, multinational, global

- but also, and increasingly so, in several spaces simultaneously. Amnesty International, to take only one example, acts in the global space through representations to the United Nations Commission on Human Rights, in the national space through pressure on governments, and in the local space through the many groups which "adopt" a political prisoner and campaign for his or her liberation.

Whatever makes citizens join forces and wherever they take action, third system associations/activities can be considered under a few broad, non-mutually exclusive and non-comprehensive clusters.

Some associations are geared to the realisation of a project intended to respond to a crisis situation, to solve a specific problem or pursue a more general objective. Objectives include organising people, especially the poor[f] and improving their daily life[g] or their environment,[h] extending technical or financial support to local initiatives,[i] promoting popular theatre,[j] linking education with production,[k] ensuring equal access to jobs, decreasing working time, opposing construction of a nuclear facility (or the deployment of missiles), reconverting the manufacture of arms into socially useful goods,[l] preventing the export of dangerous drugs to the Third World or the careless storage of toxic wastes, campaigning for the liberation of a political prisoner, sharing appropriate technologies,[m] building new North-South relations,[n] facilitating the exchange of experiences through networking and cross-cultural dialogues, or the search for alternatives. In the Third World, there is a new and growing tendency among intellectuals,[o] including women[p] or lawyers[q] to serve people.

Advocacy activities may be seen as constituting a second cluster. Associations may be formed to advocate peace,[r] a new world order, the New International Economic Order or a federalist world, a world without hunger,[s] a new approach to international security, better terms of trade for Third World countries, the recognition and effective respect of minority rights,[t] breastfeeding,[u] consumption of local products, health developments, equality of opportunities among individuals and societies, protection and enhancement of the environment, ecodevelopment, cultural pluralism and respect for the Other, development, a reform to strengthen the United Nations...

A third cluster of associations deals with **accountability** ("those who hold power must be held accountable for the consequences of its exercise")[v] and the necessary mechanisms. The Permanent Peoples' Tribunal and its predecessor, the Russel Tribunal, are examples as far as the Prince is concerned, the International Organization of Consumer Unions,[w] IBFAN[x] or Ralph Nader's Corporate Accountability Research Group and its Multinational Monitor as far as the Merchant is concerned.[y]

The three types of activities usually imply some underpinning policy-oriented research and have a broad educational role, and some associations devote themselves primarily to such functions. The association's activity often takes (exclusively or not) the form of a publication such as the Latin American *ILET Fempress*, the African *La Satellite*, the *Tribune* or the *ISIS periodicals*,[z] to choose examples in the feminist movement, or the *samizdat* in

USSR, third system activities not being limited to the West or the South.

This hazy picture may, at this stage, be complemented by a more focused look at three specific spots in the third system constellation:

Peace. In Western Europe, the largest post-1945 manifestations took place in the autumn of 1983. Half a million people marched in the streets of The Hague, 600,000 in Rome and one million in West Germany to oppose the deployment of Pershing 2 and cruise missiles. In North America, one million Americans overwhelmed New York Central Park and mid-town Manhattan on 12 June 1982 on the occasion of the United Nations General Assembly Second Special Session on Disarmament - a demonstration far larger than any of the 1960s anti-Vietnam War protests, and possibly the largest ever in New York City.

Even before the New York event, George Kennan, a senior United States establishment figure and veteran diplomat, had this definitive comment:

The recent growth and gathering strength of the anti-nuclear war movement here and in Europe is to my mind the most striking phenomenon of this beginning of the 80s. It is all the more impressive because it is so extensively spontaneous... At the heart of it lie some very fundamental and reasonable and powerful motivations: among them ... a very real exasperation with their governments... They are the expression of a deep instinctive insistence, if you don't mind, on sheer survival.... Our government will ignore this fact at its peril. This movement is too powerful, too elementary, too deeply embedded in the natural human instinct for self-preservation to be brushed aside (Kennan, 1982).

Further, as Hilkka Pietilä observed, the peace movement is no longer a

single-issue movement as the traditional peace movements were. Today the peace movement brings together and unites several different movements which all perceive arms race and nuclear weapons as a common threat. This perception is shared by conservationists, various green movements, movements for a new life style, opponents of nuclear energy, activists for Third World countries and first of all the new women's movement.

Women's Liberation. In the same paper, Hilkka Pietilä continues:

The most interesting and the most original of these movements is the women's movement. It is the most comprehensive and the least prejudiced of the movements which have started and developed their activity over recent years. It receives substance and enhancement from widening and diversifying womens' research, which opens up new perspectives for equality between men and women as well as for social transformation altogether. An analytical, cognitive women's movement as such is a peace movement. Here it differs decisively from the so-called equal rights movement, which has not questioned the basic structures and values of the present social order, and which pursued equality for women in men's world mainly on male terms.[aa]

Social orders created and dominated by men have failed. Another development, implying new structures, calls for the rejection of any mimicry. Competing with men just to do more of the same and to run the same society with the same methods, women would only reproduce outdated and inappropriate patterns. The chance of the women's liberation movement, which asserts itself everywhere, in all regions and in all spaces, is to be imaginative, innovative, alternative. Like the Third World, the young, the alienated, the exploited, the dispossessed, women represent at the same time the difference pregnant with change and the totality which prefigures a better world. They may be the midwives of another development.

Hazel Henderson has noted that

... these non-governmental organizations formed over the past fifty years by women, their proliferation in many countries and subsequent convergence on world problems and the restructuring of policies to address them, are a prototype for international action (Henderson, 1976).

Marilyn Ferguson writes that women

represent the greatest single force for political renewal in a civilization thoroughly out of balance. Just as individuals are enriched by developing both the masculine and feminine sides of the self (independence and nurturance, intellect and intuition), so the society is benefitting from a change in the balance of power between sexes.

And she quotes Gandhi who once said

if satyagraha is to be the mode of the future, then the future belongs to women (Ferguson, 1980).

Accountability. The principle of accountability and its enforcement emerges as the central theme in the effort to re-assert people's autonomous power *vis-à-vis* the Prince and the Merchant.[w] Neither appropriate mechanisms nor, even less, the formal recognition of accountability would by themselves achieve that re-assertion, but the systematic exercise of accountability would make us progress in this direction.

As an instrument of democracy (that is, strictly speaking, people's power), accountability may progressively circumscribe the power of those who hold it. The act of making Prince and Merchant accountable may instill a new sense of self-confidence among the people. It is a natural concern for citizen's associations.

An example in a specific field is provided by the Consumers Association of Penang (CAP) Malaysia. This Association monitors prices, advertisements, marketing techniques, sales of dangerous goods, inadequacy of health care, public transportation or housing. It alerts authorities and people on any abuse. It carries out research into basic needs satisfaction, fights environmental deterioration (e.g. chemical pollution, deforestation, over-fishing), provides support to local initiatives, organises educational programmes, publishes a monthly paper of broad circulation, *Utusan Konsumer*, in Malay and English, and disseminates statements in these two languages as well as in Mandarin and Tamil. More specifically, it handles complaints from people about abuses they suffer from either Prince or Merchant.

A CAP comment is relevant to this discussion:

> *In ex-colonial societies where the people have far too long been used to the passive acceptance of life's injustices, the successful lodging of a complaint changes the perception and attitude of individuals who now see that redress can be obtained if one is willing to do something positive about it. The Complaint Service thus becomes an effective means and channel through which the public is able to exercise its rights to fight business malpractices and to press for fair and better services from companies and government departments as well as to demand protection of these rights from authorities.[bb]*

PEOPLE AND THE THIRD SYSTEM

The phrase "third system" in the sense accepted here and in the practice with which it is associated was coined in September 1977. It was first embodied in the title of the "Third System Project" carried out between 1978 and 1980 by the International Foundation for Development Alternatives as a contribution to the elaboration of the United Nations International Development Strategy for the 1980's[v] (Nerfin, 1978). As implied in the definition used here, the concept extends well beyond the modest pretext of its origin.

The association with the phrase "Third World" is not only deliberate: both phrases come from the same source evoking *le Tiers Etat*, the "Third Estate" of the French *ancien régime*. Before the revolution of 1789, French society comprised three "estates," the nobility, the clergy and the third estate, i.e. the vast majority. Alfred Sauvy was the first, in 1952, to use the phrase "Third World" to refer to the periphery, or the South, a phrase which has since gained wide accceptance (Sauvy, 1982).[5] However, "third system" is conceptually closer to "third estate" than is "Third World." The latter concept is geo-political; it concerns countries. The former two are socio-political; they concern people, and that is what the third system is about.

For in the beginning were the people. As history unfolded, various social groups and individuals emerged as self-appointed rulers and leaders which, to put it schematically, managed to extract from the people - the direct producers - a tribute or plus-value. To this effect, warriors, landowners, aristocrats, clergymen, merchants, money-lenders, capitalists, generals and bureaucrats established various forms of government and economic organisation. As a result of this evolution, people are dominated, at this particular point in history, by governmental power, the Prince, and by economic power, the Merchant - sometimes united, sometimes antagonistic - but always present.

Government still fascinates, understandably so when it is sought as a tool for change at the service of people, less so when it is opposed.

The Prince may well be the object of hate or sarcasm, yet he is somehow admired. Even when a particular Prince is really bad, the very manner in which the criticism is construed implies the possibility of a good prince, a prince-philosopher. Princes of the literary kingdom, although princes in their own right, often bow to the political Prince. Consider for instance three great contemporary writers of Latin America, a continent which has had and still has its bad Princes: Miguel Angel Asturias with *Mr President*, Alejo Carpentier with *The Recourse of the Method* and even Gabriel Garcia Marquez with *The Autumn of the Patriarch*: the Prince is torn apart, and yet somewhere floats the incense of mythification.

The alternative to the Prince, for a handful, is age-old anarchy. The Prince as a person does not really matter, it is the institution which is bad, so let's get rid of it. Neither God nor Master, let us join forces and tomorrow the International will be Humankind.

The Merchant used to be close to us. The growing geographical and economic distance between producer and consumer made it at the same time more mythical in our perception and more real as a determinant of our daily lives. It has now grown into a monster/hero whose misdeeds are proportional to the services it renders. We resent its influence and its riches because we are under its influence and because its riches come from us as participants, through the market, in the process of production and consumption. For instance, we oppose transnational corporations - up to a point: I don't like Nestlé, but I don't give up coffee. I don't like ITT, but I need to communi-

---

5. That Sauvy implied that the OECD countries (the West) and CMEA countries (the European East) were the other "worlds" does not justify the use of the expressions "first" and "second" world. In this context, ordinal numbers are historically, conceptually and politically misleading. Further, it may be noted that the Chinese are using a different classification which is more action-oriented in geo-political terms. By "first" world, they mean the two superpowers, and by "second" world, smaller industrial countries in both Western and Eastern Europe.

cate with my fellow networker in Chile. I don't like Hoffmann-La Roche, but what may happen to my child without this irreplaceable drug?

One alternative to the Merchant is workers' self-management, peasants' cooperatives and equal exchange among them. But not everyone likes to be a manager, and almost everywhere self-management has begotten new managers and restarted the process of alienation. Another alternative is "the Plan" as a people-serving agent of rational production and distribution of socially useful goods and services. While it may alleviate some of the Merchant's shortcomings, the Planner still has a lot to learn, including how to recognise the plan's limits.

The persistent fascination of the Prince, the resilient reliance on the Merchant and the elusiveness of utopias suggest not only that utopias need to be revisited, but also that, however poorly they perform, neither Prince nor Merchant have outlived their usefulness.

At the present level of productivity - with its implications for surplus extraction; ideological manipulation through mass-media and the "cultural industry;" economic, social and political organisation and weaponry for both external and internal use - the fact is that some form of government, within the boundaries of the current Nation-state system, is unavoidable, and to a point, necessary. In a world dominated by two superpowers, smaller or less-powerful States still offer some protection against total subservience. Likewise unavoidable and to a point necessary is some form of economic organisation, private or public, guided by the "invisible hand" or by the Plan, mixing one way or the other transnational cor-

porations, state enterprises, national and local capitalism. When the most basic human needs remain unsatisfied, those able to foster socially-useful and ecologically-sustainable production, as well as those able to ensure some social security through redistribution, still have an essential function. Neither the withering away of the State nor generalised producers/consumers self-management are on today's agenda.

This is to say that we have to recognise that Prince and Merchant, as alienated from us and as alienating as they are, remain within the realm of necessity. But understanding necessity need not prevent liberty.

At the same time, Prince and Merchant control only parts of the power. Whether they exist *de facto* or *de jure*, whether legitimate or not, whether serving the general interest or not, they cannot possibly represent society in its totality and its differences. Moreover, they exert their powers **upon** society. Their powers are subsidiary to those of the people. Their very existence depends on the people. They are, in a sense, our creatures. People - the women and men that we are - also have power, which we can exert on Prince and Merchant as well as on ourselves. People's power is thus the only autonomous power.

Yet beyond the principles, essential as they are, stands reality. People - societies - are not homogenous. To come back to an earlier analogy, the French "third estate" was not homogenous. Opposing the nobility and high clergy were the merchants, the artisans, the peasants, the first industrial capitalists, the intellectuals, some parish priests. Their interests, beyond the abolition of absolutism, could hardly be the same. The ideology, formulated by Jean-Jacques Rousseau, Denis Diderot and others, was essentially democratic - but the bourgeoisie, assuming leadership, merely used it to take over from nobility and church, which disappeared as both governmental and economic power. By and large, the people simply changed masters. A similar scenario occurred in a different context and for different reasons, after the 1917 socialist revolution in Russia. Bureaucracy, not bourgeoisie, took over and one had to wait until the summer of 1980, in Poland, to see the people - the workers - get together and organise as an autonomous social force in a society born out of the quest for justice and socialism.

This suggests two observations. First, whatever the ideology, the social origin, or the motivations, no minority, group or individual seeking or exercising power, any power, can be given a blank cheque. Whatever provisional or lasting benefits the people may obtain from a change of power, or from power or counterpower exercised on their behalf, they will remain in a subservient situation if they do not retain their autonomous power. This is not to condemn those who aspire to, or get, governmental power - many are genuinely honest and try in earnest to achieve what they set out to do - but to pose a reflection of the nature of the Prince and a reminder that in the polity as in the economy, the division of labour breeds "disabling professions" (Illich, 1978).

Second, people, save in exceptional circumstances, do not act politically as such, *en masse*. Not all people act as

citizens, and people are not naturally good; they may be, for instance, racist, and they are easily manipulated by propaganda. Enlightened minorities (or leaders), self-propelled but society-borne, either act on the behalf of people or, better, perceiving a problem and outlining a solution, formulate a **project** in which people recognise themselves. They join forces, thus creating the **movement** through which the latent power of the people becomes patent.

The third system is thus not coterminous with the people. It brings together only those among the people who are reaching a critical consciousness of the role they may play. It is not a party or an organisation, but the movement of those associations or citizens who perceive that the essence of history is the endless effort for emancipation by which we grope to master our own destiny - an effort which is, in the final analysis, coterminous with the process of humanisation of man (in the generic sense). The third system does not seek governmental or economic power. On the contrary, its function is to help people to assert their own autonomous power *vis-à-vis* both Prince and Merchant. It endeavours to listen to those never or rarely heard and at least to offer a tribute to the unheard voices.

NETWORKING

Realities, telecommunications and perceptions[6] progressively confirm the oneness of humankind and its planet. The risk of nuclear holocaust and the conjunction of under-development and

---

6.   and also the recent discovery that we may well be, all of us on this planet, the descendants of a single female ancestor who lived in Africa 140,000 to 280,000 years ago.

mal-development also make us one. Environment and health hazards underline our interdependence. Two-thirds of the planet - its oceans - are open to global management, as is outer space. Citizens and associations working in local spaces cannot limit themselves to these spaces, however fundamental they are. Those working in the global space cannot limit themselves to their sectoral concerns, however crucial these are. Beyond spaces and themes, all need to share experiences and ideas, to feel they belong to a larger whole, to relate to others.

The other systems of power do have their own linkages, mechanisms of consultation acting in concert and joint action. Princes, whether they somehow represent their people or oppress them, have their fora. They are regional like the League of Arab States, the Association of South East Asia Nations, the Council for Mutual Economic Assistance, the Economic Community of West African States, the European Economic Community, the Gulf States Corporation or the Sistema Económico Latino Américano. They reflect specific historical circumstances, such as the Commonwealth or the Organization of the Islamic Conference. They are also global: the United Nations system of agencies, programmes and conferences. Those of the Merchants who operate across national borders have formed transnational corporations. The third system as such has nothing of this sort. And its linkages cannot be the same as those of the powers which it intends to circumscribe or influence and which it wants to make accountable.

There seem to be two possible approaches to third system global relations. The first gravitates around the United Nations system. The second -

networking - while not necessarily excluding the first one, reflects better the nature and goals of third system associations and movements.

The United Nations approach itself is as least twofold. The first branch involves some improbable journey toward a remote utopia but nevertheless deserves to be mentioned. After all, the Charter opens with the famous "We the **peoples** of the United **Nations**," and not with "We the **governments** of the united **States** of the world."

The EEC Commission, which has more power than the UN Security Council, co-exists with the European Parliament whose role may be limited but whose members, being elected, somehow speak for the people of the member countries.

Another possible analogy is offered by the International Labour Organisation, whose General Conference is composed of four representatives of each member State with individual voting power. Two are delegates of government, one of the employers and one of the workers. This does not go very far, especially since the "non-government" delegates are chosen by their respective government in agreement with each country's most representative industrial organisation.

Something along these lines, however, would be a significant improvement in the representativity of the United Nations proper, where some 700 "non-governmental organisations" maintain consultative status with the Economic and Social Council. They are a mixed bag of organisations, ranging from the International Association of the Soap and Detergent Industry to the Christian Peace Conference. Most are essential-

ly Western, and whether their relationships with the UN Economic and Social Council are "obsolete and unproductive," as some say, does not really matter (UNITAR, 1975). Furthermore, there is a persistent habit, in the
"public information" sectors of the
United Nations, to consider "NGOs" as
mere conveyor belts of intergovernmental or breaucratic wisdom distilled from
above to "public opinion" which is
seen as a passive receptacle.

It is of course not prohibited to dream
of another United Nations.

*Utopian as it may appear today -
as did so many ideas, now part of
the conventional wisdom, before
someone took the first step towards
implementing them - couldn't we
sketch out a possible UN of 2025?
Redeeming its original sin of
having been conceived, brought
into being and grown up as an organization of governments, the UN
of our children and grandchildren
will probably reflect better the
societies of the world and the actors who make them alive.*

*This could for instance be
achieved through a three-chamber
General Assembly of the United Nations. The **Prince Chamber** would
represent the governments of the
states. The **Merchant Chamber**
would represent the economic
powers, be they transnational, multinational, national or local,
belonging to the private, state or
social sectors, since at the same
time we need them and need to
regulate their activities - which is
better done with them. The **Citizen
Chamber**, where there should be
as many women as men, would,
through some mechanism ensuring
adequate representativity, speak
for the people and their associa-*

*tions. At the very least, this would
make it possible for citizens to hold
Prince and Merchant **accountable**
for the consequences of the exercise of their power...*

Perhaps some imaginative and innovative institution designers could start
working and offer to the world community some ideas on how to move
from the present state of affairs to
something more apt to enable people to
participate in the management of the
planet.

*It would be futile, at this stage, to
direct the exercise at governments.
Like most past restructuring efforts
(by far more modest), this one will,
in the short-term at least, strike the
shelves of politico-bureaucratic
lack of vision and vested interests.
The exercise should, on the contrary, not only be directed at, but
carried out with, the social actors
themselves, the women and the
young, the peasants and the city
dwellers, the producers and the
consumers, the peace marchers
and the ecological sit-in people; all
those who are vitally interested in
another development interweaving
peace, justice and a better life for
all.*[cc]

Could some steps be taken immediately, offering alternatives to the end-of-
the-day no-audience practice of
"NGOs" addressing the UN Economic
and Social Council (or other bodies)?
Could the UN Economic and Social
Council Committee on "NGOs" up-
grade its role from procedural matters
to policy matters? Could the Human
Rights Commission, the Transnational
Commission or the bodies dealing with
disarmament listen to and interact with
Amnesty International, the International Organization of Consumers Union or

the peace movements? What kind of policy and procedures for the submission and circulation of documents would ensure that relevant views are available to intergovernmental organs? Could some enlightened governments take the intitiative to send more representative delegations to the General Assembly? For instance, since each Member has five delegates, could one represent the opposition, one the business community, and one the third system? Some governments do this to some extent, but could not the practice be made more systematic and open? Could one member be elected?

In the meantime, a "major departure from the traditional relationship between the United Nations and nongovernmental organisations" must be mentioned. In October 1979, at a meeting on infant and young child feeding which took place "at the centre of WHO/UNICEF decision-making process," various groups of participants were involved on an equal footing: representatives of governments, scientists, health workers, executives of infant food manufacturers, representatives of the United Nations system and constituent-based associations from both South and North. The composition of that meeting helped make it a "qualitative leap forward in the approach to infant feeding" (Lemaresquier, 1980). And there should be no surprise that the Executive Director of UNICEF, James Grant, could write that:

we have had a remarkable amount of structural change in the past 30 years ... most of this change has been brought about by public pressure, with people ahead of governments.... The outstanding example is the national liberation movements, which have all been against

governments. The civil rights movement in the US was another case of people being ahead of the government and forcing change. And the environmental and women's movements... (Grant, 1981).

The 1979 event, whether unique happening or precedent, came after almost a decade of a new presence of associations in United Nations meetings. The turning point was the 1972 Stockholm Conference on the environment, where as many interesting and far-reaching things happened in the adjacent Forum as in the intergovernmental assembly. Since then, associations have been present and active in most major United Nations conferences, advocating their views, exchanging information, organising debates, monitoring the position of governments, lobbying delegates, publishing journals or linking up with people at large. Examples are the World Food Conference (Rome, 1974), the Seventh Special Session of the United Nations General Assembly on Development and International Cooperation (New York, 1975), Habitat (Vancouver, 1976), UNCTAD IV (Nairobi, 1976), the Conference on New and Renewable Sources of Energy (Nairobi, 1980), the Second Special Session on Disarmament (New York, 1982) and, above all, the most recent, the Women's Conference (Nairobi, 1985) where the parallel Women's Forum gathered more than 15,000 women from all over the globe.[dd]

Whatever the immediate impact of such activities, they serve another, and far-reaching, purpose, not without similarities to last century's International Exhibitions. The First International Workingmen's Association resulted from a meeting of workers in London, in 1862, on the occasion of the International Exhibition. Perhaps the United Nations conferences of the 1980's will be seen, in retrospect, as having played a similar role, facilitating contacts between people otherwise scattered, opening new space to networking.

Networking is the other approach to third system linkages. There is nothing new in its practice: since the beginning of history, some people have always been in touch with others on the basis of common values and interests. What is new is that networking becomes progressively global because of the new perceptions of the oneness of humankind, and because technology makes it possible: air travel and the photocopying machine, and the tapes, and now, in a new revolution, telecommunications.

Above all, networking already offers a concrete alternative to conventional institutions serving Prince and Merchant. These are usually designed and operated in a pyramidal manner so as to provide for hierarchical relations between a centre and a periphery, a leader and those led (even when centres or leaders are the product of some consensus). They are the vehicle of the exercise of an outer power over others. They rest on a vertical division of labour between bureaucrats and membership. They nurture disabling professions and they dispossess people. The are internally and externally competitive and foster "bigness." They seek and dispense information rather than facilitate communication. They breed conformism and dependence. They are change-resistant and self-perpetuating. As a whole, they hinder rather than enhance freedom.

In sharp contrast, networks operate horizontally. Their centres are everywhere, their peripheries nowhere. Networking simply means that a number of autonomous, equal and usually small groups link up to share knowledge, practice solidarity or act jointly and/or simultaneously in different spaces. They exercise an inner power over themselves. Based as they are on moral (as distinct from professional or institutional) motivations, networks are cooperative, not competitive. Communicating is of their essence. They ignore coordination as a specialised task. Leadership, if and when needed, is shifting. The *raison d'être* of networks is not in themselves, but in a job to be done. When there is one, they set themselves up. They adjust quickly to changing circumstances. They are resilient in adversity (for instance, that one entity is co-opted by the establishment does not affect the whole). When they are no longer useful, they disappear. They are transient. Moving outside mainstreams and beaten tracks on somewhat marginal paths, they learn from each other to look elsewhere and beyond the conventional and the immediate. Being multidimensional, they stimulate imagination and innovation. They foster solidarity and a sense of belonging. They expand the sphere of autonomy and freedom.

The source of the movement is the same everywhere - people's autonomous power - and so is its most universal goal, survival. But the latent power of people materialises only here and there. This is what happens when millions of Filipinos occupy the boulevards of Manila,[ee] when millions of Europeans assemble to oppose nuclear weapons, when Penang consumers lodge complaints against the Merchant's abuses or when the activists of Solidarnosc raise their voice. But these remain worlds apart. Networking may now be part of North American reality, and the basis for the work of the International Baby Food Network Action, but things still look as if these were only isolated islands emerging in the still unconnected archipelago of another development.

Some associations, for instance Amnesty International or the IOCU are worldwide in coverage, but their concerns are sectoral. If the objectives and activities of Lokayan in India are akin to those of IBASE in Rio de Janeiro, as are problems of the peasants in the African Sahel to those of fish-workers in the Philippines, there is no real interchange among them. Efforts are underway,[ff] but they are light-years away from the requirements, however widely these are felt.

What is sorely needed is to make any significant happening in a particular local space an event in the global space and, conversely, to intensify the sharing of experiences, to help every citizen in every association feel that s/he is not alone, that s/he belongs to a global fraternity. This implies a conscious effort toward global networking,[gg] toward global third system communication.

Global networking is now technically possible. Said Arthur Clarke in 1983:

During the coming decade, more and more businessmen, well-heeled tourists and virtually all newspersons will be carrying attaché-case-sized units that will permit direct two-way communication with their homes or offices, via the most convenient satellite. These will provide voice, telex and video facilities (still photos and, for those who read it, live TV coverage). As these units become cheaper, smaller and more universal, they will make travellers totally independent of national communications systems (Clarke, 1983).

This needs not be limited to the Prince, the Merchant and affluent people: it may and will be used by third system associations.

In a less high-tech mode, and since the written word is still available to the third system, it remains possible to multiply, intensify and indeed generalise communication through inexpensive publications.

Like many other associations mentioned in this paper, IFDA has been endeavouring to meet, however modestly, the need of third system associations to relate to each other, in whatever space they operate and whatever their cause, through its bi-monthly *Dossier* which is published in a single trilingual edition (English, French, Spanish). Dedicated to the search for another development, it publishes case studies, notes on experiences, alternative views and approaches, and information ("News From the Third System"), as provided by the network of its readers. It is global in coverage, contributors and circulation. It reflects the most current concerns on the alternative agenda, from peace to women's liberation, local self-reliance, people's empowerment, human rights, consumers' self-defense, environment, or people's North-South solidarity. Every issue systematically features authors from the principal regions and cultures of the planet. Starting from a modest mailing list of some 2,500 addresses, it is now circulated in 18,400 copies and reaches many more readers in virtually every country. This is obviously a drop of water in the ocean, and many problems are unsolved, such as those of languages,[hh] but at least the IFDA Dossier is available.

In its effort to communicate, the third system should also examine the potential of a Third World press agency, "Inter Press Service," which now has a telecommunications network extending to some 60 cities in all continents.[ii] It is trying to promote alternative information (contextual rather than limited to spot news); visibility of new actors; direct South-South and South-North links; and to create a new type of communicator. Here again, many questions remain open, including the critical financial one, but Inter-Press Service is an instrument open to the third system of which use could be made (Michanek, 1985).

Discussing the "task, substance and strategy of the social movements" in trying to stop the apocalypse, Rudolf Bahro writes:

There are various seemingly irrational responses in vogue: the New Age Movement or the Aquarian Conspiracy (Ferguson, 1980). One thing about them is correct: what is required really is a world-embracing counter-movement, and there is no Archimedian point within the existing institutions which could be used to bring about even the smallest change of course. Without forces which attack from outside, the atomic holocaust is not to be staved off... Only the most basic social movements can bring about that break in cultural continuity without which we shall be unable to save our very existence.[kk]

What Bahro says applies equally to the holocaust of dispossession - as a matter of fact, the two holocausts are but the two sides of the same coin - their causes and alternatives to them - another development. Only the movement, whatever its name, third system or otherwise, will enable life to continue on this planet - pehaps simply because it is life itself.

And what matters first is to make available to people in each and every space the instruments through which they may exercise their autonomous power. In the process of realising this potential, the role of citizens and/or asssociations is both critical and temporary. They may be seeds of change, but if seeds perish, there is no harvest. The medium may not be the message, but the process is certainly the policy if the process means enabling people to become citizens, empowering them to act autonomously, and to hold Prince, Merchant and third system associations accountable for consequences of the use of whatever power they may wield.

For, the last thing to do would be to exonerate the third system from what it requires from the others. Only full accountability will help the third system to avoid bureaucratisation, resist co-option, keep its role of countervailing power, preserve its capacity for permanent renewal, and strive to run itself by imagination; in a word, remain what it sets out to be, the servant of the people.

The formal title of this paper, presented at an ARENA/UNU Workshop on Alternative Development Perspectives in Asia, Dhyana Pura, Bali, Indonesia, March 1986, was, as requested by the or-

ganisers, *"The North-South Impasse: Potential for Creativity? - The IFDA Third System Contribution and Experience."*

REFERENCES

- Alger, Chadwick F., 1984, "Reconstructing Human Polities: Collective Security in the Nuclear Age," in Burns H. Weston (ed.), *Toward Nuclear Disarmament and Global Security: A Search for Alternatives*, Westview Press, Boulder, pp. 666-687.

- Alger, Chadwick F., 1980, "Empowering People for Global Participation," *International Transnational Associations*, No 12, December 1980, pp. 508-510.

- Alger, Chadwick F., 1979, *The Organizational Context of Development: Illuminating Paths for Wider Participation*, United Nations University, Tokyo, Doc. HSDR C-PID, mimeo.

- Alger, Chadwick F. and Saul Mendlovitz, 1984, "Grassroot Activism in the United States: Global Implications?" *Alternatives*, vol. IX, No 4, Spring 1984, pp. 447-474.

- Argüello, Manuel, 1981, *Los más pobres en la lucha*, Editorial de la Universidad Nacional, Heredia, Costa Rica.

- Capra, Fritjof, 1983, *The Turning Point: Science, Society and the Rising Culture*, Bantam Books, New York; and Fontana Pub., (1984), London.

- Capra, Fritjof and Charlene Spretnak, 1984, *Green Politics, The Global Promise*, E.P. Dutton, New York.

- Clarke, Arthur C., 1983, *Beyond the Global Village, Address on World Telecommunications Day*, United Nations, New York, 17 May 1983, mimeo.

- Dag Hammarskjöld Foundation, 1975, *What Now - Another Development; Que faire - Un autre développement; Que hacer - Otro desarrollo*, Uppsala.

- Elgin, Duane, 1981, *Voluntary Simplicity, Toward a Way of Life That is Outwardly Simple, Inwardly Rich,* William Morrow, New York. (Republished 1982 as Voluntary Simplicity, An Ecological Lifestyle that Promotes Personal and Social Renewal, Bantam Books, New York.)

- Ferguson, Marilyn, 1980, *The Aquarian Conspiracy, Personal and Social Transformations in the 1980s*, J. P. Tarcher, Los Angeles; and Granada, 1982, London.

- Galtung, Johan, 1975, "Nonterritorial Actors and the Problem of Peace," in Saul Mendlovitz (ed.), *On the Creation of a Just World Order*, The Free Press, New York, pp 151-188.

- Gibson, Tony, 1979, *People Power, Community and Work Groups in Action*, Penguin, Harmondsworth.

- Gonzales-Casanova, Pablo, 1984, *La hegemónia del pueblo y la lucha centro-américana*, Educa, San José, Costa Rica.

- Gran, Guy, 1983, *Development by People, Citizen Construction of a Just World*, Praeger, New York.

- Grant, James P., 1981, "Achieving Social and Economic Goals for the Year 2000," *Compass*, Jan-Apr, 8:1.

- Gorman, Robert F. (ed.), 1984, *Private Voluntary Organizations as Agents of Development*, Westview Press, Boulder, Colorado.

- Haddad, Ismid, *et. al.*, 1983, "NGOs, Development and Politics," *Prisma, The Indonesian Indicator*, Jun, No. 28, pp. 1-80.

- Hegedus, Zsuzsa, March 1985, *From the Refusal of Arms Race to a New Model of Security*, Paris, mimeo.

- Henderson, Hazel, 1976, "Citizen Movements for Greater Global Equality," *International Social Sciences Journal,* Vol. XXVIII, No. 4, pp. 773-788; reprinted 1978 in Creating *Alternative Futures, The End of Economics*, Berkeley Publishing Corp., New York (see especially Chapters 16 and 21).

- Hine, Virginia, Apr-May 1977, "The Basic Paradigm of a Future Socio-Cultural System," *World Issues*, pp. 19-22. Mentioned in Elgin and Ferguson (above) and reproduced in O.W. Markley and Willis W. Harman, *Changing Images of Man,* 1982, Pergamon Press, Oxford, pp. 239-247.

- Illich, Ivan, 1978, *The Right to Useful Unemployment*, Marion Boyars, London; Le chômage créateur, 1977, Le Seuil, Paris.

- Judge, A. J. N., "The Associative Society of the Future," *International Transnational Associations*, 1979:6, pp. 259-365.

- Kennan, George, "On Nuclear War" *The New York Review of Books*, 21 Jan 1982.

- Kothari, Rajni, Feb 1984, "The Non-Party Political Process," *Economic and Social Weekly*, Vol. XIX, No. 5, Bombay, pp. 216-223.

- Kothari, Rajni, "Communications for Alternative Development," *Development Dialogue* (1984:1-2) pp. 13-22.

- Lemaresquier, Thierry, "Beyond Infant Feeding: The Case for Another Relationship Between NGOs and the UN System," *Development Dialogue* (1980:1), pp. 120-125.

- Lipnack, Jessica and Jeffrey Stamps, 1982, *Networking: The First Report and Directory*, Doubleday, New York, and their *Networking Journal* and *Networking Newsletter*, published by the Networking Institute, West Newton, Massachusetts.

- Meister, Albert, 1972, *Vers une sociologie des associations*, Les Editions ouvrières, Paris.

- Melucci, A., *et. al.*, 1983, "Mouvements alternatifs et crise de l'Etat," *Revue internationale d'action communautaire*, 10/50, Autumn, p. 3-83.

- Michanek, Ernst, 1985, "Democracy as a Force for Development and the Role of Swedish Assistance," *Development Dialogue*, No.1, pp. 56-84.

- Michanek, Ernst, 1977, *Role of Swedish Non-Governmental Organizations in International Development Cooperation*, SIDA, Stockholm, mimeo.

- Naisbitt, John, 1984, *Megatrends, The New Directions Transforming our Lives*, Futura, London.

- Nerfin, Marc, 1985, "The Future of the United Nations System: Some Questions on the Occasion of an Anniversary," *Development Dialogue*, No. 1, Uppsala, Dag Hammarskjöld Foundation, pp. 5-29.

- Nerfin, Marc, 1978, "A New United Nations Development Strategy for the 80s and Beyond: the Role of the Third System," in A.J. Dolman and J. van Ettinger (eds.), *Partners in Tomorrow, Strategies for a New International Order, Presented to Jan Tinbergen on the Occasion on his 75th Birthday*, E.P. Dutton, New York, pp. 71-82.

- Padron-Castillo, Mario, 1982, *NGDOs and Grassroots Development: Limits and Possibilities*, Final Report of Third World NGOs, Lima, 15-22 March 1982, The Hague: Institute of Social Studies, mimeo.

- Padron-Castillo, Mario, 1982, *Cooperacion al desarrollo y movimiento popular: las asociaciones privadas de desarrollo*, Desco, Lima.

- Passaris, S., G. Raffi, 1984, *Les associations*, La Découverte, Paris.

- Porritt, Jonathan, 1984, *Seeing Green, The Politics of Ecology Explained*, Basil Blackwell, London.

- Rouillé d'Orfeuil, Henri, 1984, *Coopérer autrement, L'engagement des organisations non gouvernementales aujourd'hui*, L'Harmattan, Paris.

- Sauvy, Alfred, 1982, *Mondes en marhe*, Calman-Lévy, Paris.

- Schneider, Bertrand, 1985, *La révolution aux pieds nus*, Rapport au Club de Rome, Fayard, Paris.

- Sheth, D.L., 1984, "Grassroots Initiatives in India," *Economic and Political Weekly*, Vol. XIX, No. 6, February, pp. 259-262

- Sheth, D.L., 1983, "Grassroots Stirrings and the Future of Politics," *Alternatives*, Vol. IX, No. 1, March, pp. 1-24.

- Toffler, Alvin, 1980, *The Third Wave*, William Morrow and Co., New York, and 1981, Bantam Books, New York; *La troisième vague*, 1980, Danoël, Paris.

- Touraine, Alain, 1984, *Le retour de l'acteur*, Fayard, Paris.

- Union of International Associations, 1984, "The 1984 Colloquium on Associations in Africa"/Union des associations internationales, "Colloque UAI 1984, L'identité associative en Afrique" in *International Transnational Associations / Associations transnationales*, 1984 Nos. 5 and 6; 1985 Nos. 1-4.

- UNITAR, 1975, Andemicael, B. (rapporteur), *Non-Governmental Organizations in Economic and Social Development*, New York.

- Watermann, Peter, *et. al.*, 1984, *For a New Labour Internationalism*, ILERI, The Hague.

- Zielonka, Jan, 1983, *The Origin of the Social Self-Defence Movement in Poland*, KSS-KOR, Polemolo-gisch Instituut, Groningen, mimeo.

NOTES REFERRING TO THE IFDA DOSSIER:

*The **IFDA Dossier** appeared twice in 1978 (Nos 1 and 2). It was published every month in 1979 (Nos. 3-14) and every other month since January 1980. Numbers 15-20 thus correspond to 1980; 21-26 to 1981; 27-32 to 1982; 33-38 to 1983; 39-44 to 1984 and 45-50 to 1985. Every issue bears the date of the month of publication and of the following month. No. 50, published in November 1985, is thus dated Nov/Dec 1985. Indices by author, theme and association appeared in Dossiers 17, 28, 36 and 50. Dossiers 1-37, except 27, 28 and 30 as well as 44, 45 and 48 are out of stock, but the full collection and the 20,000 page background papers of* the third system project are available on microfiche from Interdocumentation AG, Post-strasse 14, 6300 Zug, Switzerland for SFR. 950.00.

a) James P. Grant, "A Children revolution for 6 Billion Dollars a Year," D.37, pp. 37-51.

b) Rajni Kothari, "Lokayan's Efforts to Overcome the New Rift," D.52, pp. 3-14; Jan Pronk "The Case for a World Public Sector," D. 54, pp. 55-66.

c) J.S. Szuszkiewic, "Can They Do It: Participation of NGOs of Third World Countries in NIEO-oriented Projects," D.10, pp. 83-95.

d) Solange Passaris, "Les enjeux de la vie associative en France," D.24, pp. 15-24.

e) Cristina Herz, "L'assemblée fédérale des verts allemands," D.47, pp. 43-46; Alexander Langer, "The Greens in Italy," ib. pp.41-42.

f) Denis Goulet, "Development as Liberation: Policy Lessons from Case Studies," D.3; G.V.S. de Silva *et. al.*, "Bhoomi Sena, A Struggle for People's Power," D.5; Jac de Bruyn et Roger Jacobs, "Le mouvement de base," D.20, pp. 97-100; Danieul Mudali, "Small Fishermen Meet at Kuantan," D.23, pp. 78-80; Fishermen Alliance in Rizal, "The Troubled Waters of Laguna Lake," D.41, pp. 51-56; Bernard Lédéa Ouedraogo, "Développer sans abîmer" (Association internationale six S) ib., pp. 23-36; "Fisherworkers Get a Chance to Speak" (International Conference of Fishworkers and Their Supporters), D.44, pp.61-62; "Philippines: Agency for Community Educational Services Foundation (ACES)," D.45, p.88. Cf. Brian McCall, "The Transition Toward Self-Reliance: Some Thoughts on the Role of People's Organizations," D.22, pp. 37-46.; Karina Constantino David, "Issues in Community Organization," D.23, pp. 5-20; Anisur Rahman, "NGO Work of Organizing the Rural Poor," D.50, pp. 15-20; Nighat Said Khan and Kamala Bhasin, "Responding to the Challenge of Rural Poverty in Asia: Role of People's Organizations," D.53, pp. 3-16 and D.54, pp. 9-20.

g) "ENDA, Environnement et développement du Tiers Monde," D.45, pp. 83-84; Lutte contre la faim en zone sahélo-somalienne," D. 47, pp. 49-54; Mariana Schkolnik, "People and Economic Organizations in Chile," ib, pp. 27-28;

Gustavo Esteva, "Mexico: Self-Help Network," D.51, pp. 73-75.

h) "India: Kalpavriksh, the Environmental Action Group," D.48, pp. 76-78, Wangari Maathai, "Kenya: The Green Belt Movement," D.49, pp. 3-12; D.53, pp. 39-41; "SINA: Settlements Information Network Africa," D.53, p. 73.

i) IBASE, "An Innovative Service for the Popular Movements," D.30, pp. 82-84; "L'Association sénégalaise de recherche et d'assistance pour le développement communautaire (AS-RADEC), D.32, pp. 89-90; Rokiatou Tall, "Afrique occidentale: L'AFO-TEC, service international d'appui à la formation et aux technologies," D.49, pp. 84-88.

j) "Philippines: Mindanao Community Theatre Network," D.50, pp. 88-89. Cf. D.30, 33, 42 and 48.

k) "Foundation for Education with Production," D.27, pp. 67-71.

l) Mike Cooley, "Beating Swords into Ploughshares, The Lucas Experiment Described," D.35, pp. 53-63, & D.33, pp. 76-77.

m) "Tool," D.47, p. 84; SATIS, "Socially Appropriate Technology International Information Services," D.48, pp. 71-74; WISE, "World Information Service on Energy," ib. p.75.

n) "An Outline of Japanese Non-governmental Organizations in Development Cooperation," D.43, pp. 81-83; "Il était une fois SOLAGRAL," D.44, pp.75-77; "France: Le GRET, un outil de communication pour un développement autocentré," D.45, p. 89; "USA: The Trickle Up Programme," D.46, p. 86; "Collectif européen Conscientisation," D.51, pp. 83-84.

o) Md Anisur Rahman, "All India Convention of People's Science Movement," D.4; "Lokayan, Dialogue of the People," D.28, pp. 84-85; D.41, pp. 37-50, Rajni Kothari, cf. note (b) supra; "Brésil: Le Centre Josué de Castro," D.43, p. 80; "Ghana: Centre for the Development of the People," D.45, p.86; "Ecuador: Red interdisciplinaria de investigación y participación," D.50, pp.83-85; "Uruguay: CIEDUR en la reconstrucción nacional," D.52, pp.77-79; "Paraguay: Educación, capacitación y tecnología campesina," D.53, p.76; "Ecuador: CATER, Centro Andino de Tecnología Rural," D.53, p.77.

p) "L'AFARD, Une association de femmes 'chercheurs'" D.21, p.12; "The Changleput Rural Women's Social Education Centre," D.42, pp.78-80; AWRAN, Asia: Women's Research and Action Network," D.49, pp. 89-90; D.50, pp. 25-37.

q) "Les services juridiques en milieu rural," D.43, pp.78-79; "Asia: The Law of Society Trust," D.46, pp.78-79; "Philippines: BATIS, Centre for People's Law," D.48, p.80; "Network of Concerned Third World Lawyers Launched," D.51, pp.76-79; "Lawasia," D.53, p.83.

r) Inga Thorsson, "The Great Peace Journey," D.50, pp.75-78; and note (aa) infra.

s) Francisco Terenzio, "World Food Assembly: The Start of a Real Process of Cooperation for the Third System?" D.46, pp.76-77; D.44, pp. 74-75; "The World Food Assembly Manifesto," D.49, pp. 77-78.

t) "The Minority Rights Group," D.31, pp. 86-87; "The International Centre for Ethnic Studies (ICES)," D.43, pp. 75-78; "DOCIP: Indigenous Populations Documentation, Research and Information Centre," D.50, p.86.

u) IBFAN, "European Mothers: Do they really have a 'free choice' on how best to feed their babies?," D.50, p.81.

v) IDFA, *Building Blocks for Alternative Development Strategies, A Progress Report from the Third System Project; Matériaux pour d'autres stratégies de développement: un rapport sur l'état d'avancement du projet tiers système; Ladrillos para estrategias alternativas de desarrollo: un informo sobre los progresos del proyecto tercer sistema* (Nyon: IFDA Dossier 17).

w) Cf. inter alia, Anwar Fazal, "Brave and Angry: The International Consumer Movement's Response to TNCs," D.21, pp. 69-75; "The New Wave of the International Consumer Movement," D.26, pp. 73-75; "Five Billion Consumers Organizing for Change," D.44, pp. 71-74. Cf note (bb) infra.

x) IBFAN, "New Actions Launched on Baby Food Issues," D.41, pp. 73-74; Milupa campaign," D.43, p. 85; Andrew Chetley, "The Power to Change: Lessons From the Baby Food Campaign," D.52, pp. 45-56.

y) Cf. The Institute for Policy Studies Network on "Meeting the Corporate Challenge," D.41, pp. 75-77 & D.44, pp. 51-54; Health Action International, D.27, p.80; Food First Information Network (FIAN), D.45, p.81; Asia-Pacific People's Environment Network (APPEN), D.42, pp. 77-78 & D.46 p. 42; Pesticide Action Network (PAN), D.50, pp. 79-80.

z) "ISIS International: A Women's Information and Communication Service," D.42, pp. 81-82; "La Satellite," D.52, pp. 73-74; "ILET Unidad de Comunicacíon Alternativa de la Mujer," D.53, pp. 74-75.

aa) Hilkka Pietilä, "Women's Peace Movement as an Innovative Proponent of the Peace Movement as a Whole," D.43, pp. 3-12. Cf. Kwee Swan Liat, "Pugwash and the Third System," D.20, pp. 107-111; Cary Sacks, "United States: Grassroots Movement for the Nuclear Freeze," D.30, pp. 85-88; Elise Boulding, "Peace Movement in the USA," D.41, pp. 3-14; Jorge Osorio V., "Los movimientos por la paz en America Latina," D.41, pp. 15-22; Hector Vera, "Mouvements pour la paix en Europe et mouvements de libération en Amérique latine," D.47, pp. 63-72.

bb) Khor Kok Peng, "Value for the People: The Potential Role of a Consumer Movement in the Third World," D.18, pp. 1-13.

cc) Marc Nerfin, "A Three-Chamber UN," D.45, pp. 2 & 32. Cf. Henry Pease Garcia, "Otro desarrollo y el tercer sistema," D.8; William N. Ellis, "A Second Level of World Government," D.16, pp. 124-126 & "New Age World Governance," D.34, pp. 43-50.

dd) D.50, pp. 25-37 & Nita Barrow, "The Women's Forum '85 in Nairobi," D.54, pp. 51-54.

ee) Marc Nerfin, "People's Power in the Philippines," D.53, pp. 2+103.

ff) F. Whitaker Ferreira, "Pour une évolution du projet des journées internationales: pourquoi est-il nécessaire de le continuer?" D.19, pp. 27-42; "CODEV, Communications for Development Foundation," D.26, p.2; "What is TIE?", D.35, pp. 86-88; "Shopfloor Internationalism and the Auto Industry," D.38, pp. 65-67; IOC/MAB, "An International Network of People and Initiatives Striving for Self-Reliance," D.36, pp. 85-87; DESCO, "Third World PDAs meet in Lima," D.37, pp. 83-86; "Asian Regional Exchange for New Alternatives (ARENA) D.43, pp. 73-74; "Argentina: The Club del Hornero Seeks Interaction," D.46, pp.81-82; "Asia: CENDHRRA, or Partnership in Action," D.47, pp. 73-76.

gg) Hazel Henderson, "Planetary Networking," D.25, pp. 91-92.

hh) Leelananda de Silva, "Unheard Voices," D.2.

ii) Roberto Savio, "Communications and Development in the 80's, D.32, pp. 75-79.

kk) Rudolf Bahro, "Who Can Stop the Apocalypse?", D.34, pp. 51-64.

INFLUENCING THE CORPORATE AND PRIVATE SECTORS

William Waldegrave
Minister of State for the Environment,
Countryside and Local Government
London, United Kingdom

SUMMARY *People's concerns must be respected and responded to by governments - whether by providing more information to allay uncertainty or by action to tackle the source of the concern directly. Greater openness in environmental matters can provide a democratic basis for action to tackle the adverse consequences of industry's activities and may bring market rewards to environmentally benign processes. The corporate and private sectors have still to fully recognise this, and must not cast the environmentalist as an unreasoning opponent of industrial growth. The public's concerns for the environment are no less rational than its preferences for any other goods or services. There is a two-way dependency: The public's ability to press successfully for tighter environmental standards depends on industry's capacity to push forward the frontiers of technological development. Protecting the environment provides new markets for the innovator, and it is in the interests of the environmentalist that market mechanisms be encouraged to bring those innovations forward.*

INTRODUCTION

R.A. Butler, a major political figure of post-war Britain, once described politics as "the art of the possible." The phrase has since become a well-worn cliché. But like most clichés, it contains a large element of truth.

The essential duty of the politician is to represent the views of the people and to do whatever he or she can to get them translated into action. The role of politicians in Government is rather more difficult: it is actually to try to turn the wishes of the people into practical, workable policies which deliver the desired results.

Politicians and governments the world over know, of course, that this is easier said than done. In today's world, governments are subject to so many different forces, over which they may often have little direct control or influence, that delivering the desired results is difficult. In the field of environmental protection we face two particular difficulties.

First, we are frequently dealing with long-term questions. All too often, by the time we become aware of an environmental problem, the action required to deal with it may take many years to implement and perhaps even longer for the resulting benefits to become apparent. This in turn makes it difficult for politicians to be seen as responding to wishes of the people. And at a time when most Governments are facing severe economic constraints, demands for additional resources for long-term projects always risk losing out to short-term projects which may appear more urgent.

The second difficulty which those who formulate environmental policy must face is that this is not a free-standing policy area. Rather, environmental protection is a dimension of the major activities and processes which bear directly on almost every aspect of our daily lives: energy generation, industry, agriculture and transport. A minister who has responsibility for environmental protection has therefore to work with, and through, these separate sectors of activity.

If, as politicians, we are to develop practical and effective policies to protect the environment, we must face up to and resolve these difficulties. The only way we can do this is by ensuring that environmental considerations form a basic input **from the outset** in all areas of economic and industrial development. My remit in this paper is to consider how we influence the private and corporate sectors of industry to do this; how we persuade them to work for development without environmental destruction. This is the essential theme of the World Conservation Strategy.

HISTORICAL BACKGROUND

Our efforts to protect the environment must be reviewed in their historical context. It has not been encouraging.

The pressures for economic development and prosperity which have so dominated the twentieth century (and in many Western countries, the nineteenth century as well) led all too often to the unrestrained exploitation of natural resources for short-term benefit. And perhaps the resource which has suffered the most severe exploitation has been the environment, as industrial processes produced waste products and emissions degrading land, water and air.

We now have the technology available for a more sustainable growth. But in leading the early industrial revolution, the United Kingdom acquired an inheritance of heavily-polluted rivers, derelict waste-lands and polluted atmosphere. We have made great progress in recovering the quality of our environment, but the process has often been slow and expensive. It is a salutory reminder that prevention is frequently cheaper than cure.

PREVENTION IS BETTER THAN CURE

In the United Kingdom our policies to protect the environment are typically the product of a combination of two forces:

* Scientific evidence that industrial processes or other activities are causing environmental damage which threaten public health or the long-term survival of ecological systems; and

* public opinion and perceptions about what does or does not constitute an "acceptable" degree of environmental damage as the price of economic development and growth.

Past efforts and resources devoted to controlling pollution had public health as their main objective. More recently, these have been devoted to cleaning up the mess caused by industrial and other processes which stared us in the face. But, as we know, public opinion has increasingly come to believe that prevention is better than cure. This is where scientific analysis and evidence, and public perceptions and values come together; for with the preventative approach science cannot always provide the hard evidence or proof we are looking for, yet public opinion may be demanding that action be taken.

This shift in public opinion was recognised by Environment Ministers of the Western Economic Summit countries when they met at Lancaster House in December 1984. They said:

We stress the importance of sustainable development, prevention rather than cure; environmental impact assessment; setting environmental standards on the basis of best technology; and development of less polluting and more cost-effective technologies.

If these objectives are to be turned into reality, environmental thinking must be built into the corporate policies of industry. The Environment Ministers, at the Lancaster House meeting, recognised this when they said:

... environmental policy should be integrated fully into other policies. It should be considered as a fundamental factor when economic decisions are taken. Environmental protection is feasible only in cooperation with the economic and technological sectors, and not in conflict with them.

Our task in Government is to persuade industry that incorporating environmental protection measures into their planning and processes is a worthwhile investment **for them**. To do that we need:

* to provide more and better information about the effects of industrial pollution on the environment;

* better presentation of the opportunities and advantages to companies of investing in environmentally benign processes;

* feedback from industry itself, so that our environmental protection policies can reflect both the reality of the situation on the ground as well as public concerns and perceptions;

* the capacity to persuade industry to recognise and respond to the concerns of the community at large.

However, where persuasion reaches the limits of its efficacy and public interest dictates, we must also be prepared to apply regulatory powers.

In recent years the theme of a preventative approach to environmental protection has increasingly been the subject of widespread debate in many countries and international fora. One of the most wide-ranging discussions of the topic was the first World Industry Conference on Environmental Management held in 1984 at Versailles, France. On that occasion, over 500 representatives from government, industry and environmental groups from more than 70 countries met to discuss ways of improving environmental quality management while pursuing economic growth and development. That Conference established that the goals of economic growth and sound environmental management were compatible and indeed had to go together if sustainable economic growth was to be achieved. And it provided an opportunity for a comprehensive exchange of views, information and experience in different aspects of environmental management, from which emerged a series of recommendations in the form of the WICEM declaration.

In the United Kingdom, the Royal Society of Arts held a conference earlier this year in London on the theme of "Industry: Caring for the Environment." This brought together representatives of Government and of a wide range of companies, including such major international companies as ICI, IBM and BP. The conference focused on the achievements and responsibilities of industry with respect to environmental protection, and provided the opportunity for companies to exchange ideas on how to build environmental considerations into industrial policy decisions.

THE LESSONS FOR INDUSTRY

A number of lessons for industry are emerging from this process of debate.

First, it is simply not enough to deal with environmental problems only when they become intolerable. It is, in fact, inefficient to regard environmental protection as a peripheral activity at the edge of commercial life; as something added on as an afterthought or cosmetic "retouch" after the major in-

dustrial decisions have been taken. It is much more efficient to build environmental protection mechanisms into industrial plans and processes at an early stage. In this way more effective environmental management can be achieved at less cost than if expensive remedial action has to be taken at a later stage in the process.

Second, if companies and organisations are to integrate environmental protection into their planning processes, they need the services of qualified, trained people who understand the context in which the industry operates. A number of companies are already moving in this direction. British Petroleum, for example, employs a special coordinator whose responsibilities include health, safety and the environment. Another British company, ICI, also employs a Group Environment Adviser, who oversees teams within the organisation, whose task it is to advise management on the environmental aspects of the company's activities. Both companies, and others like them, are acting out of enlightened self-interest; they believe that they must operate in a way which retains the confidence of the public at large and individual communities by respecting the natural environment.

Third, when companies are planning a major development or project, they should conduct systematic assessment of its impact on the environment. BP, Shell and other oil companies have pioneered environmental impact assessment in Britain to very good effect. This approach is, of course, in the interests of environmental protection. But in addition, it can only be in the company's interest to assess and then minimise the impact of its plans on the environment, for it will help secure the confidence of the community and smooth the path of development. This is particularly the case where major developments, such as oil refineries, are concerned - as the oil companies have discovered. A requirement that major developments should be subject to an environmental impact assessment has stood in the laws of the United States and a number of other countries for many years, and is now incorporated in a directive issued by the European Economic Commission, which enters into force in 1988.

Fourth, it is essential that industries should look for cost-effective technical means to get the most benefit from their operations at least cost to the environment. New technology which makes tighter controls possible at acceptable economic cost is becoming increasingly available. But as it does so the community expects it to be used. And the march of technological progress in some areas leads to expectations that improvements should be sought and achieved in others.

Some companies have done pioneering work in this field. But research is costly and many firms may often feel they do not have the resources to devote to it. In the United Kingdom we are therefore considering introducing a new scheme to help fund research and development into environmentally benign technologies and processes.

Fifth, companies need to realise that in some cases preventing pollution can actually pay, combining reductions in levels of industrial pollution together with a reduction in costs. A prominent example of this approach is that adopted by the 3M corporation. They have consciously developed a "Pollution Prevention Pays" programme.

Their search is for the most rational use of resources and energy, and the avoidance of needless environmental impact. They have attacked their problems through product reformulation, process modification equipment, equipment redesign and recovery of materials for re-use. They have found real economies from analysis of the possibilities in these areas. The result has been 52 projects introduced between 1980 and 1983, with a saving of £ 2.25 million and a major reduction in pollutant discharges.

Many other companies have found possibilities for savings in this approach. Bulmers, the British cider-makers, developed a new and more effective technique for treating its effluents which produced substantial cost reductions for the company. Many new technologies which are cleaner also reduce energy consumption, use fewer raw materials or improve working conditions. The lean burn engine for vehicles is one example. Rolls Royce's RB211-535 aero-engine which combines increased fuel efficiency with lower exhaust emissions and less noise is another. And Rockware, one of Britain's leading glass container manufacturers, set up a subsidiary in 1984 whose objective is to turn recycling of all kinds of packaging materials into profit-making ventures in their own right. By 1985, the company had already achieved savings of £200,000 a year through reduced energy bills for its glass-melting furnaces.

Sixth, multinational companies operating in different countries can seek to raise the quality of environmental management by drawing on their own worldwide operating experience. There are several benefits from such an approach. First, the company covers itself against increases in pollution control standards which may be introduced after the construction of a plant, but during its useful life. Second, it has considerable presentational benefits to the company, establishing a positive image of a modern industry setting out to live in the modern world.

This leads on to the seventh lesson for industry which is emerging from the current "environment versus development" debate. It is that an "environmentally conscious" image is an attractive advertisement in itself for a company, which can help promote its products and its standing in the market place. This is not something to be despised or dismissed: some of the major oil companies, for example, have already discovered the value of such an image and do not hesitate to promote it in their advertisements.

Not only does an environmentally-conscious **image** make good commercial sense for a company, but so do environmentally benign products. This means that companies can take advantage of the modern trend of environmental concern to develop products whose environmental qualities can be stressed in their marketing. A number of British companies have been active in this field. ICI, for example, has recently developed a range of new water-based paints. And together with Shell and other major companies they have been involved in the development of the new generation of pesticides and detergents.

THE LESSONS FOR GOVERNMENT AND SOCIETY

These are some of the main ways in which industry can contribute toward a reduction in pollution levels and a better environment, and at the same time benefit their own organisations and operations. But we cannot leave the task of improving the environmental impact of industry generally to a relatively small number of major enlightened companies. Governments have a crucial role and responsibility to create the climate in which industry as a whole is encouraged to pursue similar measures to those described above. Rather like the process of evolution by natural selection, we want to create a situation where the best practices emerge and spread through the industrial sector.

Developed countries - whether they have market or planned economies - depend upon industry for their wealth. Without economic prosperity, environmental protection inevitably slips down the list of priorities. But economic growth without regard for its impact on the environment provides a deceptive prosperity, because its true costs are being endured by others in the community. The responsibility of Governments is to **provide the framework within which economic growth can be reconciled with concern for the environment.** That means we must both encourage industry to be environmentally conscious and at the same time inform the community about the value and necessity of the industrial processes on which our economic prosperity depends.

Governments must first give clear signals to industry as to the standards it is expected to achieve. The clearest signals will be given through the regulatory role of pollution control agencies and authorities. In an era of preventative approach, high standards appear increasingly prudent. This is certainly the direction in which international influences - for example, through the European Economic Commission - are moving: influences which are shaping national policies more and more. Developing countries are also becoming more concerned to ensure that their industries work to high safety and environmental standards. It is in everyone's interests to plan for a future when industries are genuinely "good neighbours" as well as good financial investments.

The standards which Governments set will ultimately determine the pace and extent to which industrial processes generally are made cleaner. In the United Kingdom our approach to setting environmental standards focuses on the **overall** impact of emissions in a locality on each of the media - air, water or land. This gives us the flexibility to take account of, and strike a balance between, the different considerations which bear on the setting of standards: scientific evidence about the extent and nature of environmental impact; public perceptions and preferences about what is an acceptable degree of environmental impact; and what industry can realistically be expected to achieve.

We also give signals to industry through well-established arrangements for development control under the town and country planning systems. These arrangements have made a major contribution toward ensuring that a balance, acceptable to the community, can be struck between the need for industrial, commercial and other development, conservation of the landscape and of our built heritage, and the preservation of amenity. Many of the principles on which our planning system has long been based are now being in-

corporated in the recent directive on Environmental Impact Assessment issued by the European Economic Commission.

We can stimulate and encourage the wider use of environmentally-benign technologies by **harnessing market forces**. This approach rests upon the principle that the environment is a resource, and that, like any other resource, it can be managed efficiently or inefficiently. Efficiency is fostered first and foremost by the effective working of market forces, which place a value on the resource. To some extent market forces do place values on environmental resources, but in many cases market failures can and do occur. One of the main reasons why this happens is because enterprises "externalise" their costs: at its simplest, it means that the enterprise releases effluents which damage the environment, and those who use or occupy it, at no cost to itself. In economic terms, part of the "cost" of production is falling on those other than consumers of the product.

To avoid this, Governments can insist that the polluter should bear the cost of cleaning up his own effluent. He must design and run his plant to achieve environmental standards that the community will accept. He must deal permanently with any hazardous waste it produces and, if that involves extra costs, it is right that he should bear those costs and pass them on to the consumers of his goods and services. This is the approach we pursue in the United Kingdom; but it can be applied in planned economies equally well as in market economies.

The "polluter pays" principle helps stimulate the development of cleaner processes. But Governments can do more, for example by **providing direct incentives and encouragement to industry to develop environmentally-benign technology**. The United Kingdom, for example, operates a scheme of Pollution Abatement Technology Awards for companies which develop environmentally benign processes or equipment. For forward-looking companies, there are advantages in terms of prestige and a good environmentally-conscious image in winning these awards. This year, Rolls Royce won an award for their new aero-engine and ICI has won several awards. Government, industry and other organisations are jointly involved in the scheme.

There is also a rapidly growing international market in pollution abatement technology itself. As many countries raise the pollution control standards which they require industries to meet, so the demand for new technology and equipment to meet those standards is expanding. This in turn helps stimulate economic activity and employment where companies are prepared to seize the opportunities presented by that demand.

But these signals and incentives to industry have to be compatible with the perceptions of the wider community about the role of industry in our societies and about the importance of environmental protection. If we are to achieve this, two conditions must be fulfilled:

* We need a sound scientific basis to enable us to understand the impact of industrial processes on the environment and how environmental processes respond to industrial processes; to set the right standards for pollution control levels; and to monitor the achievements of those standards.

* We need to ensure a proper flow of information to the people, so that the impact of technology and industrial processes on the environment are known and understood.

The importance of a **good scientific basis** is clear. First, if we are to take effective action to protect the environment we need to understand what industrial processes are damaging it, how they are damaging it and to what extent. Secondly, if we are going to set pollution control limits which are likely to impose costs on the industries involved, we need to be as sure as we reasonably can that those costs are justified. But science cannot always provide us with clear-cut evidence, particularly in cases where damage to the environment has not yet materialised, but we strongly suspect that it may. This is where the preventative approach comes in. An example is the impact of chloro-fluorocarbons on the ozone layer. We do not know for certain what that impact is but there is evidence that it may be harmful. If the ozone layer is harmed the effect could be serious and long-lasting. That is a risk we cannot take. So the EEC has acted to limit the production of these substances. Other countries are pursuing a different approach to the same goal.

Providing more information about the impact of industrial processes on the environment is a vital step toward enabling the public to reach a judgement about the balance of advantage between the benefits of a particular industrial activity and its environmental consequences, and about the trade-off between any reduction in economic benefits which may arise from measures to reduce its environmental impact. Such considerations are of course very much in all our minds in relation to the nuclear power industry at present.

In the United Kingdom it is the Government's policy that there should be a presumption in favour of "openness" in respect of information about the environmental impact of industrial and other processes. In pursuance of that policy we have just completed and published a study on ways in which more information can be made available to the public about the extent and manner in which various industrial processes are polluting the environment. The study was conducted on the principle that the public should be able to obtain information on how far the natural environment was being degraded; that half-kept secrets fuel fear; and that secrecy could not be justified by the argument that public access to environmental data could lead to tighter controls on industry.

Finally, just as Governments must respond to the concerns of their people about the need to reduce pollution and protect the environment, so they must **sustain the image of industry as a creative rather than a destructive force**, which is essential for economic development and prosperity. In Western democracies this is best

achieved by the provision of information and free debate. This allows commentators and opinion formers to draw the public's attention to matters about which they think they should be concerned. And it allows the public to reach a view on these issues.

SUMMARY AND CONCLUSIONS

The principal lesson that we draw from the World Conservation Strategy is that we can and must achieve economic development without destroying our environment. The need for economic growth is not, as some were arguing in the 1960s and early 1970s, a thing of the past. Despite the enormous growth in prosperity of most Western countries and their inhabitants, the real and urgent need for economic development in the Third World is there for all to see - development which is often needed to provide people with the essentials of life: adequate housing, health care and enough to eat.

But that development, urgent though it is, must be guided by the concept of "sustainable livelihoods." It has to enable people to achieve a better standard of living but in a sustainable balance with the environment. That means the development should not destroy or exhaust their natural resources, leaving them worse off than before, after a brief period of relative prosperity.

Industry, governments and the wider community need to work together if the objective of sustainable growth is to be achieved and the right kind of wealth is to be created. For industry, this means adopting a preventative approach to controlling pollution by:

* building environmental considerations into corporate plans from the outset;

* employing trained and qualified people whose job it is to ensure that the environmental consequences of policies and processes are understood and evaluated at an early stage;

* looking for cost-effective technical means of maximising the efficiency of industrial processes at least environmental cost, and recognising that introducing pollution prevention technologies can reduce costs;

* recognising that a responsible approach to pollution control, together with environmentally-benign technologies and products, helps to promote public confidence in a company and to make its products more attractive to the consumer.

Governments' responsibility is ultimately to reconcile the impact of industrial development and economic growth with people's concerns about the need to protect the environment. In essence, that means it must encourage industry to be more pollution-control conscious by:

* ensuring that the right regulatory framework exists to enable industry to achieve higher but achievable standards of pollution control;

* ensuring that the economic context in which industry operates means that it - and the consumers of its products - bears the cost of pollution control, rather than the community at large;

* providing other incentives to industry to develop environmentally benign technologies and processes, and promoting their wider use.

For both industry and governments the essential prerequisite for these objectives is the provision of more and better information about the nature and impact of industrial processes on the environment. For if Government is to be able to influence industry to contribute toward a cleaner environment and if industry is to be able to respond, there must be informed public opinion and debate. Political initiatives to secure a better environment are, like all other political initiatives, concerned with the "art of the possible."

RECOMMENDATIONS AND CLOSING ADDRESS

CONCLUSIONS OF THE CONFERENCE

Dr. Martin Holdgate, Chairman of the Recommendations Committee
United Kingdom Department of the Environment
London, United Kingdom

The Recommendations Committee included Ms. Andrea Matte-Baker (Canada/Chile), Professor Adolfo Mascarenhas (Tanzania), Dr. Shimwaayi Muntemba (Zambia), Dr. Kasem Snidvongs (Thailand), and Dr. Alexandre Timoshenko from the Soviet Union. Dr. Julia Gardner and Mr. George Green, both from Canada, provided the Committee Secretariat. I would like to express my very deep and sincere appreciation for the positive, cooperative way in which the group worked together.

As a preliminary, the Committee examined first drafts of the recommendations and addressed questions and comments to the Workshops. Members of the Committee circulated among the various groups to assist in achieving a consistent approach. The Recommendations Committee then met for a prolonged final session on the eve of the last day of the Conference. We were helpfully joined for much of the time by Dr. David Munro, Secretary-General of the Conference. All of the recommendations were reviewed as they came in from Rapporteurs, and the Committee endeavoured to edit them to the required length and to achieve consistency of style.

Each recommendation or group of recommendations begins with a short preamble drawn from the relevant Workshop statements, setting out the problem addressed. The Committee arranged the material in a sequence, beginning with a very few general proposals which stemmed largely from the Plenary Sessions, particularly the opening Plenary. We felt that our Convenor, Dr. M. Swaminathan, had made some very important broad points which did not all come up again in the groups. That sequence is retained in the printed text.

The opening statements are followed by a group headed "Principles and Measures for Sustainable Development," and then by a section on "International Cooperation for Sustainable Development," followed by more concrete proposals on "The Preparation of Strategies." Lastly we collected a small number of more general action plans as "A Forward Look."

These proposals were put to the Conference at its final session. A number of amendments were moved by participants and agreed. The final text has been edited to incorporate these amendments and contain others received in writing from Workshop Chairmen, Convenors and Rapporteurs. While not every suggested change could be adopted (some were mutually contradictory), it is hoped that the result will command a broad consensus among participants and provide a clear mandate for future action.

The participants will, I hope, agree that the Ottawa Conference marked a major leap forward. The World Conservation Strategy document itself, upon which most of us still look with acclamation, broke new ground. It stressed that conservation was an essential part of development and that the safeguarding of the natural world can only be achieved within the development process. But the natural world, its biomes and ecosystems, was a dominant theme in the original World Conservation Strategy. At Ottawa, the perspective shifted. It was repeatedly stressed that the sustainable livelihoods and quality of life of people must be at the heart of our concerns. Plans and policies must be practical, equitable, and based on proper ways of valuing natural resources. But in planning to promote the development of human communities in all their rich diversity, we must not cast aside nature in the process of "civilizing."

Many cultures are grounded in a sensitivity to nature. In seeking sustainable development, we do not turn our backs on the natural world. Rather, we stress that humanity can only enjoy life to the full in harmony with nature; in harmony with other species and with the great systems of the creation of which we are part and upon which we utterly depend. This emphasis on harmony, on caring for the earth and all its peoples, on sustainable development as an expression of conservation, is the new spirit and ethic of Ottawa, and represents a forward leap as great as that provided by the World Conservation Strategy itself. We stand, in consequence, at the start of a new path: one which demands new systems of judgement, of economics, of education, of communication, and above all, of participation at all levels and between all sectors of the community. That path will be rough: it will be obstructed at many points. But it is a path along which our recommendations and conclusions at Ottawa point us.

CONFERENCE ON CONSERVATION AND DEVELOPMENT: IMPLEMENTING THE WORLD CONSERVATION STRATEGY

Conference Recommendations

1 : TOWARDS SUSTAINABLE DEVELOPMENT

General Recommendations

1. The sponsors of the World Conservation Strategy should emphasise to the world community that sustainable development is a continuous process which does not cease with the completion of any particular document and which demands the participation of groups of committed people at all levels.

2. The sponsors of the World Conservation Strategy, in partnership with other international bodies should:

* initiate discussions leading to an international code for the sustainable and equitable use of the environmental systems of the planet, on which all human life depends. These discussions should reflect the central message of the Ottawa Conference, which is that sustainable development is only practicable when it is built on an understanding of the natural world, on care for its diverse life and beauty, on concern for social systems and traditions, and on

recognition of the need for harmony among people and between people and nature;

* assist governments and other national groups, including non-governmental organisations, in the preparation of national and local codes for sustainable development, founded upon consensus and together guaranteeing the sustainable livelihood of all people.

* recognise that the concepts and practices of sustainable development must continue to evolve; especially in the light of practical experience, and that to this end it is important that machinery is established for the exchange of this experience.

3. IUCN, in association with UNEP and other international bodies, should monitor and record the changing state of the earth and its peoples, and bring to the attention of the world community instances where sustainable development is in serious jeopardy because of defects in vision, shortage of resources, imbalance between populations and their environment, or needless and significant damage resulting

from the pursuit of personal gain or political power.

4. The sponsors of the World Conservation Strategy should emphasise to governments that a sustainable growth strategy must be a conservation strategy, and that wise environmental resource management is central to the policies of economic development for which they are responsible.

5. The sponsors should also promote the concept of a quality of life index and an environmental wealth index as indicators of sustainable development that are more broadly based and more closely related to the human situation than the traditional indicators embodied in GNP. The development of new concepts of environmental economics should be pressed upon UNDP, the World Bank and aid donors, and upon national recipients and the world trading community as a means of improving judgement about investment for sustainable development.

2 : PRINCIPLES AND MEASURES FOR SUSTAINABLE DEVELOPMENT

(I) CONSERVATION STRATEGIES FOR NATURAL OPERATIONAL UNITS

Large natural units of the biosphere should be treated as "operational units" to serve as a framework for conservation and sustainable development. Such units include, for example, wetlands, grasslands, coastal marine zones, islands, mountains, and tropical forests. A primary principle of sustainable development of these units is that management should work within the context of natural patterns and cycles. Another principle is that social, economic, and cultural factors should be taken fully into account.

Recommendations

1. *Mountains*: IUCN should establish a Programme on Mountain Conservation and Sustainable Development, in cooperation with the related activities of other organisations. Particular attention should be paid to the identification of ways to ensure local community participation for satisfaction of basic needs.

2. *Islands*: Most island ecosystems are unique and include numerous endemic species with small populations, vulnerable to external impact. Their socio-economic systems depend on a relatively narrow range of natural resources. It is therefore recommended that IUCN establish a Programme on Island Conservation and Sustainable Development, paying particular attention to the smaller, most isolated, independent examples.

3. *Wetlands*: IUCN, as Secretariat for the Ramsar Convention, should work with its major conservation partners to provide long-term support for the sustainable development of wetlands. Specifically IUCN should coordinate the elaboration of a global conservation strategy for wetlands, so as to increase international commitment to conservation-based development of these resources. Simultaneously, in collaboration with national governments, local communities and conservation agencies, explicit programmes and guidelines for the sustainable utilisation of wetlands should be elaborated and implemented

through a series of regional action plans.

4. *Tropical Forests*: It is recommended that:

* The mutual interdependence of conservation and development needs to be much more forcefully demonstrated, particularly to policy and decision makers, and given a sound economic basis. The national conservation strategy process and national forestry policy reviews are the best methods yet devised of achieving this and should be further promoted by IUCN and IIED. Organisations such as WWF and WRI have a valuable role to play in further developing public awareness of the need for tropical forest management, especially through developing country NGOs.

* Development assistance agencies should make major long-term commitments to the sustained management of natural forests for the full range of goods and services that they can provide. Organisations such as ICRAF, WRI and IUCN have an important role in analysing and disseminating the techniques needed for this.

* The huge areas of wasteland and degraded tropical forest lands should become a focus of creative development assistance in order to promote sustainable production systems contributing to social and economic progress and thus lessen pressures on natural ecosystems.

* IUCN should lead a major international effort to complete the global system of National Parks and other protected areas and to further integrate them into local development processes. Compatible uses of buffer zones around protected areas should

be based upon stable production systems including forest management for the benefit of local communities.

* Priority should be given to the implementation of agreed international proposals including the UNDP/FAO/World Bank/WRI Tropical Forest Action Plan.

(II) SECTOR-BASED STRATEGIES FOR SUSTAINABLE DEVELOPMENT

Development programmes are generally planned and implemented on a sectoral basis. Such fragmentation hampers the formulation of strategies for sustainable development. Intersectoral strategies should pay particular attention to health, which is regarded as a critical factor in the development process, and the most significant basic need. There is very little chance that a development effort can be sustained by population groups who would not enjoy minimum health standards. Adequate supplies of food, energy and clean water, provided on a sustainable basis, are also essential.

Defects in the educational system are also at the root of many problems that reduce the capacity for sustainability. The concepts underlying sustainable development are not taught to students trained for industry; the discipline of Economics is particularly deficient in this respect.

Recommendations

1. Governments, international agencies, universities, NGOs and other groups should foster interaction among the economic production and resource management sectors. Such key social sectors as health, population and educa-

tion should be included. All levels within the community should be involved. Similarly, international organisations should coordinate their efforts in technical cooperation.

2. Governments and agencies funding education, as well as educational institutions, should review their teaching curricula and incorporate the principles and the methodology of environmental education, systems analysis and other multidisciplinary techniques relevant to sustainable development. Educational institutions preparing people to serve in developing countries should pay particular heed to the transferability of the concepts and the methods they teach.

3. IUCN should work with the World Health Organization to promote a long-term cooperative action programme promoting health and sustainable development.

(III) TECHNOLOGIES FOR SUSTAINABLE DEVELOPMENT

A wide range of alternatives to prevailing technical and development patterns exists, and can:

* satisfy the basic and development needs of people;

* consume fewer scarce resources;

* promote the use of abundant natural and human resources;

* minimise pollution and degradation of the ecological heritage;

* promote people's participation and social equity;

* contribute to greater self-reliance and cooperation among people;

* be consistent with diverse cultures.

Recommendation

The sponsors of the World Conservation Strategy and other international and national, governmental and non-governmental organisations should actively promote and support the identification and implementation of practical technologies appropriate for sustainable development, including those technologies which cover a range of complexities, respond to differing needs, and are applicable in both developing and industrialised countries.

(IV) ETHICS, CULTURE AND SUSTAINABLE DEVELOPMENT

A changed global situation calls for a new sense of ethics. At this juncture of human and evolutionary history it is especially important to affirm (1) the integral value and beauty of ecosystems, (2) the imperatives of social justice, and (3) their integral relationship.

The World Conservation Strategy recognises the practical importance of ethics and the arts in achieving the goal of sustainable development.

Recommendations

1. In the spirit of the World Heritage Convention and the World Charter for Nature, a section on ethics, culture and sustainable development should be included in a supplement to the World Conservation Strategy.

2. The sponsors of the World Conservation Strategy should stress that in preparation of national conservation strategies the participation of those most affected is an ethical imperative.

3. Governments and all others concerned with environmental planning,

the sustainable use of nature, and the implementation of the World Conservation Strategy have an ethical obligation to take account of the intrinsic value of all life forms and ecosystems and be as responsible, respectful and humane as possible in their use.

4. IUCN should provide the support necessary for a working group to identify the issues that must be addressed, and the resources that would be required to launch a serious global initiative in environmental ethics.

(V) ECONOMICS OF SUSTAINABLE DEVELOPMENT

Sustainable development is often imperilled by the current economic system. Sustainability must be among the criteria in the development of a future economic order and in national development planning. Imaginative action is needed by governments, the International Monetary Fund, international banks, and donor agencies to address the underlying problems of debt, terms of trade and financial flows. In the longer term, underlying social and institutional problems relating to the inappropriate uses of natural resources, the inequitable distribution of resources, and the inadequate understanding of the processes involved should be addressed.

Recommendations

In pursuing sustainable development objectives, Governments and other agencies should follow the sequence of activities set out below:

1. develop a framework that accounts for all costs and their social and regional distribution, using appropriate indicators of environmental values;

2. assess the existing natural resource base and patterns of utilisation, and estimate the economic and social consequences of renewable and non-renewable resource depletion and natural resource potential;

3. evaluate and design specific development priorities and plans, guided by World and National Conservation Strategies, with due attention to the style of development sought, appropriate consumption patterns and other key criteria;

4. act on the priorities thus derived:

* by eliminating policies (e.g. subsidies) that are unsound in narrow economic as well as environmental terms;

* by designing economic, social and institutional incentives (e.g. taxes, land tenure), appropriate science and technology policies, and investment programmes in support of these priorities;

* by reviewing and adapting the priorities on a continuing basis; and

* by cooperating in programmes designed to alleviate situations of poverty and promote basic needs.

Governments and professional institutions should, in addition:

1. secure improved systems of institutional and individual accountability;

2. develop greater flexibility toward evolving circumstances;

3. develop and disseminate new interdisciplinary concepts in economic and social theory.

(VI) INDIGENOUS PEOPLE AND SUSTAINABLE DEVELOPMENT

Indigenous people have a unique relationship to the earth, often expressed in their cultures, knowledge, practices and careful stewardship of the living earth.

Recommendations

1. The sponsors of the World Conservation Strategy should, in the future development of their thinking, reflect:

* the accrued riches of traditional conservation knowledge;

* the unique environmental ethics of many indigenous peoples, and in particular their understanding that:

    Earth is the foundation of indigenous people. It is the well of our spirituality, knowledge, languages and cultures. It is not a commodity to be bartered to maximise profit; nor should it be damaged by experimentation.

    The Earth is our historian, the cradle of our ancestors' bones. It provides us with nourishment, medicine and comfort. It is the source of our independence; it is our Mother. We do not dominate Her, but harmonize with Her.

2. The sponsors of the World Conservation Strategy should also recognise the need for cultural diversity as much as biological diversity in conservation.

3. Recognising the importance and urgency of including indigenous peoples' perspectives in the World Conservation Strategy, the sponsors of that Strategy should endorse and support an Indigenous Peoples' Conference on Conservation to be organised in concert with the World Council of Indigenous People.

4. The right of indigenous peoples to self-determination, including the right to control the use of their traditional territories and resources, should be recognised. Where resources are shared with other peoples, rights to those resources should be respected on a reciprocal basis.

National and other governments should:

* when conducting international affairs (including the negotiation and conclusion of international agreements), take into account the interests of indigenous peoples and ensure that representatives of those peoples are accorded the opportunity to participate fully in the conduct of such affairs;

* recognise that indigenous peoples, as a survival strategy, frequently occupy or move between areas and enjoy interests in more than one jurisdiction, and should do their utmost to facilitate traditional movement and, when carrying out any activities which may affect such areas or interests which lie within another jurisdiction, to consult with representatives of indigenous peoples on how adverse effects may be avoided or minimised;

* manage resources shared between indigenous peoples and others as a single unit, giving due weight to the importance to those indigenous peoples as defined by their cultures;

* establish and maintain national parks and related reserves only after purposeful negotiations with and agreement of affected indigenous peoples whose cultural aspirations, objectives, and livelihoods are sustained and whose future opportunities are retained. In this respect indigenous

peoples should not be disrupted or relocated without their full understanding and agreement.

(VII) MANAGING COMMON PROPERTY RESOURCES

Certain natural resources, for instance pasture lands, forests, soils, fisheries, wildlife and irrigation waters, are considered to be common-property (or communal) resources when their use rights are controlled by an identifiable group and are not privately owned or managed by government. Effective institutional arrangements to manage common property resources include interdependence of members, joint decision making, and formal or informal rules concerning who may use or be excluded from the resource.

Sustainable use of common-property resources requires an understanding of the historical and cultural context, and the ecological and physical nature of these resources, as well as the dynamic nature of associated common-property institutions. Many common-property institutions have a valuable role but are overlooked or underutilised in the development process.

Recommendations

Governments and others preparing strategies for the sustainable development of natural resources should:

1. include systematic analysis of resources and any existing or potential institutions to determine whether the resources are or could be managed as common property.

2. strengthen existing institutions involved in planning and implementing development goals affecting common-property resources.

3. support decision-making by communities of common-property resource users and promote and support interdisciplinary research to better understand existing common-property resource institutions and the kinds of local, national, and international measures that would increase their effectiveness.

(VIII) ENVIRONMENTAL REHABILITATION IN AFRICA[1]

Marginal and semi-arid lands in general, and the Sahelian zone in particular, have in recent years undergone a phase of progressive deterioration in their capacity to sustain life. Similar deterioration has occurred in parts of other developing regions. Despite the substantial volume of recent studies and analyses, the complex, inter-related causes of the decline remain poorly understood, while the costly efforts to halt it have thus far remained largely unsuccessful. By contrast small local initiatives and a diverse array of spontaneous responses have frequently been well adapted to the circumstances.

Recommendations

It is therefore recommended that:

1. The international aid community and governments of affected countries should together devote more resources to understanding the real causes of this degradation, as an essential foundation for effective action.

2. All those concerned should examine the major processes responsible for degradation and their links to economic, social (including popula-

1. Africa was considered as a special case, given the desperate situation in the Sahel. Many of the proposals could be applied to degraded ecosystems elsewhere.

tion), relief and development policies, ranging from local issues to global ones (particularly international terms of trade, debt and national price policies), and should ensure that rehabilitation programmes are designed to include preventative measures aimed at halting these processes.

3. All involved should use local and traditional knowledge as a basis for rehabilitation measures and should explore new initiatives and techniques in partnership with those directly affected.

4. Governments, aid agencies and NGOs should recognise the pivotal role of women, whose knowledge sustains the livelihood of their communities, and should ensure their participation at all levels of the rehabilitation process.

5. Governments and aid agencies should make a concerted effort greatly to increase funding of applied interdisciplinary research, particularly in relation to dryland farming, pastoral systems and agroforestry, and the realisation of the actual and potential socio-economic value of wild plant and animal populations.

6. Aid agencies and national governments should assist local communities in the rehabilitation of degraded areas through the implementation of integrated eco-development programmes at the community level as recommended for instance in the IUCN Sahel Action Plan.

(IX) POPULATION AND HUMAN SETTLEMENTS

Recommendations

Within the effort to address the entire character and course of development:

1. Governments should adopt, within national conservation and/or development strategies, policies

* to bring human populations into sustainable balance with their biological and physical life support systems as an important means of improving the quality of life and maintaining or restoring human dignity and self-respect; and

* to prevent wastefulness that stems from inefficiency, maldistribution and over-consumption of resources.

2. Conservation, development and population agencies should work more closely together at national and regional levels, and develop strategies which will ensure sustainable development. Local communities should be the key participants in the formulation of these strategies.

(X) WOMEN, ENVIRONMENT AND SUSTAINABLE DEVELOPMENT

The specific place of women in promoting sustainable development is increasingly appreciated. However, there is still an overall lack of serious consideration of the role of women, their contribution and potential in relation to environment and development, and there has been a failure to allocate sufficient resources to ensure their inclusion and integration.

Recommendations

1. Environmental organisations including IUCN, development agencies, and donors should actively develop, support and implement policies, strategies and plans of action which will integrate women fully into sustainable develop-

ment and natural resources conservation and management, both as part of their own process and of the full and proper implementation of the World Conservation Strategy and other conservation strategies.

2. IUCN and other international bodies should allocate sufficient resources to support assessments of the impacts on women of development and conservation projects.

(XI) ENVIRONMENTAL PLANNING AND MANAGEMENT

The goal of sustainable development is to meet human needs, including health, which is defined as a complete state of physical, social, mental and environmental well-being. Environmental planning and management is the key process both for implementing the World Conservation Strategy and for achieving these goals. The process is constrained because:

1. criteria for measuring the quality of life are inadequate;

2. information basic to the integration of environmental and human health considerations with development planning is inadequate;

3. environmental and health planning are not linked fully enough to the decision-making process;

4. environmental planning does not exist as a separate activity in many developing countries: it is consequently essential to integrate it into development plans.

Recommendation

It is recommended that IUCN, together with governments and development or-

ganisations ensure that measurable goals of and evaluative criteria for sustainable development be defined and applied. Criteria should include environmental sustainability and optimum health as measured in terms of physical, mental, social and environmental well-being. Environmental planning should be incorporated within development plans.

3 : INTERNATIONAL COOPERATION IN SUSTAINABLE DEVELOPMENT

(I) SUSTAINABLE DEVELOPMENT IN THE NORTHERN CIRCUMPOLAR REGION

Indigenous people of the northern circumpolar region are becoming increasingly apprehensive about the future. Reports of environmental degradation, examples of massive development projects at the expense of wildlife habitats, increased military activities in the North and destruction of traditional markets for products from hunters' and trappers' communities all threaten a lifestyle of harmony between people and nature, as well as the future sustainability of natural resources of the circumpolar north.

Recommendations

1. Responsible governments should pay due heed to the voice of the indigenous northern circumpolar inhabitants and ensure that they are allotted their share of decision-making processes concerning their homelands.

2. The conservation and development policies of the northern circumpolar region should be designed, from the

outset, in cooperation with the local indigenous population and communities,
whose physical survival depends on
conservation of the natural resources.

3. Due notice should be taken by the
responsible governments of the serious
damage to communities whose livelihoods depend on the sustainable use of
renewable resources being caused by
the anti-wildlife harvest movement.

4. A comprehensive northern circumpolar conservation strategy should be
developed and implemented, with the
involvement of governments, northern
indigenous peoples and resource users.

(II) DEVELOPMENT AND CONSERVATION ASSISTANCE

Development assistance can play an
important role in achieving the goals of
the World Conservation Strategy in
developing countries by enabling
recipient nations to alleviate poverty
and to protect the national resources on
which sustainable development depends. The main goal of development
assistance should be to enable people
in recipient countries to meet their own
needs in a sustainable manner. Further
changes in modalities and in donor-
recipient relations are essential if
development assistance is to play this
constructive role.

Recommendations

1. Development assistance agencies
should develop a dialogue with national governments and other organisations,
in order to support development which:

* builds on and reinforces existing cultural, social and economic institutions;

* maintains the productivity of the na-

tional resource base;

* is based upon an open, participatory
  decision-making process;

* encourages integrated, flexible and
  adaptive approaches to development;

* recognises the special role of women.

2. Development assistance agencies
should:

* employ adequate staff qualified in
  environmental and social sciences;

* require environmental and social assessments of proposed actions, including the consideration of alternatives;

* ensure that project time frames and
  economic criteria are appropriate to
  sustainability;

* whenever possible, support local institutions (village councils and
  NGOs);

* coordinate their efforts more effectively.

3. Governments of donor and recipient
nations should use all available information to identify and implement actions which promote sustainable
development. Governments and international aid agencies should also give
urgent attention to proposals for the establishment of a World Conservation
Bank.

(III) INTERNATIONAL COOPERATION FOR SUSTAINABLE DEVELOPMENT

Cooperation regarding trans-boundary
environmental issues, including monitoring, assessment, and the prevention
and mediation of disputes is crucial because of the complexity and regional or

even global dimensions of many of the underlying problems.

Recommendation

National governments and other enabling and funding institutions are urged to strengthen the appropriate inter-governmental agencies and non-governmental organisations in their international environmental monitoring, assessing, and mediating functions.

(IV) PEACE, SECURITY AND SUSTAINABLE DEVELOPMENT

The moral imperatives of conservation and militarisation are antithetical. The arms race and other military activities are hazardous to the environment and detrimental to socio-economic development. Peaceful cooperation and disarmament are prerequisites for effective environmental protection and sustainable development.

Recommendations

1. IUCN should prepare a supplement to the World Conservation Strategy on Peace, Security and Sustainable Development that explores these problems and provides appropriate policy recommendations;

2. The United Nations and Governments should intensify their efforts to reverse the present wasteful and counter-productive spiral of military expenditures with the aim of transferring a part of the resources thus released to programmes of conservation for sustainable development.

4 : PREPARATION OF STRATEGIES

(I) NATIONAL AND SUB-NATIONAL CONSERVATION STRATEGIES

National and Sub-national Conservation Strategies are the most effective means of translating the World Conservation Strategy into national and local actions and of building consensus on sustainable development. Considerable experience in initiating and preparing these strategies has been accumulated over the past six years in some 30 countries. However, the process has proved long and difficult.

Recommendations

It is recommended that:

1. IUCN and its member governments and NGOs, UNEP, WWF, FAO, Unesco, and other organisations should increase their efforts to initiate national, sub-national and local conservation strategies and support their promotion, preparation, linkage and implementation. The value of national strategies for federal States as a whole should be stressed.

2. IUCN is asked to supplement its framework document of National Conservation Strategies with additional guidelines on preparing national and sub-national conservation strategies to transfer recent experience for the benefit of those who prepare such strategies in future.

3. A network should be established to facilitate exchange of plans and experience regarding national and sub-national conservation strategies.

4. Governments should commit appropriate efforts and resources to implement national conservation strategies once these have been approved.

5. International organisations should consider the value of regional strategies, bringing together common national concerns, as has been done in Europe by the ECE and the Council of Europe.

(II) LOCAL CONSERVATION STRATEGIES

Local strategies for sustainable development are an effective means of ensuring that the basic needs of local people are met, and the quality of their lives improved through access to land, the provision of food, shelter, health services, education and employment. However the knowledge and interests of the people who actually utilise local natural resources are often ignored. Consequently, the goals and potential benefits of these strategies are not fully realised. To avoid this, it is necessary that local peoples and communities participate in the planning, implementation and evaluation process through active horizontal and vertical linkages and good communication.

Recommendations

Governments and non-governmental organisations are therefore urged to:

1. ensure the participation of local people in designing and implementing local strategies for sustainable development;

2. Strengthen local community organisations that will allow the people themselves to identify the needs and potentials of the community;

3. Provide the facilities and resource centres for information and technology gathered from local, national and international sources;

4. Develop pilot eco-development projects that will act as experimental field and educational centres for project leaders or local entrepreneurs.

(III) TECHNOLOGIES FOR SUSTAINABLE DEVELOPMENT

Recommendation

Recognising the relevance of technology to sustainable development, the sponsors of the World Conservation Strategy should elaborate and integrate a series of strategy folios on technologies for sustainable development to cover such topics as:

* sustainable rural land use;

* income-generating technologies;

* non-motorised transportation; and

* criteria for technologies for sustainable development.

(IV) RESOURCE MANAGEMENT

In many countries, improper resource allocation and management contribute dramatically to the lack of sustainability in the rural sector. Lack of access to land, water, credit, markets and technology is a further impediment. Land tenure problems need to be resolved in many such situations before sustainability can be achieved.

Recommendation

IUCN should commission a study on the impact of land tenure on sustainable development as a means of raising awareness and promoting solutions.

(V) INDIGENOUS PEOPLE AND SUSTAINABLE DEVELOPMENT

Recommendations

1. The sponsors of the World Conservation Strategy should support the preparation of a supplementary section on indigenous peoples and conservation as a guide to the development of national policies for sustainable development and international conventions and other agreements.

2. The sponsors of the World Conservation Strategy should endorse and support with resources an Indigenous Peoples' Conference on Conservation to be organised in concert with the World Council of Indigenous Peoples.

(VI) HUMAN SETTLEMENTS AND POPULATION

The desirable goal of development programmes is the achievement of equitable and sustainable development for an acceptable quality of life.

Uneven global and national development causes environmental pressures and degradation, maldistribution of populations and human settlements in relation to available resources, and problems like urban slums. This results in further deterioration of the environment. The present economic crisis has the tendency to exacerbate the problem with dire consequences for sustainable development and an acceptable quality of life. Solutions should take into account housing needs, education, employment, health care and family planning as well as the relationship with the non-urban environment.

Recommendations

1. IUCN should, in conjunction with UNEP, UNCHS and other appropriate international bodies, evaluate the socio-economic and environmental impacts of current patterns of physical, demographic and urban change and other changes in the spatial distribution and movement of populations and should develop a supplement for the World Conservation Strategy on Human Settlements and Sustainable Development.

2. The sponsors of the World Conservation Strategy should add a supplement on Population and Conservation for Sustainable Development to the World Conservation Strategy, emphasising the need to bring populations into sustainable balance with their environment, while recognising the diversity of national and local circumstances and the right of all nations to design their own strategies for balancing human numbers and resources.

(VII) WOMEN, ENVIRONMENT AND SUSTAINABLE DEVELOPMENT

The specific role of women, and particularly indigenous women, in relation to environment and development is insufficiently recognised and supported, and is not considered in the World Conservation Strategy.

Recommendation

The sponsors of the World Conservation Strategy and other conservation strategies should promote a supplement on Women, Environment and Sustainable Development to be drafted by a special task force including members from the Caucus on Women's Integration held at the Ottawa Conference on Conservation and Development.

5 : A FORWARD LOOK

(I) SPREADING THE MESSAGE

While the World Conservation Strategy has been widely commended and endorsed by government and international and national organisations, its implementation has been severely hampered because there has not been a concerted effort to bring its principles of sustainable development to key decision-makers, communities and educational audiences.

The implementation of national conservation strategies may fill this gap. They will be more effective when educational training and awareness components are adequately integrated into their development. This will require a variety of media and approaches with the specific understanding of and sensitivity to the above-mentioned target groups.

National conservation strategies should take the following important factors into account:

* Education *per se* is part of the development process and environmental principles should be incor-

porated into the overall process of learning and not treated as a separate specialisation.

* Information related to conservation must be made more readily accessible and understandable to those who need it locally, nationally and regionally;

* Environmental education and training must become a dialectic process, helping people in different positions in society to develop sound practical and ethical principles on which to base sustainable development.

Recommendations

1. The international community should develop and implement a strategy to encourage and help establish structures and processes for environmental education consistent with the principles of the World Conservation Strategy at all educational levels.

2. Designers of national, regional and local conservation strategies should incorporate education and training components into those strategies.

3. Governments and international organisations should make a concerted effort to strengthen local, national and international mechanisms for implementing environmental education. Experience of effective programmes should be shared and new programmes should be developed through cooperation. Attention should also be devoted to staff training, the production of educational materials, the establishment of educational centres at the local community level, the initiation of training processes and the development of effective networks.

(II) EVALUATING SUSTAINABLE DEVELOPMENT

The process of development needs to be monitored. Systematic evaluation procedures are required to measure the extent to which the priorities, objectives and standards of sustainable development are being met, provide the basis for adjustment if they are not, and supply essential feedback to the continuing implementation process. Provision for input from those affected should be made, and a harmonious means of conflict resolution provided.

Recommendations

1. Governmental and other agencies should promote the development of criteria and indicators by which the progress of sustainable development can be monitored. The indicators should, for instance, include sensitive measurement of cause and effect and sustainability, and be understandable by non-specialists as well as specialists. They should be suitable for scientific or general use and comparison, technically convenient and practical to employ, and adjustable in time or place without sacrifice of scientific validity or continuity of evaluation.

2. Governments and other agencies funding and initiating sustainable development projects should ensure that responsibility and accountability are clearly defined.

BUILDING THE PYRAMID

Closing Address

Dr. Mostafa K. Tolba
Executive Director, UNEP
Nairobi, Kenya

It is now just over five years since the World Conservation Strategy was unveiled. In that time we've made incredible progress. It has been a source of deep satisfaction to its principal sponsors - IUCN, WWF and UNEP - to have seen the Strategy inspire so many national conservation strategies. As with the main document, the process of drawing up a national strategy provided an opportunity for key participants to reach consensus on national conservation and development priorities. This is exactly what we intended.

But while we have cause for satisfaction, we should not yet feel altogether satisfied. When set in relief against the indices of environmental destruction, deforestation, land degradation, species extinction, achievements of the Strategy seem small indeed. In developing countries, where nine out of ten people live, there are very few signs that much is being done to halt the dismemberment of natural resources.

So while we laud the achievements of the Strategy in particular, and of the growing acceptance of conservation in general, let us keep in mind the realities - the still insignificant role that conservation plays in economic and social development, and the widespread perception among the public at large that conservation means preservation of wild animal species and little else.

In UNEP's view this Conference had two main purposes: first to update the Strategy; and second, more importantly, to decide ways we can move its precepts into action. As to the first: consensus already exists on what needs to be done. Fine tuning is required.

I believe we are also in agreement that the issue of population needs to be addressed. UNEP's position is very clear and is laid out in our 1985 State of the Environment Report. We are wary of terms like "over-population." Increase in human numbers must be considered within the context of how people use their resources, how they relate to their environment and the state of development. Only in these terms do expressions like over-population become meaningful. We endorse voluntary family planning as part of an integrated response to balance human needs and the limits of nature with development.

It is opportune that in this, the International Year of Peace, the Strategy gives more attention to the need to control the arms race. And we need to introduce a new concept of security. One that recognises how the exhaustion of the global resource base sours relations between States and raises tensions within nations.

Two other issues that come most readily to mind are a new emphasis on the need for environmental education and to increase public awareness of threats to the environment. Wherever achievements have been made - in cleaning up the Mediterranean, in tackling toxic wastes, in responding to famine - they have always been against a background of widespread public concern. I sometimes wonder whether we have learned this lesson. Knocking on the doors of ministries and accessing colleagues in development assistance agencies is not enough.

This leads me to the second and main purpose of this meeting: deciding on ways in which we can move the Recommendations of the Strategy into action.

The World Conservation Strategy was intended to be the apex of a pyramid of regional, national and local initiatives. Although we can point to national conservation strategies and to local initiatives, such as the splendid example of the Province of Alberta in devising its own Strategy, we have scarcely begun to build the pyramid. So let us not spend too much time worrying about the tip but turn most of our attention to putting the buidling blocks into place.

We find ourselves in a peculiar situation. We see around us that the decision-making process is weighted heavily against sustainable development, emphasising instead the needless destruction - or should I say "capitalisation" of our resources. We see also a large and apparently powerful environmental lobby presenting those decision-makers with a World Conservation Strategy that offers an alternative to growth through destruction. But not enough is happening.

The need is radically to increase awareness, among the public and decision-makers alike, of the very real social and economic benefits to be gained from supporting conservation. Most attention should go to those sectors which do not lend themselves well to standard cost/benefit analysis. I have in mind, for example, desertification. The world is losing productive land to the desert at about six million hectares per year. A further 20 million hectares are being reduced annually to zero economic productivity. In 1980 UNEP put the bill for stopping desertification at $4.5 billion a year. Lost production has been valued at $26 billion: a benefit/cost ratio of more than five to one.

Why then do desertification and other forms of land abuse continue? Essentially because the neo-classical economic system is hostile to resource conservation. The world continues to measure utility only in terms of capital formation. For a minority it can make economic sense to destroy a forest whose value as water provider or gene bank is discounted, or to drain a wetland that may be a vital fish nursery. The concept of sustainability is alien to most accounting systems. In Canada, as in other countries, high interest rates combined with over-capitalised production encourage farmers to squeeze every last grain of production out of the soil this year...tomorrow be damned.

It is in no one's interest to let this continue. The farmer, the consumer, the banks and the government: all of these have a stake in making sure that next year's production is no less than this year's. But when a decision-maker, a developer or a financer is presented with a proposal, he finds himself looking at a balance sheet of financial costs and benefits.

What is the financial benefit of taking no more timber than can be replaced? What is the benefit now of keeping the soil at maximum productive output? What is the benefit of keeping fish species at such a level that each year's catch will match the last? And what is the advantage of preserving the "uneconomic" species of flora and fauna upon which commercially productive species ultimately rely? All too often, of course, there just is no convenient price tag that can be put on these things. And so they tend to be ignored. Economic performance can be measured in GNP; employment in terms of what percentage of the employable population is in the workforce, and so on. But with the environment it often just does not work that way. We are used to thinking of productivity in terms of output per person/per hour when we should be gauging it in terms of output per unit of resources used.

Like many of you, I am a scientist and not an economist. It seems to me that we need to pay more heed to making our case in a language and in terms that will be readily understandable to the financiers, the planners, the industrialists; the people who lie beyond our constituency who have still to be convinced that there are real benefits to be gained from investing in conservation. We need to to make the tools of environmental management more useful to civil engineers. I am referring to environmental impact assessments; they are frequently long-winded and couched in scientific jargon. Scant attention is paid to them when the decisions are made. Too often - as most of us know well - they are relegated to a footnote.

We have made some progress with development assistance agencies, and we are slowly moving with industry and the private fianancial institutions responsible for 75 percent of all economic development. Yet, I wonder how many copies of the World Conservation Strategy exist on Wall Street, in Tokyo's business district, in the City of London?

We could make a very small beginning by changing the language and presentation of the Strategy: the text is dense, the graphics may not be very inspiring. We need to show more imagination, more enterprise in getting the message across.

What use are plans and strategies drawn up - sometimes at inordinate expense - by expatriate experts when there is no cadre of trained and motivated nationals to move them into action? The vital need is to do much more to build up indigenous capacities, to devise plans adapted to local social and economic realities and to see to it that the plans are implemented. These are the building blocks of the pyramid.

UNEP has not done nearly enough to face the issues I have touched on today. We have sometimes spread ourselves too thin to have real impact.

We have worked too long within our own constituency. The amount of time we spend talking to each other has not been matched by concrete results.

As of late we in UNEP have been concentrating on a strategy of outreach, focusing on points of leverage. We have opened a dialogue with industry, with parliamentarians, with development NGOs, with youth, religious and womens' groups. The response we have been receiving has been very encouraging.

These are among the elements which can be used in a new effort to apply the Strategy and to better deploy our resources, contacts and know-how in the building of a new command structure for its proper use.

To move ahead we intend to give priority attention in UNEP's programme to the following:

* training and environmental education;

* a campaign addressed to industry and finance institutions in language and in terms meaningful to them;

* more emphasis on the measurable benefits of conservation-based development;

* creating greater conservation awareness among the public; and

* most importantly, to help governments translate their national conservation strategies into practical sustainable development activities and help them secure resources to implement them.

The need is to make conservation more credible to decision-makers as well as to the person in the street. In the years since the Strategy was published, the environment has come down to earth. We have a case to make that conservation will create jobs and bring sustained benefits to industry as much as to the small-holder in the Third World.

We are living in the midst of a communications revolution. It is providing us with the means to reach all sectors of society. The "global village" is already upon us and we must take advantage of the possibilities this offers. We have everything except time on our side.

The Government of Canada and many of our kind host nationals from other sectors are showing us with this extraordinary meeting that they have the capacity to systematically and intelligently engage the public in debating the country's environmental future. If this momentum continues, the results will come quickly; the message will spread, and there will be peace with nature. Thank you.

ANNEXES

CONFERENCE ON CONSERVATION AND DEVELOPMENT; IMPLEMENTING THE WORLD CONSERVATION STRATEGY

Note on the Workshops

The 18 concurrent Workshops developed to complement the Plenary Sessions of the Conference were central to its effectiveness. These Workshops were designed to draft recommendations and preliminary texts to extend and enhance the content of the World Conservation Strategy and to accelerate its implementation.

Whereas recommendations focus on policy, programmes and other actions required to better achieve the goals of the World Conservation Strategy, initial work of each Workshop was designed to produce WCS supplementary folios, to elaborate themes connected to the task of implementing the World Conservation Strategy or to expand upon themes not fully treated in the original Strategy.

The papers and workshop outputs emanating from the Conference indicate that participants have taken very seriously the general mandate to consider how the World Conservation Strategy can be made more meaningful. What seems to be taking place is a seminal shift in conceptualising how to manage change so that the benefits of development are sustainable. This process is taking place because conservationists are expanding their horizons to consider the impacts of socio-economic factors on the environment, and because economists, sociologists and planners are realising the true nature of environmental opportunities and constraints.

Committed participation enabled all to leave the Conference with a broader and more clearly-defined understanding of how to achieve sustainable development. At the same time the sum of their efforts, distilled and articulated through recommendations and draft statements supplementary to the World Conservation Strategy, can provide guidance to conservationists and developers throughout the world. The reports that follow summarise the major issues discussed in each Workshop.

CONFERENCE ON CONSERVATION AND DEVELOPMENT: IMPLEMENTING THE WORLD CONSERVATION STRATEGY

Workshop Summaries

WORKSHOP 1/2

NATIONAL AND SUB-NATIONAL CONSERVATION STRATEGIES

A great deal of invaluable experience in the initiation and preparation of national and sub-national conservation strategies has been accumulated since the World Conservation Strategy was launched. The aim of this Workshop was to share this experience for the benefit of current and future preparers of conservation strategies. Participants outlined the process of strategy development in their countries and the lessons they had learned. It is proposed that Workshop proceedings form the basis of guidelines on developing national and sub-national conservation strategies as a supplement to IUCN's *NCSs: A Framework for Sustainable Development*.

Initiating national and sub-national conservation strategies is proving to be long and difficult in almost all countries. Lack of government recognition of the need for a conservation strategy and lack of public support are common obstacles. Ways of overcoming them include: assessments (for example, State of the Environment reports, environmental audits); reviews, such as USAID's *Environmental Profiles*; IUCN's *Nature of ...* Series); demonstrations of environmental degradation to decision-makers (including field trips, overflights); public hearings and information distribution to the public. Discussion should be in terms of the development and future of the country.

Restatement of the aims of a national or sub-national conservation strategy highlighted the following:

* To achieve sustainable development through the integration of development and conservation;

* to identify and respond to intersectoral conflicts and compatibilities, and determine how to combine the conservation requirements of different sectors;

* to maintain the productive and self-renewing capacities of the nation's natural resources and environment;

* to secure the nation's natural and cultural heritage;

* to build a national consensus on sustainable development.

A national or sub-national conservation strategy is a dynamic process with four main features:

* preparation of the strategy document (consisting of analysis, policy formulation, and action identification);

* project development (demonstration projects);

* consensus building;

* monitoring, evaluation, and modification. The document should be technically accurate and precise, but the language should be as simple as possible.

The strategy should be prepared by that combination of government and non-governmental agencies most likely to produce results. Since it should become policy, government leadership is preferable and full participation essential. Since it should be supported by industry, resource users and the public, their participation is desirable (the form of participation depending on relations with government).

The Steering Committee is responsible for overall direction of the conservation strategy and for ensuring full participation of all sectors. It should be high-level and sectorally representative.

The Secretariat is responsible for organising the conservation strategy.

Each of the following instruments has been found essential in at least one con-servation strategy. No strategy has used all of them.

* **Sectoral and background papers**. A wide range is needed (from within and outside government). Obtain departmental commitment, but ensure that authors write as individuals not *ex officio*. Terms of reference should ensure analysis of issues and not repetition of *status quo*;

* **Natural resources data bank**. A data bank is needed to assemble the information required for the conservation strategy document and for implementing, monitoring and evaluating the strategy;

* **Public consultation programme**. Public consultation helps to shape the strategy by obtaining the public's views on natural resources and the environment, and, by shaping it, generates public support for its implementation. Major steps should be: needs assessment/perception surveys; public debate; formal consultation on draft documents; consultation when implementing and evaluating the conservation strategy;

* **Public information programme**. An information programme gives visibility to the conservation strategy, encourages public debate, and supports public consultation;

* **Workshops**. At least two workshops are needed: one to discuss the sectoral and background papers; the other to discuss the draft strategy document;

* **Programme of demonstration projects**. Pilot projects are needed to demonstrate key aspects of the strat-

egy, to raise interest, to establish momentum, and to respond to opportunities for implementation;

* **A flexible work plan** to orchestrate the instruments.

Interactions among sectors should be analysed with respect to each sector, in terms of activities (e.g. fishing) or of resources (e.g. water). The former is easier for each sector to interpret; the latter encourages resource-based thinking. Several hundred interactions might be identified. Analysis should concentrate on those interactions which are extremely negative or positive for development aims or for maintenance of the resource. The results of analysis should be translated into sectoral actions, some of which may require special coordination by a coordinating office. Other tools for integrating conservation and development include: planning (five-year development plan or equivalent; standards, guidelines and checklists; a natural resources development plan); an integrated extension service; education and information; legislation; and demonstration projects (preferably these should achieve all three components [objectives] of conservation and be within a field of major development concern in the country).

Indicators of progress are extremely important and should be identified while the conservation strategy is being prepared. Three levels of progress should be covered:

* project funding and action taken to implement the strategy;

* field results (in terms of the three components [objectives] of conservation); and

* socio-economic results. A timeframe should be decided for each level. A body should be designated to monitor, evaluate and report progress. Its report should be organised so that it can be directly compared with the conservation strategy.

It is desirable and possible for federal countries to have national conservation strategies (NCSs). The difficulties of getting federal/provincial (state) agreement should not be exaggerated. The NCS should be a national strategy and not be limited to matters under federal jurisdiction. However, it should be made clear that the jurisdictional *status quo* would not be questioned. Agreement should be reached between the States/provinces and federal government on the scope and purpose of the national conservation strategy, and the procedures for its formulation. Representatives of the States/provinces should be fully involved in the development of the national conservation strategy. The process of preparing the national strategy should be a public one. Preparation of sub-national conservation strategies (State/provincial, regional, local) should be encouraged.

WORKSHOP 3

LOCAL CONSERVATION STRATEGIES

Unbalanced population growth, ever-increasing needs and in some instances over-consuming behaviour have led to various kinds of ecosystem imbalances. Local communities or rural populations are often mentioned when questions are raised on crises of national debts, hunger or environment degradation. However in the process of planning global, national and regional strategies for conservation and development, people at the grass-roots level are often ignored and their potentials not realised.

To be successful, development efforts at the local level must include actions that ensure sustainability of resource utilisation, maintenance of life-support systems and preservation of genetic diversity. Ecodevelopment programmes should be congruent with local needs and action strategies as much as with national ones. They should attempt to utilise all available networks and institutions in policy decisions as well as programme designing, planning, implementing and evalution. This, in essence, means to practice decentralising.

People's participation through their conscious actions and authority over the natural resources upon which their own sustenance lies are prerequisities for such a development.

Local community organisations could play a significant complementary role in transformation action of ecosystems when they require an holistic approach in programme innovation free of bureaucratic complexities. However, local community organisations in many Third World countries have scarce financial and technical resources. In authoritarian societies they are even mistrusted as elitists or subversives. Both political and material supports should be provided to local/community organisations for efforts in serving the societies concerned.

Both foreign and national experts have problems related to their own background, experience, interests and mo-

tives. However, they do possess immense potential if directed appropriately for their tasks with effective training and orientation.

Experiences from both "North" and "South" can be of great value for everyone. Appropriate methods and means should be utilised to communicate their respective experience within such societies.

Horizontal and vertical linkages and communication are needed within international, national, regional and local organisations. Such actions should be reflected in pilot projects, resource and research centres and community actions.

Even six years after the publication of the World Conservation Strategy, this perspective it is still not widely known around the world. If the people at the grass-roots level are supposed to respond to it, it is natural to expect that it reaches them in a manner they can understand. The Local Conservation Strategy Workshop suggests that a strategy folio be prepared and disseminated.

WORKSHOP 4

REGIONAL CONSERVATION STRATEGIES: SUSTAINABLE DEVELOPMENT IN THE NORTHERN CIRCUMPOLAR REGION

This Workshop included northern aboriginal people, government officials, representatives of non-government organisations and the Ministers responsible for Renewable Resources in the Yukon and Northwest Territories of Canada. Major themes emerging included recognition of the rights and status of aboriginal peoples in the circumpolar north; the necessity for community-based decision making; the overall priority on renewable resource use as the major component of sustainable development in the region, and the need for a comprehensive northern circumpolar conservation strategy.

Workshop discussion centred on defining sustainable development in the northern circumpolar region and on methods and processes through which one could ensure ongoing sustainable development in northern communities.

This was judged to require some reference to culture, community, people, wildlife, the circumpolar environment, the extended future. It was also considered that any definition of sustainable development in the circumpolar north should incorporate the principles of balanced and flexible development; a mix of development and resource use options including that for non-renewable resource development; the impacts of development in one area on the environment and resources in another area.

The meaning of sustainable development for the Arctic community of Old Crow (Yukon), was outlined by an Old Crow native and elected legislative representative for the community. This provided a concrete example of the general theme of community-based sustainable development.

Community-based land use planning, integrated resource management, community education programmes, community participation on resource management boards, the decentralisation of management responsibilities to local governments, legislative change, international cooperation and recognition, and settlement of outstanding aboriginal land claims were seen to be essential mechanisms through which sustainable development is achievable in the circumpolar north.

Two main recommendations were advanced by Workshop participants concerning the development of a comprehensive regional circumpolar conservation strategy, and recognition of the rights of northern aboriginal peoples to pursue lifestyles based on traditional renewable resource harvesting.

WORKSHOP 5

SECTORAL STRATEGIES FOR SUSTAINABLE DEVELOPMENT

The primary issue discussed in this Workshop was whether the conventional orientation in the thinking of people and planners, as well as the obvious sectoral orientation of most industrial and production activity, is or can be compatible with the goals of sustainable development.

Initial efforts of Workshop participants were directed toward identifying the most important sectors: those with the greatest capacity to absorb sustainable strategies successfully. Discussions then focused on those sectors, taking into consideration the fact that expertise among Workshop participants was concentrated in agriculture, forestry, aquaculture, health and the industrial sector. It was recognised that successful inter-sectoral planning and promotion efforts had been achieved in the past. Greatest attention was given to the Tropical Forestry Action Plan.

While the panel concluded that the sectoral orientation of most production efforts is likely to continue almost indefinitely, sustainability of development can be achieved only by creating effective bridging efforts, focusing largely on education, planning, and access by the broad mass of citizens to natural and other resources. Three recommentations were submitted toward the achivement of that goal.

WORKSHOP 6

SUSTAINABLE USES OF ENERGY

(Note: During the Conference, this Workshop was merged with Workshop 18: TECHNOLOGIES FOR SUSTAINABLE DEVELOPMENT. Refer to Summary for Workshop 18.)

WORKSHOP 7

CONSERVATION STRATEGIES FOR BIOMES: MOUNTAINS, ISLANDS, WETLANDS, FORESTS

The major task of the Workshop was to consider whether biome-based strategies are valid and useful in the context of the World Conservation Strategy.

Several speakers were invited to make brief presentations as background elements for the Workshop. The assembly then split into four sub-groups (mountains, islands, wetlands, and tropical forests), which reported on their progress in joint sessions. The last session, concerning the following principles, was agreed to be viewed as terms of reference for the Workshop recommendation on "Conservation Strategies for Natural Operational Units:"

* "Biomes" are not the best appellation for the diverse collection of natural units, including both "biomes" *sensu stricto* (e.g. grasslands, tropical moist forests) and "non-biomes" (e.g. mountains, islands, wetlands). The term "Natural Operational Unit" appears better suited to those ecological, biogeographic entities that will serve as a framework for conservation and sustainable development.

* Conservation strategies for these natural operational units should identify the major ecological relationships, processes, potentialities, and vulnerabilities of each unit. They should provide a basis for applying lessons learned in one part of the world to a similar unit found elsewhere, provide a framework for interdisciplinary cooperation both within a country and between countries, stimulate comparative studies, and promote awareness of the common problems. Finally they should enable the priorities of conservation to be clearly identified and defended on scientific grounds, which transcend national frontiers.

Such strategies should serve as frameworks to provide a perspective for action at the local ecosystem level. Interconnections and specific differences between these units need to be considered as well, particularly in planning development projects which should take account of the movement of energy, materials and populations.

* Mountain regions have been recognised internationally as being subject to serious and diverse problems on a global scale. This is due in large

part to their extreme biophysical and socio-economic diversity and political fragmentation. Moreover, their environmental degradation is assumed to produce massive downstream impacts. Collectively they occupy about 20 percent of the world's terrestrial living space and provide the life-support base for about 10 percent of the world's population. Despite much mountain research and development effort, they lack a single focus which would include the identification of means to ensure community participation to satisfy basic needs.

* Islands are not a biome in the established sense, but they have distinctive environmental features and social constraints that arise in part from their situation. Many of their natural ecosystems are unique and include numerous endemic species with small populations, vulnerable to external impact. Their socioeconomic systems also commonly depend on a relatively narrow range of natural resources. The sustainable development of smaller, more isolated, independent islands and archipelagoes is particularly difficult, and needs to blend ecological and social understanding in a special way: the transfer of continental development models is often inappropriate. The needs of island systems were not adequately recognised in the World Conservation Strategy.

* Wetlands provide a wide range of natural functions, from groundwater recharge, to coastline protection and wildlife habitat. They are subject to a still greater range of human uses: food production, supply of water, fuelwood and timber, navigation/ transport, waste disposal, recreation and tourism. Yet despite increasing awareness of these many values, wetlands have received relatively little attention in previous efforts to implement the World Conservation Strategy. This has arisen partly because of the diversity of wetland habitats, floodplains, swamps, mangroves, and lakes, whose characteristics vary depending on climate, latitude and altitude; partly because of the lack of a truly integrated approach; and because, being common to all biomes but dominant in none, wetlands are not covered by a traditional biome approach to conservation.

Although these diverse habitats have been used sustainably for centuries by various human cultures, they are today rapidly being subject to capital intensive development, from aquaculture to intensive agriculture and urbanisation, often without paying attention to far-reaching hydrological and biophysical values.

In designing steps for implementation of the World Conservation Strategy it is therefore recommended that IUCN and its major conservation partners give sustained core support to wetlands as a top conservation priority.

* Progress has been made over the past decade in improving tropical forest management, and particularly in extending systems of protected areas. As a result more efforts have been made and more knowledge accumulated than is the case for the three preceeding Natural Operational Units. In particular, the Workshop strongly supports the Tropical Forest Action Plan as the most appropriate

framework for harmonising and strengthening efforts to develop forest lands in tropical countries.

WORKSHOP 8

CONSERVATION STRATEGIES FOR ISLANDS

(Note: This Workshop was subsumed into the preceding group on Conservation Strategies for Biomes: Mountains, Islands, Wetlands, Forests.)

WORKSHOP 9

INTERNATIONAL COOPERATION FOR SUSTAINABLE DEVELOPMENT AND PEACE

There is growing awareness within the international community of the inseparability of environmental and security issues.

This Workshop opened with an expanded definition of security and went on to suggest means for resolving environmental conflict without resort to arms. Discussions followed on approaches to reducing the environmental causes of conflict and to minimising environmental disruption by military activities, both in times of war and peace. The special urgency of avoiding nuclear war is stressed in closing with a recognition of the broader significance of international efforts toward achieving sustainable development.

Warfare diverts human, financial, and natural resources from socially and environmentally constructive ends to destructive ones. To resolve environmental conflict over resources without resort to arms:

* **within the bounds of a nation** depends upon rational and equitable systems of domestic governance and upon bureaucracies responsive to the needs of all sectors of society, including ethnic minorities and nomadic groups;

* **between nations within the bounds of one of them** is provided for in principle by the United Nations Charter. Although the principle of non-aggression is firmly established in international law, associated mechanisms of arbitration and enforcement, such as those embodied in the International Court of Justice and the Security Council, require strengthening;

* **multinationally** (i.e., shared by more than one nation) requires development, adoption, and acceptance of bilateral and multilateral agreements and associated legal instruments. These should be comprehensive bodies of law that provide for protection from pollution and over-exploitation, for equitable use, for verification of compliance, and for arbitration and enforcement;

* **beyond the limits of national jurisdiction** requires the recognition that such resources must be exploited both rationally from an environmental standpoint and equitably from a social standpoint. Achievement of this dual goal cannot occur without widespread adoption of comprehensive bodies of appropriate international law.

widespread adoption of comprehensive bodies of appropriate international law.

Conflict over resources would be minimised by ensuring that adequate resources are produced and distributed equitably to meet uneven needs for a productive and dignified life. Achievement of these goals will require domestic population policies suited to the conditions of each State, measures for pollution control, programmes to rebuild degraded resources, programmes leading to sustainable diversification of income generating activities, and so forth. Existing intergovernmental and especially non-governmental institutions must be strengthened in their role of enhancing cooperation in transboundary environmental issues and in mediating disputes that arise out of these issues. Among agencies that would deserve such reinforcement are UNEP, IUCN, the International Atomic Energy Agency, and the various intergovernmental bodies established to manage shared resources, such as the International Joint Commission.

To minimise environmental disruption from military activities by the many wars that are so tragically pursued, support should be given to a number of international instruments; especially the 1977 Environmental Modification Convention; the 1925 Geneva Protocol and the 1972 Bacteriological and Toxin Weapon Convention; the 1972 World Heritage Convention; the 1959 Antarctic Treaty; and the 1977 Geneva Conventions.

To reduce environmental disruption by the military sector in peacetime, testing and weapons development must be regulated with due regard to the environment, as must military manoeuvres and routine patrolling. Special attention must be give to systems depending on nuclear energy, whether for propulsion or for other purposes. The testing and development of weapons, especially of nuclear and other weapons of mass destruction must be regulated, with the ultimate objective of a comprehensive ban on all such anti-environmental activities.

Nuclear war would be so grotesquely anti-social and anti-environmental that there exists no conceivable justification for pursuing such an activity or for threatening to do so - and thus even for possessing the means to do so. It therefore becomes a matter of extreme social and environmental urgency for everyone to strive for worldwide, effective nuclear disarmament.

Reducing tension between neighboring nations, between opposing military alliances, and in the world as a whole would reduce the frequency of armed conflicts and the likelihood of nuclear holocaust. Progress in this area would help to achieve the goals of the World Conservation Strategy for sustainable development. Indeed, cooperation in the field of environmental conservation is crucial owing to the complexity and widespread dimensions of the many associated problems. The establishment and functioning of bilateral and regional agreements for environmental assessment and protection serve as valuable confidence-building measures. They thus contribute not only to en-

vironmental conservation, but also to
the goal of peace and security.

WORKSHOP 10

DEVELOPMENT AND CONSERVATION

This Workshop addressed how the $30
billion annual flow of official development assistance (multi- or bilateral) can
be better used to promote the goals of
the World Conservation Strategy.

The Workshop considered multilateral
and bilateral flows (excluding the environmental impact of private flows -
some $70 billion annually), under three
areas of concern. First was **style of
development**. Speakers recognised
that the style could not change due to
political, strategic or practical constraints. While challenges were recognised regarding aid/trade linkages, the
tendency to promote economic dependency through aid, and the polarisation
of those who benefit from aid flows,
the group agreed to assume that the
quality of aid could be beneficial given
reforms to the aid system. It was also
recognised that great strides had been
made in modifying aid flow toward sustainable development objectives and
that this position should be con-
solidated. Alternatives to the existing
aid process for conservation assistance
were restricted to a discussion of a
proposed "world conservation bank."
Debate followed on the style of
development assistance, leading to a
resolution.

The second area of concern was the **accountability of aid agencies** to both
donor and recipient publics. Various
findings of the aid process were ex-
posed for institutional reform under

this topic. Constraints to institutional
reform were fully discussed, including
for example, the secrecy of development planning documents, and staffing
problems with respect to environmental
expertise. A major focus of the discussion was the need for accountability in
aid flows. This allows for independent
analysis of the process, and for public
pressure to improve the incorporation
of sustainable development objectives.

Also in the discussion on institutional
reform was the overriding concern to
build up **local institutions** in the
development process. All possible
agents for change should be enlisted:
existing community systems, NGOs, research institutes, local governments.
Consistent with this approach, the
group considered that the economic
climate needed to ensure sustainable
development required a catalyst for collective action rather than intervention
by the central government.

The final area of concern was the position of the "South" in the aid process.
The Workshop was not balanced in
terms of donors and recipients in
presentations, but was nevertheless able
to draft a recommendation on the
donor/recipient relationship.

WORKSHOP 11

ETHICS, CULTURE AND SUSTAINABLE DEVELOPMENT

Each position presented at the Workshop may be understood according to
the issue which it considered to be of
central significance.

The first of these stressed ecological
wholeness as the primary concern. It
addressed the degradation of nature

which results either from a narrowed capacity to appreciate nature, or from a lack of feeling for being part of nature. The biotic community is of central concern, and values are to be derived from it. Richness and diversity are to be preserved in nature: its wildness and "freeness" can instruct humanity. Holders of this position were often critical of the group's orientation as being too anthropocentric.

Another position, the central issue of which was the connection between aesthetic values and the environment, stressed the role of education as well as the role of the creative arts, in creating an ecological ethic. Aesthetic values, for this position, are integral to the appreciation as well as the renewal of nature. A vivid example was given on how art can transform our relation to nature. The case in point demonstrated how a novel about the relation of a village people to its neighboring mountain was the spur for a campaign to save the wildness of that mountain.

A similar position concerned the relation of science to ethics. Several good papers were presented on this topic, generating much discussion. A great point of dispute among the group was how it should define science. Is it universalist or is it in some way always particular to a specific region? Another question concerned the relation of science to art and aesthetics. Are they interdependent or mutually exclusive? At the root was the question of whether a new environmental ethic should be based on scientific (and hence universalist) values, or on the kind of values generated by indigenous cultures.

This question is closely related to that of how firm a hold cultural traditions must have in framing a new environmental ethic. No one held out a primary place for traditional values. It was pointed out, and generally accepted by the group, that there is no guarantee that indigenous values will be any wiser than the values of a central bureaucracy. The example of the American West was signalled as a locale where only the imposition of government values and authority save the landscape from native rapaciousness.

The last position attempted to bind social justice and ecological wholeness together. There was a recurrent debate as to whether this can in fact be done, and whether it is meaningful. Introduction of social concerns into conservation groups was necessary to encourage, to the fullest extent, participation by people who are most affected. One paper asked the conservation movement to consider its role in fostering dependency among the indigenous peoples which it attempts to help. A vigorous debate ensued on the appropriateness of these concerns, with one group member providing a point of clarification: one side of the debate was concerned that the procedure for implementing environmental action itself be ethical, while the other side held that shifting focus to this question would move attention away from the central concern, which after all was conservation itself. This led to the decision to have not only a third recommendation but a fourth, in order to achieve a balance between social concerns and ecological concerns. The Rapporteur wrote an introductory statement to the four recommendations, attempting to make a case for the use of ethics by all conservationists. It describes a new global situation characterised on one side by a new voice for local autonomy in decision-making, and on the other by a narrowed sense of appreciation for nature, each situation invoking the use of ethics.

WORKSHOP 12

ECONOMICS OF SUSTAINABLE DEVELOPMENT

Workshop discussions were directed at two categories of issues relating to the economics of sustainable development. The first included such issues as how to improve existing economic methods and tools to better reflect sustainable development values; how to encourage greater use of existing economic analytic methods (which provide better information to decision-makers on the value and potential of natural resources); patterns of utilisation; and the consequences of resource depletion. The second category related to the transformation of conventional economic theory and practice so as to integrate sustainable development and ecological values. Such a transformation was considered essential in the longer-term if the global economic order is to overcome problems relating to debt, terms of trade and financial flows.

Conventional economic theory is primarily concerned with flows (e.g., revenues/expenditures, import/export), whereas conservation values require

the accounting of natural resource, human and cultural assets and the relationships among these assets. Workshop consensus was that economic indicators that measure and value assets such as natural resource stocks must be developed and integrated into decision-making processes. It was observed that depreciation/depletion accounts are commonly used for built assets but not for natural assets; the reasons for this probably have more to do with political power structures than deficiencies in techniques of economic analysis.

If such asset indicators were used, the economic performance of nations that are depleting resources for short-term advantage would likely be weaker. The problem of evaluating the benefits and costs of depleting one type of natural asset as opposed to another was noted. This problem is compounded when such evaluations must be made between a non-renewable and a renewable resource, rather than two renewable resources. It was observed that spatial, temporal and distributional factors are important in determining the values of natural resource assets.

Definitions of sustainability were proposed. The first was an "asset" definition, which states that there is sustainability if renewable resources and the bases for such resources are not declining. A second, wider definition was also proposed, which refers to human improvement, democratic processes and the vulnerability of economic systems to externalities (e.g., oil price fluctuarions). A third ecological definition incorporated the concepts of diversity and symbiosis, which are derived from the sciences of biology and ecology.

Workshop consensus held that much progress toward sustainable development objectives could be achieved if policies (e.g., subsidies) that were unsound in narrow economic, as well as environmental, terms were eliminated. The example of the Brazilian policy to provide tax relief to cattle ranchers who clear forests for their operations was discussed. Such a policy is unjustifiable as it not only encourages wholesale destruction of natural assets, but also deprives the State of tax revenue. Greater pressure must be exerted on multilateral and bilateral agencies, and nations, to ensure that conservation and sustainable development concerns are incorporated into development plans at the country and local level.

With respect to the second set of issues, Workshop participants agreed that sustainable development is imperilled by the current economic system. Other approaches to conventional economic theory and practice, such as co-evolutionary or ecological economics, must be encouraged at educational institutions or through conferences held by credible international organisations such as IUCN.

The debt crisis faced by numerous developing nations was considered to be a crucial impediment to sustainable development. Several options available to debtor nations were considered, including outright default and negotiated settlement in which lenders would "write-down" loans in exchange for guarantees that freed-up funds would be used for sustainable development projects.

WORKSHOP 13

INDIGENOUS PEOPLES AND SUSTAINABLE DEVELOPMENT

Adoption of an indigenous philosophy relating to nature was discussed. Workshop participants felt that as a first measure there should be a clear statement of indigenous philosophy which would set forth the relationship of indigenous peoples to the earth and would serve as the guiding statement for all other actions.

A definition of "indigenous" peoples followed. The term "indigenous" also refers to "tribal," "traditional" and "aboriginal" peoples, which terms may be used interchangably. The English language or any other language used by colonisers is usually loaded with negative connotations when applied to the first peoples of a territory. Regions often have different interpretations and responses to a word, depending on the particular history of that region. However, a common understanding and relationship to the earth produces many common values and ways of relating to nature among indigenous peoples. Nevertheless, an unsatisfactory feeling remained toward the term "indigenous" peoples. This problem shall be further addressed in the preparation of a supplementary folio to the World Conservation Strategy.

The Workshop next considered possible means to incorporate indigenous peoples at all levels of development and conservation decisions which impact (frequently negatively) on indigenous peoples. Proposals to this end were:

* by incorporating indigenous peoples' roles directly into the World Conservation Strategy and other conservation initiatives, according due regard to the special role of indigenous women in the Strategy;

* by calling upon governments, NGOs, and all other institutions to recognise indigenous peoples' special relationship to nature;

* by assuring indigenous peoples a voice in the control and use of shared resources;

* by ensuring that national governments give appropriate consideration to the needs and desires of indigenous peoples whose territories would be affected by creating national parks and related reserves;

* in securing indigenous peoples' consultation and agreement in the establishment and maintenance of parks, requiring that indigenous peoples not be disrupted should they decide to remain in the park territory, nor be relocated without their agreement;

* through development of a conservation strategy by indigenous peoples based on indigenous philosophies and practices; and,

* by organising, together with the World Council of Indigenous Peoples, an Indigenous Peoples' Conference on Conservation with assistance of the principal parties to the World Conservation Strategy.

Indigenous peoples' basic right to self-determination, including their right to control the use of traditional territories, must be recognised and respected in the formulation of all conservation strategies and at all levels of planning.

Aloha 'Aina! (Love the Land!)

WORKSHOP 14

MANAGING COMMON PROPERTY RESOURCES

Property represents a secure claim on resources and property rights exist in a variety of forms worldwide. Increasingly, rights to resources are being nationalised or privatised. However, in certain situations natural resources are considered to be common or communal property, where use rights are controlled by an identifiable group of interdependent users.

Examples of resources that are frequently managed as common property include pasture lands, inshore fisheries, irrigation water, community forests, and wildlife. In some cases the common property management system has existed for centuries, evolving over time in response to changing resource pressures; in other cases the system is relatively new.

Common property management systems are characterised by interdependence of members with respect to the resource, joint decision-making, the existence of rules and conventions concerning how the resource should be used and clear definitions of who may use the resource and who may not. The essence of common property management systems is the willingness of individuals to use resources in ways that respect the rights of others in the interests of resource sustainability and the welfare of the group as a whole.

Well-functioning common property management systems provide assurances to users that the resource base will not be depleted, without giving up local control and without resort to privatisation. The fate of common property is not necessarily tragic, contrary to public opinion. Common property management systems have a valuable role to play in sustainable use of renewable resources, especially at the local level, provided they are understood in their historical, cultural, and ecological contexts.

Despite their appropriateness for sustainable local management of renewable resources, common property management arrangements are still poorly understood, especially by those who plan and implement development programmes and projects. The existence and value of common property management systems needs to be better understood. Such management systems must be identified and evaluated through research and analysis; where appropriate, their relevance to sustainable development must be recognised and legitimised; and their use as mechanisms for local management of resources must be promoted.

The establishment, or re-establishment, of local common property management systems will require the backing of governments and their willingness to support decision-making by communities of users to develop resource allocation processes and priorities of use considered equitable by the users. The international community can support this by encouraging innovation in institutional arrangements for sustainable management of renewable resources at local levels through research, experimentation and education.

WORKSHOP 15

ENVIRONMENTAL REHABILITATION

The Workshop discussed the causes of environmental degradation resulting from over-exploitation and abuses of environmental resources; the efforts undertaken to date by various organisations; their successes and failures; and opportunities for future improvements of such efforts.

Presentations were made on dryland degradation and rehabilitation, drought and related issues in social science research; biosphere reserves and their role in arid ecosystem studies; planning of range use on arid rangeland; and policies and implementation of environmental rehabilitation.

Environmental degradation can be a result of natural, economic, social, and cultural processes. In particular, it is caused by poor environmental management of resource use activities. It is therefore essential that before recommending rehabilitation of any ecosystem, assessments of these processes should be made in close collaboration with the people concerned.

Environmental rehabilitation is the effort to control, mitigate, and manage environmental degradation so that environmental resources will endure in a sustainable condition to improve the quality of life. Environmental resources include natural (ecosystem) resources, the man-made environment, and the social environment. Thus, environmental rehabilitation must serve the natural ecosystem, the man-made environment, and the people or community concerned.

There has been a tremendous range of responses to environmental degradation at international, national, and local levels. Despite the effectiveness of certain technical improvements and developments, there have also been failures and ineffective efforts.

There is a need for local groups and rural communities to be directly involved in and responsible for the management of their resources. It is also urgent to recognise the tradition of local communities in natural resource management. Local people have their own way of looking into the economic and non-economic cost-benefit practicing remedies to overcome environmental problems. There is also a need to introduce appropriate technologies that have the potential to improve rehabilitation efforts. These need to be developed through scientific, technical, and professional support to promote ecodevelopment in close collaboration with local communities, including local and national non-governmental organisations (NGOs). Therefore, the Workshop concluded that mutual learning processes are essential to ensure the success of environmental rehabilitation efforts.

WORKSHOP 16

POPULATION AND HUMAN SETTLEMENTS

After an introduction on the activities of IUCN's Population Task Force, participants outlined the following areas for consideration.

Population growth should not be regarded as a narrow sectoral issue, but as part of a broader concern, namely the relationship between sustainable development and implementation of national conservation strategies.

Population growth should be discussed in relation to:

* its impact on natural resources, and problems of reduced quality of life;

* carrying capacity of the biosphere and human numbers;

* community-based activities and the meeting of basic needs;

* the desirability of zero population growth;

* urbanisation and human settlements;

* the danger of generalisations on population concerns, and the importance of recognising regional differences;

* consideration of Third World attitudes toward population issues, and the dangers of interfering in country growth rates;

* problems associated with population distribution, lack of regard for

human dignity and self-respect, and variations (both nationally and regionally) in patterns of development;

* importance of education programmes, particularly the education of women.

In the discussions which followed, there were major disagreements between Workshop members on content of the proposed Strategy folio. The more important areas of disagreement concerned the apparent emphasis given to family planning at the expense of recognising deficiencies in development strategies and inequities in resource consumption; differences in opinion on the meaning of the term "population policy;" and fundamental disagreement on whether or not population growth *per se* was the cause of environmental degradation, food shortages, and associated socio-economic problems.

However, the Workshop reached unanimity on the two resolutions, which recognised the importance of stabilising human populations, and called for the production of two World Conservation Strategy supplementary folios, one addressing the problems of **human settlements**, and another on **population and conservation for sustainable development**.

The Workshop was unable to agree on an outline for the contents of the folio on population in the time available, and it was felt that more time was needed to discuss the extremely sensitive and complex issues involved in more detail before any recommendations could be forwarded.

The following areas were noted as topics for inclusion in the human settle-

ments folio supplement to the World Conservation Strategy:

* The process of urbanisation; metropolitan areas and the role of small and intermediate centres; population movements and their impact on the environment; social and economic impacts of urban change;

* housing and living conditions - the habitat of poverty and its impact on health (especially of children); income and jobs; decay in urban fabric; city pollution;

* disasters - floods, droughts and political changes;

* the growing gap between people's needs and governments' response; community participation - grassroots action; and

* rethinking the urban problem.

WORKSHOP 17

ENVIRONMENTAL PLANNING AND MANAGEMENT

The group examined a number of working definitions of environmental management as a new field of interdisciplinary and intersectoral action.

Agreement evolved along the following lines:

* That environmental planning and management is a synthesis of a process and value system. The World Conservation Strategy and national conservation strategies, as processes as well, should concern themselves on a priority basis with the identification of conflicts to be

resolved through development planning. At the international and national level, priority should be given to the synthesis, translation and dissemination of existing data and information concerning goods, services and hazards (rather than natural resources) which are related to proposed development projects, particularly those to be considered for international lending;

* that environmental planning should always be carried out within the broad context of environmental management, and vice-versa, that environmental management should be rooted in planning.

While the World Conservation Strategy has triggered a global re-assessment of environmental concerns, it has sometimes proved difficult to implement environmental planning and management in a manner which yields useful and usable benefits at all levels. In the area of environmental planning and management, the variability of natural or man-made ecosystems and world cultural diversity preclude the use of any one process to satisfy all needs. However, the goals of environmental planning and management are often poorly defined and little understood, as are the means for evaluating existing situations and proposed developments. These are constrained within the World Conservation Strategy by the limitations of the original definition.

To be implementable, environmental planning and management processes must consider environmental and human health perspectives of ecosystems as a goal, with sustainable development (including conservation) as a means. Development is understood to be a socio-cultural and ecological co-evolution, which requires the integration, evaluation, and monitoring of planning in an interdisciplinary and intersectoral manner.

In order to place these findings and recommendations in a broader perspective, it is suggested that environmental health provides the unifying theme, with an ecological definition of health offering a conceptual framework for action and for developing evaluative criteria for sustainable development according to the World Conservation Strategy. Such a definition is stated as: "Health is a complete state of physical, mental, social and environmental wellbeing and not merely the absence of illness, infirmity or ecological degradation."

WORKSHOP 18

TECHNOLOGIES FOR SUSTAINABLE DEVELOPMENT

This Workshop was aimed at defining strategies and promoting technology toward ends that are compatible with sustainable development. Conceptual issues and debates related to inappropriate and appropriate technologies, with discussion on efforts to introduce appropriate technologies in both industrialised and Third World countries. It was possible to gain understanding and reach conclusions about the main incentives and obstacles for such attempts, and therefore to determine clear policy implications, recommendations, and strategies (at both local and global levels) for future development and technology redirection appropriate to and compatible with aims of development that are ecologically, socially, and economically sustainable.

The discussions emphasised particular issues, concepts, and experiences of importance in participants' efforts to develop "appropriate technology;" problems encountered in implementing appropriate technology efforts; and the successes and benefits of such efforts with "lessons" from these situations.

Discussions of the issues mentioned below entailed controversies and differing viewpoints. These debates enriched the Workshop and enabled us to discern key issues and common perspectives.

There were differing views about whether issues and strategies for appropriate technology should be divided into two major "streams," with regard to "North" versus "South," developing versus developed countries, "high-tech" versus "low-tech," and urban versus rural technologies. We agreed that differences must be taken into account, but also that commonalities are shared in these areas and that drawing such stark dichotomies is not necessarily useful;

* "appropriateness" is relative; i.e. appropriate technology covers a range of scales and complexities, and must be suitable to the factors and conditions present in specific circumstances and environments;

* issues of appropriate technology also include those of technology transfer; problems can arise in transfers to the detriment of recipients;

* social, political, economic, and management dimensions are very important considerations in technology for sustainable development; these include issues of appropriateness, control of resources, equity and distribution questions, etc. Technological and design elements (i.e. engineering, efficiency, etc.) are also important;

* we must recognise limitations of appropriate technology in addressing deeper development problems;

* information access, commercialisation and marketing also constitute important dimensions;

* concepts of self-reliance, cooperation, and participation are agreed as priority "principles" in appropriate technology efforts. Using an integrated, holistic, systemic approach is a priority aspect;

* recognition and building-up of local indigenous capabilities and technologies is important in any discussion of appropriate technology;

* debate on whether "universal" priorities for appropriate technology efforts can be defined: most felt that universal priorities cannot be established which are applicable to all circumstances;

* appropriate technology is not "second class" technology; the appropriate technology approach emphasises high quality and can encourage development and growth;

* conservation and appropriate technology development can work together, and can and should work toward the goals of sustainable development.

In the discussions many dimensions were emphasised as problems to technology development and implementation of technologies. These included the following areas: lack of funds at local, national and regional levels; lack of policies to stimulate and promote "appropriate technologies;" lack of markets and commercialisation channels for such technology; generation/use of technologies that continue to generate negative effects; lack of information and knowledge about appropriate technologies; lack of technology transfer between regions, communities and nations; lack of pollution abatement and prevention technologies; poor management of wastes; dominance of inappropriate transportation systems (as examples); lack of appreciation and recognition of local knowledge and indigenous techniques, and the displacement of such technologies and knowledge; presence of deeper social, economic and political problems which aggravate technology problems - including inequitable land distribution, lack of control of resources by local people, migration, repression, illiteracy, and the like; lack of participation by local people in developing technologies (including inadequate recognition of and participation of women).

Also discussed were successes and priority dimensions which are helpful in working toward the goals of sustainable technological development.

WORKSHOP 19

SPREADING THE MESSAGE

Participants agreed early on that there was no single message to spread. There is a need at many levels to inform people about environmental concerns in language they can understand so they might learn to ask the right questions and to seek the right solu-

tions. Environmental education is clearly a key element in this process.

A number of case studies were presented under categories of Decision-makers, Youth, Rural Communities and Networking.

Although much has been achieved since the launch of the World Conservation Strategy in 1980, especially in the emergence of innovative programmes at local, regional and national levels, a great deal of work remains to be done. In particular, the underlying message in the World Conservation Strategy simply has not yet permeated those places where it can do the most good. This is particularly true of certain audiences: decision-makers - especially those in the business and industrial communities; and world youth - tomorrow's decision-makers.

Three central criticisms were raised in the course of the discussions:

* that too little emphasis has been placed on Environmental Education in the national conservation strategy process;

* that more could be done to disseminate information about the increasing number of successful environmental education projects frequently undertaken locally; and

* that the whole process of environmental learning and awareness should begin with environmentalists themselves.

There is no time to be lost in rectifying the deficiencies in implementing the World Conservation Strategy. The group considered that future action should focus on the broad areas of "Institutions" and "Information," and should bring about results at the local, regional, national and international levels, as well as among environmentalists. The international conservation community needs to focus its efforts much more clearly on getting the World Conservation Strategy message across; national authorities need to pay more attention to environmental education; and local, regional and national conservation groups need assistance in better reaching local communities. But these efforts are unlikely to be successful unless environmentalists can first develop better skills in reaching their audience.

WORKSHOP 20

EVALUATING SUSTAINABLE DEVELOPMENT

Sustainability of development depends on strategies and actions that can help to realise the potential of natural, human, and other resources in ways that maintain and enhance human well-being indefinitely while preserving genetic diversity, essential ecological processes and life support systems. Governmental and other agencies responsible for planning and management at all levels should institute systematic evaluation procedures for sustainability within a defined framework.

Evaluation should ensure that the priorities, objectives and standards of sustainability are being met, provide the basis for appropriate adjustment if they are not, and should supply essential feedback to key stages in the continuing planning and evaluation process. Assignment of responsibility and accountability to financing and initiating agencies, including the internation-

al development agencies (for both planned and in-place projects) should be included. Provision for input from those affected should be made, and a means of conflict resolution provided.

The problems of evaluating the sustainability of development were examined using case histories. From such examinations, several guiding principles for the evaluation of sustainability were derived. These principles serve as a guide to actions and behaviour in resource use and other human activities. Several criteria for evaluating the sustainability of development were also identified, including:

* ability to measure sustainability;

* measurement(s) sensitivity of cause-effect relations;

* specificity;

* understandable by non-specialists as well as specialists;

* useful in setting and/or adjusting policies;

* suitable for scientific or general use and comparison;

* technically convenient and practical to employ; and

* transferable in time or place without sacrifice of scientific validity or continuity of evaluation.

Some basic methods for evaluating (1) utilised renewable and non-renewable resources and their associated ecosystems, (2) unutilised ecosystems, and (3) life-support systems of air, water and soil are sufficiently developed to be used in the evaluation of sustainability, although "sustainability" *per se* is not always included in those present evaluations. Nor are services and hazards well accounted for. The methods used in social and economic assessments seldom consider "sustainability," and thus need to be developed. Integrated planning and management are necessary, which requires the development of methods for integrated evaluation of sustainability.

Evaluation methods rely on the use of indicators; that is, variables (assessment parameters) that provide information about something that may be continually changing. They need to encompass cause-effect-response linkages. Information provided by indicators is used to determine whether pre-defined standards of sustainability are being met, or whether at least the trends over space and time are favourable. Efforts should be directed toward defining small sets of indicators for use in evaluation. These should be supported by more extensive checklists and other evaluation information.

Evaluations of sustainability need to be done within a framework that ensures a uniform approach and continuing feedback. The skeleton of such a framework can be summarised as follows:

PHASE	ACTION
Government or lead agency strategic policy	Government or lead agency specifies that all present and planned development is to be sustainable, using information on the resource base, development potential, and human needs.
General planning	Government of lead agency specifies the particular aims and constraints to be met in plans. Alternative plans are assessed using the same standards of sustainability as above.
Intermediate level (government/agency) strategic and general planning	Similar activities undertaken by intermediate level governments or agencies on a regional or local basis if necessary.
Project design and evaluation	"Classical" resource and environmental evaluation is undertaken using integrated evaluation techniques, indicators that measure sustainability are specified, monitoring is undertaken, and projects and programmes are adjusted using monitoring results on a continuing basis.

Input from all potentially interested and/or affected parties throughout this process is assumed, and a mechanism for conflict resolution is essential.

We strongly recommend that the capability to evaluate the sustainability of existing and planned projects and programmes be developed through further in-depth investigations, workshops, etc., with the ultimate objective of developing guidelines and/or a manual for the evolution of sustainability.

CAUCUS ON WOMEN'S INTEGRATION

On 3 June 1986, during the course of Workshop Sessions, a Caucus on Women's Integration in Environmental Development gathered 80 women and men participants. The Caucus opened with an introduction of the very close relationship between women and environment/development planning activities, and the need to recognise their centrality to local resource management.

Related initiatives to further women's participation in these activities were described, for example the Environment Liaison Centre (ELC) workshops during the NGO Forum '85 (Women's Conference) in Nairobi; the network WorldWIDE (World Women in Defense of the Environment); UNEP's Committee of Women on Sustainable Development; and "Women and Environment in Forward Looking Strategies to the Year 2000" (the final document of the Women's Decade).

A proposal was introduced to draft a Supplement to the World Conservation Strategy on "Women, Environment and Sustainable Development." A draft synopsis was distributed for comments, ideas and suggestions. Everyone was invited to participate actively in the WESD project, through the sharing of experiences and contributing to the resource book to be published in 1987. Several participants presented their experiences and ideas on the project.

Out of this Caucus, a recommendation was put forward to the Final Plenary Session, concerning the drafting of a WCS supplement by a special task force including members from the Caucus.

CONFERENCE ON CONSERVATION AND DEVELOPMENT; IMPLEMENTING THE WORLD CONSERVATION STRATEGY

Author Biographies

Mr. Syed Babar Ali
President
WWF, Pakistan
Packages Ltd.
P.O. Amer Sidihu
Lahore 40, Pakistan

Mr. Syed Babar Ali, a businessman and conservationist in Pakistan, is Chairman of the WWF International Council, and President of WWF-Pakistan. He has also served as Regional Councillor for the International Union for Conservation of Nature and Natural Resources.

Ms. Margarita de Botero
President
Colegio de Villa de Leyva
Villa de Leyva, Colombia

Ms. de Botero has played prominent roles at the international level on environmental matters, and is presently a member of the World Commission on Environment and Development. At the time of the Conference, she was Director General of the Colombian Natural Resources Institution, INDERENA.

Mr. Geoffrey F. Bruce
Vice President, CIDA
Business Cooperation Branch
Hull, Quebec, Canada

Before taking up his current position, Mr. Bruce was Senior Policy Adviser for the Canadian International Development Agency (CIDA). Prior to joining that agency, he served as Canadian High Commissioner to Kenya for 12 years. Mr. Bruce was also Deputy Head of the Canadian Mission to the United Nations, and Secretary General of the Canadian Delegation to the Stockholm Conference on the Environment in 1972.

Mr. Jacques Bugnicourt
Director
ENDA
Boite Postale 3370
Dakar, Senegal

Mr. Bugnicourt was one of the founders of the ENDA Programme in Dakar (Environnement/Développement Afrique), Senegal and has extensive experience throughout Africa in education and training for sustainable development.

Dr. Françoise Burhenne-Guilmin
Head, Environmental Law Centre
International Union for Conservation
of Nature and Natural Resources
Adenauerallee 214
D-5300 Bonn 1
Federal Republic of Germany

Dr. Burhenne-Guilmin is a graduate of
the Université Libre de Bruxelles. She
is the Head of the IUCN Environmental Law Centre and a Regional Governor of the International Council of Environmental Law.

Ms. Margaret Catley-Carlson
President
Canadian International Development
Agency (CIDA)
200 Promenade du Portage
Hull, Québec
Canada K1A 0G4

Ms. Catley-Carlson has held the rank
of Assistant Secretary General of the
United Nations as Deputy Executive
Director of Operations for UNICEF.

The Hon. Ms. Victoria Chitepo
Minister of Natural Resources and
Tourism
Private Bag 7753
Harare, Zimbabwe

Ms. Chitepo is a biologist by profession and has been involved in teaching
conservation and environment at the
high school level. As Minister of
Natural Resources and tourism, she is
in the process of producing a national
conservation strategy for her country.
Ms. Chitepo currently serves on the
UNEP Committee of Senior Women
Advisers on Sustainable Development

and is the Chairperson of the IUCN
Working Group on Women and Sustainable Development.

**HRH The Prince Philip, Duke of
Edinburgh**
President, WWF International
Buckingham Palace
London SW1, United Kingdom

Since 1962, Prince Philip has visited
forty countries on behalf of WWF. He
became President of WWF International in 1981. During his visits he helps
local groups to raise funds, discusses
conservation problems with government officials and observes WWF
projects at first hand. In the United
Kingdom, as a matter of course, he
delivers lectures, gives interviews and
speaks to visiting heads of state about
conservation issues.

Dr. Jimoh Omo Fadaka
Chairman
African NGOs Environment
Network (ANEN)
Environment Liaison Centre
Post Office Box 72461
Nairobi, Kenya

Dr. Fadaka is a graduate of the London School of Economics and has extensive experience in the field of ecodevelopment and communications in
the African context. He was formerly
Senior Assistant Secretary in the Ministry of Economic Planning in Lagos and
has worked in numerous capacities
with the UN Environment Programme.
He is currently a member of the Board
of Directors of the Environment
Liaison Centre and Chairman of the
African NGOs Environment Network
in Nairobi.

Dr. M. Taghi Farvar

IUCN Senior Adviser on Sustainable
Development
Avenue du Mont-Blanc
1196 Gland, Switzerland

Dr. Farvar was formerly Director
General of Human and Environmental
Affairs in the Iranian Government and
Vice-Rector of Bu-Ali Sina University
in Iran. As a representative of his
country to UNEP's Governing Council,
he helped shape its programme when it
was being set up. He has served as
Senior Advisor on Ecodevelopment to
the UN Environment Programme, and
in Central and South America and
Africa. With extensive work in ecodevelopment theory and practice, he is
currently Senior Adviser on Sustainable Development for IUCN.

Mr. Malcolm J. Forster

Commission on Environmental Policy,
Law and Administration
International Union for Conservation
of Nature and Natural Resources
Adenauerallee 214
D-5300 Bonn 1, F.R.G.

Mr. Forster is a graduate of the University of Southampton, where he is Director of the Centre for Energy and
Natural Resources Law and a Member
of the Maritime Law Institute. He is
currently serving as Counsel to the
IUCN Commission on Environmental
Policy, Law and Administration.

Dr. José I.D.R. Furtado

Science Policy Advisor
Commonwealth Secretariat
Marlborough House, Pall Mall
London SW1 5HX, United Kingdom

Dr. Furtado is Science Policy Advisor
for the Commonwealth Secretariat. He
helped establish the Ecology Degree
Programme at the University of Malaya
where he has served as Professor of
Zoology. Dr. Furtado has published
and edited extensively in tropical ecology and is currently Chairman of the
IUCN Commission on Ecology.

Dr. Madhav Gadgil

Centre for Ecological Sciences
Indian Institute of Science
Bangalore, 560 012 India

Dr. Gadgil is a member of the Scientific Advisory Council to the Prime
Minister of India. His special interests
include common property management
systems and areas related to them.

Dr. Johan Galtung

Professor, Department of Politics
Princeton University
Princeton, New Jersey 08544, U.S.A.

Dr. Galtung, a Norwegian social scientist, is one of the founders of the Peace
Research Movement and has held the
chair of Peace and Conflict Research at
the University of Oslo. He is the
former Project Director for UNEP's
Universities Project for Goals, Processes and Indicators of Development, and
is currently a visiting professor in the
Department of Politics at Princeton
University.

Mr. Jeffrey Gritzner

National Research Council
National Academy of Sciences
2101 Constitution Avenue
Washington, D.C., U.S.A.

Mr. Gritzner is currently Senior Staff
Officer with the US National Research
Council. He has been involved in the
West African Sahel for some 22 years.
His training is essentially in the fields

of geography, geology, anthropology and agronomy.

Mr. Charles de Haes
Director General, WWF International
Avenue du Mont-Blanc
1196 Gland, Switzerland

Mr. de Haes has held the post of Director General of WWF-International since 1977. Following a career in international business, he joined WWF in 1971 as Personal Assistant to its President, H.R.H. The Prince of the Netherlands, with whom he subsequently established "The 1001 - A Nature Trust Fund," a group of influential supporters contributing to a capital fund.

Mr. Mark Halle
Conservation for Development Centre
International Union for Conservation
of Nature and Natural Resources
Avenue du Mont-Blanc
CH-1196 Gland, Switzerland

Mr. Halle is Manager of IUCN's Conservation for Development Centre at the Union's Headquarters. Following postgraduate studies at the University of Cambridge, he worked for the Conference on Security and Cooperation in Europe. Thereafter Mr. Halle joined the United Nations Environment Programme in Geneva, where he became involved with work on the World Conservation Strategy. He joined the World Wildlife Fund in 1980, moving to his present position in 1983.

Dr. Luc Hoffmann
Vice President, WWF International
Avenue de Mont-Blanc
1196 Gland, Switzerland

Dr. Hoffmann is a biologist and a director of the Hoffmann La Roche chemical company. He has been intimately involved with nature conservation on an international level all of his adult life. He founded the Tour de Valat Biological Research Station in the Camargue, France, in 1954, for which he still serves as President. Dr Hoffmann has been involved with the IUCN since 1957, serving as Vice President from 1963 to 1966. He was a founder of WWF in 1961 and, except for mandatory periods off the Board, has been a Vice-President ever since.

Dr Martin Holdgate
Chief Scientist
UK Department of the Environment
2 Marsham Street
London SW1P 3EB, United Kingdom.

Dr Holdgate was the first Director of the Central Unit on Environmental Pollution, established to coordinate United Kingdom action in that field. Dr Holdgate led the UK delegation for the Preparatory Committee of the Stockholm Conference on the Human Environment. He has been a Vice-President of the UNEP Governing Council.

Professor Peter Jacobs
Faculté de l'Aménagement
Université de Montréal
Montréal, Québec
Canada H3T 1T2

Peter Jacobs is currently Professor of Landscape Architecture at the Universities of Montreal and Harvard, and is Chairman of the Commission on Environmental Planning of the International Union for Conservation of Nature and Natural Resources. He has published and lectured widely on aspects of culture, development and the environment.

Dr . Kenneth David Kaunda
President of Zambia
State House
Lusaka, Zambia.

As a prominent African leader, Dr Kaunda has propounded a philosophy of African humanism which puts man at the centre of a development programme to eliminate poverty, hunger and all forms of injustice and inequality. In that context, he has for many years been deeply concerned about problems of environmental degradation in Africa. He has also been one of the main African leaders in the struggle against apartheid in South Africa.

Professor Robert Keith
Faculty of Environmental Studies
University of Waterloo
Waterloo, Ontario, Canada

Professor Keith is currently affiliated with the Faculty of Environmental Studies at the University of Waterloo, with extensive experience in the Canadian north. He is the current Chairman of the Canadian Arctic Resources Committee.

Mr. A.G.Kerr
Deputy Secretary
Department of Arts, Heritage and Environment
Canberra, Australia

Before taking up his current post in 1985, Mr. Kerr served as Deputy Commonwealth Ombudsman. His other government experience covers business and consumer affairs, and service within the Department of the Prime Minister.

Dr. Ashok Khosla
President
Development Alternatives
22, Palam Marg
New Delhi 110057 India

Dr. Khosla, formerly Director of Infoterra, UNEP, is currently President of Development Alternatives, a non-profit corporation designed to implement conservation for development projects in India. He is also Deputy Chairman of the IUCN Commission of Environmental Planning.

Mr. Cyrille de Klemm
21 Rue de Dantzig
75105 Paris, France

Mr. de Klemm is a graduate of the Universities of Aix-en-Provence and Paris. He has served as a consultant to numerous international organisations, including Unesco, the Council of Europe and IUCN, and lectures on environmental law at the University of Lyon. He is a member of the IUCN Commission on Environmental Planning as well as the Commission on Environmental Policy, Law and Administration.

Dr. Barbara Lausche
Commission on Environmental Policy, Law and Administration
International Union for Conservation of Nature and Natural Resources
Adenauerallee 214
D-5300 Bonn 1, F.R.G.

Dr. Lausche is an attorney and member of the senior staff, Public Policy Programme of WWF US. She has previously worked with the United States Congress Office of Technology Assessment, the International Institute for Environment and Development, the Natural Resources Defense Council and the US Environmental Protection Agency. She is a member of three IUCN Commissions.

Professor Enrique Leff
Instituto de Investigaciones Sociales
Universidad Nacional Autonoma de Mexico
Torre II de Humanidades
Cuidad Universitaria
Mexico 20, D.F.

Professor Leff specialises in environment and development research, particularly theory, concepts and methods. He is the Coordinator of the Latin America Environmental Network, and has done significant research in the area of social movements in Mexico.

Professor Le Thac Can
Director
Research Institute for Higher Education
9 Hai Ba Trung
Hanoi, Vietnam

Professor Le Thac Can is currently Vice Chairman of the National Research Programme on Resources and Environment and Director of the Research Institute for Higher Education in Hanoi. He has published diverse studies on environmental management.

Dr. Walter Lusigi
Chief Technical Adviser, Unesco
MAB Kenya Arid Lands Research Station (KALRES)
P.O. Box 147
Marsabit, Kenya

Dr. Lusigi is a wildlife and range ecologist. He worked for UNDP as a habitat ecologist before being called to the Office of the President in Kenya to start the National Environment Secretariat, after the formation of UNEP in 1973. He is presently a Regional Councillor of IUCN, a member of the IUCN Bureau, and a member of IUCN's Commissions on Ecology and Environmental Planning. He also serves as Vice Chairman of the Commission on National Parks and Protected Areas. Dr. Lusigi chaired IUCN's Task Force on Environmental Rehabilitation in the Sahel.

The Hon. D.G. Lwanga
Minister of Environmental Protection
Kampala, Uganda

Dr. Lwanga is a specialist physician, trained in the United Kingdom. He is now Minister in the new Ministry of Environmental Protection in Uganda. He played a significant role in the liberation of Uganda in January, 1986 and is thus one of those responsible for the peace that exists today.

Professor Adolfo Mascarenhas
University of Dar-es-Salaam
P.O. Box 35097
Dar-es-Salaam, Tanzania

Professor Mascarenhas is Chairman of the National Scientific Research Council and of the Tanzania Forestry Research Institute. Formerly, he was the Director of the Bureau of Resource Assessment and Land Use Planning. Professor Mascarenhas has served as an Advisor to UNICEF and WHO on water and sanitation as part of primary health care.

Professor Ophelia Mascarenhas
Director of University Library Services
University of Dar-es-Salaam
P.O.Box 35097
Dar-es-Salaam, Tanzania

One of Ms. Mascarenhas' main interests has been monitoring the interplay of modern and traditional farming methods in Tanzania. The data from projects has been used in regional and social planning. Women and development in Tanzania is another of Ms. Mascarenhas' areas of study.

The Hon. Thomas M. McMillan
Minister of the Environment, Government of Canada
Ministry of the Environment
Terrace de la Chaudière
10 rue Wellington
Ottawa K1A0H3, Canada

Before taking up his post as Minister of the Environment in 1985, Mr McMillan had served as Canada's Minister of State for Tourism. He has also been Senior Research Associate of the National Commission on Canadian Studies and Executive Officer of the Ontario Human Rights Commission.

Mr. Jeffrey A. McNeely
Director
Programme and Policy Division
International Union for Conservation of Nature and Natural Resources
Avenue du Mont-Blanc
1196 Gland, Switzerland

Mr. McNeely has extensive field experience in Thailand, Indonesia and Nepal, and has published widely in tropical ecology and national parks. He currently serves as Director of IUCN's Programme and Policy Division. Together with Paul Wachtel, he is co-author of Soul of the Tiger: Man and Wildlife in Southeast Asia (in press).

Dr. J.Geoffrey Mosley
Director
Australian Conservation Foundation
Hawthorn, Victoria
3122 Australia

Dr. Mosley is currently the Director of the Australian Conservation Foundation. He has served in numerous capacities for IUCN, most recently as Regional Councillor for Australia and Oceania.

Mr. Namukolo Mukutu
Permanent Secretary
Ministry of Lands & Natural Resources
Lusaka, Zambia

Mr. Mukutu is the Permanent Secretary of the Ministry of Lands and Natural Resources in Zambia. In 1970 he received a Bachelor of Agriculture Science degree from Massey University, New Zealand. He is a Fellow of the Economic Development Institute (World Bank) and a Member of the Association for the Advancement of Agriculture Sciences in Africa. Mr. Mukutu has previously served as Permanent Secretary in the Ministry of Agriculture and Water Development.

Dr. David A. Munro
Naivasha Consultants Ltd.
2513 Amherst Avenue
Sidney, British Columbia
Canada V8L 2H3

Dr. Munro, a biologist and administrator, was formerly responsible for various Canadian Government programmes and the Programme Division of the UN Environmental

Programme. He was formerly Director General of the International Union for Conservation of Nature and Natural Resources, and supervised the elaboration of the World Conservation Strategy. Dr. Munro is currently a consultant in environmental and renewable resource policy research and management. He is also an IUCN Regional Councillor for North America and the Caribbean, and a member of the Commission on Environmental Planning.

Mr. Constantine Mwale
Natural Resources Officer
Natural Resources Department
P.O.Box 50042
Lusaka, Zambia

Mr Mwale has worked in various capacities with the Zambian Ministry of Lands and Natural Resources for fourteen years. He is particularly concerned with promoting environmental education and carries out Environmental Impact Assessments on new projects.

Dr . John Kennedy Naysmith
Senior Advisor to the Government of Nepal
Suite 1409, Bluestar Building
G.P.O. Box 3923
Tripureswar
Kathmandu, Nepal

As well as being being an advisor to the Nepal Government, Dr Naysmith is Project Leader for the International Union for Conservation of Nature on the Nepal Conservation Strategy. He has held a number of posts in the Canadian Government including Executive Director of the National Task Force on Northern Conservation.

Mr. Marc Nerfin
President
International Foundation for
Development Alternatives
2 Place du Marché
1260 Nyon, Switzerland

Mr. Nerfin has extensive experience throughout the developing world with educational programmes designed to encourage alternative development patterns. Working with Maurice Strong, he was one of the key organisers of the 1972 Stockholm Conference on the Human Environment, and the architect of a number of important international declarations on environment, natural resources and alternative development patterns.

Professor Reuben Olembo
UN Environment Programme (UNEP)
Nairobi, Kenya

Professor Olembo, a professional geneticist, joined the UN in 1975 having served as Professor at Makerere University (Uganda) and the University of Nairobi. He is currently Director of Environmental Management and coordinates UNEP programmes in the areas of ecosystems conservation and management, desertification, and regional seas. He is the official convenor of the Ecosystems Conservation Group which links the WCS partners in conservation action, and is Chairman of the Kenyan Wildlife Fund Trustees.

Mr. Robert Prescott-Allen
PADATA Consultants
627 Aquarius
Victoria, British Columbia
Canada V9B 5B4

Robert Prescott-Allen participated in the organisation and writing of the World Conservation Strategy for IUCN